Recaps

Each major section within a chapter ends with a list of key points. Students are able to quickly review what they've read before moving on to the next section.

RECAP

1. Opportunity costs are the benefits that are forgone due to a choice. When you choose one thing, you must give up—forgo—others.
2. Opportunity costs are an individual concept but can be used to demonstrate scarcity and choice for a society as a whole.
3. The production possibilities curve represents all combinations of goods and services that can be produced using limited resources efficiently to their full capabilities.
4. Points inside the production possibilities curve represent the underutilization or inefficient use of resources—more goods and services could be produced by using the limited resources more fully or efficiently.
5. Points outside the production possibilities curve represent combinations of goods and services that are unattainable given the limitation of resources. More resources would have to be obtained, or a more efficient means of production through the development of technology or innovative management techniques would have to be discovered, to produce quantities of goods and services outside the current production possibilities curve.

Economic Insight Boxes

These boxes provide in-depth treatment of contemporary economic issues, helping students to make connections between economic concepts and the world they live in.

Government Creates a Market for Fishing Rights

Economic Insight

There is no practical way to establish ownership rights of ocean fish stocks. Traditionally, fish have been free for the taking—a common pool resource. Theory teaches that such underpricing leads to overconsumption. In the halibut fisheries off Alaska, fishing fleets caught so many halibut that the survival of the stock was threatened. No single fishing boat had an incentive to harvest fewer fish since the impact on its own future catch would be minimal and others would only increase their take. This is an example of what is known as "the tragedy of the commons."

Officials tried limiting the length of the fishing season. But this effort only encouraged new capital investment such as larger and faster boats with more effective (and expensive) fishing equipment. In order to control the number of fish caught, the season was shortened in some areas from 4 months to 2 days by the early 1990s. Most of the halibut caught had to be frozen rather than marketed fresh, and halibut caught out of season had to be discarded.

In late 1992, the federal government proposed a new approach: assigning each fisherman a permit to catch a certain number of fish. The total number of fish for which permits are issued will reflect scientific estimates of the number of fish that can be caught without endangering the survival of the species. Also, the permits will be transferable—they can be bought and sold. By making the permits transferable, the system in effect creates a market where one did not exist previously. The proposed system will encourage the most profitable and efficient boats to operate at full capacity by buying permits from less successful boats, ensuring a fishing fleet that uses labor and equipment efficiently. Moreover, the transferable permits system establishes a market price for the opportunity to fish—a price that better reflects the true social cost of using this common resource.

Source: *Economic Report of the President, 1993*, p. 207.

Economically Speaking

This feature pairs current newspaper articles with original commentary by Boyes and Melvin. *Economically Speaking* prepares students to think critically about the economic principles, models, and policies they read about in the news, and provides a springboard for further research and discussion.

Economically Speaking

Car Sector Braces for Stiffer Competition

The Malaysian automotive sector is bracing for the stiffer competition that will come in 2005 when tariff barriers come down for the sector under the Asian Free Trade

But to assume that the underdog would definitely be trampled upon by the stronger team would not be a correct statement, even dimunitive David beat the brawn

ensure that the products they sell are at least of similar standards, quality and performance with the competitors.

Otherwise, they would be

Commentary

Free trade means that restrictions such as tariffs and barriers are eliminated. A tariff is a tax applied to imported goods or services that raises the price of foreign-made items. The tariff allows inefficient local producers to compete locally with more efficient foreign producers. But when the tariff is reduced or eliminated, the local producers must be as efficient as the foreign producers in order to compete with them. Malaysia's automobile industry fears it may not be as efficient. It is hoping that the loyalty of the local population coupled with

consumers can consume less than they could with trade. Malaysian consumers would be restricted to the nation's own PPC, represented by point *A* or any point on or inside the PPC. Trade restrictions would mean that Malaysian consumers have an opportunity cost of amount *A* to *B*; they forgo the additional amount of goods and services that trade would allow. There is no doubt that free trade will benefit Malaysian consumers. But, the transition from a restricted trade to free trade, from *A* to *B*, may involve the loss of jobs in one area of the economy

3.2°
4.°

Microeconomics

FIFTH EDITION

William Boyes
Arizona State University

Michael Melvin
Arizona State University

Houghton Mifflin Company   Boston   New York

To our families
W. B.   M. M.

Sponsoring Editor: Ann West
Associate Editor: Jennifer DiDomenico
Senior Project Editor: Bob Greiner
Senior Production/Design Coordinator: Carol Merrigan
Senior Manufacturing Coordinator: Marie Barnes
Marketing Manager: Barbara Lebuhn

PHOTO CREDITS

(Text Credits follow the Glossary section.)

Library of Congress Catalog Card Number: 2001088496

ISBN: 0-618-12795-X

1 2 3 4 5 6 7 8 9 —VH— 05 04 03 02 01

Preface

In the first edition of *Microeconomics* we integrated the global perspective with the traditional economic principles to give students a framework to understand the globally developing economic world. Events since then have made this approach even more imperative. The Soviet Union has disintegrated, newly independent nations have emerged, and markets have been established where none had existed before. Students and instructors embraced the idea that the economies of countries are interrelated and that this should be made clear in the study of economics. *Microeconomics* gives students the tools they need to make connections between the economic principles they learn and the now-global world they live in.

Current users of *Microeconomics* report that their students find the book "very interesting," "really easy to understand," and "easy to learn from." We have also discovered that this book has well served students from many different backgrounds and with varying future plans—from those who major in business, psychology, education, engineering, English, and other fields to those who choose to pursue economics.

Now, in the fifth edition, we continue to refine and improve the text as a teaching and learning instrument while expanding its international base by updating and adding examples related to global economics throughout.

CHANGES IN THE FIFTH EDITION

The fifth edition of *Microeconomics* has been thoroughly updated and refined. A detailed account of all the additions, deletions, and modifications can be found in the Transition Guide in the *Instructor's Resource Manual* and on the web site at: college.hmco.com.

Revised Microeconomic Coverage

The microeconomic material includes further refinements to enable students to see the forest while wandering around the trees. In addition, a new chapter, Chapter 13 on "The New Economy," explores the economics of the Internet and other high-tech phenomena, with emphasis on the economics of information and networks. Chapters 15 and 16 in the fourth edition, which covered the labor market and wage differentials, have been combined to form one cohesive labor market chapter.

Modern Topics and Features Throughout

Modern topics continue to be the emphasis of the text. The economics of personnel, strategic behavior, and the economics of information are maintained but are restructured and reemphasized. The effects of corruption on economic growth and development is now included in the economic development chapter to mirror the current policy emphasis in multinational organizations on this topic.

Each chapter contains approximately fifteen exercises that challenge students, test their retention and understanding of the material, and extend their knowledge. Internet Exercises on the accompanying web site, at least three per chapter, ask students to investigate a topic, make comparisons, and use Internet researching skills to answer questions keyed to the Chapter topics. For example, in Chapter 1, students can access our web site and examine statistics of people attending college in the United States. Students are then asked several questions about the data.

SUCCESSFUL FEATURES RETAINED FROM THE FOURTH EDITION

In addition to the considerable updating and revising we've done for the fifth edition, there are several features preserved from the previous edition that we think instructors will find interesting.

Enhanced Student Relevance

With all the demands on today's students, it's no wonder that they resist spending time on a subject unless they see how the material relates to them and how they will benefit from mastering it. We incorporate features throughout the text that show economics as the relevant and necessary subject we know it to be.

Real-World Examples Students are rarely intrigued by unknown manufacturers or service companies. Our text talks about people and firms that students recognize. We describe business decisions made by McDonald's and Pizza Hut, by Kodak and Fuji, and by the local video store or café. We discuss the policies of U.S. presidents and other world leaders. These examples grab students' interest. Reviewers have repeatedly praised the use of novel examples to convey economic concepts.

Economic Insight Boxes These brief boxes bring in contemporary material from current periodicals and journals to illustrate or extend the discussion in the chapter. By reserving interesting but more technical sidelights for boxes, we lessen the likelihood that students will be confused or distracted by issues that are not critical to understanding the chapter. By including excerpts from articles, we help students learn to move from theory to real-world examples. And by including plenty of contemporary issues, we guarantee that students will see how economics relates to their own lives. New topics covered in the fifth edition include features of the new $20 bill, currency trading around the world, and winner-takes-all and market inefficiency.

Economically Speaking Boxes The objective of the principles course is to teach students how to translate to the real world the predictions that come out of economic models and to translate real-world events into an economic model in order to analyze and understand what lies behind the events. The Economically Speaking boxes present students with examples of this kind of analysis. Students read an article that appears on the left-hand page of a two-page spread at the end of each chapter. The commentary on the right-hand page shows how the facts and events in the article translate into a specific economic model or idea, thereby demonstrating the relevance of theory. Nearly two-thirds of the articles and commentaries are new to the fifth edition, covering such current events as the 2000/2001 gas price increases, the effects of a "hard landing" in the U.S. on Asia, surpluses in the U.S. budget, and college dropouts and dotcoms.

An Effective and Proven System of Teaching and Learning Aids

This text is designed to make teaching easier by enhancing student learning. Tested pedagogy motivates students, emphasizes clarity, reinforces relationships, simplifies review, and fosters critical thinking. And, as we have discovered from reviewer and user feedback, this pedagogy works.

In-Text Referencing System Sections are numbered for easy reference and to reinforce hierarchies of ideas. Numbered section heads serve as an outline of the chapter, allowing instructors flexibility in assigning reading, and making it easy for students to find topics to review. Each item in the key terms list and summary at the end of the chapter refers students back to the appropriate section's number.

The section numbering system appears throughout the Boyes/Melvin ancillary package; the *Test Banks, Study Guides,* and *Instructor's Resource Manual* are organized according to the same system.

Fundamental Questions These questions help to organize the chapter and highlight those issues that are critical to understanding. Each related fundamental question also appears in the margin by the text discussion and, with brief answers, in the chapter summaries. A fuller discussion and answer to each of these questions may be found in the *Study Guides* available as supplements to this text. The fundamental questions also serve as one of several criteria used to categorize questions in the *Test Banks.*

Preview This motivating lead-in sets the stage for the chapter. Much more than a road map, it helps students identify real-world issues that relate to the concepts that will be presented.

Recaps Briefly listing the main points covered, a recap appears at the end of each major section within a chapter. Students are able to quickly review what they have just read before going on to the next section.

Summary The summary at the end of each chapter is organized along two dimensions. The primary organizational device is the list of fundamental questions. A brief synopsis of the discussion that helps students to answer those questions is arranged by section below each of the questions. Students are encouraged to create their own links among topics as they keep in mind the connections between the big picture and the details that make it up.

Comments Found in the text margins, these comments highlight especially important concepts, point out common mistakes, and warn students of common pitfalls. They alert students to parts of the discussion that they should read with particular care.

Key Terms Key terms appear in bold type in the text. They also appear with their definition in the margin and are listed at the end of the chapter for easy review. All key terms are included in the Glossary at the end of the text.

Friendly Appearance

Economics can be intimidating; this is why we've tried to keep *Microeconomics* looking friendly and inviting. The one-column design and ample white space in this text provide an accessible backdrop. Over 150 figures rely on well-developed pedagogy and consistent use of color to reinforce understanding. Striking colors were chosen to enhance readability and provide visual interest. Specific curves were assigned specific colors, and families of curves were assigned related colors.

Annotations on the art point out areas of particular concern or importance. Students can see exactly which part of a graph illustrates a shortage or a surplus, a change in consumption or consumer surplus. Tables that provide data from which graphs are plotted are paired with their graphs. Where appropriate, color is used to show correlations between the art and the table, and captions clearly explain what is shown in the figures and link them to the text discussion.

The color photographs not only provide visual images but make the text appealing. These vibrant photos tell stories as well as illustrate concepts, and lengthy captions explain what is in the photos, again to draw connections between the images and the text discussion.

Thoroughly International Coverage

Students understand that they live in a global economy; they can hardly shop, watch the news, or read a newspaper without stumbling on this basic fact. International examples are presented in every chapter but are not merely added on, as is the case with many other texts. By introducing international effects on demand and supply in Chapter 3 and then describing in a non-technical manner the basics of the foreign exchange market and the balance of payments in Chapter 7, we are able to incorporate the international sector into the economic models and applications wherever appropriate thereafter. Because the international content is incorporated from the beginning, students develop a far more realistic picture of the national economy; as a result they don't have to alter their thinking to allow for international factors later on. The three chapters that focus on international topics at the end of the text allow those instructors who desire to delve much more deeply into international issues to do so.

The global applicability of economics is emphasized by *using traditional economic concepts to explain international economic events and using international events to illustrate economic concepts that have traditionally been illustrated with domestic examples.* Instructors need not know the international institutions to introduce international examples since the topics through which they are addressed are familiar, for example, price ceilings, price discrimination, expenditures on resources, marginal productivity theory, and others. (See the back endpapers for some examples.)

Unique international elements of microeconomic coverage in the text include:

- The introduction of exchange rates as a determinant of demand and supply in Chapter 3
- Extensive analyses of the effects of trade barriers, tariffs, and quotas
- An examination of strategic trade
- An examination of dumping as a special case of price discrimination
- The identification of problems faced by multinational firms
- A comparison of behavior, results, and institutions among nations with respect to consumption, production, firm size, government policies toward business, labor markets, health care, income distribution, environmental policy, and other issues

Modern Microeconomic Organization and Content

All too often microeconomics is presented as a succession of facts, graphs, and theories whose connections are not easily grasped or appreciated. Because students don't see the big picture, they find microeconomics difficult and unrelated to their lives. We give students a context for organizing and understanding the material covered and point out how it relates to their everyday experience. We also draw students' interest by extending the application of economic principles to important social issues of the day—families, aging, health care, college and occupational choice, and discrimination.

Part II presents basic concepts such as elasticity, consumer behavior, and costs of production. Parts III and IV both begin with overview chapters (Chapter 9 on product markets and Chapter 15 on resource markets). These overviews give students a chance to look at the big picture before delving into details they often find confusing. Chapter 9, for instance, gives students an intuitive overview of the market structures before they explore each type of structure in more detail in succeeding chapters. Chapter 9 lightens the load that the more-detailed chapters have to bear, easing students into the market structure material. The traditional topics are covered in the separate market structure chapters, Chapters 10 to 12, but the coverage is also modern, including such topics as strategic behavior, price discrimination, nonprice competition, and the economics of information. Having fought their way first through the cost curves and then the market structures, students often complain that they do not see the relevance of that material to real-world situations. The intuitive overview chapter alleviates some of that frustration. New material on technological change and financial capital is included in Chapter 13. The coverage of environmental issues is expanded and given prominent positioning as Chapter 18.

A COMPLETE TEACHING AND LEARNING PACKAGE

In today's market no book is complete without a full complement of ancillaries. Those instructors who face huge classes find good transparencies (acetates) to be critical instructional tools. Others may find that computer simulations and tutorials are invaluable. Still others use projection technology and want *PowerPoint* slides. All of these are available. And to foster the development of consistent teaching and study strategies, the ancillaries pick up pedagogical features of the text—like the fundamental questions—wherever appropriate.

Transparencies   Available to adopters are over 100 color acetates showing the most important figures in the text. Over 10 percent of these figures have one to three overlays, which in addition to adding clarity and flexibility to the discussion, allow instructors to visually demonstrate the dynamic nature of economics.

Instructor's Resource Manual (*IRM*)   Patricia Diane Nipper has produced a manual that will streamline preparation for both new and experienced faculty. Preliminary sections cover class administration, alternative syllabi, and an introduction to the use of cooperative learning in teaching the principles of economics.

The *IRM* also contains a detailed chapter-by-chapter review of all the changes made in the fifth edition. This Transition Guide should help instructors more easily move from the use of the fourth edition to this new edition.

Each chapter of the *IRM* contains:

- Overview and objectives that *(1) describe the content and unique features of the chapter and (2) provide a list of concrete objectives that students will need to master in order to succeed with later chapters.*
- The fundamental questions
- The key terms
- A lecture outline with *teaching strategies*—general techniques and guidelines, essay topics, and other hints to enliven your classes
- Opportunities for discussion
- Answers to every end-of-chapter exercise
- Answers to *Study Guide* homework questions
- Active learning exercises

Study Guides   Janet L. Wolcutt and James E. Clark of the Center for Economic Education at Wichita State University have revised the *Macroeconomics* and *Microeconomics Study Guides* to give students the practice they need to master this course. Initially received by students and instructors with great enthusiasm, the guides maintain their warm and lively style to keep students on the right track. For each chapter:

- Fundamental questions are answered in one or several paragraphs. For students who have trouble formulating their own answers to these questions after reading the text, the *Study Guides* provide an invaluable model.

- Key terms are listed.

- A Quick Check Quiz is organized by section, so any wrong answers send the student directly to the relevant material in the text.

- Practice Questions and Problems, which is also organized by section, includes a variety of question formats—multiple choice, true/false, matching, and fill in the blank. They test understanding of the concepts and ask students to construct or perform computations.

- Thinking About and Applying . . . uses newspaper headlines or some other real-life applications to test students' ability to reason in economic terms.

- A Homework page at the end of each chapter contains five (two factual, two applied, and one synthesis/analysis) questions that can be answered on the sheet and turned in for grading. Answers are included in the *IRM*.

- Sample tests appear at the end of each *Study Guide* part and consist of 25 to 50 questions similar to *Test Bank* questions. Taking the sample tests helps students determine whether they are prepared for exams.

- Answers are provided for all questions except the Homework questions. Students are referred back to the relevant sections in the main text for each question.

Test Banks Test Banks for both *Macroeconomics* and *Microeconomics* are available. More than 8,000 test items, approximately 30% of which are new to this edition, provide a wealth of material for classroom testing. Features include:

- Multiple choice, true/false, and essay questions in every chapter

- Questions new to this edition are marked for easy identification

- An increased number of analytical, applied, and graphical questions

- The identification of all test items according to topic, question type (factual, interpretive, or applied), level of difficulty, and applicable fundamental question

- A *Study Guide* section of the test bank that includes five test items taken directly from the *Study Guide* and five test items that parallel *Study Guide* questions, for the instructor who is interested in rewarding students for working through the *Study Guide*

Computerized Test Bank A new sophisticated and user-friendly program called HMTesting is available to help instructors quickly create tests from over 7,000 test bank items according to various selection criteria, including random selection. The program prints graphs as well as the text part of each question. Instructors can scramble the answer choices, edit questions, add their own questions to the pool, and customize their exams in various other ways. HMTesting provides a complete testing solution, including classroom administration and online testing features in addition to test generation. This program is available for Windows and Macintosh users.

Tutorial and Simulation Software Tutorial/simulation software, extensively revised to parallel this fifth edition, is now packaged with every new student copy of the text. A tutorial for each text chapter provides an opportunity for students to review graphing concepts and models and chapter-specific content and then to test themselves on what they've learned. A glossary and context-sensitive help are always available. The simulation component of the software includes over 60 years of data on more than twenty key economic indicators, allowing students to plot data, compare various measurement instruments, and print out their results.

HMClassPrep CD-ROM This supplement contains all the resources you need to prepare lessons based on the fifth edition of the text, including lecture outlines and teaching strategies, chapter overviews and objectives, and in-class discussion ideas. This wealth of resources is organized by chapter and resource type for easy reference and class planning.

PowerPoint Slides All the figures from the text are provided on electronic slides created for Microsoft's popular *PowerPoint* presentation software. *PowerPoint* allows instructors to create customized lecture presentations that can be displayed on computer-based projection systems. The slides are produced as a complete presentation, but using *PowerPoint,* presenters can also insert their own slides into the presentation or use specific slides in sets that they create themselves. The slides are available to instructors on the website and on the Instructor ClassPrep CD-ROM.

WebSite The fifth edition website provides an extended learning environment for students and a rich store of teaching resources for instructors. To jump directly to the Boyes text site, go to *college.hmco.com,* choose *Instructor* or *Student,* and then type "Boyes" in the "Jump to Textbook Sites" box. Instructors will need a username and password (available from their Houghton Mifflin sales representative) to get onto the password protected parts of the site. Included on the student site are key economic links for every chapter, extended web-based assignments, and on-line quizzes—all intended to help students test their mastery of the chapter content. The instructor site contains economic and teaching resource links, teaching tips, answers to end-of-chapter exercises, and access to demonstrations of other components of the teaching package.

Smarthinking Online Tutoring Service
Instructors adopting the fifth edition of Boyes/Melvin *Microeconomics* can choose to provide their students with free access to Smarthinking. If this option is chosen, students with Internet access may interact live online with an experienced Smarthinking "e-structor" (online tutor) between 9 P.M. and 1 A.M. EST, every Sunday through Thursday. Smarthinking provides state-of-the-art communication tools, such as chat technology and virtual whiteboards designed for easy rendering of economic formulas and graphs, to help your students practice key concepts and learn to think economically.

WebCT e-Pack and Blackboard Course Cartridge These resources provide text-specific student study aids in customizable, Internet-based education platforms. Both platforms provide a full array of content delivery and course management features for instructors who wish to incorporate educational technology in their traditional classrooms or for those who are creating distance learning courses.

ACKNOWLEDGMENTS

Writing a text of this scope is a challenge that requires the expertise and efforts of many. We are grateful to our friends and colleagues who have so generously given their time, creativity, and insight to help us create a text that best meets the needs of today's students.

We'd especially like to thank the many reviewers of *Microeconomics* listed on the following pages. Their

comments have proved invaluable in revising this text. In particular, we wish to thank Chin-Chyuan Tai of Averett College, who reviewed the text for accuracy in the last stages of production.

Unsolicited feedback from current users has also been greatly appreciated. We'd like to thank Nancy Roberts and Elmer Gooding of Arizona State University, and John Somers of Portland Community College for their very useful feedback.

Thanks go to Eugenio Dante Suarez for his work on the *Test Banks* for this edition and the fourth edition. Thanks also to Bob Cunningham of Alma College and Davis Folsom and Rick Boulware of University of South Carolina, Beaufort, who reviewed the *Test Banks* for accuracy. The important contributions of Melissa Hardison on the third edition *Test Banks,* Bettina Peiers and Karen Thomas-Brandt on the second edition *Test Banks,* and Michael Couvillion on the first edition *Test Banks* must also be acknowledged.

We would also like to thank James E. Clark and Janet L. Wolcutt of Wichita State University for their continued contributions to the *Study Guides* and Patricia Diane Nipper of Southside Virginia Community College for her work on the fifth and previous editions of the *Instructor's Resource Manual.* Thanks also to Chin-Chyuan Tai of Averett College for reviewing this important supplement. Thanks, too, go to Paul S. Estenson of Gustavus Adolphus College and Edward T. Merkel of Troy State University for their contribution in preparing the second edition *Instructor's Resource Manual.*

We want to thank the many people at Houghton Mifflin Company who devoted countless hours to making this text the best it could be, including Ann West, Jennifer DiDomenico, Bob Greiner, Carol Merrigan, Marie Barnes, Tonya Lobato, and Angma Jhala. We are grateful for their enthusiasm, expertise, and energy.

Finally, we wish to thank our families and friends. The inspiration they provided through the conception and development of this book cannot be measured but certainly was essential.

Our students at Arizona State University continue to help us improve the text through each edition; their many questions have given us invaluable insight into how best to present this intriguing subject. It is our hope that this textbook will bring a clear understanding of economic thought to many other students as well. We welcome any feedback for improvements.

W. B.   M. M.

REVIEWERS

David Black
University of Toledo
Toledo, OH

Gary Bogner
Baker College-Muskegon
Muskegon, MI

Rick Boulware
University of South Carolina,
Beaufort
Beaufort, SC

Bradley Braun
University of Central Florida
Orlando, FL

William S. Brewer
Genesee Community College
Batavia, NY

Gregory Brown
Martin Community College
Williamston, NC

Kristin Carrico
Umpqua Community College
Roseburg, OR

Jill L. Caviglia
Salisbury State University
Salisbury, MD

Kenneth W. Christianson, Jr.
Ithaca College
Ithaca, NY

Valerie A. Collins
Colorado Mountain College
Glenwood Springs, CO

Wilfrid W. Csaplar, Jr.
Southside Virginia Community
College
Keysville, VA

Bob Cunningham
Alma College
Alma, MI

Stephen B. Davis
Valley City State University
Valley City, ND

Lynne Pierson Doti
Chapman University
Orange, CA

Raymond J. Egan
WA
(Retired, formerly at Pierce
College)

Martha Field
Greenfield Community College
Greenfield, MA

Fred Fisher
Colorado Mountain College, CO

Davis Folsom
University of South Carolina,
Beaufort
Beaufort, SC

Bradley Garton
Laramie County Community
College
Laramie, Wyoming

Omer Gokcekus
North Carolina Central University
Durham, NC

R.W. Hafer
Southern Illinois University–
Edwardsville
Edwardsville, IL

Michael Harsh
Randolph-Macon College

Arleen Hoag
Owens Community College
Toledo, OH

James Johnson
Black Hawk College
Moline, IL

Jeff Keil
J. Sargent Reynolds Community
College

Donna Kish-Goodling
Muhlenburg College
Allentown, PA

Ali Kutan
SIUE
Edwardsville, IL

Nikiforos Laopodis
Villa Julie College, MD

John D. Lathrop
New Mexico Junior College
Hobbs, NM

Paul Lockard
Black Hawk College
Moline, IL

Glenna Lunday
Western Oklahoma State College
Les Manns
Doane College

Dan Marburger
Arkansas State University
Jonesborough, AK

Buddy Miller
Carteret Community College
Morehead City, NC

Charles Okeke
Community College of Southern
Nevada
Las Vegas, NV

Robert Payne
Baher College
Port Huron, MI

Dick Risinit
Reading Area Community College

Robert S. Rycroft
Mary Washington College
Fredericksburg, VA

Charles Saccardo
Bentley College, MA

Charles Sackrey
Bucknell University
Lewisburg, PA

J. Richard Sealscott
Northwest State Community
College

Steve Seteroff
Chapman University Bangor
Academic Center, WA
City University, WA

Richard Skolnik
SUNY-Oswego
Oswego, NY

Scott F. Smith
University at Albany
Albany, NY

Thom Smith
Hill College
Hillsboro, TX

John Somers
Portland Community College–
Sylvania
Portland, Oregon

John J. Spitzer
State University of New York
College at Brockport
Brockport, NY

Chin-Chyuan Tai
Averett College
Danville, VA

Rob Verner
Ursuline College
Pepper Pike, OH

Mark E. Wohar
University of Nebraska
Omaha, NE

Darrel A. Young
University of Texas
Austin, TX

Girma Zelleke
Kutztown University
Kutztown, PA

Brief Contents

Contents

CHAPTER 4   The Market System and the Private Sector   74

CHAPTER 5   The Public Sector   100

Contents

PART THREE **Product Markets**   **196**

CHAPTER 9 **Profit Maximization**   **198**

CHAPTER 10 **Perfect Competition**   **216**

CHAPTER 11 **Monopoly**   **236**

Contents   **xix**

PART FIVE   Current Issues Involving the Public Sector and the Market Economy   416

CHAPTER 19   Aging, Social Security, and Health Care   418

CHAPTER 20   Income Distribution, Poverty and Government Policy   440

PART SIX   Issues in International Trade and Finance   464

CHAPTER 21   World Trade Equilibrium   466

Contents

CHAPTER 22   International Trade Restrictions   486

CHAPTER 23   Exchange-Rate Systems and Practices   504

Glossary   G-1

Index   I-1

Microeconomics

Part One

Introduction to the
Price System

Chapter 1

Economics: The World Around You

? Fundamental Questions

1. **What is economics?**

2. **What is the economic way of thinking?**

Y ou are a member of a very select group: you are attending college. Only about 19 percent of the American population has a college degree (bachelor's or associate's), and about 50 percent of people between the ages of 18 and 22 are currently attending college.

Preview

Why aren't more people attending college? Part of the reason may be the increased costs of college; the direct expenses associated with college have risen much more rapidly than average income. Yet, attending college and acquiring an education is more valuable today than in the past. Technological change and increased international trade have placed a premium on a college education; more and more jobs require the skills acquired in college. As a result, the wage disparity between college-educated and non-college-educated workers is rising fairly rapidly. Over their lifetimes, college-educated people earn nearly twice as much as people without college degrees.

Why are you attending college? Perhaps you've never really given it a great deal of thought—your family always just assumed that college was a necessary step after high school; perhaps you analyzed the situation and decided that college was better than the alternatives. Whichever approach you took, you were practicing economics. You were examining alternatives and making choices. This is what economics is about.

The objective of economics is to understand why the real world is what it is. This is not an easy proposition, for the real world is very complex. After all, what happens in the real world is the result of human behavior, and humans are not simple creatures. Nonetheless, there are some fundamental regularities of human behavior that can help to explain the world we observe.

One such regularity is that people behave in ways that make themselves and those they care about better off and happier. Even without knowing that having a college education means your income will be higher than if you do not earn a college degree, you and your family knew or suspected that the college degree would mean a better lifestyle and a more secure or more prestigious job for you. However, what makes one person happy may not make others happy.

Knowing that it is the person without a college degree who is first laid off or unemployed during a recession, that the riskier jobs are held by those without a college degree, and that a person without a college degree is six times more likely to fall into poverty than a person with a college degree, we might be inclined to argue that the 50 percent of young people not attending college are making the wrong choice. But we can't say that. We don't know their circumstances; we don't know what makes them happy. We only know that they do not believe the benefits of college outweigh the costs; otherwise they would be in college.

Knowing that most people behave in ways that make themselves better off and that most people compare costs and benefits in coming to a decision is powerful stuff. It allows us to explain much of the real world and to predict how that world might change if certain events occur.

This knowledge of human behavior is the subject matter of economics. To study economics is to seek answers not only for why people choose to go to college but also for why economies go through cycles, at times expanding and creating new jobs and at other times dipping into recessions; for why some people are thrown out of jobs to join the ranks of the unemployed while others are drawn out of the ranks of the unemployed into new jobs; for why some people live on welfare; for why some nations are richer than others; for why the illegal drug trade is so difficult to stop; for why health care is so expensive; or, in general, for why the world is what it is.

This chapter is the introduction to our study of economics. In it we present some of the terminology commonly used in economics and outline what the study of economics is. ▨

1. THE DEFINITION OF ECONOMICS

People have unlimited wants—they always want more goods and services than they have or can purchase with their incomes. Whether they are wealthy or poor, what they have is never enough. Since people do not have everything they want, they must use their limited time and income to select those things they want most and forgo, or relinquish, the rest. The choices they make and the manner in which the choices are made explain much of why the real world is what it is.

Economic Insight

1.a. Scarcity

Neither the poor nor the wealthy have unlimited time, income, or wealth, and both must make choices to use these limited items in a way that best satisfies their wants. Because wants are unlimited and incomes, time, and other items are not, scarcity exists everywhere. **Scarcity** of something means that there is not enough of that item to satisfy everyone who wants it; it means that if a good has no cost, that is, at a zero price, the amount of the good that people want is greater than the amount that is available. Anything for which this condition holds is called an **economic good**. An economic good refers to *goods and services*—where goods are physical products, such as books or food, and services are nonphysical products, such as haircuts or golf lessons.

If there is enough of an item to satisfy wants, even at a zero price, the item is said to be a **free good**. It is difficult to think of examples of free goods. At one time people referred to air as free, but with air pollution control devices and other costly activities directed toward the maintenance of air quality standards, "clean" air, at least, is not a free good, as noted in the Economic Insight "'Free' Air?"

If people would pay to have less of an item, that item is called an **economic bad**. It is not so hard to think of examples of bads: pollution, garbage, and disease fit the description.

Some goods are used to produce other goods. For instance, to make chocolate chip cookies, we need flour, sugar, chocolate chips, butter, our own labor, and an oven. To distinguish between the ingredients of a good and the good itself, we call the ingredients **resources**. (Resources are also called **factors of production** and **inputs**; the terms are interchangeable.) The ingredients of the cookies are the resources, and the cookies are the goods.

As illustrated in Figure 1(a), economists have classified resources into three categories: land, labor, and capital.

1. **Land** includes all natural resources, such as minerals, timber, and water, as well as the land itself.
2. **Labor** refers to the physical and intellectual services of people, including the training, education, and abilities of the individuals in a society.

---

scarcity: when less of something is available than is wanted at the zero price.

economic good: any item that is scarce

free good: a good for which there is no scarcity

economic bad: any item for which we would pay to have less

resources, factors of production, or **inputs:** goods used to produce other goods, i.e., land, labor and capital

land: all natural resources, such as minerals, timber, and water, as well as the land itself

labor: the physical and intellectual services of people, including the training, education, and abilities of the individuals in a society

Figure 1

Flow of Resources and Income

Three types of resources are used to produce goods and services: land, labor, and capital. See 1(a). The owners of resources are provided income for selling their services. Landowners are paid rent; laborers receive wages; and capital receives interest. See 1(b). Figure 1(c) links Figures 1(a) and 1(b). People use their resources to acquire income with which they purchase the goods they want. Producers use the money received from selling the goods to pay for the use of the resources in making goods. Resources and income flow between certain firms and certain resource owners as people allocate their scarce resources to best satisfy their wants.

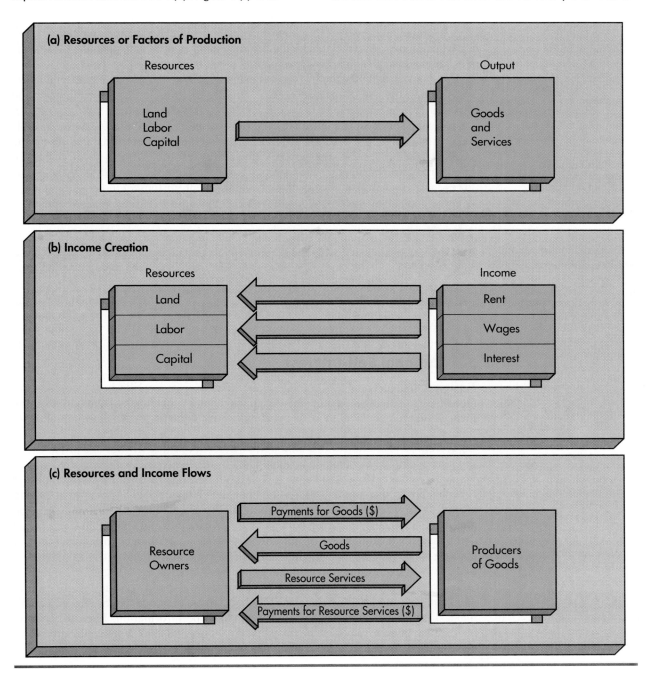

(a) **Resources or Factors of Production**

Resources — Land, Labor, Capital → Output — Goods and Services

(b) **Income Creation**

Resources — Land, Labor, Capital ← Income — Rent, Wages, Interest

(c) **Resources and Income Flows**

Resource Owners — Payments for Goods ($) → Producers of Goods
Goods ←
Resource Services →
← Payments for Resource Services ($)

capital: products such as machinery and equipment that are used in production

3. **Capital** refers to products such as machinery and equipment that are used in production. Capital is a manufactured or created product used solely for the production of the goods and services that are consumed by individuals. You will often hear the term *capital* used to describe the financial backing for some project or the stocks and bonds used to finance some business. This common usage is not incorrect but should be distinguished from the physical entity— the machinery and equipment and the buildings, warehouses, and factories. Thus we refer to the stocks and bonds as *financial capital* and to the physical entity as capital.

People obtain income by selling their resources or the use of their resources, as illustrated in Figure 1(b). Owners of land receive *rent*; people who provide labor services are paid *wages*; and owners of capital receive *interest*.

Figures 1(a) and 1(b) are linked because the income that resource owners acquire from selling the use of their resources provides them the ability to buy goods and services. And producers use the money received from selling their goods to pay for the resource services. In Figure 1(c), the flows of money are indicated along the outside arrows, and the flows of goods or resource services are indicated along the inside arrows. The resource services flow from resource owners to producers of goods in return for income; the flows of goods go from the producers of the goods to resource owners in return for the money payment for these goods.

1.b. Choices

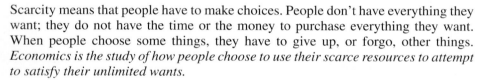

1. What is economics?

Scarcity means that people have to make choices. People don't have everything they want; they do not have the time or the money to purchase everything they want. When people choose some things, they have to give up, or forgo, other things. *Economics is the study of how people choose to use their scarce resources to attempt to satisfy their unlimited wants.*

1.c. Rational Self-Interest

rational self-interest: how people choose the options that give them the greatest amount of satisfaction

Rational self-interest is the term economists use to describe how people make choices. It means that people will make the choices that, at the time and with the information they have at their disposal, will give them the greatest amount of satisfaction.

You chose to attend college although 50 percent of those in your age group chose not to attend. All of you made rational choices based on what you perceived was in your best interest. How could it be in your best interest to do one thing and in another person's best interest to do exactly the opposite? Each person has unique goals and attitudes and faces different costs. Although your weighing of the alternatives came down on the side of attending college, another person weighed similar alternatives and came down on the side of not attending college. Both decisions were rational because in both cases the individual compared alternatives and selected the option that the *individual* thought was in his or her best interest.

It is important to note that rational self-interest depends on the information at hand and the individual's perception of what is in his or her best interest. People will make different choices even when facing the same information. Even though the probability of death in an accident is nearly 20 percent less if seat belts are worn, many people choose not to use them. Are these people rational? The answer is yes.

Having only a few minutes before his economics class begins, and having to reach the building located on the lower peninsula, the student grabs his hang glider and prepares to jump off the cliff. The student knows that instead of attending class, he might continue hang gliding, hike Guatemala's mountains, or sail its beautiful waters. However, he has compared benefits and costs of attending class versus not attending; he decided to attend class.

Perhaps they do not want their clothes wrinkled or perhaps seat belts are just too inconvenient or perhaps they think the odds of getting in an accident are just too small to worry about. Whatever the reason, these people are choosing the option that at the time gives them the greatest satisfaction. *This is rational self-interest.* Economists sometimes use the term *bounded rationality* to emphasize the point that people do not have perfect knowledge or perfect insight. In this book we simply use the term *rational* to refer to the comparison of costs and benefits.

Economists think that most of the time most human beings are weighing alternatives, looking at costs and benefits, and making decisions in a way that they believe makes them better off. This is not to say that economists look upon human beings as androids lacking feelings and able only to carry out complex calculations like a computer. Rather, economists believe that the feelings and attitudes of human beings enter into people's comparisons of alternatives and help determine how people decide something is in their best interest.

Human beings are self-interested, *not selfish.* People do contribute to charitable organizations and help others; people do make individual sacrifices because those sacrifices benefit their families or people they care about; soldiers do risk their lives to defend their country. All these acts are made in the name of rational self-interest.

RECAP

1. Scarcity exists when people want more of an item than exists at a zero price.
2. Goods are produced with resources (also called factors of production and inputs). Economists have classified resources into three categories: land, labor, and capital.

3. Choices have to be made because of scarcity. People cannot have or do everything they desire all the time.

4. People make choices in a manner known as rational self-interest; people make the choices that at the time and with the information they have at their disposal will give them the greatest satisfaction.

2. What is the economic way of thinking?

2. THE ECONOMIC APPROACH

Economists often refer to the "economic approach" or to "economic thinking." By this, they mean that the principles of scarcity and rational self-interest are used in a specific way to search out answers to questions about the real world.

2.a. Positive and Normative Analysis

positive analysis: analysis of what is

In applying the principles of economics to questions about the real world, it is important to avoid imposing your opinions or value judgments on others. Analysis that does not impose the value judgments of one individual on the decisions of others is called **positive analysis.** If you demonstrate that unemployment in the automobile industry in the United States rises when people purchase cars produced in other countries instead of cars produced in the United States, you are undertaking positive analysis. However, if you claim that there ought to be a law to stop people from buying foreign-made cars, you are imposing your value judgments on the decisions and desires of others. That is not positive analysis. It is, instead, **normative analysis.** *Normative means "what ought to be"; positive means "what is."* If you demonstrate that the probability of death in an automobile accident is 20 percent higher if seat belts are not worn, you are using positive analysis. If you argue that there should be a law requiring seat belts to be worn, you are using normative analysis.

normative analysis: analysis of what ought to be

Conclusions based on opinion or value judgments do not advance one's understanding of events.

2.b. Scientific Method

As stated before, economists want to understand the real world and to be able to predict the results of certain events. These goals are hardly unique to economics—they are the same goals most scientists strive toward. A chemist may want to predict the results of combining certain chemicals, and an astronomer may want to predict the results of black holes on galaxy behavior. Similarly, an economist may want to predict the result of an increase in the tuition and fees of college or the result of an increase in taxes. The economist uses much the same methodology as the chemist and astronomer to examine the real world—the **scientific method.** There are five steps in the scientific method, as noted in Figure 2: (1) recognize the problem or issue, (2) cut away unnecessary detail by making assumptions, (3) develop a model or story of the problem or issue, (4) make predictions, and (5) test the model.

scientific method: a manner of analyzing issues that involves five steps: recognizing the problem, making assumptions, building a model, making predictions, and testing the model

The first step in the scientific method, the recognition of the problem, means that an issue is identified—rise in unemployment, accelerated inflation, failure of a business, growth of social security taxes, increased cocaine addiction, the AIDS epi-

Figure 2

The Five Steps of the Scientific Method

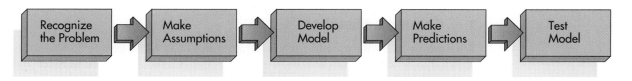

demic, the purchase of one cereal over another, the choice of one job over another, and on and on. Once the issue is identified, the next step is to explain it. This step may seem simple enough, but often it is not. Each problem in economics is so complex that the task of explaining it seems impossible. Thousands, even hundreds of thousands, of details are involved in something as apparently straightforward as deciding why people choose one college over another. The location of the college relative to the home, the appearance of the college, the friendliness of the admissions officers, the reputation of the football team, the occupations of parents, whether friends are attending college, the weather during the day the college was visited, and whether the student was feeling well the day applications were submitted are all details involved in the decision. Economists, like sociologists, political scientists, and paleontologists, cannot often take into account all the details surrounding an event they want to study. They have to reduce the complexity of the real world to manageable proportions using models and assumptions.

theory or **model:** a simplification or abstraction of the real world that enables scientists to organize their thoughts

A **theory,** or **model,** is merely a simplification, or abstraction, of the real world that enables scientists to organize their thoughts. A paper airplane is a model of a real airplane; a computer simulation of space is a model of the galaxies. Each model can illustrate certain aspects of the real world but is not intended to capture every aspect of the real world. Good economic models are those that explain or predict well; poor models are those that do not explain or predict well.

assumptions: statements accepted as true without proof

ceteris paribus: other things being equal, or everything else held constant

An economic model uses assumptions to simplify the problem at hand. **Assumptions** are statements taken for granted or accepted as true without proof. One of the most commonly used assumptions is *everything else held constant,* referred to quite often in its Latin form, ***ceteris paribus***. We might say that fewer people attend college as the tuition of college rises, *ceteris paribus*. This means that if only the tuition and number of people attending college are allowed to change, then a higher tuition means fewer people attend college. If we did not make the assumption of everything else held constant, then the statement could be grossly in error. If, for instance, incomes quadrupled while tuition rose a mere 5 percent, we could observe more people attending college even as the tuition rose. Similarly, if the income-earning potential of those with a college degree increased significantly, we might observe that more people attended college even as the tuition rose. Assumptions allow us to focus on the relationship between the variables in which we are interested, in this case tuition and the number of people attending college.

An economic model (or theory) is a tool used in the attempt to understand the real world. As with any theory, it must undergo **tests** to see whether it is consistent with the facts—whether it can be used to make accurate predictions.

tests: trials or measurements used to determine whether a theory is consistent with the facts

2.c. Common Mistakes

Why are so many items sold for $2.99 rather than $3? Most people attribute this practice to ignorance on the part of others: "People look at the first number and round to it—they see $2.99 but think $2." Although this reasoning may be correct, no one admits to such behavior when asked. A common error in the attempt to understand human behavior is to argue that other people do not understand something or are stupid. Instead of relying on rational self-interest to explain human behavior, ignorance or stupidity is called on.

fallacy of composition: the mistaken assumption that what applies in the case of one applies to the case of many

Another common mistake in economic analysis, called the **fallacy of composition,** is the error of attributing what applies in the case of one to the case of many. If one person in a theater realizes a fire has begun and races to the exit, that one person is better off. If we assume that a thousand people in a crowded theater would be better off behaving exactly like the single individual, we would be committing the mistake known as the fallacy of composition.

association as causation: the mistaken assumption that because two events seem to occur together, one causes the other

The mistaken interpretation of **association as causation** occurs when unrelated or coincidental events that occur at about the same time are believed to have a cause-and-effect relationship. For example, the result of the football Super Bowl game is sometimes said to predict how the stock market will perform. According to this "theory," if the NFC team wins, the stock market will rise in the new year, but if the AFC team wins, the market will fall. This bit of folklore is a clear example of confusion between causation and association. Simply because two events seem to occur together does not mean that one causes the other. Clearly, a football game cannot cause the stock market to rise or fall.

2.d. Microeconomics and Macroeconomics

Economics is the study of how people choose to allocate their scarce resources among their unlimited wants and involves the application of certain principles—scarcity, choice, rational self-interest—in a consistent manner using the scientific method. The study of economics is usually separated into two general areas, microeconomics and macroeconomics. **Microeconomics** is the study of economics at the level of the individual economic entity: the individual firm, the individual consumer, and the individual workers. In **macroeconomics,** rather than analyzing the behavior of an individual consumer, we look at the sum of the behaviors of all consumers, which is called the consumer sector, or household sector. Similarly, instead of examining the behavior of an individual firm, in macroeconomics we examine the sum of the behaviors of all firms, called the business sector.

microeconomics: the study of economics at the level of the individual

macroeconomics: the study of the economy as a whole

RECAP

1. The objective of economics is to understand why the real world is what it is.
2. Positive analysis refers to what is, while normative analysis refers to what ought to be.

3. The scientific method consists of five steps: recognition of the problem, assumptions, model, predictions, and tests of the model.

4. Assumptions are a means of simplifying the analysis; they are statements accepted as true without proof.

5. Assuming that others are ignorant, the fallacy of composition, and interpreting association as causation are three commonly made errors in economic analysis.

6. The study of economics is typically divided into two parts, macroeconomics and microeconomics.

SUMMARY

? 1. What is economics?

1. The objective of economics is to understand why the real world is what it is. *Preview*

2. The resources that go into the production of goods are land, labor, and capital. *§1.a*

3. Economics is the study of how people choose to allocate scarce resources to satisfy their unlimited wants. *§1.b*

4. Scarcity is universal; it applies to anything people would like more of than is available at a zero price. Because of scarcity, choices must be made, and choices are made in a way that is in the decision-maker's rational self-interest. *§1.a, 1.b, 1.c*

5. People make choices that, at the time and with the information at hand, will give them the greatest satisfaction. *§1.c*

? 2. What is the economic way of thinking?

6. Positive analysis is analysis of what is; normative analysis is analysis of what ought to be. *§2.a*

7. The scientific method consists of five steps: recognition of the problem, assumptions, model, predictions, and tests of the model. *§2.b*

8. Assumptions are a means of simplifying the analysis. *§2.b*

9. Assuming that others are ignorant, the fallacy of composition, and interpreting association as causation are three commonly made errors in economic analysis. *§2.c*

10. The study of economics is typically divided into two parts, macroeconomics and microeconomics. *§2.d*

KEY TERMS

scarcity *§1.a*

economic good *§1.a*

free good *§1.a*

economic bad *§1.a*

resources, factors of production, or inputs *§1.a*

land *§1.a*

labor *§1.a*

capital *§1.a*

rational self-interest *§1.c*

positive analysis *§2.a*

normative analysis *§2.a*

scientific method *§2.b*

theory or model *§2.b*

assumptions *§2.b*

ceteris paribus *§2.b*

tests *§2.b*

fallacy of composition *§2.c*

association as causation *§2.c*

microeconomics *§2.d*

macroeconomics *§2.d*

EXERCISES

1. Which of the following are economic goods? Explain why each is or is not an economic good.
   a. Steaks
   b. Houses
   c. Cars
   d. Garbage
   e. T-shirts

2. Many people go to a medical doctor every time they are ill; others never visit a doctor. Explain how a "model" of human behavior can include such opposite behaviors.

3. Erin has purchased a $35 ticket to a "Grateful Dead" concert. She is invited to a sendoff party for a friend who is moving to another part of the country. The party is scheduled for the same day as the concert. If she had known about the party before she bought the concert ticket, she would have chosen to attend the party. Will Erin choose to attend the concert? Explain.

4. It is well documented in scientific research that smoking is harmful to our health. Smokers have higher incidences of coronary disease, cancer, and other catastrophic illnesses. Knowing this, about 30 percent of young people begin smoking and about 25 percent of the U.S. population smokes. Are the people who choose to smoke irrational? What do you think of the argument that we should ban smoking in order to protect these people from themselves?

5. Indicate which of the following statements is true or false. If the statement is false, change it to make it true.
   a. Positive analysis imposes the value judgments of one individual on the decisions of others.
   b. *Ceteris paribus* is Latin for "let the buyer beware."
   c. Rational self-interest is the same thing as selfishness.
   d. An economic good is scarce if it has a positive price.
   e. An economic bad is an item that has a positive price.
   f. A resource is an ingredient used to make factors of production.

6. Are the following statements normative or positive? If a statement is normative, change it to a positive statement.
   a. The government should provide free tuition to all college students.
   b. An effective way to increase the skills of the work force is to provide free tuition to all college students.
   c. The government must provide job training if we are to compete with other countries.

7. In the *New York Times Magazine* in 1970, Milton Friedman, a Nobel Prize–winning economist, argued that "the social responsibility of business is to increase profits." How would Friedman's argument fit with the basic economic model that people behave in ways they believe are in their best self-interest?

8. Two economists crossed the street one day when one spied a twenty-dollar bill on the sidewalk. The first economist pointed out to the second economist that there was a twenty-dollar bill on the sidewalk. The second said, "No, there isn't a twenty-dollar bill there. If it were a twenty-dollar bill, somebody would have picked it up." In what sense does this joke describe the scientific methodology used by economists?

9. Use economics to explain why men's and women's restrooms tend to be located near each other in airports and other public buildings.

10. Use economics to explain why diamonds are more expensive than water, when water is necessary for survival and diamonds are not.

11. Use economics to explain why people leave tips (a) at a restaurant they visit often and (b) at a restaurant they visit only once.

12. Use economics to explain why people contribute to charities.

13. Use economics to explain this statement: "Increasing the speed limit has, to some degree, compromised highway safety on interstate roads but enhanced safety on noninterstate roads."

For Internet exercises and web resources related to this chapter, go to
http://college.hmco.com.

Pumped Up Over Cheap Gas

Two women duked it out. Two men crashed their cars. Another woman wrote a letter to her grandmother, read 150 pages in a paperback and sat for 3 and one-half hours. Why? Cheap gas.

Circle K sold 49-cent gas for two hours Saturday at two new stores at Priest Drive and Elliot Road in south Tempe and Chandler Boulevard and Desert Foothills Parkway in Phoenix.

The stores are Circle K's first to open in the Valley in five years, an event the corporation celebrated by dropping gasoline prices lower than they've been since Gerald Ford was president.

"I remember when I was little going with my mom when there were gasoline wars. That's what it reminds me of," said Ann Vry, spokeswoman for Circle K. "People would get very excited about filling up their tanks." Whitney Hamilton of Gilbert knows the feeling. She got in the

Tempe line at 6:30 a.m.; the special began at 10. "I was in line before there was a line," said Hamilton, who read and wrote her grandmother. "I've never seen them (gas prices) this low. I don't think I'll ever see them this low again."

Vera Lujan drove the 15 or so miles from her central Phoenix home to Tempe, arriving at 8 a.m. Seven cars were ahead of her. "I was already on empty, so I put in $1 and drove over," Lujan said. "I know. It's weird."

About 300 cars were in line at the Tempe store when the cheap gas began. Crowds were lighter in Phoenix, where only about 25 cars waited at any given time.

Circle K officials estimated that they filled up at least 12 cars every five minutes. A 15-gallon limit on the fill-ups was enforced.

"I think I burned more gas than I'm going to get," Ben Valdez of

Tempe said as he approached the pumps after waiting 90 minutes.

Some of those waiting could have used a lesson in patience.

"There've been a few little temper raises," Tempe police Officer Dick Steely said, including a fistfight that broke out when one woman tried to cut in front of another.

John Fecther of Tempe came for the gas but saw the long lines and tried to make a U-turn away from the area. He was hit by another vehicle.

"I was going to get the heck out of here," he said as he filled out a police report. "People are crazy. What are you going to save? $4 or $5? I guess to some people that's a lot of money."

Source: "Pumped Up Over Cheap Gas," from *The Arizona Republic,* January 22, 1995, p. B1. Used with permission. Permission does not imply endorsement.

The Arizona Republic/January 22, 1995

Commentary

Economics is the study of human behavior. How then does economics explain the rush to purchase cheap gas? Economists claim that decisions are the process of comparing costs and benefits. In this article, people have chosen to drive to the Circle K store and spend time in line in order to purchase 15 gallons of gasoline at a price of $.49. Thus, people looked at their costs of driving to the station and spending time in line and decided that these costs were less than the benefits they derived from the cheap gas. So let's look at this decision.

The usual price for gasoline at this time in this market was $1.09 a gallon. Thus, each gallon purchased at the cheap price, $.49, means a savings of $.60. Since 15 gallons could be purchased, the most one could save on the gas purchase would be $9.00.

Did the savings outweigh the costs?

At one station, 300 cars were in line. Since 12 cars were served each five minutes, the wait at that station was about 2 hours and 5 minutes. If one gallon of gas was consumed waiting in line and another gallon driving to and from the station, then the savings would be 13 gallons at $.60 or $7.80. Thus, it would seem that those people choosing to purchase the gas believed that more than 2 hours of their time was worth less than $7.80.

However, the time waiting was not the only possible cost of purchasing the gas. The story indicates that some people got into fights and another was in an accident. The possibility of a mishap could also be considered a cost. In addition, the wear and tear on the car from starting and stopping or idling could be considered. The frustration of waiting and in observing other people attempting to crowd or cheat in line could also be a cost. And, whatever else a person could have been doing for that 2 to 3 hours is a cost.

There might be benefits we haven't considered yet. For some people, the joy of being in a large group might be a benefit. These same people might drive anywhere that large groups form. For other people, the demonstration of how important cheap gas is, is the important point, not the money savings. These people are price shoppers—always on the lookout for the best price. For still others, getting out of the house with a good excuse and having some time for reading or reflection might be a benefit.

Whatever factors go into the calculation of costs and benefits, it seems that for many people, the benefits of the cheap gas outweighed the costs. John Fecther said that he was attempting to get out of there after seeing the long lines. John had made a comparison of costs and benefits, apparently assuming that there would be shorter lines. Once he altered his calculation of costs, he changed his mind. He said, "People are crazy. What are you going to save—$4 or $5? I guess that's a lot of money for some people." Is Mr. Fecther right? Was it the $4 or $5 savings that enticed people? Would Mr. Fecther have driven to another appliance store a mile or two away if he was shopping for a dishwasher and learned that he could save $4 or $5 at the other store? Probably not. Why then did he decide to go purchase the cheap gas, even thinking the lines would be shorter?

Working with Graphs

According to the old saying, one picture is worth a thousand words. If that maxim is correct, and, in addition, if producing a thousand words takes more time and effort than producing one picture, it is no wonder that economists rely so extensively on pictures. The pictures that economists use to explain concepts are called *graphs*. The purpose of this appendix is to explain how graphs are constructed and how to interpret them.

1. READING GRAPHS

The three kinds of graphs used by economists are shown in Figures 1, 2, and 3. Figure 1 is a *line graph*. It is the most commonly used type of graph in economics. Figure 2 is a *bar graph*. It is probably used more often in popular magazines than any other kind of graph. Figure 3 is a *pie graph,* or *pie chart*. Although it is less popular than the bar and line graphs, it appears often enough that you need to be familiar with it.

1.a. Relationships Between Variables

Figure 1 is a line graph showing the ratio of the median income of people who have completed four or more years of college to the median income of those who have completed just four years of high school. The line shows the value of a college education in terms of the additional income earned relative to the income earned without a college degree on a year-to-year basis. You can see that the premium for completing college has risen in recent years.

Figure 2 is a bar graph indicating the unemployment rate by educational attainment. The blue refers to high school dropouts, the red refers to those with four years of high school, and the green refers to those with four or more years of college. One set of bars is presented for males and one set for females. The bars are arranged in order, with the highest incidence of unemployment depicted first, the next highest second, and the lowest located third. This arrangement is made only for ease in reading and interpretation. The bars could be arranged in any order. The graph illustrates that unemployment strikes those with less education more than it does those with more education.

Figure 3 is a pie chart showing the percentage of the U.S. population completing various years of schooling. Unlike line and bar graphs, a pie chart is not actually a picture of a relationship between two variables. Instead, the pie represents the whole, 100 percent of the U.S. population, and the pieces of the pie represent parts

Figure 1

Ratio of Median Incomes of College- to High School–Educated Workers

Figure 1 is a line graph showing the ratio of the median income of people who have completed four or more years of college to the median income of those who completed four years of high school. The line shows the income premium for educational attainment, or the value of a college education in terms of income, from year to year. The rise in the line since about 1979 shows that the premium for completing college has risen. Source: *Statistical Abstract of the United States, 1996* (Washington, D.C.: U.S. Government Printing Office).

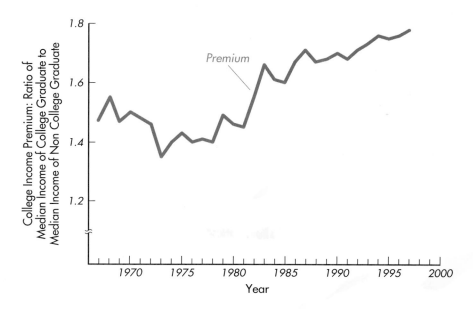

Figure 2

Unemployment and Education

Figure 2 is a bar graph indicating the unemployment rate by educational attainment. The blue refers to high school dropouts, the red refers to those with four years of high school, and the green refers to those with four or more years of college. One set of bars is presented for males and one set for females. The bars are arranged in order, with the highest incidence of unemployment shown first, the next highest second, and the lowest third. This arrangement is made only for ease in reading and interpretation. The bars could be arranged in any order. Source: U.S. Census Bureau; www.census.gov/population.

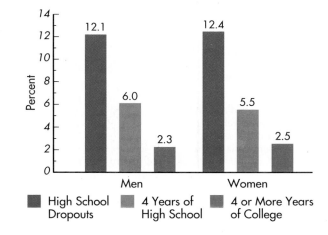

Figure 3

Educational Attainment

Figure 3 is a pie chart showing the percentage of the U.S. population completing various years of schooling. Unlike line and bar graphs, a pie chart is not actually a picture of a relationship between two variables. Instead, the pie represents the whole, 100 percent of the U.S. population, and the pieces of the pie represent parts of the whole—the percentage of the population completing one to four years of elementary school only, five to seven years of elementary school, and so on up to four or more years of college. Source: U.S. Census Bureau, Sept. 15, 2000; www.census.gov/population.

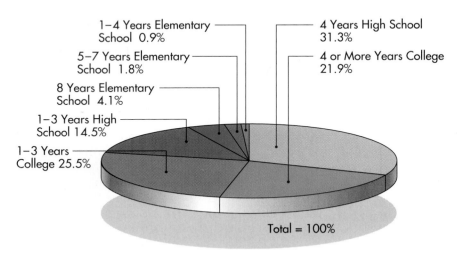

1–4 Years Elementary School 0.9%

5–7 Years Elementary School 1.8%

8 Years Elementary School 4.1%

1–3 Years High School 14.5%

1–3 Years College 25.5%

4 Years High School 31.3%

4 or More Years College 21.9%

Total = 100%

of the whole—the percentage of the population completing one to four years of elementary school only, five to seven years of elementary school, and so on, up to four or more years of college.

Because a pie chart does not show the relationship between variables, it is not as useful for explaining economic concepts as line and bar graphs. Line graphs are used more often than bar graphs to explain economic concepts.

1.b. Independent and Dependent Variables

independent variable: the variable whose value does not depend on the value of other variables

dependent variable: the variable whose value depends on the value of the independent variable

Most line and bar graphs involve just two variables, an **independent variable** and a **dependent variable.** An independent variable is one whose value does not depend on the values of other variables; a dependent variable, on the other hand, is one whose value does depend on the values of other variables. The value of the dependent variable is determined after the value of the independent variable is determined.

In Figure 2, the *independent* variable is the educational status of the man or woman, and the *dependent* variable is the incidence of unemployment (percentage of group that is unemployed). The incidence of unemployment depends on the educational attainment of the man or woman.

1.c. Direct and Inverse Relationships

If the value of the dependent variable increases as the value of the independent variable increases, the relationship between the two types of variables is called a **direct,**

18   Part One / Introduction to the Price System or **positive, relationship.** If the value of the dependent variable decreases as the value of the independent variable increases, the relationship between the two types of variables is called an **inverse,** or **negative, relationship.**

In Figure 2, unemployment and educational attainment are inversely, or negatively, related: as people acquire more education, they are less likely to be unemployed.

2. CONSTRUCTING A GRAPH

Let's now construct a graph. We will begin with a consideration of the horizontal and vertical axes, or lines, and then we will put the axes together. We are going to construct a *straight-line curve.* This sounds contradictory, but it is common terminology. Economists often refer to the demand or supply *curve,* and that curve may be a straight line.

2.a. The Axes

It is important to understand how the *axes* (the horizontal and vertical lines) are used and what they measure. Let's begin with the horizontal axis, the line running across the page in a horizontal direction. Notice in Figure 4(a) that the line is divided into equal segments. Each point on the line represents a quantity, or the value of the variables being measured. For example, each segment could represent one year or 10,000 pounds of diamonds or some other value. Whatever is measured, the value increases from left to right, beginning with negative values, going on to zero, which is called the *origin,* and then moving on to positive numbers.

A number line in the vertical direction can be constructed as well, also shown in Figure 4(a). Zero is the origin, and the numbers increase from bottom to top. Like the horizontal axis, the vertical axis is divided into equal segments; the distance between 0 and 10 is the same as the distance between 0 and −10, between 10 and 20, and so on.

In most cases, the variable measured along the horizontal axis is the independent variable. This isn't always true in economics, however. Economists often measure the independent variable on the vertical axis. Do not assume that the variable on the horizontal axis is independent and the variable on the vertical axis is dependent.

Putting the horizontal and vertical lines together lets us express relationships between two variables graphically. The axes cross, or intersect, at their origins, as shown in Figure 4(a). From the common origin, movements to the right and up, in the area—called a quadrant—marked I, are combinations of positive numbers; movements to the left and down, in quadrant III, are combinations of negative numbers; movements to the right and down, in quadrant IV, are negative values on the vertical axis and positive values on the horizontal axis; and movements to the left and up, in quadrant II, are positive values on the vertical axis and negative values on the horizontal axis.

Economic data are typically positive numbers: the unemployment rate, the inflation rate, the price of something, the quantity of something produced or sold, and so on. Because economic data are usually positive numbers, the only part of the coordinate system that usually comes into play in economics is the upper right portion, quadrant I. That is why economists may simply sketch a vertical line down to the origin and then extend a horizontal line out to the right, as shown in Figure 4(b). Once in a while, economic data are negative—for instance, profit is negative when costs exceed revenues. When data are negative, quadrants II, III, and IV of the coordinate system could be used.

Figure 4

The Axes, the Coordinate System, and the Positive Quadrant

Figure 4(a) shows the vertical and horizontal axes. The horizontal axis has an origin, measured as zero, in the middle. Negative numbers are to the left of zero, positive numbers to the right. The vertical axis also has an origin in the middle. Positive numbers are above the origin, negative numbers below. The horizontal and vertical axes together show the entire coordinate system.

Positive numbers are in quadrant I, negative numbers in quadrant III, and combinations of negative and positive numbers in quadrants II and IV.

Figure 4(b) shows only the positive quadrant. Because most economic data are positive, often only the upper right quadrant, the positive quadrant, of the coordinate system is used.

(a) The Coordinate System

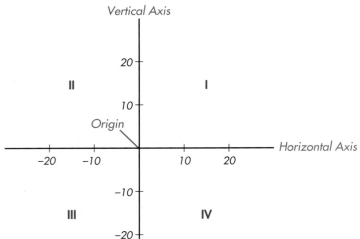

(b) The Positive Quadrant

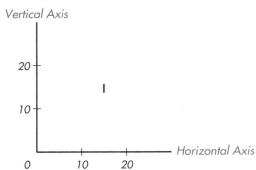

2.b. Constructing a Graph from a Table

Now that you are familiar with the axes, that is, the coordinate system, you are ready to construct a graph using the data in the table in Figure 5. The table lists a series of possible price levels for a personal computer (PC) and the corresponding number of PCs people choose to purchase. The data are only hypothetical; they are not drawn from actual cases.

The information given in the table is graphed in Figure 5. We begin by marking off and labeling the axes. The vertical axis is the list of possible price levels. We begin at zero and move up the axis at equal increments of $1,000. The horizontal axis is the number of PCs sold. We begin at zero and move out the axis at equal increments of 1,000 PCs. According to the information presented in the table, if the price is $10,000, no one buys a PC. The combination of $10,000 and 0 PCs is point *A* on the graph. To plot this point, find the quantity zero on the horizontal axis (it is at the origin), and then move up the vertical axis from zero to a price level of $10,000. (Note that we have measured the units in the table and on the graph in thousands.) At a price of $9,000, there are 1,000 PCs purchased. To plot the combination

Figure 5

The information given in the table is graphed below. We begin by marking off and labeling the axes. The vertical axis is the list of possible price levels. The horizontal axis is the number of PCs purchased. Beginning at zero, the axes are marked at equal increments of 1,000. According to the information presented in the table, if the price level is $10,000, no PCs are purchased. The combination of $10,000 and 0 PCs is point *A* on the graph. At a price of $9,000, there are 1,000 PCs purchased. This is point *B*. The final step in constructing a line graph is to connect the points that are plotted. When the points are connected, the straight line slanting downward shows the relationship between the price of PCs and the number of PCs purchased.

Point	Price per PC (thousands of dollars)	Number of PCs Purchased (thousands)
A	$10	0
B	9	1
C	8	2
D	7	3
E	6	4
F	5	5
G	4	6
H	3	7
I	2	8
J	1	9
K	0	10

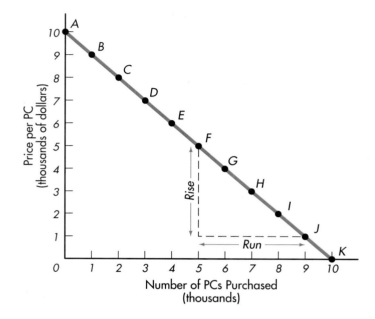

of $9,000 and 1,000 PCs, find 1,000 units on the horizontal axis and then measure up from there to a price of $9,000. This is point *B*. Point *C* represents a price of $8,000 and 2,000 PCs. Point *D* represents a price of $7,000 and 3,000 PCs. Each combination of price and PCs purchased listed in the table is plotted in Figure 5.

The final step in constructing a line graph is to connect the points that are plotted. When the points are connected, the straight line slanting downward from left to right in Figure 5 is obtained. It shows the relationship between the price of PCs and the number of PCs purchased.

2.c. Interpreting Points on a Graph

Let's use Figure 5 to demonstrate how points on a graph may be interpreted. Suppose the current price of a PC is $6,000. Are you able to tell how many PCs are being purchased at this price? By tracing that price level from the vertical axis over to the curve and then down to the horizontal axis, you find that 4,000 PCs are purchased. You can also find what happens to the number purchased if the price falls from $6,000 to $5,000. By tracing the price from $5,000 to the curve and then down to the horizontal axis, you discover that 5,000 PCs are purchased. Thus, according to the graph, a decrease in the price from $6,000 to $5,000 results in 1,000 more PCs being purchased.

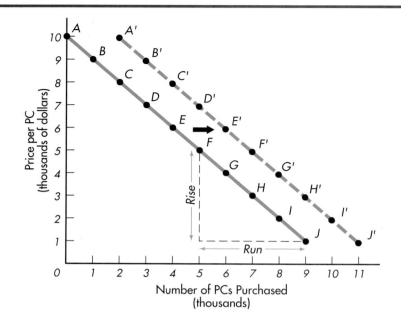

Figure 6

Shift of Curve

An increase in income allows more people to purchase PCs at each price. At a price of $8,000, for instance, 4,000 PCs are purchased rather than 2,000.

2.d. Shifts of Curves

Graphs can be used to illustrate the effects of a change in a variable not represented on the graph. For instance, the curve drawn in Figure 5 shows the relationship between the price of PCs and the number of PCs purchased. When this curve was drawn, the only two variables that were allowed to change were the price and the number of computers. However, it is likely that people's incomes determine their reaction to the price of computers as well. An increase in income would enable more people to purchase computers. Thus, at every price more computers would be purchased. How would this be represented? As an outward shift of the curve, from points *A, B, C,* etc., to *A', B', C',* etc., as shown in Figure 6.

Following the shift of the curve, we can see that more PCs are purchased at each price than was the case prior to the income increase. For instance, at a price of $8,000 the increased income allows 4,000 PCs to be purchased rather than 2,000. The important point to note is that if some variable that influences the relationship shown in a curve or line graph changes, then the entire curve or line changes—that is, it shifts.

3. SLOPES

A curve may represent an inverse, or negative, relationship or a direct, or positive, relationship. The slope of the curve reveals the kind of relationship that exists between two variables.

3.a. Positive and Negative Slopes

slope: the steepness of a curve, measured as the ratio of the rise to the run

The **slope** of a curve is its steepness, the rate at which the value of a variable measured on the vertical axis changes with respect to a given change in the value of the variable measured on the horizontal axis. If the value of a variable measured on one axis goes up when the value of the variable measured on the other axis goes down, the variables have an inverse (or negative) relationship. If the values of the variables rise or fall together, the variables have a direct (or positive) relationship. Inverse relationships are represented by curves that run downward from left to right; direct relationships by curves that run upward from left to right.

Slope is calculated by measuring the amount by which the variable on the vertical axis changes and dividing that figure by the amount by which the variable on the horizontal axis changes. The vertical change is called the *rise,* and the horizontal change is called the *run.* Slope is referred to as the *rise over the run:*

$$\text{Slope} = \frac{\text{rise}}{\text{run}}$$

The slope of any inverse relationship is negative. The slope of any direct relationship is positive.

Let's calculate the slope of the curve in Figure 5. Price (P) is measured on the vertical axis, and quantity of PCs purchased (Q) is measured on the horizontal axis. The rise is the change in price (ΔP), the change in the value of the variable measured on the vertical axis. The run is the change in quantity of PCs purchased (ΔQ), the change in the value of the variable measured on the horizontal axis. The symbol Δ means "change in"; it is the Greek letter delta, so ΔP means "change in P" and ΔQ means "change in Q." Remember that slope equals the rise over the run. Thus the equation for the slope of the straight-line curve running downward from left to right in Figure 5 is

$$\text{Slope} = \frac{\Delta P}{\Delta Q}$$

As the price (P) declines, the number of PCs purchased (Q) increases. The rise is negative, and the run is positive. Thus, the slope is a negative value.

The slope is the same anywhere along a straight line. Thus, it does not matter where we calculate the changes along the vertical and horizontal axes. For instance, from 0 to 9,000 on the horizontal axis—a change of 9,000—the vertical change is a negative $9,000 (from $10,000 down to $1,000). Thus, the rise over the run is −9,000/9,000, or −1. Similarly, from 5,000 to 9,000 in the horizontal direction, the corresponding rise is $5,000 to $1,000, or −$4,000, so that the rise over the run is −4,000/4,000, or −1.

Remember that direct, or positive, relationships between variables are represented by lines that run upward from left to right. These lines have positive slopes. Figure 7 is a graph showing the number of PCs that producers offer for sale at various price levels. The curve represents the relationship between the two variables, number of PCs offered for sale and price. It shows that as price rises, so does the number of PCs offered for sale. The slope of the curve is positive. The change in the rise (the vertical direction) that comes with an increase in the run (the horizontal direction) is positive. Because the graph is a straight line, you can measure the rise and run using any two points along the curve and the slope will be the same. We find the slope by calculating the rise that accompanies the run. Moving from 0 to 4,000 PCs gives us a run of 4,000. Looking at the curve, we see that the corresponding rise is 2,000. Thus, the rise over the run is 2,000/4,000, or .50.

3.b. Equations

Graphs and equations can be used to illustrate the same topics. Some people prefer to use equations rather than graphs, or both equations and graphs, to explain a

Figure 7

Personal Computers Offered for Sale and Price

Figure 7 is a graph showing the number of PCs offered for sale at various price levels. The curve shows that as price rises, so does the number of PCs purchased. We move from 0 to 4,000, giving us a run of 4,000. The corresponding rise is 2,000. Thus, the rise over the run is 2,000/4,000, or .50.

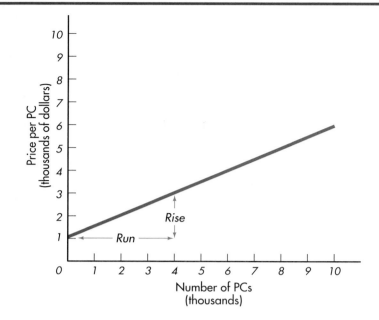

concept. Since a few equations are used in this book, we need to briefly discuss how they demonstrate the same things as a graph.

The general equation of a straight line has the form $Y = a + bX$, where Y is the dependent variable, X is the independent variable, a defines the intercept (the value of Y when $X = 0$), and b is the slope. If b is negative, the line slopes downward. If b is positive, the line slopes upward. In the case of Figure 5, the price, P, is the independent variable, and the number of PCs purchased, Q, is the dependent variable. The number of PCs purchased depends on the price. In equation form, substituting Q for Y and P for X, the relationship between price and PCs purchased is $Q = a + bP$. We already know that the slope, b, is negative. For each $1,000 decline in price, 1,000 more PCs are purchased. The slope, b, is -1. The value of a represents the value of Q when P is zero. When the price is zero, 10,000 PCs are purchased. Thus, $a = 10,000$. The equation of Figure 5 is $Q = 10,000 - 1P$.

The equation can be used to tell us how many PCs will be purchased at any given price. Suppose the price is $P = $4,000$. Substituting $4,000 for P in the equation yields

$$Q = 10,000 - 1(4,000)$$
$$= 6,000$$

SUMMARY

1. There are three commonly used types of graphs: the line graph, the bar graph, and the pie chart. *§1.a*

2. An independent variable is a variable whose value does not depend on the values of other variables. The values of a dependent variable do depend on the values of other variables. *§1.b*

3. A direct, or positive, relationship occurs when the value of the dependent variable increases as the value of the independent variable increases. An indirect, or negative, relationship occurs when the value of the dependent variable decreases as the value of the independent variable increases. *§1.c*

4. Most economic data are positive numbers, so often only the upper right quadrant of the coordinate system is used in economics. *§2.a*

5. A curve shifts when a variable that affects the dependent variable and is not measured on the axes changes.

6. The slope of a curve is the rise over the run: the change in the variable measured on the vertical axis over the corresponding change in the variable measured on the horizontal axis. *§3.a*

7. The slope of a straight-line curve is the same at all points along the curve. *§3.a*

8. The equation of a straight line has the general form $Y = a + bX$, where Y is the dependent variable, X the independent variable, a the value of Y when X equals zero, and b the slope. *§3.b*

KEY TERMS

independent variable *§1.b*

dependent variable *§1.b*

direct, or positive, relationship *§1.c*

inverse, or negative, relationship *§1.c*

slope *§3.a*

EXERCISES

1. On the right are two sets of figures: the total quantity of Mexican pesos (new pesos) in circulation (the total amount of Mexican money available) and the peso price of a dollar (how many pesos are needed to purchase one dollar). Values are given for the years 1987 through 1999 for each variable.

   a. Plot each variable by measuring time (years) on the horizontal axis and, in the first graph, pesos in circulation on the vertical axis and, in the second graph, peso price of a dollar on the vertical axis.
   b. Plot the combinations of variables by measuring pesos in circulation on the horizontal axis and peso prices of a dollar on the vertical axis.
   c. In each of the graphs in parts a and b, what are the dependent and independent variables?
   d. In each of the graphs in parts a and b, indicate whether the relationship between the dependent and independent variables is direct or inverse.

Year	Pesos in Circulation (billions)	Peso Price of a Dollar
1987	12,627	1.3782
1988	21,191	2.2731
1989	29,087	2.4615
1990	47,439	2.8126
1991	106,227	3.0184
1992	122,220	3.0949
1993	143,902	3.1156
1994	145,429	3.3751
1995	150,572	6.4194
1996	206,180	7.5994
1997	276,281	8.5850
1998	331,537	9.9680
1999	371,322	9.4270

2. Plot the data listed on the right:

   a. Use price as the vertical axis and quantity as the horizontal axis and plot the first two columns.
   b. Show what quantity is sold when the price is $550.
   c. Directly below the graph in part a, plot the data in columns 2 and 3. Use total revenue as the vertical axis and quantity as the horizontal axis.
   d. What is total revenue when the price is $550? Will total revenue increase or decrease when the price is lowered?

Price	Quantity Sold	Total Revenue
$1,000	200	200,000
900	400	360,000
800	600	480,000
700	800	560,000
600	1,000	600,000
500	1,200	600,000
400	1,400	560,000
300	1,600	480,000
200	1,800	360,000
100	2,000	200,000

Chapter 2

Choice, Opportunity Costs, and Specialization

1. What are opportunity costs? Are they part of the economic way of thinking?

2. What is a production possibilities curve?

3. Why does specialization occur?

4. What are the benefits of trade?

Preview

I n the previous chapter we learned that scarcity forces people to make choices. There are costs involved in any choice. As the old saying goes, "There is no free lunch." In every choice, alternatives are forgone, or sacrificed.

All choices have both costs and benefits. This chapter explains how to calculate these costs and benefits and what they imply for the behavior of individuals and society as a whole. ■

1. OPPORTUNITY COSTS

A choice is simply a comparison of alternatives: to attend college or not to attend college, to change jobs or not to change jobs, to purchase a new car or to keep the old one. An individual compares the costs and benefits of each option and chooses the option expected to provide the most happiness or net benefit. Of course, when one option is chosen, the benefits of the alternatives are forgone. You choose not to attend college and you forgo the benefits of attending college; you buy a new car and forgo the benefits of having the money to use in other ways. *Economists refer to the forgone opportunities or forgone benefits of the next best alternative as* **opportunity costs**—the highest-valued alternative that must be forgone when a choice is made.

opportunity costs: the highest-valued alternative that must be forgone when a choice is made

The cost of any item or activity includes the opportunity cost involved in its purchase.

Opportunity costs are part of every decision and activity. Your opportunity costs of reading this book are whatever else you could be doing—perhaps watching TV, talking with friends, working, or listening to music. Your opportunity costs of attending college are whatever else you could be doing—perhaps working full-time or traveling around the world. Each choice means giving up something else.

1.a. The Opportunity Cost of Going to College

Suppose you decided to attend a college where the tuition and other expenses add up to $4,290 per year. Are these your total costs of attending college? If you answer yes, you are ignoring opportunity costs. Remember that you must account for forgone opportunities. If instead of going to college you could have worked full-time and earned $20,800, the actual cost of college is the $4,290 of direct expenses plus the $20,800 of forgone salary, or $25,090. This calculation assumes you would not work part-time or during the summer.

1.b. Tradeoffs and Decisions at the Margin

Life is a continuous sequence of decisions, and every single decision involves choosing one thing over another or trading off something for something else. A **tradeoff** means giving up one good or activity in order to obtain some other good or activity. Each term you must decide whether to register for college or not. You could work full-time and not attend college, attend college and not work, or work part-time and attend college. The time you devote to college will decrease as you devote more time to work. You trade off hours spent at work for hours spent in college; in other words, you compare the benefits you think you will get from going to college this term with the costs of college this term. Once you decide to go to college, you must decide how much to study. Once you sit down and begin studying, you are deciding whether to continue studying or to do something else. "What should I do for the next hour, study or watch TV?" The "next" hour is the additional, or what economists call the marginal, hour. Making choices involves comparing the **marginal costs** and the **marginal benefits.** *Marginal* means "change," so a decision involves the comparison of a change in benefits and a change in costs.

tradeoff: the giving up of one good or activity in order to obtain some other good or activity

marginal cost: additional cost

marginal benefit: additional benefit

1.c. The Production Possibilities Curve

Societies, like individuals, face scarcities and must make choices. And societies, like individuals, forgo opportunities each time they make a particular choice and must compare the marginal costs and marginal benefits of each alternative.

The tradeoffs facing a society can be illustrated in a graph known as the **production possibilities curve (PPC).** The production possibilities curve shows the maximum quantity of goods and services that can be produced using limited resources to

production possibilities curve (PPC): a graphical representation showing the maximum quantity of goods and services that can be produced using limited resources to the fullest extent possible

the fullest extent possible. Figure 1 shows a production possibilities curve based on the information (see the table in Figure 1) about the production of defense goods and services and nondefense goods and services by a nation such as the United States. Defense goods and services include guns, ships, bombs, personnel, and so forth, that are used for national defense. Nondefense goods and services include education, housing, and food that are not used for national defense. All societies allocate their scarce resources in order to produce some combination of defense and nondefense goods and services. Because resources are scarce, a nation cannot produce as much of everything as it wants. When it produces more health care, it must forgo the production of education or automobiles; when it devotes more of its resources to the military area, fewer are available to devote to health care.

If we could draw or even visualize many dimensions, we could draw a PPC that had a specific good measured along the axis in each dimension. Since we can't, we typically just draw a two-dimensional graph and thus can have just two classes of goods.

Figure 1

The Production Possibilities Curve

With a limited amount of resources, only certain combinations of defense and nondefense goods and services can be produced. The maximum amounts that can be produced, given various tradeoffs, are represented by points A_1 through E_1. Point F_1 lies inside the curve and represents the underutilization of resources. More of one type of goods and less of another could be produced, or more of both types could be produced. Point G_1 represents an impossible combination. There are insufficient resources to produce quantities lying beyond the curve.

Point	Defense Goods and Services (millions of units)	Nondefense Goods and Services (millions of units)
A_1	200	0
B_1	175	75
C_1	130	125
D_1	70	150
E_1	0	160
F_1	130	25
G_1	200	75

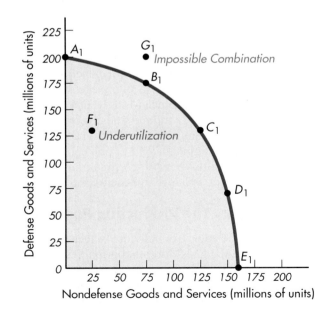

In Figure 1 the two classes are defense-type goods and nondefense-type goods. But we could just as easily draw a PPC for health care and all other goods or for education and all other goods. These PPCs would look like Figure 1 except that the axes would measure units of health care and other goods or units of education and other goods.

A production possibilities curve shows that more of one type of good can be produced only by reducing the quantity of other types of goods that are produced; it shows that a society has scarce resources; and it shows what the marginal costs and marginal benefits of alternative decisions are. In what way does the PPC show these things? We can answer that question by looking more carefully at Figure 1. In this figure, units of defense goods and services are measured on the vertical axis; units of nondefense goods and services on the horizontal axis. If all resources are allocated to producing defense goods and services, then 200 million units can be produced, but the production of nondefense goods and services will cease. The combination of 200 million units of defense goods and services and 0 units of nondefense goods and services is point A_1, a point on the vertical axis. At 175 million units of defense goods and services, 75 million units of nondefense goods and services can be produced (point B_1). Point C_1 represents 125 million units of nondefense goods and services and 130 million units of defense goods. Point D_1 represents 150 million units of nondefense goods and services and 70 million units of defense goods and services. Point E_1, a point on the horizontal axis, shows the combination of no production of defense goods and services and 160 million units of nondefense goods and services.

The production possibilities curve represents the maximum, or the outer limit, of what can be produced.

The production possibilities curve shows the *maximum* output that can be produced with a limited quantity and quality of resources. The PPC is a picture of the tradeoffs facing society. Only one combination of goods and services can be produced at any one time. All other combinations are forgone.

1.c.1. Points Inside the Production Possibilities Curve
Suppose a nation produces 130 million units of defense goods and services and 25 million units of nondefense goods and services. That combination, Point F_1 in Figure 1, lies inside the production possibilities curve. A point lying inside the production possibilities curve indicates that resources are not being fully or efficiently used. If the existing work force is employed only 20 hours per week, it is not being fully used. If two workers are used when one would be sufficient—say, two people in each Domino's Pizza delivery car—then resources are not being used efficiently. If there are resources available for use, society can move from point F_1 to a point on the PPC, such as point C_1. The move would gain 100 million units of nondefense goods and services with no loss of defense goods and services.

1.c.2. Points Outside the Production Possibilities Curve
Point G_1 in Figure 1 represents the production of 200 million units of defense goods and services and 75 units of nondefense goods and services. Point G_1, however, represents the use of more resources than are available—it lies outside the production possibilities curve. Unless more resources can be obtained and/or the quality of resources improved so that the nation can produce more with the same quantity of resources, there is no way the society can currently produce 200 million units of defense goods and 75 million units of nondefense goods.

1.c.3. Shifts of the Production Possibilities Curve
If a nation obtains more resources, points outside its current production possibilities curve become attainable. Suppose a country discovers new sources of oil within its borders and is able to greatly increase its production of oil. Greater oil supplies would enable the country to increase production of all types of goods and services.

Figure 2 shows the production possibilities curve before (PPC_1) and after (PPC_2) the discovery of oil. PPC_1 is based on the data given in the table in Figure 1. PPC_2 is based on the data given in the table in Figure 2, which shows the increase in production of goods and services that results from the increase in oil supplies. The first combination of goods and services on PPC_2, point A_2, is 220 million units of defense goods and 0 units of nondefense goods. The second point, B_2, is a combination of 200 million units of defense goods and 75 million units of nondefense goods. C_2 through F_2 are the combinations shown in the table in Figure 2. Connecting these points yields the bowed-out curve, PPC_2. Because of the availability of new supplies of oil, the nation is able to increase production of all goods, as shown by the *shift* from PPC_1 to PPC_2. A comparison of the two curves shows that more goods and services for both defense and nondefense are possible along PPC_2 than along PPC_1.

The outward shift of the PPC can be the result of an increase in the quantity of resources, but it also can occur because the quality of resources improves. For

Figure 2

A Shift of the Production Possibilities Curve

Whenever everything else is not constant, the curve shifts. In this case, an increase in the quantity of a resource enables the society to produce more of both types of goods. The curve shifts out, away from the origin.

Combination	Defense Goods and Services (millions of units)	Nondefense Goods and Services (millions of units)
A_2	220	0
B_2	200	75
C_2	175	125
D_2	130	150
E_2	70	160
F_2	0	165

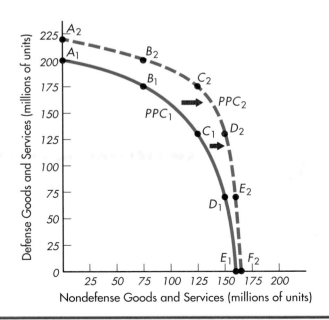

Part One / Introduction to the Price System

instance, a technological breakthrough could conceivably improve the way that communication occurs, thereby requiring fewer people and machines and less time to produce the same quantity and quality of goods. The work force could become more literate, thereby requiring less time to produce the same quantity and quality of goods. Each of these quality improvements in resources could lead to an outward shift of the PPC.

The outward shift of the PPC illustrates that the capacity, or potential, of the economy has grown. However, being able to produce more of all goods doesn't mean that a society will do that. A society might produce at a point on the PPC, inside the PPC, or even attempt to produce at a point outside the PPC.

Knowing that the opportunity costs include the entire PPC plus the forgone production of those resources not fully or efficiently used, why would a society produce at a point inside the PPC? Almost as puzzling is why a society might try to produce beyond its capacity, something it cannot sustain, when the opportunity costs include not only the entire PPC but the possible damage to the society's "internal organs" due to overheating. The answers to these questions are far from straightforward; in fact, a significant part of macroeconomics is devoted to answering them.

RECAP

1. Opportunity costs are the benefits that are forgone due to a choice. When you choose one thing, you must give up—forgo—others.
2. Opportunity costs are an individual concept but can be used to demonstrate scarcity and choice for a society as a whole.
3. The production possibilities curve represents all combinations of goods and services that can be produced using limited resources efficiently to their full capabilities.
4. Points inside the production possibilities curve represent the underutilization or inefficient use of resources—more goods and services could be produced by using the limited resources more fully or efficiently.
5. Points outside the production possibilities curve represent combinations of goods and services that are unattainable given the limitation of resources. More resources would have to be obtained, or a more efficient means of production through the development of technology or innovative management techniques would have to be discovered, to produce quantities of goods and services outside the current production possibilities curve.

2. SPECIALIZATION AND TRADE

No matter which combination of goods and services a society chooses to produce, other combinations of goods are forgone. The PPC illustrates what these forgone combinations are.

2.a. Marginal Opportunity Cost

The shape of the PPC illustrates the ease with which resources can be transferred from one activity to another. If it becomes increasingly more difficult or costly to move resources from one activity to another, the PPC will have the bowed-out shape of Figure 1. With each successive increase in the production of nondefense goods, we see that some amount of defense goods has to be given up. The incremental amounts of defense production given up with each increase in the production of non-defense goods are known as marginal opportunity costs. **Marginal opportunity cost** is the amount of one good or service that must be given up to obtain one additional unit of another good or service, no matter how many units are being produced.

The bowed-out shape shows that for each additional nondefense good, more and more defense goods have to be forgone. According to the table and graph in Figure 3, we see that moving from point A to point B on the PPC means increasing nondefense production from 0 to 25 million units and decreasing defense production from 200 million to 195 million units, resulting in a marginal opportunity

marginal opportunity cost: the amount of one good or service that must be given up to obtain one additional unit of another good or service, no matter how many units are being produced

---

Figure 3

The Production Possibilities Curve and Marginal Opportunity Costs

With a limited amount of resources, only certain combinations of defense and nondefense goods and services can be produced. The maximum amounts that can be produced are represented by points A through H. With each increase of non-defense production, marginal opportunity costs increase. This occurs as a result of specialization. The first resources switched from defense to nondefense production are those that are least specialized in the production of defense goods. But as more and more nondefense goods are produced, the more specialized resources have to be switched as well. This means higher opportunity costs; increasing amounts of defense goods have to be forgone.

Combination	Defense Goods and Services (millions of units)	Marginal Opportunity Costs (defense units forgone per 25 units of nondefense units gained)	Nondefense Goods and Services (millions of units)
A	220		0
		5	
B	195		25
		7	
C	188		50
		13	
D	175		75
		20	
E	155		100
		30	
F	125		125
		50	
G	75		150
		75	
H	0		160

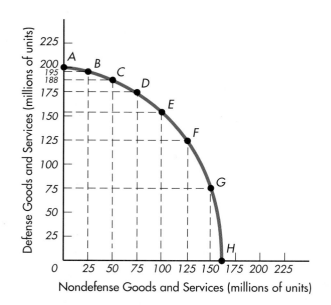

---

cost of 5 million units of defense goods and services for each 25 million units of nondefense goods and services. Moving from point *B* to point *C* means increasing nondefense production from 25 to 50 million units, decreasing defense production from 195 to 188 million units and creating a marginal opportunity cost of 7 million units. Moving from point *C* to point *D* causes an increase in nondefense production from 50 to 75 million units, a decrease in defense production from 188 million to 175 million units, and a marginal opportunity cost of 13 million units. As you can see from the table for Figure 3, marginal opportunity costs increase with each successive increase of nondefense production. In other words, it gets more and more costly to produce nondefense goods. The increased marginal opportunity costs occur as a result of specialization. The first resources switched from defense to nondefense production are those that are least specialized in the production of defense goods. Switching these resources is less costly (less has to be given up) than switching the specialists. An accountant can do accounting in either defense- or nondefense-related industries equally well; an expert rocket physicist cannot work as efficiently in health care as in the defense area. But as more and more nondefense goods are produced, the more specialized resources have to be switched as well. This means higher opportunity costs, and increasing amounts of defense goods have to be forgone.

2.b. Specialize Where Opportunity Costs Are Lowest

3. Why does specialization occur?

Individuals, firms, and nations select the option with the lowest opportunity costs.

Few of us are jacks-of-all-trades. How do we decide where to devote our energies? The answer is to *specialize in those activities that require us to give up the smallest amount of other things*; in other words, specialize where costs are lowest. A plumber does plumbing and leaves teaching to the teachers. The teacher teaches and leaves electrical work to the electrician. A country such as Grenada, which has abundant rich land suitable for the cultivation and production of nutmeg and other spices, specializes in spice production. If we specialize, however, how do we get the other things we want? The answer is that we trade, or exchange goods and services.

2.b.1. Trade By specializing in activities in which opportunity costs are lowest and then trading, each country or individual will end up with more than if each tried to produce everything. Consider a simple hypothetical example, as given in Figure 4, which concerns two countries, Haiti and the Dominican Republic, that share an island. Assume Haiti and the Dominican Republic must decide how to allocate their resources between food production and health care. Haiti's daily production possibilities curve is plotted using the data in columns 2 and 3 of the table. If Haiti devotes all of its resources to health care, then it would be able to provide 1,000 people adequate care each day but would have no resources with which to produce food. If it devotes half of its available resources to each activity, then it would provide 500 people adequate health care and produce 7 tons of food. Devoting all of its resources to food production would mean that Haiti could produce 10 tons of food but would have no health care. The Dominican Republic's production possibilities curve is plotted using the data in columns 4 and 5 of the table. If the Dominican Republic devotes all of its resources to health care, it could provide adequate care to 500 people daily but would be unable to produce any food. If it devotes half of its resources to each activity then it could provide 300 people health care and produce 5 tons of food; and if it devotes all of its resources to food production, it could produce 10 tons of food but no health care.

Suppose that Haiti and the Dominican Republic each want 500 people per day provided adequate health care. By itself, the Dominican Republic would be unable

Figure 4

The Benefits of Trade

The trade point of providing health care to 500 people and 2 tons of food is beyond the Dominican Republic's PPC; similarly, the trade point of providing health care to 500 people and 8 tons of food is beyond Haiti's PPC. However, through specialization and trade, these points are achieved by the two nations.

Allocation of Resources to Health Care	Haiti Health Care (no. of people provided care)	Food (tons)	Dominican Republic Health Care (no. of people provided care)	Food (tons)
100%	1,000	0	500	0
50	500	7	300	5
0	0	10	0	10

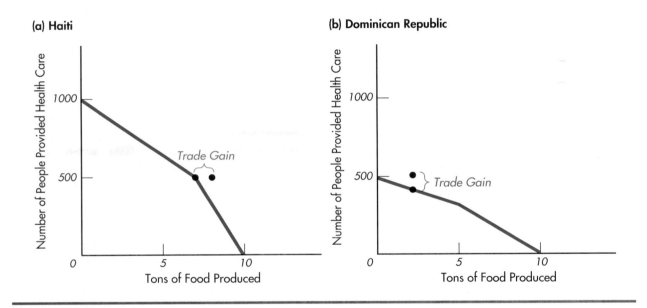

(a) Haiti

Trade Gain

(b) Dominican Republic

Trade Gain

to grow any food if it devoted resources to health care for 500 people. However, if the Dominican Republic and Haiti could agree to some type of exchange, perhaps the Dominican Republic could get some food and give the 500 people the health care. But who produces what? The answer depends on opportunity costs. If the Dominican Republic decides to provide health care to 500 people, it must forgo 10 tons of food; Haiti, on the other hand, must forgo only 3 tons of food if it decides to provide health care to 500 people. Haiti's opportunity cost for devoting its resources to providing 500 people health care, 3 tons of food, is lower than the Dominican Republic's, 10 tons. Conversely, if the Dominican Republic produces 10 tons of food, it forgoes providing health care for only 500 people while Haiti forgoes health care for 1,000 people. Clearly, the Dominican Republic's opportunity costs of producing food are lower than Haiti's.

Given the differences in opportunity costs, it would make sense for Haiti to devote its resources to health care and for the Dominican Republic to devote its resources to food production. In this case, Haiti would provide 1,000 people health care and produce no food and the Dominican Republic would produce 10 tons of food but no health care. The two nations would then trade. The Dominican Republic might give 8 tons of food to Haiti in exchange for health care for 500 people. Under this scheme, where each country gets health care for 500 people, the Dominican Republic would be better off by the 2 tons of food it would also get, while Haiti would be better off by the 8 rather than 7 tons of food it would get if it provided the 500 people health care using its own resources. Each is made better off by specialization and trade.

Specialization and trade enable nations to acquire combinations of goods that lie beyond their own resource capabilities. This is shown in Figure 4: the trade point of 500 people being provided health care and 2 tons of food is beyond the Dominican Republic's PPC. Similarly, the trade point of 500 people being provided health care and 8 tons of food is beyond Haiti's PPC. The same result applies to individuals and firms. Even though one person, one firm, or one nation is limited to the combinations of goods it can produce using its own resources along or inside its own PPC, through specialization and trade more goods can be acquired. This is why people, firms, and nations trade; this is why there are buyers and sellers.

2.c. Comparative Advantage

We have seen that the choice of which area or activity to specialize in is made on the basis of opportunity costs. Economists refer to the ability of one person or nation to do something with a lower opportunity cost than another as **comparative advantage.** In the example shown in Figure 4, the Dominican Republic had a comparative advantage in food production and Haiti had a comparative advantage in health-care provision. Devoting all resources to health care, Haiti can provide 1,000 people health care while the Dominican Republic can provide only 500 people health care. Devoting all resources to food production, both Haiti and the Dominican Republic can produce 10 tons of food. Clearly, Haiti is better at health care and no worse at food production. Haiti's comparative advantage is in producing health care—it gives up three tons of food for providing 500 people health care while the Dominican Republic gives up ten tons of food for providing 500 people health care. Conversely, the Dominican Republic has a comparative advantage in food production. It gives up providing 500 people health care if it produces ten tons of food while Haiti gives up providing 1,000 people health care if it produces ten tons of food. Haiti has a *comparative advantage* in health care and the Dominican Republic has a *comparative advantage* in food production. It is the relative amount given up not the absolute amount that can be produced that determines comparative advantage. Even if Haiti could produce eleven tons of food while the Dominican Republic could produce only ten, the Dominican Republic's comparative advantage would be in food production.

Comparative advantage applies to every case of trade or exchange. You may be better at both computer programming and literature than your roommate, but you may be much better at computer programming and only slightly better at literature. You, then, have a comparative advantage in computers. Your roommate has a comparative advantage as well, in literature. Remember, comparative advantage depends on opportunity costs. Just because you are better than your roommate at both

comparative advantage: the ability to produce a good or service at a lower opportunity cost than someone else

The fruit of the prickly pear cactus is popular in salads and drinks. Recently, the extract from the cactus leaves has been found to relieve some of the symptoms of diabetes. Physicians in Mexico and Japan prescribe the extract as a substitute for insulin in some cases and as an enhancement to insulin in others. Though the prickly pear cactus grows in the southwestern United States as well, the harvesting of the cacti occurs mainly in Mexico because most of the prickly pear cactus forests are in Mexico, and the labor-intensive harvesting process is less costly in Mexico than it would be in the United States. Mexico has a comparative advantage in the harvesting of the cacti.

activities, you do not have the same opportunity costs in both. Like Haiti and the Dominican Republic, you and your roommate are better off specializing and then trading (helping each other) than if both of you do all the studying all by yourselves. You both get better grades and have more time to devote to other activities.

2.d. Specialization and Trade Occur Everywhere

Each of us will specialize in some activity, earn an income, and then trade our output (or income) for other goods and services we want. Specialization and trade ensure that we are better off than doing everything ourselves. *Specialization according to comparative advantage followed by trade allows everyone to acquire more of the goods they want.*

4. What are the benefits of trade?

Individuals specialize in the activity in which their opportunity costs are lowest.

RECAP

1. Marginal opportunity cost is the amount of one good or service that must be given up to obtain one additional unit of another good or service.
2. The rule of specialization is: the individual (firm, region, or nation) will specialize in the production of the good or service that has the lowest opportunity cost.
3. Comparative advantage exists whenever one person (firm, nation) can do something with lower opportunity costs than some other individual (firm, nation) can.
4. Specialization and trade enable individuals, firms, and nations to get more than they could without specialization and trade.

SUMMARY

? 1. What are opportunity costs? Are they part of the economic way of thinking?

1. Opportunity costs are the forgone opportunities of the next best alternative. Choice means both gaining something and giving up something. When you choose one option you forgo all others. The benefits of the next best alternative are the opportunity costs of your choice. *§1*

? 2. What is a production possibilities curve?

2. A production possibilities curve represents the tradeoffs involved in the allocation of scarce resources. It shows the maximum quantity of goods and services that can be produced using limited resources to the fullest extent possible. *§1.c*

3. The bowed-out shape of the PPC occurs because of specialization and increasing marginal opportunity costs. *§2.a*

? 3. Why does specialization occur?

4. Comparative advantage accounts for specialization. We specialize in the activities in which we have the lowest opportunity costs, that is, in which we have a comparative advantage. *§2.c*

? 4. What are the benefits of trade?

5. Specialization and trade enable those involved to acquire more than they could by not specializing and engaging in trade. *§2.d*

KEY TERMS

opportunity costs *§1*

tradeoff *§1.b*

marginal cost *§1.b*

marginal benefit *§1.b*

production possibilities curve (PPC) *§1.c*

marginal opportunity cost *§2.a*

comparative advantage *§2.c*

EXERCISES

1. In most presidential campaigns, candidates promise more than they can deliver. Clinton and Gore promised more and better health care, a better environment, only minor reductions in defense, better education, and a better and improved system of roads, bridges, sewer systems, water systems, and so on. What economic concept were the candidates ignoring?

2. Janine is an accountant who makes $30,000 a year. Robert is a college student who makes $8,000 a year. All other things being equal, who is more likely to stand in a long line to get a concert ticket?

3. Back in the 1960s, President Lyndon Johnson passed legislation that increased expenditures for both the Vietnam War and social problems in the United States. Since the U.S. economy was operating at its full employment level when President Johnson did this, he appeared to be ignoring what economic concept?

4. The following numbers measure the tradeoff between grades and income.

Total Hours	Hours Studying	GPA	Hours Working	Income
60	60	4.0	0	$ 0
60	40	3.0	20	$100
60	30	2.0	30	$150
60	10	1.0	50	$250
60	0	0.0	60	$300

a. Calculate the opportunity cost of an increase in the number of hours spent studying in order to earn a 3.0 grade point average (GPA) rather than a 2.0 GPA.

b. Is the opportunity cost the same for a move from a 0.0 GPA to a 1.0 GPA as it is for a move from a 1.0 GPA to a 2.0 GPA?

c. What is the opportunity cost of an increase in salary from $100 to $150?

5. Suppose a second individual has the following trade-offs between income and grades:

Total Hours	Hours Studying	GPA	Hours Working	Income
60	50	4.0	10	$ 60
60	40	3.0	20	$120
60	20	2.0	40	$240
60	10	1.0	50	$300
60	0	0.0	60	$360

a. Define comparative advantage.

b. Does either individual (the one in exercise 4 or the one in exercise 5) have a comparative advantage in both activities?

c. Who should specialize in studying and who should specialize in working?

6. A doctor earns $250,000 per year while a professor earns $40,000. They play tennis against each other each Saturday morning, each giving up a morning of relaxing, reading the paper, and playing with their children. They could each decide to work a few extra hours on Saturday and earn more income. But they choose to play tennis or to relax around the house. Are their opportunity costs of playing tennis different?

7. Plot the PPC of a nation given by the following data.

Combination	Health Care	All Other Goods
A	0	100
B	25	90
C	50	70
D	75	40
E	100	0

a. Calculate the marginal opportunity cost of each combination.

b. What is the opportunity cost of combination C?

c. Suppose a second nation has the following data. Plot the PPC and then determine which nation has the comparative advantage in which activity. Show whether the two nations can gain from specialization and trade.

Combination	Health Care	All Other Goods
A	0	50
B	20	40
C	40	25
D	60	5
E	65	0

8. A doctor earns $200 per hour, a plumber $40 per hour, and a professor $20 per hour. Everything else the same, which one will devote more hours to negotiating the price of a new car?

9. Perhaps you've heard of the old saying "There is no such thing as a free lunch." What does it mean? If someone invites you to a lunch and offers to pay for it, is it free to you?

10. You have waited 30 minutes in a line for the Star Tours ride at Disneyland. You see a sign that says, "From this point on your wait is 45 minutes." You must decide whether to continue in line or to move elsewhere. On what basis do you make the decision? Do the 30 minutes you've already stood in line come into play?

11. The university is deciding between two meal plans. One plan charges a fixed fee of $600 per semester and allows students to eat as much as they want. The other plan charges a fee based on the quantity of food consumed. Under which plan will students eat the most?

12. Evaluate this statement: "You are a natural athlete, an attractive person who learns easily and communicates well. Clearly, you can do everything better than your friends and acquaintances. As a result, the term *specialization* has no meaning for you. Specialization would cost you rather than benefit you."

13. During China's Cultural Revolution in the late 1960s and early 1970s, many people with a high school or college education were forced to move to farms and work in the fields. Some were common laborers for eight or more years. What does this policy say about specialization and the PPC? Would you predict that the policy would lead to an increase in output?

14. In elementary school and through middle school most students have the same teacher throughout the day and for the entire school year. Then, beginning in high school different subjects are taught by different teachers. In college, the same subject is often taught at different levels—freshman, sophomore, junior-senior, or graduate—by different faculty. Is education taking advantage of specialization only from

high school on? Comment on the differences between elementary school and college and the use of specialization.

15. The top officials in federal government and high-ranking officers of large corporations often have chauffeurs to drive them around the city or from meeting to meeting. Is this simply one of the perquisites of their position, or is the use of chauffeurs justifiable on the basis of comparative advantage?

Car Sector Braces for Stiffer Competition

The Malaysian automotive sector is bracing for the stiffer competition that will come in 2005 when tariff barriers come down for the sector under the Asian Free Trade Area (AFTA) scheme.

When that day comes, Malaysia will open its successful but small players to an environment filled with great predators. The chances for survival do exist but staying alive in the so-called liberalised world where there will be a "level playing field" for all players will be tough.

"A level playing field is like a football match. The field is level but it'll be like Malaysia versus Brazil," said DRB-Hicom chairman Tan Sri Mohd Saleh Sulong recently. "It's a one sided argument."

Saleh's argument hits the mark as far as the automotive industry is at. Considering the stellar qualities of the Brazilians compared with Malaysia's not too well endowed national team, we are looking at a potential drubbing.

But to assume that the underdog would definitely be trampled upon by the stronger team would not be a correct statement, even dimunitive David beat the brawn of Goliath.

"We are already in the game. Whether we like it or not, we have to compete with these players." Saleh had said to reporters who visited the company's integrated automotive plant in Pekan, Pahang, recently.

In the case of competition in the automotive sector, local players can take heart that Malaysians would show loyalty to Malaysian-made vehicles as long as they are of the same quality.

This will tip the scale for the local carmakers of surviving the stiff competition when tariffs are removed under the Afta programmes in year 2003. In Malaysia, the removal has been postponed to 2005.

But support should not be taken for granted by national carmakers. It is their responsibility to ensure that the products they sell are at least of similar standards, quality and performance with the competitors.

Otherwise, they would be shortchanging their loyal fans and once cheated, it will be difficult to gain back their trust. The outcome will be ugly, similar to a football match, booing their own team due to disgust towards the players' below par performance.

This is a situation where the national carmakers must avoid at all costs. Without the support of the locals coupled with pressure from the international car giants, the national carmakers are doomed.

FADZIL GHAZALI

Source: "Car Sector Braces for Stiffer Competition," from the *New Straits Times Press* (Malaysia), *Berhad Business Times* (Malaysia), July 4, 2000. Copyright 2000.

New Straits Times Press, Berhard Business Times/July 4, 2000

Commentary

Free trade means that restrictions such as tariffs and barriers are eliminated. A tariff is a tax applied to imported goods or services that raises the price of foreign-made items. The tariff allows inefficient local producers to compete locally with more efficient foreign producers. But when the tariff is reduced or eliminated, the local producers must be as efficient as the foreign producers in order to compete with them. Malaysia's automobile industry fears it may not be as efficient. It is hoping that the loyalty of the local population coupled with some government intervention will enable it to survive.

Free trade can be difficult for some. For whom? For those working in an industry that has no comparative advantage. If another nation can produce automobiles more efficiently than Malaysia can, then free trade will drive the Malaysian automobile industry out of business. Those employed in the Malaysian automobile industry will have to switch to other industries. This switch, or transition, to other industries is difficult and costly for those involved. But, the result is economic growth, more income, and the ability to purchase more than could be produced just by Malaysia.

We learned in this chapter that nations could gain by specializing where their opportunity costs are lowest and then trading. Trade allows a society to acquire goods and services beyond its own PPC. Suppose that the following figure represents Malaysia's PPC. With trade, Malaysia could gain some amount, say A to B. Not allowing trade means consumers can consume less than they could with trade. Malaysian consumers would be restricted to the nation's own PPC, represented by point A or any point on or inside the PPC. Trade restrictions would mean that Malaysian consumers have an opportunity cost of amount A to B; they forgo the additional amount of goods and services that trade would allow. There is no doubt that free trade will benefit Malaysian consumers. But, the transition from a restricted trade to free trade, from A to B, may involve the loss of jobs in one area of the economy and the increase in jobs in another area of the economy. The people employed in the losing area will feel the effect of trade negatively while those employed in the gaining area will feel the benefits of trade.

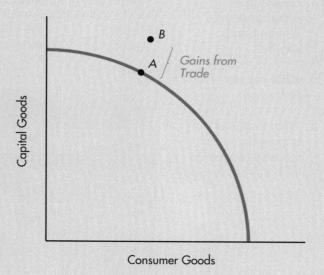

Preview

People (and firms and nations) can get more if they specialize in certain activities and then trade with one another to acquire the goods and services they desire than if they do everything themselves. But how are the specialized producers to get together or to know who specializes in what? We could allow the government to decide, or we could rely on first-come, first-served, or even simply luck. Typically it is the market mechanism—buyers and sellers interacting via prices—we rely on to ensure that gains from trade occur. To see why, consider the following situation and then carry out the exercise.

I. At a sightseeing point, reachable only after a strenuous hike, a firm has established a stand where bottled water is sold. The water, carried in by the employees of the firm, is sold to thirsty hikers in 6-ounce bottles. The price is $1 per bottle. Typically only 100 bottles of the water are sold each day. On a particularly hot day,

200 hikers each want to buy at least one bottle of water. Indicate what you think of each of the following means of distributing the water to the hikers by responding to each allocation approach with one of the following five responses:

a. Completely fair
b. Acceptable
c. Unfair
d. Very unfair
e. Totally unfair

1. Increasing the price until the quantity of water bottles hikers are willing and able to purchase exactly equals the number of water bottles available for sale
2. Selling the water for $1 per bottle on a first-come, first-served basis
3. Having the local authority (government) buy the water for $1 per bottle and distribute it according to its own judgment
4. Selling the water for $1 per bottle following a random selection procedure or lottery

The following is a similar situation but involves a different product.

II. A physician has been providing medical services at a fee of $100 per patient and typically sees thirty patients per day. One day the flu bug has been so vicious that the number of patients attempting to visit the physician exceeds sixty. Indicate what you think of each of the following means of distributing the physician's services to the sick patients by responding with one of the following five answers:

a. Completely fair
b. Acceptable
c. Unfair
d. Very unfair
e. Totally unfair

1. Raising the price until the number of patients the doctor sees is exactly equal to those patients willing and able to pay the doctor's fee
2. Selling the services for $100 per patient on a first-come, first-served basis
3. Having the local authority (government) pay the physician $100 per patient and choose who is to receive the services according to its own judgment
4. Selling the physician's services for $100 per patient following a random selection procedure or lottery

How did you answer the exercises? Did you notice that in fact, each allocation mechanism is unfair in the sense that someone gets the good or service and someone does not? With the market system, it is those without income or wealth who must do without. Under the first-come, first-served system it is those who arrive later who do without. Under the government scheme it is those not in favor or those who do not match up with the government's rules who do without. And, with a random procedure, it is those who do not have the lucky ticket or correct number who are left out.

Since each allocation mechanism is in a sense unfair, how do we decide which to use? One way might be by the incentives each creates.

A market arises when buyers and sellers exchange a well-defined good or service. In stock markets, buyers and sellers exchange their "goods," or stocks, solely through electronic connections. Shoppers at a flower market can examine the day's assortment and make their choices.

With the first-come, first-served allocation scheme, the incentive is to be first. You have no reason to improve the quality of your products or to increase the value of your resources. Your only incentive is to be first. Supply will not increase. Why would anyone produce when all everyone wants is to be first? As a result, growth will not occur and standards of living will not rise. A society based on first-come, first-served would die a quick death.

A government scheme provides an incentive either to be a member of government and thus help determine the allocation rules or to perform according to government dictates. There are no incentives to improve production and efficiency, to improve quantities supplied, and thus no reason for the economy to grow. We have seen how this system fared with the collapse of the Soviet Union.

The random allocation provides no incentives at all; simply hope that manna from heaven falls on you.

With the market system, the incentive is to acquire purchasing ability—to obtain income and wealth. This means you must provide goods that have high value to others and provide resources that have high value to producers—to enhance your worth as an employee by acquiring education or training and to enhance the value of the resources you own.

The market system also provides incentives for quantities of scarce goods to increase. In the case of the water stand in scenario I, if the price of the water increases and the owner of the water stand is earning significant profits, others may carry or truck water to the top of the hill and sell it to thirsty hikers; the amount of water available thus increases. In the case of the doctor in scenario II, other doctors may think that opening an office near the first might be a way to earn more; the amount of physician services available increases. Since the market system creates the incentive for the amount supplied to increase, economies grow and expand and standards of living improve. The market system also ensures that resources are allocated to where they are most highly valued. If the price of an item rises, consumers may switch over to another item, or another good or service, that can serve about the same purpose. When consumers switch, production of the alternative good rises and thus resources used in its production must increase as well. The resources then are reallocated from lower-valued uses to higher-valued uses. ■

1. MARKETS

1. What is a market?

The supermarket, the stock market, and the market for foreign exchange are similar in that well-defined goods and services are exchanged. A market may be a specific location, such as the supermarket or the stock market, or it may be the exchange of particular goods or services at many different locations, such as the foreign exchange market.

1.a. Market Definition

market: a place or service that enables buyers and sellers to exchange goods and services

A **market** makes possible the exchange of goods and services. A market may be a formally organized exchange, such as the New York Stock Exchange, or it may be loosely organized like the market for used bicycles or automobiles. A market may be confined to one location, as in the case of a supermarket or the stock market, or it may encompass a city, a state, a country, or the entire world. The market for agricultural products, for instance, is international, but the market for labor services is mostly local or national.

1.b. Barter and Money Exchanges

The purpose of markets is to facilitate the exchange of goods and services between buyers and sellers. In some cases money changes hands; in others only goods and services are exchanged. The exchange of goods and services directly, without money, is called **barter.** Barter occurs when a plumber fixes a leaky pipe for a lawyer in exchange for the lawyer's work on a will or when a Chinese citizen provides fresh vegetables to a U.S. visitor in exchange for a pack of U.S. cigarettes.

barter: the direct exchange of goods and services without the use of money

Most markets involve money because goods and services can be exchanged more easily with money than without it. When IBM purchases microchips from Yakamoto of Japan, IBM and Yakamoto don't exchange goods directly. Neither firm may have what the other wants. Barter requires a **double coincidence of wants:** IBM must have what Yakamoto wants, and Yakamoto must have what IBM wants. The **transaction costs** (the costs associated with making an exchange) of finding a double coincidence of wants for barter transactions are typically very high. Money reduces these transaction costs. To obtain the microchips, all IBM has to do is provide dollars to Yakamoto. Yakamoto is willing to accept the money since it can spend it to obtain the goods that it wants.

double coincidence of wants: the situation that exists when A has what B wants and B has what A wants

transaction costs: the costs involved in making an exchange

1.c. Relative Price

relative price: the price of one good expressed in terms of the price of another good

When people agree to trade or exchange, they must agree on the rate of exchange, or the price. The price of an exchange is a **relative price**—the price of one good expressed in terms of the price of another good. In a barter exchange a relative price is established between the goods traded. When the lawyer exchanges 2 hours of work for 1 hour of the plumber's work, the relative price established is 2/1. In a money exchange the relative price is more implicit. You pay a money price of $1 for a carton of milk. But, with that purchase you are forgoing everything else you could get for that dollar. Thus, the carton of milk is worth 1/3 of a $3 box of Quaker Oats 100% Natural cereal, 1/200 of a $200 used Diamond Back mountain bike, 20 sticks of $.05/stick Trident gum, and so on. These are the relative prices of the milk. Relative prices are a measure of what you must give up to get one unit of a good or service and are, therefore, a measure of opportunity costs. Since opportunity costs are what decisions are based on, when economists refer to the price of something, it is the relative price they have in mind.

RECAP

1. A market is not necessarily a specific location or store. Instead, the term *market* refers to buyers and sellers communicating with each other regarding the quality and quantity of a well-defined product, what buyers are willing and able to pay for a product, and what sellers must receive in order to produce and sell a product.

2. Barter refers to exchanges made without the use of money.

3. Money makes it easier and less expensive to exchange goods and services.

4. The price of a good or service is a measure of what you must give up to get one unit of that good or service.

2. DEMAND

2. What is demand?

Demand and supply determine the price of any good or service. To understand how a price level is determined and why a price rises or falls, it is necessary to know how demand and supply function. We begin by considering demand alone, then supply, and then we put the two together. Before we begin, we discuss some economic terminology that is often confusing.

Economists distinguish between the terms **demand** and **quantity demanded.** When they refer to the *quantity demanded,* they are talking about the amount of a product that people are willing and able to purchase at a *specific* price. When they refer to *demand,* they are talking about the amount that people would be willing and able to purchase at *every possible* price. Demand is the quantities demanded at every price. Thus, the statement that "the demand for U.S. white wine rose after a 300 percent tariff was applied to French white wine" means that at each price for U.S. white wine, more people were willing and able to purchase U.S. white wine. And the statement that "the quantity demanded of white wine fell as the price of white wine rose" means that people were willing and able to purchase less white wine because the price of the wine rose.

demand: the amount of a product that people are willing and able to purchase at every possible price

quantity demanded: the amount of a product that people are willing and able to purchase at a specific price

2.a. The Law of Demand

law of demand: the quantity of a well-defined good or service that people are willing and able to purchase during a particular period of time decreases as the price of that good or service rises and increases as the price falls, everything else held constant

Consumers and merchants know that if you lower the price of a good or service without altering its quality or quantity, people will beat a path to your doorway. This simple truth is referred to as the **law of demand.**

According to the law of demand, people purchase more of something when the price of that item falls. More formally, the law of demand states that the quantity of some item that people are willing and able to purchase, during a particular period of time, decreases as the price rises, and vice versa.

The more formal definition of the law of demand can be broken down into five phrases:

1. The quantity of a well-defined good or service that
2. people are willing and able to purchase
3. during a particular period of time
4. decreases as the price of that good or service rises and increases as the price falls,
5. everything else held constant

The first phrase ensures that we are referring to the same item, that we are not mixing different goods. A watch is a commodity defined and distinguished from other goods by several characteristics: quality, color, and design of the watch face, to name a few. The law of demand applies to the well-defined good, in this case, a watch. If one of the characteristics should change, the good would no longer be well defined—in fact, it would be a different good. A Rolex watch is different from a Timex watch; Polo brand golf shirts are different goods than generic brand golf shirts; Mercedes-Benz automobiles are different goods than Yugo automobiles.

The second phrase indicates that people must not only *want* to purchase some good, they must be *able* to purchase that good in order for their wants to be counted as part of demand. For example, Sue would love to buy a membership to the Paradise Valley Country Club, but because the membership costs $35,000, she is not able to purchase the membership. Though willing, she is not able. At a price of $5,000, however, she is willing and able to purchase the membership.

The third phrase points out that the demand for any good is defined for a specific period of time. Without reference to a time period, a demand relationship would not make any sense. For instance, the statement that "at a price of $3 per Happy Meal, 13 million Happy Meals are demanded" provides no useful information. Are the 13 million meals sold in one week or one year? Think of demand as a rate of purchase at each possible price over a period of time—2 per month, 1 per day, and so on.

The fourth phrase points out that price and quantity demanded move in opposite directions; that is, as the price rises, the quantity demanded falls, and as the price falls, the quantity demanded rises.

determinants of demand: factors other than the price of the good that influence demand—income, tastes, prices of related goods and services, expectations, and number of buyers

Demand is a measure of the relationship between the price and quantity demanded of a particular good or service, when the determinants of demand do not change. The **determinants of demand** are income, tastes, prices of related goods and services, expectations, and the number of buyers. If any one of these items changes, demand changes. The final phrase, everything else held constant, ensures that the determinants of demand do not change.

2.b. The Demand Schedule

demand schedule: a table or list of the prices and the corresponding quantities demanded of a particular good or service

A **demand schedule** is a table or list of the prices and the corresponding quantities demanded of a particular good or service. The table in Figure 1 is a demand schedule for video rentals (movies). It shows the number of videos that a consumer named Bob would be willing and able to rent at each price during the year, everything else held constant. As the rental price of the videos gets higher relative to the prices of other goods, Bob would be willing and able to rent fewer videos.

At the high price of $5 per video, Bob indicates that he will rent only 10 videos during the year. At a price of $4 per video, Bob tells us that he will rent 20 videos during the year. As the price drops from $5 to $4 to $3 to $2 and to $1, Bob is willing and able to rent more videos. At a price of $1, Bob would rent 50 videos during the year, nearly 1 per week.

Figure 1

Bob's Demand Schedule and Demand Curve for Videos

The number of videos that Bob is willing and able to rent at each price during the year is listed in the table, or demand schedule. The demand curve is derived from the combinations given in the demand schedule. The price-quantity combination of $5 per video and 10 videos is point *A*. The combination of $4 per video and 20 videos is point *B*. Each combination is plotted, and the points are connected to form the demand curve.

Combination	Price per Video (constant-quality units)	Quantity Demanded per Year (constant-quality units)
A	$5	10
B	$4	20
C	$3	30
D	$2	40
E	$1	50

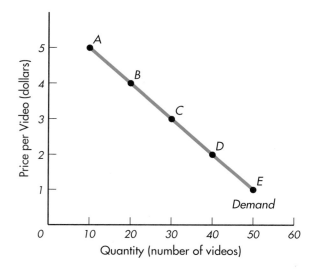

2.c. The Demand Curve

demand curve: a graph of a demand schedule that measures price on the vertical axis and quantity demanded on the horizontal axis

A **demand curve** is a graph of the demand schedule. The demand curve shown in Figure 1 is plotted from the information given in the demand schedule. Price is measured on the vertical axis, quantity per unit of time on the horizontal axis. The demand curve slopes downward because of the inverse relationship between the rental price of the videos and the quantity an individual is willing and able to purchase (rent). Point *A* in Figure 1 corresponds to combination *A* in the table: a price of $5 and 10 videos demanded. Similarly, points *B, C, D,* and *E* in Figure 1 represent the corresponding combinations in the table. The line connecting these points is Bob's demand curve for videos.

All demand curves slope down because of the law of demand: as price falls, quantity demanded increases. The demand curves for bread, electricity, automobiles, colleges, labor services, and any other good or service you can think of slope down. You might be saying to yourself, "That's not true. What about the demand for Mercedes-Benz cars or Gucci bags? As their price goes up, they become more prestigious and

When speaking of the demand curve or demand schedule, we are using constant-quality units. The quality of a good does not change as the price changes along a demand curve.

the quantity demanded actually rises." To avoid confusion in such circumstances, we say "everything else held constant." With this statement we are assuming that tastes don't change and that, therefore, the goods *cannot* become more prestigious as the price changes. Similarly, we do not allow the quality or the brand name of a product to change as we define the demand schedule or demand curve. We concentrate on the one quality or the one brand; so when we say that the price of a good has risen, we are talking about a good that is identical at all prices.

2.d. From Individual Demand Curves to a Market Curve

Bob's demand curve for video rentals is plotted in Figure 1. Unless Bob is the only renter of the videos, his demand curve is not the total, or market demand, curve. Market demand is the sum of all individual demands. To derive the market demand curve, then, the individual demand curves of all consumers in the market must be added together. The table in Figure 2 lists the demand schedules of three individuals, Bob, Helen, and Art. Because in this example the market consists only of Bob, Helen, and Art, their individual demands are added together to derive the market demand. The market demand is the last column of the table.

Bob's, Helen's, and Art's demand schedules are plotted as individual demand curves in Figure 2(a). In Figure 2(b) their individual demand curves have been added together to obtain the market demand curve. (Notice that we add in a horizontal direction—that is, we add quantities at each price, not the prices at each quantity.) At a price of $5, we add the quantity Bob would buy, 10, to the quantity Helen would buy, 5, to the quantity Art would buy, 15, to get the market quantity demanded of 30. At a price of $4, we add the quantities each of the consumers is willing and able to buy to get the total quantity demanded of 48. At all prices, then, we add the quantities demanded by each individual consumer to get the total, or market quantity, demanded.

2.e. Changes in Demand and Changes in Quantity Demanded

When one of the determinants of demand—income, tastes, prices of related goods, expectations, or number of buyers—is allowed to change, the demand for a good or service changes as well. What does it mean to say that demand changes? Demand is the entire demand schedule, or demand curve. When we say that demand changes, we are referring to a change in the quantities demanded at each and every price.

For example, if Bob's income rises, then his demand for video rentals rises. At each and every price, the number of videos Bob is willing and able to rent each year rises. This increase is shown in the last column of the table in Figure 3. A change in demand is represented by a shift of the demand curve, as shown in Figure 3(a). The shift to the right, from D_1 to D_2, indicates that Bob is willing and able to rent more videos at every price.

When the price of a good or service is the only factor that changes, the quantity demanded changes but the demand curve does not shift. Instead, as the price of the rentals is decreased (increased), everything else held constant, the quantity that people are willing and able to purchase increases (decreases). This change is merely a movement from one point on the demand curve to another point on the same demand curve, not a shift of the demand curve. *Change in the quantity demanded* is the phrase economists use to describe the change in the quantities of a particular good or service that people are willing and able to purchase as the price of that good or service changes. A change in the quantity demanded, from point *A* to point *B* on the demand curve, is shown in Figure 3(b).

Figure 2

The Market Demand Schedule and Curve for Videos

The market is defined to consist of three individuals: Bob, Helen, and Art. Their demand schedules are listed in the table and plotted as the individual demand curves shown in Figure 2(a). By adding the quantities that each demands at every price, we obtain the market demand curve shown in Figure 2(b). At a price of $1 we add Bob's quantity demanded of 50 to Helen's quantity demanded of 25 to Art's quantity demanded of 27 to obtain the market quantity demanded of 102. At a price of $2 we add Bob's 40 to Helen's 20 to Art's 24 to obtain the market quantity demanded of 84. To obtain the market demand curve, for every price we sum the quantities demanded by each market participant.

	Quantities Demanded per Year by			
Price per Video	**Bob**	**Helen**	**Art**	**Market Quantity Demanded**
$5	10 +	5 +	15 =	30
$4	20	10	18	48
$3	30	15	21	66
$2	40	20	24	84
$1	50	25	27	102

(a) Individual Demand Curves

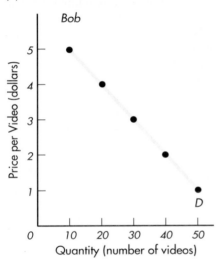
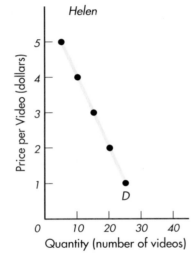
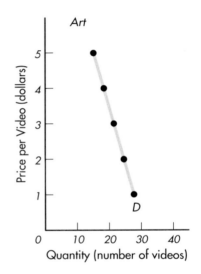

(b) Market Demand Curve

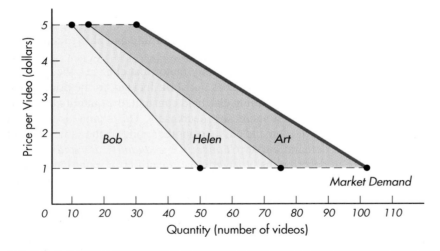

Figure 3

A Change in Demand and a Change in the Quantity Demanded

According to the table, Bob's demand for videos has increased by 5 videos at each price level. In Figure 3(a), this change is shown as a shift of the demand curve from D_1 to D_2. Figure 3(b) shows a change in the quantity demanded. The change is an increase in the quantity that consumers are willing and able to purchase at a lower price. It is shown as a movement along the demand curve from point A to point B.

Price per Video	Quantities Demanded per Year	
	Before	After
$5	10	15
$4	20	25
$3	30	35
$2	40	45
$1	50	55

(a) Change in Demand

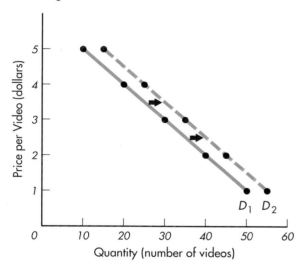

(b) Change in Quantity Demanded

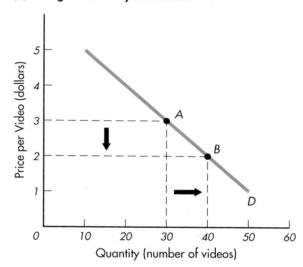

The demand curve shifts when income, tastes, prices of related goods, expectations, or the number of buyers changes. Let's consider how each of these determinants of demand affects the demand curve.

2.e.1. Income The demand for any good or service depends on income. The higher someone's income is, the more goods and services that person can purchase at any given price. The increase in Bob's income causes his demand to increase. This change is shown in Figure 3(a) by the shift to the right from the curve labeled D_1 to the curve labeled D_2. Increased income means a greater ability to purchase goods and services. At every price, more videos are demanded along curve D_2 than along curve D_1.

2.e.2. Tastes The demand for any good or service depends on individuals' tastes and preferences. For decades, the destination of choice for college students in the East and Midwest during spring break was Fort Lauderdale, Florida. In the early 1990s, many students decided that Mexico offered a more exciting destination than

Fort Lauderdale. Regardless of the prices of the Fort Lauderdale and Mexican vacations, tastes changed so that more students went to Mexico. The demand curve for the Mexican vacation shifted to the right while that for the Fort Lauderdale vacation shifted to the left.

2.e.3. Prices of Related Goods and Services

Goods and services may be related in two ways. **Substitute goods** can be used for each other, so that as the price of one rises, the demand for the other rises. Bread and crackers, BMWs and Acuras, video rentals and theater movies, universities and community colleges, electricity and natural gas are, more or less, pairs of substitutes. As the price of cassette tapes rises, everything else held constant, the demand for CDs will rise and the demand curve for CDs will shift to the right. As the price of theater movies increases, the demand for video rentals will rise and the demand curve for the videos will shift to the right.

Complementary goods are used together, and as the price of one rises, the demand for the other falls. Bread and margarine, beer and peanuts, cameras and film, shoes and socks, CDs and CD players, video rentals and VCRs are examples of pairs of complementary goods. As the price of cameras rises, people tend to purchase fewer cameras, but they also tend to purchase less film. As the price of VCRs rises, people tend to purchase fewer VCRs, but they also demand fewer video rentals. The demand curve for a complementary good shifts to the left when the price of the related good increases.

2.e.4. Expectations

Expectations about future events can have an effect on demand today. People make purchases today because they expect their income level to be a certain amount in the future, or they expect the price of certain items to be higher in the future.

2.e.5. Number of Buyers

Market demand consists of the sum of the demands of all individuals. The more individuals there are with income to spend, the greater the market demand is likely to be. For example, the populations of Florida and Arizona are much larger during the winter than they are during the summer. The demand for any particular good or service in Arizona and Florida rises (the demand curve shifts to the right) during the winter and falls (the demand curve shifts to the left) during the summer.

2.f. International Effects

The law of demand says the amount of a good or service that people are willing and able to purchase during a particular period of time falls as the price rises and rises as the price falls. It does not indicate whether those people are residents of the United States or some other country. The demand for a product that is available to residents of other countries as well as to residents of the United States will consist of the sum of the demands by U.S. and foreign residents. However, because nations use different monies or currencies, the demand will be affected by the rate at which the different currencies are exchanged. As pointed out in the Economic Insight "The Foreign Exchange Market," an **exchange rate** is the rate at which monies of different countries are exchanged. If the exchange rate changes, then the foreign price of a good produced in the United States will change. To illustrate this, let's consider an example using Levi's blue jeans sold to both U.S.

---

substitute goods: goods that can be used in place of each other; as the price of one rises, the demand for the other rises

complementary goods: goods that are used together; as the price of one rises, the demand for the other falls

A change in demand is represented by a shift of the demand curve.

exchange rate: the rate at which monies of different countries are exchanged

---

The Foreign Exchange Market

Most countries have their own national currency. Germany has the deutsche mark, France the franc, England the pound sterling, Japan the yen, the United States the dollar, and so on. The citizens of each country use their national currency to carry out transactions. For transactions among nations to occur, however, some exchange of foreign currencies is necessary.

Americans buy Toyotas and Nissans from Japan, while U.S. computer companies sell pocket calculators to businesses in Mexico. Some Americans open bank accounts in Switzerland, while U.S. real estate companies sell property to citizens in England. These transactions require the acquisition of a foreign currency. An English business that wants to buy property in the United States will have to exchange pounds sterling for dollars. A U.S. car distributor that imports Toyotas will have to exchange dollars for yen in order to pay the Toyota manufacturer.

The exchange of currency and the determination of the value of national currencies occur in the foreign exchange market. This is not a tightly organized market operating in a building in New York. Usually, the term *foreign exchange market* refers to the trading that occurs among large international banks. Such trading is global and is done largely through telephone and computer communication systems. If, for example, a foreign exchange trader at First Chicago Bank calls a trader at Bank of Tokyo to buy $1 million worth of Japanese yen, that is a foreign exchange market transaction. Banks buy and sell currencies according to the needs and demands of their customers. Business firms and individuals rely largely on banks to buy and sell foreign exchange for them.

The price of one currency expressed in terms of another currency is called a *foreign exchange rate,* or just *exchange rate.* You can think of an exchange rate as the number of dollars it

costs to purchase one unit of another country's currency. For instance, how many dollars does it take to purchase one unit of Japan's currency, the yen? One yen (¥) costs about $.009, or nine-tenths of a cent. The list that follows shows the number of U.S. dollars it took to purchase one unit of several different nations' currencies in December 2000.

Number of U.S. Dollars Needed to Purchase One

Australian dollar	.5205
Belgian franc	.0211
Canadian dollar	.6426
French franc	.1299
German mark	.4357
Italian lira	.00044
Japanese yen	.00917
Dutch guilder	.3867
Spanish peseta	.00512
Swedish krona	.0985
Swiss franc	.5593
United Kingdom pound	1.4255

and Japanese customers. The Japanese currency is the yen (¥). In January 2000, it took 130 yen to purchase one dollar. Suppose that a pair of Levi's blue jeans is priced at $20 in the United States. That dollar price in terms of yen is ¥2,600. The exchange rate between the yen and the dollar means that ¥2,600 converts to $20; ¥2,600 = $20 × 130¥/$. In July of 1999 the exchange rate was ¥124 per dollar. If the U.S. price of the blue jeans was $20, in Japan, the yen value of the blue jeans would be $20 × ¥124/$ = ¥2,480. The blue jeans were more expensive in Japan because of the exchange rate change, even though the U.S. price of blue jeans did not change. The demand for U.S. blue jeans would have declined from July 1999 to January 2000 simply because of the exchange rate change. Thus, changes in exchange rates can affect the demand for goods. At constant U.S. prices, demand curves for U.S. goods will shift around as exchange rates change and foreign purchases fluctuate.

1. According to the law of demand, as the price of any good or service rises (falls), the quantity demanded of that good or service falls (rises), during a specific period of time, everything else held constant.

2. A demand schedule is a listing of the quantity demanded at each price.

3. The demand curve is a downward-sloping line plotted using the values of the demand schedule.

4. Market demand is the sum of all individual demands.

5. Demand changes when one of the determinants of demand changes. A demand change is a shift of the demand curve.

6. The quantity demanded changes when the price of the good or service changes. This is a change from one point on the demand curve to another point on the same demand curve.

7. The determinants of demand are income, tastes, prices of related goods and services, expectations, and number of buyers.

8. The exchange rate also is a determinant of demand when a good is sold in both the United States and other countries.

3. What is supply?

supply: the amount of a good or service that producers are willing and able to offer for sale at each possible price during a period of time, everything else held constant

quantity supplied: the amount sellers are willing to offer at a given price, during a particular period of time, everything else held constant

law of supply: the quantity of a well-defined good or service that producers are willing and able to offer for sale during a particular period of time increases as the price of the good or service increases and decreases as the price decreases, everything else held constant

3. SUPPLY

Why is the price of hotel accommodations higher in Phoenix in the winter than in the summer? Demand AND supply. Why is the price of beef higher in Japan than in the United States? Demand AND supply. Why did the price of the dollar in terms of the Japanese yen rise in 1999? Demand AND supply. Both demand and supply determine price; neither demand nor supply alone determine price. We now discuss supply.

3.a. The Law of Supply

Just as demand is the relation between the price and the quantity demanded of a good or service, supply is the relation between price and quantity supplied. **Supply** is the amount of the good or service producers are willing and able to offer for sale at each possible price during a period of time, everything else held constant. **Quantity supplied** is the amount of the good or service producers are willing and able to offer for sale at a *specific* price, during a period of time, everything else held constant. According to the **law of supply,** as the price of a good or service rises, the quantity supplied rises, and vice versa.

The formal statement of the law of supply consists of five phrases:

1. The quantity of a well-defined good or service that
2. producers are willing and able to offer for sale
3. during a particular period of time
4. increases as the price of the good or service increases and decreases as the price decreases,
5. everything else held constant

The first phrase is the same as the first phrase in the law of demand. The second phrase indicates that producers must not only *want* to offer the product for sale but must be *able* to offer the product. The third phrase points out that the quantities producers will offer for sale depend on the period of time being considered. The fourth phrase points out that more will be supplied at higher than at lower prices. The final phrase ensures that the **determinants of supply** do not change. The determinants of supply are those factors that influence the willingness and ability of producers to offer their goods and services for sale other than the price of the good or service—the prices of resources used to produce the product, technology and productivity, expectations of producers, the number of producers in the market, and the prices of related goods and services. If any one of these should change, supply changes.

determinants of supply: factors other than the price of the good that influence supply—prices of resources, technology and productivity, expectations of producers, number of producers, and the prices of related good and services

supply schedule: a table or list of prices and corresponding quantities supplied of a particular good or service

supply curve: a graph of a supply schedule that measures price on the vertical axis and quantity supplied on the horizontal axis

3.b. The Supply Schedule and Supply Curve

A **supply schedule** is a table or list of the prices and the corresponding quantities supplied of a good or service. The table in Figure 4 presents MGA's supply schedule of videos. The schedule lists the quantities that MGA is willing and able to supply at each price, everything else held constant. As the price increases, MGA is willing and able to offer more videos for rent.

A **supply curve** is a graph of the supply schedule. Figure 4 shows MGA's supply curve of videos. The price and quantity combinations given in the supply schedule correspond to the points on the curve. For instance, combination A in the table cor-

---

Figure 4

MGA's Supply Schedule and Supply Curve for Videos

The quantity that MGA is willing and able to offer for sale at each price is listed in the supply schedule and shown on the supply curve. At point *A*, the price is $5 per video and the quantity supplied is 60 videos. The combination of $4 per video and 50 videos is point *B*. Each price-quantity combination is plotted, and the points are connected to form the supply curve.

Combination	Price per Video (constant-quality units)	Quantity Supplied per Year (constant-quality units)
A	$5	60
B	$4	50
C	$3	40
D	$2	30
E	$1	20

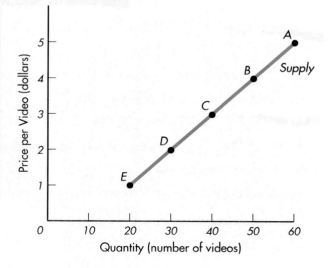

responds to point A on the curve; combination B in the table corresponds to point B on the curve, and so on for each price-quantity combination.

The supply curve for MGA slopes upward. This means that MGA is willing and able to supply more at higher prices than it is at lower prices. Recall from Chapter 2 that as society puts more and more resources into the production of any specific item, the opportunity cost of each additional unit of production rises because more-specialized resources are transferred to activities in which they are relatively less productive. So also MGA finds that as it increases production, the opportunity costs of additional production rise. Hence, the only way that MGA, or any producer, is willing and able to produce more is if the price rises sufficiently to cover these increasing opportunity costs.

3.c. From Individual Supply Curves to the Market Supply

To derive market supply, the quantities that each producer supplies at each price are added together, just as the quantities demanded by each consumer are added together to get market demand. The table in Figure 5 lists the supply schedules of three video rental stores: MGA, Motown, and Blockmaster. For our example, we assume that these three are the only video rental stores. (We are also assuming that the brand names are not associated with quality or any other differences.)

The supply schedule of each producer is plotted in Figure 5(a). Then in Figure 5(b) the individual supply curves have been added together to obtain the market supply curve. At a price of $5, the quantity supplied by MGA is 60, the quantity supplied by Motown is 30, and the quantity supplied by Blockmaster is 12. This means a total quantity supplied in the market of 102. At a price of $4, the quantities supplied are 50 by MGA, 25 by Motown, and 9 by Blockmaster for a total market quantity supplied of 84. The market supply schedule is the last column in the table. The plot of the price and quantity combinations listed in this column is the market supply curve. The market supply curve slopes up because each of the individual supply curves has a positive slope. The market supply curve tells us that the quantity supplied in the market increases as the price rises.

3.d. Changes in Supply and Changes in Quantity Supplied

A change in the quantity supplied is a movement along the supply curve. A change in the supply is a shift of the supply curve.

When we draw the supply curve, we allow only the price and quantity supplied of the good or service we are discussing to change. Everything else that might affect supply is assumed not to change. If any of the determinants of supply—the prices of resources used to produce the product, technology and productivity, expectations of producers, the number of producers in the market, and the prices of related goods and services—changes, the supply schedule changes and the supply curve shifts.

3.d.1. Prices of Resources

If labor costs—one of the resources used to produce video rentals—rise, higher rental prices will be necessary to induce each store to offer as many videos as it did before the cost of the resource rose. The higher cost of resources causes a decrease in supply, meaning a leftward shift of the supply curve, from S_1 to S_2 in Figure 6(a).

Two interpretations of a leftward shift of the supply curve are possible. One comes from comparing the old and new curves in a horizontal direction; the other comes from comparing the curves in a vertical direction. In the vertical direction, the decrease in supply informs us that sellers want a higher price to produce any

Figure 5

The Market Supply Schedule and Curve for Videos

The market supply is derived by summing the quantities that each producer is willing and able to offer for sale at each price. In this example, there are three producers: MGA, Motown, and Blockmaster. The supply schedules of each are listed in the table and plotted as the individual supply curves shown in Figure 5(a). By adding the quantities supplied at each price, we obtain the market supply curve shown in Figure 5(b). For instance, at a price of $5, MGA offers 60 units, Motown 30 units, and Blockmaster 12 units, for a market supply quantity of 102. The market supply curve reflects the quantities that each producer is able and willing to supply at each price.

Price per Video	Quantities Supplied per Year by			Market Quantity Supplied
	MGA	Motown	Blockmaster	
$5	60 +	30 +	12 =	102
$4	50	25	9	84
$3	40	20	6	66
$2	30	15	3	48
$1	20	10	0	30

(a) Individual Supply Curves

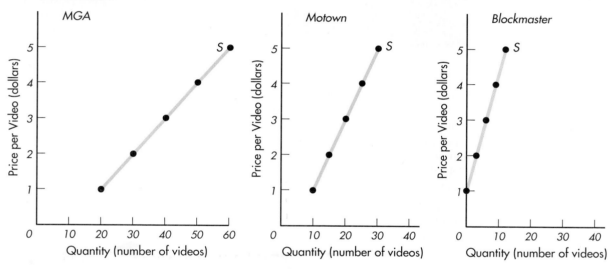

(b) Market Supply Curve

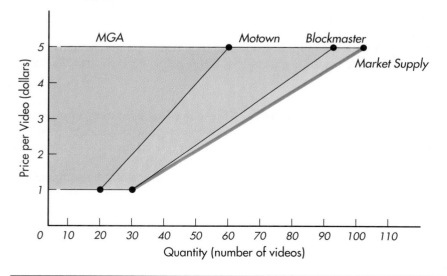

Before computers and x-ray fluorescence equipment were invented, curators of museums and authenticators of art had to destroy portions of art to determine the age and components of the art. Now, as shown in the Prado Museum in Madrid, the high-tech equipment is used to study the inorganic pigments in paint and determine when, where, and how the art was created, all without damaging any aspect of the art.

given quantity. Compare, for example, point A on curve S_1 with point C on curve S_2. Points A and C represent the same quantity but different prices. Sellers will offer 66 videos at a price of $3 per video according to supply curve S_1. But if the supply curve shifts to the left, then the sellers want more ($3.50) for 66 units.

In the horizontal direction, the decrease in supply means that sellers will offer less for sale at any given price. This can be seen by comparing point B on curve S_2 with point A on curve S_1. Both points correspond to a price of $3, but along curve S_1, sellers are willing to offer 66 units for rent, while curve S_2 indicates that sellers will offer only 57 videos for rent.

If resource prices declined, then supply would increase. That combination would be illustrated by a rightward shift of the supply curve. If a firm purchases supplies from other nations, exchange rate changes can affect the firm's costs and thus its supply curve. For instance, suppose a U.S. firm purchases lumber from Canada. At an exchange rate of 1 Canadian dollar per 1 U.S. dollar, 1,000 Canadian dollars worth of supplies costs 1,000 U.S. dollars. In 1998, with the Canadian dollar worth only .6992 U.S. dollars, the supplies worth 1,000 Canadian dollars cost only 699.20 U.S. dollars. Since the cost of supplies has declined for the U.S. firm, its supply curve shifts out.

3.d.2. Technology and Productivity

If resources are used more efficiently in the production of a good or service, more of that good or service can be produced for the same cost, or the original quantity can be produced for a lower cost. As a result, the supply curve shifts to the right, as in Figure 6(b).

The move from horse-drawn plows to tractors or from mainframe computers to personal computers meant that each worker was able to produce more. The increase in output produced by each unit of a resource is called a *productivity increase.*

Figure 6

A Shift of the Supply Curve

Figure 6(a) shows a decrease in supply and the shift of the supply curve to the left, from S_1 to S_2. The decrease is caused by a change in one of the determinants of video supply—an increase in the price of labor. Because of the increased price of labor, producers are willing and able to offer fewer videos for rent at each price than they were before the price of labor rose. Supply curve S_2 shows that at a price of $3 per video, suppliers will offer 57 videos. That is 9 units less than the 66 videos at $3 per video indicated by supply curve S_1. Conversely, to offer a given quantity, producers must receive a higher price per video than they previously were getting: $3.50 per video for 66 videos (on supply curve S_2) instead of $3 per video (on supply curve S_1).

Figure 6(b) shows an increase in supply. A technological improvement or an increase in productivity causes the supply curve to shift to the right, from S_1 to S_2. At each price, a higher quantity is offered for sale. At a price of $3, 66 units were offered, but with the shift of the supply curve, the quantity of units for sale at $3 apiece increases to 84. Conversely, producers can reduce prices for a given quantity—for example, charging $2 per video for 66 units.

(a) Decrease in Supply

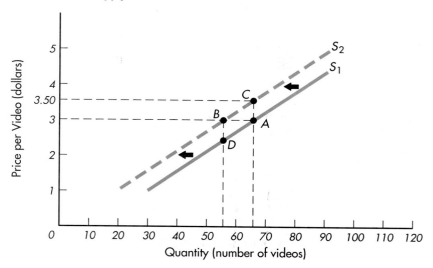

(b) Increase in Supply

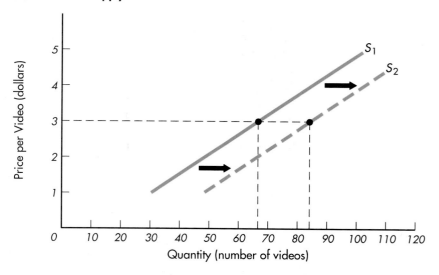

productivity: the quantity of output produced per unit of resource

Productivity is defined as the quantity of output produced per unit of resource. Improvements in technology cause productivity increases, which lead to an increase in supply.

3.d.3. Expectations of Producers

Sellers may choose to alter the quantity offered for sale today because of a change in expectations regarding the determinants of supply. A supply curve illustrates the quantities that suppliers are willing and able to supply at every possible price level. If suppliers expect something to occur to resource supplies or the cost of resources, then suppliers may alter the quantities they are willing and able to supply at every possible price. The key point is that the supply curve will shift if producers expect something to occur that will alter the anticipated profits at every possible price level, not just a change in one price. For instance, the expectation that demand will decline in the future does not lead to a shift of the supply curve; it leads instead to a decline in quantity supplied as the new demand curve intersects the supply curve at a lower level of prices and output.

3.d.4. Number of Producers

When more people decide to produce a good or service, the market supply increases. More is offered for sale at each and every price, causing a rightward shift of the supply curve.

3.d.5. Prices of Related Goods or Services

The opportunity cost of producing and selling any good or service is the forgone opportunity to produce any other good or service. If the price of an alternative good changes, then the opportunity cost of producing a particular good changes. This could cause the supply curve to change. For instance, if the video store can offer videos or arcade games with equal ease, an increase in the price of the arcade games could induce the store owner to offer more arcade games and fewer videos. The supply curve of videos would then shift to the left.

3.e. International Effects

Many firms purchase supplies from other nations, or even locate factories and produce in other nations. Events in other parts of the world can influence their costs and thus the amounts they are willing to supply. Nike purchases its shoes from manufacturers in other parts of the world, particularly Asia. Suppose the manufacturing costs in Malaysia are 78 ringgit. In 1997 the exchange rate was .3150 U.S. dollars to the ringgit, so that manufacturing costs in terms of dollars were \$24.57 (.3150 $\times$ 78). In December 2000, the exchange rate had risen to .2632 U.S. dollars to the ringgit. With the same manufacturing costs of 78 ringgit, the dollar costs had fallen to \$20.52 (.2632 $\times$ 78). Thus, the costs to Nike had fallen over the years without any changes in production. This means the supply curve of Nike shoes shifted out.

A *change in supply* occurs when the quantity supplied at each and every price changes or there is a shift in the supply curve—like the shift from S_1 to S_2 in Figure 7(a). A change in one of the determinants of supply brings about a change in supply.

When only the price changes, a greater or smaller quantity is supplied. This is shown as a movement along the supply curve, not as a shift of the curve. A change in price is said to cause a *change in the quantity supplied*. An increase in quantity supplied is shown in the move from point A to point B on the supply curve of Figure 7(b).

Figure 7

A Change in Supply and a Change in the Quantity Supplied

In Figure 7(a), the quantities that producers are willing and able to offer for sale at every price decrease, causing a leftward shift of the supply curve from S_1 to S_2. In Figure 7(b), the quantities that producers are willing and able to offer for sale increase, due to an increase in the price of the good, causing a movement along the supply curve from point A to point B.

(a) Change in Supply

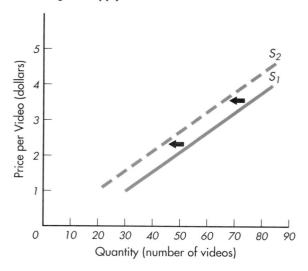

(b) Change in Quantity Supplied

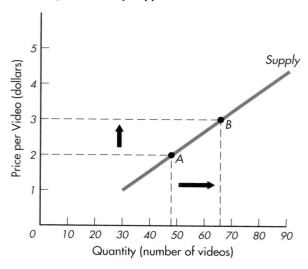

RECAP

1. According to the law of supply, the quantity supplied of any good or service is directly related to the price of the good or service, during a specific period of time, everything else held constant.

2. Market supply is found by adding together the quantities supplied at each price by every producer in the market.

3. Supply changes if the prices of relevant resources change, if technology or productivity changes, if producers' expectations change, if the number of producers changes, or if the prices of related goods and services change.

4. Changes in supply are reflected in shifts of the supply curve. Changes in the quantity supplied are reflected in movements along the supply curve.

4. EQUILIBRIUM: PUTTING DEMAND AND SUPPLY TOGETHER

The demand curve shows the quantity of a good or service that buyers are willing and able to purchase at each price. The supply curve shows the quantity that producers are willing and able to offer for sale at each price. Only where the two curves intersect is the quantity supplied equal to the quantity demanded. This intersection is the point of **equilibrium.**

equilibrium: the price and quantity at which quantity demanded and quantity supplied are equal

4.a. Determination of Equilibrium

Figure 8 brings together the market demand and market supply curves for video rentals. The supply and demand schedules are listed in the table and the curves are

Figure 8

Equilibrium

Equilibrium is established at the point where the quantity that suppliers are willing and able to offer for sale is the same as the quantity that buyers are willing and able to purchase. Here, equilibrium occurs at the price of $3 per video and the quantity of 66 videos. It is shown as point *e* at the intersection of the demand and supply curves. At prices above $3, the quantity supplied is greater than the quantity demanded, and the result is a surplus. At prices below $3, the quantity supplied is less than the quantity demanded, and the result is a shortage. The area shaded brown shows all prices at which there is a surplus—where quantity supplied is greater than the quantity demanded. The surplus is measured in horizontal direction at each price. The area shaded blue represents all prices at which a shortage exists—where the quantity demanded is greater than the quantity supplied. The shortage is measured in a horizontal direction at each price.

Price per Video	Quantity Demanded per Year	Quantity Supplied per Year	Status
$5	30	102	Surplus of 72
$4	48	84	Surplus of 36
$3	66	66	Equilibrium
$2	84	48	Shortage of 36
$1	102	30	Shortage of 72

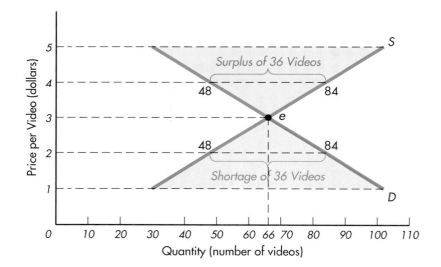

4. How is price determined by demand and supply?

disequilibrium: a point at which quantity demanded and quantity supplied are not equal at a particular price

surplus: a quantity supplied that is larger than the quantity demanded at a given price; it occurs whenever the price is greater than the equilibrium price

shortage: a quantity supplied that is smaller than the quantity demanded at a given price; it occurs whenever the price is less than the equilibrium price

5. What causes price to change?

plotted in the graph in Figure 8. Notice that the curves intersect at only one point, labeled *e*, a price of $3 and a quantity of 66. The intersection point is the equilibrium price, the only price at which the quantity demanded and quantity supplied are the same. You can see that at any other price the quantity demanded and quantity supplied are not the same. These are called **disequilibrium** points.

Whenever the price is greater than the equilibrium price, a **surplus** arises. For example, at $4, the quantity of videos demanded is 48 and the quantity supplied is 84. Thus, at $4 per video there is a surplus of 36 videos—that is, 36 videos are not rented. Conversely, whenever the price is below the equilibrium price, the quantity demanded is greater than the quantity supplied and there is a **shortage.** For instance, if the price is $2 per video, consumers will want and be able to pay for more videos than are available. As shown in the table in Figure 8, the quantity demanded at a price of $2 is 84 but the quantity supplied is only 48. There is a shortage of 36 videos at the price of $2.

Neither a surplus nor a shortage exists for long if the price of the product is free to change. Producers who are stuck with videos sitting on the shelves getting brittle and out of style will lower the price and reduce the quantities they are offering for rent in order to eliminate a surplus. Conversely, producers whose shelves are empty even as consumers demand videos will acquire more videos and raise the rental price to eliminate a shortage. Surpluses lead to decreases in the price and the quantity supplied and increases in the quantity demanded. Shortages lead to increases in the price and the quantity supplied and decreases in the quantity demanded.

Note that a shortage is not the same thing as scarcity. A shortage exists only when the quantity that people are willing and able to purchase at a particular price is more than the quantity supplied *at that price.* Scarcity occurs when more is wanted at a zero price than is available.

4.b. Changes in the Equilibrium Price: Demand Shifts

Equilibrium is the combination of price and quantity at which the quantities demanded and supplied are the same. Once an equilibrium is achieved, there is no incentive for producers or consumers to move away from it. An equilibrium price changes only when demand and/or supply changes—that is, when the determinants of demand or determinants of supply change.

Let's consider a change in demand and what it means for the equilibrium price. Suppose that experiments on rats show that watching videos causes brain damage. As a result, a large segment of the human population decides not to rent videos. Stores find that the demand for videos has decreased, as shown in Figure 9 by a leftward shift of the demand curve, from curve D_1 to curve D_2.

Once the demand curve has shifted, the original equilibrium price of $3 per video at point e_1 is no longer equilibrium. At a price of $3, the quantity supplied is still 66, but the quantity demanded has declined to 48 (look at the demand curve D_2 at a price of $3). There is, therefore, a surplus of 18 videos at the price of $3.

With a surplus comes downward pressure on the price. This downward pressure occurs because producers acquire fewer videos to offer for rent and reduce the rental price in an attempt to rent the videos sitting on the shelves. Producers continue reducing the price and the quantity available until consumers rent all copies of the videos that the sellers have available, or until a new equilibrium is established. That new equilibrium occurs at point e_2 with a price of $2.50 and a quantity of 57.

The decrease in demand is represented by the leftward shift of the demand curve. A decrease in demand results in a lower equilibrium price and a lower equilibrium

Figure 9

The Effects of a Shift of the Demand Curve

The initial equilibrium price ($3 per video) and quantity (66 videos) are established at point e_1, where the initial demand and supply curves intersect. A change in the tastes for videos causes demand to decrease, and the demand curve shifts to the left. At $3 per video, the initial quantity supplied, 66 videos, is now greater than the quantity demanded, 48 videos. The surplus of 18 units causes producers to reduce production and lower the price. The market reaches a new equilibrium, at point e_2, $2.50 per video and 57 videos.

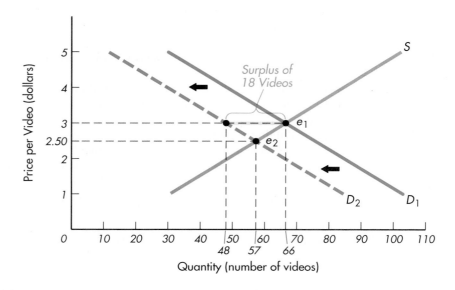

quantity as long as there is no change in supply. Conversely, an increase in demand would be represented as a rightward shift of the demand curve and would result in a higher equilibrium price and a higher equilibrium quantity as long as there is no change in supply.

4.c. Changes in Equilibrium Price: Supply Shifts

The equilibrium price and quantity may be altered by a change in supply as well. If the price of relevant resources, technology and productivity, expectations of producers, the number of producers, or the prices of related products change, supply changes.

Let's consider an example. Petroleum is a key ingredient in videotapes. Suppose the quantity of oil available is reduced by 40 percent, causing the price of oil to rise. Every video manufacturer has to pay more for oil, which means that the rental stores must pay more for each videotape. To purchase the videos and offer them for rent, the rental stores must receive a higher rental price in order to cover their higher costs. This is represented by a leftward shift of the supply curve in Figure 10.

The leftward shift of the supply curve, from curve S_1 to curve S_2, leads to a new equilibrium price and quantity. At the original equilibrium price of $3 at point e_1, 66

Figure 10

The Effects of a Shift of the Supply Curve

The initial equilibrium price and quantity are $3 and 66 units, at point e_1. When the price of labor increases, suppliers are willing and able to offer fewer videos for rent at each price. The result is a leftward (upward) shift of the supply curve, from S_1 to S_2. At the old price of $3, the quantity demanded is still 66, but the quantity supplied falls to 48. The shortage is 18 videos. The shortage causes suppliers to acquire more videos to offer for rent and to raise the rental price. The new equilibrium, e_2, the intersection between curves S_2 and D, is $3.50 per video and 57 videos.

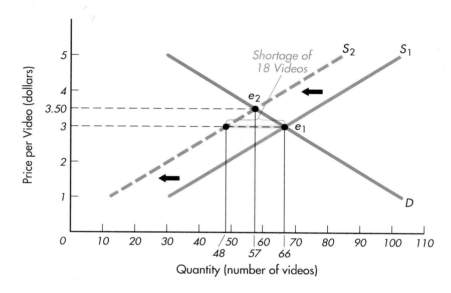

videos are supplied. After the shift in the supply curve, 48 videos are offered for rent at a price of $3 apiece, and there is a shortage of 18 videos. The shortage puts upward pressure on price. As the price rises, consumers decrease the quantities that they are willing and able to rent, and sellers increase the quantities that they are willing and able to supply. Eventually, a new equilibrium price and quantity is established at $3.50 and 57 videos at point e_2.

The decrease in supply is represented by the leftward shift of the supply curve. A decrease in supply with no change in demand results in a higher price and a lower quantity. Conversely, an increase in supply would be represented as a rightward shift of the supply curve. An increase in supply with no change in demand would result in a lower price and a higher quantity.

4.d. Equilibrium in Reality

6. What happens when price is not allowed to change with market forces?

We have examined a hypothetical (imaginary) market for video rentals in order to represent what goes on in real markets. We have established that the price of a good or service is defined by an equilibrium between demand and supply. We noted that an equilibrium could be disturbed by a change in demand, a change in supply, or simultaneous changes in demand and supply. The important point of this discussion is to demonstrate that when not in equilibrium, the price and the quantities demanded and/or supplied change until equilibrium is established. The market is always attempting to reach equilibrium.

Looking at last year's sweaters piled up on the sale racks, waiting over an hour for a table at a restaurant, finding that the VCR rental store doesn't have a copy of the movie you want to rent in stock, or hearing that 5 or 6 percent of people willing and able to work are unemployed may make you wonder whether equilibrium is ever established. In fact, it is not uncommon to observe situations where quantities demanded and supplied are not equal. But this observation does not cast doubt on the usefulness of the equilibrium concept. Even if all markets do not clear, or reach equilibrium, all the time, we can be reasonably assured that market forces are operating so that the market is moving toward an equilibrium. The market forces exist even when the price is not allowed to change, as illustrated in the following section.

price floor: a situation where the price is not allowed to decrease below a certain level

4.d.1. Price Ceilings and Price Floors   A **price floor** is a situation where the price is not allowed to decrease below a certain level. Consider Figure 11 representing the market for sugar. The equilibrium price of sugar is $.10 a pound, but because the government has set a price floor of $.20 a pound, as shown by the solid yellow line, the price is not allowed to move to its equilibrium level. A surplus of 250,000 pounds of sugar results from the price floor. Sugar growers produce 1 million pounds of sugar and consumers purchase 750,000 pounds of sugar.

We saw previously that whenever the price is above the equilibrium price, market forces work to decrease the price. The price floor interferes with the functioning of the market; a surplus exists because the government will not allow the price to drop. How does the government ensure that the price floor remains in force? It has to purchase the excess sugar. The government must purchase the surplus so that its price floor of $.20 per pound remains in force.

What would occur if the government had set the price floor at $.09 a pound? Since at $.09 a pound a shortage of sugar would result, the price would rise. A price

Figure 11

A Price Floor

The equilibrium price of sugar is $.10 a pound, but because the government has set a price floor of $.20 a pound, as shown by the solid yellow line, the price is not allowed to move to its equilibrium level. A surplus of 250,000 pounds of sugar results from the price floor. Sugar growers produce 1 million pounds of sugar and consumers purchase 750,000 pounds of sugar.

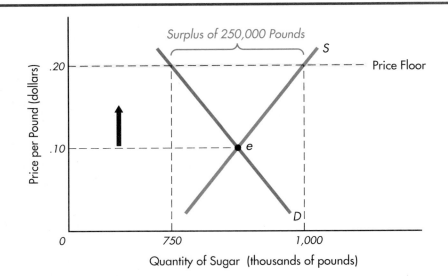

Figure 12

Rent Controls

A demand and supply graph representing the market for apartments in New York City is shown. The equilibrium price is $3,000 a month. The government has set a price of $1,500 a month. The government's price ceiling is shown by the solid yellow line. At the government's price, 3,000 apartments are available but consumers want 6,000. There is a shortage of 3,000 apartments.

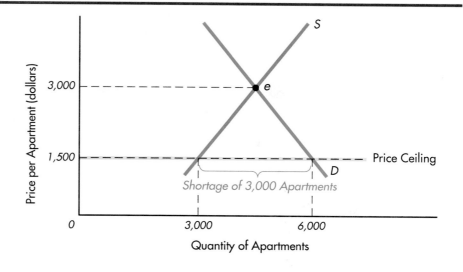

price ceiling: a situation where the price is not allowed to rise above a certain level

floor only keeps the price from falling, not rising. So the price rises to its equilibrium level of $.10. Only if the price floor is set above the equilibrium price is it an effective price floor.

A **price ceiling** is the situation where a price is not allowed to rise to its equilibrium level. Los Angeles, San Francisco, and New York are among over 125 U.S. cities that have *rent controls*. A rent control law places a ceiling on the rents that landlords can charge for apartments. Figure 12 is a demand and supply graph representing the market for apartments in New York. The equilibrium price is $3,000 a month. The government has set a price of $1,500 a month as the maximum that can be charged. The price ceiling is shown by the solid yellow line. At the rent control price of $1,500 per month, 3,000 apartments are available but consumers want 6,000 apartments. There is a shortage of 3,000 apartments.

The shortage means that not everyone willing and able to purchase the apartment will be allowed to. Since the price is not allowed to ration the apartments, something else will have to. It may be that those willing and able to stand in line the longest get the apartments. Perhaps bribing an important official might be the way to get an apartment. Perhaps relatives of officials or important citizens will get the apartments. Whenever a price ceiling exists, a shortage results and some rationing device other than price will arise.

Had the government set the rent control price at $4,000 per month, the price ceiling would not have had an effect. Since the equilibrium is $3,000 a month, the price would not have risen to $4,000. Only if the price ceiling is below the equilibrium price will it be an effective price ceiling.

Price ceilings are not uncommon features in the United States or in other economies. China had a severe housing shortage for 30 years because the price of housing was kept below equilibrium. Faced with unhappy citizens and realizing the cause of the shortage, officials began to lift the restrictions on housing prices in 1985. The shortage has diminished. In the former Soviet Union, prices on all goods and services were defined by the government. For most consumer items, the price was set below equilibrium; shortages existed. The long lines of people waiting to purchase food or clothing were the result of the price ceilings on all goods and services. In the United States, price ceilings on all goods and services have been imposed at times. During the First and Second World Wars and during the Nixon administration of the early 1970s, wage and price controls were imposed. These were price ceilings on all goods and services. As a result of the ceilings, people were unable to purchase many of the products they desired. The Organization of Petroleum Exporting Countries (OPEC) restricted the quantity of oil in the early 1970s and drove its price up considerably. The U.S. government responded by placing a price ceiling on gasoline. The result was long lines at gas stations—shortages of gasoline.

Price floors are quite common features in economies as well. The agricultural policies of most of the developed nations are founded on price floors—the government guarantees that the price of an agricultural product will not fall below some level. Price floors result in surpluses, and this has been the case with agricultural products as well. The surpluses in agricultural products in the United States have resulted in cases where dairy farmers dumped milk in the river, where grain was given to other nations at taxpayer expense, and where citrus ranchers picked and then discarded thousands of tons of citrus, all to reduce huge surpluses.

There are many reasons other than price ceilings and price floors why we observe excess supplies or demands in the real world. In most cases, the excess demands or supplies are due to the difficulty of changing prices rapidly or to the desires of either the demanders or suppliers not to have prices change rapidly. We shall consider many such cases in the text. The important part of the discussion in this chapter is to keep in mind that unless the price is not allowed to change, surpluses and shortages will put pressure on the price to move to its equilibrium level.

RECAP

1. Equilibrium occurs when the quantity demanded and quantity supplied are equal: it is the price-quantity combination where the demand and supply curves intersect.

2. A price that is above the equilibrium price creates a surplus. Producers are willing and able to offer more for sale than buyers are willing and able to purchase.

3. A price that is below the equilibrium price leads to a shortage, because buyers are willing and able to purchase more than producers are willing and able to offer for sale.

4. When demand changes, price and quantity change in the same direction— both rise as demand increases and both fall as demand decreases.

5. When supply changes, price and quantity change but not in the same direction. When supply increases, price falls and quantity rises. When supply decreases, price rises and quantity falls.

6. When both demand and supply change, the direction of the change in price and quantity depends on the relative sizes of the changes of demand and supply.

7. A price floor is a situation where a price is set above the equilibrium price. This creates a surplus.

8. A price ceiling is a case where a price is set below the equilibrium price. This creates a shortage.

SUMMARY

❓ 1. What is a market?

1. A market is where buyers and sellers trade a well-defined good or service. *§1*

❓ 2. What is demand?

2. Demand is the quantities that buyers are willing and able to buy at alternative prices. *§2*

3. The quantity demanded is a specific amount at one price. *§2*

4. The law of demand states that as the price of a well-defined commodity rises (falls), the quantity demanded during a given period of time will fall (rise), everything else held constant. *§2.a*

5. Demand will change when one of the determinants of demand changes, that is, when income, tastes, prices of related goods and services, expectations, or number of buyers change. In addition, the demand may change when exchange rates change. A demand change is illustrated as a shift of the demand curve. *§2.e, 2.f*

❓ 3. What is supply?

6. Supply is the quantities that sellers will offer for sale at alternative prices. *§3.a*

7. The quantity supplied is the amount sellers offer for sale at one price. *§3.a*

8. The law of supply states that as the price of a well-defined commodity rises (falls), the quantity supplied during a given period of time will rise (fall), everything else held constant. *§3.a*

9. Supply changes when one of the determinants of supply changes, that is, when prices of resources, technology and productivity, expectations of producers, the number of producers, or the prices of related goods or services change. A supply change is illustrated as a shift of the supply curve. *§3.d*

❓ 4. How is price determined by demand and supply?

10. Together, demand and supply determine the equilibrium price and quantity. *§4*

❓ 5. What causes price to change?

11. A price that is above equilibrium creates a surplus, which leads to a lower price. A price that is below equilibrium creates a shortage, which leads to a higher price. *§4.a*

12. A change in demand or a change in supply (a shift of either curve) will cause the equilibrium price and quantity to change. *§4.b, 4.c*

13. Markets are not always in equilibrium, but forces work to move them toward equilibrium. *§4.d*

❓ 6. What happens when price is not allowed to change with market forces?

14. A price floor is a situation where a price is not allowed to decrease below a certain level—it is set above the equilibrium price. This creates a surplus. A price ceiling is a case where a price is not allowed to rise—it is set below the equilibrium price. This creates a shortage. *§4.d*

KEY TERMS

market *§1.a*

barter *§1.b*

double coincidence of wants *§1.b*

transaction costs *§1.b*

relative price *§1.c*

demand *§2*

quantity demanded *§2*

law of demand *§2.a*

determinants of demand *§2.a*

demand schedule *§2.b*

demand curve *§2.c*

substitute goods *§2.e.3*

complementary goods *§2.e.3*

exchange rate *§2.f*

supply *§3.a*

quantity supplied *§3.a*

law of supply *§3.a*

determinants of supply *§3.a*

EXERCISES

1. Illustrate each of the following events using a demand and supply diagram for bananas.

   a. Reports surface that imported bananas are infected with a deadly virus.
   b. Consumers' incomes drop.
   c. The price of bananas rises.
   d. The price of oranges falls.
   e. Consumers expect the price of bananas to decrease in the future.

2. Answer true or false and if the statement is false, change it to make it true. Illustrate your answers on a demand and supply graph.

   a. An increase in demand is represented by a movement up the demand curve.
   b. An increase in supply is represented by a movement up the supply curve.
   c. An increase in demand without any changes in supply will cause the price to rise.
   d. An increase in supply without any changes in demand will cause the price to rise.

3. Using the following schedule, define the equilibrium price and quantity. Describe the situation at a price of $10. What will occur? Describe the situation at a price of $2. What will occur?

Price	Quantity Demanded	Quantity Supplied
$ 1	500	100
$ 2	400	120
$ 3	350	150
$ 4	320	200
$ 5	300	300
$ 6	275	410
$ 7	260	500
$ 8	230	650
$ 9	200	800
$10	150	975

4. Suppose the government imposed a minimum price of $7 in the schedule of exercise 3. What would occur? Illustrate.

5. In exercise 3, indicate what the price would have to be to represent an effective price ceiling. Point out the surplus or shortage that results. Illustrate a price floor and provide an example of a price floor.

6. A common feature of skiing is waiting in lift lines. Does the existence of lift lines mean that the price is not working to allocate the scarce resource? If so, what should be done about it?

7. Why don't we observe barter systems as often as we observe the use of currency?

8. A severe drought in California has resulted in a nearly 30 percent reduction in the quantity of citrus grown and produced in California. Explain what effect this event might have on the Florida citrus market.

9. The prices of the Ralph Lauren Polo line of clothing are considerably higher than comparable quality lines. Yet, it sells more than a J. C. Penney brand line of clothing. Does this violate the law of demand?

10. In December, the price of Christmas trees rises and the quantity of trees sold rises. Is this a violation of the law of demand?

11. In recent years, the price of artificial Christmas trees has fallen while the quality has risen. What impact has this event had on the price of cut Christmas trees?

12. Many restaurants don't take reservations. You simply arrive and wait your turn. If you arrive at 7:30 in the evening, you have at least an hour wait. Notwithstanding that fact, a few people arrive, speak quietly with the maitre d', hand him some money, and are promptly seated. At some restaurants that do take reservations, there is a month wait for a Saturday evening, three weeks for a Friday evening, two weeks for Tuesday through Thursday, and virtually no wait for Sunday or Monday evening. How do you explain these events using demand and supply?

13. Evaluate the following statement: "The demand for U.S. oranges has increased because the quantity of U.S. oranges demanded in Japan has risen."

14. In December 1992, the federal government began requiring that all foods display information about fat content and other ingredients on food packages. The displays had to be verified by independent laborato- ries. The price of an evaluation of a food product could run as much as $20,000. What impact do you think this law had on the market for meat?

15. Draw a PPC. Which combination shown by the PPC will be produced? Does the combination that is produced depend on how goods and services are allocated?

Economically Speaking

A Sleuth for Landlords with Eviction in Mind

The silver Cadillac trolled by the stately red brick home a few times and then stopped in front. Two men in black suits and sunglasses stepped out of the car, drawing nervous glances from a crew of gardeners silently pruning bushes in an exclusive Westchester County neighborhood overlooking Long Island Sound.

After fishing something out of the trunk, one of the men, the stocky, bald fellow with the handlebar mustache, began walking toward the house. A private investigator named Vincent Parco, he wasn't playing games. His client wanted results, not excuses.

Suddenly, he reached into his bulging coat pocket. He pulled out a small video camera. He began filming the house, zooming in on the number on the mailbox and the license plates on the minivan in the driveway.

Mr. Parco is not the kind of P.I. who snaps photographs of married men in love nests with women who are not their wives. His specialty is getting the goods on people who two-time their landlords.

The owner of the house, he said, also had a rent-controlled apartment on East 83rd Street in Manhattan. The landlord of that building hired Mr. Parco in hopes of proving that the tenant has no right to remain in the apartment at below-market rent. Under state and city rent laws, those who benefit from rent regulation must use their apartments as their primary residences. Basically, that means they must live there at least half the time. . . .

In the case of an occupied apartment, if a landlord can prove in Housing Court that a tenant is spending less than 183 nights per year in the apartment, the landlord has a chance of evicting the tenant. Or he may simply have enough leverage to persuade the tenant to accept a modest buyout offer.

Then the landlord can try to deregulate the place and convert it to a condominium or co-op, or put it on the open rental market, often for many times the previous rent. . . .

Some landlord groups estimate that 20 percent of those who lease rent-regulated apartments do not use the apartment as their primary residence. These include the pied-a-terre set as well as tenants illegally subletting, those with suspected connections to prostitution, gambling and drugs, and those who use the apartments for commercial or professional purposes. . . .

COREY KILGANNON

Source: From the *New York Times,* March 26, 2000, p. 4. Copyright 2000 the New York Times Company.

New York Times/**March 26, 2000**

Commentary

Rent controls, at their simplest, can be represented as a price ceiling (see figure, below left). A rent control could be represented as a maximum, or ceiling price, of P_m, which is less than the equilibrium price P_1. This price ceiling creates a shortage: At the rent-control price P_m, the quantity of housing units demanded is Q_d while the quantity of housing units supplied is only Q_s. The difference, $Q_d - Q_s$, is the number of families willing and able to rent a house at price P_m but for whom there are no homes available.

How is this excess demand resolved? Two things occur. One is that something other than price serves as the allocator. Common replacements for price are: first-come, first-served; preferences of the landlord; or black market or under-the-table payoffs. The second is that the landlord decreases the maintenance on the existing rentals, and new rental units are not brought to the market. As the landlord experiences a lower return on the rental housing, he or she has a lower incentive to devote resources to the upkeep of the unit. As a result, the quality of the housing deteriorates. Unable to secure what he or she considers a fair return, the landlord has no incentive to make improvements or maintain the property.

Not only does rent control lead to deterioration but the lower return on the rental housing means that some landlords may convert their units to condominiums or to commercial properties and sell them. Over time, the supply of rental housing declines. The supply curve shifts in, to S_2 in the figure, below right, creating greater excess demand.

In the case of rent controls in New York, the inability of price to do the rationing of scarce apartments has created a cottage industry—the market for sleuths who discover tenants who are not using the rent-controlled apartment as specified by law. This industry would not exist if there were no rent controls. The cost of the industry is initially borne by the landlords whose costs of doing business rise, and thus, the supply curve shifts in further, driving rents even higher.

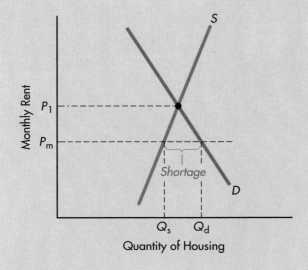

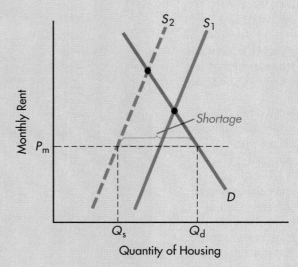

Chapter 4

The Market System and the Private Sector

? Fundamental Questions

1. **In a market system, who decides what goods and services are produced and how they are produced, and who obtains the goods and services that are produced?**

2. **What is a household, and what is household income and spending?**

3. **What is a business firm, and what is business spending?**

4. **How does the international sector affect the economy?**

5. **How do the three private sectors—households, businesses, and the international sector—interact in the economy?**

Preview

You decide to buy a new Toyota, so you go to a Toyota dealer and exchange money for the car. The Toyota dealer has rented land and buildings and hired workers in order to make cars available to you and other members of the public. The employees earn incomes paid by the Toyota dealer and then use their incomes to buy food from the grocery store. This transaction generates revenue for the grocery store, which hires workers and pays them incomes that they then use to buy groceries and Toyotas. Your expenditure for the Toyota is part of a circular flow. Revenue is received by the Toyota dealer, who pays employees, who, in turn, buy goods and services.

Of course, the story is complicated by the fact that the Toyota is originally manufactured and purchased in Japan and then shipped to the United States before it can be sold by the local Toyota dealer. Your purchase of the Toyota creates revenue for the local dealer as well as for the manufacturer in Japan, who pays Japanese autoworkers to produce Toyotas. Furthermore, when you buy your Toyota, you must

pay a tax to the government, which uses tax revenues to pay for police protection, national defense, the legal system, and other services. Many people in different areas of the economy are involved.

An economy is made up of individual buyers and sellers. Economists could discuss the neighborhood economy that surrounds your university, the economy of the city of Chicago, or the economy of the state of Massachusetts. But typically it is the national economy, the economy of the United States, that is the center of their attention. To clarify the operation of the national economy, economists usually group individual buyers and sellers into three sectors: households, businesses, and government. Omitted from this grouping, however, is an important source of activity, the international sector. Since the U.S. economy affects, and is affected by, the rest of the world, to understand how the economy functions, we must include the international sector.

We begin this chapter by examining the way that buyers and sellers interact in a market system. The impersonal forces of supply and demand operate to answer the following questions: Who determines what is produced and how they are produced? Who gets the output that is produced? The answers are given by the market system and involve the private-sector participants: households, business firms, and the international sector. Government also plays a major role in answering these questions, but we leave government and its role for the next chapter.

Following the discussion of the market system, we examine basic data and information on each individual sector with the objective of answering some general questions: What is a household, and how do households spend their incomes? What is a business firm, and how does a corporation differ from a partnership? What does it mean if the United States has a trade deficit?

After describing the three sectors that make up the private sector of the national economy, we present a simple economic model to illustrate the interrelationships linking all the individual sectors into the national economy. ■

1. THE MARKET SYSTEM

1. In a market system, who decides what goods and services are produced and how they are produced, and who obtains the goods and services that are produced?

As we learned in Chapter 2, the production possibilities curve represents all possible combinations of goods and services that a society can produce if its resources are used fully and efficiently. Which combination, that is, which point on the PPC, will society choose? In a price or market system, the answer is given by demand and supply.

1.a. Consumer Sovereignty

In recent years, time-starved Americans spent about as much time eating out as they did eating at home. In the 1950s and 1960s, this trend was just beginning. Consumers wanted more and more restaurants and fast-food outlets. As a result, McDonald's, Wendy's, Big Boy, White Castle, Pizza Hut, Godfather's Pizza, and other fast-food outlets flourished. The trend toward eating away from home reached fever pitch in the late 1970s, when the average number of meals per person eaten out (excluding brown-bag lunches and other meals prepared at home but eaten elsewhere) exceeded one per day.

In the 1980s, people wanted the fast food but didn't want to go get it. By emphasizing delivery, Domino's Pizza and a few other fast-food outlets became very successful. In the 1990s, the takeout taxi business—where restaurant food is delivered to homes—grew 10 percent per year. However, the star of this story is not Domino's, Pizza Hut, or other restaurants. It is the consumer. In a market system, if consumers are willing and able to pay for more restaurant meals, more restaurants appear. If consumers are willing and able to pay for food delivered to their homes, food is delivered to their homes.

Why does the consumer wield such power? The name of the game for business is profit, and the only way business can make a profit is by satisfying consumer wants. The consumer, not the politician or the business firm, ultimately determines what is to be produced. A firm that produces something that no consumers want will not remain in business very long. **Consumer sovereignty**—the authority of consumers to determine what is produced through their purchases of goods and services—dictates what goods and services will be produced. Supermarkets and grocery stores are responding to the consumer as well, by putting fast-food restaurants, like Pizza Hut and Taco Bell, inside their stores.

1.b. Profit and the Allocation of Resources

When a good or service seems to have the potential to generate a profit, someone with entrepreneurial ability will put together the resources needed to produce that good or service. An individual with entrepreneurial ability aims to earn a profit by renting land, hiring labor, and using capital to produce a good or service that can be sold for more than the sum of rent, wages, and interest. If the potential profit turns into a loss, the entrepreneur may stop buying resources and turn to some other occupation or project. The resources used in the losing operation would then be available for use in an activity where they would be more highly valued.

To illustrate how resources get allocated in the market system, let's look at the market for fast foods. Figure 1 shows a change in demand for meals eaten in restaurants. The initial demand curve, D_1, and supply curve, S, are shown in Figure 1(a). With these demand and supply curves, the equilibrium price (P_1) is \$8, and the equilibrium quantity (Q_1) is 100 units (meals). At this price-quantity combination, the number of meals demanded equals the number of meals sold; equilibrium is reached, so we say the market clears (there is no shortage or surplus).

The second part of the figure shows what happened when consumer tastes changed, and people preferred to have food delivered to their homes. This change in tastes caused the demand for restaurants to decline and is represented by a leftward shift of the demand curve, from D_1 to D_2, in Figure 1(b). The demand curve shifted to the left because fewer in-restaurant meals were demanded at each price. Consumer tastes, not the price of in-restaurant meals, changed first. (A price change would have led to a change in the quantity demanded and would be represented by a move *along* demand curve D_1.) The change in tastes caused a change in demand and a leftward shift of the demand curve. The shift from D_1 to D_2 created a new equilibrium point. The equilibrium price (P_2) decreased to \$6, and the equilibrium quantity (Q_2) decreased to 80 units (meals).

While the market for in-restaurant food was changing, so was the market for delivered food. People substituted meals delivered to their homes for meals eaten in restaurants. Figure 2(a) shows the original demand for food delivered to the home. Figure 2(b) shows a rightward shift of the demand curve, from D_1 to D_2, representing increased demand for home delivery. This demand change resulted in a higher market-clearing price for food delivered to the home, from \$10 to \$12.

The changing profit potential of the two markets induced existing firms to switch from in-restaurant service to home delivery and for new firms to offer delivery from the start. Domino's Pizza, which is a delivery-only firm, grew from a one-store operation to become the second largest pizza chain in the United States. Pizza Hut, which at first did not offer home delivery, had to play catch-up; and by 1992, about two-thirds of Pizza Hut's more than 5,000 restaurants were delivering pizza.

Figure 1

A Demand Change in the Market for In-Restaurant Food

In Figure 1(a), the initial market-clearing price (P_1) and market-clearing quantity (Q_1) are shown. In Figure 1(b), the market-clearing price and quantity change from P_1 and Q_1 to P_2 and Q_2 as the demand curve shifts to the left because of a change in tastes. The result of decreased demand is a lower price and a lower quantity produced.

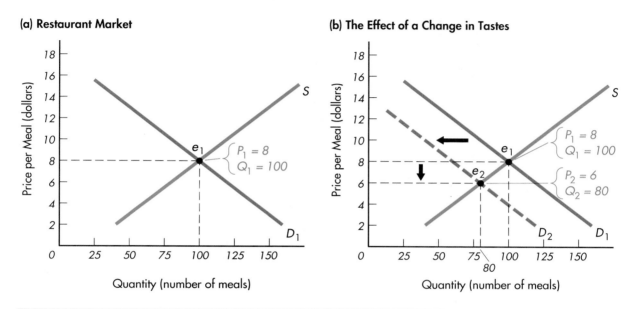

(a) Restaurant Market

(b) The Effect of a Change in Tastes

As the market-clearing price of in-restaurant fast food fell (from $8 to $6 in Figure 1), the quantity of in-restaurant meals sold also declined (from 100 to 80) because the decreased demand, lower price, and resulting lower profit induced some firms to decrease production. In the delivery business, the opposite occurred. As the market-clearing price rose (from $10 to $12 in Figure 2[b]), the number of meals delivered also rose (from 50 to 60). The increased demand, higher price, and resulting higher profit induced firms to increase production.

Why did the production of delivered foods increase while the production of meals at restaurants decreased? Not because of government decree. Not because of the desires of the business sector, especially the owners of restaurants. The consumer—consumer sovereignty—made all this happen. Businesses that failed to respond to consumer desires and failed to provide the desired good at the lowest price failed to survive.

1.c. The Flow of Resources

After demand shifted to home-delivered food, the resources that had been used in the restaurants were available for use elsewhere. A few former waiters, waitresses, and cooks were able to get jobs in the delivery firms. Some of the equipment used in eat-in restaurants—ovens, pots, and pans—was purchased by the delivery firms; and some of the ingredients that previously would have gone to the eat-in restaurants

Figure 2

A Demand Change in the Market for Delivered Food

In Figure 2(a), the initial market-clearing price (P_1) and quantity (Q_1) are shown. In Figure 2(b), the demand for delivered food increases, thus driving up the market-clearing price (P_2) and quantity (Q_2), as the demand curve shifts to the right, from D_1 to D_2.

(a) Delivery Market

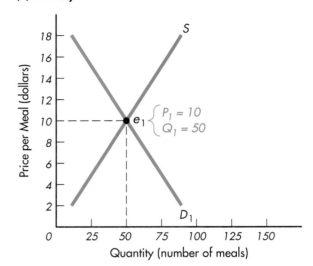

(b) The Effect of a Change in Tastes

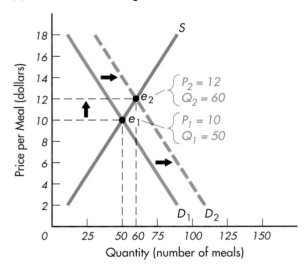

were bought by the delivery firms. A few former employees of the eat-in restaurants became employed at department stores, at local pubs, and at hotels. Some of the equipment was sold as scrap; other equipment was sold to other restaurants. In other words, the resources moved from an activity where their value was relatively low to an activity where they were more highly valued. No one commanded the resources to move. They moved because they could earn more in some other activity.

Adam Smith described this phenomenon in his 1776 treatise *The Wealth of Nations,* saying it was as if an invisible hand reached out and guided the resources to their most-valued use. That invisible hand is the self-interest that drives firms to provide what consumers want to buy, leads consumers to use their limited incomes to buy the goods and services that bring them the greatest satisfaction, and induces resource owners to supply resource services where they are most highly valued. (There is more about Smith in the Economic Insight "Adam Smith.")

Competitive firms produce in the manner that minimizes costs and maximizes profits.

Firms produce the goods and services and use the resources that enable them to generate the highest profits. If one firm does this better than others, then that firm earns a greater profit than others. Seeing that success, other firms copy or mimic the first firm. If a firm cannot be as profitable as the others, it will eventually go out of business or move to another line of business where it can be successful. In the process of firms always seeking to lower costs and make higher profits, society finds that the goods and services buyers want are produced in the least costly manner. Consumers not only get the goods and services they want and will pay for, but they get these products at the lowest possible price.

1.d. The Determination of Income

Ownership of resources determines who gets what goods and services in a market system.

Consumer demands dictate *what* is produced, and the search for profit defines *how* goods and services are produced. *For whom* are the goods and services produced, that is, who gets the goods and services? In a price or market system, those who have the ability to pay for the products get the products. Your income determines your ability to pay, but where does income come from? Income is obtained by selling the services of resources. When you sell your labor services, your money income reflects your wage rate or salary level. When you sell the services of the capital you own, you receive interest; and when you sell the services of the land you own, you receive rent. A person with entrepreneurial ability earns profit as a payment for services. Thus, we see that buyers and sellers of goods and services and resource owners are linked together in an economy: the more one buys, the more income or revenue the other receives. In the remainder of this chapter, we learn more about the linkages among the sectors of the economy. We classify the buyers and the resource owners into the household sector; the sellers or business firms are the business sector; households and firms in other countries, who may also be buyers and sellers of this country's goods and services, are the international sector. These three sectors—

Adam Smith

Economic Insight

Adam Smith was born in 1723 and reared in Kirkcaldy, Scotland, near Edinburgh. He went to the University of Glasgow when he was 14, and three years later began studies at Oxford, where he stayed for six years. In 1751, Smith became professor of logic and then moral philosophy at Glasgow. From 1764 to 1766, he tutored the future duke of Buccleuch in France, and then he was given a pension for the remainder of his life. Between 1766 and 1776, Smith completed *The Wealth of Nations.* He became commissioner of customs for Scotland and spent his remaining years in Edinburgh. He died in 1790.

Economists date the beginning of their discipline from the publication of *The Wealth of Nations* in 1776. In this major treatise, Smith emphasizes the role of self-interest in the functioning of markets, specialization, and division of labor.

According to Smith, the fundamental explanation of human behavior is found in the rational pursuit of self-interest. Smith uses it to explain how men choose occupations, how farmers till their lands, and how leaders of the American Revolution were led by it to rebellion. Smith did not equate self-interest with selfishness but broadened the definition of self-interest, believing that a person is interested "in the fortune of others and renders their happiness necessary to him, though he derives nothing from it, except the pleasure of seeing it." On the basis of self-interest, Smith constructed a theory of how markets work: how goods, once produced, are sold to the highest bidders, and how the quantities of the goods that are produced are governed by their costs and selling prices. But Smith's insight showed that this self-interest resulted in the best situation for society as a whole. In a celebrated and often-quoted

passage from the treatise Smith says:

> But man has almost constant occasion for the help of his brethren, and it is in vain for him to expect it from their benevolence only. He will be more likely to prevail if he can interest their self-love in his favour, and show them that it is for their own advantage to do for him what he requires of them. . . . It is not from the benevolence of the butcher, the brewer, or the baker, that we can expect our dinner, but from their regard to their own interest.

Source: *An Inquiry into the Nature and Causes of the Wealth of Nations,* edited and with an introduction, notes, marginal summary, and index by Edwin Cannan. (Chicago: University of Chicago Press, 1976). Reprinted by permission of the University of Chicago Press.

private sector: households, businesses, and the international sector

public sector: the government

households, business firms, and the international sector—constitute the **private sector** of the economy. In this chapter we focus on the interaction among the components of the private sector. In the next chapter we focus on the **public sector,** government, and examine its role in the economy.

RECAP

1. In a market system, consumers are sovereign and decide by means of their purchases what goods and services will be produced.

2. In a market system, firms decide how to produce the goods and services that consumers want. In order to earn maximum profits, firms use the least-cost combinations of resources.

3. Income and prices determine who gets what in a market system. Income is determined by the ownership of resources.

2. What is a household, and what is household income and spending?

household: one or more persons who occupy a unit of housing

2. HOUSEHOLDS

A **household** consists of one or more persons who occupy a unit of housing. The unit of housing may be a house, an apartment, or even a single room, as long as it constitutes separate living quarters. A household may consist of related family members, like a father, mother, and children, or it may comprise unrelated individuals, like three college students sharing an apartment. The person in whose name the house or apartment is owned or rented is called the *householder.*

2.a. Number of Households and Household Income

There are more than 103 million households in the United States. The breakdown of households by age of householder is shown in Figure 3. Householders between 35 and 44 years old make up the largest number of households. Householders between 45 and 54 years old have the largest median income. The *median* is the middle value—half of the households in an age group have an income higher than the median and half have an income lower than the median. Figure 3 shows that households in which the householder is between 45 and 54 years old have a median income of about $54,000, substantially higher than the median incomes of other age groups. Typically, workers in this age group are at the peak of their earning power. Younger households are gaining experience and training; older households include retired workers.

The size distribution of households in the United States is shown in Figure 4. Thirty-three percent of all households, or 34,262,000 are two-person households. The stereotypical household of husband, wife, and two children accounts for only 14 percent of all households. There are relatively few large households in the United States. Of the more than 103 million households in the country, only 1,261,000 (1 percent) have seven or more persons.

2.b. Household Spending

consumption: household spending

Household spending is called **consumption.** Householders consume housing, transportation, food, entertainment, and other goods and services. Household spending (also called *consumer spending*) per year in the United States is shown in Figure 5, along with household income. The pattern is one of steady increase. Spending by the household sector is the largest component of total spending in the economy—rising to over $6 trillion in 1999.

Figure 3

Age of Householder, Number of Households, and Median Household Income in the United States

The graph reveals that householders aged 35 to 44 make up the largest number of households, and householders aged 45 to 54 earn the highest median annual income. Source: U.S. Department of Commerce, *Money Income in the United States,* September, 1999.

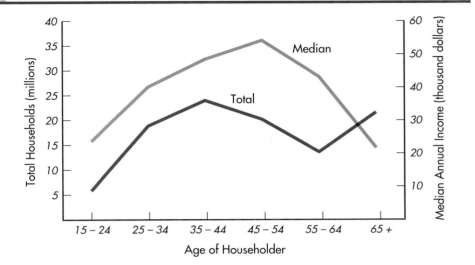

RECAP

1. A household consists of one or more persons who occupy a unit of housing.
2. An apartment or house is rented or owned by a householder.
3. As a group, householders between the ages of 45 and 54 have the highest median incomes.
4. Household spending is called *consumption.*

Figure 4

Size Distribution of Households in the United States

As the pie chart illustrates, two-person households make up a larger percentage of the total number of households than any other group, a total of 33 percent. Large households with seven or more persons are becoming a rarity, accounting for only 1 percent of the total number of households. Source: U.S. Department of Commerce, *Money Income in the United States,* September 1999.

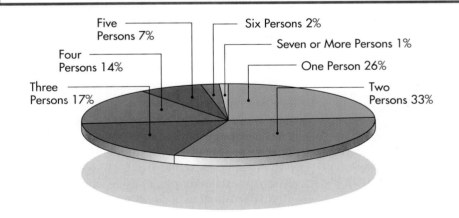

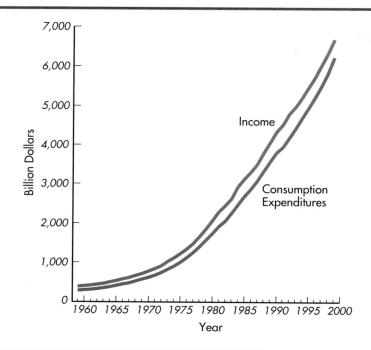

Figure 5

Household Spending and Income

Household spending (consumption) and income each year from 1959 to 1999 are shown. Both show a pattern of steady increase. Source: U.S. Department of Commerce (Bureau of Economic Analysis and Bureau of the Census).

3. What is a business firm, and what is business spending?

business firm: a business organization controlled by a single management

sole proprietorship: a business owned by one person who receives all the profits and is responsible for all the debts incurred by the business

partnership: a business with two or more owners who share the firm's profits and losses

corporation: a legal entity owned by shareholders whose liability for the firm's losses is limited to the value of the stock they own

3. BUSINESS FIRMS

A **business firm** is a business organization controlled by a single management. The firm's business may be conducted at more than one location. The terms *company, enterprise,* and *business* are used interchangeably with *firm.*

3.a. Forms of Business Organizations

Firms are organized as sole proprietorships, partnerships, or corporations. A **sole proprietorship** is a business owned by one person. This type of firm may be a one-person operation or a large enterprise with many employees. In either case, the owner receives all the profits and is responsible for all the debts incurred by the business.

A **partnership** is a business owned by two or more partners who share both the profits of the business and responsibility for the firm's losses. The partners could be individuals, estates, or other businesses.

A **corporation** is a business whose identity in the eyes of the law is distinct from the identity of its owners. State law allows the formation of corporations. A corporation is an economic entity that, like a person, can own property and borrow money in its own name. The owners of a corporation are shareholders. If a corporation cannot pay its debts, creditors cannot seek payment from the shareholders' personal wealth. The corporation itself is responsible for all its actions. The shareholders' liability is limited to the value of the stock they own.

Many firms are global in their operations even though they may have been founded and may be owned by residents of a single country. Firms typically first

multinational business: a
firm that owns and operates
producing units in foreign
countries

enter the international market by selling products to foreign countries. As revenues from these sales increase, the firms realize advantages by locating subsidiaries in foreign countries. A **multinational business** is a firm that owns and operates producing units in foreign countries. The best-known U.S. corporations are multinational firms. Ford, IBM, PepsiCo, and McDonald's all own operating units in many different countries. Ford Motor Company, for instance, is the parent firm of sales organizations and assembly plants located around the world. As transportation and communication technologies progress, multinational business activity will grow.

3.b. Business Statistics

Figure 6(a) shows that in the United States there are far more sole proprietorships than partnerships or corporations. Figure 6(a) also compares the revenues earned by each type of business. The great majority of sole proprietorships are small businesses, with revenues under $25,000 a year. Similarly, over half of all partnerships also have revenues under $25,000 a year, but only 23 percent of the corporations are in this category.

Figure 6(b) shows that the 68 percent of sole proprietorships that earn less than $25,000 a year account for only about 9 percent of the revenue earned by proprietorships. The 0.4 percent of proprietorships with revenue of $1 million or more account for about 19 percent. Even more striking are the figures for partnerships and corporations. The 58 percent of partnerships with the smallest revenue account for only 0.4 percent of the total revenue earned by partnerships. At the other extreme, the 5 percent of partnerships with the largest revenue account for 88 percent of total partnership revenue. The 23 percent of corporations in the smallest range account for less than 0.1 percent of total corporate revenue, while the 18 percent of corporations in the largest range account for 94 percent of corporate revenue.

The message of Figure 6 is that big business is important in the United States. There are many small firms, but large firms and corporations account for the greatest share of business revenue. Although there are only about one-third as many corporations as sole proprietorships, corporations have more than fifteen times the revenue of sole proprietorships.

3.c. Firms Around the World

Big business is a dominant force in the United States. Many people believe that because the United States is the world's largest economy, U.S. firms are the largest in the world. Figure 7 shows that this is not true. Of the ten largest corporations in the world (measured by sales), four are Japanese. Big business is not just a U.S. phenomenon.

3.d. Entrepreneurial Ability

The emphasis on bigness should not hide the fact that many new firms are started each year. Businesses are typically begun as small sole proprietorships. Many of them are forced to go out of business within a year or two. Businesses survive in the long run only if they provide a good or service that people want enough to yield a profit for the entrepreneur. Although there are fabulous success stories, the failure rate among new firms is high. Thorough research of the market and careful planning play a large part in determining whether a new business succeeds but so can luck, as the Economic Insight "The Successful Entrepreneur" confirms.

Figure 6

Number and Revenue of Business Firms

As Figure 6(a) illustrates, most sole proprietorships and partnerships are small firms, with nearly 70 percent of all proprietorships falling into the less-than-$25,000 revenue category, and nearly 60 percent of all partnerships falling into the same lowest revenue category. Corporations are more likely to be larger—18 percent have revenues exceeding $1 million. Figure 6(b) shows that most sole proprietorship revenues are earned by the larger proprietorships, those in the $100,000 to $499,000 category. By contrast, the small number of partnerships in the top revenue category is enough to account for 88 percent of all partnership revenues. (Note: totals do not always equal 100%.)
Source: *Economic Report of the President, 2000.*

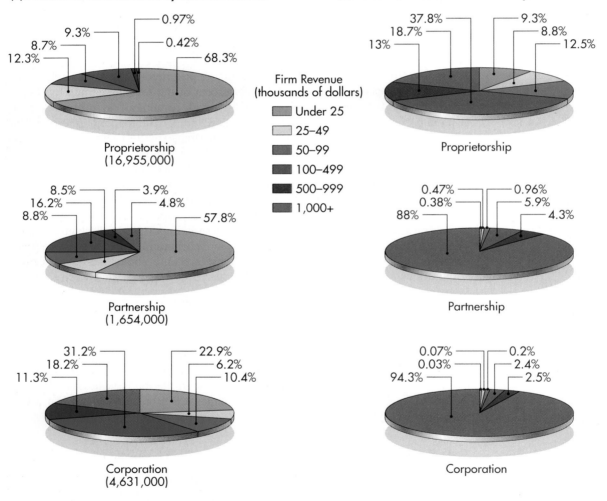

(a) Number of Business Firms by Revenue Amount

Proprietorship
(16,955,000)
0.97% · 0.42% · 68.3% · 9.3% · 8.7% · 12.3%

Partnership
(1,654,000)
8.5% · 3.9% · 4.8% · 57.8% · 16.2% · 8.8%

Corporation
(4,631,000)
31.2% · 22.9% · 6.2% · 10.4% · 18.2% · 11.3%

Firm Revenue
(thousands of dollars)
- Under 25
- 25–49
- 50–99
- 100–499
- 500–999
- 1,000+

(b) Percent of Total Business Firms by Revenue Amount

Proprietorship
37.8% · 9.3% · 8.8% · 18.7% · 12.5% · 13%

Partnership
0.47% · 0.96% · 0.38% · 5.9% · 88% · 4.3%

Corporation
0.07% · 0.2% · 0.03% · 2.4% · 94.3% · 2.5%

The Successful Entrepreneur (Sometimes It's Better to Be Lucky Than Good)

Entrepreneurs do not always develop an abstract idea into reality when starting a new firm. Sometimes people stumble onto a good thing by accident and then are clever enough and willing to take the necessary risk to turn their lucky find into a commercial success.

In 1875, a Philadelphia pharmacist on his honeymoon tasted tea made from an innkeeper's old family recipe. The tea, made from sixteen wild roots and berries, was so delicious that the pharmacist asked the innkeeper's wife for the recipe. When he returned to his pharmacy, he created a solid concentrate of the drink that could be sold for home consumption.

The pharmacist was Charles Hires, a devout Quaker, who intended to sell "Hires Herb Tea" to hard-drinking Pennsylvania coal miners as a nonalcoholic alternative to beer and whiskey. A friend of Hires suggested that miners would not drink anything called "tea" and recommended that he call his drink "root beer."

The initial response to Hires Root Beer was so enthusiastic that Hires soon began nationwide distribution. The yellow box of root beer extract was a familiar sight in homes and drugstore fountains across the United States. By 1895, Hires, who started with a $3,000 loan, was operating a business valued at half a million dollars (a lot of money in 1895) and bottling ready-to-drink root beer across the country.

Hires, of course, is not the only entrepreneur clever enough to turn a lucky discovery into a business success. In 1894, in Battle Creek, Michigan, a sanitarium handyman named Will Kellogg was helping his older brother prepare wheat meal to serve to patients in the sanitarium's dining room. The two men would boil wheat dough and then run it through rollers to produce thin sheets of meal. One day they left a batch of the dough out overnight. The next day, when the dough was run through the rollers, it broke up into flakes instead of forming a sheet.

By letting the dough stand overnight, the Kelloggs had allowed moisture to be distributed evenly to each individual wheat berry. When the dough went through the rollers, the berries formed separate flakes instead of binding together. The Kelloggs toasted the wheat flakes and served them to the patients. They were an immediate success. In fact, the brothers had to start a mail-order flaked-cereal business because patients wanted flaked cereal for their households.

Kellogg saw the market potential for the discovery and started his own cereal company (his brother refused to join him in the business). He was a great promoter who used innovations like four-color magazine ads and free-sample promotions. In New York City, he offered a free box of corn flakes to every woman who winked at her grocer on a specified day. The promotion was considered risqué, but Kellogg's sales in New York increased from two railroad cars of cereal a month to one car a day.

Will Kellogg, a poorly paid sanitarium worker in his mid-forties, became a daring entrepreneur after his mistake with wheat flour led to the discovery of a way to produce flaked cereal. He became one of the richest men in America because of his entrepreneurial ability.

Source: *Entrepreneurs* by Joseph and Suzy Fucini. Hall and Company, 1985.

That many new businesses fail is a fact of economic life. In the U.S. economy, anyone with an idea and sufficient resources has the freedom to open a business. However, if buyers do not respond to the new offering, the business fails. Only firms that satisfy this "market test" survive. Entrepreneurs thus try to ensure that as wants change, goods and services are produced to satisfy those wants.

3.e. Business Spending

investment: spending on capital goods to be used in producing goods and services

Investment is the expenditure by business firms for capital goods—machines, tools, and buildings—that will be used to produce goods and services. The economic meaning of *investment* is different from the everyday meaning, "a financial

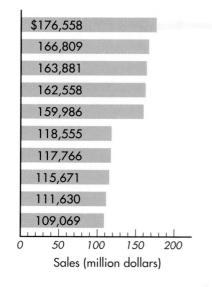

Figure 7

The World's Ten Largest Public Companies

As shown in the chart, large firms are not just a U.S. phenomenon. Source: *Fortune* Global 500, ©2000 Time Inc. All rights reserved.

Rank	Firm (country)	Sales (million dollars)
1	General Motors (U.S.)	$176,558
2	Wal-Mart Stores (U.S.)	166,809
3	Exxon Mobil (U.S.)	163,881
4	Ford Motor (U.S.)	162,558
5	DaimlerChrysler (Germany/U.S.)	159,986
6	Mitsui (Japan)	118,555
7	Mitsubishi (Japan)	117,766
8	Toyota Motor (Japan)	115,671
9	General Electric (U.S.)	111,630
10	Itochu (Japan)	109,069

transaction such as buying bonds or stocks." In economics, the term *investment* refers to business spending for capital goods.

Investment spending in 1999 was $1,577 billion, an amount equal to roughly one-fourth of consumption, or household spending. Investment spending between 1959 and 1999 is shown in Figure 8. Compare Figures 5 and 8 and notice the different patterns of spending. Investment increases unevenly, actually falling at times and then rising very rapidly. Even though investment spending is much smaller than consumption, the wide swings in investment spending mean that business expenditures are an important factor in determining the economic health of the nation.

RECAP

1. Business firms may be organized as sole proprietorships, partnerships, or corporations.
2. Large corporations account for the largest fraction of total business revenue.
3. Many new firms are started each year, but the failure rate is high.
4. Business investment spending fluctuates widely over time.

4. How does the international sector affect the economy?

4. THE INTERNATIONAL SECTOR

Today, foreign buyers and sellers have a significant effect on economic conditions in the United States, and developments in the rest of the world often influence U.S. buyers and sellers. We saw in Chapter 3, for instance, how exchange rate changes can affect the demand for U.S. goods and services.

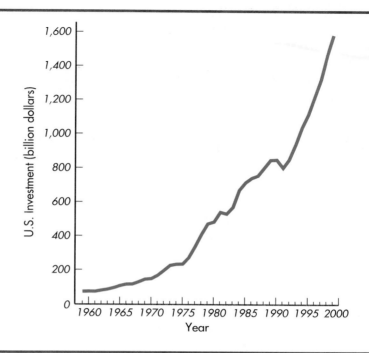

Figure 8

U.S. Investment Spending

Business expenditures on capital goods have been increasing erratically since 1959. Source: *Economic Report of the President, 2000.*

4.a. Types of Countries

The nations of the world may be divided into two categories: industrial countries and developing countries. Developing countries greatly outnumber industrial countries (see Figure 9). The World Bank (an international organization that makes loans to developing countries) groups countries according to per capita income (income per person). Low-income economies are those with per capita incomes of $755 or less. Middle-income economies have per capita incomes of $756 to $9,265. High-income economies—oil exporters and industrial market economies—are distinguished from the middle-income economies and have per capita incomes of greater than $9,266. Some countries are not members of the World Bank and so are not categorized, and information about a few small countries is so limited that the World Bank is unable to classify them.

It is readily apparent from Figure 9 that low-income economies are heavily concentrated in Africa and Asia. Countries in these regions have a low profile in U.S. trade, although they may receive aid from the United States. U.S. trade is concentrated with its neighbors Canada and Mexico, along with the major industrial powers. Nations in each group present different economic challenges to the United States.

4.a.1. The Industrial Countries   The World Bank uses per capita income to classify twenty-three countries as "industrial market economies." They are listed in the bar chart in Figure 10. The twenty-three countries listed in Figure 10 are among

Figure 9

World Economic Development

The colors on the map identify low-income, middle-income, and high-income economies. Countries have been placed in each group on the basis of GNP per capita and, in some instances, other distinguishing economic characteristics. Source: *World Development Report, 2000.*

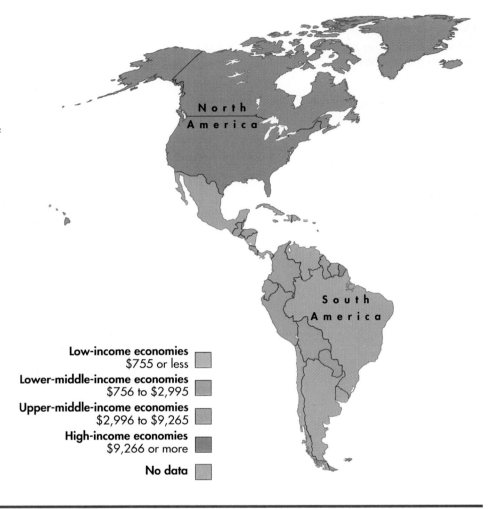

Low-income economies
$755 or less

Lower-middle-income economies
$756 to $2,995

Upper-middle-income economies
$2,996 to $9,265

High-income economies
$9,266 or more

No data

the wealthiest countries in the world. Not appearing on the list are the high-income oil-exporting nations like Libya, Saudi Arabia, Kuwait, and the United Arab Emirates. The World Bank considers those countries to be "still developing."

The economies of the industrial nations are highly interdependent. As conditions change in one country, business firms and individuals looking for the best return or interest rate on their funds may shift large sums of money between countries. As the funds flow from one country to another, economic conditions in one country spread to other countries. As a result, the industrial countries, particularly the major economic powers like the United States, Germany, and Japan, are forced to pay close attention to each other's economic policies.

4.a.2. The Developing Countries   The developing countries provide a different set of problems for the United States than do the industrial countries. In the

1980s, the debts of the developing countries to the developed nations reached tremendous heights. For instance, at the end of 1989, Brazil owed foreign creditors $111.3 billion, Mexico owed $95.6 billion, and Argentina owed $64.7 billion. In each case, the amounts owed were more than several times the annual sales of goods and services by those countries to the rest of the world. The United States had to arrange loans at special terms and establish special trade arrangements in order for those countries to be able to buy U.S. goods.

imports: products that a country buys from other countries

exports: products that a country sells to other countries

The United States tends to buy, or *import,* primary products such as agricultural produce and minerals from the developing countries. Products that a country buys from another country are called **imports.** The United States tends to sell, or *export,* manufactured goods to developing countries. Products that a country sells to another country are called **exports.** The United States is the largest producer and exporter of grains and other agricultural output in the world. The efficiency of U.S. farming

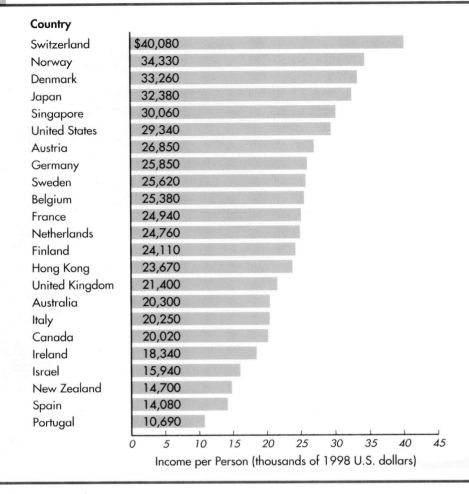

Figure 10

The Industrial Market Economies

The bar chart lists some of the wealthiest countries in the world. Source: World Bank, *World Development Report, 1999, 2000.*

Country	Income per Person (thousands of 1998 U.S. dollars)
Switzerland	$40,080
Norway	34,330
Denmark	33,260
Japan	32,380
Singapore	30,060
United States	29,340
Austria	26,850
Germany	25,850
Sweden	25,620
Belgium	25,380
France	24,940
Netherlands	24,760
Finland	24,110
Hong Kong	23,670
United Kingdom	21,400
Australia	20,300
Italy	20,250
Canada	20,020
Ireland	18,340
Israel	15,940
New Zealand	14,700
Spain	14,080
Portugal	10,690

Income per Person (thousands of 1998 U.S. dollars)

relative to farming in much of the rest of the world gives the United States a comparative advantage in many agricultural products.

4.b. International-Sector Spending

Economic activity of the United States with the rest of the world includes U.S. spending on foreign goods and foreign spending on U.S. goods. Figure 11 shows how U.S. exports and imports are spread over different countries. Notice that two countries, Canada and Japan, account for roughly one-third of U.S. exports and more than one-third of U.S. imports. Trade with the industrial countries is approximately twice as large as trade with the developing countries, and U.S. trade with eastern Europe is trivial.

When exports exceed imports, a **trade surplus** exists. When imports exceed exports, a **trade deficit** exists. Figure 11 shows that the United States is importing much more than it exports.

The term **net exports** refers to the difference between the value of exports and the value of imports: net exports equals exports minus imports. Figure 12 traces U.S.

trade surplus: the situation that exists when imports are less than exports

trade deficit: the situation that exists when imports exceed exports

net exports: the difference between the value of exports and the value of imports

The United States and Europe have been waging a "banana war" as a result of European quotas on banana imports. To support banana growers in former European colonies in Africa, Asia, and the Caribbean, the European Union (EU) imposed quotas on banana imports in 1993. This resulted in European banana prices rising to much higher levels than in other countries like the United States and it also harmed U.S. firms that saw their market share of the European banana business decline significantly. The World Trade Organization (WTO) ruled that the quota should be eliminated, but the EU refused to do so. As a result, the WTO gave the United States permission to impose 100 percent tariffs on certain imports from the EU. At the time this book went to print, the controversy still raged.

Figure 11

Direction of U.S. Trade

This chart shows that a trade deficit exists for the United States, since U.S. imports greatly exceed U.S. exports. The chart also shows that trade with western Europe, Japan, and Canada accounts for about half of U.S. trade. Source: *Economic Report of the President, 2000.*

Eastern Europe
Other Countries
  (except eastern Europe)
Oil Exporters

Industrial Countries:
Western Europe
Japan
Canada
Other

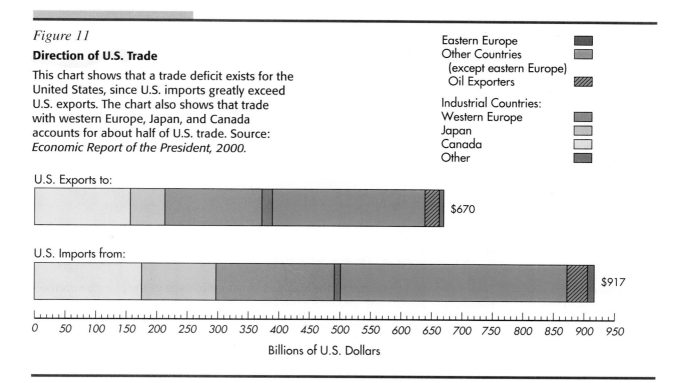

U.S. Exports to:

$670

U.S. Imports from:

$917

0 50 100 150 200 250 300 350 400 450 500 550 600 650 700 750 800 850 900 950

Billions of U.S. Dollars

Figure 12

U.S. Net Exports

Prior to the late 1960s, the
United States generally
exported more than it
imported and had a trade
surplus. Since 1976, net
exports have been
negative, and the United
States has had a trade
deficit. Source: *Economic
Report of the President,
2000.*

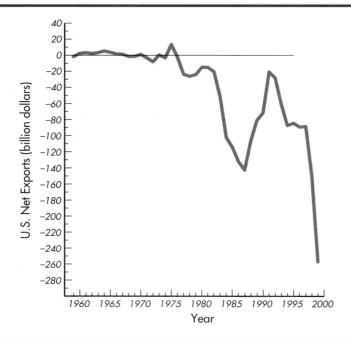

net exports over time. Positive net exports represent trade surpluses; negative net
exports represent trade deficits. The trade deficits (indicated by negative net exports)
starting in the 1980s were unprecedented. Reasons for this pattern of international
trade are discussed in later chapters.

RECAP

1. The majority of U.S. trade is with the industrial market economies.
2. Exports are products sold to foreign countries; imports are products bought
   from foreign countries.
3. Exports minus imports equal net exports.
4. Positive net exports signal a trade surplus; negative net exports signal a trade
   deficit.

5. LINKING THE SECTORS

5. How do the three
   private sectors—
   households,
   businesses, and the
   international
   sector—interact in
   the economy?

Now that we have an idea of the size and structure of each of the private sectors—
households, businesses, and international—let's discuss how the sectors interact.

5.a. Households and Firms

Households own all the basic resources, or factors of production, in the economy.
Household members own land and provide labor, and they are the entrepreneurs,
stockholders, proprietors, and partners who own business firms.

Part One / Introduction to the Price System

Figure 13

The Circular Flow: Households and Firms

The diagram indicates that income is equal to the value of output. Firms hire resources from households. The payments for these resources represent household income. Households spend their income for goods and services produced by the firms. Household spending represents revenue for firms. Households save some of their income. This income reenters the circular flow as investment spending. Financial intermediaries like banks take in the saving of households and then lend this money to business firms for investment spending.

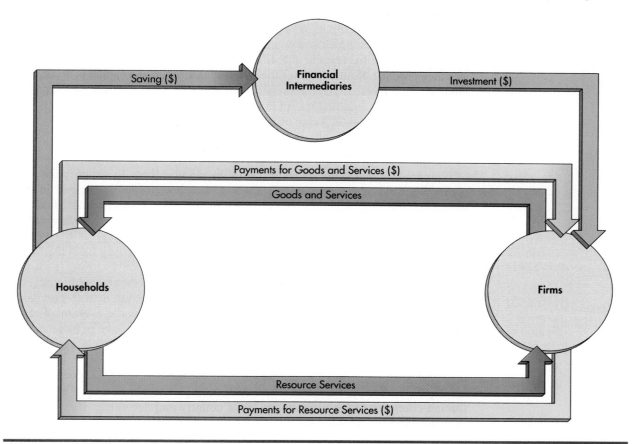

Households and businesses interact with each other by means of buying and selling. Businesses employ the services of resources in order to produce goods and services. Business firms pay households for their resource services.

Households sell their resource services to businesses in exchange for money payments. The flow of resource services from households to businesses is shown by the blue-green line at the bottom of Figure 13. The flow of money payments from firms to households is shown by the gold line at the bottom of Figure 13. Households use the money payments to buy goods and services from firms. These money payments are the firms' revenues. The flow of money payments from households to firms is shown by the gold line at the top of the diagram. The flow of goods and services from firms to households is shown by the blue-green line at the top of Figure 13. There is, therefore, a flow of money and goods and services from one sector to the

financial intermediaries:
institutions that accept
deposits from savers and
make loans to borrowers

circular flow diagram: a
model showing the flow of
output and income from
one sector of the economy
to another

other. The payments made by one sector are the receipts taken in by the other sector. Money, goods, and services flow from households to firms and back to households in a circular flow.

Households do not spend all of the money they receive. They save some fraction of their income. In Figure 13, we see that household saving is deposited in **financial intermediaries** like banks, credit unions, and saving and loan firms. A financial intermediary accepts deposits from savers and makes loans to borrowers. The money that is saved by the households reenters the economy in the form of investment spending as business firms borrow for expansion of their productive capacity.

The **circular flow diagram** represented in Figure 13 indicates that income is equal to the value of output. Money flows to the household sector are the sum of the payments to the resource owners, including the payments to entrepreneurs. Money flows to firms are the revenue that firms receive when they sell the goods and services they produce. Revenue minus the costs of land, labor, and capital is profit. Profit represents the payment to entrepreneurs and other owners of corporations, partnerships, and sole proprietorships. In this simple economy, household income is equal to business revenue—the value of goods and services produced.

5.b. Households, Firms, and the International Sector

Figure 14 includes foreign countries in the circular flow. To simplify the circular flow diagram, let's assume that households are not directly engaged in international trade and that only business firms are buying and selling goods and services across international borders. This assumption is not far from the truth for the industrial countries and for many developing countries. We typically buy a foreign-made product from a local business firm rather than directly from the foreign producer.

A line labeled "net exports" connects firms and foreign countries in Figure 14, as well as a line labeled "payments for net exports." Notice that neither line has an arrow indicating the direction of flow as do the other lines in the diagram. The reason is that net exports of the home country may be either positive (a trade surplus) or negative (a trade deficit). When net exports are positive, there is a net flow of goods from the firms of the home country to foreign countries and a net flow of money from foreign countries to the firms of the home country. When net exports are negative, the opposite occurs. A trade deficit involves net flows of goods from foreign countries to the firms of the home country and net money flows from the domestic firms to the foreign countries. If exports and imports are equal, net exports are zero because the value of exports is offset by the value of imports.

Figure 14 shows the circular flow linking the private sectors of the economy. This model is a simplified view of the world, but it highlights the important interrelationships. The value of output equals income, as always; but spending may be for foreign as well as domestic goods. Domestic firms may produce for foreign as well as domestic consumption.

RECAP

1. The circular flow diagram illustrates how the main sectors of the economy fit together.
2. The circular flow diagram shows that the value of output is equal to income.

Figure 14

The Circular Flow: Households, Firms, and Foreign Countries

The diagram assumes that households are not directly engaged in international trade. The flow of goods and services between countries is represented by the line labeled "net exports." Neither the net exports line nor the line labeled "payments for net exports" has an arrow indicating the direction of the flow because the flow can go from the home country to foreign countries or vice versa. When the domestic economy has positive net exports (a trade surplus), goods and services flow out of the domestic firms toward foreign countries and money payments flow from the foreign countries to the domestic firms. With negative net exports (a trade deficit), the reverse is true.

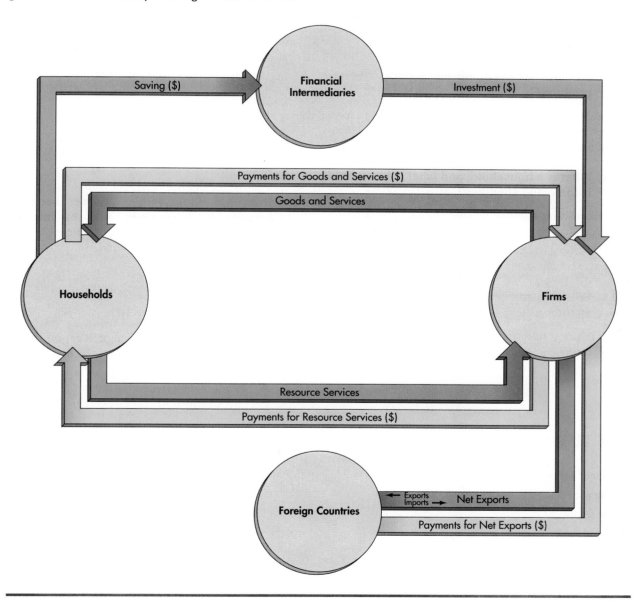

SUMMARY

? 1. In a market system, who decides what goods and services are produced?

1. In a market system, consumers are sovereign and decide by means of their purchases what goods and services will be produced. *§1.a*

? 2. How are goods and services produced?

2. In a market system, firms decide how to produce the goods and services that consumers want. In order to earn maximum profits, firms use the least-cost combinations of resources. *§1.c*

? 3. Who obtains the goods and services that are produced?

3. Income and prices determine who gets what in a market system. Income is determined by the ownership of resources. *§1.d*

? 4. What is a household, and what is household income and spending?

4. A household consists of one or more persons who occupy a unit of housing. *§2*

5. Household spending is called *consumption* and is the largest component of spending in the economy. *§2.b*

? 5. What is a business firm, and what is business spending?

6. A business firm is a business organization controlled by a single management. *§3*

7. Businesses may be organized as sole proprietorships, partnerships, or corporations. *§3.a*

8. Business investment spending—the expenditure by business firms for capital goods—fluctuates a great deal over time. *§3.e*

? 6. How does the international sector affect the economy?

9. The international trade of the United States occurs predominantly with the other industrial economies. *§4.a*

10. Exports are products sold to the rest of the world. Imports are products bought from the rest of the world. *§4.a.2*

11. Exports minus imports equal net exports. Positive net exports mean that exports are greater than imports and a trade surplus exists. Negative net exports mean that imports exceed exports and a trade deficit exists. *§4.b*

? 7. How do the three private sectors— households, businesses, and the international sector—interact in the economy?

12. The resources combined to produce goods and services are also known as factors of production. They consist of land, labor, capital, and entrepreneurial ability. *§5.a*

13. The total value of output produced by the factors of production is equal to the income received by the owners of the factors of production. *§5.a*

KEY TERMS

consumer sovereignty *§1.a*

private sector *§1.d*

public sector *§1.d*

household *§2*

consumption *§2.b*

business firm *§3*

sole proprietorship *§3.a*

partnership *§3.a*

corporation *§3.a*

multinational business *§3.a*

investment *§3.e*

imports *§4.a.2*

exports *§4.a.2*

trade surplus *§4.b*

trade deficit *§4.b*

net exports *§4.b*

financial intermediaries *§5.a*

circular flow diagram *§5.a*

EXERCISES

1. What is consumer sovereignty? What does it have to do with determining what goods and services are produced? Who determines how goods and services are produced? Who receives the goods and services in a market system?

2. Is a family a household? Is a household a family?

3. What is the median value of the following series? 4, 6, 8, 3, 9, 10, 10, 1, 5, 7, 12

4. Which sector (households, business, or international) spends the most? Which sector spends the least? Which sector, because of volatility, has importance greater than is warranted by its size?

5. What does it mean if net exports are negative?

6. Why does the value of output always equal the income received by the resources that produced the output?

7. Total spending in the economy is equal to consumption plus investment plus government spending plus net exports. If households want to save and thus do not use all of their income for consumption, what will happen to total spending? Because total spending in the economy is equal to total income and output, what will happen to the output of goods and services if households want to save more?

8. People sometimes argue that imports should be limited by government policy. Suppose a government quota on the quantity of imports causes net exports to rise. Using the circular flow diagram as a guide, explain why total expenditures and national output may rise after the quota is imposed. Who is likely to benefit from the quota? Who will be hurt?

9. Draw the circular flow diagram linking households, business firms, and the international sector. Use the diagram to explain the effects of a decision by the household sector to increase saving.

10. Suppose there are three countries in the world. Country A exports $11 million worth of goods to country B and $5 million worth of goods to country C; country B exports $3 million worth of goods to country A and $6 million worth of goods to country C; and country C exports $4 million worth of goods to country A and $1 million worth of goods to country B.

    a. What are the net exports of countries A, B, and C?
    b. Which country is running a trade deficit? A trade surplus?

11. Over time, there has been a shift away from outdoor drive-in movie theaters to indoor movie theaters. Use supply and demand curves to illustrate and explain how consumers can bring about such a change when tastes change.

12. Figure 3 indicates that the youngest and the oldest households have the lowest household incomes. Why should middle-aged households have higher incomes than the youngest and oldest?

13. The chapter provides data indicating that there are many more sole proprietorships than corporations or partnerships. Why are there so many sole proprietorships? Why is the revenue of the average sole proprietorship less than that of the typical corporation?

14. List the four sectors of the economy along with the type of spending associated with each sector. Order the types of spending in terms of magnitude and give an example of each kind of spending.

15. The circular flow diagram of Figure 14 excludes the government sector. Draw a new version of the figure that includes this sector with government spending and taxes added to the diagram. Label your new figure and be sure to include arrows to illustrate the direction of flows.

Zooming in on Wills

Prince William has been ably shielded from the press—but that will change when he turns 18.

When Prince William finally leaves Eton at the end of the month he may well reflect in years to come that his schooldays were the best time of his life. At least behind the walls of Britain's most famous public school William was afforded protection from the prying lens of the media.

All that will change when he hangs up his light-blue colours and makes his first hesitant step into adulthood on June 29 in the full glare of the media.

The boy who will be King will have to run the gauntlet of thousands of flash bulbs every time he sets foot in public. For William, the days of a shielded existence are over, for good, at the relatively young age of 18. . . .

Prince Charles was the first royal whose many courtships were splashed over newsstands all around the world. Diana, Princess of Wales, was accorded film star status. It means that William, unlike his father, will at least know what to expect, having lived through the media feeding frenzy for most of his life.

St. James's Palace is working on a strategy with the Press Complaints Commission (PCC) to try to give William some protection. But even Lord Wakeham, chairman of the PCC and one of the wiliest political operators of his generation, knows it will be impossible to find an answer.

Wakeham issued a warning shot to the press this week to heed the fact that while William comes of age on Wednesday (June 21) he remains a schoolboy until June 29. Wakeham reiterated the PCC code, which forbids intrusive photographs of any schoolchildren—even ones destined to be King.

At first glance it may have seemed a pointless statement as William has only days left at Eton. But as interest mounts in his coming of age, one member of the PCC observed: "Even two days, let alone seven, can seem like a lifetime once the tabloid press is in full flow." . . .

And even if the British tabloids exercise restraint there will be no such obligation on the Continent. From all over the world picture desks are requesting photographs from St. James's Palace and stories from their British correspondents. They are prepared to run the snatched paparazzi pictures, which the British media is supposed to have given commitments not to publish. The Internet will create even more temptation even if the photographs have been obtained by the forbidden telephoto lens.

Whether they like it or not St. James's Palace has to concede that William has become the badly needed glamour in the royal household—which tragically died in a Paris underpass in August 1997. Having inherited his mother's dazzling looks William is destined for superstar status. The fact that he is the image of Diana has intensified the international interest.

William, like his father in his day, will be called the world's most eligible bachelor. There will be a six-figure price tag on the picture of the first girlfriend, the first kiss, William smoking, or drinking. . . .

As one former Fleet Street tabloid editor says: "Everyone will start off with good intentions. But when the paparazzi offer the first exclusive photographs of William with a pretty blonde it will be page one, three, four, five, and the rest. They will be worth a fortune."

The Palace has been warned.

ANDREW PIERCE

The Times (London)/June 16, 2000

Commentary

Standing in line at the grocery store you notice the headlines on the tabloid, "Aliens take body of Roseanne" and you wonder how anyone could pay for these tabloids. Some people not only wonder about that but, as this article notes, think that these tabloids are invading the privacy of citizens. Even though there is a British Press Complaints Commission aimed at regulating the tabloid press, there is still an expectation that Prince William, like his mother, Princess Diana, before him, will be hounded by the tabloids when he is out of school. Who determines whether these newspapers and magazines are appropriate or not? Who defines whether the tabloids are pulling us into the sewer?

In a market system, it is consumers who determine whether the magazines and newspapers exist. If the producers of the newspapers and magazines cannot cover their costs with their revenues from sales and advertisements, then the producers will change what they do. They will either alter the coverage or presentation of stories or they will get out of the business altogether.

In a market system, products are provided if they result in a profit to producers. This means the customer must be willing and able to pay for them. If stories about baseball have no interest to readers, then consumers will not purchase magazines that focus on baseball. As a result, magazines will have to alter what they do present in order to attempt to retain their sales. *Sports Illustrated* would have to have stories about other sports, swimsuits, and other topics instead of baseball.

If people do not want to read tabloids and they are unwilling to purchase the newspapers, then the tabloids will not exist. Only if people are willing and able to pay the price sufficient for the newspaper publishers to make a profit will the newspapers be published. No one is forcing anyone to read the tabloids.

Suppose that the market for tabloids is represented in the demand and supply diagram shown below. Suppose that for some reason, perhaps the tragedy of Princess Diana's death, that the willingness to purchase tabloids decreases. This is illustrated by an inward shift of the demand curve, from D_1 to D_2. The magazine and newspaper prices will decline, from P_1 to P_2. In addition, fewer magazines and newspapers are purchased—quantity sold falls from Q_1 to Q_2.

A decline in sales of the tabloids is not necessarily a good or a bad thing. All it really is, is a change in tastes and preferences and a shift of the demand curve. For some reason, people are not willing and able to purchase as many of the tabloids as they did before. There is no "good" or "bad" to this fact. It is simply a positive statement.

The lesson here is that the consumer does reign supreme in a market system. No profit-maximizing firm will ignore customer desires. Firms may try new cost-reducing approaches or revenue enhancing techniques, but whether the tabloids are published depends on whether customers are willing and able to buy them.

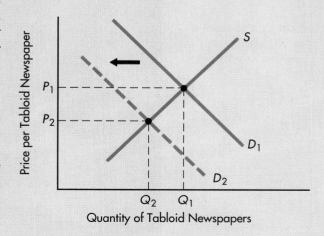

Chapter 5

The Public Sector

? Fundamental Questions

1. How does the government interact with the other sectors of the economy?

2. What is the economic role of government?

3. Why is the public sector such a large part of a market economy?

4. What does the government do?

5. How do the sizes of public sectors in various countries compare?

Preview

From conception to death, we are affected by the activities of the government. Many mothers receive prenatal care through government programs. We are born in hospitals that are subsidized or run by the government. We are delivered by doctors who received training in subsidized colleges. Our births are recorded on certificates filed with the government. Ninety percent of us attend public schools. Many of us live in housing that is directly subsidized by the government or whose mortgages are insured by the government. Most of us at one time or another put savings into accounts that are insured by the government. Virtually all of us, at some time in our lives, receive money from the government—from student loan programs, unemployment compensation, disability insurance, social security, or Medicare. Twenty percent of the work force is employed by the government. The prices of wheat, corn, sugar, and dairy products are controlled or strongly influenced by the government. The prices we pay for

cigarettes, alcohol, automobiles, utilities, water, gas, and a multitude of other goods are directly or indirectly influenced by the government. We travel on public roads and publicly subsidized or controlled airlines, airports, trains, and ships. Our legal structure provides a framework in which we all live and act; the national defense ensures our rights of citizenship and protects our private property. By law, the government is responsible for employment and the general health of the economy.

According to virtually any measure, government in the United States has been a growth industry since 1930. The number of people employed by the local, state, and federal governments combined grew from 3 million in 1930 to over 19 million today; there are now more people employed in government than there are in manufacturing. Annual expenditures by the federal government rose from $3 billion in 1930 to approximately $1.8 trillion today, and total government (federal, state, and local) expenditures now equal about $2.9 trillion annually. In 1929, government spending constituted less than 2.5 percent of total spending in the economy. Today, it is around 20 percent. The number of rules and regulations created by the government is so large that it is measured by the number of telephone-book-sized pages needed just to list them, and that number is more than 67,000. The cost of all federal rules and regulations is estimated to be somewhere between $4,000 and $17,000 per U.S. household each year, and the number of federal employees required to police these rules is about 125,000.

There is no doubt that the government (often referred to as the *public sector*) is a major player in the U.S. economy. But in the last few chapters we have been learning about the market system and how well it works. If the market system works so well, why is the public sector such a large part of the economy? In this chapter we discuss the public sector and the role government plays in a market economy. ■

1. THE CIRCULAR FLOW

1. How does the government interact with the other sectors of the economy?

Government in the United States exists at the federal, state, and local levels. Local government includes county, regional, and municipal units. Economic discussions tend to focus on the federal government because national economic policy is set at that level. Nevertheless, each level affects us through its taxing and spending decisions, and laws regulating behavior.

To illustrate how the government sector affects the economy, let's add government to the circular flow model presented in the previous chapter. Government at the federal, state, and local levels interacts with both households and firms. Because the government employs factors of production to produce government services, households receive payments from the government in exchange for the services of the factors of production. The flow of resource services from households to government is illustrated by the blue-green line flowing from the households to government in Figure 1. The flow of money from government to households is shown by the gold line flowing from government to households. We assume that government, like a household, does not trade directly with foreign countries but obtains foreign goods from domestic firms that do trade with the rest of the world.

Households pay taxes to support the provision of government services, such as national defense, education, and police and fire protection. In a sense, then, the household sector is purchasing goods and services from the government as well as from private businesses. The flow of tax payments from households and businesses to government is illustrated by the gold lines flowing from households and businesses to government, and the flow of government services to households and businesses is illustrated by the purple lines flowing from government.

Figure 1

The Circular Flow: Households, Firms, Government, and Foreign Countries

The diagram assumes that households and government are not directly engaged in international trade. Domestic firms trade with firms in foreign countries. The government sector buys resource services from households and goods and services from firms. This government spending represents income for the households and revenue for the firms. The government uses the resource services and goods and services to provide government services for households and firms. Households and firms pay taxes to the government to finance government expenditures.

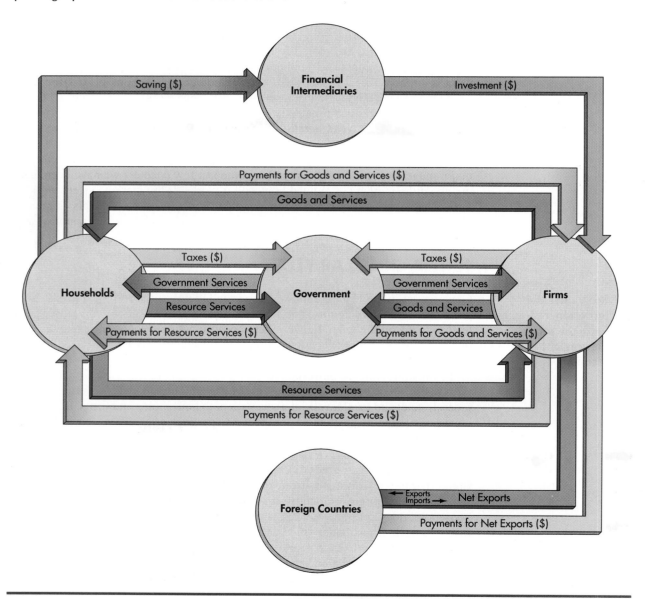

The addition of government brings significant changes to the model. Households have an additional place to sell their resources for income, and businesses have an additional market for goods and services. The value of *private* production no longer equals the value of household income. Households receive income from government in exchange for providing resource services to government. The total value of output in the economy is equal to the total income received, but government is included as a source of income and a producer of services.

RECAP

1. The circular flow diagram illustrates how the main sectors of the economy fit together.
2. Government interacts with both households and firms. Households get government services and pay taxes; they provide resource services and receive income. Firms sell goods and services to government and receive income.

2. THE ROLE OF GOVERNMENT IN THE MARKET SYSTEM

2. What is the economic role of government?

We have learned that consumers use their limited incomes to buy the goods and services that give them the greatest satisfaction, that resource owners offer the services of their resources to the highest bidder, and that firms produce the goods and services and use the resources that enable them to generate the highest profits. In other words, everyone—consumers, firms, resource suppliers—attempts to get the most benefits for the least cost.

This apparently narrow, self-interested behavior is converted by the market into a social outcome in which no one can be made better off without making someone else worse off. Any resource allocation that could make someone better off and no one any worse off would increase efficiency. When all such allocations have been realized, so that the *only* way to make one person better off would harm someone else, then we have realized the best allocation society can achieve. As Adam Smith noted in 1776, self-interested individuals, wholly unaware of the effects of their actions, act as if driven by an *invisible hand* to produce the greatest social good.

2.a. Government as the Guardian of Efficiency

economic efficiency: a situation where no one in society can be made better off without making someone else worse off

technical efficiency: producing at a point on the PPC

Economic efficiency is the name given to the events described by Adam Smith. Efficiency can mean many things to many different people. Even within economics there are different definitions of efficiency. We have already talked about the production possibilities curve and efficiency; operating at a point on the PPC is called *productive* or **technical efficiency.** A firm is said to be operating efficiently when it produces a given quantity and quality of goods at the lowest possible cost. Consumers are said to be efficient when they are getting the greatest bang for the buck, using their scarce resources to get the greatest benefits. *Economic efficiency* encompasses all of these definitions of efficiency. When *one person cannot be made better off without harming someone else,* then we say economic efficiency prevails.

Somewhat amazingly, economic efficiency occurs in a market system simply through the self-interested individual actions of participants in that system. Efficiency is not the result of some despot controlling the economy and telling people what they can and cannot do. The market system results in efficiency because people own their resources and goods and will exchange their goods or resources for others only if the exchange makes them better off. The higher profits go, the more income is earned by people with entrepreneurial ability. In order to earn profits, entrepreneurs have to provide, at the lowest possible cost, the goods and services that consumers want and are able to buy. This means that the least-cost combination of resources is used by each firm, but it also means that resources are employed in their most highly valued uses. Any reallocation of resources results in a situation that is worse—some resources will not be used where they are most highly valued, and some consumers will be less satisfied with the goods and services they can purchase.

As we saw in the Preview, the government plays a significant role in the U.S. economy; governmental influence is even larger in other market economies and is especially large in a socialist economy like Cuba. Why, if the actions of individuals in the market system result in the best social outcome, does the government play such a large role?

?

3. Why is the public sector such a large part of a market economy?

There are two justifications given for the government's role in a market economy beyond ensuring private property rights. One is based on cases where the market may not always result in economic efficiency. The second is based on the idea that people who do not like the market outcome use the government to change the outcome. Sections 2.b through 2.f are brief discussions of some cases where the market system may fail to achieve economic efficiency. Section 2.g is a brief discussion of cases where people manipulate the market outcome.

2.b. Information and the Price System

As you learned in Chapters 3 and 4, a market is a place or service that allows buyers and sellers to exchange information on what they know about a product, what buyers are willing and able to pay for a product, and what sellers want to receive in order to produce and sell a product. A market price is a signal indicating when more or less of a good is desired. When the market price rises, buyers know that the quantity demanded at the prior equilibrium price exceeded the quantity supplied.

A market price is only as good an indicator as the information that exists in the market. It takes time for people to gather information about a product. It takes time to go to a market and purchase an item. It takes time for producers to learn what people want and bring together the resources necessary to produce that product. Thus, people are not likely to be perfectly informed, nor will everyone have the same information. This means that not all markets will adjust instantaneously or even at the same speed to a change in demand or supply. It also means that some people may pay higher prices for a product than others pay. Some people may be swindled by a sharp operator, and some firms may fail to collect debts owed them.

market imperfection: a lack of efficiency that results from imperfect information in the marketplace

When information is not perfect, **market imperfections** may result. As a result of market imperfections, least-cost combinations of resources may not be used, or resources may not be used where they have the highest value. Often in such cases, people have argued for the government to step in with rules and regulations concerning the amount of information that must be provided. The government requires, for example, that specific information be provided on the labels of food products, that warning labels be placed on cigarettes and alcohol products, and that statements about the condition of a used car be made available to buyers. The government also declares certain actions by firms or consumers to be fraudulent or illegal. It also tests and licenses pharmaceuticals and members of many professions—medical doctors, lawyers, beauticians, barbers, nurses, and others.

Government plays an active role in regulating some professions. Physicians and other health professionals are licensed by the government with the intent to ensure that health-care providers are properly trained.

2.c. Externalities

The market system works efficiently only if the market price reflects the full costs and benefits of producing and consuming a particular good or service. Recall that people make decisions on the basis of their opportunity costs and the market price is a measure of what must be forgone to acquire some good or service. If the market price does not reflect the full costs, then decisions cannot reflect opportunity costs. For instance, when you use air conditioners, you contaminate the ozone layer with Freon but you don't pay the costs of that contamination. When you drive, you don't pay for all of the pollution created by your car. When you have a loud, late-night party, you don't pay for the distractions you impose on your neighbors. When firms dump wastes or create radioactive by-products, they don't pay the costs. When homeowners allow their properties to become rundown, they reduce the value of neighboring properties but they don't pay for the loss of value. When society is educated, it costs less to produce signs, ballots, tax forms, and other information tools. Literacy enables a democracy to function effectively, and higher education may stimulate scientific discoveries that improve the welfare of society. When you acquire an education, however, you do not get a check in the amount of savings your education will create for society. All these side effects—some negative, some positive—which are not covered by the market price are called **externalities.**

externalities: costs or benefits of a transaction that are borne by someone not directly involved in the transaction

Externalities are the costs or benefits of a market activity borne by someone who is not a direct party to the market transaction. When you drive, you pay only for gasoline and car maintenance. You don't pay for the noise and pollutants that your car emits. You also don't pay for the added congestion and delays that you impose on other drivers. Thus, the *market* price of driving understates the *full* cost of driving to society; as a result, people drive more frequently than they would if they had to pay the full cost.

The government is often called upon to intervene in the market to resolve externality problems. Government agencies, such as the Environmental Protection Agency, are established to set and enforce air quality standards, and taxes are imposed to obtain funds to pay for external costs or subsidize external benefits.

Thus, the government provides education to society at below-market prices because the positive externality of education benefits everyone.

2.d. Public Goods

The market system works efficiently only if the benefits derived from consuming a particular good or service are available only to the consumer who buys the good or service. You buy a pizza, and only you receive the benefits of eating that pizza. What would happen if you weren't allowed to enjoy that pizza all by yourself? Suppose your neighbors have the right to come to your home when you have a pizza delivered and share your pizza. How often would you buy a pizza? There is no way to exclude others from enjoying the benefits of some of the goods you purchase. These types of goods are called **public goods,** and they create a problem for the market system.

public goods: goods whose consumption cannot be limited only to the person who purchased the good

Radio broadcasts are public goods. Everyone who tunes in a station enjoys the benefits. National defense is also a public good. You could buy a missile to protect your house, but your neighbors, as well as you, would benefit from the protection it provided. A pizza, however, is not a public good. If you pay for it, only you get to enjoy the benefits. Thus, you have an incentive to purchase pizza. You don't have that incentive to purchase public goods. If you and I both benefit from the public good, who will buy it? I'd prefer that you buy it so that I receive its benefits at no cost. Conversely, you'd prefer that I buy it. The result may be that no one will buy it.

Fire protection provides a good example of the problem that occurs with public goods. Suppose that as a homeowner you have the choice of subscribing to fire protection services from a private firm or having no fire protection. If you subscribe and your house catches fire, the fire engines will arrive as soon as possible and your house may be saved. If you do not subscribe, your house will burn. Do you choose to subscribe? You might say to yourself that as long as your neighbors subscribe, you need not do so. The fact that your neighbors subscribe means that fires in their houses won't cause a fire in yours, and you do not expect a fire to begin in your house. If many people made decisions in this way, fire protection services would not be available because not enough people would subscribe to make the services profitable.

private property right: the limitation of ownership to an individual

The problem with a public good is the communal nature of the good. No one has a **private property right** to a public good. If you buy a car, you must pay the seller an acceptable price. Once this price is paid, the car is all yours and no one else can use it without your permission. The car is your private property, and you make the decisions about its use. In other words, you have the private property right to the car. Public goods are available to all because no one individual owns them or has property rights to them.

free ride: the enjoyment of the benefits of a good by a producer or consumer without having to pay for it

When goods are public, people have an incentive to try to obtain a **free ride**—the enjoyment of the benefits of a good without paying for the good. Your neighbors would free-ride on your purchases of pizza if you didn't have the private property rights to the pizza. People who enjoy public radio and public television stations without donating money to them are getting free rides from those people who do donate to them. People who benefit from the provision of a good whether they pay for it or not have an incentive not to pay for it.

Typically, in the absence of private property rights to a good, people call on the government to claim ownership and provide the good. For instance, governments act as owners of police departments and specify how police services are used. The Economic Insight "Government Creates a Market for Fishing Rights" provides one example of government specifying private property rights.

Government Creates a Market for Fishing Rights

There is no practical way to establish ownership rights of ocean fish stocks. Traditionally, fish have been free for the taking—a common pool resource. Theory teaches that such underpricing leads to overconsumption. In the halibut fisheries off Alaska, fishing fleets caught so many halibut that the survival of the stock was threatened. No single fishing boat had an incentive to harvest fewer fish since the impact on its own future catch would be minimal and others would only increase their take. This is an example of what is known as "the tragedy of the commons."

Officials tried limiting the length of the fishing season. But this effort only encouraged new capital investment such as larger and faster boats with more effective (and expensive) fishing equipment. In order to control the number of fish caught, the season was shortened in some areas from 4 months to 2 days by the early 1990s. Most of the halibut caught had to be frozen rather than marketed fresh, and halibut caught out of season had to be discarded.

In late 1992, the federal government proposed a new approach: assigning each fisherman a permit to catch a certain number of fish. The total number of fish for which permits are issued will reflect scientific estimates of the number of fish that can be caught without endangering the survival of the species. Also, the permits will be transferable—they can be bought and sold. By making the permits transferable, the system in effect creates a market where one did not exist previously. The proposed system will encourage the most profitable and efficient boats to operate at full capacity by buying permits from less successful boats, ensuring a fishing fleet that uses labor and equipment efficiently. Moreover, the transferable permits system establishes a market price for the opportunity to fish—a price that better reflects the true social cost of using this common resource.

Source: *Economic Report of the President, 1993*, p. 207.

2.e. Monopoly

If only one firm produces a good that is desired by consumers, then that firm might produce a smaller amount of the good in order to charge a higher price. In this case, resources might not be used in their most highly valued manner and consumers might not be able to purchase the goods they desire. A situation where there is only one producer of a good is called a **monopoly.** The existence of a monopoly can imply the lack of economic efficiency. The government is often called on to regulate the behavior of firms that are monopolies or even to run the monopolies as government enterprises.

monopoly: a situation where there is only one producer of a good

2.f. Business Cycles

People are made better off by economic growth. Economic growth increases the number of jobs and draws people out of poverty and into the mainstream of economic progress. Economic stagnation, on the other hand, throws the relatively poor out of their jobs and into poverty. These fluctuations in the economy are called **business cycles.** People call on the government to protect them against the periods of economic ill health and to minimize the damaging effects of business cycles. Government agencies are established to control the money supply and other important parts of the economy, and government-financed programs are implemented to offset some of the losses that result during bad economic times. The U.S. Congress requires that the government provide economic growth and minimize unemployment. History has shown that this is easier said than done.

business cycles: fluctuations in the economy between growth and stagnation

2.g. The Public Choice Theory of Government

The efficiency basis for government intervention in the economy discussed in sections 2.b through 2.f implies that the government is a cohesive organization functioning in much the same way that a benevolent dictator would. This organization intervenes in the market system only to correct the ills created by the market. Not all economists agree with this view of government. Many claim that the government is not a benevolent dictator looking out for the best interests of society but is instead merely a collection of individuals who respond to the same economic impulses we all do—that is, the desire to satisfy our own interests.

Economic efficiency does not mean that everyone is as well off as he or she desires. Economic efficiency merely means that someone or some group cannot be made better off without harming some other person or group of people. People always have an incentive to attempt to make themselves better off. If their attempts result in the transfer of benefits to themselves and away from others, however, economic efficiency has not increased. Moreover, the resources devoted to enacting the transfer of benefits are not productive; they do not create new income and benefits but merely transfer income and benefits. Such activity is called **rent seeking.** Rent seeking refers to cases where people devote resources to attempting to create income transfers to themselves. Rent seeking includes the expenditures on lobbyists in Congress, the time and expenses that health-care professionals devote to fighting nationalized health care, the time and expenses farmers devote to improving their subsidies, and millions of other examples.

A group of economists, referred to as **public choice** economists, argue that government is more the result of rent seeking than it is market failure. The study of public choice focuses on how government actions result from the self-interested behaviors of voters and politicians. Whereas the efficiency justification of government argues that it is only in cases where the market does not work that the government steps in, the public choice theory says that the government may be brought into the market system whenever someone or some group can benefit, even if efficiency is not served.

According to the public choice economists, price ceilings or price floors may be enacted for political gain rather than market failure; government spending or taxing policies may be enacted not to resolve a market failure but instead to implement an income redistribution from one group to another; government agencies such as the Food and Drug Administration may exist not to improve the functioning of the market but to enact a wealth transfer from one group to another. Each such instance of manipulation leads to a larger role for government in a market economy. Moreover, government employees have the incentive to increase their role and importance in the economy and therefore transfer income or other benefits to themselves.

The government sector is far from a trivial part of the market system. Whether the government's role is one of improving economic efficiency or the result of rent seeking is a topic for debate, and in later chapters we discuss this debate in more detail. For now, it is satisfactory just to recognize how important the public sector is in the market system and what the possible reasons for its prevalence are.

rent seeking: the use of resources to transfer income from one group to another

public choice: the study of how government actions result from the self-interested behaviors of voters and politicians

RECAP

1. The government's role in the economy may stem from the inefficiencies that exist in a market system.
2. The market system does not result in economic efficiency when there are market imperfections such as imperfect information or when the costs or benefits of the transaction are borne by parties not directly involved in the transaction. Such cases are called externalities. Also, the market system may not be efficient when private ownership rights are not well defined. The government is called upon to resolve these inefficiencies that exist in the market system.

3. The government is asked to minimize the problems that result from business cycles.

4. The public choice school of economics maintains that the government's role in the market system is more the result of rent seeking than of reducing market inefficiencies.

4. What does the government do?

3. OVERVIEW OF THE UNITED STATES GOVERNMENT

When Americans think of government policies, rules, and regulations, they typically think of Washington, D.C., because their economic lives are regulated and shaped more by policies made there than by policies made at the local and state levels. Who actually is involved in economic policymaking? Important government institutions that shape U.S. economic policy are listed in Table 1. This list is far from inclusive, but it includes the agencies with the broadest powers and greatest influence.

Economic policy involves macroeconomic issues like government spending and control of the money supply and microeconomic issues aimed at providing public goods like police and military protection, correcting externalities like pollution, and maintaining a competitive economy.

Table 1

U.S. Government Economic Policymakers and Related Agencies

Institution	Role
Fiscal policymakers	
President	Provides leadership in formulating fiscal policy
Congress	Sets government spending and taxes and passes laws related to economic conduct
Monetary policymaker	
Federal Reserve	Controls money supply and credit conditions
Related agencies	
Council of Economic Advisers	Monitors the economy and advises the president
Office of Management and Budget	Prepares and analyzes the federal budget
Treasury Department	Administers the financial affairs of the federal government
Commerce Department	Administers federal policy regulating industry
Justice Department	Enforces legal setting of business
Comptroller of the Currency	Oversees national banks
International Trade Commission	Investigates unfair international trade practices
Federal Trade Commission	Administers laws related to fair business practices and competition

3.a. Microeconomic Policy

Government provides public goods to avoid the free-rider problem that would occur if private firms provided the goods.

One reason for government's microeconomic role is the free-rider problem associated with the provision of public goods. If an army makes all citizens safer, then all citizens should pay for it. But even if one person does not pay taxes, the army still protects this citizen from foreign attack. To minimize free riding, the government collects mandatory taxes to finance public goods. Congress and the president determine the level of public goods needed and how to finance them.

Government taxes or subsidizes some activities that create externalities.

Microeconomic policy also deals with externalities. Activities that cause air or water pollution impose costs on everyone. For instance, a steel mill may generate air pollutants that have a negative effect on the surrounding population. A microeconomic function of government is to internalize the externality—that is, to force the steelmaker to bear the full cost to society of producing steel. In addition to assuming the costs of hiring land, labor, and capital, the mill should bear the costs associated with polluting the air. Congress and the president determine which externalities to address and the best way of taxing or subsidizing each activity in order to ensure that the amount of the good produced and its price reflect the true value to society.

Government regulates industries where free market competition may not exist and polices other industries to promote competition.

Another of government's microeconomic roles is to promote competition. Laws to restrict the ability of business firms to engage in practices that limit competition exist and are monitored by the Justice Department and the Federal Trade Commission. Some firms, such as public utilities, are monopolies and face no competition. The government defines the output, prices, and profits of many monopolies. In some cases, the monopolies are government-run enterprises.

3.b. Macroeconomic Policy

The focus of the government's macroeconomic policy is monetary and fiscal policy. **Monetary policy** is policy directed toward control of money and credit. The major player in this policy arena is the Federal Reserve, commonly called "the Fed." The **Federal Reserve** is the central bank of the United States. It serves as a banker for the U.S. government and regulates the U.S. money supply.

monetary policy: policy directed toward control of money and credit

Federal Reserve: the central bank of the United States

The Federal Reserve System is run by a seven-member Board of Governors. The most important member of the board is the chairman, who is appointed by the president for a term of four years. The board meets regularly (from ten to twelve times a year) with a group of high-level officials to review the current economic situation and set policy for the growth of U.S. money and credit. The Federal Reserve exercises a great deal of influence on U.S. economic policy.

fiscal policy: policy directed toward government spending and taxation

Fiscal policy, the other area of macroeconomic policy, is policy directed toward government spending and taxation. In the United States, fiscal policy is determined by laws that are passed by Congress and signed by the president. The relative roles of the legislative and executive branches in shaping fiscal policy vary with the political climate, but usually it is the president who initiates major policy changes. Presidents rely on key advisers for fiscal policy information. These advisers include Cabinet officers such as the secretary of the Treasury and the secretary of state as well as the director of the Office of Management and Budget. In addition, the president has a Council of Economic Advisers made up of three economists—usually a chair, a macroeconomist, and a microeconomist—who, together with their staff, monitor and interpret economic developments for the president. The degree of influence wielded by these advisers depends on their personal relationship with the president.

Government has the responsibility of minimizing the damage from business cycles.

3.c. Government Spending

Federal, state, and local government spending for goods and services is shown in Figure 2. Except during times of war in the 1940s and 1950s, federal expenditures

Figure 2

Federal, State, and Local Government Expenditures for Goods and Services

In the 1950s and early 1960s, federal government spending was above state and local government spending. In 1969, state and local expenditures rose above federal spending and have remained higher ever since. Source: Data are from the *Economic Report of the President, 2000.*

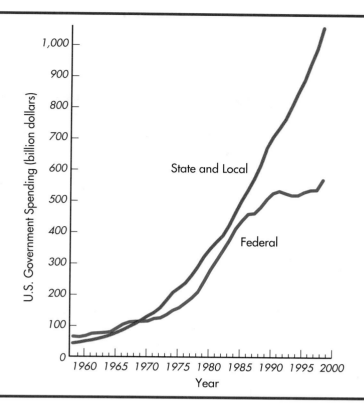

were roughly similar in size to state and local expenditures until 1969. Since 1969, state and local spending has been growing more rapidly than federal spending.

Combined government spending on goods and services is larger than investment spending but much smaller than consumption. In 1999, combined government spending was about $1,630 billion, investment spending was about $1,623 billion, and consumption was about $6,250 billion.

Besides government expenditures on goods and services, government also serves as an intermediary, taking money from some taxpayers and transferring this income to others. Such **transfer payments** are a part of total government expenditures, so the total government budget is much larger than the expenditures on goods and services reported in Figure 2. In 1999, total expenditures of federal, state, and local government for goods and services were about $1,630 billion. In this same year, transfer payments paid by all levels of government were about $1,018 billion.

The magnitude of federal government spending relative to federal government revenue from taxes has become an important issue in recent years. Figure 3 shows that the federal budget was roughly balanced until the early 1970s. The budget is a measure of spending and revenue. A balanced budget occurs when federal spending is approximately equal to federal revenue. This was the case through the 1950s and 1960s. If federal government spending is less than tax revenue, a **budget surplus** exists. By the early 1980s, federal government spending was much larger than revenue, so a large **budget deficit** existed. The federal budget deficit grew very rapidly to almost $280 billion by the early 1990s before beginning to drop and turning to surplus by 1998. When spending is greater than revenue, the excess spending must be covered by borrowing, and this borrowing can have effects on investment and consumption as well as on economic relationships with other countries.

transfer payment: income transferred from a citizen, who is earning income, to another citizen by the government

budget surplus: the excess that results when government spending is less than revenue

budget deficit: the shortage that results when government spending is greater than revenue

Figure 3

U.S. Federal Budget Deficits

The budget deficit is equal to the excess of government spending over tax revenue. If taxes are greater than government spending, a budget surplus (shown as a negative deficit) exists. Source: Data are from the *Economic Report of the President, 2000.*

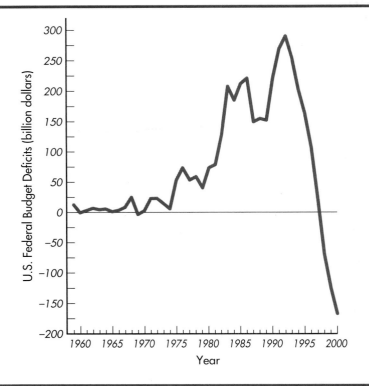

RECAP

1. The microeconomic functions of government include correcting externalities, redistributing income from high-income groups to lower-income groups, enforcing a competitive economy, and providing public goods.

2. Macroeconomic policy attempts to control the economy through monetary and fiscal policy.

3. The Federal Reserve conducts monetary policy. Congress and the president formulate fiscal policy.

4. Government spending is larger than investment spending but much smaller than consumption spending.

5. When government spending exceeds tax revenue, a budget deficit exists. When government spending is less than tax revenue, a budget surplus exists.

4. GOVERNMENT IN OTHER ECONOMIES

5. How do the sizes of public sectors in various countries compare?

The government plays a role in every economy, and in most the public sector is a much larger part of the economy than it is in the United States. In some economies, referred to as **centrally planned,** or nonmarket, economies, the public sector is the principal component of the economy. There are significant differences between the market system and the centrally planned systems. In market economies, people can own businesses, be private owners of land, start new businesses, and purchase what they want as long as they can pay the price. They may see their jobs disappear as business

centrally planned economy: an economic system in which the government determines what goods and services are produced and the prices at which they are sold

conditions worsen, but they are free to take business risks and to reap the rewards if taking these risks pays off. Under centrally planned systems, people are not free to own property other than a house, a car, and personal belongings. They are not free to start a business. They work as employees of the state. Their jobs are guaranteed regardless of whether their employer is making the right or wrong decisions and regardless of how much effort they expend on the job. Even though they might have money in their pockets, they may not be able to buy many of the things they want. Money prices are often not used to ration goods and services, so people may spend much of their time standing in lines to buy the products available on the shelves of government stores. Waiting in line is a result of charging a money price lower than equilibrium and imposing a quantity limit on how much a person can buy. The time costs, along with the money price required to buy goods, will ration the limited supply.

The Soviet Union implemented a centrally planned economy in the 1920s, following its October 1917 revolution. During, and especially following, World War II, the Soviet system expanded into eastern Europe, China, North Korea, and Vietnam. At the peak of Soviet influence, about one-third of the world's population lived in countries generally described as having centrally planned economic systems. The 1980s and 1990s ushered in a new world order, however. The Soviet Union's economy failed and ultimately led to the fall of the Communist governments in eastern Europe, the disintegration of the Soviet Union, the end of the Cold War, and the reunification of West and East Germany.

4.a. Overview of Major Market Economies

Figure 4 shows the size of government and the type of economy for several countries. The United States is representative of nations that are market economies with relatively small public sectors. Cuba is representative of nations that are primarily centrally planned. Germany, Japan, and the United Kingdom are market economies but the public sector plays a larger role than it does in the United States.

4.a.1. France The public sector in France is much larger than it is in the United States. France is a market economy in which a national economic plan has been used

Figure 4

The Economic Systems

The closer a country is to a market economy without a public sector, the closer to the lower-left area of the diagram it is placed. Conversely, the more the country is a centrally planned economy, the closer to the upper-right area of the diagram it is placed.

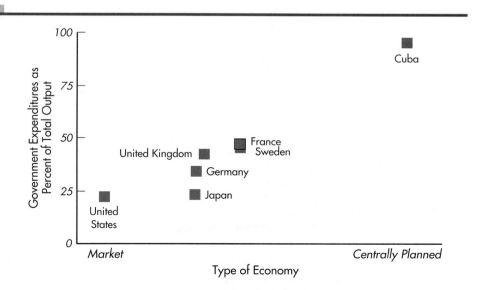

In Germany, the telephone company, Deutsche Telekom, is owned by private stockholders as well as the German government. When Telekom was "privatized" a few years ago, the government sold shares of stock to the public but retained a big share for itself. Such government involvement in seemingly private enterprise occurs in many industrial as well as developing countries.

to influence resource allocation. The French plan, however, does not order firms to do things. The plan is indicative; it offers suggested targets. The state uses its budget and its ownership of firms to attempt to further the implementation of the plan. Government ownership is concentrated in banking, coal, gas and electricity, transportation, and auto and aircraft production. The government-sector share of the economy is quite large; total government expenditures are nearly 50 percent of total output.

4.a.2. United Kingdom The role of the public sector in the United Kingdom is significant but not exceptional by European standards. Great Britain is an island economy with a land area slightly greater than that of the state of Minnesota and a population of just over 59 million persons. The resource base of the economy is quite limited, and the British economy is tied very closely to other economies. The British concept of an appropriate role for the public sector in economic affairs is more limited than that prevailing in France. Government spending is about 40 percent of total output in the United Kingdom.

4.a.3. Germany There is no significant planning apparatus in Germany, and the public sector owns few businesses, but the public sector intervenes a great deal to foster social programs. For instance, the government regulates business hours, supports minimum prices for brand-name articles, imposes rent controls, regulates the hiring and firing of employees, regulates vacations, and has a series of other laws protecting workers and renters. State expenditures are about 30 percent of total output. The unification of the East and West German economies and the merging of two different types of systems has led to additional government intervention.

4.a.4. Japan Japan is a capitalist economy whose postwar rate of economic growth is the highest among the major industrialized countries. Japan is a small country with adequate labor but generally limited supplies of natural resources and land. Like Great Britain, Japan is an island economy. With a population of approximately 126 million and a land area slightly smaller than that of the state of California, Japan is densely populated. The public sector appears on the surface to have a relatively small role in the Japanese economy: government spending as a percent of total output is only about 20 percent. But this statistic understates the reality. The public sector plays a very important role through the Japanese industrial families known as *keiretsu*. The government wields its influence on the keiretsu through various ministries. For example, the Ministry of International Trade and Industry (MITI) is responsible for international trade, domestic production, and domestic industrial structure. The MITI guides and influences economic decisions by promoting key sectors of the economy and carefully phasing out other, low-productivity sectors. The MITI uses government funds for research and development and to provide assistance for organizational change, such as mergers. Economic planning has not been an important element in the Japanese economy. Japan has had a planning agency since the late 1940s and has assembled numerous plans, but the plans are neither binding nor involuntarily implemented.

4.a.5. Sweden   The Swedish economic system and its performance are of interest because Sweden is viewed as a system that has been able, over an extended period of time, to sustain economic progress through the efficiency of the market while at the same time ensuring that incomes are equally distributed. Sweden is a relatively small but highly industrialized country. It has a total area of roughly 450,000 square kilometers (somewhat larger than the state of California) and a population of just over 8.9 million. Foreign trade is of vital importance to Sweden, accounting for more than 80 percent of its total output. The Swedish economy looks like a market economy in the production of goods and services, but the government accounts for nearly 45 percent of total purchases in Sweden.

RECAP

1. No economy is purely private. The public sector plays a role in every economy.
2. A market economy relies on prices and individual actions to solve economic problems. In centrally planned economies, the government decides what is produced, how it is produced, and who gets what.

SUMMARY

? 1. How does the government interact with the other sectors of the economy?

1. The circular flow diagram illustrates the interaction among all sectors of the economy—households, businesses, the international sector, and the public sector. *§1*

? 2. What is the economic role of government?

2. The market system results in economic efficiency. Economic efficiency means that in an economy one person cannot be made better off without harming someone else. *§2.a*

3. The market system does not result in economic efficiency when there are market imperfections, externalities, or public goods. Market imperfections occur when information is imperfect. *§2.b–2.g*

? 3. Why is the public sector such a large part of a market economy?

4. Two general reasons are given for the government's participation in the economy: the government may resolve the inefficiencies that occur in a market system, or the government may be the result of rent seeking. *§2.b–2.g*

5. Economic efficiency means that some people cannot be made better off without others being made worse off. Some people do not like the result of the market outcome and want to alter it. In such cases, resources are devoted to creating a transfer of income. This is called rent seeking. *§2.g*

? 4. What does the government do?

6. The government carries out microeconomic and macroeconomic activities. The microeconomic activities include resolving market imperfections, externalities, and public goods problems. The macroeconomic activities are directed toward monetary and fiscal policies and minimizing disruptions due to business cycles. *§3*

7. Governments often provide public goods and services such as fire protection, police protection, and national defense. Governments place limits on what firms and consumers can do in certain types of situations. Governments tax externalities or otherwise attempt to make price reflect the full cost of production and consumption. *§3.a*

8. Governments carry out monetary and fiscal policies to attempt to control business cycles. In the United States, monetary policy is the province of the Federal Reserve, and fiscal policy is up to the Congress and the president. *§3.b*

? 5. How do the sizes of public sectors in various countries compare?

9. Market systems rely on the decisions of individuals. Centrally planned systems rely on the government to answer economic questions for all individuals. *§4*

10. The size and influence of the public sector ranges from the market economies of the United States and Canada to the centrally planned economy of Cuba. *§4.a*

KEY TERMS

economic efficiency *§2.a*

technical efficiency *§2.a*

market imperfection *§2.b*

externalities *§2.c*

public goods *§2.d*

private property right *§2.d*

free ride *§2.d*

monopoly *§2.e*

business cycles *§2.f*

rent seeking *§2.g*

public choice *§2.g*

monetary policy *§3.b*

Federal Reserve *§3.b*

fiscal policy *§3.b*

transfer payments *§3.c*

budget surplus *§3.c*

budget deficit *§3.c*

centrally planned economy *§4*

EXERCISES

1. Illustrate productive or technical efficiency using a production possibilities curve. Can you illustrate economic efficiency? Are you able to show the exact point where economic efficiency would occur?

2. Why would an externality be referred to as a market failure? Explain how your driving on a highway imposes costs on other drivers. Why is this an externality? How might the externality be resolved or internalized?

3. What is the difference between a compact disk recording of a rock concert and a radio broadcast of that rock concert? Why would you spend $12 on the CD but refuse to provide any support to the radio station?

4. "The American buffalo disappeared because they were not privately owned." Evaluate this statement.

5. Which of the following economic policies are the responsibility of the Federal Reserve? Congress and the president?

   a. An increase in the rate of growth of the money supply
   b. A decrease in the rate of interest
   c. An increase in taxes on the richest 2 percent of Americans
   d. A reduction in taxes on the middle class
   e. An increase in the rate of growth of spending on health care

6. "The Department of Justice plans to file a lawsuit against major airlines, claiming they violated price-fixing laws by sharing plans for fare changes through a computer system, officials said Friday." Is this a microeconomic or macroeconomic policy?

7. People sometimes argue that imports should be limited by government policy. Suppose a government quota on the quantity of imports causes net exports to rise. Using the circular flow diagram as a guide, explain why total expenditures and national output may rise after the quota is imposed. Who is likely to benefit from the quota? Who will be hurt? Explain why the government would become involved in the economy through its imposition of quotas.

8. Most highways are "free" ways: there is no toll charge for using them. What problem does free access create? How would you solve this?

9. Explain why the suggested government action may or may not make sense in each of the following scenarios.

   a. People purchase a VCR with a guarantee provided by its maker, only to find that within a year the company has gone out of business. Consumers demand that the government provide the guarantee.

   b. Korean microchip producers are selling the microchips at a price that is below the cost of making the microchips in the United States. The U.S. government must impose taxes on the Korean microchips imported into the United States.

   c. The economy has slowed down, unemployment has risen, and interest rates are high. The government should provide jobs and force interest rates down.

   d. Fully 15 percent of all United States citizens are without health insurance. The government must provide health care for all Americans.

   e. The rising value of the dollar is making it nearly impossible for U.S. manufacturers to sell their products to other nations. The government must decrease the value of the dollar.

   f. The rich got richer at a faster rate than the poor got richer during the 1990s. The government must increase the tax rate on the rich to equalize the income distribution.

   g. The AIDS epidemic has placed such a state of emergency on health care that the only solution is to provide some pharmaceutical firm with a monopoly on any drugs or solutions discovered for HIV or AIDS.

10. Many nations of eastern Europe are undergoing a transition from a centrally planned to a market economic system. An important step in the process is to define private property rights in countries where they did not exist before. What does this mean? Why is it necessary to have private property rights?

11. Using the circular flow diagram, illustrate the effects of an increase in taxes imposed on the household sector.

12. Using the circular flow diagram, explain how the government can continually run budget deficits, that is, spend more than it receives in revenue from taxes.

13. Suppose you believe that government is the problem, not the solution. How would you explain the rapid growth of government during the past few decades?

14. The government intervenes in the private sector by imposing laws that ban smoking in all publicly used buildings. As a result, smoking is illegal in bars, restaurants, hotels, dance clubs, and other establishments. Is such a ban justified by economics?

15. In reference to exercise 14, we could say that before a ban is imposed, the owners of businesses owned the private property right to the air in their establishments. As owners of this valuable asset they would ensure it is used to earn them the greatest return. Thus, if their customers desired nonsmoking, then they would provide nonsmoking environments. How then does the ban on smoking improve things? Doesn't it merely transfer ownership of the air from the business owners to the nonsmokers?

A Big "Nein" to Deutsche Telekom; Telecommunications: Germany Still Doesn't Have a Completely Open Market

Deutsche Telekom has become crazed over spending the loose change in its pockets. A few weeks ago, the company was reported to be considering an acquisition of Sprint. This week, Deutsche Telekom announced that it was buying VoiceStream Wireless for a deal valued at $50.5 billion.

This deal makes no sense financially: VoiceStream had a net loss last year of $455 million on revenue of $475 million. To acquire VoiceStream's 2.3 million wireless subscribers, Deutsche Telekom will pay more than $20,000 per subscriber. A return of 10% on this investment over 10 years would require a yearly profit of more than $3,200 per wireless customer. This is impossible, particularly for VoiceStream, which has losses nearly as large as its revenues. Wishful thinking, hopes for the future and faith are fine for religion, but are no way to run a business, as Deutsche Telekom soon will learn if this deal goes through. But if the Germans want to throw away their money, let them.

There are policy reasons, however, to oppose this acquisition because Deutsche Telekom is, in effect, a subsidiary of the German government and is actively expanding and acquiring other telecommunication firms in Germany and around the globe. These acquisitions are being done in the name of globalization, but that is simply a politically correct term for the colonialism and imperialism of the past.

Many countries have claimed to privatize the former government monopolization of telecommunications. Yet much of the stock of the "privatized" telecommunication firms is owned by the government. In the case of Germany, more than half of the stock of Deutsche Telekom is owned by the government. This is partial privatization.

One problem with partial privatization is that it is in the best interests of the government to maximize the value of the stock of the partially owned telecommunications company. This means that the partially privatized company is treated favorably by the government. Another problem is that governments are reluctant to sell their remaining ownership and totally privatize, since such a massive sale would decrease the value of all the shares on the open market. Thus, governments are motivated to manipulate the value of such stocks. The stock of Deutsche Telekom thus is overvalued, since much of it is held by the German government and is not on the open market. It is this overvalued stock that will fund the proposed acquisition of VoiceStream.

Even partial privatization is to be preferred to the old system of complete government ownership and control of telecommunications. Yet the solution to the evils of partial privatization is total privatization, such as what happened with British Telecom. But France, Germany, Japan and Sweden are dragging their feet in achieving complete privatization of their former government monopolies of telecommunications. In the meantime, they should not be allowed market entry into countries that are completely privatized.

Partial privatization is not consistent with open markets and competition. Until Germany completely privatizes Deutsche Telekom, the company should not be allowed to have dominant ownership of any telecommunications firm in the United States— even if it [is] about to lose its lederhosen in this deal.

A. MICHAEL NOLL

Source: *Los Angeles Times*, July 26, 2000, p. 9. Copyright 2000 Times Mirror Company.

Los Angeles Times/July 26, 2000

Commentary

Chapter 5 indicated that there is a legitimate role for government in a market economy. In particular, government is justified to be involved in the production of products involving market imperfections like externalities. However, in many countries, government has operated firms that could be better operated by private business. As a result, in recent years there has been a trend toward the *privatization* of such firms. The privatization of government-owned enterprises is generally intended to increase efficiency by providing the activity being privatized the same incentives that private business firms face. The outcome of such privatization is expected to minimize the costs of production for a given level and quality of output.

The article indicates that the German telephone company, Deutsche Telekom, has been *partially* privatized but that the German government still owns more than half of the company's stock. So private ownership does not exist in the usual sense of the term. This policy of partial privatization has been followed in many countries where privatization is politically controversial. Why should the government retain ownership of a substantial portion of a seemingly private firm? Politics is the short answer. Those who have benefited from the government control of the firm usually have an interest in maintaining government control, and if the government owns more than half of the firm's outstanding stock, then the government exercises majority control of the firm. Perhaps labor unions fear that private ownership will mean fewer jobs at lower wages. In the case of Telekom, there may have been some services that were provided at less than the true cost of produc-

tion, and those households and/or firms which received service at a subsidized rate fear privatization may end their subsidy. Such groups provide political support for less than full privatization.

Privatization is likely to continue around the world as more and more governments seek to minimize their role in the economy and allow private business to respond to free market incentives in the production of goods. This article reminds us that partial privatization, where government retains some ownership of formerly government-operated enterprises, is not without controversy. The partially privatized firm may not have to compete with other firms on an equal basis but may be given favorable treatment by the government that increases its market value beyond that of a fully privatized firm.

This outcome is not a certainty, however, as the shares that are sold to the public may be worth less in a partially privatized firm than a fully privatized firm if the public believes that the government involvement will hinder the efficiency of the firm and its ability to earn profits. The author assumes that the ownership of more than half of Deutsche Telekom by the German government has increased the value of the outstanding stock held by the public beyond what a fully privatized firm would have reached. While that may or may not be true in this case, it certainly will not be a general rule that will always occur. After all, how many people would believe that government can do a better job of running a business than private citizens—managers and employees—who will be compensated on the basis of the firm's performance and profitability?

Part Two

Product Market Basics

Chapter 6

Elasticity: Demand and Supply

1. How do we measure how much consumers alter their purchases in response to a price change?
2. Why are measurements of elasticity important?
3. How does a business determine whether to increase or decrease the price of the product it sells in order to increase revenues?
4. Why might senior citizens or children receive price discounts relative to the rest of the population?
5. What determines whether consumers alter their purchases a little or a lot in response to a price change?
6. How do we measure how much changes in income, changes in the prices of related goods, or changes in advertising expenditures affect consumer purchases?
7. How do we measure how much producers respond to a price change?

Preview

Let's begin by trying to gain some perspective on what we have been doing and what we will be doing in the next few chapters. In the previous five chapters we defined economics, opportunity costs, and the "economic way of thinking." The economic way of thinking is to recognize that people are self-interested and as a result do those things they expect will make them happiest. We say that people compare the costs and benefits of some activity, but it is the incremental or marginal costs and marginal benefits that are important. It is the next minute, the next day, the next dollar, the next month's income that matter in people's decisions.

People compare marginal benefits and marginal costs. If marginal benefits are larger than the marginal costs of some activity, then people do that activity. If the marginal benefits are less than the marginal costs, then people do not do that activity. One of the things people do is trade or exchange. But, as we discovered, they

trade only if they believe that the trade will make them better off. This is what the gains from trade are all about; all parties to a trade can gain and have to think they will gain or else they will not trade.

The interaction of traders—of buyers and sellers—is represented by demand and supply. A market is a situation or place where buyers and sellers interact—demand and supply. Within a market, demand and supply determine the market price—the price at which buyers and sellers agree to trade.

In the previous chapters we examined how markets work to allocate scarce goods, services, and resources. We need to do more, however, if we are to understand why the world is what it is. We have to have a more in-depth understanding of markets, of demand and supply. We begin that process here. In this and the following chapters, we examine demand. We delve into the incentives and motivations of consumers. We examine how consumers behave when the price of a good or service changes, when income changes, or, in general, when marginal benefits or marginal costs change. After examining consumer behavior in more detail, we turn to supply. Suppliers are firms of one form or another, so to understand supply, we have to examine how firms behave. We look at sales, revenue, costs, and profits and see what firms do to try to be successful. ▪

1. How do we measure how much consumers alter their purchases in response to a price change?

1. THE PRICE ELASTICITY OF DEMAND

Suppose you are in charge of setting the price of McDonald's Big Mac. McDonald's has not been doing well lately. Burger King has been grabbing more and more of the fast-food hamburger market. You have correctly reasoned that you should lower the price of the Big Mac to increase sales. The problem is you don't know how much to lower it. Should the price be $2.99 or $1.99 or $.99? The answer depends on how consumers respond to the price change. Economists have devised measures of how much consumers alter their purchases in response to price changes. These measures are called elasticities.

1.a. The Definition of Price Elasticity

The price elasticity of demand is a measure of the magnitude by which consumers alter the quantity of some product they purchase in response to a change in the price of that product. The more price-elastic demand is, the more responsive consumers are to a price change—that is, the more they will adjust their purchases of a product when the price of that product changes. Conversely, the less price-elastic demand is, the less responsive consumers are to a price change.

price elasticity of demand: the percentage change in the quantity demanded of a product divided by the percentage change in the price of that product

The **price elasticity of demand** is the percentage change in the quantity demanded of a product divided by the percentage change in the price of that product:

$$\frac{\%\Delta Q^{D}}{\%\Delta P}$$

For instance, if the quantity of videotapes that are rented falls by 3 percent whenever the price of a videotape rental rises by 1 percent, the price elasticity of demand for videotape rentals is 3.

According to the law of demand, whenever the price of a good rises, the quantity demanded of that good falls. Thus, the price elasticity of demand is always negative, which can be confusing when referring to a "very high elasticity"—actually, a large negative number—or to a "low elasticity"—a small negative number. To avoid this confusion, economists use the absolute value of the price elasticity of demand and thus ignore the negative sign. Absolute value, denoted as | |, turns the negative number into a positive one. Thus, denoting the price elasticity of demand as e_d, we have

$$e_d = |-3\%/1\%| = |-3| = 3$$

Demand can be elastic, unit-elastic, or inelastic. When the price elasticity of demand is greater than 1, demand is said to be *elastic*. For instance, the demand for videotape rentals, according to the example of $e_d = 3$, is elastic. When the price elasticity of demand is 1, demand is said to be *unit-elastic*. For example, if the price of private education rises by 1 percent and the quantity of private education purchased falls by about 1 percent, the price elasticity of demand is

$$e_d = |-1\%/1\%| = 1$$

When the price elasticity of demand is less than 1, demand is said to be *inelastic*. In this case, a 1 percent rise in price brings forth a smaller than 1 percent decline in quantity demanded. For example, if the price of gasoline rises by 1 percent and the quantity of gasoline purchased falls by .2 percent, the price elasticity of demand is

$$e_d = |-.2\%/1\%| = .2$$

1.b. Demand Curve Shapes and Elasticity

perfectly elastic demand curve: a horizontal demand curve indicating that consumers can and will purchase all they want at one price

A **perfectly elastic demand curve** is a horizontal line that shows that consumers can purchase any quantity they want at the single prevailing price. In Figure 1(a), a perfectly elastic demand curve represents the demand for the wheat harvested by a single farmer in Canada. The Canadian farmer is only one small producer of wheat who, because he is just one among many, is unable to charge a price that differs from the price of wheat in the rest of the world. If this farmer's wheat is even slightly more expensive than wheat elsewhere, consumers will shift their purchases away from

Grocery shopping in many nations does not resemble the once-a-week trip to the supermarket most households in the United States make. This Indian woman and her child make a daily trip to the stores and shops looking for the best produce and the best bargains. Having more time available to devote to grocery shopping means that the price elasticity of demand for the grocery items is higher. A small price change may induce the woman to make a trip to another store; a small price change for someone without the time to make additional trips to the store will not affect purchases.

Figure 1

The Price Elasticity of Demand

Figure 1(a), a perfectly elastic demand curve, represents the demand for one farmer's wheat. Because there are so many other suppliers, buyers purchase wheat from the least expensive source. If this farmer's wheat is priced ever so slightly above other farmers' wheat, buyers will switch to another source. Also, because this farmer is just one small producer in a huge market, he can sell everything he wants at the market price. Figure 1(b), a perfectly inelastic demand curve, represents the demand for insulin by a diabetic. A certain quantity is necessary to satisfy the need regaardless of the price. Figure 1(c) shows two straight-line demand curves, D_1 and D_3, and a curved demand curve, D_2. These demand curves are neither perfectly elastic nor perfectly inelastic.

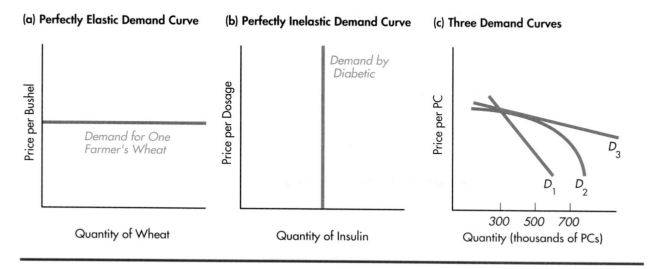

(a) Perfectly Elastic Demand Curve   **(b) Perfectly Inelastic Demand Curve**   **(c) Three Demand Curves**

this farmer and buy the wheat produced by other farmers in Canada and the rest of the world. A perfectly elastic demand means that even the smallest price change will cause consumers to change their consumption by a huge amount, in fact, totally switching purchases to the producer with the lowest prices.

perfectly inelastic demand curve: a vertical demand curve indicating that there is no change in the quantity demanded as the price changes

A **perfectly inelastic demand curve** is a vertical line illustrating the idea that consumers cannot or will not change the quantity of a good they purchase when the price of the product is changed. Perhaps insulin to a diabetic is a reasonably vivid example of a good whose demand is perfectly inelastic. Of course, this behavior holds only over a certain price range. Eventually, the price rises enough that even the diabetic will have to decrease the quantity demanded. Figure 1(b) shows a perfectly inelastic demand curve.

In between the two extreme shapes of demand curves are the demand curves for most products. Figure 1(c) shows two downward-sloping straight-line demand curves, D_1 and D_3, and one downward-sloping curved demand curve, D_2. Although demand curves can have virtually any shape—curve or straight line—the straight-line shape is used to illustrate the demand for most goods and services.

The price elasticity of demand declines as we move down a straight-line demand curve.

1.b.1. Price Elasticity Along a Straight-Line Demand Curve   The price elasticity of demand varies along a straight-line downward-sloping demand curve, declining as we move down the curve. The reason that elasticity changes along the straight-line demand curve is due to the way that elasticity is calculated, not to some intuitive economic explanation.

Figure 2

The Price Elasticity of Demand Varies Along a Straight-Line Demand Curve

Figure 2 shows that the price elasticity of demand varies along a straight-line demand curve. As we move down the demand curve, the price elasticity varies from elastic to unit-elastic to inelastic.

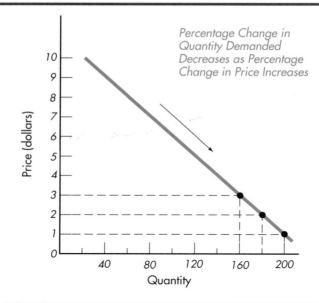

Along a straight-line demand curve, equal changes in price mean equal changes in quantity. For instance, if price changes by $1 in Figure 2, quantity demanded changes by 20 units; as price changes from $1 to $2, quantity demanded falls from 200 to 180; as price changes from $2 to $3, quantity demanded falls from 180 to 160; and so on. Each $1 change in price means a 20-unit change in quantity demanded. But those same amounts (constant amounts of $1 and 20 units) do not translate into constant percentage changes.

A $1 change at the top of the demand curve is a significantly different percentage change from a $1 change at the bottom of the demand curve. A $1 change from $10 is a 10 percent change, but a $1 change from $2 is a 50 percent change. Thus, as we move down the demand curve from higher to lower prices, a given dollar change becomes a larger and larger percentage change in price. The opposite is true of quantity changes. As we move downward along the demand curve, the same change in quantity becomes a smaller and smaller percentage change. A 10-unit change from 20 is a 50 percent change, while a 10-unit change from 200 is a 5 percent change. As we move down the straight-line demand curve, the percentage change in quantity demanded declines while the percentage change in price increases. Because the price elasticity of demand is the ratio of the percentage change in quantity demanded to the percentage change in price, the price elasticity of demand moves close to zero as we move down the straight-line demand curve.

The downward-sloping straight-line demand curve is divided into three parts by the price elasticity of demand: the *elastic region*, the *unit-elastic point*, and the *inelastic region*. The demand is elastic from the top of the curve to the unit-elastic point. At all prices below the unit-elastic point, the price elasticity of demand lies between 1 and 0. This is the inelastic portion of the curve.

The terms elastic *and* inelastic *refer to a price range, not to the entire demand curve.*

Elastic	$e_d > 1$
Unit-elastic	$e_d = 1$
Inelastic	$0 < e_d < 1$

2. Why are measurements of elasticity important?

1.c. The Price Elasticity of Demand Is Defined in Percentage Terms

By measuring the price elasticity of demand in terms of percentage changes, economists are able to compare how consumers respond to changes in the prices of different products. For instance, the impact of a 1 percent increase in the price of gasoline (measured in gallons) can be compared to the impact of a 1 percent change in the price of videotape rentals (measured in number of rentals). Or the impact of a 1 percent increase in the price of college tuition can be compared to the impact of a 1 percent rise in the price of a Big Mac.

Percentage changes ensure that we are comparing apples to apples, not apples to oranges. What sense could be made of a comparison between the effects on quantity demanded of a $1 rise in the price of college tuition, from $5,000 to $5,001, and a $1 rise in the price of Big Macs, from $2 to $3? The dollar change would mean that tuition increases by 0.02 percent, and the hamburger price increases by 50 percent.

1.d. Average or Arc Elasticity

One of the problems of measuring elasticity is that the value depends on the base, or the starting point. An increase from $5 to $6 is a 20 percent change [($6 − $5)/$5 = 1/5], but a decrease from $6 to $5 is a 16.67 percent change [($5 − $6)/$6 = 1/6]. The result differs according to whether we start from $5 or $6—that is, according to whether the base is $5 or $6. Because the value of the price elasticity of demand varies depending on the base, economists use the average price and average quantity demanded to calculate elasticity. The elasticity obtained when the midpoint, or average, price and quantity are used is often called the **arc elasticity**. The formula used to calculate arc elasticity is

arc elasticity: the price elasticity of demand measured over a price range using the midpoint, or average, as the base

$$e_d = \frac{|(Q_2 - Q_1)/[(Q_1 + Q_2)/2]|}{|(P_2 - P_1)/[(P_1 + P_2)/2]|}$$

Let's use this formula to calculate an elasticity. At a price of $6 per ticket, the average moviegoer demands 2 tickets per month. At a price of $4 per ticket, the average moviegoer purchases 6 tickets per month. Thus,

$$P_1 = \$6 \qquad Q_1 = 2$$
$$P_2 = \$4 \qquad Q_2 = 6$$

The *change* in quantity demanded is $Q_2 - Q_1 = 6 - 2 = 4$. The *percentage change* is the change divided by the base. The base is the average, or midpoint between the two quantities, the sum of the two quantities divided by 2: $(Q_1 + Q_2)/2 = (6 + 2)/2 = 4$. With 4 as the base, the percentage change in quantity is 4/4, or 100 percent. We can say that the quantity of movie tickets sold rose by an average of 100 percent as the price of a ticket declined from $6 to $4.

The change in price is −$2, from $6 to $4, and the average price is $(P_1 + P_2)/2 = (\$6 + \$4)/2 = \$5$. The percentage change in price is −$2/$5 = −40 percent.

Because the numerator of the price elasticity of demand is 100 percent and the denominator is −40 percent, the price elasticity is

$$e_d = |100/-40| = 2.5$$

According to these calculations, the price elasticity of demand for movie tickets, over the price range from $6 to $4, is 2.5. We can say that demand is elastic over this price range.

1. The price elasticity of demand is a measure of the degree to which consumers will alter the quantities of a product they purchase in response to changes in the price of that product.

2. Because the quantity demanded always declines as price rises, the price elasticity of demand is always a negative number. To avoid confusion when discussing price elasticity of demand, we use the absolute value—that is, the negative sign is ignored.

3. The price elasticity of demand is a ratio of the percentage change in the quantity demanded to the corresponding percentage change in the price.

4. When the price elasticity of demand is greater than 1, demand is said to be *elastic*. When the price elasticity of demand is equal to 1, demand is said to be *unit-elastic*. When the price elasticity of demand is less than 1, demand is said to be *inelastic*.

5. The elasticity obtained by using average price and average quantity demanded is called the *arc elasticity*.

2. THE USE OF PRICE ELASTICITY OF DEMAND

The price elasticity of demand may be a manager's best friend. It informs her whether to raise or lower prices, whether to charge different customers different prices, whether to charge different prices at different times of the day, and whether it is better to focus on prices, to advertise, or to carry out business strategies that do not focus on prices.

2.a. Total Revenue and Price Elasticity of Demand

3. How does a business determine whether to increase or decrease the price of the product it sells in order to increase revenues?

A manager concerned with increasing revenue must know what the current price elasticity of demand is for the firm's product. There is a close relationship between price elasticity of demand and total revenue. **Total revenue** (TR) equals the price of a product multiplied by the quantity sold: $TR = P \times Q$. If P rises by 10 percent and Q falls by more than 10 percent, then total revenue declines as a result of the price rise. If P rises by 10 percent and Q falls by less than 10 percent, then total revenue rises as a result of the price rise. And if P increases by 10 percent and Q falls by 10 percent, total revenue does not change as the price changes. Thus, total revenue increases as price is increased if demand is inelastic, decreases as price is increased if demand is elastic, and does not change as price is increased if demand is unit-elastic.

total revenue (TR):
$TR = P \times Q$

$$\text{Elastic:} \quad \uparrow P \Rightarrow \downarrow TR$$
$$\downarrow P \Rightarrow \uparrow TR$$
$$\text{Inelastic:} \uparrow P \Rightarrow \uparrow TR$$
$$\downarrow P \Rightarrow \downarrow TR$$

Whenever the price elasticity of demand for a product is in the elastic region, the product supplier must decrease price in order to increase revenue. For instance, the price elasticity of demand for airline travel has been found to be near 2.4. This means that, over some price range, for each 1 percent increase in the price of an airline ticket, the quantity of tickets demanded will decline by 2.4 percent.

In the spring of 2000, a trip could be made from New York to Los Angeles for $250 each way, if you included a Saturday night stay. If the airlines had increased the fare by 10 percent, to $275 each way, they would have sold 24 percent (2.4 × 0.10) fewer tickets. As a result, their total revenue would have fallen. The revenue from selling 3,000 tickets per day for the trip between New York and Los Angeles at a fare of $250 was $750,000 per day. At a fare of $275, the quantity of tickets demanded would have declined by 720 to 2,280 per day (3,000 × 0.24 = 720), and revenue would have fallen to $627,000 per day. As long as the price elasticity of demand exceeds 1, total revenue is decreased if the price is increased.

As long as demand is elastic, price must be decreased to increase total revenue. But by how much should the price be lowered? Since the price elasticity of demand declines as the price falls along a straight-line demand curve, eventually price reaches a point where demand becomes unit-elastic. Further price decreases at this stage would cause total revenue to fall. Thus, *total revenue* can be maximized by setting the price where demand is unit-elastic.

The table in Figure 3 is a demand schedule for airline tickets listing the price and quantity of tickets sold and the total revenue ($P \times Q$). Figure 3(a) shows a straight-line demand curve representing the demand for air travel. Total revenue is plotted in Figure 3(b), directly below the demand curve. You can see that total revenue rises as price falls in the elastic range of the demand curve, while in the inelastic range of the demand curve, total revenue declines as price falls. *The unit-elastic point is the price at which revenue is at a maximum.* Remember that this is revenue, not profit, we are discussing. A firm may or may not want to maximize revenue, as noted in the Economic Insight "Price, Revenue, and Profit." To increase revenue:

1. If in elastic range of demand, lower price.
2. If in inelastic range of demand, raise price.

2.b. Price Discrimination

Ads and marquees proudly proclaim that "Kids stay free" or that "Senior discounts apply," and it is well known that airlines sell vacation travelers tickets for significantly less than the business traveler pays. The price elasticity of demand might explain why firms will not always increase revenue if they lower their prices, but what explains why firms charge different customers different prices for the same product? It is exactly the same principle. When demand is elastic, a price decrease causes total revenue to increase; and when demand is inelastic, a price increase causes total revenue to rise. If different groups of customers have different price elasticities of demand for the same product and if the groups are easily identifiable and can be kept from trading with each other, then the seller of the product can increase total revenue by charging each group a different price. Charging different prices to different customers for the same product is called **price discrimination**. Price discrimination occurs when senior citizens purchase movie tickets at a lower price than younger citizens or when business travelers pay more for airline tickets than vacation travelers.

Senior citizens are frequently offered movie tickets at lower prices than younger people. The reason for the discount is that, on average, older people are more inclined than younger people to respond to a change in the price of admission to a movie.

Suppose everyone pays the same ticket price of $5 and the price elasticity of demand by senior citizens is 2.0, while that by nonsenior citizens is 0.5. Lowering the price of a movie ticket by 10 percent would cause senior citizens to increase their purchases of movie tickets by 20 percent, but nonsenior citizens would increase

As long as the price elasticity of demand exceeds 1, total revenue is decreased if the price is increased.

4. Why might senior citizens or children receive price discounts relative to the rest of the population?

price discrimination: charging different customers different prices for the same product

Figure 3

Total Revenue and Price Elasticity

The demand schedule provides data for plotting the straight-line demand curve, Figure 3(a), and the total revenue curve, Figure 3(b). In the elastic region of the demand curve, a price decrease will increase total revenue. At the unit-elastic point, a price decrease will not change total revenue. In the inelastic region of the demand curve, a price decrease will decrease total revenue.

Price per Ticket	Quantity of Tickets Sold per Day	Total Revenue
$1,000	200	$200,000
$ 900	400	$360,000
$ 800	600	$480,000
$ 700	800	$560,000
$ 600	1,000	$600,000
$ 500	1,200	$600,000
$ 400	1,400	$560,000
$ 300	1,600	$480,000
$ 200	1,800	$360,000
$ 100	2,000	$200,000

(a) Air Travel Demand Curve

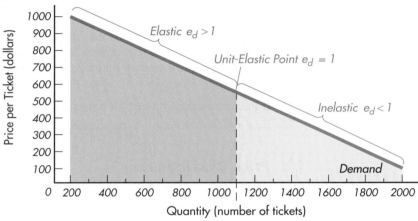

(b) Total Revenue for Airline

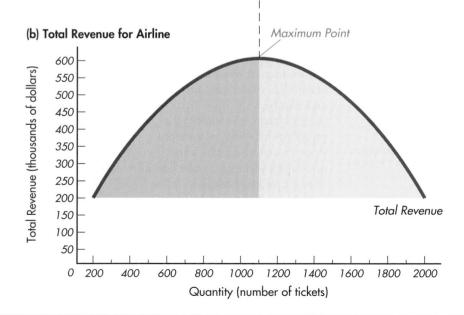

Price, Revenue, and Profit

Profit is defined as revenue minus costs. If revenue rises but costs rise more, then profit declines. Whether a price reduction leads to more profits depends on how revenue and costs respond to the price change. With the price elasticity of demand we are looking only at the response of revenue to price changes. We do not know what costs are doing, and thus we do not know what is happening to profit. (We examine costs in the chapter "Supply: The Costs of Doing Business.")

Many people confuse revenue and profit; and sometimes even business people embark on a strategy of increasing revenue but lose sight of the "bottom line," that is, profit. Stan Shih had a strategy of making his Taiwan-based computer firm, founded in 1983, one of the top five companies by 1995. Shih's firm, known as Acer, entered the United States by purchasing companies in Silicon Valley. It began producing a low-cost line of PCs known as Acros in 1992. Sales were expected to reach $100 million in the first year. The sales goal was reached, but the company was not particularly pleased. According to Peter A. Janssen, Acer America's marketing vice president, "The revenues are huge. The problem is profitability."[1]

A similar situation befuddled the 3DO Company, a Redwood City video game software and hardware developer. The 3DO Company tripled its revenues but still lost $9.4 million during the last quarter of 1994. The company increased advertising in order to increase revenues, but the advertising expenditures rose more than revenues did.[2]

[1]Statement by Janssen reported in *Business Week*, May 18, 1992, p. 129.
[2]Reported in the *San Francisco Chronicle*, February 10, 1995, p. B2.

---

their purchases by only 5 percent. Total revenue from senior citizens would rise, but that from nonsenior citizens would fall. It would make more sense for the theater to lower the price for senior citizens but not for younger people.

Airline discounts are constructed on the basis of the price elasticity of demand as well. Vacationers know their schedules well in advance and can take advantage of the least expensive means of travel. Business travelers are more constrained. They often do not know their schedules days in advance, and they usually want to travel on Monday through Friday. The airlines recognize that the demand for air travel by vacationers is much more elastic than the demand by business travelers. As a result, airlines offer discounts to travelers who purchase tickets well in advance and stay over a Saturday night. For instance, in the spring of 1998, a cross-country roundtrip fare was $840 unless the trip included an overnight stay on Saturday. Then the fare dropped to $360. If tickets were purchased two weeks in advance, the fare dropped to $240.

RECAP

1. If the price elasticity of demand is greater than 1, revenue and price changes move in the opposite direction. An increase in price causes a decrease in revenue, and a decrease in price causes an increase in revenue. If the price elasticity of demand is less than 1, revenue and price move in the same direction. If the price elasticity of demand is 1, revenue does not change as price changes.

2. When the price elasticity of demand for one product differs among different groups of easily identified customers, firms can increase revenues by charging each group a different price. The groups with elastic demands will receive lower prices than those with inelastic demands.

3. DETERMINANTS OF THE PRICE ELASTICITY OF DEMAND

5. What determines whether consumers alter their purchases a little or a lot in response to a price change?

The degree to which the price elasticity of demand is inelastic or elastic depends on the following factors, which differ among products and among consumers:

- The existence of substitutes
- The importance of the product in the consumer's total budget
- The time period under consideration

3.a. The Existence of Substitutes

Consumers who can switch from one product to another without losing quality or some other attribute associated with the original product will be sensitive to a price change. Their demand will be elastic. Such consumers will purchase a substitute rather than the original product whenever the relative price of the original product rises.

A senior citizen discount is offered at movie theaters because of the different price elasticities of demand by senior citizens and nonsenior citizens. Why are their elasticities different? More substitutes may be available to senior citizens than to younger folks. Retirees have more time to seek out alternative entertainment activities than do people who are working full-time. Retirees can go to movies during the early part of the day or on weekdays when the theater runs a special.

In contrast, diabetics have no substitutes that replace insulin, and business travelers have few substitutes for the airlines. As a result, their demands are relatively inelastic. The more substitutes there are for a product, the greater the price elasticity of demand.

The more substitutes there are for a product, the greater the price elasticity of demand.

3.b. The Importance of the Product in the Consumer's Total Budget

Because a new car and a European vacation are quite expensive, even a small percentage change in their prices can take a significant portion of a household's income. As a result, a 1 percent increase in price may cause many households to delay the purchase of a car or vacation. Coffee, on the other hand, accounts for such a small portion of a household's total weekly expenditures that a large percentage increase in the price of coffee will probably have little effect on the quantity of coffee purchased. The demand for vacations is most likely quite a bit more elastic than the demand for coffee. The greater the portion of the consumer's budget a good constitutes, the more elastic is the demand for the good.

The greater the portion of the consumer's budget a good constitutes, the more elastic the demand for the good.

3.c. The Time Period Under Consideration

If we are speaking about a day or an hour, then the demand for most goods and services will have a low price elasticity. If we are referring to a year or to several years, then the demand for most products will be more price-elastic than in a shorter period. For instance, the demand for gasoline is very nearly perfectly inelastic over a period of a month. No good substitutes are available in so brief a period. Over a ten-year period, however, the demand for gasoline is much more elastic. The additional time allows consumers to alter their behavior to make better use of gasoline

The longer the period under consideration, the more elastic the demand for the good.

and to find substitutes for gasoline. The longer the period under consideration, the more elastic is the demand for any product.

RECAP

1. The price elasticity of demand depends on how readily and easily consumers can switch their purchases from one product to another.
2. Everything else held constant, the greater the number of close substitutes, the greater the price elasticity of demand.
3. Everything else held constant, the greater the proportion of a householder's budget a good constitutes, the greater is the householder's price elasticity of demand for that good.
4. Everything else held constant, the longer the time period under consideration, the greater is the price elasticity of demand.

6. How do we measure how much changes in income, changes in the prices of related goods, or changes in advertising expenditures affect consumer purchases?

4. OTHER DEMAND ELASTICITIES

A price change leads to a movement along the demand curve. When something that affects demand, other than price, changes, the demand curve shifts. How far the demand curve shifts is measured by elasticity—elasticity of the variable whose value changes. As we saw in Chapter 3, "Markets, Demand and Supply, and the Price System," demand is determined by income, prices of related goods, expectations, tastes, number of buyers, and international effects. A change in any one of these will cause the demand curve to shift, and a measure of elasticity exists for each of these demand determinants. The *income elasticity of demand* measures the percentage change in demand caused by a 1 percent change in income, the *cross-price elasticity of demand* measures the percentage change in demand caused by a 1 percent change in the price of a related good, the *advertising elasticity of demand* measures the percentage change in demand caused by a 1 percent change in advertising expenditures (change in tastes), and so on.[1] Each elasticity is calculated by dividing the percentage change in demand by the percentage change in the variable under consideration.

4.a. The Cross-Price Elasticity of Demand

cross-price elasticity of demand: the percentage change in the quantity demanded for one good divided by the percentage change in the price of a related good, everything else held constant

The **cross-price elasticity of demand** measures the degree to which goods are substitutes or complements (for a discussion of substitutes and complements, see Chapter 3). The cross-price elasticity of demand is defined as the percentage change

---

[1]Notice that we should define the cross-price elasticity as the percentage change in demand rather than percentage change in quantity demanded because it is the entire demand curve that is changing. However, common usage defines the formula as the percentage change in quantity demanded for good j divided by the percentage change in the price of good k. Thus for both cross-price and income elasticities, we follow the common usage.

in the quantity demanded for one good divided by the percentage change in the price of a related good, everything else held constant:

$$\text{Cross-price elasticity of demand} = \frac{\text{percentage change in quantity demanded for good j}}{\text{percentage change in the price of good k}}$$

When the cross-price elasticity of demand is positive, the goods are substitutes; and when the cross-price elasticity of demand is negative, the goods are complements. If a 1 percent *increase* in the price of a movie ticket leads to a 5 percent *increase* in the quantity of videotapes that are rented, movies and videotapes are substitutes. If a 1 percent rise in the price of a movie ticket leads to a 5 percent *drop* in the quantity of popcorn consumed, movies and popcorn are complements.

4.b. The Income Elasticity of Demand

The income elasticity of demand measures the magnitude of consumer responsiveness to income changes. The **income elasticity of demand** is defined as the percentage change in quantity demanded for a product divided by the percentage change in income, everything else held constant:

$$\text{Income elasticity of demand} = \frac{\text{percentage change in quantity demanded for good j}}{\text{percentage change in income}}$$

Goods whose income elasticity of demand is greater than zero are **normal goods**. Products often called necessities have lower income elasticities than products known as luxuries. Gas, electricity, health-oriented drugs, and physicians' services might be considered necessities. Their income elasticities are about 0.4 or 0.5. On the other hand, people tend to view dental services, automobiles, and private education as luxury goods. Their elasticities are 1.5 to 2.0.

income elasticity of demand: the percentage change in the quantity demanded for a good divided by the percentage change in income, everything else held constant

normal goods: goods for which the income elasticity of demand is positive

What used to fill an entire room now can be held on a lap. The laptop, or notebook, computer is capable of carrying out calculations that only twenty years ago required a computer of 10 feet by 12 feet. When initially introduced, the personal computer and the laptop version appealed primarily to high-income earners—the income elasticity of demand was high. The machine was looked on as an expensive toy. Today, the computer is virtually a necessity and the income elasticity of demand is significantly lower than it was even five years ago. The laptop goes everywhere, even with a marine biologist who uses the laptop to record and analyze data while sitting in a rubber boat off the coast of Fiji .

Consumers could have a negative income elasticity of demand for some goods: less of those goods would be consumed as income rose. Such goods are called **inferior goods**. It is difficult to think of examples of inferior goods. Some people claim that potatoes, rice, and hamburger are inferior goods because people who have very low levels of income eat large quantities of these goods but give up those items and begin eating fruit, fish, and higher-quality meats as their incomes rise. The problem with calling these products inferior is that many higher-income households consume large quantities of potatoes, rice, and hamburger.

R E C A P

1. The cross-price elasticity of demand is the percentage change in the quantity demanded for one product divided by the percentage change in the price of a related product, everything else held constant. If the cross-price elasticity of demand is positive, the goods are substitutes. If the cross-price elasticity of demand is negative, the goods are complements.

2. The income elasticity of demand is the percentage change in the quantity demanded for one product divided by the percentage change in income, everything else held constant. If the income elasticity of a good is greater than zero, the good is called a *normal good*. If the income elasticity of a good is negative, the good is called an *inferior good*.

3. Elasticities can be calculated for any determinant of demand. Although income and related goods elasticities were calculated in the text, other elasticities like international development, service, quality, and expectations could have been calculated.

7. How do we measure how much producers respond to a price change?

5. SUPPLY ELASTICITIES

Elasticity is a measure of responsiveness. The response of buyers to price changes is measured by the price elasticity of demand. The response of sellers to price changes can also be measured by elasticity. The *price elasticity of supply* is a measure of how sellers adjust the quantity of a good they offer for sale when the price of that good changes.

5.a. The Price Elasticity of Supply

The **price elasticity of supply** is the percentage change in the quantity supplied of a good divided by the percentage change in the price of that good, everything else held constant. The price elasticity of supply is usually a positive number because the quantity supplied typically rises when the price rises. Supply is said to be elastic over a price range if the price elasticity of supply is greater than 1 over that price range. It is said to be inelastic over a price range if the price elasticity of supply is less than 1 over that price range.

$$\text{Price elasticity of supply} = \frac{\text{percentage change in the quantity supplied}}{\text{percentage change in the price}}$$

Different shapes the supply curve may take are illustrated in Figure 4. Figure 4(a) is a vertical line, representing a product for which the quantity supplied cannot increase no matter the price. There are some special types of goods for which

Figure 4

The Price Elasticity of Supply

There are some special types of goods for which supply cannot change no matter the length of time allowed for change. For such goods, the price elasticity of supply is zero and the supply curve is vertical, as shown in Figure 4(a). Figure 4(b) is a perfectly elastic supply curve, a horizontal line. A perfectly elastic supply curve says that the quantity supplied is unlimited at the given price; a small—infinitesimal—price change would lead to an infinite change in quantity supplied. For most goods, the supply curve lies between the perfectly inelastic and perfectly elastic extremes. In Figure 4(c) three supply curves are drawn. Curve S_1 is steeper than the others but less steep than a perfectly inelastic curve. Curve S_2 is a curved supply curve. Curve S_3 is flatter than the others but not as flat as the perfectly elastic curve.

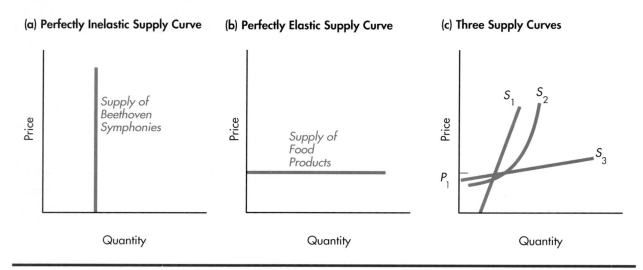

(a) Perfectly Inelastic Supply Curve **(b) Perfectly Elastic Supply Curve** **(c) Three Supply Curves**

supply cannot change no matter the length of time allowed for change—land surface, Monet paintings, Beethoven symphonies. For such goods, the price elasticity of supply is zero. Figure 4(b) shows a perfectly elastic supply curve, a horizontal line. There are some goods for which the quantity supplied at the current price can be whatever anyone wants given sufficient time. The production of food, for instance, has increased tremendously during the past century while the price has remained about the same. For most goods, the supply curve lies between the perfectly inelastic and perfectly elastic extremes. In Figure 4(c), three supply curves are drawn illustrating different shapes the supply curve might have. Curve S_1 is steeper than the others but less steep than a perfectly inelastic curve. Curve S_2 is a curved supply curve, and curve S_3 is flatter than the others but not as flat as the perfectly elastic curve.

5.b. The Long and Short Runs

short run: a period of time short enough that the quantities of at least one of the resources cannot be varied

The shape of the supply curve depends primarily on the length of time being considered. Economists view time in terms of two distinct periods, the short run and the long run. The **short run** is a period of time long enough for existing firms to change the quantity of output they produce by changing the quantities of *some* of the

long run: a period of time long enough that the quantities of all resources can be varied

resources used to produce their output but not long enough for the firms to change the quantities of *all* of the resources. In the short run, firms are not able to build new factories or retrain workers. The **long run** is a period of time long enough for existing firms to change the quantities of all the resources they use and for new firms to begin producing the product. The chronological time for short and long runs varies from industry to industry. The long run for oil refining may be as long as seven to eight years; for personal computers, perhaps a year; for basket making, probably no longer than a day or two.

Usually, the greater the time period allowed, the more readily firms will increase their quantities supplied in response to a price change. Thus, supply curves applicable to shorter periods of time tend to be more inelastic than supply curves that apply to longer periods of time. If firms have to change their production techniques or switch from the production of one good to another in order to change the quantities they supply, they can respond less in a week to a price change than they could in a year. A baker who can switch from producing cupcakes to muffins within a day has large price elasticities of supply for cupcakes and for muffins; a small increase in the price of muffins relative to cupcakes will cause the bakery to increase significantly the quantity of muffins baked and reduce the quantity of cupcakes baked. An automobile manufacturing plant that requires several months or years to switch from one type of car to another, however, will have a relatively inelastic supply.

In Figure 4(c), supply curve S_1 represents a shorter-run supply curve. For a given price change, the quantity supplied would change by a small amount, shown by moving along S_1 from point P_1. Curve S_2 represents a firm that is able to increase quantity supplied substantially in the short run if it is currently producing a small amount. But, if it is producing a larger amount, it cannot increase output very much in the short run, perhaps because increased production would require an expansion of the current factory. Curve S_3 represents a longer-run supply curve. The change in output in response to a price change is greater along S_3 than along either of the other curves.

5.c. Price Elasticities of Demand and Supply

Who actually pays a tax levied on some item or some business? Is it the business, or does the consumer ultimately pay? The answer seems straightforward enough: "Clearly, the consumer pays the tax since the consumer takes the item to the checkout counter and forks over the money." Social security is a tax levied one-half on the employer and one-half on the employee. Who pays the social security tax? This too seems straightforward—"They both pay half." The answers are not that easy, however. Who pays the tax depends on the price elasticities of demand *and* supply.

Suppose that the price elasticity of supply for the item being taxed is large and the demand for that item is price-inelastic. In this case, the firm can raise the price without losing sales, which means that the tax can be added to the price and the firm will not lose sales. Moreover, the firm can switch from producing the taxed good to producing a nontaxed good relatively easily. Since the firm will not lose sales as a result of the tax, the firm does not need to worry about lowering the price and thus paying a portion of the tax. Regardless of whether the tax is imposed on the firm or on the consumer, it is the consumer who actually pays the tax. We say that the **tax incidence** falls on the consumer. Consider cigarettes, for example. If smokers will buy the same quantity of cigarettes even if the price rises by 20 percent, then an

tax incidence: a measure of who pays a tax

8 percent tax levied on cigarettes will not affect sales. Firms would not need to reduce price to keep sales the same.

If, on the other hand, supply is price-inelastic and demand price-elastic, then a price increase means a revenue decrease for the firm. Since the firm cannot raise price without losing sales and cannot readily switch to producing another good, the firm must incorporate the tax in the original price and offer the same total cost to consumers after the tax is levied as before the tax. Hence, the firm will lower the price of the product enough that the price plus the new tax will just about equal the original (before tax) price. In this case, it is the business that pays the tax; the tax incidence falls on the business. If the price elasticity of demand for potato chips were high and the price elasticity of supply low, then an 8 percent tax on potato chips would reduce sales unless the business reduced the price of the chips. Because the business has to lower the price to maintain its sales, it actually pays the tax. The incidence falls on business.

In general, the more elastic the demand and the less elastic the supply, everything else held constant, the more the incidence falls on businesses and the less on consumers.

RECAP

1. The price elasticity of supply is the percentage change in the quantity supplied of one product divided by the percentage change in the price of that product, everything else held constant. The price elasticity of supply increases as the time period under consideration increases.

2. The long run is a period of time just long enough that the quantities of all resources can be varied. The short run is a period of time just short enough that the quantity of at least some of the resources cannot be varied.

3. The interaction of demand and supply determines the price and quantity produced and sold; the relative size of demand and supply price elasticities determines how the market reacts to changes. For instance, the size of supply relative to demand price elasticities determines the incidence of a tax.

SUMMARY

? How do we measure how much consumers alter their purchases in response to a price change?

1. The price elasticity of demand is a measure of the responsiveness of consumers to changes in price. It is defined as the percentage change in the quantity demanded of a good divided by the percentage change in the price of the good. *§1.a*

2. The price elasticity of demand is always a negative number because price and quantity demanded are inversely related. To avoid confusion about what large or small elasticity means, the price elasticity of demand is calculated as the absolute value of the percentage change in the quantity demanded of a good

divided by the percentage change in the price of the good. *§1.a*

3. As the price is lowered along a straight-line demand curve, the price elasticity of demand declines. *§1.b.1*

4. The straight-line demand curve consists of three segments: the top part, which is elastic; the unit-elastic region; and the bottom part, which is inelastic. *§1.b.1*

5. The price elasticity of demand is calculated as the arc, or average, elasticity to avoid the problems created in choosing a starting point, or base. *§1.d*

6. Comparing the price elasticity of demand for various products/services allows economists to see how consumers respond to price changes. In other words, it can tell us how big a difference price makes in a particular purchasing decision.

? **How does a business determine whether to increase or decrease the price of the product it sells in order to increase revenues?**

7. If the price elasticity of demand is greater than 1, total revenue and price changes move in opposite directions. An increase in price causes a decrease in total revenue, and a decrease in price causes an increase in total revenue. If demand is inelastic, total revenue and price move in the same direction. *§2.a*

? **Why might senior citizens or children receive price discounts relative to the rest of the population?**

8. When the price elasticity of demand for one product differs among different groups of easily identifiable customers, firms can increase total revenue by resorting to price discrimination. The customers with the more elastic demands will receive lower prices than the customers with less elastic demands. *§2.b*

? **What determines whether consumers alter their purchases a little or a lot in response to a price change?**

9. Everything else held constant, the greater the number of close substitutes, the greater the price elasticity of demand. *§3.a*

10. Everything else held constant, the greater the proportion of a household's budget a good constitutes, the greater the household's elasticity of demand for that good. *§3.b*

11. Everything else held constant, the longer the time period under consideration, the greater the price elasticity of demand. *§3.c*

? **How do we measure whether changes in income, changes in the prices of related goods, or changes in advertising expenditures affect consumer purchases?**

12. Elasticities can be calculated for any variable that affects demand. *§4*

13. The cross-price elasticity of demand is defined as the percentage change in the quantity demanded for one good divided by the percentage change in the price of a related good, everything else held constant. *§4.a*

14. The income elasticity of demand is defined as the percentage change in the quantity demanded of a good divided by the percentage change in income, everything else held constant. *§4.b*

? **How do we measure whether producers respond to a price change?**

15. The price elasticity of supply is defined as the percentage change in the quantity supplied of a good divided by the percentage change in the price of that good, everything else held constant. *§5.a*

16. The short run is a period of time short enough that the quantities of at least some of the resources cannot be varied. The long run is a period of time just long enough that the quantities of all resources can be varied. *§5.b*

17. The incidence of a tax depends on the price elasticities of demand and supply. In general, the more elastic the demand and the less elastic the supply, everything else held constant, the more the incidence falls on businesses and the less on consumers. *§5.c*

KEY TERMS

price elasticity of demand *§1.a*

perfectly elastic demand curve *§1.b*

perfectly inelastic demand curve *§1.b*

arc elasticity *§1.d*

total revenue (*TR*) *§2.a*

price discrimination *§2.b*

cross-price elasticity of demand *§4.a*

income elasticity of demand *§4.b*

normal goods *§4.b*

inferior goods *§4.b*

price elasticity of supply §5.a

short run §5.b

long run §5.b

tax incidence §5.c

EXERCISES

Use the following hypothetical demand schedule for movies to do exercises 1–4.

Quantity Demanded	Price	Elasticity
100	$ 5	
80	$10	
60	$15	
40	$20	
20	$25	
10	$30	

1. a. Determine the price elasticity of demand at each quantity demanded using the starting price and quantity as the bases. Next, do the same using the ending price and quantity as the bases; then, use the average price and quantity.
   b. Redo exercise 1a using price changes of $10 rather than $5.
   c. Plot the price and quantity data given in the demand schedule. Indicate the price elasticity value at each quantity demanded using the average price and quantity demanded as the bases. Explain why the elasticity value gets smaller as you move down the demand curve.

2. Below the demand curve plotted in exercise 1, plot the total revenue curve, measuring total revenue on the vertical axis and quantity on the horizontal axis.

3. What would a 10 percent increase in the price of movie tickets mean for the revenue of a movie theater if the price elasticity of demand were 0.1, 0.5, 1.0, and 5.0?

4. Using the demand curve plotted in exercise 1, illustrate what would occur if the income elasticity of demand were 0.05 and income rose by 10 percent. If the income elasticity of demand was 3.0 and income rose by 10 percent, what would occur?

5. Which is easier: to list five substitutes for each of the products listed under the elastic portion of Table 1 or five substitutes for the goods listed under the inelastic portion? Explain.

6. Are the following pairs of goods substitutes or complements? Indicate whether their cross-price elasticities are negative or positive.
   a. Bread and butter
   b. Bread and potatoes
   c. Socks and shoes
   d. Tennis racket and golf clubs
   e. Bicycles and automobiles
   f. Foreign investments and domestic investments
   g. Cars made in Japan and cars made in the United States

7. Suppose the price elasticity of demand for movies by teenagers is 0.2 and that by adults is 2.0. What policy would the movie theater implement to increase total revenue? Use hypothetical data to demonstrate your answer.

8. Explain how consumers will react to a job loss. What will be the first goods they will do without?

9. Explain why senior citizens can obtain special discounts at movie theaters, drugstores, and other businesses.

10. Calculate the income elasticity of demand from the following data (use the midpoint or average):

Income	Quantity Demanded
$15,000	20,000
$20,000	30,000

   a. Explain why the value is a positive number.
   b. Explain what would happen to a demand curve as income changes if the income elasticity were 2.0. Compare that outcome to the situation that would occur if the income elasticity of demand were 0.2.

11. The poor tend to have a price elasticity of demand for movie tickets that is greater than 1. Why don't you see signs offering "poor people discounts" similar to the signs offering "senior citizen discounts"?

12. Suppose a tax is imposed on a product that has a completely inelastic supply curve. Who pays the tax?

13. Explain why a 40 percent across-the-board tax on businesses might not benefit the consumers.

14. Explain what must occur for the strategies suggested by the following headlines to be successful:
    a. "Ford to go nationwide with plan for one-price selling of Escorts."
    b. "P. F. Flyers cut sneaker prices to $20 a pair in a move to triple 1999 sales to 10 million pairs."
    c. "Honda plans to launch a less expensive 'value-priced' Accord."
    d. "Procter & Gamble cuts prices of Dash detergent 30 to 40 percent."

15. Suppose the demand for insulin consists of two types of consumers, those who must have a dose each day and those who are able to go without the drug for several weeks. Suppose the price elasticity of demand for the first group is 0.01 and that for the second group is 4.0. Explain how the firms producing insulin might price the insulin.

Equal-Pricing Bill Passed

The City Council yesterday took action that would make it easier for women to get equal billing—literally—with men for identical services such as haircuts, dry cleaning and shoe repairs.

By a 48–0 vote, the council passed legislation empowering the city's Consumer Affairs Department to issue summonses and collect fines from businesses that post gender-based prices for identical goods and services. The measure now goes to Mayor Rudolph Giuliani for consideration.

If the measure becomes law, violators would be subject to civil penalties ranging from $50 to $250 for a first offense; $100 to $500 for subsequent violations.

"We want to persuade all businesses to charge everyone the same price for the same service," said Council Speaker Peter Vallone. "It's the fair thing to do."

Councilwoman Karen Koslowitz (D-Forest Hills), head of the council's Consumer Affairs Committee, said the bill would make enforcement of existing anti-price-discrimination codes easier. Under current law, a woman who believes she has been the victim of price discrimination must file a complaint with the city Human Rights Commission, which then holds hearings.

"Under the new law, if Consumer Affairs inspectors go into a business and see different prices posted for men and women, they can issue a summons immediately, no ifs, ands or buts," said Bernice Spitzer, the committee's spokeswoman.

Some business associations have objected to the legislation. For example, Peter Atha of the Neighborhood Cleaners Association-International, testified that women were sometimes charged more than men because their blouses and shirts are too small to fit on pressing machines and have to be hand-pressed.

A study released by the council last year showed that women paid 13.5 percent more than men to launder shirts, 10.7 percent more for identical garment alterations done by a dry cleaner and that nearly half of the haircutters surveyed charged women more than men for a basic haircut.

Source: Reprinted with permission. Newsday, Inc. 1997.

***Newsday* (New York)/December 18, 1997**

Commentary

It doesn't cost a laundry any more to launder a woman's shirt than a man's or a woman's pants than a man's. Yet, it is very common for laundries to charge more for the woman's clothes than the man's. It doesn't cost haircutters any more to cut a woman's hair than a man's. Yet, for the same haircut, a woman will be charged significantly more than a man. A new pair of heels on a woman's loafers is no more costly to install than a new pair of heels on a man's loafers. Yet, the repair on a woman's shoes is typically more expensive than on a man's. Why? According to many people, it is blatant discrimination. Businesses charge women more simply because they are women.

The question raised by this view is why another business doesn't advertise that women will be charged exactly the same as men and thereby attract female business. If a laundry located on the corner charges women more than men for the same clothing items, a laundry located across the street charging women and men the same would attract women customers. How then could the discriminating laundry stay in business?

Perhaps the answer isn't that blatant discrimination is occurring. Perhaps something else is going on. We have to look at either the costs of carrying out the activity or the demand. Most people argue that the costs are typically no different. In the article, Peter Atha of the Cleaners Association indicated that it is more costly to launder women's clothes. But this argument seems pretty weak. Women provide more business to cleaners, so why wouldn't the equipment be gauged according to women's clothes so that laundering men's would be the more costly? We can probably rule out cost differences as accounting for the differences in prices charged men and women.

What about demand? Is the demand different? Women are a greater part of the demand for laundry services, shoe repair services, and haircutting services than men are. It seems that the price elasticity of demand for these services is lower for women than men. If so, the price differentials would make perfect economic sense. If the price elasticity of demand for these services is lower for women than it is for men, the businesses would increase their revenue by lowering the price to men and raising it to women. This would account for the price discrimination. The question would be why the price elasticity of demand is lower for women than for men.

Price elasticity depends on the number of substitutes and the importance of the product in an individual's budget. Are there fewer substitutes for these services for women than men? Is the cost of these services a greater portion of the budget of women than of men? If these questions can be answered yes, then demand differences can be said to account for the pricing differences. If not, then we are back to square one.

Consumer Choice

? **Fundamental Questions**

1. How do consumers allocate their limited incomes among the billions of goods and services that exist?

2. Why does the demand curve slope down?

3. What is consumer surplus?

Preview

Several students who had just completed their final exam in economics were joking that any lab animal could be trained to get an A in economics. It would only have to answer "demand and supply" to every question. The students' sarcasm demonstrated both their grasp and lack of understanding of economics. There is no doubt that demand and supply are at the heart of economics, but unless you know why demand and supply behave as they do, can you be confident about what they imply? Can firms be sure they will sell more if they lower the price of their product? Should producers confidently assume that when income grows, demand will increase?

In this chapter we take a close look at demand. We examine how and why consumers make choices and what factors influence their choices. In the next chapter, "Supply: The Costs of Doing Business," we turn to the supply side and

To illustrate the relation between marginal and total utility, we have plotted the data from Table 1 in Figure 1(a). The total utility curve rises as quantity rises until the fifth hour of listening. After 5 hours, the total utility curve declines. The reason total utility rises at first is that each additional hour provides a little more utility. The marginal utility of the first hour is 200; the marginal utility of the second hour is 98; of the third, 50; of the fourth, 10; and of the fifth, zero. By the fifth hour, total utility is $200 + 98 + 50 + 10 + 0 = 358$.

We have plotted marginal utility in Figure 1(b), directly below the total utility curve of Figure 1(a). Marginal utility declines with each successive unit, reaches zero, and then turns negative. As long as marginal utility is positive, total utility rises. When marginal utility becomes negative, total utility declines. Marginal utility is zero at the point where total utility is at its maximum (unit 5 in this case).

1.c. Diminishing Marginal Utility and Time

The concept of diminishing marginal utility makes sense only if we define the *period of time* during which consumption is occurring. If Gabrielle listened to the music over a period of several days, we would not observe diminishing marginal utility until she had listened more than 5 hours. Usually, the shorter the time period, the more quickly marginal utility diminishes. Once the time period has been defined, diminishing marginal utility will apply; it applies to everyone and to every good and service, except perhaps to income itself, as discussed in the Economic Insight "Does Money Buy Happiness?"

1.d. Consumers Are Not Identical

All consumers experience diminishing marginal utility, but the rate at which marginal utility declines is not identical for all consumers. The rate at which marginal utility diminishes depends on an individual's tastes and preferences. Gabrielle clearly enjoys country and western music. For a person who dislikes it, the first hour might yield disutility or negative utility.

1.e. An Illustration: "All You Can Eat"

The principle of diminishing marginal utility says something about "all you can eat" specials. It says that you will stop eating when marginal utility is zero. At some restaurants consumers who pay a fixed charge may eat as much as they desire. The only restriction is that the restaurant does not allow "doggy bags." Because diminishing marginal utility eventually sets in, all consumers eventually stop eating when their marginal utility is zero. This is the point at which their total utility is at a maximum: one more bite would be distasteful and would decrease utility. The restaurant must determine what fixed price to charge. Knowing that no consumer will eat forever—that each will stop when his or her marginal utility is zero—the restaurant must set a price that yields a profit from the average consumer.

RECAP

1. Utility is a concept used to represent the degree to which goods and services satisfy wants.
2. Total utility is the total satisfaction that a consumer obtains from consuming a particular good or service.
3. Marginal utility is the utility that an additional unit of a good or service yields.

Figure 1

Total and Marginal Utility

Figure 1(a) shows the total utility obtained from listening to country and western music. Total utility reaches a maximum and then declines as additional listening becomes distasteful. For the first hour, the marginal and total utilities are the same. For the second hour, the marginal utility is the additional utility provided by the second unit. The total utility is the sum of the marginal utilities of the first and second units. The second unit provides less utility than the first unit, the third less than the second, and so on, in accordance with the law of diminishing marginal utility. But total utility, the sum of marginal utilities, rises as long as marginal utility is positive. Figure 1(b) shows marginal utility. When marginal utility is zero, total utility is at its maximum. When marginal utility is negative, total utility declines.

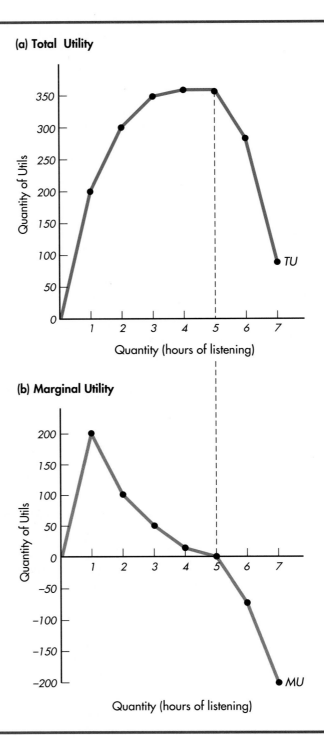

(a) Total Utility

(b) Marginal Utility

Does Money Buy Happiness?

Diminishing marginal utility affects consumer purchases of every good. Does diminishing marginal utility affect income as well? This question has been a topic of economic debate for years. The case for progressive taxation—the more income you have, the greater the percentage of each additional dollar that you pay in taxes—is based on the idea that the marginal utility of income diminishes. In theory, if each additional dollar brings less utility to a person, the pain associated with giving up a portion of each additional dollar will decline. And as a result of taxing the rich at a higher rate than the poor, the total pain imposed on society from a tax will be less than it would be if the same tax rate were applied to every dollar.

Economists have attempted to confirm or disprove the idea of the diminishing marginal utility of income, but doing so has proved difficult. Experiments have even been carried out on the topic. In one experiment, laboratory rats were trained to work for pay. They had to hit a bar several times to get a piece of food or a drink of water. After a while, after obtaining a certain amount of food and water, the rats reduced their work efforts, choosing leisure instead of more food and water. Thus, the rats did react as if their "income"—food and water—had a diminishing marginal utility.

Economists have also turned to the literature of psychology. Psychologists have carried out many surveys to measure whether people are more or less happy under various circumstances. One

Source: Adapted from David G. Myers, *The Pursuit of Happiness* (New York: William Morrow, 1992).

survey back in the 1960s asked people in different income brackets whether they were unhappy, pretty happy, or very happy. The results indicated that the higher income is, the happier people are. More recent studies by David Myers and John Stossel of ABC News examine why people are happy and find some results that contradict the earlier study. Although citizens of the more wealthy nations tend to be happier than citizens of the less wealthy nations, this relationship is not very strong. More important than wealth is the history of democracy; the longer a nation has been democratic, the happier are its citizens. Within any one country, there is only a modest link between well-being and being well-off. "Once we're comfortable, more money therefore provides

diminishing returns. The second helping never tastes as good as the first," says Myers. "The second fifty thousand dollars of income means much less than the first." Myers uses a figure something like the accompanying one to illustrate his findings. Notice how income and percentage who are happy both rise until a 1990 income level of about $7,000 per person after tax is reached. After that income level, as income rises, the percentage who are happy does not change much.

Sources: John Stossel, "The Mystery of Happiness: Who Has It and How to Get It," ABC News, April 15, 1996, and replayed since; David G. Myers, *The Pursuit of Happiness* (New York: William Morrow, 1992); and N. M. Bradburn and D. Caplovitz, *Reports on Happiness* (Chicago: Aldine, 1965), p. 9.

4. Total utility increases until dissatisfaction sets in. When another unit of a good would yield disutility, the consumer has been filled up with the good—more will not bring greater satisfaction.

5. According to the principle of diminishing marginal utility, marginal utility declines with each additional unit of a good or service that the consumer obtains. When marginal utility is zero, total utility is at its maximum.

2. UTILITY AND CHOICE

1. How do consumers allocate their limited incomes among the billions of goods and services that exist?

Can we simply conclude that people will consume goods until the marginal utility of each good is zero? No, we cannot, for we would be ignoring scarcity and opportunity costs. No one has enough income to purchase everything until the marginal utility of each item is zero. Because incomes are limited, purchasing one thing means not purchasing other things. Gabrielle, our country and western music fancier, might be able to get more utility by purchasing some other good than by buying more music to listen to.

2.a. Consumer Choice

To illustrate the effect of opportunity costs on consumption, let's turn again to Gabrielle. Gabrielle has a budget of $10 to spend on CDs, gasoline, and movies. She has found a place selling used CDs. She also goes to a discount gas station and a discount movie theater. We want to know how many units of each she will purchase. The answer is in Table 2.

The price (*P*) of each secondhand CD is $2; the price of each gallon of gas is $1; the price of each movie is $3. The marginal utility (*MU*) provided by each unit and the ratio of the marginal utility to the price (*MU/P*) are presented at the top of the table. In the lower part of the table are the steps involved in allocating income among the three goods.

The first purchase involves a choice among the first unit of each of the three goods. The first CD yields a marginal utility (*MU*) of 200 and costs $2; thus, per dollar of expenditure, the first CD yields 100 utils (*MU/P* = 100). The first gallon of gas yields a marginal utility per dollar of expenditure of 200. The first movie yields a marginal utility per dollar of expenditure of 50; it yields 150 utils and costs $3. Which does Gabrielle choose?

To find the answer, compare the ratios of the marginal utility per dollar of expenditure (*MU/P*), *not* the marginal utility of each good (*MU*). The ratio of marginal utility to price puts the goods on the same basis (utility per dollar) and allows us to make sense of Gabrielle's decisions. Looking only at marginal utilities would not do this. For instance, another diamond might yield 10,000 utils and another apple might yield only 100 utils; but if the diamond costs $100,000 and the apple costs $1, the marginal utility per dollar of expenditure on the apple is greater than the marginal utility per dollar of expenditure on the diamond, and thus a consumer is better off purchasing the apple.

As indicated in Table 2, Gabrielle's first purchase is the gallon of gas. It yields the greatest marginal utility per dollar of expenditure (she needs gas in her car to be able to go anywhere); and because it costs $1, Gabrielle has $9 left to spend.

Table 2

The Logic of Consumer Choice

CD (P = $2)			Gas (P = $1)			Movie (P = $3)		
Units	MU	MU/P	Units	MU	MU/P	Units	MU	MU/P
1	200	100	1	200	200	1	150	50
2	98	49	2	150	150	2	90	30
3	50	25	3	50	50	3	60	20
4	10	5	4	30	30	4	30	10
5	0	0	5	0	0	5	9	3
6	−70	−35	6	−300	−300	6	0	0
7	−200	−100	7	−700	−700	7	−6	−2

Steps	Choices		Decision	Remaining Budget
1st purchase	1st CD:	MU/P = 100	Gas	$10 − $1 = $9
	1st gas:	MU/P = 200		
	1st movie:	MU/P = 50		
2nd purchase	1st CD:	MU/P = 100	Gas	$9 − $1 = $8
	2nd gas:	MU/P = 150		
	1st movie:	MU/P = 50		
3rd purchase	1st CD:	MU/P = 100	CD	$8 − $2 = $6
	3rd gas:	MU/P = 50		
	1st movie:	MU/P = 50		
4th purchase	2nd CD:	MU/P = 49	Gas	$6 − $1 = $5
	3rd gas:	MU/P = 50		
	1st movie:	MU/P = 50		
5th purchase	2nd CD:	MU/P = 49	Movie	$5 − $3 = $2
	4th gas:	MU/P = 30		
	1st movie:	MU/P = 50		
6th purchase	2nd CD:	MU/P = 49	CD	$2 − $2 = 0
	4th gas:	MU/P = 30		
	2nd movie:	MU/P = 30		

Note: Purchases made with $10: 2 CDs, 3 gallons of gas, and 1 movie ticket.

The second purchase involves a choice among the first CD, the second gallon of gas, and the first movie. The ratios of marginal utility per dollar of expenditure are 100 for the CD, 150 for the gas, and 50 for a movie. Thus, Gabrielle purchases the second gallon of gas and has $8 left.

For the third purchase Gabrielle must decide between the first CD, the first movie, and the third gallon of gas. Because the CD yields a ratio of 100 and both the gas and the movie yield ratios of 50, she purchases the CD. The CD costs $2, so she has $6 left to spend.

A utility-maximizing consumer like Gabrielle always chooses the purchase that yields the greatest marginal utility per dollar of expenditure. If two goods offer the same marginal utility per dollar of expenditure, the consumer will be indifferent between the two—that is, the consumer won't care which is chosen. For example, Table 2 indicates that for the fourth purchase another gallon of gas or a movie would yield 50 utils per dollar. The consumer is completely indifferent between the two and so arbitrarily selects gas. The movie is chosen for the fifth purchase. With the sixth purchase, the total budget is spent. For $10, Gabrielle ends up with 2 CDs, 3 gallons of gas, and 1 movie.

In this example, Gabrielle is portrayed as a methodical, robotlike consumer who calculates how to allocate her scarce income among goods and services in a way that ensures that each additional dollar of expenditure yields the greatest marginal utility. This picture is more than a little far-fetched, but it does describe the result if not the process of consumer choice. People do have to decide which goods and services to purchase with their limited incomes, and people do select the options that give them the greatest utility.

2.b. Consumer Equilibrium

With $10, Gabrielle purchases 2 CDs, 3 gallons of gas, and 1 movie ticket. For the second CD, the marginal utility per dollar of expenditure is 49; for the third gallon of gas, it is 50; and for the first movie, it is 50. Is it merely a fluke that the marginal utility per dollar of expenditure ratios are nearly equal? No. *In order to maximize utility, consumers must allocate their limited incomes among goods and services in such a way that the marginal utilities per dollar of expenditure on the last unit of each good purchased will be as nearly equal as possible.* This is called the **equimarginal principle** and also represents **consumer equilibrium**. It is consumer equilibrium because the consumer will not change from this point unless something changes income, marginal utility, or price.

In our example, the ratios are not identical at consumer equilibrium—49, 50, 50—but they are as close to equal as possible because Gabrielle (like all consumers) had to purchase whole portions of the goods. Consumers cannot spend a dollar on any good or service and always get the fractional amount a dollar buys—one-tenth of a tennis lesson or one-third of a bottle of water. Instead, consumers have to purchase goods and services in whole units—1 piece or 1 ounce or 1 package—and pay the per unit price.

The equimarginal principle is simply common sense. Consumers spend an additional dollar on the good that gives the greatest satisfaction. At the prices given in Table 2, with an income of $10, and with the marginal utilities given, Gabrielle maximizes her utility by purchasing 2 CDs, 3 gallons of gas, and 1 movie ticket. Everything else held constant, no other allocation of the $10 would yield Gabrielle more utility.

Consumers are in equilibrium when they have no incentive to reallocate their limited budget or income. With *MU* standing for marginal utility and *P* for price, the general rule for consumer equilibrium is

$$\frac{MU_{CD}}{P_{CD}} = \frac{MU_{gas}}{P_{gas}} = \frac{MU_{movie}}{P_{movie}} = \ldots = \frac{MU_x}{P_x}$$

MU_x/P_x is the marginal utility per dollar of expenditure on any good other than CDs, gas, or movies. It represents the opportunity cost of spending $1 on CDs, gas, or movies.

equimarginal principle or **consumer equilibrium:** to maximize utility, consumers must allocate their scarce incomes among goods so as to equate the marginal utilities per dollar of expenditure on the last unit of each good purchased

1. To maximize utility, consumers must allocate their limited incomes in such a way that the marginal utilities per dollar obtained from the last unit consumed are equal among all goods and services; this is the equimarginal principle.

2. As long as the marginal utilities per dollar obtained from the last unit of all products consumed are the same, the consumer is in equilibrium and will not reallocate income.

3. Consumer equilibrium, or utility maximization, is summarized by a formula that equates the marginal utilities per dollar of expenditure on the last item purchased of all goods:

$$MU_a/P_a = MU_b/P_b = MU_c/P_c = MU_x/P_x$$

3. THE DEMAND CURVE AGAIN

We have shown how consumers make choices—by allocating their scarce incomes among goods in order to maximize their utility. The next step is to relate consumer choices to the demand curve.

3.a. The Downward Slope of the Demand Curve

The demand curve or schedule can be derived from consumer equilibrium by altering the price of one good or service.

2. Why does the demand curve slope down?

Recall from Chapter 3 that as the price of a good falls, the quantity demanded of that good rises. This inverse relation between price and quantity demanded arises from diminishing marginal utility and consumer equilibrium.

Consumers allocate their income among goods and services in order to maximize their utility. A consumer is in equilibrium when the total budget is expended and the marginal utilities per dollar of expenditure on the last unit of each good are the same. A change in the price of one good will disturb the consumer's equilibrium; the ratios of marginal utility per dollar of expenditure on the last unit of each good will no longer be equal. The consumer will then reallocate her income among the goods in order to increase total utility.

In the example presented in Table 2, the price of a CD is $2, the price per gallon of gas is $1, and the price of a movie ticket is $3. Now suppose the price of the CD falls to $1 while the prices of gas and movies and Gabrielle's budget of $10 remain the same. Common sense tells us that Gabrielle will probably alter the quantities purchased by buying more CDs. To find out if she does—and whether the equimarginal principle holds—her purchases can be traced step by step as we did previously.

In Table 3, only the *MU/P* ratio for CDs is different from the corresponding figure at the top of Table 2. At the old consumer equilibrium of 2 CDs, 3 gallons of gas, and 1 movie, the marginal utility per dollar of expenditure (*MU/P*) on each good is

CD: 98/$1 = 98/$1   Gas: 50/$1 = 50/$1   Movie: 150/$3 = 50/$1

Clearly, the ratios are no longer equal. In order to maximize utility, Gabrielle must reallocate her budget among the goods. When all $10 is spent, Gabrielle finds that she has purchased 3 CDs, 4 gallons of gas, and 1 movie ticket. The lower price of CDs has induced her to purchase an additional CD. Gabrielle's behavior illustrates what you already know: the quantity demanded of CDs increases as the price of the CD decreases.

Table 3

A Price Change

CD (P = $1)			Gas (P = $1)			Movie (P = $3)		
Units	MU	MU/P	Units	MU	MU/P	Units	MU	MU/P
1	200	**200**	1	200	200	1	150	50
2	98	**98**	2	150	150	2	90	30
3	50	**50**	3	50	50	3	60	20
4	10	**10**	4	30	30	4	30	10
5	0	**0**	5	0	0	5	9	3
6	−70	**−70**	6	−300	−300	6	0	0
7	−200	**−200**	7	−700	−700	7	−6	−2

If the price of the CD is increased to $3, we find that Gabrielle demands only 1 CD. The three prices and the corresponding quantities of CDs purchased give us Gabrielle's demand for CDs, which is shown in Figure 2. At $3 she is willing and able to buy 1 CD; at $2 she is willing and able to buy 2 CDs; and at $1 she is willing and able to buy 3 CDs.

3. What is consumer surplus?

3.b. Consumer Surplus

An individual's demand curve measures the value that the individual consumer places on each unit of the good being considered. For example, the value that Gabrielle places on the first CD is the price she would be willing and able to pay for it. The price Gabrielle would be willing to pay for one CD is $3, as shown in Figure 2. At a price of $2, Gabrielle purchases two CDs. She is willing to pay $3 for the first and $2 for the second, but she gets both for $2 each. She gets a bonus because the value she places on the CD is higher than the price she has to pay for it. This bonus is called *consumer surplus.*

consumer surplus: the difference between what the consumer is willing to pay for a unit of a good and the price that the consumer actually has to pay

Consumer surplus is a measure of the difference between what a consumer is willing and able to pay and the market price of a good. At a market price of $2, Gabrielle's consumer surplus is equal to ($3 − $2) + ($2 − $2) = $1. At a price of $1, Gabrielle is willing and able to purchase 3 CDs, but only the third CD is worth only $1 to her. The first two are worth more than the $1 she has to pay for them. When she purchases the CDs, she gets a bonus of ($3 − $1) + ($2 − $1) + ($1 − $1) = $3.

3.c. Shifts of Demand and the Determination of Market Demand

Individual demand comes from utility maximization. Individuals allocate their scarce incomes among goods in order to get the greatest utility; this occurs when consumer equilibrium is reached, represented in symbols as $MU_a/P_a = MU_b/P_b = \cdots = MU_x/P_x$. As the price of a good or service is changed, consumer equilibrium

Figure 2

Consumer Surplus and the Demand for CDs

Gabrielle is willing and able to pay $3 for the first CD. She is willing to pay $2 for the second CD. If the market price of CDs is $2, she can buy both the first and the second CDs for $2 each; and she receives a bonus on the first, paying less for it than she is willing and able to pay. This bonus, the consumer surplus, is indicated by the blue area. At a price of $1, the consumer surplus is both the blue and yellow areas.

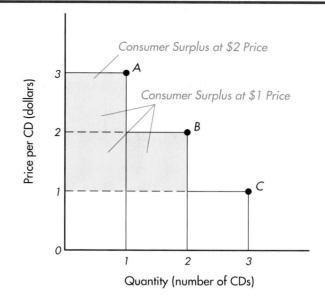

is disturbed. In response to the price change, individuals alter their purchases so as to achieve maximum utility.

When the price of one good falls while everything else is held constant, two things occur: (1) other goods become relatively *more* expensive so consumers buy more of the less expensive good and less of the more expensive goods, and (2) the good purchased prior to the price change now costs less so the consumer can buy more of all goods.

When a good becomes relatively less expensive, it yields more satisfaction per dollar than before, so consumers buy more of it than before as they decrease their expenditures on other goods. This is the *substitution effect* of a price change.

The substitution effect indicates that following a decrease in the price of a good or service, an individual will purchase more of the now less expensive good and less of other goods.

Figure 3 shows that at the price of $2 per CD, Gabrielle spends $4 on CDs. When the price falls to $1, she spends only $2 for those two CDs. As a result, Gabrielle can purchase more of all goods, including the good whose price has fallen. This is the *income effect* of a price change.

The income effect of a price change indicates that an individual's income can buy more of all goods when the price of one good declines, everything else held constant.

The process of changing the price of one good or service while income, tastes and preferences, and the prices of related goods are held constant, defines the individual's demand for that good or service. Should income, tastes and preferences, or prices of related goods and services change, then the individual's demand will change. More or less income means more or less goods and services can be purchased. A change in income affects the ratios of *MU/P* and disturbs consumer equilibrium. When the price of a related good changes, the ratio of marginal utility to price for that good changes, thus disturbing consumer equilibrium. And changes in tastes and preferences, represented as changes in the *MU*s, also alter consumer equilibrium. For each change in a determinant of demand, a new demand curve for a good or service is derived; the demand curve will have shifted.

Figure 3

Gabrielle's Demand Curve for CDs

The demand curve shows that Gabrielle purchases 1 CD at a price of $3, 2 CDs at a price of $2, and 3 CDs at a price of $1.

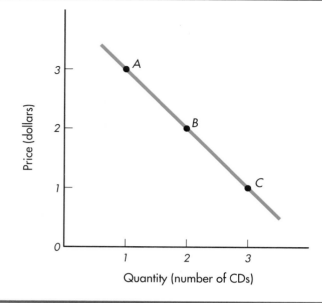

Consumer equilibrium shows that the nonprice determinants of demand have their effects through the MUs or the prices of other goods and services.

The market demand curve is the sum of all the individual demand curves. This means that anything that affects the individual curves also affects the market curve. In addition, when we combine the individual demand curves into a market demand curve, the number of individuals to be combined determines the position of the market demand curve. Changes in the number of consumers alters the market demand curve. We thus say that the determinants of demand are tastes and preferences, income, prices of related goods, international effects, and number of consumers.

Halloween has changed from what was once a child's holiday to the second most popular holiday in the United States. Spending on Halloween supplies exceeds spending for every holiday except Christmas. The increased tastes for Halloween fun have led to an increased demand for costumes. In terms of economic theory, marginal utility for each dollar of spending on Halloween costumes has risen.

Also, recall that diminishing marginal utility is defined for consumption during a specific period of time. Since consumer equilibrium and thus the demand curve depend on diminishing marginal utility, the demand curve is also defined for consumption over a specific period of time. Changes in the time period or changes in expectations will therefore also alter demand.

<table>
<tr><td>RECAP</td><td>
1. The principle of diminishing marginal utility and the equimarginal principle account for the inverse relation between the price of a product and the quantity demanded.

2. Consumer surplus is the excess of the amount consumers are willing and able to pay for an item over the price they actually pay.

3. A price change triggers the substitution effect and the income effect.

4. The substitution effect occurs because once a good becomes less expensive, it yields more satisfaction per dollar than before and consumers buy more of it than before. They do this by decreasing their purchases of other goods. The income effect of the price change occurs because a lower price raises real income (total utility) and the consumer purchases more of all goods.

5. The market demand curve is the summation of all individual demand curves.

6. Economists derive the market demand curve for a good by assuming that individual incomes are fixed, that the prices of all goods except the one in question are constant, that each individual's tastes remain fixed, that expectations do not change, that the number of consumers is constant, and that the time period under consideration remains unchanged. A change in any one of these determinants causes the demand curve to shift.
</td></tr>
</table>

SUMMARY

❓ How do consumers allocate their limited incomes among the billions of goods and services that exist?

1. Consumer equilibrium refers to the utility-maximizing situation in which the consumer has allocated his or her budget among goods and services in such a way that the marginal utilities per dollar of expenditure on the last unit of any good are the same for all goods. It is represented in symbols as

$$MU_a/P_a = MU_b/P_b \cdots = MU_x/P_x \qquad §2.b$$

2. Utility is a measure of the satisfaction received from possessing or consuming a good. *§1.a*

3. *Diminishing marginal utility* refers to the decline in utility received from each additional unit of a good that is consumed during a particular period of time.

The more of some good a consumer has, the less desirable is another unit of that good. *§1.b*

4. Even if a good is free a consumer will eventually reach a point where one more unit of the good would be undesirable or distasteful, and he or she will not consume that additional unit. *§1.e*

5. The demand curve slopes down because of diminishing marginal utility and consumer equilibrium. *§3.a*

6. The income and substitution effects of a price change occur because of diminishing marginal utility and the equimarginal principle. When the price of one good falls while all other prices remain the same, it yields more satisfaction per dollar than before, so consumers buy more of it than before. *§3.b*

7. Market demand is the summation of individual demands. *§4.a*

KEY TERMS

utility *§1.a*

diminishing marginal utility *§1.b*

marginal utility *§1.b*

disutility *§1.b*

total utility *§1.b*

equimarginal principle *§2.b*

consumer equilibrium *§2.b*

consumer surplus *§3.b*

EXERCISES

1. Using the following information, calculate total utility and marginal utility.

   a. Plot the total utility curve.
   b. Plot marginal utility directly below total utility.
   c. At what marginal utility value does total utility reach a maximum?

Number of utils for the 1st unit	300
Number of utils for the 2nd unit	250
Number of utils for the 3rd unit	220
Number of utils for the 4th unit	160
Number of utils for the 5th unit	100
Number of utils for the 6th unit	50
Number of utils for the 7th unit	20
Number of utils for the 8th unit	0
Number of utils for the 9th unit	-250

2. Is it possible for marginal utility to be negative and total utility positive? Explain.

3. Suppose Mary is in consumer equilibrium. The marginal utility of good A is 30 and the price of good A is $2.

   a. If the price of good B is $4, the price of good C is $3, the price of good D is $1, and the price of all other goods and services is $5, what is the marginal utility of each of the goods Mary is purchasing?
   b. If Mary has chosen to keep $10 in savings, what is the ratio of *MU* to *P* for savings?

4. Using the following utility schedule, derive a demand curve for pizza.

   a. Assume income is $10, the price of each slice of pizza is $1, and the price of each glass of beer is $2. Then change the price of pizza to $2 per slice.
   b. Now change income to $12 and derive a demand curve for pizza.

Slices of Pizza	Total Utility	Glasses of Beer	Total Utility
1	200	1	500
2	380	2	800
3	540	3	900
4	600	4	920
5	630	5	930

5. Using utility explain the following commonly made statements:

   a. I couldn't eat another bite.
   b. I'll never get tired of your cooking.
   c. The last drop tastes as good as the first.
   d. I wouldn't eat broccoli if you paid me.
   e. My kid would eat nothing but junk food if I allowed her.
   f. Any job worth doing is worth doing well.

6. How would guests' behavior likely differ at a BYOB (bring your own bottle) party and one at which the host provides the drinks? Explain your answer.

7. A round of golf on a municipal golf course usually takes about 5 hours. At a private country club golf course a round takes less than 4 hours. What accounts for the difference? Would the time spent playing golf be different if golfers paid only an admission fee (membership fee) and no monthly dues or if they paid only a charge per round and no monthly dues?

8. To increase marginal utility, you must decrease consumption (everything else held constant). This statement is correct even though it sounds strange. Explain why.

9. Suppose that the marginal utility of good A is 4 times the marginal utility of good B, but the price of good A is only 2 times larger than the price of good B. Is this point consumer equilibrium? If not, what will occur?

10. Last Saturday you went to a movie and ate a large box of popcorn and two candy bars and drank a medium soda. This Saturday you went to a movie and ate a medium box of popcorn and one candy bar and drank a large soda. Your tastes and preferences did not change. What could explain the different combinations of goods you purchased?

11. Peer pressure is an important influence on the behavior of youngsters. For instance, many preteens begin smoking because their friends pressure them into being "cool" by smoking. Using utility theory, how would you explain peer pressure?

12. Many people who earn incomes below some level receive food stamps from the government. Econo-mists argue that these people would be better off if the government gave them the cash equivalent of the food stamps rather than the food stamps. What is the basis of the economists' argument?

13. Suppose you are in consumer equilibrium and have chosen to work 10 hours a day, leaving the other 14 hours each day for leisure activities (leisure includes sleeping and anything other than working on the job).

   a. How might you change your behavior if your wage rate per hour rises?
   b. What are the income and substitution effects of the price change?
   c. What would occur if the income effect is larger than the substitution effect?

14. What is the impact on charitable giving of a reduction in the tax rate on income? Will the lower tax rate lead to more or to less charitable giving?

Sudden Wealth Syndrome

Too much too young: the curse of Sudden Wealth Syndrome may be the problem you wish you had, but the wired world's wealthy have real difficulties coming to terms with their new-found mega-fortunes. . . .

But once the initial euphoria of immense wealth wears off, they begin to notice that their open-top Porsches are stuck in traffic under the baking sun, that they can only sleep in one bed even if their house has 40, and that all the cash in the world cannot buy calm. . . .

Many find it hard to believe that a smattering of computer proficiency mixed with a dash of prescient timing can really be all it took to concoct such magnificent riches. This often leads to a troubling sense of "I-don't-deserve-it."

Gerald Spencer, who made around pounds 50m for being the programming hotshot behind the Excite search engine, says: "Do I deserve the money I have? I struggle with that a lot. On one level, I'd like to believe I have certain skills that have made me successful. But how can being a little more competent at computer science than most people make you so much richer?". . .

Psychologists such as Goldbart and DiFuria, who have become minor celebrities, have hundreds of such clients on their books. They first spotted the trend of woeful wealth several years ago when the internet economy was just taking off. "We kept seeing clients come in with issues of wealth, and they were getting younger and younger," DiFuria recalls. "I had very successful men who'd say they'd stop when they reached $3m, and then it was $15m, and then $50m."

Goldbart adds: "They bought the BMW and they have the $3m house. And they still wake up in the morning and say, 'I don't feel good about myself.' " This often translates into deep insecurity about how people relate to you. Christopher Mogil is a director of More Than Money, a group which "assists" people in handling new wealth. He says: "There are a lot of challenges that people face when they come into wealth they didn't expect. Your relationships with friends change. You ask yourself whether people are interested in you or your money.". . .

While the rich have always had problems, it is the speedy accumulation of wealth, and the youth of its owners, which sets the internet fortunes apart. Silicon Valley is full of millionaires still shy of 30, but often these people lack the necessary maturity to deal with their good fortune. . . .

Other experts agree that very few people are psychologically and emotionally prepared for the life-altering effects of large amounts of money, and that they need all the help money can buy. . . .

While the poor or merely comfortably-off may dismiss such problems, the phenomenon is so widespread that it has created a mini-industry of its own. Silicon Valley psychologists are almost as much in demand as lawyers, while several special organisations have sprung up to teach internet millionaires how to give to charity.

Even financial institutions are starting to realise the scale of the problem. Charles Schwab, the online broker, and Merrill Lynch, the American investment bank, arrange seminars for their high-tech millionaires on how to cope with their good fortune, focusing on everything from inheritance taxes to stock options. . . .

ANDY GOLDBERG

Daily Telegraph **(London)/June 8, 2000**

Commentary

"The underlying assumption is that if you have all the money in the world, you'll be happy and fulfilled. That's simply not true." Does this contradict economics? Isn't the basic assumption in economics that more is better than less, that more money is better than less money? The answer is no, more is not always better than less. More disease, more filth, more garbage, more pollution, more of many things are not better than less. With respect to goods, we do assume that more is better than less as long as there is no problem in storing or keeping the goods and services and as long as our tastes do not change. The chocolate cake example used in the text where our consumer ate so much that he or she got sick, illustrates nicely that more is preferred to less as long as there are no storage costs: it is simply impossible to "store" an infinite amount of cake, that is, to eat it. Eventually, more cake is not desired. This is the law of diminishing marginal utility in operation. It says that during a given period of time, as we get more of an additional good, the marginal amount of that good will provide us less additional happiness than a previous amount did.

In the Economic Insight "Does Money Buy Happiness?" it was shown that up to some income level, money and expressed happiness seem to rise together but then as money continues to rise, happiness does not. The article says the same thing. People want more money—more money enables people to purchase more of everything—and so more money equates to more happiness. This seems to occur up to a point. Once someone has a bunch of money, however, additional amounts do not mean very much.

What does more income do? It shifts the budget constraint out; it enables people to purchase more of everything. The consumer equilibrium formula

$$MU_a/P_a = MU_b/P_b = MU_c/P_c = \cdots MU_z/P_z$$

states that a consumer will purchase additional amounts of items until the consumer's budget is spent and the marginal utility of each dollar of expenditures is nearly equal across all purchases. With more income, more of everything can be purchased. The consumer still purchases by spending the budget on each good and service up to the point where the last dollar spent on each item yields the same additional utility. So the question is, do people also experience diminishing marginal utility with money? The answer has to be no as long as there are no costs to storage and tastes do not change.

An underlying theme in the article is that money can't buy happiness. Yet, it was stated several times that it is time and maturity that is creating the problems of becoming rich, not money. It was noted in the article that very few people are psychologically and emotionally prepared for the life-altering effects of large amounts of money. It does not tell us what happens to these people, whether the challenge of succeeding disappears or whether they change relationships and alter friendships or whether work loses its appeal. The article does note that *they need all the help money can buy.* Interesting phrase, the one noted in italics, that these rich people need all the help money can buy. What this says is that the money does enable the new rich to seek out more happiness. So, what can we conclude? Does money create unhappiness or does it enable people to purchase happiness?

Indifference Analysis

Indifference analysis is an alternative approach to utility theory for explaining consumer choice but does not require us to rely on the concept of utility.

1. INDIFFERENCE CURVES

In Figure 1, four combinations of CDs and gallons of gasoline are listed in the table and plotted in Figure 1(a). Preferring more to less, the consumer will clearly prefer C to the other combinations. Combination C is preferred to B because C offers one more CD and the same amount of gas as B. Combination C is preferred to A because C offers 1 more CD and 1 more gallon of gas than A. And combination C is preferred to D because one more CD is obtained with no loss of gas. Combinations B and D are preferred to A; however, it is not obvious whether B is preferred to D or D is preferred to B.

Let's assume that the consumer has no preference between B and D. We thus say that the consumer is **indifferent** between combination B (2 CDs and 1 gallon of gas) and combination D (1 CD and 2 gallons of gas). Connecting points B and D, as in Figure 1(b), produces an indifference curve. An **indifference curve** shows all the combinations of two goods that the consumer is indifferent among, or, in other words, an indifference curve shows all the combinations of goods that will give the consumer the same level of total utility.

The quantity of goods increases as the distance from the origin increases. Thus, any combination lying on the indifference curve (like B or D) is preferred to any combination falling below the curve, or closer to the origin (like A). Any combination appearing above the curve, or farther from the origin (like C), is preferred to any combination lying on the curve.

indifferent: lacking any preference

indifference curve: a curve showing all combinations of two goods that the consumer is indifferent among

1.a. The Shape of Indifference Curves

The most reasonable shape for an indifference curve is a downward slope from left to right, indicating that as less of one good is consumed, more of another good is consumed. Indifference curves are not likely to be vertical, horizontal, or upward sloping. They do not touch the axes, and they do not touch each other.

An indifference curve that is a vertical line, like the one labeled I_v in Figure 2(a), would mean that the consumer is indifferent to combinations B and A. For most goods this will not be the case because combination B provides more of one good with no less of the other good.

Figure 1

Indifference Curve

Four combinations of two goods, CDs and gasoline, are presented to the consumer in Figure 1(a). Preferring more to less, the consumer will clearly prefer *C* to *A, B,* and *D*. Points *B* and *D* are preferred to *A*, but the consumer has no clear preference between *B* and *D*. The consumer is indifferent between *B* and *D*. Figure 1(b) shows that all combinations of goods among which the consumer is indifferent lie along an indifference curve.

Combination	CDs	Gallons of Gasoline
A	1	1
B	2	1
C	2	2
D	1	2

(a) Combinations of CDs and Gasoline

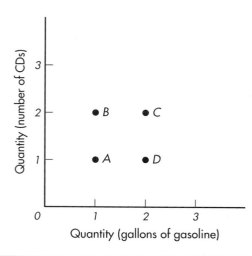

(b) Indifference Curve

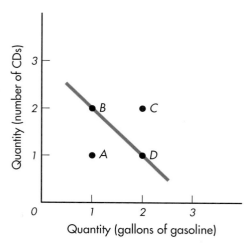

Similarly, horizontal indifference curves, such as line I_h in Figure 2(b), are ruled out for most goods. People are not likely to be indifferent between combinations *A* and *B* along the horizontal curve since *B* provides more of one good with no less of the other good than *A*.

An upward-sloping curve, such as I_u in Figure 2(c), would mean that the consumer is indifferent between a combination of goods that provides less of everything and a combination that provides more of everything (compare points *A* and *B*). Rational consumers tend to prefer more to less.

1.b. The Slope of Indifference Curves

The slope, or steepness, of indifference curves is determined by consumer preferences. The amount of one good that a consumer must give up to get an additional unit of the other good and remain equally satisfied changes as the consumer trades off one good for the other. The less a consumer has of a good, the more the consumer values an additional unit of that good. This preference is shown by an indifference curve that bows in toward the origin, like the curve shown in Figure 3. A consumer who has 4 CDs and 1 gallon of gasoline (point *D*) may be willing to give up 2 CDs for 1 more gallon of gasoline, moving from *D* to *E*. But a consumer who has only

Figure 2

Unlikely Shapes of Indifference Curves

A vertical indifference curve, as in Figure 2(a), would violate the condition that more is preferred to less, as would a horizontal indifference curve, as in Figure 2(b), or an upward-sloping curve, as in Figure 2(c). Thus, indifference curves are not likely to have any of these shapes.

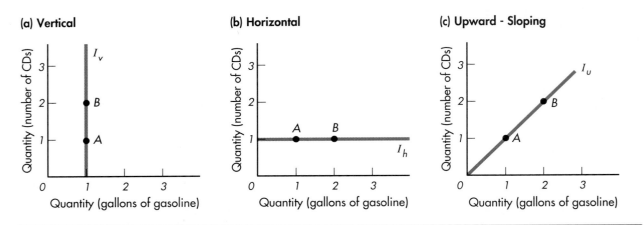

2 CDs may be willing to give up only 1 CD to get that additional gallon of gasoline. This preference is shown as the move from *E* to *F*.

1.c. Indifference Curves Cannot Cross

Indifference curves do not intersect. If the curves crossed, two combinations of goods that are clearly not equally preferred by the consumer would seem to be

Figure 3

Bowed-In Indifference Curve

Indifference curves slope down from left to right and bow in toward the origin. They bow in because consumers value a good relatively more if they have less of it, *ceteris paribus*. At the top of the curve, where a little gasoline and many CDs are represented by point *D*, the consumer is willing to give up 2 CDs to get 1 gallon of gasoline. But lower down on the curve, such as at point *E*, the consumer has more gasoline and fewer CDs than at point *D* and thus is willing to give up fewer CDs to get 1 more gallon of gasoline.

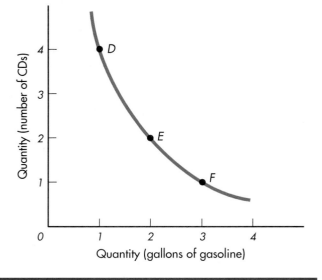

Figure 4

Indifference Curves Do Not Cross

If two indifference curves intersected, such as at point *B*, then the consumer would be indifferent to all points on each curve. But point *C* clearly provides more CDs than point *A* and no less gasoline, so the consumer will prefer *C* to *A*. If the consumer prefers more to less, the indifference curves will not cross.

Figure 5

Indifference Map

Indifference curves cover the entire positive quadrant. As we move away from the origin, more is preferred to less: I_5 is preferred to I_4, I_4 is preferred to I_3, and so on.

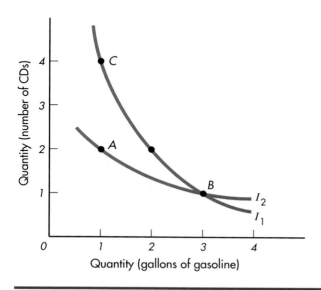

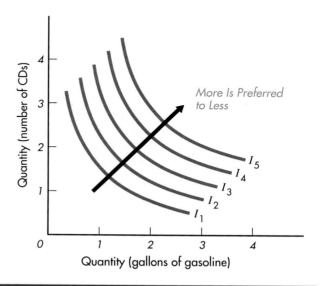

equally preferred. According to Figure 4, the consumer is indifferent between *A* and *B* along indifference curve I_2 and indifferent between *B* and *C* along indifference curve I_1. Thus, the consumer appears to be indifferent among *A*, *B*, and *C*. Combination *C*, however, offers more CDs and no less gasoline than combination *A*. Clearly, the consumer, preferring more to less, will prefer *C* to *A*. Thus, indifference curves are not allowed to cross.

1.d. An Indifference Map

indifference map: a complete set of indifference curves

An **indifference map,** located in the positive quadrant of a graph, indicates the consumer's preferences among all combinations of goods and services. The farther from the origin an indifference curve is, the more the combinations of goods along that curve are preferred. The arrow in Figure 5 indicates the ordering of preferences: I_2 is preferred to I_1; I_3 is preferred to I_2 and I_1; I_4 is preferred to I_3, I_2, and I_1; and so on.

2. BUDGET CONSTRAINT

The indifference map reveals only the combinations of goods and services that a consumer prefers or is indifferent among—what the consumer is *willing* to buy. It does not tell us what the consumer is *able* to buy. Consumers' income levels or

budget line: a line showing all the combinations of goods that can be purchased with a given level of income

budgets limit the amount that they can purchase. Let's suppose a consumer has allocated $6 to spend on gas and CDs. Figure 6 shows the **budget line,** a line giving all the combinations of goods that a budget can buy at given prices.

Anywhere along the budget line in Figure 6(a), the consumer is spending $6. When the price of CDs is $1 and the price of gas is $1 per gallon, the consumer can choose among several different combinations of CDs and gas that add up to $6. If only CDs are purchased, 6 CDs can be purchased (point *A*). If only gas is purchased, 6 gallons of gas can be purchased (point *G*). At point *B*, 5 CDs and 1 gallon of gas can be purchased. At point *C*, 4 CDs and 2 gallons of gas can be purchased. At point *F*, 1 CD and 5 gallons of gas can be purchased.

Figure 6

The Budget Line

In Figure 6(a), a budget line is drawn for a consumer with a $6 budget to be spent on CDs and gallons of gasoline costing $1 each. The consumer can purchase 6 CDs and no gas, 5 CDs and 1 gallon of gas, and so on. In Figure 6(b), the budget line shifts outward because the budget is increased from $6 to $7 and the consumer can purchase more. In Figure 6(c), the initial budget line (Y_1) runs from 6 to 6. When the price of CDs increases from $1 to $2, the budget line ($Y_2$) rotates down along the CD axis. Spending the entire $6 budget on CDs allows the consumer to buy only 3 CDs rather than the 6 that were obtained at the per unit price of $1.

(a) Initial Budget Line

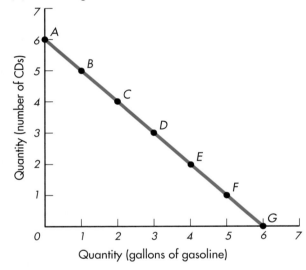

(b) Shift Due to Income Increase

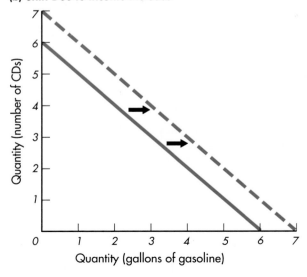

(c) Shift (Rotation) Due to Relative Price Change

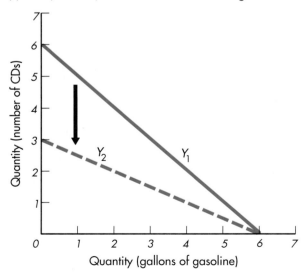

An increase in the consumer's income or budget is shown as an outward shift of the budget line. Figure 6(b) shows an increase in income from $6 to $7. The budget line shifts out to the line running from 7 to 7. A change in income or in the consumer's budget causes a parallel shift of the budget line.

A change in the price of one of the goods causes the budget line to rotate. For example, with a budget of $6 and the prices of both CDs and gas at $1, we have the budget line Y_1 of Figure 6(c). If the price of CDs rises to $2, only 3 CDs can be purchased if the entire budget is spent on CDs. As a result, the budget line (Y_2) is flatter, running from 3 on the vertical axis to 6 on the horizontal axis. Conversely, a rise in the price of gas would cause the budget line to become steeper.

3. CONSUMER EQUILIBRIUM

Putting the budget line on the indifference map allows us to determine the one combination of goods and services that the consumer is both *willing* and *able* to purchase. Any combination of goods that lies on or below the budget line is within the consumer's budget. Which combination will the consumer choose in order to yield the greatest satisfaction (utility)?

The budget line in Figure 7 indicates that most of the combinations along indifference curve I_1 and point C on indifference curve I_2 are attainable. Combinations along indifference curve I_3 are preferred to combinations along I_2, but the consumer is *not able* to buy combinations along I_3 because they cost more than the consumer's budget. Therefore, point C represents the maximum level of satisfaction, or utility, available to the consumer. Point C is the point where the budget line is tangent to (just touches) the indifference curve.

The demand curve for a good can be derived from indifference curves and budget lines by changing the price of one of the goods, leaving everything else the same, and finding the consumer equilibrium points. Budget line Y_1, running from 6 on the vertical axis to 6 on the horizontal axis in Figure 8(a), is the initial budget, in which

Figure 7

Consumer Equilibrium

The consumer maximizes satisfaction by purchasing the combination of goods that is on the indifference curve farthest from the origin but attainable given the consumer's budget. The combinations along I_1 are attainable, but so are the combinations that lie above I_1. Combinations beyond the budget line, such as those along I_3, cost more than the consumer's budget. Point C, where the indifference curve I_2 just touches, or is tangent to, the budget line, is the chosen combination and the point of consumer equilibrium.

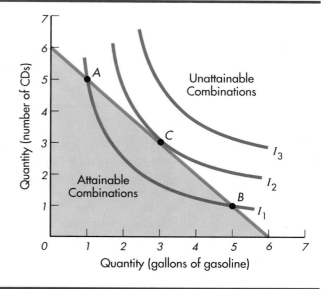

Figure 8

The Demand Curve

By changing the price of one of the goods and leaving everything else the same, we can derive the demand curve. Figure 8(a) shows that as the price of a gallon of gasoline increases from $1 to $2, the budget line rotates in toward the CD axis. Consumer equilibrium occurs at point E instead of at point C. The consumer is purchasing only 2 gallons of gasoline at the $2 per gallon price, whereas the consumer purchased 3 gallons of gasoline at the $1 per gallon price. Plotting the price of gasoline and the number of gallons of gasoline directly below, in Figure 8(b), yields the demand curve for gasoline.

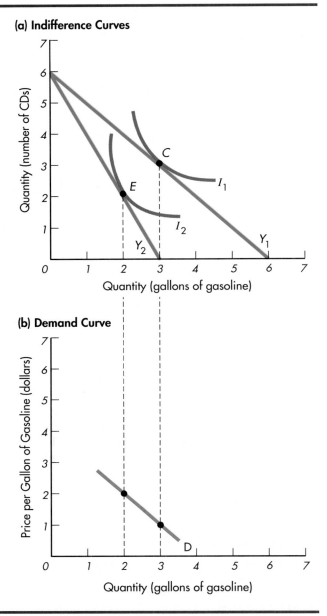

(a) Indifference Curves

(b) Demand Curve

the price of each CD is $1 and the price of each gallon of gas is $1. We then increase the price of each CD to $2 and draw the second budget line, Y_2, running from 6 CDs to 3 gallons of gas. For each budget (income) line, we draw the indifference curve that is tangent. For Y_1 it is curve I_1; for Y_2 it is curve I_2. The original consumer equilibrium is point C, the tangency between the initial budget line and curve I_1. The point at which the new budget line is just tangent to an indifference curve is the new consumer equilibrium point. This is point E.

At point C, 3 gallons of gas are purchased; at point E, 2 gallons of gas are purchased. By plotting the combinations of price and quantity demanded below the indifference curves, as in Figure 8(b), we trace out the demand curve for gasoline.

SUMMARY

1. Indifference curves show all combinations of two goods that give the consumer the same level of total utility. *§1*

2. An indifference map is a complete set of indifference curves filling up the positive quadrant of a graph. *§1.d*

3. The indifference curve indicates what the consumer is willing to buy. The budget line indicates what the consumer is able to buy. Together they determine the combination of goods the consumer is willing and able to buy. *§1, 2*

4. Consumer equilibrium occurs at the point where the budget line just touches, or is tangent to, an indifference curve. *§3*

5. The demand curve can be derived from the indifference curves and budget lines. A change in the relative price causes the budget line to rotate and become tangent to an indifference curve at a different quantity of goods. As the price of one good rises relative to the price of another, the quantity demanded of the higher-priced good falls. *§3*

KEY TERMS

indifferent *§1*

indifference curve *§1*

indifference map *§1.d*

budget line *§2*

EXERCISES

1. Use these combinations for exercises a and b:

Combination	Clothes	Food
A	1 basket	1 pound
B	1 basket	2 pounds
C	1 basket	3 pounds
D	2 baskets	1 pound
E	2 baskets	2 pounds
F	2 baskets	3 pounds
G	3 baskets	1 pound
H	3 baskets	2 pounds
I	3 baskets	3 pounds

   a. If more is preferred to less, which combinations are clearly preferred to other combinations? Rank the combinations in the order of preference.

   b. Some clothes-food combinations cannot be clearly ranked. Why not?

2. Explain why two indifference curves cannot cross.

3. Using the data that follow, plot two demand curves for cake. Then explain what could have led to the shift of the demand curve.

I. Price of Cake	Quantity of Cake Demanded	II. Price of Cake	Quantity of Cake Demanded
$1	10	$1	14
$2	8	$2	10
$3	4	$3	8
$4	3	$4	6
$5	1	$5	5

Chapter 8

Supply: The Costs of Doing Business

? Fundamental Questions

1. **What is the law of diminishing marginal returns?**

2. **What is the relationship between costs and output in the short run?**

3. **What is the relationship between costs and output in the long run?**

Preview

In 1955, Akio Morita, the founder of Sony Corporation, began selling a small transistor radio in the United States. "I saw the United States as a natural market," he said. Morita showed the radio to Bulova, a large watch and appliance firm. Bulova offered to purchase a huge amount of radios but with one condition: Sony would have to put Bulova's name on the radio; Sony would be a so-called OEM (original equipment manufacturer) supplier. Morita refused, stating that in a few years the name Sony would be as well known as Bulova.

Morita soon received another large purchase offer, nearly 100,000 radios, from a chain store. He knew Sony did not have the capacity to produce that many radios. "Our capacity was less than a thousand radios a month." An order of 100,000 would mean hiring and training new employees and expanding facilities even more. Morita sat down and drew a curve that looked something like the lopsided letter U shown

170

Part Two / Product Market Basics

Figure 1

Morita's Cost Curve for Transistor Radios

Visualizing Sony's production capabilities, Akio Morita saw that per unit costs would fall initially and then rise quite rapidly.

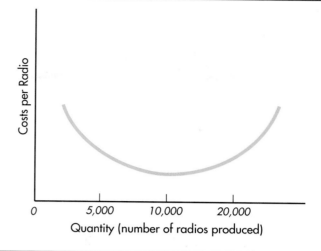

in Figure 1. The cost for 5,000 would be the beginning of the curve. For 10,000 the costs would fall (and Sony could offer a lower price), and that was at the bottom of the U. For 30,000 the cost would begin to climb. For 50,000 the cost per unit would be higher than for 5,000, and for 100,000 units, the cost would be much more per unit than the first 5,000.

Morita explained to the chain store buyer, "If we had to double our production—more labor, more materials, etc.—to complete an order for 100,000 radios and if we could not get a repeat order the following year, we would be in big trouble." The buyer, initially stunned, was eventually persuaded and ended up buying 10,000 radios. That decision was crucial for Sony. Had Morita succumbed to the lure of the larger order and expanded production and costs, it could have led to early failure. Today, however, Sony is one of the world's largest corporations with sales exceeding $30 billion a year.[1]

1. FIRMS AND PRODUCTION

The terms *company, enterprise,* and *business* are used interchangeably with *firm*. Recall from Chapter 4 that firms can be organized as sole proprietorships, partnerships, or corporations and can be national or multinational companies. In our discussion of the costs of doing business, we use *firm* to refer to all types of business organizations. Thus, we speak of a firm as an institution in which resources—land, labor, and capital—are combined to produce a product or service. The terms *produce* and *production* are also used broadly; they refer not only to manufacturing but also to the retailer who buys goods from a wholesaler and offers the goods to the customers.

---

[1]Story paraphrased from Slomo Maital, *Executive Economics* (New York: Free Press, 1994), pp. 66–75; "The World's Best Brand," *Fortune,* May 31, 1993, p. 31; and "Sony Corp.: Globalization," *Harvard Business School Case Study 391–071,* 1990.

Figure 2

The Circular Flow

The flow of goods and services and money between the household and business sectors is pictured. Businesses sell goods and services to households. The money received is total revenue. The difference between total revenue and the payment for land, labor, and capital is profit. The resources—land, labor, and capital—flow from the household to the business sector. The payment for these resources flows from the business sector to the household sector.

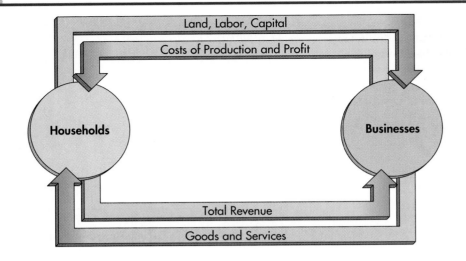

1.a. The Relationship Between Output and Resources

The simplest circular flow diagram from Chapter 4 is reproduced here as Figure 2. It shows that money flows from the household sector to the business sector in payment for goods and services. The flow of money from the household sector to the business sector is the firm's total revenue. In turn, money flows from the business sector to households as payment for the use of their resources—land, labor, and capital. After the owners of land, labor, and capital have been paid, the owner of the business receives what is left, the profit. Clearly, the amount of profit received by the owner of the business depends on the output produced by the firm and the quantities and costs of land, labor, and capital used by the firm to produce the output. Owners of businesses want to produce output at the lowest possible cost. Doing so requires a business owner to compare all combinations of resources (inputs) that can be used to produce output and select the least-cost combination.

Let's use a hypothetical firm, Pacific Western Airlines (PWA), to discuss the relationship between inputs and output. The number (in thousands) of passenger-miles that results when PWA employs alternative combinations of mechanics and airplanes is shown in Table 1. One mechanic can generate 30 (thousand) passenger-miles if PWA has 5 airplanes, 100 (thousand) passenger-miles if PWA has 10 airplanes, 250 (thousand) passenger-miles if PWA has 15 airplanes, and so on. With a second mechanic, output is increased with each quantity of airplanes: 2 mechanics and 5 airplanes now generate 60 (thousand) passenger-miles, and so on.

Pacific Western Airlines could produce about the same amount, say 340 (thousand) to 360 thousand passenger-miles, with several different combinations of mechanics and airplanes—3 mechanics with 10 airplanes, 2 mechanics with 15 airplanes, or 1 mechanic with 20 airplanes. And several other output levels can be produced with a number of different combinations of mechanics and airplanes. Which

Number of Mechanics	Capital (number of airplanes)							
	5	10	15	20	25	30	35	40
0	0	0	0	0	0	0	0	0
1	30	100	250	340	410	400	400	390
2	60	250	360	450	520	530	520	500
3	100	360	480	570	610	620	620	610
4	130	440	580	640	690	700	700	690
5	130	500	650	710	760	770	780	770
6	110	540	700	760	800	820	830	840
7	100	550	720	790	820	850	870	890
8	80	540	680	800	830	860	880	900

Table 1

Alternative Quantities (in thousands) of Output That Can Be Produced by Different Combinations of Resources

combination does PWA choose? That depends on whether PWA is making choices for the short run or for the long run. In the long run, or planning period, the firm may consider any and all combinations of resources. In the short run, or production period, the choices open to the firm are limited. Recall that the short run is a period of time just short enough that at least one resource cannot be changed—it is fixed. Suppose that PWA had previously leased or purchased 10 airplanes and cannot change the number of planes for at least a year. In this case, the fixed resource is airplanes. The options open to PWA in the short run thus are only those under the column labeled "10" airplanes shown in Table 1. Pacific Western Airlines can vary the number of mechanics but not the number of airplanes in the short run.

The **total physical product TPP** (also called total product) schedule and curve shows how the quantity of the variable resource (mechanics) and the output produced are related. In Figure 3(a), columns 1 and 3 of Table 1 are reproduced and plotted. With total output measured on the vertical axis and the number of mechanics measured on the horizontal axis, the combinations of output and mechanics trace out the *TPP* curve. Both the table and the *TPP* curve in Figure 3(a) show that as additional units of the variable resource are used, total output at first rises, initially quite rapidly and then more slowly, and then declines. As the first units of the variable resource (mechanics) are used, each additional mechanic can provide many passenger-miles for the airline. But after a time, there are "too many chefs stirring one broth" and each additional mechanic adds only a little to total passenger-miles flown and, eventually, actually detracts from the productivity of the other mechanics.

total physical product (TPP): the maximum output that can be produced when successive units of a variable resource are added to fixed amounts of other resources

1.b. Diminishing Marginal Returns

This relationship between quantities of a variable resource and quantities of output is called the **law of diminishing marginal returns.** According to the law of diminishing marginal returns, when successive equal amounts of a variable resource are combined with a fixed amount of another resource, output will initially accelerate, then decelerate, and eventually will usually decline. Looking at Table 1, you can see the law of diminishing marginal returns at each quantity of airplanes. Just increase the number of mechanics for any given quantity of airplanes and output will rise at first rapidly but then more slowly. Similarly, if you fix the quantity of mechanics and then vary the number of airplanes, you will also observe the law of diminishing

law of diminishing marginal returns: when successive equal amounts of a variable resource are combined with a fixed amount of another resource, marginal increases in output that can be attributed to each additional unit of the variable resource will eventually decline

Figure 3

Total, Average, and Marginal Product

The table provides plotting data for the graphs. Total, average, and marginal product schedules and curves are shown. The total product schedule, shown in Figure 3(a), is taken from the table by fixing one resource, airplanes, at 10.

The average and marginal product schedules are calculated from the total product schedule. Average is total output divided by number of mechanics; marginal is the change in the total output divided by the change in the number of mechanics.

Number of Mechanics	Total Output	Average Physical Product	Marginal Physical Product
0	0	–	–
1	100	100	100
2	250	125	150
3	360	120	110
4	440	110	80
5	500	100	60
6	540	90	40
7	550	78.6	10
8	540	67.5	– 10

(a) The Total Physical Product Curve

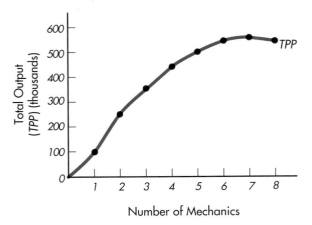

(b) The Average Physical Product Curve

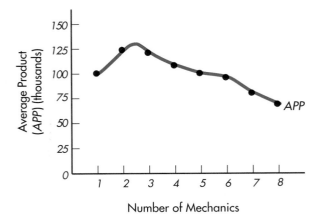

(c) The Marginal Physical Product Curve

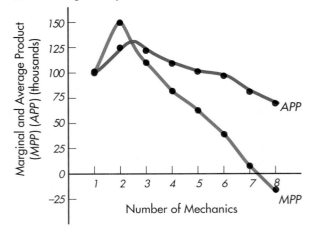

marginal returns. With 1 mechanic, for instance, as the number of airplanes is increased, output rises from 30 to 100 to 250 to 340, and so on. The first increases are large, but the output rises less rapidly and eventually declines as the number of airplanes is increased.

The law of diminishing marginal returns shows up more clearly with the average product and marginal product curves, also called **average physical product (*APP*)** and **marginal physical product (*MPP*)** curves. The average product schedule, shown in the third column of the table in Figure 3(b), is calculated by dividing total output by the number of mechanics:

$$APP = \frac{\text{total output}}{\text{number of mechanics}}$$

Plotting *APP* gives us Figure 3(b), a curve that rises quite rapidly and then slowly declines. The marginal product schedule is the change in total output divided by the change in the quantity of variable resources. In this example, *MPP* is calculated by dividing the change in total output by the change in the number of mechanics:

$$MPP = \frac{\text{change in output}}{\text{change in number of mechanics}}$$

The *MPP* schedule is column 4 in the table. The graph of the *MPP* schedule is shown in Figure 3(c); it is drawn on top of the *APP* curve so that we can compare *MPP* and *APP*. The *MPP* curve rises initially more rapidly than *APP*, then falls more rapidly than *APP*, and eventually reaches zero. When *MPP* is zero or negative, the additional variable resources are actually detracting from the production of other resources, causing output to decline.

According to the law of diminishing marginal returns, when successive equal amounts of a variable resource are combined with a fixed amount of another resource, output will rise, initially accelerating and then decelerating, and eventually may decline. Diminishing marginal returns are not unique to the airline industry. In every instance where increasing amounts of one resource are combined with

average physical product (APP): output per unit of resource

marginal physical product (MPP): the additional quantity that is produced when one additional unit of a resource is used in combination with the same quantities of all other resources

1. **What is the law of diminishing marginal returns?**

Business owners combine quantities of land, labor, and capital to produce goods and services in the most profitable way. Technological improvements help them produce a larger quantity of goods and services at lower cost, thereby increasing profitability. Here, an Egyptian woman supervises several automatic sewing machines. One woman can produce the same quantity with the automatic machines 100 times faster than when the sewing was done by hand. Employing more people may speed up production; eventually, however, employing more people will not speed up production and could actually retard production as the workers interfere with each other's tasks.

fixed amounts of other resources, the additional output that can be produced initially increases but eventually decreases.

For instance, diminishing marginal returns limit the effort to improve passenger safety during collisions by installing air bags in cars. The first air bag added to a car increases protection considerably. The second adds an element of safety, particularly for the front-seat passenger. But additional air bags provide little additional protection and eventually would lessen protection as they interfered with each other. As successive units of the variable resource, air bags, are placed on the fixed resource, the car, the additional amount of protection provided by the air bags declines.

The law of diminishing marginal returns also applies to studying. On a typical day, during the first hour you study a subject you probably get a great deal of information. During the second hour you may also learn a large amount of new material, but eventually another hour of studying will produce no benefits and could be counterproductive.

Diminishing marginal returns occur because the efficiency of variable resources depends on the quantity of the fixed resources. If the airline mechanics must stand around waiting for tools or for room to work on the jet engines, then an additional mechanic will allow few, if any, additional passenger-miles to be flown. The limited capacity of the fixed resources—the number of planes, tools, and hangar space—causes the efficiency of the variable resource—the mechanics—to decline. Similarly, we often see diminishing marginal returns at restaurants. We walk into a restaurant and see lots of empty tables but are told that there is a 15-minute wait to be seated. The problem is that the number of servers (the fixed resource) is not sufficient to provide quality service to all the tables (the variable resource). The restaurant gives each server one table to serve, then two, then three, and so on, until the quality of the service begins to decline. Without more servers, some tables will have to be left empty.

1.b.1. Average and Marginal   Average and marginal relationships behave the same way with respect to each other no matter whether they refer to physical product, cost, utility, grade points, or anything else. For instance, think of the grade point average (GPA) that you get each semester as your *marginal* GPA and your cumulative, or overall, GPA as your *average* GPA. You can see the relation between marginal and average by considering what will happen to your cumulative GPA if this semester's GPA is less than your cumulative GPA. Suppose your GPA this semester is 3.0 for 16 hours of classes and your cumulative GPA, not including this semester, is 3.5 for 48 hours of classes. Your marginal (this semester's) GPA will be less than your average GPA. Thus, when your marginal GPA is added to your average GPA, the average GPA falls, from 3.5 to 3.375. *As long as the marginal is less than the average, the average falls.* If your GPA this semester is 4.0 instead of 3.0, your average GPA will rise from 3.5 to 3.625. *As long as the marginal is greater than the average, the average rises.*

Whenever marginal is less than average, the average is falling, and whenever marginal is greater than average, the average is rising.

If the average is falling when marginal is below average and rising when marginal is above average, then marginal and average can be the same only when the average is neither rising nor falling. If your GPA this semester is 3.5 and your cumulative GPA up to this semester was 3.5, then your new GPA will be 3.5. Average and marginal are the same when the average is constant. This occurs only when the average curve is at its maximum or minimum point.

In Figure 4 the relationship between average physical product and marginal physical product is illustrated. You can see in both the table and the figure that as long as

Figure 4

Marginal and Average Physical Product

When the marginal is above the average, the average is rising; when the marginal is below the average, the average is falling. The *MPP* = *APP* at the maximum of the *APP*, between 2 and 3 mechanics.

Number of Mechanics	Total Output	Average Physical Product	Marginal Physical Product
0	0	–	–
1	100	100	100
2	250	125	150
3	360	120	110
4	440	110	80
5	500	100	60
6	540	90	40
7	550	78.6	10
8	540	67.5	– 10

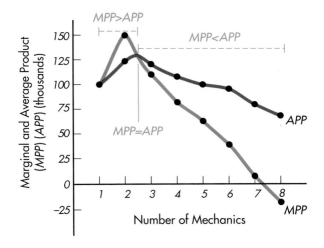

the *MPP* is greater than the *APP*, the *APP* is rising; whenever the *MPP* is less than the *APP*, the *APP* is falling. Thus, the *MPP* and *APP* are equal at the peak or top of the *APP* curve. This occurs between 2 and 3 mechanics.

RECAP

1. According to the law of diminishing marginal returns, as successive units of a variable resource are added to the fixed resources, the additional output produced will initially rise but will eventually decline.

2. Diminishing marginal returns occur because the efficiency of variable resources depends on the quantity of the fixed resources.

3. As long as the marginal is less than the average, the average falls. As long as the marginal is greater than the average, the average rises.

2. FROM PRODUCTION TO COSTS

Every firm (and every individual and nation as well) is faced with the law of diminishing marginal returns. The law is, in fact, a physical property, not an economic one, but is important to economics because it defines the relationship between costs and output in the short run.

2.a. The Calculation of Costs

The total, average, and marginal physical product schedules and curves show the relationship between quantities of resources (inputs) and quantities of output. To examine the costs of doing business rather than the physical production relationships, we must define the costs of each unit of resources. Suppose, in our airline example, the cost per mechanic, the variable resource, is $1,000 per mechanic, and this is the only cost PWA has. Then, the total costs are those listed in column 3 of the table in Figure 5, calculated by multiplying $1,000 by the number of mechanics necessary to produce the output listed in column 2.

The total cost schedule is plotted on a graph where output is measured on the horizontal axis and total cost on the vertical axis, as shown in Figure 5(a). The total cost curve indicates that as output rises in the short run, costs rise, initially rapidly, then more slowly, and finally more and more rapidly.

Figure 5(b) is the total physical product curve of Figure 3(a). You might notice a resemblance between the total cost curve and the total physical product curve. In fact, they are like mirror images, both shaped by the law of diminishing marginal returns.[2]

Since total cost and total physical product have the same shape (except for being mirror images), then average physical product and average cost and marginal physical product and marginal cost should also have the same shapes except for being mirror images. **Average total cost (*ATC*)** is the per unit cost and is derived by dividing total cost by the quantity of output:

average total cost (*ATC*): per unit cost

$$ATC = \frac{\text{total cost}}{\text{total output}}$$

marginal cost (*MC*): the additional cost of producing one more unit of output

Marginal cost (*MC*) is the change in cost caused by a change in output and is derived by dividing the change in total cost by the change in the quantity of output:

$$MC = \frac{\text{change in total cost}}{\text{change in quantity of output}}$$

The average total cost schedule is listed in column 3 and the marginal cost schedule in column 4 of the table in Figure 6. Notice that these schedules are calculated with respect to output. It is the *relationship* between costs and output produced that is focused on with the cost schedules and curves.

2.b. The U Shape of Cost Curves

In Figure 6(a) the average cost schedule is plotted next to the *APP* curve of Figure 3(b). In Figure 6(b), the marginal cost schedule is plotted next to the *MPP* curve of Figure 3(c). Can you see the resemblances between the curves? Whereas the *MPP* and *APP* curves might be described as hump shaped, the *MC* and *ATC* curves can be

---

[2]You might see the resemblance more clearly if the total cost curve is rotated so that output is the vertical axis and cost the horizontal axis.

Figure 5

Total Costs

Figure 5(a) is the total cost curve, columns 2 and 3 of the table. Figure 5(b) is the total product curve, reproduced from Figure 3(a). Both curves illustrate diminishing marginal returns.

Number of Mechanics	Total Output (thousands)	Total Cost (thousands)
0	0	$ 0
1	100	$1,000
2	250	$2,000
3	360	$3,000
4	440	$4,000
5	500	$5,000
6	540	$6,000
7	550	$7,000
8	540	$8,000

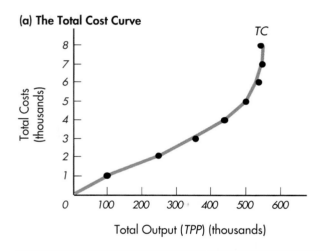

(a) The Total Cost Curve

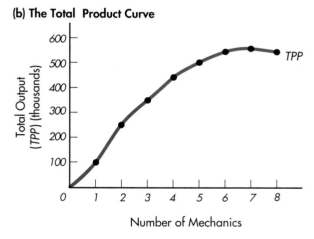

(b) The Total Product Curve

described as U shaped. In Figure 6(c), the *MC* and *ATC* curves are put on the same graph next to the *MPP* and *APP* curves of Figure 4. You can see that the relationship between marginal and average applies to both product and cost curves: whenever the marginal is above the average, the average is rising, and whenever the marginal is below the average, the average is falling; note also that *MPP* = *APP* at the maximum point of the *APP* curve while *MC* = *ATC* at the minimum point on the *ATC* curve.

The purpose of comparing the product and cost curves is to emphasize the importance of the law of diminishing marginal returns to short-run costs. Diminishing returns defines the relationship between costs and output in the short run for every firm, no matter whether that firm is a billion-dollar-a-year corporation or a small proprietorship. Obviously, the size or scale of the companies will differ, but the U-shape of the cost curves will not. *Every firm will face a U-shaped cost curve in the short run because of the law of diminishing marginal returns.*

2. What is the relationship between costs and output in the short run?

Figure 6

Average and Marginal Costs

Figure 6(a) shows the average total cost curve and the *APP* curve. Figure 6(b) shows the marginal cost curve and the *MPP* curve. The cost curves are described as U shaped, the product curves as hump shaped. The shapes of the curves are due to the law of diminishing marginal returns. Figure 6(c) shows the relationship between average and marginal curves.

Quantity of Output (thousands)	Total Cost (thousands)	Average Cost (thousands)	Marginal Cost (thousands)
100	$1,000	$10	$ 10
250	$2,000	$ 8	$ 6.7
360	$3,000	$ 8.33	$ 9.1
440	$4,000	$ 9	$ 12.5
500	$5,000	$10	$ 16.7
540	$6,000	$11.1	$ 25
550	$7,000	$12.7	$100

(a) Compare *APP* with *ATC*

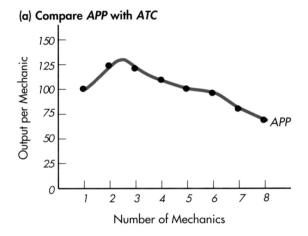

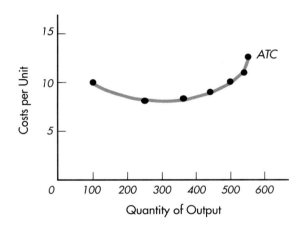

To this point we have used a very simplified situation to describe costs. We placed a cost on the mechanics but on nothing else. Everything has costs. For PWA, the leased airplanes are costs; the buildings, other employees, utilities, and so on are also costs. In the next section we turn to a more in-depth look at costs.

RECAP

1. Costs are derived by putting dollar figures on the resources used in production.
2. Average total cost is the cost per unit of output—total cost divided by the number of units of output produced.
3. Marginal cost is the change in costs divided by the change in output.
4. The relationship between costs and output in the short run is defined by the law of diminishing marginal returns.
5. The cost curves (*TC, ATC, MC*) and the product curves (*TPP, APP, MPP*) are like mirror images of each other, all reflecting the law of diminishing marginal returns.

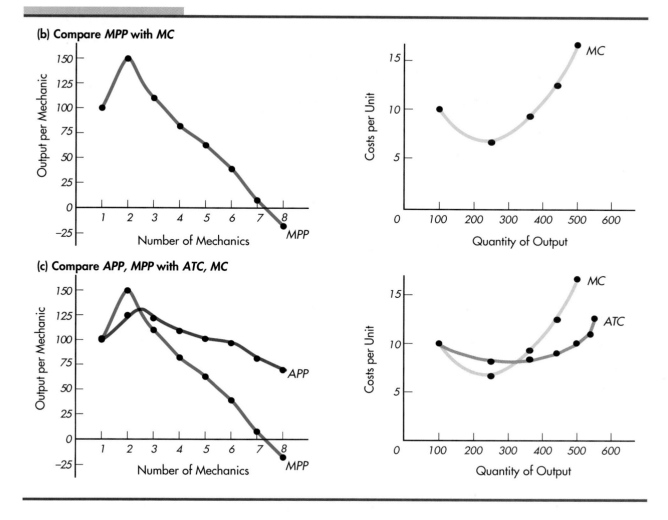

(b) Compare *MPP* with *MC*

(c) Compare *APP, MPP* with *ATC, MC*

6. The U-shape of the cost curves indicates that as output is increased, a great deal of output can be produced by each additional unit of a variable resource initially. But eventually, the increase in output slows and may decline as more and more units of the variable resource are added.

7. The relationship between marginal and average applies to both product and cost curves. When marginal is above average, average is rising, and when marginal is below average, average is falling. The *MPP* = *APP* at the maximum of *APP; MC* = *ATC* at the minimum of *ATC*.

3. COST SCHEDULES AND COST CURVES

A firm must pay for the variable resources, such as the mechanics for PWA, but it has other costs as well—it must pay for the fixed resource. In our discussion of costs and production to this point, we have ignored these other costs. Let's now introduce fixed costs and take another look at the cost curves.

3.a. An Example of Costs

Let's suppose that the costs for PWA of transporting passengers each week are shown in the table in Figure 7. Column 1 lists the total quantity (Q) of output produced (measured in hundred million passenger-miles). Notice that we have listed the data by equal increments of output, from 1 to 2 to 3 and so on (hundred millions of passenger-miles) to make it easier to focus on the relationship between output and costs.

total fixed costs (TFC):
costs that must be paid whether a firm produces or not

Column 2 lists the **total fixed costs (TFC),** costs that must be paid whether the firm produces or not. Fixed costs are $10,000—this is what must be paid whether

---

Figure 7

The Marginal and Average Cost Curves

The table provides plotting data for the figure, which shows the average fixed, average variable, average total, and marginal costs. Average fixed costs (*AFC*) decline steadily from the first unit of output. Average variable costs (*AVC*) initially decline but then rise as output rises. Average total costs (*ATC*), the sum of average fixed and average variable costs, decline and then rise as output rises. The distance between the *ATC* and *AVC* curves is *AFC*. The *MC* curve crosses the *AVC* curve at its minimum point, point *A*, and crosses the *ATC* curve at its minimum, point *B*. (Note: Total output is measured in hundred million passenger-miles. The *TFC*, *TVC*, and *TC* are measured in thousands of dollars. The *AFC*, *AVC*, *ATC*, and *MC* are measured in thousands of dollars per hundred-million passenger-miles.

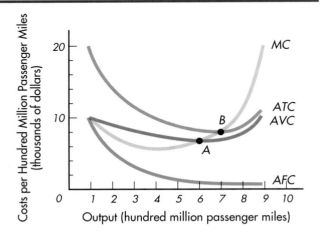

(1) Total Output (Q)	(2) Total Fixed Costs (TFC)	(3) Total Variable Costs (TVC)	(4) Total Costs (TC)	(5) Average Fixed Costs (AFC)	(6) Average Variable Costs (AVC)	(7) Average Total Costs (ATC)	(8) Marginal Costs (MC)	
0	$10	$ 0	$10					
1	$10	$10	$20	$10	$10	$20	$10	
2	$10	$18	$28	$ 5	$ 9	$14	$ 8	
3	$10	$25	$35	$ 3.33	$ 8.33	$11.6	$ 7	
4	$10	$30	$40	$ 2.5	$ 7.5	$10	$ 5	
5	$10	$35	$45	$ 2	$ 7	$ 9	$ 5	
6	$10	$42	$52	$ 1.66	$ 7	$ 8.66	$ 7	Point *A*
7	$10	$50.6	$60.6	$ 1.44	$ 7.2	$ 8.6	$ 8.6	Point *B*
8	$10	$60	$70	$ 1.25	$ 7.5	$ 8.75	$ 9.4	
9	$10	$80	$90	$ 1.1	$ 8.8	$10	$20	

1 or 1 billion passenger-miles are produced. The fixed costs in this example might represent the weekly portion of the annual payment for the planes, which are the resource whose quantity is fixed. Column 3 lists the **total variable costs (*TVC*),** costs that rise or fall as production rises or falls. The costs of resources such as employees, fuel, water, and meals rise as output rises. **Total costs (*TC*),** the sum of total variable and total fixed costs, are listed in column 4. Although the distinction between variable and fixed costs is important to economists, many businesspeople focus more on overhead and direct costs. The relation between these concepts is discussed in the Economic Insight "Overhead." (Overhead is not the same as fixed costs. Overhead refers to costs that are not directly attributable to production, such as administrative costs. Overhead costs may vary, however. For instance, more production may bring with it more paperwork and administration.)

Average costs—average total, average fixed, and average variable costs—are derived by dividing the corresponding total costs by the quantity of output—number of passenger-miles. *Average fixed costs (AFC)* decline as output rises because the total fixed cost, $10,000, is divided by a larger and larger number as output rises. *Average variable costs (AVC)* and *average total costs (ATC)* first decline and then rise, according to the law of diminishing marginal returns. When there are fixed resources and fixed costs, the firm is operating in the short run. For this reason, average total cost is often referred to as the **short-run average total cost (*SRATC*).** Marginal costs (*MC*), the additional costs that come from producing an additional unit of output, are listed in column 8. Marginal costs initially fall and then rise as output rises.

Overhead

Economic Insight

Economists classify costs as fixed or variable. Fixed costs do not change as the volume of production changes. Variable costs, on the other hand, depend on the volume of production. In business, costs are often classified into overhead and direct operating costs. Overhead costs are those that are not directly attributable to the production process. They include such items as taxes, insurance premiums, managerial or administrative salaries, paperwork, the cost of electricity not used in the production process, and others. Overhead costs can be either fixed or variable. Insurance premiums, taxes, and managerial salaries are fixed costs. They must be paid regardless of how much is produced. Electricity used to operate the production process is a variable cost, increasing as the quantity of output produced is increased.

Statements like "We need to spread the overhead" sound somewhat like the concept of declining average fixed costs—fixed cost per unit of output declines as output rises. But overhead may also include variable costs. Thus, the need to "spread the overhead" refers to reducing the total costs that are not directly attributable to the production process. The more a firm can keep its overhead costs the same and increase its volume of production, the more overhead costs look and act like fixed costs. The higher the percentage of overhead costs that are fixed, the more closely related the economists' and the business person's classifications will be. But the two are not—and are not meant to be—the same.

The different classifications provide different information. The economist is interested in the decision to produce, whether to produce, and how much to produce at all. This is the information provided by fixed and variable costs. The business person is interested in attributing costs to different activities, that is, in determining whether the business is running as cost-efficiently as it can. The classification of costs into overhead and direct provides this information.

The average and marginal cost schedules are plotted in Figure 7. The *AVC* curve reaches a minimum at the 5 to 6 hundred million passenger-mile level. The *ATC* curve lies above the *AVC* curve by the amount of the average fixed costs. The *ATC* curve declines until the 7 hundred million passenger-mile point and then rises. The *MC* curve begins below the *AVC* and *ATC* curves and declines until the 5 hundred million passenger-mile point, where it begins to climb. The *MC* curve passes through the *AVC* curve at the minimum value of the *AVC* curve and then continues rising until it passes through the *ATC* curve at the minimum point of the *ATC* curve. The marginal cost curve intersects the average cost curves at the minimum points of the average cost curves.

The MC *curve intersects the* AVC *curve at the minimum point of the* AVC *curve; the* MC *curve intersects the* ATC *curve at the minimum point of the* AVC *curve.*

The role of each of the three types of costs—fixed, variable, and marginal—should be relatively obvious. In the short run, firms can do nothing about fixed costs—they are fixed. It is variable costs that are important in the short run. Firms can alter their variable costs. Average variable costs are the per unit variable costs. Marginal costs play the most important role; they are the incremental costs, the change in costs resulting from a small decline or increase in output. They inform the executive whether the last unit of output produced—the last passenger carried on the plane—increased costs a huge amount, a small amount, or not at all. Thus, the executive can decide whether to produce that last unit. We will see how the costs come into play more clearly in the following chapters.

RECAP

1. Total fixed costs (*TFC*) are costs that do not vary as the quantity of goods produced varies. An example of a fixed cost is the rent on a building. Rent has to be paid whether or not the firm makes or sells any goods.

2. Total variable costs (*TVC*) are costs that change as the quantity of goods produced changes. The cost of materials is usually variable. For instance, the cost of leather for making boots or cloth for manufacturing clothing changes as the quantity produced changes. The fuel required to fly planes will increase as more passengers are transported.

3. Total costs (*TC*) are the sum of fixed and variable costs:

$$TC = TFC + TVC$$

4. Average total costs (*ATC*) are total costs divided by the total quantity of the good that is produced, Q:

$$ATC = \frac{TC}{Q}$$

5. Average fixed costs (*AFC*) are total fixed costs divided by the quantity produced:

$$AFC = \frac{TFC}{Q}$$

6. Average variable costs (*AVC*) are total variable costs divided by the quantity produced:

$$AVC = \frac{TVC}{Q}$$

7. Marginal costs (*MC*) are the incremental costs that come from producing one more or one less unit of output:

$$MC = \frac{\text{change in } TC}{\text{change in } Q}$$

8. Short-run average total cost (*SRATC*) is the total cost divided by the total quantity of output when at least one resource cannot be changed.

4. THE LONG RUN

3. What is the relationship between costs and output in the long run?

A firm can choose to relocate, build a new plant, or purchase additional planes only in the long run, or planning stage. A manager can choose any size of plant or building and any combination of other resources when laying out the firm's plans because all resources are variable in the long run. In essence, during the long run the manager compares all short-run situations.

Table 2, which is based on Table 1, shows the quantities of output that can be produced by alternative combinations of mechanics and airplanes at our hypothetical airline, PWA. You may recall that we specified that PWA had leased 10 airplanes and thus had to constrain itself to producing those combinations under the column labeled "10" in the short run. In the long run, the firm faces no fixed resources—everything is variable. PWA has a choice of how many airplanes to lease and thus has the choice of any combination of resources shown in Table 2.

The law of diminishing marginal returns does not apply when all resources are variable. Diminishing returns applies only when quantities of variable resources are combined with a fixed resource. In the long run everything is variable. Consider the combinations of resources and the resulting output levels colored green in Table 2. A single mechanic combined with 5 airplanes can produce 30 (thousand) passenger-miles. Doubling both mechanics and airplanes (to 2 mechanics and 10 airplanes) means that 250 (thousand) passenger-miles can be produced. Doubling both resources again, to 4 mechanics and 20 airplanes, means that 640 (thousand) passenger-miles can be produced. Doubling the resources once again, to 8 mechanics and 40 airplanes, results in 900 (thousand) passenger-miles being flown. For the

Table 2

The Long Run or Planning Period (passenger-miles in thousands)

Number of Mechanics	Capital (number of airplanes)							
	5	10	15	20	25	30	35	40
0	0	0	0	0	0	0	0	0
1	30	100	250	340	410	400	400	390
2	60	250	360	450	520	530	520	500
3	100	360	480	570	610	620	620	610
4	130	440	580	640	690	700	700	690
5	130	500	650	710	760	770	780	770
6	110	540	700	760	800	820	830	840
7	100	550	720	790	820	850	870	890
8	80	540	680	800	830	860	880	900

first few times the quantities of both resources were doubled, output rose by more than the resources. But eventually, the output increase was less than double as the resources were doubled. This need not have been the case. Output could have continued to rise more rapidly than the resources, or it could have risen at a constant amount, or it could have declined throughout. Unlike the short run, where the relationship between inputs and output is defined by the law of diminishing marginal returns, the long run is not guided by a physical law.

4.a. Economies of Scale and Long-Run Cost Curves

When all resources are changed, we say that the scale of the firm has changed. **Scale** means size. In the long run, a firm has many sizes to choose from—those given in Table 2 for PWA, for instance. The short run requires that scale be fixed—only a variable resource is changed. For each size or scale, therefore, there is a set of short-run average- and marginal-cost curves. For each quantity of airplanes (each column in Table 2), PWA has a set of average and marginal U-shaped cost curves. Figure 8(a) shows several short-run cost curves along which a firm could produce. Each short-run cost curve is drawn for a particular quantity of the capital resource—that is, a specific column in Table 2. Once the quantity of the capital resource is selected, the firm brings together different combinations of the other resources with the fixed capital resource. If a small quantity of the capital resource is selected, the firm might operate along $SRATC_1$. If the firm selects a slightly larger quantity of the capital resource, then it will be able to operate anywhere along $SRATC_2$. With a still larger quantity, the firm can operate along $SRATC_3$, $SRATC_4$, $SRATC_5$, or some other short-run average total cost curve.

In the long run, the firm can choose any of the $SRATC$ curves. All it needs to do is choose the level of output it wants to produce and then select the least-cost combination of resources with which to reach that level. Least-cost combinations are represented in Figure 8(b) by a curve that just touches each $SRATC$ curve. This curve is the **long-run average-total-cost** curve (**LRATC**—the lowest cost per unit of output for every level of output when all resources are variable). If the firm had chosen to acquire or use a quantity of fixed resources indicated by $SRATC_3$ in Figure 8(b), then it could produce Q_4 only at point A. Only by increasing its quantity of fixed resources could the firm produce at point B on $SRATC_4$.

You can see in Figure 8(b) that the long-run average-total-cost curve does *not* connect the minimum points of each of the short-run average-cost curves ($SRATC_1$, $SRATC_2$, etc.). The reason is that the minimum point of a short-run average-total-cost curve is not necessarily the lowest-cost method of producing a given level of output. For instance, point A on $SRATC_3$ is much higher than point B on $SRATC_4$, but output level Q_4 could be produced at either A or B. When the quantities of all resources can be varied, the choices open to the manager are much greater than when only one or a few of the resources are variable.

The long-run average-total-cost curve gets its shape from economies and diseconomies of scale. If producing each unit of output becomes less costly as the amount of output produced rises, there are **economies of scale**—unit costs decrease as the quantity of production increases and all resources are variable. If the cost per unit rises as output rises, there are **diseconomies of scale**—unit costs increase as the quantity of production increases and all resources are variable. Economies of scale account for the downward-sloping portion of the long-run average-cost curve. Diseconomies of scale account for the upward-sloping portion.

If the cost per unit of output is constant as output rises, there are **constant returns to scale.** Figures 9(a), 9(b), and 9(c) show three possible shapes of a long-run

Figure 8

The Short-Run and Long-Run Average-Cost Curves

The long-run average-cost curve represents the lowest costs of producing any level of output when all resources are variable. Short-run average-cost curves represent the lowest costs of producing any level of output in the short run, when at least one of the resources is fixed. Figure 8(a) shows the possible *SRATC* curves facing a firm. Figure 8(b) shows the *LRATC* curve, which connects the minimum cost of producing each level of output. Notice that the *SRATC* curves need not indicate the lowest costs of producing in the long run. If the short run is characterized by $SRATC_3$, then quantity Q_4 can be produced at point *A*. But if some of the fixed resources are allowed to change, managers can shift to $SRATC_4$ and produce at point *B*.

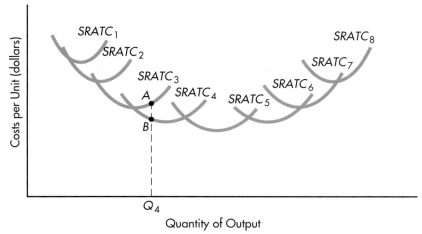

(a) Short-Run Average-Total-Cost Curves

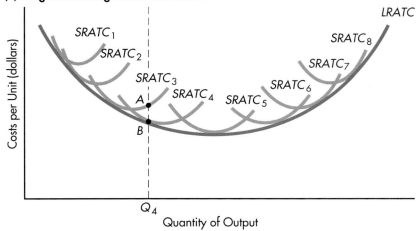

(b) Long-Run Average-Total-Cost Curve

average-cost curve. Figure 9(a) is the usual U shape, indicating that economies of scale are followed by constant returns to scale and then diseconomies of scale. Figure 9(b) is a curve indicating only economies of scale. Figure 9(c) is a curve indicating only constant returns to scale. Each of these long-run average-total-cost curves would connect several short-run average-total-cost curves, as shown in Figure 9(d), 9(e), and 9(f).

4.b. The Reasons for Economies and Diseconomies of Scale

Firms that can specialize more as they grow larger may be able to realize economies of scale. Specialization of marketing, sales, pricing, and research, for example, allows some employees to focus on research while others focus on marketing and still others focus on sales and on pricing.

Figure 9

Long-Run and Short-Run Cost Curves

In Figure 9(a), a U-shaped *LRATC* curve is shown. The downward-sloping portion is due to economies of scale, the horizontal portion to constant returns to scale, and the upward-sloping portion to diseconomies of scale. In Figure 9(b), only economies of scale are experienced.

In Figure 9(c), only constant returns to scale are experienced. The *LRATC* curve connects the lowest cost for each level of output given by the *SRATC* curves. Three such short-run cost curves for each *LRATC* curve are illustrated in Figure 9(d), 9(e), and 9(f).

(a) Economies, Constant Returns, and Diseconomies

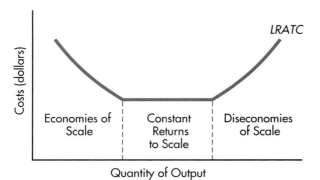

(d) Economies, Constant Returns, and Diseconomies

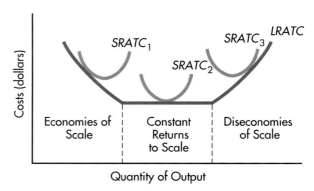

(b) Economies of Scale

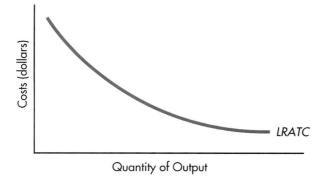

(e) Economies of Scale

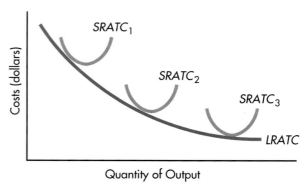

(c) Constant Returns to Scale

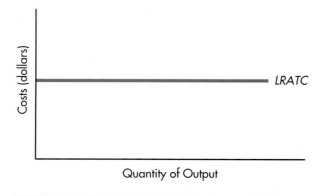

(f) Constant Returns to Scale

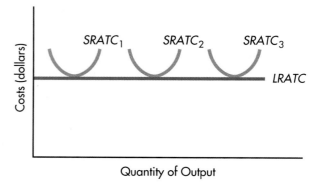

Economies of scale may also result from the use of large machines that are more efficient than small ones. Large blast furnaces can produce more than twice as much steel per hour as smaller furnaces, but they do not cost twice as much to build or operate. Large electrical-power generators are more efficient (more output per quantity of resource) than small ones.

Size, however, does not automatically improve efficiency. The specialization that comes with large size often requires the addition of specialized managers. A 10 percent increase in the number of employees may require an increase greater than 10 percent in the number of managers. A manager to supervise the other managers is needed. Paperwork increases. Meetings are held more often. The amount of time and labor that are not devoted to producing output grows. In other words, the overhead increases. In addition, it becomes increasingly difficult for the CEO to coordinate the activities of each division head and for the division heads to communicate with one another. In this way, size can cause diseconomies of scale.

4.c. The Minimum Efficient Scale

The law of diminishing marginal returns applies to every resource, every firm, and every industry. Whether there are economies of scale, diseconomies of scale, constant returns to scale, or some combination of these depends on the industry under consideration. No law dictates that an industry will have economies of scale eventually followed by diseconomies of scale, although that seems to be the typical pattern. Theoretically, it is possible for an industry to experience only diseconomies of scale, only economies of scale, or only constant returns to scale.

Most industries experience both economies and diseconomies of scale. For example, Mrs. Fields Cookies trains the managers of all Mrs. Fields outlets at its headquarters in Park City, Utah. The training period is referred to as Cookie College. By spreading the cost of Cookie College over more than 700 outlets, Mrs. Fields Cookies is able to achieve economies of scale. However, the company faces some diseconomies because the cookie dough is produced at one location and distributed to the outlets in premixed packages. The dough factory can be large, but the distribution of dough produces diseconomies of scale that worsen as outlets are opened farther and farther away from the factory.

minimum efficient scale (MES): the minimum point of the long-run average-cost curve; the output level at which the cost per unit of output is the lowest

If the long-run average-total-cost curve reaches a minimum, the level of output at which the minimum occurs is called the **minimum efficient scale (MES).** The *MES* varies from industry to industry; it is significantly smaller, for instance, in the production of shoes than it is in the production of cigarettes. A shoe is made by stretching leather around a mold, sewing the leather, and fitting and attaching the soles and insoles. The process requires one worker to operate just two or three machines at a time. Thus, increasing the quantity of shoes made per hour requires more building space, more workers, more leather, and more machines. The cost per shoe declines for the first few shoes made per hour, but rises thereafter. Cigarettes, on the other hand, can be rolled in a machine that can produce several thousand per hour. Producing 100 cigarettes an hour is more costly per cigarette than producing 100,000 per hour.

4.d. The Planning Horizon

The long run is referred to as a planning horizon because the firm has not committed to a fixed quantity of any resource and has all options available to it. In determining the size or scale to select, the manager must look at expected demand and expected costs of production and then select the size that appears to be the most profitable. Once a scale is selected, the firm is operating in the short run since at least

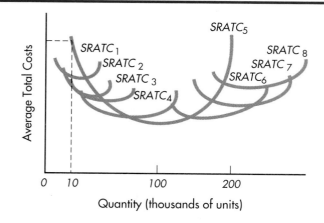

Figure 10

Morita's Problem

Had Sony chosen to produce at $SRATC_5$ it would have been constrained to operate along $SRATC_5$ in the short run. A decrease in production to 10,000 units would have meant rising up the short-run cost curve and producing at very high per unit costs.

one of the resources is fixed. Sony, for instance, was constrained to a rather small production facility for transistor radios back in the 1950s, as discussed in the Preview. This means that it was operating along a specific short-run average-cost curve. To produce 100,000 radios would have meant moving far up the right side of the U so that per unit costs would have been extremely high. If Akio Morita had anticipated several more huge purchase orders in future years, he might have committed to produce 100,000 radios and increased the scale of Sony. Expanding the scale of Sony would have meant moving down along the long-run average-cost curve, perhaps from the current position of $SRATC_1$ in Figure 10 to $SRATC_5$. Once having committed to the scale of $SRATC_5$, Sony would again be operating in the short run. Increases and decreases in production would be a move along $SRATC_5$. You can see what Morita was worried about. Suppose that production dropped back to the 10,000 radios per year level. Then, being constrained to operate along $SRATC_5$, Sony would have experienced huge per unit costs.

RECAP

1. Many industries are characterized by U-shaped long-run average-cost curves but need not be. There is no law dictating a U-shaped *LRATC* curve.

2. The long-run average-total-cost curve gets its U shape from economies and diseconomies of scale, unlike the short-run cost curves, which get their U shape from diminishing marginal returns.

3. The minimum efficient scale (*MES*) is the size of a firm that is at the minimum point of a long-run average-cost curve.

4. The *MES* varies from industry to industry. Some industries, like the electric-power industry, have large economies of scale and a large *MES*. Other kinds of industries, like the fast-food industry, have a relatively small *MES*.

5. Economies of scale may result from specialization and technology. Diseconomies of scale may occur because coordination and communication become more difficult as size increases.

SUMMARY

1. A firm is a business organization that brings together land, labor, capital, and business ownership to produce a product or service. *§1*

2. The short run is a period of time just short enough that the quantity of at least one of the resources cannot be altered. *§1.a*

3. The total physical product curve is a picture of the short-run relationship between resources (inputs) and output when one resource is variable. *§1.a*

? What is the law of diminishing marginal returns?

4. According to the law of diminishing marginal returns, when successive equal amounts of a variable resource are combined with a fixed amount of another resource, there will be a point beyond which the extra or marginal product that can be attributed to each additional unit of the variable resource will decline. *§1.a, 1.b*

? What is the relationship between costs and output in the short run?

5. The total-cost curve is the mirror image of the *TPP* curve. Similarly, *MC* is the mirror image of *MPP*, and *AC* is the mirror image of *APP*. Their shapes are due to the law of diminishing marginal returns. *§2.a, 2.b*

6. Fixed costs are costs that do not vary as the quantity of goods produced varies. *§3.a*

7. Variable costs rise as the quantity of goods produced rises. *§3.a*

8. Total costs are the sum of fixed and variable costs. *§3.a*

9. Average total costs are the costs per unit of output—total costs divided by the quantity of output produced. *§3.a*

10. Average costs fall when marginal costs are less than average and rise when marginal costs are greater than average. *§3.a.1*

11. The U shape of short-run average-total-cost curves is due to the law of diminishing marginal returns. *§2.b, 3.b*

? What is the relationship between costs and output in the long run?

12. The U shape of long-run average-total-cost curves is due to economies and diseconomies of scale. *§4.a*

13. Economies of scale result when increases in output lead to decreases in unit costs and the quantities of all resources are variable. *§4.a*

14. Diseconomies of scale result when increases in output lead to increases in unit costs and the quantities of all resources are variable. *§4.a*

15. Constant returns to scale occur when increases in output lead to no changes in unit costs and the quantities of all resources are variable. *§4.a*

16. The minimum efficient scale (*MES*) occurs at the minimum point of the long-run average-total-cost curve. *§4.c*

17. The long run is the planning horizon where all resources are variable. Once a size or scale is selected, the firm is operating in the short run. *§4.d*

KEY TERMS

total physical product (*TPP*) *§1.a*

law of diminishing marginal returns *§1.b*

average physical product (*APP*) *§1.b*

marginal physical product (*MPP*) *§1.b*

average total costs (*ATC*) *§2.a*

marginal cost (*MC*) *§2.a*

total fixed costs (*TFC*) *§3.a*

total variable costs (*TVC*) *§3.a*

total costs (*TC*) *§3.a*

average fixed costs (*AFC*) *§3.a*

average variable costs (*AVC*) *§3.a*

short-run average total cost (*SRATC*) *§3.a*

scale *§4.a*

long-run average total cost (*LRATC*) *§4.a*

economies of scale *§4.a*

diseconomies of scale *§4.a*

constant returns to scale *§4.a*

minimum efficient scale (*MES*) *§4.c*

EXERCISES

1. Use the following information to list the total fixed costs, total variable costs, average fixed costs, average variable costs, average total costs, and marginal costs.

Output	Costs	TFC	TVC	AFC	AVC	ATC	MC
0	$100						
1	$150						
2	$225						
3	$230						
4	$300						
5	$400						

2. Use the following table to answer the questions listed below.

Output	Cost	TFC	TVC	AFC	AVC	ATC	MC
0	$ 20						
10	$ 40						
20	$ 60						
30	$ 90						
40	$120						
50	$180						
60	$280						

  a. List the total fixed costs, total variable costs, average fixed costs, average variable costs, average total costs, and marginal costs.
  b. Plot each of the cost curves.
  c. At what quantity of output does marginal cost equal average total cost and average variable cost?

3. Use Table 2 in the chapter to demonstrate the law of diminishing marginal returns. Where does the law apply if there are 20 airplanes in the short run? What occurs if there are only 10 airplanes? Plot the *APP* curve for 20 airplanes and for 10 airplanes.

4. Use Table 2 in the chapter to demonstrate the law of diminishing marginal returns if the fixed resource is mechanics. Plot the *APP* curve for 1 mechanic and for 4 mechanics.

5. Describe some conditions that might cause large firms to experience inefficiencies that small firms would not experience.

6. What is the minimum efficient scale? Why would different industries have different minimum efficient scales?

7. Describe the relation between marginal and average costs. Describe the relation between marginal and average fixed costs and between marginal and average variable costs.

8. Explain why the *APP* curve rises when *MPP* is greater than *APP* and falls when *MPP* is less than *APP*.

9. Explain why the short-run marginal-cost curve must intersect the short-run average-total-cost and average-variable-cost curves at their minimum points. Why doesn't the marginal-cost curve also intersect the average-fixed-cost curve at its minimum point?

10. Explain the relationship between the shapes of the production curves and the cost curves. Specifically, compare the marginal-physical-product curve and the marginal-cost curve, and the average-physical-product curve and the average-total-cost curve.

11. Consider a firm with a fixed-size production facility as described by its existing cost curves.
  a. Explain what would happen to those cost curves if a mandatory health insurance program is imposed on all firms.
  b. What would happen to the cost curves if the plan required the firm to provide a health insurance program for each employee worth 10 percent of the employee's salary?
  c. How would that plan compare to one that requires each firm to provide a $100,000 group program that would cover all employees in the firm no matter the number of employees?

12. Explain the fallacy of the following statement: "You made a real blunder. The $600 you paid for repairs is worth more than the car."

13. Explain the statement "We had to increase our volume to spread the overhead."

14. Three college students are considering operating a tutoring business in economics. This business would require that they give up their current jobs at the student recreation center, which pay $6,000 per year. A fully equipped facility can be leased at a cost of $8,000 per year. Additional costs are $1,000 a year for insurance and $.50 per person per hour for materials and supplies. Their services would be priced at $10 per hour per person.

a. What are fixed costs?
b. What are variable costs?
c. What is the marginal cost?
d. How many students would it take to break even?

15. Express Mail offers overnight delivery to customers. It is attempting to come to some conclusion on whether to expand its facilities or not. Currently its fixed costs are $2 million per month and its variable costs are $2 per package. It charges $12 per package and has a monthly volume of 2 million packages. If it expands, its fixed costs will rise by $1 million and its variable costs will fall to $1.50 per package. Should it expand?

Monopoly: Old Concept in a New Era

A watershed event in economic history appears to be unfolding, and the controversy over Microsoft's business practices promises to be a defining moment in the epoch's early stages.

The dawning of the information age is a watershed event because technology is ushering in an era of high fixed costs and low marginal costs.

"Staggering start-up costs," said Dallas Federal Reserve bank chief economist W. Michael Cox, "(go to) design products, recruit workers, purchase equipment and establish a marketplace presence. But once in production, delivering additional goods or services is often rather cheap."

Treasury Secretary Lawrence Summers acknowledged the significance of this phenomenon in a recent speech when he said, "The only incentive to produce anything is the possession of temporary monopoly power, because without that power the price will be bid down to the marginal cost and the high initial fixed costs cannot be recouped. (Therefore) the constant pursuit of that monopoly power becomes the central driving thrust of the new economy."

Thus, his remarks suggest, this way of doing business will become critical to economic growth. It was a remarkable admission from a leading economic spokesman for an administration committed to bringing down Microsoft for alleged abuses of monopolistic power.

The marginal cost of anything is the cost of producing one additional unit, and economic theory generally holds that in a competitive economy the selling price of a good is determined by its marginal cost.

But what if the marginal cost is zero? Stephen J. Entin, an economist who heads the Institute for Research on the Economics of Taxation, recently addressed the Microsoft antitrust case in this context.

The initial government complaint against Microsoft centered on the allegation that Netscape was harmed because Microsoft gave away its Explorer net browser as part of Windows. This alleged predatory act undermined Netscape's market domination and ability to charge for its browser.

Entin contends that because the marginal cost of producing one more copy of a browser is almost nothing and there are no barriers to entry in the browser market, "it was inevitable that some competitor or other would emerge to drive the price to zero."

In the new economy, Entin predicts, any monopoly power will be the short-lived result of temporary technical or marketing power that will prove as brief as Netscape's rule over the browser market.

Therefore, Entin says, it shouldn't concern either government trustbusters or the courts. When all is said and done, this may be the lesson of the Microsoft prosecution as high-tech progress overtakes the legal process.

Meanwhile, whatever challenges this new economy might pose for those trying to profit from it or control it, it promises to be a Big Rock Candy Mountain for consumers. Peter Huber, a senior fellow at the Manhattan Institute, has gone so far as to envision an end of poverty because what were once scarcities will trend toward unlimited supply at zero cost.

Jerry Heaster, "Monopoly: Old Concept in a New Era," *The Kansas City Star,* June 14, 2000, C1.

The Kansas City Star/June 14, 2000

Commentary

"The marginal cost of anything is the cost of producing one additional unit, and economic theory generally holds that in a competitive economy the selling price of a good is determined by its marginal cost. But what if the marginal cost is zero?" A firm maximizes its profit by producing (and selling) a quantity where $MR = MC$. If MC is zero, or at least very small, then profit will be maximized at a large quantity—where MR is also zero or very near zero. This is shown in the following figure; $MR = MC$ at a price that is very near zero.

The firm produces (and sells) the quantity Q at the price P. This figure would illustrate the temporary monopoly created by the large fixed costs (notice how the marginal cost curve slopes down from a relatively high level near zero output) because the eco-

nomic profit would be substantial. As other firms realize the economic profit earned by this firm with a temporary monopoly, they enter the business. As a result, the temporary monopoly is lost. The demand curve becomes more elastic as more substitutes become available to consumers. This is illustrated by the second graph, with the flatter demand and marginal-revenue curves and the identical marginal-cost curve. Now, the quantity sold by the initial firm is less and the price is less. Notice that the price is very nearly the same as the marginal cost. This is the result of perfect competition—price will be equal to marginal cost—consumers pay only the marginal cost of producing the product. That is the Big Rock Candy Mountain mentioned in the article; consumers will benefit from these cost conditions.

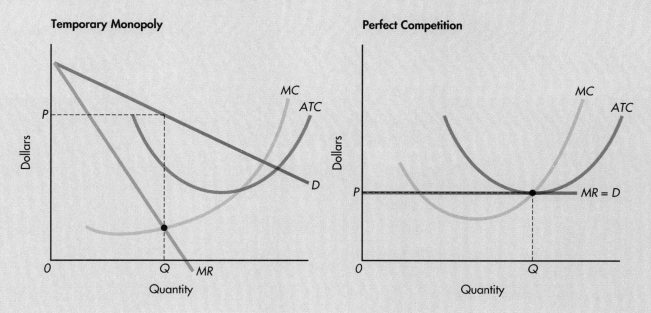

Part Three

Product Markets

Chapter 9

Profit Maximization

? Fundamental Questions

1. What is the role of economic profit in allocating resources?

2. Why do economists and accountants measure profit differently?

3. How do firms decide how much to supply?

4. What is a market structure?

5. What are price makers and price takers?

Preview

A firm is a combination of resources used to produce a good or service. The firm adds value to the resources it uses if it pays the resources for their use and still has something left over. In 2000 Microsoft bought materials worth $4 billion. Its wage and salary bill was around $9 billion, and the cost of the capital that the company used—premises, factories, machinery, and equipment—was about $4 billion. Thus, it cost Microsoft $17 billion to produce its output. Sales were $23 billion—$6 billion more than it cost to produce the output. This figure of $6 billion is a measure of the value that Microsoft added, the difference between the value of its output and the full cost of its inputs. ■

1. PROFIT MAXIMIZATION

adding value: creating output that is more valuable than the resources used to create the output

Adding value is an objective not only for for-profit institutions but for not-for-profit institutions as well. The purpose of a for-profit firm is to maximize profit. The purpose of a charitable organization, university, or tennis or golf club is to create an output that is more valuable than the cost of the inputs used to produce the output. For instance, St. Mary's Food Bank is a nonprofit firm whose wage and salary bill was $2.5 million and whose cost of capital was $1.2 million in 1997. Its charitable contributions were $3.7 million, exactly the cost of the resources it used. Its added value was the amount by which the value of the services it provided exceeded the cost of inputs. Adding value is the purpose of business activity. In the long run, organizations that fail to add value will not survive. Inefficient decisions and allocations will eventually be replaced or overturned by more efficient ones.

1. **What is the role of economic profit in allocating resources?**

1.a. Economic Profit

Measuring added value is easier for for-profit firms than for not-for-profit organizations. Nevertheless, for both types of organizations, added value is what remains from the value of output once the costs of the inputs used in the organization have been fully accounted for. Inputs consist of three general groups: land, labor, and capital, and the cost of each is:

Rent to landowners

Wages and salaries to workers for their labor services

Interest to the owners of capital (investors)

In each case, the cost is an opportunity cost—the amount necessary to keep the resource owners from moving the resources to an alternative use. For instance, if a landowner can rent her land to another firm at a higher rate, then she will. She has to be paid the opportunity cost of the land. Similarly, if you could earn more for doing the same job elsewhere, you would take that job. An employee must be paid at least what he could earn elsewhere.

debt: loans

equity: shares of stock

The cost of capital is also an opportunity cost. Capital is aquired through loans (**debt**) and sales of ownership rights (shares of stock—**equity**—for a public company). The cost of debt is the interest that is paid on the debt. The cost of equity is the alternative returns that the investors (owners) could have gotten had they not chosen to invest in this particular activity or company—the investors' opportunity cost. For instance, since shareholders of Microsoft could invest in other businesses, the return from the best of these alternative investments, a return that was forgone when Microsoft stock was purchased, is the cost of investing in Microsoft. And Microsoft must pay these shareholders at least what they expect to get from alternative investments or the shareholders will take their money elsewhere.

2. **Why do economists and accountants measure profit differently?**

Added value is the return to shareholders (or owners) that exceeds the return they expected to get in an alternative investment. Economists refer to this as **economic profit** and distinguish between it and **accounting profit.** The profit figure reported in annual reports, income statements, and other financial statements is accounting profit. Accounting profit is the value of output less the cost of inputs but *not including* the opportunity cost of the owner's (shareholder's) capital. Economic profit is

economic profit: total revenue less total costs including all opportunity costs

accounting profit: total revenue less total costs except for the opportunity cost of capital

the difference between the value of output and the opportunity cost of all inputs *including* the opportunity cost of the owner's or shareholder's capital.[1]

$$\text{Accounting profit} = \text{revenue} - \text{cost of land} - \text{cost of labor} - \text{cost of debt capital}$$

$$\text{Economic profit} = \text{accounting profit} - \text{cost of equity capital}$$

Wal-Mart, for instance, reported a profit of $8,913 million in 2000. This is Wal-Mart's accounting profit. Subtracting Wal-Mart's cost of capital from its accounting profit indicates that its economic profit was $1,528 million, only 17 percent of its accounting profit.

Coca-Cola had $2.4 billion in accounting profits in 2000. It had $18 billion of investor-supplied capital and its cost of capital was 12.62 percent. The economic profit for Coca-Cola in 2000 was

$$\text{Economic profit} = \text{accounting profit} - \text{opportunity cost of capital}$$
$$= \$2.4 \text{ billion} - \$15 \text{ billion} (0.1262)$$
$$= \$2.4 \text{ billion} - \$2.2 \text{ billion}$$
$$= \$.13 \text{ billion}$$

1.a.1. Negative Economic Profit

Economists refer to a firm that subtracts value (whose cost of equity capital is greater than its accounting profit) as having **negative economic profit.** Negative economic profit means the resources would have a higher value in another use. A firm that continually subtracts value will not exist in the long run. Suppose you were an investor in General Motors Corporation (GM). Having experienced 4 percent annual returns over the last ten years, lower returns than you anticipated, you look at your alternatives. You realize that you could have earned more by selling your shares of stock in GM and purchasing shares in another firm. If many GM shareholders did this, GM could no longer acquire the use of resources. It would have to go out of business. Why has GM not gone out of business? Because not enough investors have decided they could do better investing in another firm. However, for more than 1 percent of the total firms in the United States each year, investors choose to invest elsewhere and the firms do go out of business. For a short period, firms can earn negative economic profit and remain in business. In 2000, such well-known companies as AOL, Hewlett-Packard, Pepsico, Walt Disney, Motorola, and Boeing had negative economic profit. If their owners anticipated a continuing pattern of negative economic profit, they would take their money elsewhere.

negative economic profit: total revenue is less than total costs when total costs include all opportunity costs

1.a.2. Zero Economic Profit

A firm that neither adds value nor subtracts it is a firm whose revenue is sufficient to pay the cost of inputs but with nothing left over after paying those inputs. Economists refer to this as **zero economic profit** or **normal accounting profit.** If Microsoft had revenue of $8.75 billion and costs of $6.75 billion, it would have an accounting profit of $2 billion. But if the shareholders could have earned 10 percent in an alternative activity and they have invested $20 billion in Microsoft, then Microsoft's economic profit would be zero; its added value would be zero.

zero economic profit: total revenue is equal to total costs when total costs include all opportunity costs

normal accounting profit: zero economic profit

---

[1]If the firm is a private firm, then the equity capital includes the owner's own dollars put into the business and the uncompensated time the owner puts into the business.

Zero economic profit might sound bad, but it is not. A zero economic profit simply means that the owners could not do better elsewhere; the firm is earning a positive accounting profit. The investors have no incentive to sell Microsoft and purchase something else since they would expect to earn no more than they do with Microsoft.

positive economic profit: total revenue is greater than total costs when total costs include all opportunity costs

1.a.3. Positive Economic Profit
If a firm is returning more to its owners than the owners' opportunity cost, the firm is said to be earning **positive economic profit.** Positive economic profit is a powerful signal in the market place. Other investors see the positive economic profit and want to get in on it as well. As a result, they take their funds from whatever use they are currently in and invest them in existing and new firms that will compete with the profitable firm. Additional firms producing the good or service mean that supply increases; this will lower the price of that good or service and reduce the positive economic profit. Entry will stop once economic profit is zero.

1.a.4. Role of Economic Profit
Economic profit serves as a beacon, attracting resources when it is positive and directing resources to other uses when it is negative. When a firm earns a positive economic profit, it is making enough to pay the opportunity cost of all the resources it uses, including the opportunity cost of the investors. The investors are doing better than they would have expected to do in any other investment. Conversely, when a firm earns a negative economic profit, the investors are not being paid their opportunity cost and they will take their investments elsewhere. When economic profit is zero, the firm is earning just enough to pay all the resources their opportunity costs. Thus, investors are getting as much as they would have expected to get in any other investment. The firm earning zero economic profit will neither drive investors away nor attract additional investors.

1.b. Accountants and Economic Profit

Accountants do not present economic profit in income statements and balance sheets. Why not? Partly because they have not been convinced it is necessary but more importantly because of the difficulty of calculating the cost of capital.

The cost of equity capital is the amount that the investors would have to be paid not to move their funds to another firm, that is, the opportunity cost to investors of leaving their money with a particular firm. That amount is sure to vary from investor to investor. My opportunity cost is not the same as yours. But even ignoring this problem and focusing on the average investor, the cost of capital is not easily measured. As a result, few firms report economic profits along with their accounting profits. But, more and more firms are beginning to offer investors some information on economic profit.

RECAP

1. Added value refers to the difference between the value of output and the full cost of inputs.
2. Added value is the same as economic profit.
3. Accounting profit is total revenue less total costs. It does not include the opportunity cost of the owner's capital.
4. Economic profit is accounting profit less the opportunity cost of the owner's capital.

5. Economic profit can be positive, negative, or zero. A positive economic profit means that the revenue exceeds the full cost of inputs, that is, that inputs are earning more than their opportunity cost. A negative economic profit means that the inputs are not earning their opportunity costs. A zero economic profit means that the inputs are just earning their opportunity costs.

6. Economic profit is not straightforward to measure because the opportunity cost of capital depends on investor alternatives.

7. The cost of capital is the amount a firm would have to pay investors to have them invest in this firm rather than another.

8. Adding value is the objective of a firm's owners.

9. For the for-profit firm, the objective of adding value is the same as maximizing profit. For the not-for-profit firm, the objective of adding value depends on how output is valued.

A cab driver in Tokyo dusts the rear seat of his cab prior to picking up passengers. Taxicabs are tightly regulated in Japan, having to serve specific districts and maintain specified quality standards. A particular company may have a government-created monopoly in a certain part of the city. Nevertheless, each cab company attempts to compete with other cab and limousine companies by providing extra service. Cleanliness and order are emphasized. Many cab drivers wear white gloves; others use feather dusters on the seats before each customer enters the cab; still others provide special music and other services.

2. MARGINAL REVENUE AND MARGINAL COST

A firm's decision to supply a good or service depends on expected profit. An entrepreneur or manager of a firm looks at the demand for the firm's product and at its costs of doing business and determines whether a profit potential exists. To analyze the firm's decisions, we must put the demand for the firm's product together with the firm's costs.

3. How do firms decide how much to supply?

2.a. Demand and Cost Curves

Consider Figure 1, in which the average-total and marginal-cost curves, derived in the previous chapter, are drawn along with a downward-sloping demand curve. The

Figure 1

Revenue, Cost, and Profit

In Figure 1 the demand curve is drawn along with the average-total and marginal-cost curves. A point of output, Q_1, is arbitrarily chosen to illustrate what total costs, total revenue, and total profit would be at that output point. The price, P_1, is given by the demand curve, tracing Q_1 up to the demand curve. Total revenue, $P_1 \times Q_1$, is given by the rectangle labeled *ABCD*. The total costs are given by seeing how much it costs per unit of output to produce Q_1. That quantity, *BE*, multiplied by the total quantity *AB*, provides the total cost area, *ABEF*. Total profit is total revenue minus total costs, *ABCD* − *ABEF* = *FECD*.

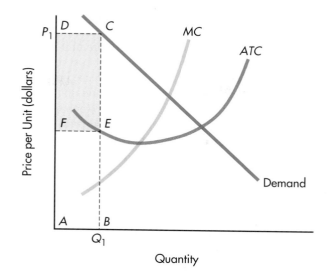

demand curve could also be horizontal or vertical. The shape of the demand curve characterizes the environment in which the firm is selling.

With the downward-sloping demand curve, the firm knows that total revenue first rises and then declines as price is lowered down along the demand curve. Maximum revenue is the point where the price elasticity of demand is 1. But this point is not necessarily the profit-maximizing point. How do we find the profit-maximizing point?

Profit is the difference between total revenue and total costs. Consider the profit the firm shown in Figure 1 earns at price P_1 selling output Q_1. Total revenue is price times quantity, or $P_1 \times Q_1$, the rectangle *ABCD*. At quantity Q_1 total cost is given by *ABEF*, found by determining the average total cost (cost per unit of output) at Q_1 and multiplying that by the quantity Q_1. Profit at quantity Q_1, then, is the difference between the rectangle *ABCD* and the rectangle *ABEF*. Profit at Q_1 is given by *ABCD* − *ABEF* = *FECD*.

The profit given by the rectangle *FECD* in Figure 1 is the profit the firm would earn by producing and selling quantity Q_1. The area *FECD* is not necessarily the maximum profit—the firm might earn more producing more or less than Q_1. To find the quantity at which profit is maximized, we could compare total revenue and total cost for each output level. There is an easier way, however: to find the quantity of output at which profit is a maximum, simply compare marginal cost and marginal revenue.

2.b. Profit Maximum: Marginal Revenue Equals Marginal Cost

Marginal cost is the additional cost of producing one more unit of output. *Marginal revenue* is the additional revenue obtained from selling one more unit of output. If the production of one more unit of output increases costs less than it increases revenue—that is, if marginal cost is less than marginal revenue—then producing (and selling) that unit will increase profit. Conversely, if the production of one more unit costs more than the revenue obtained from the sale of the unit, then producing that unit will decrease profit. When marginal revenue is greater than marginal cost, producing more will increase profit. Conversely, when marginal revenue is less than marginal cost, producing more will lower profit. Thus, *profit is at a maximum when marginal revenue equals marginal cost.*

Profit is maximized at the output level where marginal revenue and marginal cost are equal (MR = MC).

The profit-maximizing rule, *MR = MC*, is illustrated in Table 1, which lists output, total revenue, total cost, marginal revenue, marginal cost, and profit for an individual firm selling custom-made mountain bicycles. The first column is the total quantity (*Q*) of bikes produced. In column 2 is the total revenue (*TR*) generated by selling each quantity, and in column 3 is the total cost (*TC*) of producing each quantity. Fixed costs, the costs the firm encounters even when it produces nothing, amount to $1,000, as listed in column 3, row 1. Marginal revenue (*MR*), the change in total revenue that comes with the production of an additional bike, is listed in the fourth column. The marginal revenue of the first bike produced is the change in revenue that the firm receives for increasing its production and sales from zero to 1 unit; the marginal revenue of the first bike is listed in the row of bike number 1. The marginal revenue of the second bike produced is the change in revenue that the firm receives for increasing its production and sales from 1 to 2 bikes; the marginal revenue of that second bike is listed in the row of bike number 2. Marginal cost (*MC*), the additional cost of producing an additional bike, is listed in column 5. The marginal cost of the first bike is the additional cost of producing the first bike; the marginal cost of the second bike is the increase in costs that results from increasing production from 1 to 2 bikes. Total profit, the difference between total revenue and total cost (*TR* − *TC*), is listed in the last column.

Table 1

Profit Maximization

(1) Total Output (Q)	(2) Total Revenue (TR)	(3) Total Cost (TC)	(4) Marginal Revenue (MR)	(5) Marginal Cost (MC)	(6) Profit (TR − TC)
0	$ 0	$1,000			−$1,000
1	$ 1,700	$2,000	$1,700	$1,000	−$ 300
2	$ 3,300	$2,800	$1,600	$ 800	$ 500
3	$ 4,800	$3,500	$1,500	$ 700	$1,300
4	$ 6,200	$4,000	$1,400	$ 500	$2,200
5	$ 7,500	$4,500	$1,300	$ 500	$3,000
6	$ 8,700	$5,200	$1,200	$ 700	$3,500
7	$ 9,800	$6,000	$1,100	$ 800	$3,800
8	$10,800	$7,000	$1,000	$1,000	$3,800
9	$11,700	$9,000	$ 900	$2,000	$2,700

The first bike costs $2,000 to produce ($1,000 of fixed costs and $1,000 of variable costs); the marginal cost (additional cost) of the first bike is $1,000. When sold, the bike brings in $1,700 in revenue, so the marginal revenue is $1,700. Since marginal revenue is greater than marginal cost, the firm is better off producing that first bike than not producing it.

The second bike costs an additional $800 (column 5) to produce and brings in an additional $1,600 (column 4) in revenue. With the second bike, marginal revenue exceeds marginal cost. Thus the firm is better off producing 2 bikes than none or 1.

Profit continues to rise as production rises until the eighth bike is produced. The marginal cost of producing the seventh bike is $800, and the marginal revenue from selling the seventh bike is $1,100. The marginal cost of producing the eighth bike is $1,000, and the marginal revenue from selling that eighth bike is also $1,000. The marginal cost of producing the ninth bike, $2,000, exceeds the marginal revenue obtained from the ninth bike, $900. Profit declines if the ninth bike is produced. The firm increases profit by producing the seventh bike and reduces profit by producing the ninth bike. Thus, the firm can maximize profit by producing 8 bikes, the quantity at which marginal revenue and marginal cost are equal.[2]

Supply rule: Produce and offer for sale the quantity at which marginal revenue equals marginal cost (MR = MC).

2.b.1. The Marginal-Revenue Curve

The example of the mountain bikes shows us that the only thing we need to add to Figure 1 to be able to point out the profit-maximizing point is the marginal-revenue curve. Drawing the marginal-revenue curve is really quite simple. The first step is to recognize that the demand curve is also the average-revenue curve; it shows the revenue per unit. Thus, the marginal-revenue curve and the demand curve are related to each other in the same way any average and marginal curves are related. That is, when the average is declining, the marginal is also declining and lies below the average. Thus, when the demand curve is downward sloping, the marginal-revenue curve is also downward sloping but lies below the demand curve.

The steeper the demand curve, the steeper the marginal-revenue curve; the marginal-revenue curve for a perfectly inelastic demand curve is the same vertical line as the demand curve. The flatter the demand curve, the flatter the marginal-revenue curve; the marginal-revenue curve for the perfectly elastic demand curve is the same as the demand curve. In between these two extremes, the marginal-revenue curve lies below the demand curve and slopes down.

For the downward-sloping demand curve, we can be more specific in drawing the marginal-revenue curve than to simply note that it slopes down and lies below the demand curve. Recall that the marginal-revenue curve is positive as long as total revenue is rising and is negative as total revenue declines. Since total revenue rises in the price-elastic region of the demand curve, marginal revenue is positive in that region. Total revenue reaches its peak at the unit-elastic point of the demand curve and then turns down; marginal revenue is zero at the unit-elastic point. And total revenue declines in the inelastic region of the demand curve, so marginal revenue must be negative in the inelastic region. Thus, the marginal-revenue curve slopes down and crosses the horizontal axis at the quantity where the demand curve is unit-elastic.

---

[2]You might notice that profit is at the maximum level for quantities of 7 and 8 bikes. This occurs because we are dealing with integers, 1, 2, 3, and so on, when discussing output. There would be a unique quantity for which profit is at its maximum level if we could divide the quantities into small units instead of having to deal with integers. That unique quantity would be where $MR = MC$. Thus, we always choose the quantity at which marginal revenue and marginal cost are the same as the profit-maximizing quantity.

Figure 2

Profit Maximum with $MR = MC$

The demand, *ATC*, and *MC* curves from Figure 1 are redrawn. In addition, the *MR* curve is added. The curve *MR* is drawn by recognizing that demand is average revenue, and since average revenue is falling, marginal revenue must also be falling and lie below average. In addition, marginal revenue crosses the horizontal axis at the output level where the price elasticity of demand is unity. Profit is then found where $MR = MC$. This is quantity Q_m and price P_m. Total profit is the rectangle *GHIJ*.

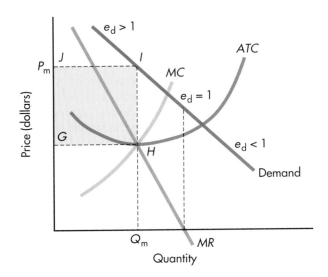

In Figure 2 we have redrawn Figure 1 and added the marginal-revenue curve. Now we can easily find the profit-maximizing point. It is the point at which $MR = MC$. In Figure 2, the profit-maximizing point is given by price P_m and the quantity Q_m, and total profit is given by the rectangle *GHIJ*.

RECAP

1. The average- and marginal-cost curves and the demand and marginal-revenue curves together characterize the producing and selling environments of a firm.

2. The demand curve is also the average-revenue curve. Thus, the marginal-revenue and demand curves are related to each other, as are any average and marginal curves. When demand declines, marginal revenue declines and lies below demand.

3. The profit-maximizing rule is to produce where marginal revenue equals marginal cost.

3. SELLING ENVIRONMENTS OR MARKET STRUCTURE

We know that every firm, no matter its size, no matter its location, no matter what it does, has a relationship in the short run between costs and output dictated by the law of diminishing marginal returns. Thus, the cost curves can have only one shape—the U shape. Demand is another matter. Every single firm has a unique demand curve for its goods and services. But the similarities of the shapes of the demand curve for similar type firms enable us to discuss just four very general selling environments—perfect competition, monopolistic competition, oligopoly, and monopoly.

3.a. Characteristics of the Market Structures

4. What is a market structure?

Economists analyzing the behavior of firms assume that firms can be classified into one of four market structure models. Once a market structure is defined, economists can then examine the behavior of firms within it. A market structure is a *model*—a simplification of reality. Few if any industries fit neatly into one market structure or another. Economists use the four models to describe how firms might behave under certain conditions. They can then modify the models to improve their understanding of how firms behave in real life.

The market structure in which a firm produces and sells its product is defined by three characteristics:

 The number of firms that make up the market

 The ease with which new firms may enter the market and begin producing the good or service

 The degree to which the products produced by the firms are different

In some industries, such as agriculture, there are millions of individual firms. In others, such as in the photofinishing supplies industry, there are very few firms. It is relatively easy and inexpensive to enter the desktop publishing business, but it is much more costly and difficult to start a new airline.

3.b. Market Structure Models

Table 2 summarizes the characteristics of the four market structures.

3.b.1. Perfect Competition
Perfect competition is a market structure characterized by a very large number of firms, so large that whatever any *one* firm does

Table 2

Summary of Market Structures and Predicted Behavior

Market Structure	Characteristics			Behavior	
	Number of Firms	Entry Condition	Product Type	Price Strategy	Promotion Strategy
Perfect competition	Very large number	Easy	Standardized	Price taker	None
Monopoly	One	No entry possible	Only one product	Price maker	Little
Monopolistic competition	Large number	Easy	Differentiated	Price maker	Large amount
Oligopoly	Few	Impeded	Standardized or differentiated	Interdependent	Little or large amount

has no effect on the market; firms that produce an identical (standardized or nondifferentiated) product; and easy entry. Because of the large number of firms, consumers have many choices of where to purchase the good or service, and there is no cost to the consumer of going to a different store. Because the product is standardized, consumers do not prefer one store to another or one brand to another. In fact, there are no brands—only identical, generic products. Because each firm is such a small part of the market, each is unable to do anything other than choose how much to sell at the prevailing market price. In other words, the demand curve for the individual firm in perfect competition is a horizontal line, as shown in Figure 3(a).

3.b.2. Monopoly Monopoly is a market structure in which there is just one firm and entry by other firms is not possible. Because there is only one firm, consumers have only one place to buy the good, and there are no close substitutes.

The demand curve facing the single firm in a monopoly is the market demand because the firm is the only supplier in the market. Figure 3(b) shows the demand curve facing the firm in a monopoly. Being the only producer, the firm in a monopoly must carefully consider what price to charge. Unlike a price increase in a perfectly competitive market, a price increase in a monopoly will not drive every customer to another producer. But if the price is too high, revenue will decline as consumers decide to forgo the product supplied by that one firm. A firm operating in any market but perfect competition is not a price taker. Economists have used different names to refer to a firm that is not a price taker, sometimes using **price maker**, other times **price setter**, and still other times **price searcher**. All three

5. What are price makers and price takers?

price maker, price setter, or **price searcher:** a firm that sets the price of the product it sells

---

Figure 3

The Demand Curve Facing an Individual Firm

The demand curve for the individual firm in perfect competition is a horizontal line at the market price, as shown in Figure 3(a).

Figure 3(b) shows the market demand, which is the demand curve faced by the monopoly firm. The firm is the only supplier and thus faces the entire market demand.

Figure 3(c) shows the downward-sloping demand curve faced by the firm in monopolistic competition. The curve slopes downward because of the differentiated nature of the products in the industry.

(a) Firm in Perfect Competition

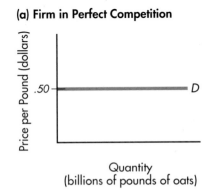

(b) Firm in Monopoly

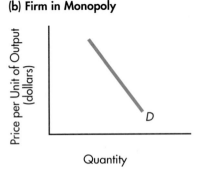

(c) Firm in Monopolistic Competition

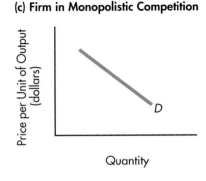

terms are meant to imply the same thing: that the firm determines the quantity it produces and the price at which it sells the products.

3.b.3. Monopolistic Competition
A monopolistically competitive market structure is characterized by a large number of firms, easy entry, and differentiated products. Product differentiation distinguishes a perfectly competitive market from a monopolistically competitive market (in both, entry is easy and there are a large number of firms).

Even though there are many firms in a monopolistically competitive market structure, the demand curve faced by *any one firm* slopes downward, as in Figure 3(c). Because each product is slightly different from all other products, each firm is like a minimonopoly—the only producer of that specific product. The greater the differentiation among products, the less price-elastic the demand.

3.b.4. Oligopoly
In an oligopoly, there are few firms—more than one but few enough so that each firm alone can affect the market. Automobile producers constitute one oligopoly, steelmakers another. Entry into an oligopoly is more difficult than entry into a perfectly competitive or monopolistically competitive market, but in contrast to monopoly, entry can occur. The products offered by the firms in an oligopoly may be differentiated or nondifferentiated. Oligopolistic firms are *interdependent*, and this interdependence distinguishes oligopoly from the other market structures.

The oligopolist faces a downward-sloping demand curve, but the shape of the curve depends on the behavior of competitors. Oligopoly is the most complicated of the market structure models to examine because there are so many behaviors firms might display. Because of its diversity, many economists describe oligopoly as the most realistic of the market structure models.

3.c. Demand and Profit Maximization

Does a perfectly competitive firm maximize profit in a different manner than a monopolist or monopolistically competitive firm? The answer is not really. Each firm maximizes profit by finding the quantity where marginal revenue equals marginal cost ($MR = MC$) and then setting the price according to demand. For the perfectly competitive firm, the only decision is what quantity to produce because the individual firm has no control over price; price is determined by the entire market (all firms and all consumers). The output choice of the perfectly competitive firm is shown in Figure 4(a). As with all firms, the perfectly competitive firm selects to produce and offer for sale the amount where the MC curve crosses the MR curve. The difference is that for the perfectly competitive firm, marginal revenue, demand, and price are identical. For firms in all other selling environments, the process of maximizing profit is what we described earlier. The firm finds the quantity where $MR = MC$. It then determines what price consumers are willing and able to pay to purchase the quantity of output offered by the firm [indicated by tracing a vertical line up to demand, as shown in Figure 4(b)]. That price is the profit-maximizing price, $P.*$

1. Economists have identified four market structures: perfect competition, monopoly, monopolistic competition, and oligopoly.
2. Perfect competition is a market structure in which many firms are producing a nondifferentiated product and entry is easy.

3. Monopoly is a market structure in which only one firm supplies the product and entry cannot occur.

4. Monopolistic competition is a market structure in which many firms are producing differentiated products and entry is easy.

5. Oligopoly is a market structure in which a few firms are producing either standardized or differentiated products and entry is possible but not easy. The distinguishing characteristic of oligopoly is that the firms are interdependent.

Once again note that when $MR = MC$ the firm can't do better; it is maximizing its added value. Consider the data shown in Table 3. Column 1 is output, column 2 is the marginal cost of each output level, and column 3 is the marginal revenue.

The first unit of output costs $30 but, when sold, brings in $100, so the firm earns a profit of $70 on the first suit. The second unit costs another $50 but brings in another $90 when sold, so the second unit increases profit by $40. The third unit costs an additional $80 and brings in an additional $80 when sold. The third unit neither increases nor decreases profit. The fourth unit costs another $120 but brings in only $70 when sold and the fifth unit costs $110 more than the revenue the firm obtains by selling it. The firm makes additional profit by producing and selling units 1 and 2 and makes no additional profit but loses nothing producing and selling the third unit. The fourth and fifth take profit away. The firm clearly will produce and sell either 2 or 3 units. If the firm produced 2 and saw the additional profit of that second unit, it would produce the third unit. When the firm sees that the addi-

---

Figure 4

Profit Maximizing Price and Quantity for Price Taker and Price Maker

Figure 4(a) shows the profit-maximizing quantity Q* and price P* for the price taker while Figure 4(b) shows the profit maximizing quantity Q* and price P* for the price maker. In both cases, the quantity is determined by finding where $MC = MR$ and the price is determined by demand at that quantity.

(a) Price Taker

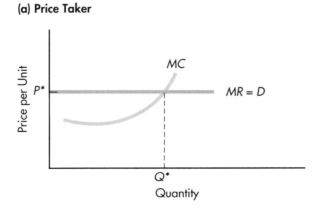

(b) Price Maker

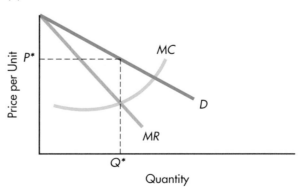

Table 3	Output	MC	MR
Marginal Revenue and Marginal Cost	0		
	1	$ 30	$100
	2	$ 50	$ 90
	3	$ 80	$ 80
	4	$120	$ 70
	5	$170	$ 60

tional profit of the third unit is zero, it knows that to produce the fourth unit would reduce profit. Thus, the firm produces 3 units. Notice that is also the quantity where $MR = MC$.

Now that we understand the profit maximization process, we'll discuss firm behavior in each of the market structures in more detail. We'll begin in the next chapter with perfect competition and then turn to monopoly, monopolistic competition, and finally oligopoly.

SUMMARY

? What is the role of economic profit in allocating resources?

1. Economic profit indicates whether resources will remain in their current activity or will be distributed to a different activity. When economic profit is positive, all resources including the firm's investors and owners are getting paid more than what they could have expected to get in another activity. Others seeing this will redirect their time and investments to that activity. Conversely, when economic profit is negative, all resources are not getting paid their opportunity costs. Resource owners will take their resources and place them into an activity promising to pay more. *§1.a*

? Why do economists and accountants measure profit differently?

2. The basic assumption about the behavior of firms is that firms maximize profit. Although some firms may deviate from profit maximization, the assumption of profit maximization is a useful simplification of reality. *§1*

3. Accountants measure only the direct costs. Economists measure all opportunity costs. *§1.a*

4. Normal profit is a zero economic profit. Above-normal profit is positive economic profit. Below-normal profit is a negative economic profit. *§1.a.1*

? How do firms decide how much to supply?

5. The supply rule for all firms is to supply the quantity at which the firm's marginal revenue and marginal cost are equal. *§2.b*

? What is a market structure?

6. A market structure is a model of the producing and selling environments in which firms operate. The three characteristics that define market structure are number of firms, the ease of entry, and whether the products are differentiated. *§3.a*

7. A perfectly competitive market is a market in which a very large number of firms are producing an identical product and entry is easy. *§3.b.1*

8. A monopoly is a market in which there is only one firm and entry by others cannot occur. *§3.b.2*

9. A monopolistically competitive market is a market in which a large number of firms are producing differentiated products and entry is easy. *§3.b.3*

10. The demand curve facing a monopolistically competitive firm is downward sloping because of the differentiated nature of the products offered by the firm. *§3.b.3*

11. An oligopoly is a market in which a few firms are producing either differentiated or nondifferentiated products and entry is possible but not easy. The distinguishing characteristic of an oligopoly is that the firms are interdependent. *§3.b.4*

12. The demand curve facing a firm in an oligopoly is downward sloping. The elasticity depends on the actions and reactions to price changes by fellow oligopolists in the industry. *§3.b.4*

? What are price makers and price takers?

13. The demand curve facing a perfectly competitive firm is a horizontal line at the market price. The firm takes the price determined in its market as its price. *§3.b.1*

14. A firm that determines the quantity it produces and the price at which it sells the products, is a price maker. *§3.b.2*

15. The marginal-revenue curve for all firms except those in perfect competition is downward sloping and lies below the demand curve. The marginal-revenue curve for the perfectly competitive firm is the same as the demand curve, a horizontal or perfectly elastic curve. *§3.c*

KEY TERMS

adding value *§1*
debt *§1.a*
equity *§1.a*
economic profit *§1.a*
accounting profit *§1.a*

negative economic profit *§1.a.1*
zero economic profit *§1.a.2*
normal accounting profit *§1.a.2*
positive economic profit *§1.a.3*
price maker, price setter, or price searcher *§3.b.2*

EXERCISES

1. Can accounting profit be positive and economic profit negative? Can accounting profit be negative and economic profit positive? Explain.

2. Use the following information to calculate accounting profit and economic profit.

   Sales $100
   Employee expenses $40
   Inventory expenses $20
   Value of owner's labor in any other enterprise $40

3. Calculate accounting profit and economic profit for each of the following firms (amounts are in millions of dollars).

	General Motors	Barclay's Bank	Microsoft
Sales	$50,091	$5,730	$2,750
Wages and salaries	$29,052	$3,932	$ 400
Cost of capital-equity	$12,100	$ 750	$ 35
Interest on debt	$ 7,585	$ 275	$ .5
Cost of materials	$ 6,500	$ 556	$1,650

4. Which type of market characterizes most businesses operating in the United States today?

5. Since a firm in monopoly has no competitors producing close substitutes, does the monopolist set exorbitantly high prices?

6. Advertising to create brand preferences is most common in what market structures?

7. Draw a perfectly elastic demand curve on top of a standard U-shaped average-total-cost curve. Now add in the marginal-cost and marginal-revenue curves. Find the profit-maximizing point, $MR = MC$. Indicate the firm's total revenues and total cost.

8. Give ten examples of differentiated products. Then list as many nondifferentiated products as you can.

9. Describe profit maximization in terms of marginal revenue and marginal cost.

10. Use the information in the table to calculate total revenue, marginal revenue, and marginal cost. Indicate the profit-maximizing level of output. If the price was $3 and fixed costs were $5, what would variable costs be? At what level of output would the firm produce?

Output	Price	Total Costs	Total Revenue ($P \times Q$)
1	$5	$10	
2	$5	$12	
3	$5	$15	
4	$5	$19	
5	$5	$24	
6	$5	$30	
7	$5	$45	

11. If agriculture is an example of perfect competition, why are there so many brands of dairy products at the grocery store?

12. Using demand curves, illustrate the effect of product differentiation on the part of haircutters.

13. Why might society prefer perfect competition over monopoly?

14. Try to classify the following firms into one of the four market structure models. Explain your choice.
   a. Rowena's Gourmet Foods (produces and sells a line of specialty foods)
   b. Shasta Pool Company (swimming pool and spa building)
   c. Merck (pharmaceutical)
   d. America West Airlines
   e. UDC Homebuilders
   f. Legal Seafoods (restaurant chain)

15. Draw two sets of cost curves. For the first set, assume fixed costs are huge and there are large economies of scale (large *MES*). For the second set, assume fixed costs are small and the economies of scale are small (small *MES*). Now, on each set of cost curves place a downward-sloping demand curve. Find the profit-maximizing point in each case.

Cutting Edge: Focus on New Technology

No such thing as a free lunch? Tell it to Web surfers on the Internet, where everything from computers and pet food to cold, hard cash is being given away.

Borrowing a page from television and other advertiser-supported media, scores of Web sites are giving away products and services in hope they will attract enough advertisers and shoppers to become profitable. . . .

Although free product samples, trial subscriptions and other come-ons have long been a staple of American commerce, the Internet giveaways are testing the staying power of fledgling Web companies, some of which are into their fourth or fifth year of bleeding red ink.

Indeed, last week EMachines, based in Irvine, said it could no longer afford to provide free Internet access to its customers.

The deals also often come with strings attached. According to the Federal Trade Commission, more than 90% of online merchants gather some kind of data about their visitors. And some operators, such as grocery service Streamline.com, ask that customers provide such personal data as the number and ages of children in a household.

Nevertheless, the proliferation of deals on the Net is transforming consumer shopping psychology. With price comparisons and contests just a mouse click away, con-sumers are acquiring a penchant for bargain hunting that Jack Benny would envy. . . .

Petsmart.com Inc.'s chief executive, Tom McGovern, for instance, has vowed that his company will never succumb to "the narcotic of free shipping." But he did confess to doing a little bargain hunting himself. Last year, he sprang for an offer for More.com to deliver razor blades for just the $1 product price. The health and fitness Web site pledges not to raise the price on its blades for as long as McGovern continues to order the product. . . .

"Any site that thinks it's going to have an advertising-driven strategy is probably misguided," said Alan Alper, who follows e-commerce for Gomez Advisors Inc. in Lincoln, Mass. "The bottom line is: There isn't a free lunch. You have to be selling something."

Of course, giveaways have proved popular—and profitable—in the old media.

"Who Wants to Be a Millionaire" is a hit on ABC, and the Fox challenger "Greed" has also scored well in the ratings. Still, experts marvel at the breadth of giveaways and promotions on the Internet by companies with far shallower pockets than the television networks.

"Loss leaders are not a new phenomenon . . . but what's so interesting is that merchants on the Web have taken it to a much further extreme," said Shane Greenstein, an associate professor of management at Northwestern University.

"The only reason these giveaways would make sense would be if consumers were loyal," Greenstein said, "But then the question arises, why would you expect consumer loyalty in cyberspace when we don't see that in the non-virtual world?"

Indeed, the proliferation of Web merchants has some consumers, such as Boston University professor Bruce D. Weinberg, playing one against another.

In recent months, Weinberg has been testing grocers in Boston, where four online firms compete to make home deliveries. One, Streamline.com, last year offered Weinberg $75 off the first order and delivered the groceries to his door for no additional charge. The company has since reduced the discount to $50, but Weinberg remains amazed at the generous deal.

"They bring the stuff to your door, sit it down on your counter and take back the returns—I don't know how they can afford to do it," Weinberg said. "I've just been blown away by the deals online. This is a great time to be a consumer."

Jube Shiver, Jr., "The Cutting Edge: Focus on Technology," *Los Angeles Times,* February 7, 2000, C1.

Los Angeles Times/February 7, 2000

Commentary

Microsoft Corporation harmed rivals by giving away its Internet Explorer browser rather than charging a price for it, at least that is what the case against Microsoft claimed. The complaint was that Microsoft undercut or sold below its cost of supplying that browser in order to drive Netscape out of business. Giving away products is becoming increasingly common in the New Economy.

Why would a firm give away its product? The reason depends on the existence of high fixed costs and very small marginal costs. Recall that fixed costs are the costs that cannot be changed in the short run. In many instances these costs are the costs necessary to enter a business or to introduce a product. Marginal costs are the additional costs of producing one more unit of the good or service being supplied.

Consider the production of a music CD. To produce the first CD, it is necessary to acquire and assemble the studio, the band, and the recovering equipment. The band is paid a performance fee, the equipment is purchased, and the studio is rented. Thus, if the production company were only to create one CD, the cost of that CD would be very high. But none of these expensive items are necessary to produce the second CD. All those expensive items are fixed costs to the music producer—they won't change as additional CDs are produced. The only thing necessary for the second CD is the duplicating equipment and the plastic disk. Thus, each additional CD costs pennies to produce. This means that the marginal cost of the first CD is very high, that of the second and subsequent ones have marginal costs that are near zero.

This kind of high fixed costs and small marginal costs is illustrated in the figure. The first CD's fixed costs are very high. The marginal cost curve drops

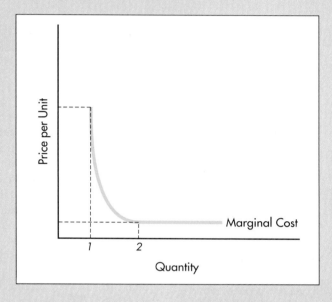

rapidly from the level of the huge fixed costs to near zero as additional CDs are produced.

Suppose it costs ten million dollars to create that first music CD and that the cost of the second CD is one dollar while the cost of the third CD, the fourth, and so on is only five cents—the cost of the plastic. How much should the production firm charge for a CD? Should it charge a high price, say the level of the fixed costs? If it does that and other firms are offering the same good or service, the firm will lose its market. The firm has to charge something close to its marginal cost in order not to lose out to rivals.

Many firms reason that because the price they can charge is so low, it is better to give the product away so as to entice consumers to purchase other more profitable goods or services. This is what Microsoft did. This is what AOL and other Internet service providers did. This, according to the article, is what the New Economy is all about.

Perfect Competition

Preview

Agriculture is often used as a real-life example of the perfectly competitive market structure, and indeed, many individual farmers are *price takers*, unable to affect the price of the product. Agriculture is a worldwide industry consisting of hundreds of millions of individual producers. To enter the industry in the low-income developing countries, all one needs is a small plot of land, seed, and access to water and tools. In the developed industrial nations, however, the average farm exceeds 400 acres and relies on combines and tractors costing several hundred thousand dollars, as well as on fertilizers and other materials. Nonetheless, the product is indistinguishable, and each individual firm is a very small part of the entire market. The grain from one farm is indistinguishable from that of another farm, and no single farm is able to increase the price of its grain and still sell the grain. Agriculture is not alone. In general, anything

that is a commodity—identical products sold by a number of sellers—is exchanged in a perfectly competitive market. ■

1. THE PERFECTLY COMPETITIVE FIRM IN THE SHORT RUN

We begin our analysis of perfect competition by taking the viewpoint of an individual farmer who is currently in business, having already procured the necessary land, tools, equipment, and employees to operate a farm. After we discuss how much the individual farmer decides to produce and how the price of the farmer's produce is determined, we discuss the entry and the exit processes. We examine how someone begins a business and how someone leaves or exits the business. We then alter our perspective and look at the market as a whole. Let's start our discussion by reviewing the characteristics of a perfectly competitive market.

1.a. The Definition of Perfect Competition

1. What is perfect competition?

Perfect competition is a firm behavior when many firms produce identical products and entry is easy.

A market that is perfectly competitive exhibits the following characteristics:

1. There are many sellers. No one firm can have an influence on market price. Each firm is such a minute part of the total market that however much the firm produces—nothing at all, as much as it can, or some amount in between—it will have no effect on the market price.

2. The products sold by the firms in the industry are identical. The product sold by one firm can be substituted perfectly for the product sold by any other firm in the industry. Products are not differentiated by packaging, advertising, or quality.

3. Entry is easy and there are many potential entrants. There are no huge economies of scale relative to the size of the market. Laws do not require producers to obtain licenses or pay for the privilege of producing. Other firms cannot take action to keep someone from entering the business. Firms can stop producing and can sell or liquidate the business without difficulty.

4. Buyers and sellers have perfect information. Buyers know the price and quantity at each firm. Each firm knows what the other firms are charging and how they are behaving.

1.b. The Demand Curve of the Individual Firm

2. What does the demand curve facing the individual firm look like, and why?

A firm in a perfectly competitive market structure is said to be a *price taker* because the price of the product is determined by market demand and supply, and the individual firm simply has to accept that price. In 2000 the world market price of corn was about $1 per bushel, and nearly 20 billion bushels worldwide were produced. Approximately 46 percent of all the corn harvested in the world comes from the United States. Nevertheless, the average farm in the United States produces an extremely small percentage of the total quantity harvested each year.

What would occur if one U.S. farmer decided to set the price of corn at $1.20 per bushel when the market price was $1 per bushel? According to the model of a perfectly competitive market, no one would purchase the higher-priced corn because the identical product could be obtained without difficulty elsewhere for $1 per bushel. In this instance, what the model predicts is what actually occurs in the real-world corn market. The grain silo owner who buys the farmers' grain would simply pass on that farm's grain and move to the next truckful of grain at $1 per bushel. By setting a price above the market price, the individual farmer may sell nothing.

The individual firm in a perfectly competitive industry is a price taker because it cannot charge more than the market price and it will not charge less.

Is an individual farmer likely to set a price of $.80 per bushel when the market price is $1 per bushel? Not in a perfectly competitive market. All of the produce from a single farm can be sold at the market price. Why would a farmer sell at $.80 per bushel when he or she can get $1 per bushel? The individual farm is a price taker because it cannot charge more than the market price and it will not charge less.

You could think of price takers as being the sellers in a big auction. The potential buyers bid against each other for the product until a price is determined. The product is then sold at that price. The seller has no control over the price.

Market demand and supply are shown in Figure 1(a). The demand curve of a single firm is shown in Figure 1(b). The horizontal line at the market price is the demand curve faced by an individual firm in a perfectly competitive market structure. It shows that the individual firm is a price taker—that the demand curve is per-

---

Figure 1

Market Demand and Supply and Single-Firm Demand for Corn

Market demand and supply are shown in Figure 1(a). The equilibrium price is $1 per bushel, and 20 billion bushels are produced and sold. The equilibrium price defines the horizontal, or perfectly elastic, demand curve faced by the individual perfectly competitive firm in Figure 1(b).

(a) Market

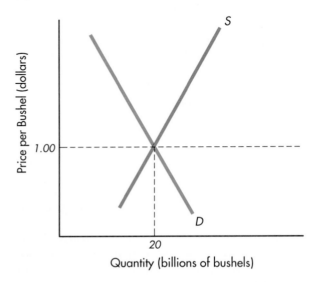

(b) Individual Firm

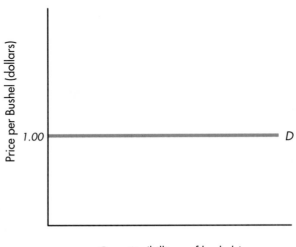

fectly elastic. The question facing the individual firm in a perfectly competitive industry is how much to produce, not what price to charge.

1.c. Profit Maximization

3. How does the firm maximize profit in the short run?

Profit maximization occurs at the output level where MR = MC.

4. At what point does a firm decide to suspend operations?

MR = MC is the profit-maximizing or loss-minimizing output level.

We know that profit is maximized when *MR* = *MC*. Profit rises when the revenue brought in by the sale of one more unit (one more bushel) is greater than the cost of producing that unit. Conversely, if the cost of producing one more unit is greater than the amount of revenue brought in by selling that unit, profit declines with the production of that unit. Only when marginal revenue and marginal cost are the same is profit at a maximum, as illustrated in Figure 2.[1]

With a price of $1 per bushel, the individual farm maximizes profit by producing 9 bushels. We can illustrate how much profit the individual firm in perfect competition earns or whether it makes a loss, by calculating total costs at the quantity where *MR* = *MC* and comparing that with total revenue.

In Figure 2, the price per bushel of $1 exceeds the cost per bushel (average total cost, $.8733) by the distance *BC* ($.1267) when 9 bushels are produced. This amount ($.1267) is the profit per bushel. The total profit is the rectangle *ABCD* (highlighted in the table).

Figure 3 illustrates what occurs to the individual firm in a perfectly competitive market as the market price changes. The only curve in Figure 3 that changes as a result of the price change is the perfectly elastic demand curve (which is also the price line and the marginal-revenue curve). Let's assume that the market price changes to $.70 per bushel so that the individual farm's demand curve shifts down. Whether the firm is making a profit is determined by finding the new quantity at which the new marginal-revenue curve, *MR₂*, *equals the marginal-cost curve, at point F*, and then tracing a vertical line from point *F* to the *ATC* curve at point *G*. The distance *FG* is the profit or loss per unit of output. If the demand curve is above the *ATC* curve at that point, the firm is making a profit. If the *ATC* curve exceeds the price line, as is the case in Figure 3, the firm is suffering a loss.

A profit cannot be made as long as the price is less than the average-cost curve, because the cost per bushel (*ATC*) exceeds the revenue per bushel (price). At a price of $.70 per bushel, marginal revenue and marginal cost are equal as the sixth bushel is produced (see Figure 3 and the highlighted bar in the table), but the average total cost is greater than the price. The cost per bushel (*ATC*) is $.8667, which is higher than the price or revenue per bushel of $.70. Thus, the firm makes a loss, shown as the rectangle *EFGH* in Figure 3.

Recall that an economic loss means that opportunity costs are not being covered by revenues; that is, the owners could do better in another line of business. An economic loss means that a firm is confronted with the choice of whether to continue

---

[1]Marginal revenue and marginal cost could be equal at small levels of production and sales, such as with the first bushel, but profit would definitely not be at its greatest level. The reason is that marginal cost is falling with the first unit of production—the marginal cost of the second unit is less than the marginal cost of the first unit. Since marginal revenue is the same for both the first and second units, profit actually rises as quantity increases. Profit maximization requires that marginal revenue equal marginal cost *and that marginal cost be rising*. Since marginal revenue and marginal cost are the same for the ninth bushel and marginal cost is rising, the ninth bushel is the profit-maximizing level of output.

Figure 2

Profit Maximization

The profit-maximization point for a single firm is shown for a price of $1 per bushel. Marginal revenue and marginal cost are equal at the profit-maximization point, 9 bushels. At quantities less than 9 bushels, marginal revenue exceeds marginal cost, so increased production would raise profits. At quantities greater than 9, marginal revenue is less than marginal cost, so reduced production would increase profits. The point at which profit is maximized is shown by the highlighted row in the table. The profit per unit is the difference between the price line and the average-total-cost curve at the profit-maximizing quantity. Total profit ($1.14) is the rectangle ABCD, an area that is equal to the profit per unit times the number of units.

Total Output (Q)	Price (P)	Total Revenue (TR)	Total Cost (TC)	Total Profit (TR − TC)	Marginal Revenue (MR)	Marginal Cost (MC)	Average Total Cost (ATC)
0	$1	$ 0	$ 1.00	−$1.00			
1	$1	$ 1	$ 2.00	−$1.00	$1	$1.00	$2.00
2	$1	$ 2	$ 2.80	−$ .80	$1	$ .80	$1.40
3	$1	$ 3	$ 3.50	−$ .50	$1	$ .70	$1.1667
4	$1	$ 4	$ 4.00	$ .00	$1	$ .50	$1.00
5	$1	$ 5	$ 4.50	$ .50	$1	$ .50	$ .90
6	$1	$ 6	$ 5.20	$ .80	$1	$ .70	$ .8667
7	$1	$ 7	$ 6.00	$1.00	$1	$ .80	$ .8571
8	$1	$ 8	$ 6.86	$1.14	$1	$ .86	$ .8575
9	$1	$ 9	$ 7.86	$1.14	$1	$1.00	$ .8733
10	$1	$10	$ 9.36	$ .64	$1	$1.50	$ .936
11	$1	$11	$12.00	−$1.00	$1	$2.64	$1.09

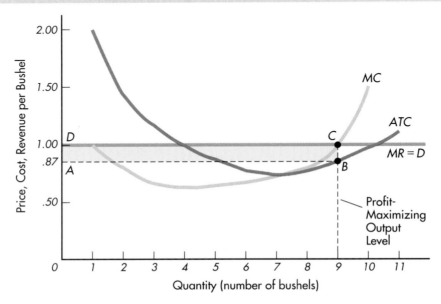

Figure 3

Loss Minimization

In Figure 3 the price changed from $1 per bushel to $.70 per bushel. The profit-maximization, or loss-minimization, point is the level of output where $MR = MC$. If, at this output level, the price is less than the corresponding average-cost curve, the firm makes a loss. At a price of $.70 per bushel, a loss is incurred—the loss-minimizing level of output is 6 bushels, as shown by the highlighted bar in the table. The total loss is the rectangle *EFGH*.

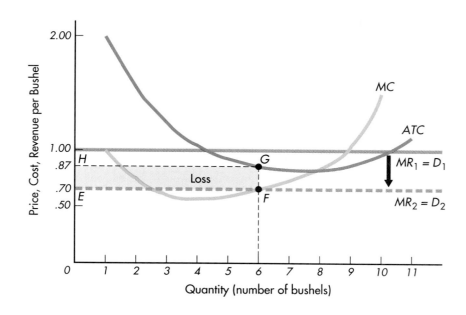

Total Output (Q)	Price (P)	Total Revenue (TR)	Total Cost (TC)	Total Profit (TR − TC)	Marginal Revenue (MR)	Marginal Cost (MC)	Average Total Cost (ATC)
0	$.70	$0	$ 1.00	−$1.00			
1	$.70	$ .70	$ 2.00	−$1.30	$.70	$1.00	$2.00
2	$.70	$1.40	$ 2.80	−$1.40	$.70	$ .80	$1.40
3	$.70	$2.10	$ 3.50	−$1.40	$.70	$ .70	$1.1667
4	$.70	$2.80	$ 4.00	−$1.20	$.70	$ .50	$1.00
5	$.70	$3.50	$ 4.50	−$1.00	$.70	$ .50	$ .90
6	$.70	$4.20	$ 5.20	−$1.00	$.70	$ .70	$ .8667
7	$.70	$4.90	$ 6.00	−$1.10	$.70	$ .80	$ .8571
8	$.70	$5.60	$ 6.86	−$1.26	$.70	$ .86	$ .8575
9	$.70	$6.30	$ 7.86	−$1.56	$.70	$1.00	$ .8733
10	$.70	$7.00	$ 9.36	−$2.36	$.70	$1.50	$ .936
11	$.70	$7.70	$12.00	−$4.30	$.70	$2.64	$1.09

producing, shut down temporarily, or shut down permanently. The decision depends on which alternative has the lowest opportunity cost.

1.d. Short-Run Break-Even and Shutdown Prices

5. When will a firm shut down permanently?

In the short run, certain costs, such as rent on land and equipment, must be paid whether or not any output is produced. These are the firm's fixed costs. If a firm has purchased equipment and buildings but does not produce, the firm still has to pay for the equipment and buildings. Thus, the decision about whether to produce or to temporarily suspend operations depends on which option promises the lesser costs. In order to continue producing in the short run, the firm must earn sufficient revenue to pay all of the *variable* costs (the costs that change as output changes), because then the excess of revenue over variable costs will enable the firm to pay some of its fixed costs. If all of the variable costs cannot be paid for out of revenue, then the firm should suspend operations temporarily because by continuing to produce, the firm must pay its fixed costs as well as those variable costs in excess of revenue.

Does suspending operations mean quitting the business altogether—shutting down permanently? It may, but it need not. The decision depends on the long-term outlook. If the long-term outlook indicates that revenue will exceed costs, then production is warranted. However, if the outlook is for continued low prices and the inability to cover costs, a firm would be better off quitting the business altogether.

To see how producing at a loss can at times be better than not producing at all, let's return to the individual farm in Figure 4. At a price of \$.70 per bushel, the output at which $MR = MC$ is 6 bushels, as shown by the highlighted bar in the table. At 6 bushels, total revenue is \$4.20 and total cost is \$5.20. The farm loses \$1 by producing 6 bushels. The question is whether to produce at all. If production is stopped, the fixed cost of \$1 must still be paid. Thus, the farmer is indifferent between producing 6 bushels and losing \$1 or shutting down and losing \$1. Should the price be less than the minimum point of the average-variable-cost curve (AVC), as would occur at any price less than $P = \$.70$ per bushel, the farm is not earning enough to cover its variable costs (see Figure 4 and accompanying table). By continuing to produce, the farm will lose more than it would lose if it suspended operations or shut down until the outlook improved. The minimum point of the average-variable-cost curve is the **shutdown price.** If the market price is less than the minimum point of the AVC curve, then the firm will incur fewer losses if it does not produce than if it continues to produce in the short run.

shutdown price: the minimum point of the average-variable-cost curve

At prices above the minimum point of the average-variable-cost curve, the excess of revenue over variable cost means that some fixed costs can be paid. A firm is better off producing than shutting down because by producing it is able to earn enough revenue to pay all the variable costs and some of the fixed costs. If the firm does not produce, it will still have to pay all of the fixed costs. When the price equals the minimum point of the average-total-cost curve, the firm is earning just enough revenue to pay for all of its costs, fixed and variable. This point is called the **break-even price.** At the break-even price, economic profit is zero—all costs are being covered, including opportunity costs. Because costs include the opportunity costs of the resources already owned by the entrepreneur—his or her own labor and capital—zero economic profit means that the entrepreneur could not do better in another activity. Zero economic profit is normal profit, profit just sufficient to keep the entrepreneur in this line of business.

6. What is the break-even price?

break-even price: a price that is equal to the minimum point of the average-total-cost curve

Figure 4

Shutdown Price

When the firm is making a loss, it must decide whether to continue producing or suspend operations and not produce. The decision depends on which alternative has higher costs. When the price is equal to or greater than the minimum point of the average-variable-cost curve, $.70, the firm is earning sufficient revenue to pay for all of the variable costs. When the price is less than the minimum point of the average-variable-cost curve, the firm is not covering all of its variable costs. In that case the firm is better off shutting down its operations. For this reason, the minimum point of the *AVC* curve is called the *shutdown price*. The *break-even price* is the minimum point of the *ATC* curve because at that point all costs are being paid.

Total Output (Q)	Price (P)	Total Revenue (TR)	Total Cost (TC)	Total Profit (TR − TC)	Marginal Revenue (MR)	Marginal Cost (MC)	Average Total Cost (ATC)	Average Variable Cost (AVC)
0	$.70	$0	$ 1.00	−$1.00				
1	$.70	$ .70	$ 2.00	−$1.30	$.70	$1.00	$2.00	$1.00
2	$.70	$1.40	$ 2.80	−$1.40	$.70	$ .80	$1.40	$ .90
3	$.70	$2.10	$ 3.50	−$1.40	$.70	$ .70	$1.1667	$ .833
4	$.70	$2.80	$ 4.00	−$1.20	$.70	$ .50	$1.00	$ .75
5	$.70	$3.50	$ 4.50	−$1.00	$.70	$ .50	$ .90	$ .70
6	$.70	$4.20	$ 5.20	−$1.00	$.70	$ .70	$ .8667	$ .70
7	$.70	$4.90	$ 6.00	−$1.10	$.70	$ .80	$ .8571	$ .714
8	$.70	$5.60	$ 6.86	−$1.26	$.70	$ .86	$ .8575	$ .7325
9	$.70	$6.30	$ 7.86	−$1.56	$.70	$1.00	$ .8733	$ .7622
10	$.70	$7.00	$ 9.36	−$2.36	$.70	$1.50	$ .936	$ .836
11	$.70	$7.70	$12.00	−$4.30	$.70	$2.64	$1.09	$1.00

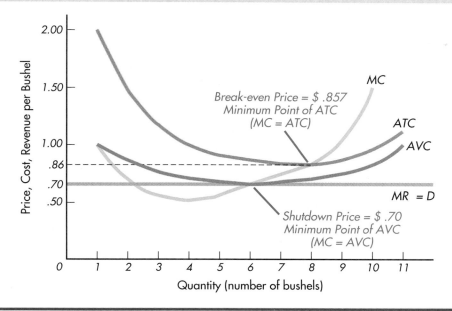

The shutdown price is the price that is equal to the minimum point of the *AVC* curve. The break-even price is the price that is equal to the minimum point of the *ATC* curve.

In the examples just discussed, the firm continues to operate at a loss because variable costs are being covered and the long-term outlook is favorable. Many firms decide to operate for a while at a loss, then suspend operations temporarily, and finally shut down permanently. A firm will shut down permanently if all costs cannot be covered in the long run. In the long run, the minimum point of the *ATC* curve is the permanent shutdown point. Price must exceed the minimum point of the *ATC* curve in the long run if the firm is to remain in business. Of the 80,000 businesses that shut down permanently in 1997, most went through a period in which they continued to operate even though variable costs were not being covered by revenue.

1.e. The Firm's Supply Curve in the Short Run

7. What is the firm's supply curve in the short run?

As long as revenue equals or exceeds variable costs, an individual firm will produce the quantity at which marginal revenue and marginal cost are equal. This means that the individual firm's supply curve is the portion of the *MC* curve that lies above the *AVC* curve. An individual firm's supply curve shows the quantity that a firm will produce and offer for sale at each price. When the price is less than the minimum point of the *AVC* curve, a firm incurs fewer losses from not producing than from producing. The firm thus produces and supplies nothing, and there is no supply curve. When the price is greater than the minimum point of the *AVC* curve, the firm will produce and offer for sale the quantity yielded at the point where the *MC* curve and the *MR* line intersect for each price. The supply curve is thus the *MC* curve. The portion of the *MC* curve lying above the minimum point of the *AVC* curve is the individual firm's supply curve in the short run.

In our example of an individual farm illustrated in Figure 4, nothing is produced at a price of $.50 per bushel. At $.70 per bushel, the farm produces 6 bushels in the short run; at $1 per bushel, the farm produces 9 bushels. The higher the price, the greater the quantity produced and offered for sale.

8. What is the firm's supply curve in the long run?

A firm may continue to produce and offer its products for sale even if it is earning a negative economic profit, as long as it earns enough revenue to pay its variable costs and expects revenue to grow enough to pay all costs eventually. If the business does not improve and losses continue to pile up, the firm will shut down permanently. In the long run, the firm must be able to earn enough revenue to pay all of its costs. If it does not, the business will not continue to operate. If the firm does earn enough to pay its costs, the firm will produce and offer for sale the quantity of output yielded at the point where $MR = MC$. This means that the firm's supply curve is the portion of its *MC* curve that lies above the minimum point of the *ATC* curve.

RECAP

1. The firm maximizes profit or minimizes losses by producing at the output level at which *MR* and *MC* are equal.

2. In order to remain in business, the firm must earn sufficient revenue to pay for all of its variable costs. The shutdown price is the price that is just equal to the minimum point of the *AVC* curve.

3. The firm's break-even price is the price that is just equal to the minimum point of the *ATC* curve.

4. The portion of the marginal-cost curve lying above the minimum point of the *AVC* curve is the firm's short-run supply curve.

5. The portion of the marginal-cost curve lying above the minimum point of the *ATC* curve is the firm's long-run supply curve.

2. THE LONG RUN

In the short run, at least one of the resources cannot be altered. This means that new firms cannot be organized and begin producing. Thus the supply of firms in an industry is fixed in the short run. In the long run, of course, all quantities of resources can be changed. Buildings can be built or purchased and machinery accumulated and placed into production. New firms may arise as entrepreneurs not currently in the industry see that they could earn more than they are currently earning and decide to expand into new businesses.

Exit and entry are long-run phenomena.

Entry and exit can both occur in the long run. On average, 4.5 percent of the total number of farms go out of business each year, and more than half of them file for bankruptcy. The numbers leaving the business increased substantially in the 1980s as the costs of doing business rose and agricultural prices fell. On average, 6.5 percent of existing farms left the agricultural industry each year in the 1980s. In the 1990s, the rate declined to about the previous average.

How does exit occur? Entrepreneurs may sell their businesses and move to another industry, or they may use the bankruptcy laws to exit the industry. A sole proprietor or partnership may file Chapter 13 personal bankruptcy; a corporation may file Chapter 7 bankruptcy or a Chapter 11 reorganization; a farmer may file

The price taker can do nothing but accept the market price and sell at that price. When times are bad, the market price may be so low that some of the price takers must exit the market. In this photo, farmers are gathered at an auction as several must liquidate and leave the business. Others attend the auction to purchase equipment at bargain basement prices.

Chapter 12. From the mid-1970s to the present, the average birthrate for all industries (the percent of total businesses that begin during a year) has been just over 11.2 percent, and the average death rate (the percent of total businesses that disappear during a year) has been 9.6 percent.

2.a. The Market Supply Curve and Exit and Entry

When additional firms enter the industry and begin producing the product, the market supply curve shifts out.

When firms leave the industry, the market supply curve shifts in.

Recall from Chapter 3 that the market supply curve shifts when the number of suppliers changes. In the corn-producing business, when new farms enter the market, the total quantity of corn supplied at each price increases. In other words, entry causes the market supply curve to shift out to the right.

Conversely, exit means fewer producers and lower quantities supplied at each price, and a leftward or inward shift of the market supply curve. Suppose some existing farms are not covering their costs and believe the future is not bright enough to warrant continued production. As a result, they shut down their operations and sell their equipment and land. As the number of farms in the industry declines, everything else held constant, the market supply curve shifts to the left—as long as those remaining in the business produce the same quantity, or less, as they did before the farms exited.

2.b. Normal Profit in the Long Run

One of the principal characteristics of the perfectly competitive market structure is that entry and exit can occur easily. Thus, entry and exit occur whenever firms are earning more or less than a *normal profit* (zero economic profit). When a normal profit is being earned, there is no entry or exit. This condition is the long-run equilibrium.

The process of establishing the long-run position is shown in Figure 5. The market demand and supply curves for corn are shown in Figure 5(a), and the cost and revenue curves for a representative firm in the industry are shown in Figure 5(b). Let's assume that the market price is $1. Let's also assume that at $1 per bushel, the demand curve facing the individual farm (the price line) is equal to the minimum point of the ATC curve. The quantity produced is 9 bushels. The individual farm and the industry are in equilibrium. There is no reason for entry or exit to occur, and no reason for individual farms to change their scale of operation.

To illustrate how the process of reaching the long-run equilibrium occurs in the perfectly competitive market structure, let's begin with the market in equilibrium at $S_1 = D_1$. Then let's suppose a major agricultural disaster strikes Russia and Russia turns to the United States to buy agricultural products. As a result of the increased Russian demand, the total demand for U.S. corn increases, as shown by the rightward shift of the demand curve to D_2 in Figure 5(a). In the short run, the market price rises to $1.50 per bushel, where the new market demand curve intersects the initial market supply curve, S_1. This raises the demand curve for the individual farm to the horizontal line at $1.50 per bushel. In the short run, the individual farms in the industry increase production (by adding variable inputs) from 9 bushels to 10 bushels, the point in Figure 5(b) where $MC = MR_2 = \$1.50$, and earn economic profit of the amount shown by the yellow rectangle.

The above-normal profit attracts others to the farming business. The result of the new entry and expansion is a rightward shift of the market supply curve. How far does the market supply curve shift? It shifts until the market price is low enough that firms in the industry earn normal profit. Let us suppose that the costs of doing busi-

Figure 5

Economic Profit in the Long Run

Market demand and supply determine the price and the demand curve faced by the single perfectly competitive firm. At a price of $1 per bushel, the individual farm is earning normal profit. After an agricultural disaster in Russia increases the demand for U.S. corn, the price rises to $1.50. At $1.50 per bushel, the single farm makes a profit equal to the yellow rectangle. Above-normal profits induce new farms to begin raising corn and existing farms to increase their production.

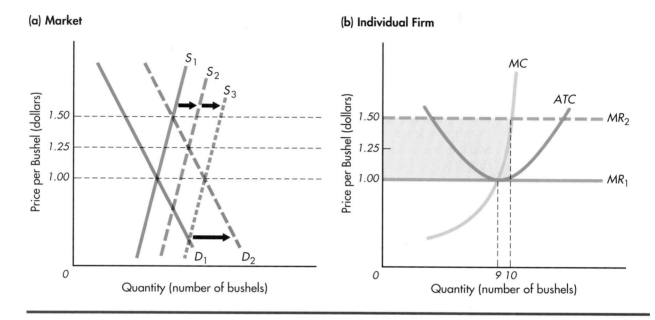

(a) Market

(b) Individual Firm

ness do not rise as the market expands. Then, if the market supply curve shifts to S_2, the new market price, $1.25, is less than the former price of $1.50 but still high enough for firms to earn above-normal profits. These profits are sufficient inducement for more firms to enter, causing the supply curve to shift farther right. The supply curve continues to shift until there is no incentive for additional firms to enter—that is, until firms are earning the normal profit, where price is equal to the minimum ATC, shown as S_3 in Figure 5(a). When the adjustment stops, firms are just earning the normal profit.

In the long run, perfectly competitive firms earn normal profits.

2.c. The Predictions of the Model of Perfect Competition

According to the model of perfect competition, whenever above-normal profits are earned by existing firms, entry occurs until a normal profit is earned by all firms. Conversely, whenever economic losses occur, exit takes place until a normal profit is made by all remaining firms.

It is so important to keep in mind the distinctions between economic and accounting terms that we repeatedly remind you of them. A *zero economic profit* is a

9. What are the long-run equilibrium results of a perfectly competitive market?

normal accounting profit, or just *normal profit.* It is the profit just sufficient to keep a business owner or investors in a particular line of business, the point where revenue exactly equals total opportunity costs. Business owners and investors earning a normal profit are earning enough to cover their opportunity costs—they could not do better by changing—but are not earning more than their opportunity costs. A *loss* refers to a situation where revenue is not sufficient to pay all of the opportunity costs. A firm can earn a positive accounting profit and yet be experiencing a loss, not earning a normal profit.

The long-run equilibrium position of the perfectly competitive market structure shows firms producing at the minimum point of their long-run average-total-cost curves. If the price is above the minimum point of the *ATC* curve, then firms are earning above-normal profit and entry will occur. If the price is less than the minimum of the *ATC* curve, exit will occur. Only when price equals the minimum point of the *ATC* curve will neither entry nor exit take place.

Producing at the minimum of the *ATC* curve means that firms are producing with the lowest possible costs. They could not alter the way they produce and produce less expensively. They could not alter the resources they use and produce less expensively.

Firms produce at a level where marginal cost and marginal revenue are the same. Since marginal revenue and price are the same in a perfectly competitive market, firms produce where marginal cost equals price. This means that firms are employing resources until the marginal cost to them of producing the last unit of a good just equals the price of the last unit. Moreover, since price is equal to marginal cost, consumers are paying a price that is as low as it can get; the price just covers the marginal cost of producing that good or service. There is no waste—no one could be made better off without making someone else worse off. Economists refer to this result as **economic efficiency.**

economic efficiency: when the price of a good or service just covers the marginal cost of producing that good or service and people are getting the goods they want

2.c.1. Producer Surplus
Efficiency is the term economists give to the situation where firms are producing with as little cost as they can (minimum point of the *ATC* curve) and consumers are getting the products they desire at a price that is equal to the marginal cost of producing those goods. To say that a competitive market is efficient is to say that all market participants get the greatest benefits possible from market exchange.[2]

How do we measure the benefits of the market? In the chapter on consumer choice, we discussed the concept of consumer surplus, indicating that it is a measure of the difference between what consumers would be willing to pay for a product and the price they actually have to pay to buy the product. Consumer surplus is a measure of the benefits consumers receive from market exchange. A similar measure exists for the firm. It is called **producer surplus.** Producer surplus indicates the difference between the price firms would have been willing to accept for their products and the price they actually receive.

producer surplus: the difference between the price firms would have been willing to accept for their products and the price they actually receive

---

[2]Economists have classified efficiency into several categories. *Productive efficiency* refers to the firm's using the least-cost combination of resources to produce any output level. This output level may not be the goods consumers want, however. *Allocative efficiency* is the term given to the situation where firms are producing the goods consumers most want and consumers are paying a price just equal to the marginal cost of producing the goods. Allocative efficiency may occur when firms are not producing at their most efficient level. Economic efficiency exists when both productive and allocative efficiency occur.

Figure 6

Producer and Consumer Surpluses

Since the firm is willing to sell the product at the marginal cost and since the firm receives the market price, the difference between the two is a bonus to the firm, a bonus of market exchange. This bonus is producer surplus. Figure 6 illustrates total producer surplus in a competitive market, the sum of the producer surplus received by each firm in the market. Producer surplus is the area below the price line and above the supply curve. Also pictured is total consumer surplus. Recall that consumer surplus is the difference between what the consumer would be willing to pay for a good, the demand curve, and the price actually paid. The sum of producer and consumer surplus represents the total benefits that come from exchange in a market: benefits that accrue to the consumer plus those that accrue to the firm.

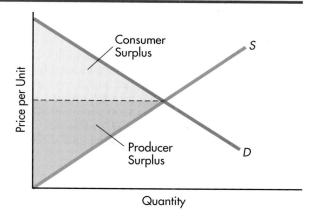

Since the firm is willing to sell the product at the marginal cost, as long as marginal cost is greater than average variable cost, and since the firm receives the market price, the difference between the two is a bonus to the firm, a bonus resulting from market exchange. This bonus is producer surplus.

Consumer surplus = area above equilibrium price and below the demand curve

Producer surplus = area below equilibrium price and above the supply curve

Figure 6 illustrates consumer and producer surplus in a competitive market. The sum of producer and consumer surplus represents the total benefits that come from exchange in a market: benefits that accrue to the consumer plus those that accrue to the firm.

The primary result of perfect competition is that things just do not get any better: total consumer and producer surplus is at a maximum. Any interference with the market exchange reduces the total surplus. Consider rent control on apartments, for instance. The market for rental apartments is pictured in Figure 7. As shown in Figure 7, the market solution would yield a monthly rent of $400. The consumer surplus would be the area *ABC*; the producer surplus would be the area *ABD*. Now, suppose the city imposes a rent control at $300 per month. The producer surplus changes to area *EFD* while the consumer surplus changes to *EFHC*. Clearly the total surplus has been reduced. The question policymakers must decide is whether the additional benefits to consumers offset the losses to producers.

Figure 7

Rent Control and Market Efficiency

The market for rental apartments is pictured in this graph; the market solution would yield a monthly rent of $400. The consumer surplus would be the area *ABC*; the producer surplus would be the area *ABD*. Now, suppose the city imposes rent control at $300 per month. The producer surplus changes to area *EFD* while the consumer surplus changes to *EFHC*. The total surplus has been reduced by the rent control.

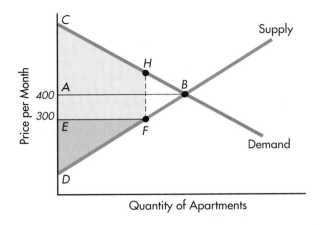

RECAP

1. Entry occurs when firms are earning above-normal profit or positive economic profit.

2. A temporary shutdown occurs when firms are not covering their variable costs in the short run. In the long run, exit occurs when firms are not covering all costs.

3. The short-run market supply curve is the horizontal sum of the supply curves of all individual firms in the industry.

4. In a perfectly competitive market, firms produce goods at the least cost, and consumers purchase the goods they most desire at a price that is equal to the marginal cost of producing the good. There is no waste—no one could be made better off without making someone else worse off. Economists refer to this result as economic efficiency.

5. Producer surplus is the benefit the firm receives for engaging in market exchange; it is the difference between the price the firm would be willing to sell its goods for and the price the firm actually receives.

6. Consumer surplus is the area below the demand curve and above the equilibrium price; producer surplus is the area above the supply curve and below the equilibrium price.

SUMMARY

❓ What is perfect competition?

1. Perfect competition is a market structure in which there are many firms that are producing an identical product and where entry and exit are easy. *§1.a*

❓ What does the demand curve facing the individual firm look like, and why?

2. The demand curve of the individual firm is a horizontal line at the market price. Each firm is a price taker. *§1.b*

? How does the firm maximize profit in the short run?

3. The individual firm maximizes profit by producing at the point where $MR = MC$. *§1.c*

? At what point does a firm decide to suspend operations?

4. A firm will shut down operations temporarily if price does not exceed the minimum point of the average-variable-cost curve. *§1.c*

? When will a firm shut down permanently?

5. A firm will shut down operations permanently if price does not exceed the minimum point of the average-total-cost curve in the long run. *§1.d*

? What is the break-even price?

6. The firm breaks even when revenue and cost are equal—when the demand curve (price) just equals the minimum point of the average-total-cost curve. *§1.d*

? What is the firm's supply curve in the short run?

7. The firm's short-run supply curve is the portion of its marginal-cost curve that lies above the minimum point of the average-variable-cost curve. *§1.e*

? What is the firm's supply curve in the long run?

8. The firm produces at the point where marginal cost equals marginal revenue, as long as marginal revenue exceeds the minimum point of the average-total-cost curve. Thus, the firm's long-run supply curve is the portion of its marginal-cost curve that lies above the minimum point of the average-total-cost curve. *§1.e*

? What are the long-run equilibrium results of a perfectly competitive market?

9. In the long run, all firms operating in perfect competition will earn a normal profit by producing at the lowest possible cost, and all consumers will buy the goods and services they most want at a price equal to the marginal cost of producing the goods and services. *§2.c*

10. Producer surplus is the difference between what a firm would be willing to produce and sell a good for and the price the firm actually receives for the good. Consumer surplus is the difference between what an individual would be willing to pay for a good and what the individual actually has to pay. Total consumer and producer surpluses are at a maximum in a perfectly competitive market. *§2.c.1*

KEY TERMS

shutdown price *§1.d*
break-even price *§1.d*

economic efficiency *§2.c*
producer surplus *§2.c.1*

EXERCISES

1. Cost figures for a hypothetical firm are given in the following table. Use them for the exercises below. The firm is selling in a perfectly competitive market.

Output	Fixed Cost	AFC	Variable Cost	AVC	Total Cost	ATC	MC
1	$50		$ 30				
2	$50		$ 50				
3	$50		$ 80				
4	$50		$120				
5	$50		$170				

a. Fill in the blank columns.
b. What is the minimum price needed by the firm to break even?
c. What is the shutdown price?
d. At a price of $40, what output level would the firm produce? What would its profits be?

2. Label the curves in the following graph.

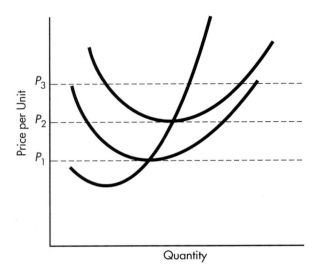

a. At each market price, P_1, P_2, and P_3, what output level would the firm produce?
b. What profit would be earned if the market price was P_1?
c. What are the shutdown and break-even prices?

3. Why might a firm continue to produce in the short run even though the market price is less than its average total cost?

4. Explain why the demand curve facing the individual firm in a perfectly competitive industry is a horizontal line.

5. Explain what occurs in the long run in a constant-cost industry, an increasing-cost industry, and a decreasing-cost industry when the market demand declines (shifts in).

6. What can you expect from an industry in perfect competition in the long run? What will price be? What quantity will be produced? What will be the relation between marginal cost, average cost, and price?

7. Assume that the market for illegal drugs is an example of a perfectly competitive market structure. Describe what the perfectly competitive market model predicts for illegal drugs in the long run. What

is likely to be the impact of the U.S. government's war on drugs in the short run? In the long run?

8. If no real-life industry meets the conditions of the perfectly competitive model exactly, why do we study perfect competition? What is the relevance of the model to the decision by Estée Lauder to switch careers? Why might it shed some light on pollution, acid rain, and other social problems?

9. Using the model of perfect competition, explain what it means to say, "Too much electricity is generated," or "Too little education is produced." Would the firm be producing at the bottom of the *ATC* curve if too much or too little was being produced?

10. Private swimming pools can be dangerous. There are serious accidents each year in those areas of the United States where backyard pools are common. Should pools be banned? In other words, should the market for swimming pools be eliminated? Answer this in terms of producer and consumer surplus.

11. Discuss whether the following are examples of perfectly competitive industries.
    a. The U.S. stock market
    b. The automobile industry
    c. The consumer electronics market
    d. The market for college students

12. Macy's was making millions of dollars in profits when it declared bankruptcy. Explain Macy's decision.

13. Entry and exit of firms occur in the long run but not the short run. Why? What is meant by the long run and the short run? Would you say that entry is more or less difficult than exit?

14. Use the following data for the exercises below.

Price	Quantity Supplied	Quantity Demanded
$20	30	0
$18	25	5
$16	20	10
$14	15	15
$12	10	20
$10	5	25
$ 8	0	30

a. What is the equilibrium price and quantity?
b. Draw the demand and supply curves. If this represents perfect competition, are the curves individual-firm or market curves? How is the quantity supplied derived?

c. Show the consumer surplus. Show the producer surplus.

d. Suppose that a price ceiling of $12 was imposed. How would this change the consumer and producer surplus? Suppose a price floor of $16 was imposed. How would this change the consumer and producer surplus?

15. Explain the following statement: "The market can better determine the value of polluting than the politicians. Rather than assign an emission fee to a polluting firm, simply allow firms to purchase the rights to pollute."

Internet Exercises/ Resources

For Internet exercises and web resources related to this chapter, go to **http://college.hmco.com.**

Food Marketers Show a Taste for Video Growth

CHICAGO—Video rental and sales in the supermarket industry have, in the last several years, gone from an afterthought to a major moneymaker. That was the consensus of video suppliers, fixturing companies, and manufacturers at the Food Marketing Institute's annual Supermarket Industry Convention, held May 2–6 at McCormick Place here.

"Video is no longer a loss leader in supermarkets," said Stewart Gershenbaum, VP of the Midwest division for JD Store Equipment of Lombard, Ill. "The change has accrued over the last three years. Before, supermarkets weren't marketing video the way they should—all the space they'd devote to video was 20 feet of wall. Now they're operating 5,000-square-foot, and larger, video sections." The St. Louis-based Schnucks supermarket chain, for instance, said Gershenbaum, "has a store-within-a-store setup, and it's the biggest video entity in St. Louis." . . .

Executives of Selectrak Family Video of Hillside, Ill., which leases video management programs to 200 stores across the country, reported an increase in rental revenues this past year—a testament, they say, to the increasing viability of video in supermarkets. "Unlike the rest of the industry, which reports flat rentals, ours continue to rise," said marketing coordinator Tamara Sokolec.

Selectrak provides fixtures, racking, custom computer setups, and free marketing support to its clients. "Over the last year, we've put a great deal of effort into marketing," said Sokolec, who attributed Selectrak's rental increase to that stepped-up marketing effort. . . .

For many supermarkets, video rental vending machines are the way to go. Michael Malet, president of Lakeland, Fla.-based Keyosk Corp. (headquartered in Irvine, Calif.), said 200–300 supermarkets around the country use Keyosk's Video Rental Center vending machines. Typical clients are "stores which don't have the space for a video section, or which don't want to hire extra staff for a video section," he said.

According to Malet, one major California supermarket chain, Hughes Markets, has switched from staffed video centers to Keyosk vending machines over the last year. "The machines are simple to operate and to service," Malet noted. "Our field people don't need to be technicians."

Companies that deal exclusively in sell-through report significant numbers in the supermarket arena, as well as those involved in rental. "We've doubled our supermarket business over the last couple of years," said David Sutton, president of Front Row Entertainment of Edison, N.J., which manufactures and distributes budget sell-through video.

"The programs we offer are lucrative for supermarkets," Sutton continued. "Our titles are $3.99–$8.99, with full exchange privileges, and we offer 30–60-day promotions."

Cabin Fever Entertainment, a video manufacturer based in Greenwich, Conn., made its first FMI appearance this year. "Supermarkets are a growing business for video companies," said national sales director Dick Zima, who said Cabin Fever's 80-title product line has become available in supermarkets just during the past year.

Zima said Cabin Fever has been "utilizing parent company U.S. Tobacco's accounts to expand into supermarkets. There's a huge potential consumer base."

Source: Moira McCormick, "Food Marketers Show a Taste for Video Growth," *Billboard,* May 23, 1992, p. 49. (c) 1995 BPI Communications, Inc. Used with permission from *Billboard Magazine.*

Billboard/May 23, 1992

Commentary

Video rental stores have become a staple of the American retail landscape. Their widespread proliferation has increased the number of outlets available to consumers, but owners of these video stores are beginning to realize only meager profits. The rapid growth in the number of video rental stores suggests an ease of entry that characterizes a perfectly competitive industry. Having video rental outlets on virtually every corner means there are a large number of sellers. The rising interest in offering video rentals by supermarkets increases the number of sellers even further. And, with the new ways to display videos, the space required to open a video rental outlet has diminished considerably, allowing even more entry into the industry. All of these facts imply that each video rental store is a price taker and can be analyzed according to the model of a firm in an industry that is perfectly competitive.

The graph on the left depicts the demand and supply curves for the video rental market, and the graph on the right illustrates the corresponding cost and marginal-revenue curves for a typical video rental store. The market supply and demand curves labeled S_1 and D_1 represent the situation a few years ago, when video store owners realized above-normal profit. The rental price of $4 that resulted from the intersection of S_1 and D_1 (at point e_1 in the graph on the left) allowed the typical video store to enjoy a profit (represented by the rectangle $ABCD$ in the graph on the right). This profit occurred because the point at which marginal revenue intersected marginal cost was above the average-total-cost curve.

Everyone wants to get in on a good thing, however, and the presence of above-normal profit led to market entry. New video rental stores opened and existing supermarkets expanded their video offerings. This led to an outward shift of the market supply curve to S_2. The new market-supply curve intersects demand at the lower price of $3 per rental (point e_2 in the graph on the left). At this price, the marginal revenue of the typical firm crosses the marginal-cost curve at the bottom of the average-total-cost curve (point F in the graph on the right). The price each firm receives from the video rentals is lower than the initial price, and firms no longer make positive economic profits.

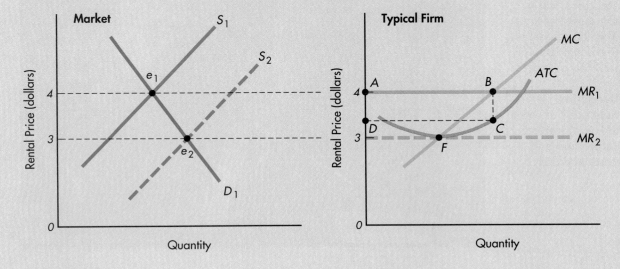

Chapter 11

Monopoly

? **Fundamental Questions**

1. What is monopoly?

2. How is a monopoly created?

3. What does the demand curve for a monopoly firm look like, and why?

4. Why would someone want to have a monopoly in some business or activity?

5. Under what conditions will a monopolist charge different customers different prices for the same product?

6. How do the predictions of the models of perfect competition and monopoly differ?

Preview

The Justice Department of the United States found the Microsoft Corporation guilty of attempting to monopolize the personal computer operating system and applications market. The claim was that Microsoft acted unfairly to attempt to be the only firm selling an operating system; that is, Microsoft acted unfairly to become a monopoly. What is a monopoly? Why does the word conjure up images of dastardly deeds and inspire governments to call it illegal? The purpose of this chapter is to answer these questions. ■

Bill Gates

1. THE MARKET STRUCTURE OF MONOPOLY

1. What is monopoly?

There are widespread beliefs about monopoly that demand our attention. One such belief is that a monopolist can earn unseemly profits by charging outrageously high prices. Another is that a monopolist does not have to respond in any way to customer desires. And a third is that it is impossible for a monopolist to make a loss. We'll discuss these beliefs in this chapter. We begin by defining what a monopolist is.

1.a. Market Definition

monopoly: a market structure in which there is a single supplier of a product

monopoly firm (monopolist): a single supplier of a product for which there are no close substitutes

Monopoly is a market structure in which there is a single supplier of a product. A **monopoly firm (monopolist)** may be large or small, but whatever its size, it must be the *only supplier* of the product. In addition, a monopoly firm must sell a product for which there are *no close substitutes*. The greater the number of close substitutes for a firm's products, the less likely it is that the firm has a monopoly.

You purchase products from monopoly firms every day, perhaps without realizing it. Congress created the U.S. Postal Service to provide first-class mail service. No other firm is allowed to provide that service. The currency you use is issued and its quantity is controlled by a government entity known as the Federal Reserve. It is illegal for any organization or individual other than the Federal Reserve to issue currency.

2. How is a monopoly created?

1.b. The Creation of Monopolies

Glaxo-Wellcome's profits doubled in the three years following the introduction of AZT. Glaxo-Wellcome was a monopoly supplier of AZT, and it was earning above-normal profits on AZT. But if a product is valuable and the owners are getting rich from selling it, won't others develop substitutes and also enjoy the fruits of the market? Yes, unless something impedes entry. The name given to that something is **barrier to entry.** There are three general classes of barriers to entry:

barrier to entry: anything that impedes the ability of firms to begin a new business in an industry in which existing firms are earning above-normal profits

- Natural barriers, such as economies of scale
- Actions on the part of firms that create barriers to entry
- Governmentally created barriers

1.b.1. Economies of Scale   Economies of scale can be a barrier to entry. There are economies of scale in the generation of electricity. The larger the generating plant, the lower the cost per kilowatt-hour of electricity produced. A large generating plant can produce each unit of electricity much less expensively than several small generating plants. Size thus constitutes a barrier to entry since to be able to enter and compete with existing large-scale public utilities, a firm needs to be large so that it can produce each kilowatt-hour as inexpensively as the large-scale plants.

1.b.2. Actions by Firms   Entry is barred when one firm owns an essential resource. The owners of the desiccant clay mine in New Mexico had a monopoly position because they owned the essential resource, clay. Inventions and discoveries are essential resources, at least until others come up with close substitutes. Microsoft owned the important resources known as Windows. Was Microsoft a monopoly?

1.b.3. Government   Barriers to entry are often created by governments. The U.S. government issues patents, which provide a firm a monopoly on certain products, inventions, or discoveries for a period of 17 years. Such is the case with the

Glaxo-Wellcome monopoly. The company was granted a patent on AZT and thus was, by law, the only supplier of the drug. Domestic government policy also restricts entry into many industries. The federal government issues broadcast licenses for radio and television and grants airlines landing rights at certain airports. City governments limit the number of taxi companies that can operate, the number of cable television companies that can provide service, and the number of garbage collection firms that can provide service. State and local governments issue liquor licenses and restrict the number of electric utility companies. These are just a few of the government-created monopolies in the United States.

1.c. Types of Monopolies

natural monopoly: a monopoly that arises from economies of scale

The word *monopoly* is often associated with other terms such as *natural monopoly*, *local monopoly*, *regulated monopoly*, and *monopoly power*. A **natural monopoly** is a firm that has become a monopoly because of economies of scale and demand conditions. The adjective *natural* indicates that the monopoly arises from cost and demand conditions, not from government action. If costs decline as the quantity produced rises, only very large producers will be able to stay in business. Their lower costs will enable them to force smaller producers, who have higher costs, out of business. Large producers can underprice smaller producers, as illustrated in Figure 1. The larger firm, operating along ATC_2, can set a price anywhere between P_1 and P_2 and thereby drive the smaller firm, operating along ATC_1, out of business. If the market can support only one producer or if the long-run average-total-cost curve continually slopes downward, the monopoly that results is said to be natural. Electric utilities are often considered to be natural monopolies because there are large economies of scale in the generation of electricity. One large power plant can generate electricity at a lower per-kilowatt-hour cost than can several small power plants. The transmission of electricity is different, however. There are diseconomies of scale in the transmission of electricity. The farther electricity has to be transmit-

---

Figure 1

Economies of Scale

A large firm producing along ATC_2 can produce output much less expensively per unit than a small firm operating along ATC_1. The large firm, therefore, can set a price that is below the minimum point of the small firm's average-total-cost curve yet still earn profit. Any price between P_1 and P_2 will provide a profit for the large firm and a loss for the small firm.

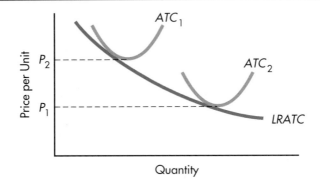

---

ted, the higher the per-kilowatt-hour costs. Together, generation and transmission imply an MES that is sufficiently large for a local monopoly but not for a national or international monopoly.

A **local monopoly** is a firm that has a monopoly within a specific geographic area. An electric utility may be the sole supplier of electricity in a municipality or local area. A taxicab company may have a monopoly for service to the airport or within a city. Cable TV companies may have monopolies within municipalities. An airline may have a monopoly over some routes.

A **regulated monopoly** is a monopolist whose prices and production rates are controlled by a government entity. Electric utility companies, telephone companies, cable TV companies, and water companies are or have been regulated monopolies. A state corporation or utility commission sets their rates, determines the costs to be allowed in the production of their services, and restricts entry by other firms.

Monopoly power is market power, the ability to set prices. It exists whenever the demand curve facing the producer is downward sloping. Monopolies exercise monopoly power, but so do all firms except those operating in perfectly competitive markets. A firm that has monopoly power is a price maker rather than a price taker.

local monopoly: a monopoly that exists in a limited geographic area

regulated monopoly: a monopoly firm whose behavior is monitored and prescribed by a government entity

monopoly power: market power, the ability to set prices

RECAP

1. A monopoly firm is the sole supplier of a product for which there are no close substitutes.
2. A monopoly firm remains the sole supplier because of barriers to entry.
3. Barriers to entry may be economic, such as economies of scale, they may be due to the exclusive ownership of an essential resource, or they may be created by government policy.
4. A natural monopoly is a monopoly that results through economies of scale. A regulated monopoly is a monopoly whose pricing and production are controlled by the government. A local monopoly is a firm that has a monopoly in a specific geographic region.
5. Monopoly power, or market power, is the ability to set prices.

---

3. What does the demand curve for a monopoly firm look like, and why?

2. THE DEMAND CURVE FACING A MONOPOLY FIRM

In any market, the industry demand curve is a downward-sloping line because of the law of demand. Although the industry demand curve is downward sloping, the demand curve facing an individual firm in a perfectly competitive market is a horizontal line at the market price. This is not the case for the monopoly firm. Because a monopoly firm is the sole producer, it *is* the industry, so its demand curve is the industry demand curve.

2.a. Marginal Revenue

The demand curve facing the monopoly firm is the industry demand curve.

In the early 1990s, a small U.S. company introduced a wireless VCR that could operate from more than one television set and didn't even have to be placed in the same room as the television. For a few years, this company had a monopoly on the wireless VCR. Let's consider the pricing and output decisions of the firm, using hypothetical cost and revenue data.

Suppose a wireless VCR sells for $1,500, and at that price the firm is selling 5 VCRs per day, as shown in Figure 2. If the monopoly firm wants to sell more, it must move down the demand curve. Why? Because of the law of demand. People will do without the wireless VCR rather than pay more than they think it's worth. As the price declines, sales increase. The table in Figure 2 shows that if the monopoly firm lowers the price to $1,350 per unit from $1,400, it will sell 8 VCRs per day instead of 7.

What is the firm's marginal revenue? To find marginal revenue, the total revenue earned at $1,400 per VCR must be compared to the total revenue earned at $1,350 per VCR—the change in total revenue must be calculated. At $1,400 apiece, 7 VCRs are sold each day and total revenue each day is

$$\$1,400 \text{ per VCR} \times 7 \text{ VCRs} = \$9,800$$

At $1,350 apiece, 8 VCRs are sold and total revenue is

$$\$1,350 \text{ per VCR} \times 8 \text{ VCRs} = \$10,800$$

The difference, change in total revenue, is $1,000. Thus, marginal revenue is

$$\frac{\Delta TR}{\Delta Q} = \frac{\$1,000}{1 \text{ VCR}} = \$1,000$$

The change in revenue is the difference between the increased revenue due to increased quantity sold, the yellow area in Figure 2, and the decreased revenue due to a lower price, the blue area in Figure 2.

Marginal revenue is less than price for a monopoly firm.

The price is $1,350 per VCR, but marginal revenue is $1,000 per VCR. Price and marginal revenue are not the same for a monopoly firm. This is a fundamental difference between a monopolist and a perfect competitor. For a perfect competitor, price and marginal revenue are the same.

Public utilities, such as nuclear power plants, are regulated monopolies in the United States and are government-run enterprises in other parts of the world. With private ownership, it is the stockholders or owners who reap the benefits of profits and could bear the burden of losses. Until the 1990s, the utilities were guaranteed by government regulation not to have losses. Beginning in 1992, government regulation has been relaxed so that utilities must compete or prepare for competition from other electricity generating companies.

Figure 2

Demand Curve for a Monopolist

As the VCR price is reduced, the quantity demanded increases. But because the price is reduced on all quantities sold, not just on the last unit sold, marginal revenue declines faster than price.

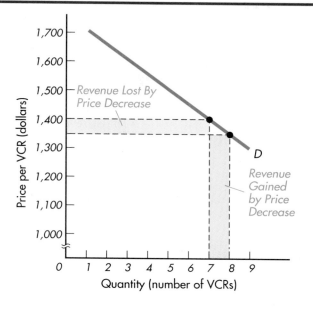

Quantity per Day	Price	Total Revenue	Marginal Revenue
1	$1,700	$ 1,700	$1,700
2	$1,650	$ 3,300	$1,600
3	$1,600	$ 4,800	$1,500
4	$1,550	$ 6,200	$1,400
5	$1,500	$ 7,500	$1,300
6	$1,450	$ 8,700	$1,200
7	$1,400	$ 9,800	$1,100
8	$1,350	$10,800	$1,000
9	$1,300	$11,700	$ 900

Marginal revenue is less than price and declines as output rises because the monopolist must lower the price in order to sell more units. When the price of a VCR is $1,400, the firm sells 7 VCRs. When the price is dropped to $1,350, the firm sells 8 units. The firm does not sell the first 7 VCRs for $1,400 and the eighth one for $1,350. It might lose business if it tried to do that. The customer who purchased the good at $1,350 could sell the product for $1,375 to a customer about to pay $1,400, and the firm would lose the $1,400 sale. Customers who would have paid $1,400 could decide to wait until they too can get the $1,350 price. As long as customers know about the prices paid by other customers and as long as the firm cannot easily distinguish among customers, the monopoly firm is not able to charge a different price for each additional unit. All units are sold at the same price, and in order to sell additional units, the monopolist must lower the price on all units. As a result, marginal revenue and price are not the same.

2.a.1. Marginal and Average Revenue
Recall from the chapter "Elasticity: Demand and Supply" that whenever the marginal is greater than the average, the average rises, and whenever the marginal is less than the average, the average falls. Average revenue is calculated by dividing total revenue by the number of units of output sold:

$$AR = \frac{P \times Q}{Q} = P$$

At a price of $1,500 per VCR, average revenue is

$$\frac{\$7,500}{5} = \$1,500$$

Average revenue at a price of $1,450 per VCR is

$$\frac{\$8,700}{6} = \$1,450$$

Average revenue is the same as price; in fact, *the average-revenue curve is the demand curve*. Because of the law of demand, where quantity demanded rises as price falls, average revenue (price) always falls as output rises (the demand curve slopes downward). Because average revenue falls as output rises, marginal revenue must always be less than average revenue. For the monopolist (or any firm facing a downward-sloping demand curve), marginal revenue always declines as output increases, and the marginal-revenue curve always lies below the demand curve.

Also recall from previous chapters that the marginal-revenue curve is positive in the elastic region of the demand curve ($e_d > 1$), is zero at the output level where the demand curve is unit-elastic ($e_d = 1$), and is negative in the inelastic portion of the demand curve ($e_d < 1$).[1] This is illustrated in Figure 3 (repeated from the chapter "Elasticity: Demand and Supply").

RECAP

1. The demand curve facing a monopoly firm is the market demand curve.
2. For the monopoly firm, price is greater than marginal revenue. For the perfectly competitive firm, price and marginal revenue are equal.
3. As price declines, total revenue increases in the elastic portion of the demand curve, reaches a maximum at the unit-elastic point, and declines in the inelastic portion.
4. The marginal-revenue curve of the monopoly firm lies below the demand curve.
5. For both the perfectly competitive firm and the monopoly firm, price = average revenue = demand.

3. PROFIT MAXIMIZATION

The objective of the monopoly firm is to maximize profit. Where does the monopolist choose to produce, and what price does it set? Recall from the chapter "Profit Maximization," that all profit-maximizing firms produce at the point where marginal revenue equals marginal cost.

---

[1]The slope of the demand curve is one-half the slope of the marginal-revenue curve. Consider the demand formula $P = a - bQ$; total revenue is $PQ = aQ - bQ^2$, so marginal revenue is $MR = a - 2bQ$.

Figure 3

Downward-Sloping Demand Curve and Revenue

The straight-line downward-sloping demand curve in Figure 3(a) shows that the price elasticity of demand becomes more inelastic as we move down the curve. In the elastic region, revenue increases as price is lowered, as shown in Figure 3(b); in the inelastic region, revenue decreases as price is lowered. The revenue-maximizing point, the top of the curve in Figure 3(b), occurs where the demand curve is unit-elastic, shown in Figure 3(a).

(a) Demand and Price Elasticity

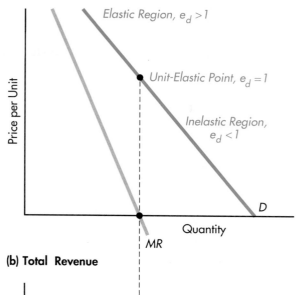

(b) Total Revenue

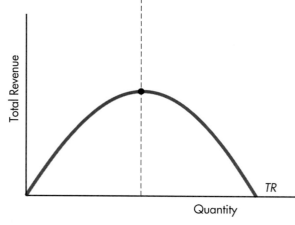

3.a. What Price to Charge?

A schedule of revenues and costs for the wireless VCR producer accompanies Figure 4. Total revenue (*TR*) is listed in column 3; total cost (*TC*), in column 4. Total profit (*TR* − *TC*), shown in column 5, is the difference between the entries in column 3 and those in column 4. Marginal revenue (*MR*) is listed in column 6, marginal cost (*MC*) in column 7, and average total cost (*ATC*) in column 8.

The quantity of output to be produced is the quantity that corresponds to the point where *MR* = *MC*. How high a price will the market bear at that quantity? The market is willing and able to purchase the quantity given by *MR* = *MC* at the corresponding price on the demand curve. As shown in Figure 4(a), the price is found by drawing a vertical line from the point where *MR* = *MC* up to the demand curve and

Figure 4

Profit Maximization for the VCR Producer

The data listed in the table are plotted in Figure 4(a). The firm produces where $MR = MC$, 8 units; charges a price given by the demand curve directly above the production of 8 units, a price of $1,350 per VCR; and earns a profit (yellow rectangle). In Figure 4(b), the firm is shown to be operating at a loss (blue rectangle). It produces output Q at price P, but the average total cost exceeds the price.

(1) Total Output (Q)	(2) Price (P)	(3) Total Revenue (TR)	(4) Total Cost (TC)	(5) Total Profit (TR − TC)	(6) Marginal Revenue (MR)	(7) Marginal Cost (MC)	(8) Average Total Cost (ATC)
0	$1,750	$ 0	$1,000	−$1,000			
1	$1,700	$ 1,700	$2,000	−$ 300	$1,700	$1,000	$2,000
2	$1,650	$ 3,300	$2,800	$ 500	$1,600	$ 800	$1,400
3	$1,600	$ 4,800	$3,500	$1,300	$1,500	$ 700	$1,167
4	$1,550	$ 6,200	$4,000	$2,200	$1,400	$ 500	$1,000
5	$1,500	$ 7,500	$4,500	$3,000	$1,300	$ 500	$ 900
6	$1,450	$ 8,700	$5,200	$3,500	$1,200	$ 700	$ 867
7	$1,400	$ 9,800	$6,000	$3,800	$1,100	$ 800	$ 857
8	$1,350	$10,800	$7,000	$3,800	$1,000	$1,000	$ 875
9	$1,300	$11,700	$9,000	$2,700	$ 900	$2,000	$1,000

(a) Making a Profit

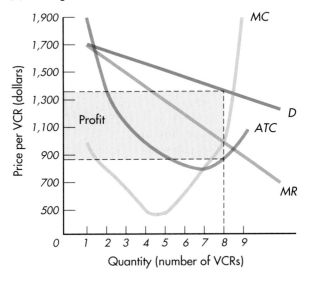

(b) Operating at a Loss

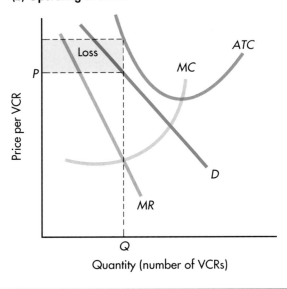

then extending a horizontal line over to the vertical axis. That price is $1,350 when output is 8.

3.b. Monopoly Profit and Loss

4. Why would someone want to have a monopoly in some business or activity?

The profit that the monopoly firm generates by selling 8 VCRs at a price of $1,350 is shown in Figure 4(a) as the colored rectangle. The vertical distance between the *ATC* curve and the demand curve, multiplied by the quantity sold, yields total profit.

Just like any other firm, a monopoly firm could experience a loss. A monopoly supplier of sharpeners for disposable razor blades probably would not be very successful, and the U.S. Postal Service has failed to make a profit in five of the last ten years. Unless price exceeds average costs, the firm loses money. A monopolist producing at a loss is shown in Figure 4(b)—the price is less than the average total cost.

Like a perfectly competitive firm, a monopolist will suspend operations in the short run if its price does not exceed the average variable cost at the quantity the firm produces. And, like a perfectly competitive firm, a monopolist will shut down permanently if revenue is not likely to equal or exceed all costs in the long run (unless the government subsidizes the firm, as it does in the case of the U.S. Postal Service). In contrast, however, if a monopolist makes a profit, barriers to entry will keep other firms out of the industry. As a result, the monopolist can earn above-normal profits in the long run.

A monopolist can earn above-normal profits in the long run.

3.c. Monopoly Myths

There are a few myths about monopoly that we have debunked here. The first myth is that a monopolist can charge any price it wants and will reap unseemly profits by continually increasing the price. We know that a monopolist maximizes profit by producing the quantity that equates marginal revenue and marginal cost. We also know that a monopolist can only price and sell the quantities given by the demand curve. If the demand curve is very inelastic, as would be the case for a lifesaving pharmaceutical, then the price the monopolist would charge will be high. Conversely, if demand is very price-elastic, the monopolist will experience losses by charging exorbitant prices. A second myth is that a monopolist is not sensitive to customers. The monopolist can stay in business only if it earns at least a normal profit. Ignoring customers, producing a good no one will purchase, setting prices that all customers think are exorbitant, and providing terrible service or products customers do not want will not allow a firm to remain in business for long. The monopolist faces a demand curve for its product and must search for a price and quantity that are dictated by that demand curve. The third myth is that the monopolist cannot make a loss. A monopolist is no different than any other firm in that it has costs of doing business and it must earn sufficient revenues to pay those costs. If the monopolist sets too high a price or provides a product few want, revenues may be less than costs and losses may result.

RECAP

1. Profit is maximized at the output level where $MR = MC$.
2. The price charged by the monopoly firm is the point on the demand curve that corresponds to the quantity where $MR = MC$.
3. A monopoly firm can make profits or experience losses. A monopoly firm can earn above-normal profit in the long run.

4. The monopoly firm will shut down in the short run if all variable costs aren't covered. It will shut down in the long run if all costs aren't covered.

4. PRICE DISCRIMINATION

Up to now we have assumed that the monopolist charges all customers the same price. Under certain conditions, a firm operating in markets that are not perfectly competitive can increase profits by charging different customers different prices. This is called **price discrimination.** The objective of the firm is to charge each customer exactly what each is willing to pay and in this way extract the total consumer surplus.

price discrimination: the practice of selling the same thing to different customers at different prices

5. Under what conditions would a monopolist charge different customers different prices for the same product?

4.a. Necessary Conditions for Price Discrimination

You read in section 2a that the monopoly firm has to sell all of its products at a uniform price; otherwise, one customer could sell to another, thereby reducing the monopoly firm's profits. However, if customers do not come into contact with each other or are somehow separated by the firm, the firm may be able to charge each customer the exact price that he or she is willing to pay. By doing this, the firm is able to collect a great deal more of the consumer surplus than it would receive if it charged all customers the same price. Although a firm does not have to be a monopolist to price-discriminate, the monopolist can more easily separate customers than the oligopolist or monopolistic competitor.

When different customers are charged different prices for the same product or when customers are charged different prices for different quantities of the same product, price discrimination is occurring. Price discrimination occurs when price changes result not from cost changes but from the firm's attempt to extract more of the consumer surplus. Certain conditions are necessary for price discrimination to occur:

- The firm cannot be a price taker (perfect competitor).
- The firm must be able to separate customers according to price elasticities of demand.
- The firm must be able to prevent resale of the product.

4.b. Examples of Price Discrimination

Examples of price discrimination are not hard to find. Senior citizens often pay a lower price than the general population at movie theaters, drugstores, and golf courses. It is relatively easy to identify senior citizens and to ensure that they do not resell their tickets to the general population.

Tuition at state schools is different for in-state and out-of-state residents. It is not difficult to find out where a student resides, and it is very easy to ensure that in-state students do not sell their place to out-of-state students.

Airlines discriminate between business passengers and others. Passengers who do not fly at the busiest times, who purchase tickets in advance, and who can stay at their destination longer than a day pay lower fares than business passengers, who cannot make advance reservations and who must travel during rush hours. It is relatively easy for the airlines to separate business from nonbusiness passengers and to ensure that the latter do not sell their tickets to the former.

Electric utilities practice a form of price discrimination by charging different rates for different quantities of electricity used. The rate declines as the quantity purchased increases. A customer might pay $.07 per kilowatt-hour for the first 100 kilowatt-hours, $.06 for the next 100, and so on. Many utility companies have different rate structures for different classes of customers as well. Businesses pay less per kilowatt-hour than households.

Grocery coupons, mail-in rebates, trading stamps, and other discount strategies are also price-discrimination techniques. Shoppers who are willing to spend time cutting out coupons and presenting them receive a lower price than those not willing to spend that time. Shoppers are separated by the amount of time they are willing to devote to coupon clipping. Is it possible that the popcorn at the movies is also a price-discrimination tactic? If the excess price of the popcorn and other foodstuffs at the movies was simply translated to an admission ticket, the movie theater would lose those customers who do not purchase popcorn. By charging a high price for the popcorn, the movie theater is distinguishing those customers who have a lower price elasticity of demand for the entire package of the movie and the popcorn from those with a higher elasticity of demand.

4.c. The Theory of Price Discrimination

How does price discrimination work? Suppose there are two classes of buyers for movie tickets, senior citizens and everybody else, and each class has a different elasticity of demand. The two classes are shown in Figure 5. Profit is maximized when $MR = MC$. Because the same firm is providing the goods in two submarkets, MC is the same for senior citizens and the general public, but the demand curves differ. Because the demand curves of the two groups differ, there are two MR curves: MR_{sc} for senior citizens, in Figure 5(a), and MR_{gp} for the general population, in Figure 5(b). Profit is maximized when $MR_{sc} = MC$ and when $MR_{gp} = MC$. The price is found by drawing a vertical line from the quantities where $MR = MC$ up to the respective demand curves, D_{sc} and D_{gp}.

Notice that the price to the general population, P_{gp}, is higher than the price to the senior citizens, P_{sc}. The reason is that the senior citizens' demand curve is more elastic than the demand curve of the general population. Senior citizens are more sensitive to price than is the general population, so to attract more of their business, the merchant has to offer them a lower price.

By discriminating, a monopoly firm makes greater profits than it would make by charging both groups the same price. If both groups were charged the same price, P_{gp}, the monopoly firm would lose sales to senior citizens who found the price too high, Q_{sc} to Q_2. And if both groups were charged P_{sc}, so few additional sales to the general population would be made that revenues would fall.

4.d. Dumping

Price discrimination is a strategy used by many firms that sell their products in different countries. A derogatory name for this policy is **dumping.** Dumping occurs when an identical good is sold to foreign buyers for a lower price than is charged to domestic buyers. International dumping is a controversial issue. Producers in a country facing foreign competitors are likely to appeal to their domestic government for protection from the foreign goods being dumped in their market. Typically, the appeal for government assistance is based on the argument that the dumping firms are practicing **predatory dumping**—dumping intended to drive rival firms out of

dumping: setting a higher price on goods sold domestically than on goods sold in foreign markets

predatory dumping: dumping to drive competitors out of business

Figure 5

Price Discrimination

There are two classes of buyers for the same product. Figure 5(a) shows the elasticity of demand for senior citizens. Figure 5(b) shows the elasticity of demand for the general population. The demand of the senior citizens is more elastic than that of the general population. As a result, faced with the same marginal cost, the firm charges senior citizens a lower price than it charges the rest of the population. The quantity sold to senior citizens is Q_{sc}, the intersection between MC and MR_{sc}, and the price charged is P_{sc}. The quantity sold to the general population is Q_{gp}, and the price charged is P_{gp}.

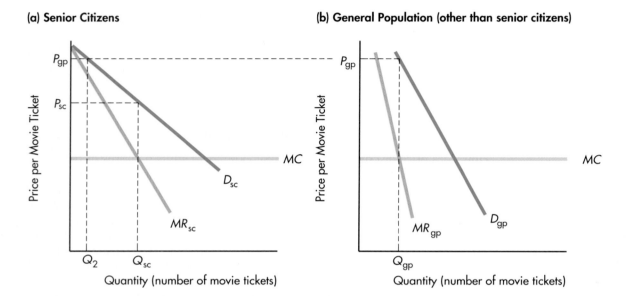

(a) Senior Citizens

(b) General Population (other than senior citizens)

business. A successful predator firm raises prices after the rival is driven from the market.

Canadian electronics manufacturers might accuse Japanese firms of dumping if the Japanese firms are selling electronics in Canada for less than they charge in Japan. The Canadian manufacturers may appeal to the Canadian government, asserting that the Japanese firms are engaged in predatory dumping to drive the Canadian firms out of business and warning that the Japanese firms will then raise the price of electronics products in Canada without fear of competition by the domestic Canadian firms. Claims of predatory dumping are often emotional and stir up the nationalistic sympathy of the rest of the domestic economy.

The U.S. government frequently responds to charges of dumping brought against foreign firms by U.S. industry. The government has pursued claims of predatory dumping against South African manufacturers of steel plate; German, Italian, and French winemakers; Japanese manufacturers of semiconductors; Singapore manufacturers of typewriters; Korean shipbuilders; Chinese motor bike producers; and many other manufacturers.

One famous case involved Sony Corporation of Japan. In the United States, Sony was selling Japanese-made TV sets for $180 while charging buyers in Japan $333 for the same model. The U.S. television producers claimed that Sony was dumping TV sets in the U.S. market and seriously damaging U.S. television manufacturers. (Although U.S. producers disliked the low price of Japanese competitors, U.S. consumers benefited.) The U.S. government threatened to place high tariffs on Japanese television sets entering the United States unless Japan raised the price of Japanese televisions sold in the United States. The threat worked, and the price of Japanese TVs exported to the United States increased.

Charges of predatory dumping make good news stories, but it is also true that dumping is to be expected when producers with the ability to set prices (as is the case for firms operating in markets that are not perfectly competitive) face segmented markets that have different price elasticities of demand. Conceptually, dumping is no different from what happens when a car dealer charges one buyer a higher price than another for the same car. If both buyers were aware of the range of prices at which the dealer would sell the car, or if both buyers had exactly the same price elasticity of demand, they would pay exactly the same price.

The Japanese electronics manufacturer realizes that the electronics market in Japan is separate from the electronics market in Canada or the United States. If the price elasticity of demand for electronics is different in each country, the Japanese manufacturer will maximize profit by charging a different price in each country.

RECAP

1. Price discrimination occurs when a firm charges different customers different prices for the same product or charges different prices for different quantities of the same product.

2. Three conditions are necessary for price discrimination to occur: (1) the firm must have some market power, (2) the firm must be able to separate customers according to price elasticities of demand, and (3) the firm must be able to prevent resale of the product.

3. Dumping is setting a higher price on goods sold in the domestic market than on goods sold in the foreign market. Dumping is another name for price discrimination in sales to customers that occurs in different countries.

5. COMPARISON OF PERFECT COMPETITION AND MONOPOLY

6. How do the predictions of the models of perfect competition and monopoly differ?

The perfectly competitive market structure results in economic efficiency because price is equal to marginal cost and firms are producing at the bottom of the average-total-cost curve. The monopoly market structure does not yield efficiency.

5.a. Costs of Monopoly: Inefficiency

In the long run, the perfectly competitive firm operates at the minimum point of the long-run average-total-cost curve and the firm's price is equal to its marginal cost. Profit is the normal level. A monopolist does not operate at the minimum point of the average-total-cost curve and does not set price equal to marginal cost.

Figure 6

Monopoly and Perfect Competition Compared

Figure 6(a) shows a perfectly competitive industry; it produces at the point where industry demand, *D*, and industry supply, *S*, intersect. The quantity produced by the industry is Q_{pc}; the price charged is P_{pc}. Consumer surplus is the triangle $P_{pc}BA$. Figure 6(b) shows what happens if the industry is monopolized. The single firm faces the industry demand curve, *D*, and has the marginal-revenue curve *MR*. The intersection of the marginal-cost curve and the marginal-revenue curve indicates the quantity that will be produced, Q_m. The price charged for Q_m is P_m. Thus, the monopoly firm produces less and charges more than the perfectly competitive industry. Consumer surplus, shown as the triangle P_mCA, is smaller in the monopoly industry. The area $P_{pc}ECP_m$ is the consumer surplus in perfect competition that is transferred from consumer to producer. The producer surplus is area $OFCP_m$. The deadweight loss is the area *CFB*.

(a) The Perfectly Competitive Market

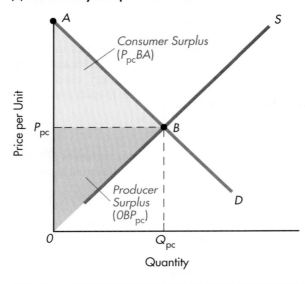

(b) Monopoly

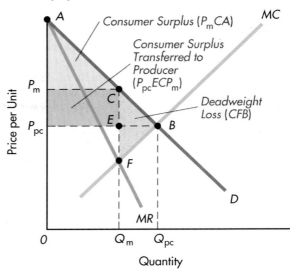

Because entry does not occur, a monopoly firm may earn above-normal profit in the long run.

Figure 6(a) shows a perfectly competitive market. The market demand curve is *D*; the market supply curve is *S*. The market price determined by the intersection of *D* and *S* is P_{pc}. At P_{pc} the perfectly competitive market produces Q_{pc}. Consumers are able to enjoy the consumer surplus indicated by the triangle $P_{pc}BA$, by purchasing the quantity Q_{pc} at the price P_{pc}. Firms receive the producer surplus indicated by triangle OBP_{pc} by producing the quantity Q_{pc} and selling that quantity at price P_{pc}.

Let's assume that all of the firms in a perfectly competitive industry are merged into a single monopoly firm and that the monopolist does not close or alter plants and does not achieve any economies of scale. In other words, what would occur if a perfectly competitive industry is transformed into a monopoly—just one firm determines price and quantity produced? The industry demand curve becomes the monopoly firm's demand curve, and the industry supply curve becomes the monopoly firm's marginal-cost curve. This is illustrated in Figure 6(b).

The monopoly firm restricts quantity produced to Q_m, where $MR = MC$, and charges a price P_m as indicated on the demand curve shown in Figure 6(b). *The monopoly firm thus produces a lower quantity than does the perfectly competitive industry, Q_m compared to Q_{pc}, and sells that smaller quantity at a higher price, P_m compared to P_{pc}.* In addition, the consumer surplus in monopoly is the triangle P_mCA, which is smaller than the consumer surplus under perfect competition, $P_{pc}BA$. The rectangle $P_{pc}ECP_m$ is part of consumer surplus in perfect competition. In monopoly, that part of consumer surplus is transferred to the firm. The total producer surplus is area $OFCP_m$.

Thus, firms are better off (more producer surplus) while consumers are worse off (less consumer surplus) under monopoly compared to perfect competition. Consumers are worse off by area $P_{pc}BCP_m$ and firms are better off by area $P_{pc}ECP_m$ less area EFB. The triangle CFB is lost by both consumers and firms and goes to no one. This loss is the reduction in consumer surplus and producer surplus that is not transferred to the monopoly firm or to anyone else; it is called a **deadweight loss.** If a monopoly firm can produce output at the same cost as the perfectly competitive industry, there is a loss to society in going from perfect competition to monopoly; that loss is called a deadweight loss also.

deadweight loss: the reduction of consumer surplus without a corresponding increase in profit when a perfectly competitive firm is monopolized

5.b. The Deadweight Loss May Be Overstated

The deadweight loss just described may, in reality, be overstated. A monopolist may face the potential of rivals if profit gets too high or may have to worry about government intervention.

5.b.1. Potential Competition
The Intel Corporation has to be concerned that rival firms will take away its virtual monopoly of the computer chip market. As a result, Intel chips such as the P-6 are not priced as high, and more are sold than might be the case if the firm did not fear entry. The lower the price relative to what it could be, the less the deadweight loss. Monopoly firms may keep the price lower and produce more output than is suggested by the theory of monopoly because these firms fear that if their profit is too high, it could bring about entry and competition in the future. The fear of potential entry is called **potential competition.**

potential competition: possible entry or rivalry capable of forcing existing producers to behave as if the competition actually existed

5.b.2. Government Intervention
Another constant fear for the monopoly firm is that the government will intervene. Since the 1930s, the governments of most of the developed nations have scrutinized business operations in an attempt to discourage the formation of monopolies. Many proposed mergers have been prohibited because of the fear that monopoly might result. The activities of large firms are watched especially closely. This pressure may lessen the deadweight losses of monopoly.

5.b.3. Economies of Scale
Underlying the preceding comparison of perfect competition and monopoly is the assumption that cost conditions will not change. However, it seems unrealistic to assume that the acquisition or merger of many firms would not change the cost structure in the industry. If there are economies of scale, the large-scale firm will be able to produce the product at a lower cost per unit than the many smaller firms. As a result, the deadweight losses imposed on society by a monopoly firm may be diminished.

5.c. The Deadweight Loss May Be Understated

The deadweight losses imposed by monopoly firms may be smaller than suggested by the comparison of perfect competition and monopoly, but it is also possible that they could actually be larger than the comparison suggests. The monopoly could operate less efficiently, and resources could be taken away from productive activities and devoted to maintaining a monopoly.

5.c.1. Higher Costs and X-Inefficiency

As you have learned, a monopoly firm does not operate at the minimum point on the average-total-cost curve, but a perfectly competitive firm does. Thus, the monopolist not only imposes a deadweight loss but also produces at a higher cost per unit than does the perfectly competitive firm. The high cost may go even higher if the monopolist becomes inefficient because of a lack of competition or potential competition.

Many monopolies are created and maintained by the government. The resulting monopoly firms do not have to worry about potential competition or government intervention. Monopoly firms may not feel the need to operate efficiently because they face no competition from entering firms. Many economists have argued that because monopoly firms have no fear of competition, they operate less efficiently than would competitive firms producing the same output. The inefficiency that occurs in the absence of fear of entry and rivalry is called **X-inefficiency.** The X-inefficiency is represented by an upward shift of the average-total-cost curve.

The greater X-inefficiency is, the greater the cost to society when a perfectly competitive industry is monopolized. As the average costs of production rise because of X-inefficiency, consumer surplus falls without a corresponding increase in the monopolist's profit. The additional loss in consumer surplus due to X-inefficiency is an increase in deadweight losses.

X-inefficiency: the tendency of a firm not faced with competition to become inefficient

5.c.2. Rent Seeking

Monopolists devote significant resources to preserving their monopoly positions. Liquor licenses are valuable because they bestow a local monopoly on the recipients. Similarly, radio and television broadcasting rights provide above-normal profits to the holders of those rights. To protect their above-normal profits and ensure political support for their monopoly positions, the owners provide significant amounts of money to lobbyists, lawyers, and political action committees (PACs). Activities that are undertaken simply to create a transfer from one group to another are known as **rent seeking.** Rent-seeking expenditures do not add to productive activity. A lawyer working to take $100 from the consumer and give it to the monopoly firm is giving up some other productive activity. The opportunity cost of the lawyer's time is a deadweight loss to society.

The potential for rent seeking is indicated in Figure 7 as the above-normal profit, the rectangle *EBCF*. It would be worthwhile for the owners of the monopoly firm to devote resources up to the amount of their profit in order to maintain their monopoly. Any profit that remains in excess of the amount spent on rent seeking would still be above-normal profit to the owners. When profit, *EBCF* in Figure 7, is used to pay for the nonproductive lobbying activities, it becomes part of the deadweight loss.

rent seeking: the use of resources simply to transfer wealth from one group to another without increasing production or total wealth

5.c.3. Innovation

If a monopoly firm tends to be more or less innovative than a perfectly competitive firm would be, the costs imposed on society by the monopoly may be smaller or larger than the comparison with perfect competition would suggest. If profits that can be obtained with a successful invention are quickly competed

Figure 7

Rent Seeking

A monopoly firm earns an above-normal profit. The managers of the firm are willing to expend all of the profit to retain the monopoly. The amount of the profit used to maintain the monopoly is rent seeking.

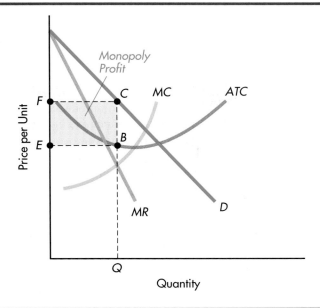

away, there might be less incentive to innovate than there would be if above-normal profits could exist for a number of years. This argument forms the basis of patent laws. A patent confers a monopoly on a firm or individual for a certain product or part for 17 years.

The counterargument is that entrepreneurs are always looking for ways to earn additional profit and protect against additional losses. If an entrepreneur is unwilling to spend money for research and development, competitors will quickly put the firm out of business because they will innovate and be able to produce products less expensively or produce better products than the firm that fails to innovate.

5.d. Supply and the Monopoly Firm

For the firm in perfect competition, the variable supply curve is that portion of the marginal-cost curve that lies above the average-cost curve, and the market supply curve is the sum of all the individual firms' supply curves. The supply curve for the firm selling in any of the other market structures is not as straightforward to derive and, therefore, neither is the market supply curve. The reason is that firms selling in market structures other than perfect competition are price makers rather than price takers. This means that the hypothetical experiment of varying the price of a product and seeing how the firm selling that product reacts makes no sense.

In the case of the monopolist, the firm supplies a quantity determined by setting marginal revenue equal to marginal cost, but it also sets the price to go along with this quantity. Varying the price will not change the decision rule since the firm will choose to produce its profit-maximizing output level and set the price accordingly. There is, therefore, only one quantity and price at which the monopolist will operate. There is a supply point, not a supply curve. Moreover, because the monopolist is the only firm in the market, its supply curve (or supply point) is also the market supply curve (or point).

The complications of the price makers do not alter the supply rule: a firm will produce and offer for sale a quantity that equates marginal revenue with marginal cost. This supply rule applies to all firms, regardless of the market structure in which the firm operates.

RECAP

1. A monopoly firm produces a smaller quantity and charges a higher price than a perfectly competitive industry if the two industries have identical costs.

2. The consumer surplus is smaller if an industry is operated by a monopoly firm than it is if an industry is operated by perfectly competitive firms. Profits are larger in the monopoly case.

3. The costs to society that result when a perfectly competitive industry becomes a monopoly are a reduction of consumer surplus as well as producer surplus that is not transferred to anyone. This loss is called a *deadweight loss*.

4. The deadweight loss imposed by monopoly firms may be overstated because the monopoly fears that entry or government intervention could occur.

5. The deadweight loss imposed by monopoly firms may be understated if monopoly firms tend to operate inefficiently and devote resources to maintaining their monopoly positions.

6. If a monopoly firm is more innovative than perfectly competitive firms, the deadweight loss of monopoly will be smaller than indicated by a direct comparison of the pricing and output decisions of the two. Conversely, if the monopoly firm is less innovative, the deadweight loss will be larger.

SUMMARY

? What is monopoly?

1. Monopoly is a market structure in which there is a single supplier of a product. A monopoly firm, or monopolist, is the only supplier of a product for which there are no close substitutes. *§1.a*

? How is a monopoly created?

2. Natural barriers to entry (such as economies of scale), barriers erected by firms in the industry, and barriers erected by government may create monopolies. *§1.b, 1.b.1, 1.b.2, 1.b.3*

3. The term *monopoly* is often associated with natural monopoly, local monopoly, regulated monopoly, and monopoly power. *§1.c*

? What does the demand curve for a monopoly firm look like, and why?

4. Because a monopolist is the only producer of a good or service, the demand curve facing a monopoly firm is the industry demand curve. *§2*

5. Price and marginal revenue are not the same for a monopoly firm. Marginal revenue is less than price. *§2.a*

6. The average-revenue curve is the demand curve. *§2.a.1*

7. A monopoly firm maximizes profit by producing the quantity of output yielded at the point where marginal revenue and marginal cost are equal. *§3.a*

8. A monopoly firm sets a price that is on the demand curve and that corresponds to the point where marginal revenue and marginal cost are equal. *§3.a*

? Why would someone want to have a monopoly in some business or activity?

9. A monopoly firm can make above-normal or normal profit or even a loss. If it makes above-normal profit, entry by other firms does not occur and the monopoly firm can earn above-normal profit in the long run. Exit occurs if the monopoly firm cannot cover costs in the long run. *§3.b*

Under what conditions would a monopolist charge different customers different prices for the same product?

10. Price discrimination occurs when the firm is not a price taker, can separate customers according to their price elasticities of demand for the firm's product, and can prevent resale of the product. *§4.a*

11. *Dumping* is a derogatory name given to the price discrimination used by firms selling in more than one nation. *§4.d*

How do the predictions of the models of perfect competition and monopoly differ?

12. A comparison of monopoly and perfectly competitive firms implies that monopoly imposes costs on society. These costs include less output's being produced and that output's being sold at a higher price. *§5.a*

13. The deadweight losses of monopoly may not be as large as the comparison with perfect competition suggests if (1) monopoly firms are more innovative, (2) the threat of potential competition or of government intervention causes the monopoly firm to lower price and increase quantity, or (3) the monopoly firm operates more efficiently than a perfectly competitive firm would. *§5.b*

14. The deadweight losses of monopoly may be larger than the comparison with perfect competition suggests if (1) the monopoly firm operates inefficiently because of a lack of competition, (2) rent seeking occurs, or (3) the monopolist is less innovative than the perfect competitor. *§5.c*

KEY TERMS

monopoly *§1.a*

monopoly firm (monopolist) *§1.a*

barrier to entry *§1.b*

natural monopoly *§1.c*

local monopoly *§1.c*

regulated monopoly *§1.c*

monopoly power *§1.c*

price discrimination *§4*

dumping *§4.d*

predatory dumping *§4.d*

deadweight loss *§5.a*

potential competition *§5.b.1*

X-inefficiency *§5.c.1*

rent seeking *§5.c.2*

EXERCISES

1. About 85 percent of the soup sold in the United States is Campbell's brand. Is Campbell Soup Company a monopoly firm?

2. Price discrimination is practiced by movie theaters, motels, golf courses, drugstores, and universities. Are they monopolies? If not, how can they carry out price discrimination?

3. Why is it necessary for the seller to be able to keep customers from reselling the product in order for price discrimination to occur? There are many products for which you get a discount for purchasing large quantities. For instance, most liquor stores will provide a discount on wine if you purchase a case. Is this price discrimination? If so, what is to keep one cus-

tomer from purchasing cases of wine and then reselling single bottles at a price above the case price but below the liquor store's single-bottle price?

4. Many people have claimed that there is no good for which substitutes are not available. If so, does this mean there is no such thing as monopoly?

5. Suppose that at a price of $6 per unit, quantity demanded is 12 units. Calculate the quantity demanded when the marginal revenue is $6 per unit. (*Hint:* The price elasticity of demand is unity at the midpoint of the demand curve.)

6. In the following figure, if the monopoly firm faces ATC_1, which rectangle measures total profit? If the

monopoly firm faces ATC_2, what is total profit? What information would you need in order to know whether the monopoly firm will shut down or continue producing in the short run? In the long run?

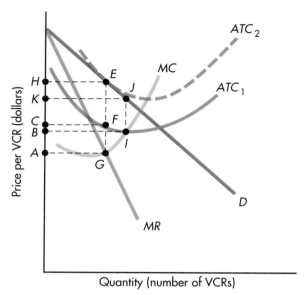

7. In recent years, U.S. car manufacturers have charged lower car prices in western states in an effort to offset the competition by the Japanese cars. This two-tier pricing scheme has upset many car dealers in the eastern states. Many have called it discriminatory and illegal.

   a. What conditions are necessary for this pricing scheme to be profitable to the U.S. companies?

   b. Is this pricing scheme the same as dumping?

8. Consider the following demand schedule. Does it apply to a perfectly competitive firm? Compute marginal and average revenue.

Price	Quantity
$100	1
$ 95	2
$ 88	3
$ 80	4
$ 70	5
$ 55	6
$ 40	7
$ 22	8

9. Suppose the marginal cost of producing the good in question 8 is a constant $10 per unit of output. What quantity of output will the firm produce?

10. Do you agree or disagree with this statement: "A monopoly firm will charge an exorbitant price for its product"? Explain your answer.

11. Do you agree or disagree with this statement: "A monopoly firm will run a much less safe business than a perfect competitor"? Explain your answer.

12. The pistachio nut growers of California petitioned the U.S. government to restrict the flow of Iranian pistachios because of dumping. Iranian pistachios were being sold in the United States at a price that was lower than it cost to produce the nuts in California. If you were an economist with the U.S. government, would you support the petition of the California growers?

13. State colleges and universities have two levels of tuition or fees. The less expensive is for residents of the state, the more expensive for nonresidents. Assume the universities are profit-maximizing monopolists and explain their pricing policy. Now, explain why the colleges and universities give student aid and scholarships.

14. Several electric utilities are providing customers with a choice of billing procedures. Customers can select a time-of-day meter that registers electric usage throughout the day, or they can select a regular meter that registers total usage at the end of the day. With the time-of-day meter, the utility is able to charge customers a much higher rate for peak usage than for nonpeak usage. The regular meter users pay the same rate for electric usage no matter when it is used. Why would the electric utility want customers to choose the time-of-day meter?

15. Suppose that a firm has a monopoly on a good with the following demand schedule:

Price	Quantity
$10	0
$ 9	1
$ 8	2
$ 7	3
$ 6	4
$ 5	5
$ 4	6
$ 3	7
$ 2	8
$ 1	9
$ 0	10

a. What price and quantity will the monopolist produce at if the marginal cost is a constant $4?

b. Calculate the deadweight loss from having the monopolist produce, rather than a perfect competitor.

Conflict Diamonds; Americans Can Stop the Damage They Do

This is a story about diamonds—"conflict diamonds." These stones come from war-ravaged Angola, Sierra Leone and Congo. Far from being anyone's best friend, they have proven a powerful enemy of the innocent thousands killed, wounded and maimed in those wars.

Why is this of concern to Americans? Because Americans buy 65 percent of all retail diamonds. Because if Americans begin to insist on proof that those diamonds are not washed with African blood, they can become a powerful force for bringing peace to these horribly brutalized peoples.

Rep. Tony Hall, D-Ohio, has introduced legislation that would require certificates on all diamonds, detailing their place of origin. The United Nations and the British government are pushing for tighter controls as well. Opinions differ on whether Hall's approach is practical, but his legislation sends a strong message to the diamond industry: Find ways to clean up your trade or we will.

"Diamonds are forever," says diamond cartel DeBeers. But human lives and human limbs aren't. Consider Maria, an 8-month-old baby girl in Sierra Leone. In an act of unfathomable cruelty, her arm was hacked off by the "rebel" terrorists of the Revolutionary United Front (RUF). The RUF mob has sought to impose its will on Sierra Leone by chopping off thousands of civilian hands, feet and ears. Thousands more people have simply been slaughtered and left to rot in village streets. Men, women, children, civilian, soldier; it makes no difference to the RUF.

What's the diamond connection? The RUF has kept itself well supplied with arms, vehicles, food and other supplies by mining and smuggling hundreds of millions of dollars worth of illicit diamonds into a world market that is determined to see no evil.

It's the same in Angola, where illicit diamonds have funded the 25-year-old war waged by Jonas Savimbi and his UNITA forces. By one estimate, UNITA earned $4 billion from its illegal sales of diamonds between 1992 and 1998. It used that money to undermine the Angola peace process and to purchase new arms.

The international diamond industry has taken several steps to stop the trade in illicit diamonds, but they are puny steps. Much more could be done, beginning with an acknowledgment of responsibility.

Take the DeBeers cartel. It mines 50 percent of the world's diamonds and purchases about 80 percent of those offered for sale on open markets. More than $4 billion in diamonds are stockpiled in DeBeers offices; it buys and sells in quantities designed to keep diamond prices at an artificially high rate. All told, it controls 85 percent of the world trade. (Where is trust buster Joel Klein when we need him?)

DeBeers insists it is impossible to tell where uncut diamonds originate (others disagree) but simultaneously insists it buys no conflict diamonds. How can those statements both be true? Well, DeBeers says, it has closed its offices in the controversial areas of Angola, Sierra Leone and Congo.

But here's how it works. The Ivory Coast diamond industry closed down in the 1980s, but Belgium recorded imports of more than 1.5 million carats in gemstones from the Ivory Coast annually in the mid-'90s. Those stones were most likely smuggled to the Ivory Coast from Angola and Sierra Leone.

Liberia produces about 100,000 carats a year. But between 1994 and 1998, more than 31 million carats were exported to the world diamond center in Antwerp. These too were smuggled stones, fueling not only the violence in their countries of origin, but in Liberia.

Sierra Leone officially exported only 8,500 carats in 1998, but Belgium recorded 770,000 carats coming from that country. You've got to ask: Why did Belgium take them, and where did they go?

The answers seem pretty straightforward: Belgium let them in because Antwerp is afraid of losing market share to Tel Aviv and Mumbai (formerly Bombay). And it's impossible to believe many of those stones didn't end up with DeBeers. Otherwise, the price would have tumbled.

If this trade in illicit diamonds caused harm only to soldiers, it would be bad enough. But for every soldier killed in these African wars, death and injury comes to scores of innocents like baby Maria.

What can you do? Push Congress and this year's crop of congressional candidates to put pressure on the international diamond trade. Because the United States is the premier retail market for diamonds, it has the clout to force a cleanup. Belgium and the major diamond trading companies seem determined to turn a blind eye. The United States must force that eye open.

Source: "Conflict Diamonds; Americans Can Stop the Damage They Do," *Star Tribune* (Minneapolis, MN), June 12, 2000, p. 10A. Copyright 2000 *Star Tribune*.

Star Tribune **(Minneapolis, MN)/June 12, 2000**

Commentary

One of the most famous monopolies is DeBeers, the diamond suppliers. DeBeers is not actually a monopolist—the only seller—but has been the dominant firm for nearly 70 years. The South African company controls over 60 percent of the $7 billion a year global market for uncut diamonds. Over the years, it has used its dominance of the industry to determine prices by buying up surplus diamonds. The policy dates back to 1934 when the Great Depression caused a slump in diamond prices and the chairman then of DeBeers, Sir Ernest Oppenheimer, offered to buy all the rough stones on the market. Had prices continued to fall, the move would have probably led to DeBeers's bankruptcy. But the price recovered and Sir Ernest's gamble laid the foundation for the company's dominance of the diamond industry for the remainder of the century. DeBeers spent billions of dollars to accumulate a large stockpile of diamonds which were never sold. At the end of 1999, the DeBeers's diamond mountain, hoarded in its London vaults, was worth around $4 billion. The diamonds were used to maintain or manipulate the price. But that practice is changing. DeBeers announced that it is giving up its traditional role of buyer of last resort of every stone on the market. The reason given for the change is what are called conflict diamonds, diamonds sold by various forces in Africa to fuel civil wars. DeBeers announced it will not purchase or trade in conflict diamonds.

While the policy might have some emotional or ethical appeal, the real reason DeBeers is ending its buyer of last resort strategy is to reduce its declining economic profits. DeBeers knows that if conflict, or blood, diamonds become an emotional consumer issue, they could trigger a public opinion backlash similar to the one that crippled the fur trade. Moreover, rivals such as BHP, the Australian group, and Rio Tinto of the United Kingdom are gaining more and more market share. DeBeers's strategy is two-pronged: one to attempt to reduce the supply of diamonds and one to increase the demand.

DeBeers's strategy on conflict diamonds is most likely motivated by more than just fears of a consumer boycott. If DeBeers can position itself as a producer and distributor of clean diamonds, it will keep a tight grip on the market without the expense of maintaining a stockpile. The company is proposing measures that will make it the only buyer of rough diamonds that are licensed. Moreover, by reducing the supply of licensed stones DeBeers will be able to sell its stockpile without disrupting prices. On the demand side, DeBeers spent $170 million last year to advertise the gems under its famous slogan, "A diamond is forever," and it has begun to place a certificate of guarantee on the stones that they are not from rebel-controlled areas. It has asked its buyers to join in the advertising campaign and to support its efforts at restricting the supply of diamonds from war-torn Africa.

It is difficult for a monopolist to give up that monopoly power and those positive economic profits. DeBeers doesn't plan to do so without a fight.

Chapter 12

Monopolistic Competition and Oligopoly

? Fundamental Questions

1. What is monopolistic competition?

2. What behavior is most common in monopolistic competition?

3. What is oligopoly?

4. In what form does rivalry occur in an oligopoly?

5. Why does cooperation among rivals occur most often in oligopolies?

Preview

To understand much of firms' behavior, one or more of the characteristics of perfect competition and monopoly must be altered. These alterations give us the models of monopolistic competition and oligopoly. ▪

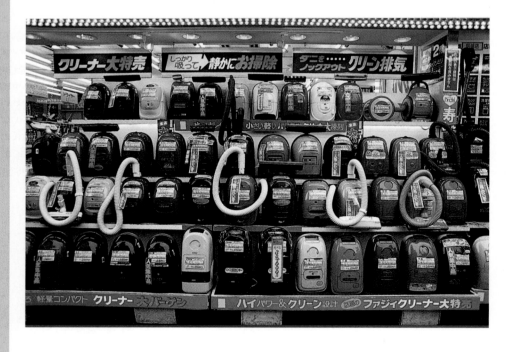

1. MONOPOLISTIC COMPETITION

1. What is monopolistic competition?

Monopolistic competition is a market structure in which (1) there are a large number of firms, (2) the products produced by the firms are differentiated, and (3) entry and exit occur easily. The definitions of *monopolistic competition* and *perfect competition* overlap. In both structures, there are a large number of firms. The difference is that each firm in monopolistic competition produces a product that is slightly different from all other products, whereas in perfect competition the products are standardized. The definition of *monopolistic competition* also overlaps with that of *monopoly*. Because each firm in monopolistic competition produces a unique product, each has a "mini" monopoly over its product. Thus, like a monopolist, the firm in a monopolistically competitive market structure has a downward-sloping demand curve, marginal revenue is below the demand curve, and price is greater than marginal cost. What distinguishes monopolistic competition from monopoly is ease of entry. Any time firms in monopolistic competition are earning above-normal profit, new firms enter and entry continues until firms are earning normal profit. In monopoly, a firm can earn above-normal profit in the long run. Table 1 summarizes differences among perfect competition, monopoly, and monopolistic competition.

1.a. Profits and Entry

Monopolistically competitive firms produce differentiated products.

Firms in monopolistic competition tend to use product differentiation more than price to compete. They attempt to provide a product for each market niche. Even though the total market might not be expanding, they divide the market into smaller and smaller segments by introducing variations of products. You can think of a market demand curve for clothes, but within that market there are many niches and many demand curves. In fact, there are separate demand curves for each product—Gap Kids, The Gap, J. Crew, The Limited, Limited Express, and so on. Each individual demand curve is quite price-elastic because of the existence of many close substitutes.

When a new product is introduced, the demand curve for all closely related products shifts in toward the origin because less of the total market is available for each product. New products are introduced as long as there are above-normal profits.

1.a.1. In the Short Run Figure 1(a) shows the cost and revenue curves of a monopolistically competitive firm providing a single product in the short run. As with all profit-maximizing firms, production occurs at the quantity where $MR = MC$. The

	Perfect Competition	Monopoly	Monopolistic Competition
Number of firms	Many	One	Many
Type of product	Undifferentiated	One	Differentiated
Entry conditions	Easy	Difficult or impossible	Easy
Demand curve for firm	Horizontal (perfectly elastic)	Downward sloping	Downward sloping
Price and marginal cost	$MC = P$	$MC < P$	$MC < P$
Long-run profit	Zero	Yes	Zero

Table 1

Summary of Perfect Competition, Monopoly, and Monopolistic Competition

For many years about the only choice of a toy for young girls was a Barbie. That has changed. In the doll category, the American Girls dolls initiated a new industry—dolls with a story attached. The American Girls were so successful that several copycat companies have emerged. The dolls represent the market process in action.

price the firm charges, P_1, is given by the demand curve at the quantity where $MR = MC$. Price P_1 is above average total cost, as indicated by the distance AB. Thus, the firm is earning above-normal profit, shown as the rectangle $CBAP_1$.

If the firms in a monopolistically competitive market are earning normal profit, the marginal-revenue and marginal-cost curves for each firm intersect at quantity Q_1 in Figure 1(b), and the price is P_1. The price is the same as the average total cost at Q_1, so a normal profit is obtained. If the firm is earning a loss, then the average-total-cost curve lies above the demand curve at the quantity produced, as shown in Figure 1(c). At Q_1, the firm is earning a loss, the rectangle P_1BAC. The firm must decide whether to temporarily suspend production of that product or continue producing because the outlook is favorable. The decision depends on whether revenue exceeds variable costs.

1.a.2. In the Long Run Whenever existing firms in a market structure without barriers to entry are earning above-normal profit, new firms enter the business and, in some cases, existing firms expand until all firms are earning the normal profit. In a perfectly competitive industry, the new firms supply a product that is identical to the product being supplied by existing firms. *In a monopolistically competitive industry, entering firms produce a close substitute, not an identical or standardized product.*

As the introduction of new products by new or existing firms occurs, the demand curves for existing products shift in until a normal profit is earned. For each firm and each product, the demand curve shifts in, as shown in Figure 2, until it just touches the average-total-cost curve at the price charged and output produced, P_2 and Q_2. When profit is at the normal level, expansion and entry cease.

When firms are earning a loss on a product and the long-run outlook is for continued losses, the firms will stop producing that product. Exit means that fewer differentiated products are produced, and the demand curves for the remaining products shift out. This continues until the remaining firms are earning normal profits.

Figure 1

A Monopolistically Competitive Firm

A monopolistically competitive firm faces a downward-sloping demand curve. The firm in Figure 1(a) maximizes profit by producing Q_1, where $MR = MC$, and charging a price, P_1, given by the demand curve above Q_1. Profit is the rectangle $CBAP_1$. In Figure 1(b) the firm is earning a normal profit because where $MR = MC$, price is P_1 on the demand curve above Q_1 and is equal to average total cost. In Figure 1(c) the firm is earning the loss of rectangle P_1BAC. At the profit-maximizing (loss-minimizing) output level, Q_1, average total cost exceeds price.

(a) Above Normal Profit

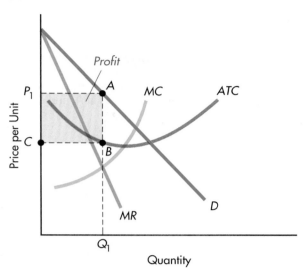

(b) Normal Profit

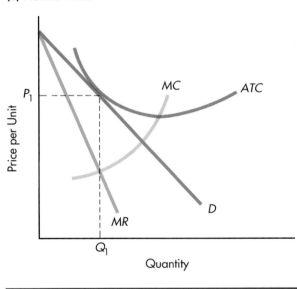

(c) Economic Loss

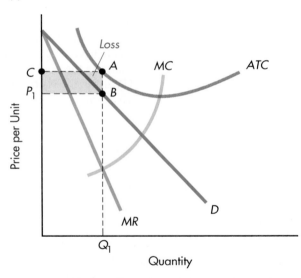

1.b. Monopolistic Competition versus Perfect Competition

Figure 3 shows both a perfectly competitive firm in long-run equilibrium and a monopolistically competitive firm in long-run equilibrium. The perfectly competitive firm, shown as the horizontal demand and marginal-revenue curve, $MR_{pc} = D_{pc}$, produces at the minimum point of the long-run average-total-cost curve at Q_{pc}; and the price, marginal cost, marginal revenue, and average total costs are P_{pc}. The long-run equilibrium for a monopolistically competitive firm is shown with the demand curve D_{mc} and marginal-revenue curve MR_{mc}. The monopolistically competitive firm produces at Q_{mc}, where $MR_{mc} = MC$, and charges a price determined by drawing a

Figure 2

Entry and Normal Profit

In the long run, the firm in monopolistic competition earns a normal profit. Entry shifts the firm's demand curve in from D_1 to D_2. Entry, which takes the form of a differentiated product, continues to occur as long as above-normal profits exist. When the demand curve just touches the average-total-cost curve, as at P_2 and Q_2, profit is at the normal level.

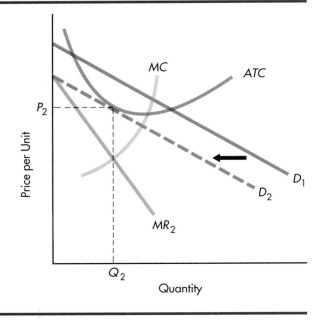

Monopolistically competitive firms produce less and charge a higher price than perfectly competitive firms.

vertical line up from the point where $MR_{mc} = MC$ to the demand curve. That price is just equal to the point where the long-run average-total-cost curve touches the demand curve, P_{mc}. In other words, at Q_{mc} the monopolistically competitive firm is just earning the normal profit.

The difference between a perfectly competitive firm and a monopolistically competitive firm is clear in Figure 3. Because of the downward-sloping demand curve

Figure 3

Perfect and Monopolistic Competition Compared

The perfectly competitive firm produces at the point where the price line, the horizontal MR curve, intersects the MC curve. This is the bottom of the ATC curve in the long run, quantity Q_{pc} at price P_{pc}. The monopolistically competitive firm also produces where $MR = MC$. The downward-sloping demand curve faced by the monopolistically competitive firm means that the quantity produced, Q_{mc}, is less than the quantity produced by the perfectly competitive firm, Q_{pc}. The price charged by the monopolistically competitive firm is also higher than that charged by the perfectly competitive firm, P_{mc} versus P_{pc}. In both cases, however, the firms earn only a normal profit.

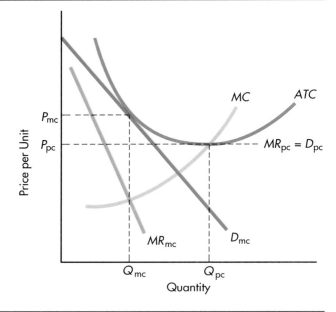

facing the monopolistically competitive firm, the firm does not produce at the minimum point of the long-run average-total-cost curve, Q_{pc}. Instead, it produces a smaller quantity of output, Q_{mc}, at a higher price, P_{mc}. The difference between P_{mc} and P_{pc} is the additional amount consumers pay for the privilege of having differentiated products. If consumers placed no value on product choice—if they desired generic products—they would not pay anything extra for product differentiation, and the monopolistically competitive firm would not exist.

Even though price does not equal marginal cost and the monopolistically competitive firm does not operate at the minimum point of the average-total-cost curve, the firm does earn normal profit in the long run. And although the monopolistically competitive firm does not strictly meet the conditions of economic efficiency (since price is not equal to marginal cost), the inefficiency is not due to the firm's ability to restrict quantity and increase price but instead results directly from consumers' desire for variety. It is hard to argue that society is worse off with monopolistic competition than it is with perfect competition since the difference is due solely to consumer desires. Yet variety is costly and critics of market economies argue that the cost is not worthwhile. Would the world be a better place if we had a simpler array of products to choose from, if there was a simple generic product—one type of automobile, say—for everyone?

Monopolistic competition does not yield economic efficiency because consumers are willing and able to pay for variety.

1.c. Nonprice Competition

2. What behavior is most common in monopolistic competition?

A firm in a monopolistically competitive market structure attempts to differentiate its product from the products offered by its rivals. Successful product differentiation reduces the price elasticity of demand. The demand curve, shown as the rotation from D_1 to D_2 in Figure 4, becomes steeper. McDonald's, for example, has successfully used advertising to differentiate its product.

Numerous characteristics may serve to differentiate products: quality, color, style, safety features, taste, packaging, purchase terms, warranties, and guarantees. A firm might change its hours of operation—for example, a supermarket might offer

Figure 4

Advertising, Prices, and Profits

A successful differentiation program will reduce the price elasticity of demand, shown as a steeper demand curve, D_2, compared to D_1. The successful differentiation enables the firm to charge a higher price.

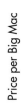
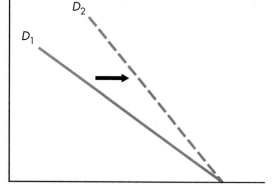

service 24 hours a day—to call attention to itself. Firms can also use location to differentiate their products. A firm may locate where traffic is heavy and the cost to the consumer of making a trip to the firm is minimal. If location is used for differentiation, however, why do fast-food restaurants tend to group together? Where you find a McDonald's you usually find a Taco Bell or a Wendy's nearby. The model of monopolistic competition explains this behavior. Suppose that five identical consumers—A, B, C, D, and E—are spread out along a line as shown in Figure 5. Consumer C is the median consumer, residing equidistantly from consumers B and D and equidistantly from consumers A and E. Assume that the five consumers care about the costs incurred in getting to a fast-food restaurant and are indifferent between the food offered. McDonald's is the first fast-food provider to open near these five consumers. Where does it locate? It locates as close to consumer C as possible because that location minimizes the total distance of all five consumers from McDonald's.

Taco Bell wants to open in the same area. If it locates near consumer D, then Taco Bell will pull customers D and E from McDonald's but will have no chance to attract A, B, or C. Conversely, if it locates near consumer A, only A will go to Taco Bell. Only if Taco Bell locates next door to McDonald's will it have a chance to gather a larger market share than McDonald's. As other fast-food firms enter, they too will locate close to McDonald's.

A prediction that comes from the theory of monopolistic competition is that an innovation or successful differentiation in any area—style, quality, location—leads initially to above-normal profit but eventually brings in copycats that drive profit back down to the normal level. In a monopolistically competitive market structure, innovation and above-normal profit for one firm are followed by entry and normal profit. Differentiation and above-normal profit then occur again. They induce entry, which again drives profit back to the normal level. The cycle continues until product differentiation no longer brings above-normal profit.

Figure 5

Location Under Monopolistic Competition

Five customers—A, B, C, D, and E—reside along a straight line. Customer C is in the middle, equidistant from B and D and from A and E. McDonald's decides to locate a restaurant at the spot that is closest to all five customers. This is the median position, where consumer C resides.

Other fast-food firms locate nearby because any other location will increase the total distance of some consumers from the fast-food restaurant, thereby causing some customers to go elsewhere.

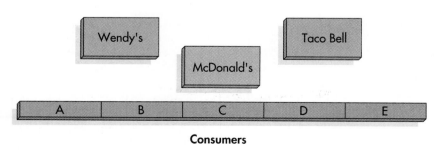

Consumers

RECAP

1. The market structure called *monopolistic competition* is an industry in which many sellers produce a differentiated product and entry is easy.
2. In the short run, a firm in monopolistic competition can earn above-normal profit.
3. In the long run, a firm in a monopolistically competitive market structure will produce at a higher cost and lower output than a firm in a perfectly competitive market structure will. In both market structures, firms earn only a normal profit.
4. Monopolistic competitors may engage more in nonprice competition than in price differentiation.

?

3. What is oligopoly?

2. OLIGOPOLY AND INTERDEPENDENCE

Oligopoly is a market structure characterized by (1) few firms, (2) either standardized or differentiated products, and (3) difficult entry. Oligopoly may take many forms. It may consist of one dominant firm coexisting with many smaller firms or a group of giant firms (two or more) that dominate the industry coexisting with other small firms. Whatever the number of firms, the characteristic that describes oligopoly is *interdependence*; an individual firm in an oligopoly does not decide what to do without considering what the other firms in the industry will do. When a large firm in an oligopoly changes its behavior, the demand curves of the other firms are affected significantly.

In monopolistically competitive and perfectly competitive markets, what one firm does affects each of the other firms so slightly that each firm essentially ignores the others. Each firm in an oligopoly, however, must closely watch the actions of the other firms because the action of one can dramatically affect the others. This interdependence among firms leads to actions not found in the other market structures.

?

4. In what form does rivalry occur in an oligopoly?

strategic behavior: the behavior that occurs when what is best for A depends on what B does, and what is best for B depends on what A does

game theory: a description of oligopolistic behavior as a series of strategic moves and countermoves

2.a. Oligopoly and Strategic Behavior

Because of the great variety of behavior possible under oligopoly, economists have been unable to agree on a single description of how oligopolistic firms behave. The only uniform description of the behavior of oligopolistic firms is *strategic*.

Strategic behavior occurs when what is best for A depends on what B does and what is best for B depends on what A does. It is much like a card game—bridge, say—where strategies are designed depending on the cards the players are dealt. Underbidding, overbidding, bluffing, deceit, and other strategies are carried out. In fact, the analogy between games and firm behavior in oligopoly is so strong that economists have applied **game theory** to their analyses of oligopoly. Game theory, developed in the 1940s by John von Neumann and Oskar Morgenstern, describes oligopolistic behavior as a series of strategic moves and countermoves. In this section we briefly discuss some of the theories of oligopolistic behavior.

2.a.1. The Kinked Demand Curve All firms know the law of demand. Thus, they know that sales will rise if price is lowered because people will purchase more of all goods (the income effect) and will substitute away from the more expensive goods to purchase more of the less expensive goods (the substitution effect). But the firms in an oligopoly may not know the shape of the demand curve for their product

Illicit drugs constitute about 4 percent of worldwide trade. Many governments attempt to stop the trade by confiscating supplies and arresting traders. The greatest demand for drugs comes from the United States and the greatest spending on drug interdiction takes place by the United States.

Game theory can illustrate ways in which oligopolistic firms interact. Game theory considers each firm a participant in a game where the winners are the firms with the greatest profit.

because the shape depends on how the rivals react to one another. They have to predict how their competitors will respond to a price change in order to know what their demand curve looks like.

Let's consider the auto industry. Suppose General Motors's costs have fallen (its marginal-cost curve has shifted down) and the company is deciding whether to lower the prices on its cars. If GM did not have to consider how the other car companies would respond, it would simply lower the price in order to be sure that the new MC curve intersected the MR curve, as illustrated in Figure 6(a). But GM suspects that the demand and marginal-revenue curves in Figure 6(a) do not represent its true market situation. Instead GM believes that if it lowers the prices on its cars from their current level of P_1, the other auto companies will follow suit. If they also lower the price on their cars, the substitution effect for the GM cars does not occur; sales of GM cars might increase a little but only because of the income effect. In other words, GM does not capture the market as indicated in Figure 6(b) by D_1 but finds the quantity demanded increasing along D_2 (below price P_1). Also GM suspects that should it increase the price of its cars, none of the other auto companies would raise theirs. In this case, the price increase would mean substantially reduced sales because of both the income and substitution effects. The quantity demanded decreases, as indicated along D_1. Consequently, the demand curve for GM is a combination of D_1 and D_2. It is D_1 above P_1 and D_2 below P_1, a demand curve with a *kink*.

What should GM do? It should price where $MR = MC$. But the resulting marginal-revenue curve is given by a combination of MR_1 and MR_2. The MR_1 curve slopes down gently until reaching the quantity associated with the kink. As we move below

Figure 6

The Kinked Demand Curve

If competitors follow price changes, the demand curve faced by an oligopolistic firm is the curve D_1 in Figures 6(a) and 6(b). If competitors do not follow price changes, the demand curve faced by the firm is D_2 in 6(b). If competitors match price decreases but not price increases, then the firm faces a combination of the two demand curves. If competitors do not follow a price increase, then above the current price, P_1, the relevant demand curve is D_1. If competitors do follow a price decrease, then below price P_1 the relevant demand curve is D_2. The demand curve is the shaded combinations of the two demand curves; it has a kink at the current price. The resulting marginal-revenue curve is also a combination of the two marginal-revenue curves. The marginal-revenue curve is MR_1 to the left of the kink in the demand curve and MR_2 to the right of the kink. Between the two marginal-revenue curves is a gap. The firm produces where $MR = MC$. If the MC curve intersects the MR curve in the gap, the resulting price is P_1 and the resulting quantity produced is Q_1. If costs fall, as represented by a downward shift of MC_1 to MC_2, the price and quantity produced do not change.

(a) Competitors Follow Price Changes

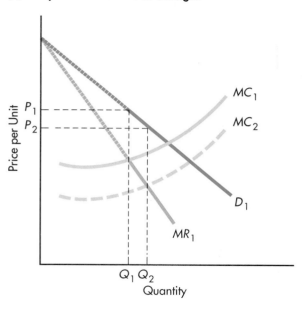

(b) Competitors Do Not Follow Price Changes

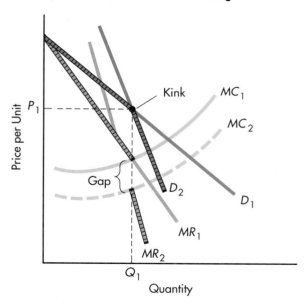

the kink, the MR_2 curve becomes the appropriate marginal-revenue curve. Thus, the shaded portions of the two marginal-revenue curves combine to give the firm's marginal-revenue curve. Notice how GM's marginal-cost curves, MC_1 and MC_2, intersect the combined MR curves at the same price and quantity, P_1 and Q_1. Thus, GM's strategy is to do nothing: *not* to change price even though costs have changed.

The firms in an oligopoly might avoid price competition altogether and devote resources to nonprice competition. Even with nonprice competition, however, strategic behavior comes into play, as noted in the next section.

2.a.2. Dominant Strategy Consider the situation in which firms must decide whether to devote more resources to advertising. When a firm in any given industry advertises its product, its demand increases for two reasons. First, people who had not used that type of product before learn about it, and some will buy it. Second, other people who already consume a different brand of the same product may switch brands. The first effect boosts sales for the industry as a whole, while the second redistributes existing sales within the industry.

Consider the cigarette industry as an example and assume that the matrix in Figure 7 illustrates the possible actions that two firms might undertake and the results of those actions. The top left rectangle represents the payoffs, or results, if both A and B advertise; the bottom left is where A advertises but B does not; the top right is the payoffs when B advertises but A does not; and the bottom right is the payoffs if neither advertises. If firm A can earn higher profits by advertising than by not advertising, whether or not firm B advertises, then firm A will surely advertise. This is referred to as a **dominant strategy**—a strategy that produces the best results no matter what strategy the opposing player follows. Firm A compares the left side of the matrix to the right side and sees that it earns more by advertising no matter what firm B does. If B advertises and A advertises, then A earns 70, but if A does not advertise it earns 40. If B does not advertise, then A earns 100 by advertising and only 80 by not advertising. The dominant strategy for firm A is to advertise. And according to Figure 7, the dominant strategy for firm B also is to advertise. Firm B will earn 80 by advertising and 50 by not advertising if A advertises. Firm B will earn 100 advertising, but only 90 not advertising if A does not advertise. But notice that both firms would be better off if neither advertised; firm A would earn 80 instead of 70, and firm B would earn 90 instead of 80. Yet, the firms cannot afford to *not* advertise because they would lose more if the other firm advertised and they didn't. This situation is known as the prisoner's dilemma; see the Economic Insight "The Prisoner's Dilemma" for a more complete description.

None of the cigarette manufacturers wants to do much advertising, for example. Yet strategic behavior suggests that they must. Firm A advertises, so firm B does also. Each ups the advertising ante. How can this expensive advertising competition be controlled? Each firm alone has no incentive to do it, since unilateral action will

dominant strategy: a strategy that produces better results no matter what strategy the opposing firm follows

Figure 7

Dominant Strategy Game

Figure 7 illustrates the dominant strategy game. The dominant strategy for firm A is to advertise. No matter what firm B does, firm A is better off advertising. If firm B does not advertise, firm A earns 80 not advertising and 100 advertising. If firm B does advertise, firm A earns 40 not advertising and 70 advertising. Similarly, firm B is better off advertising no matter what firm A does. Both A and B have dominant strategies—advertise.

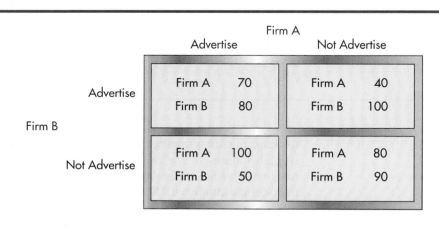

The Prisoner's Dilemma

Strategic behavior characterizes oligopoly. Perhaps the most well-known example of strategic behavior occurs in what is called the prisoner's dilemma.

Two people have been arrested for a crime, but the evidence against them is weak. The sheriff keeps the prisoners separated and offers each a special deal. If one prisoner confesses, that prisoner can go free as long as only he confesses, and the other prisoner will get ten or more years in prison. If both prisoners confess, each will receive a reduced sentence of two years in jail. The prisoners know that if neither confesses, they will be cleared of all but a minor charge and will serve only two days in jail. The problem is they do not know what deal the other is offered or if the other will take the deal.

The options available to the two prisoners are shown in the four cells of the figure. Prisoner B's options are shown along the horizontal direction and prisoner A's along the vertical direction. In the upper left cell is the result if both prisoners confess. In the

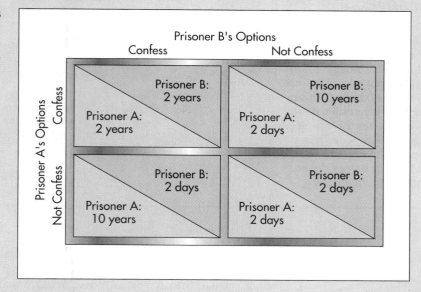

lower left is the result if prisoner A does not confess but prisoner B does; in the upper right cell is the result of A's confessing but prisoner B's not confessing; and in the lower right cell is the result when neither prisoner confesses. The dominant strategy for both prisoners is to confess and to receive two years of jail time.

If the prisoners had been loyal to each other, each would have received a much smaller penalty. Because both chose to confess, each is worse off than would have been the case if each had known what the other was doing. Yet, in the context of the interdependence of the decisions, each made the best choice.

---

mean a significant loss of market share. But if they can ban advertising together or if the government passes a law banning cigarette advertising, all of the cigarette companies will be better off. In fact, a ban on cigarette advertising on television has been in effect since January 1, 1971. The ban was intended by the government as a means of reducing cigarette smoking—of helping the consumer. Yet who does this ban really benefit?

2.a.3. Nondominant Strategy   There are many situations in which not every firm has a dominant strategy. Suppose that the payoffs for the two cigarette firms are such that firm A is better off advertising no matter what firm B does, but firm B is better off advertising only if firm A advertises. Then, in contrast to the prisoner's dilemma, the best strategy for firm B depends on the particular strategy chosen by firm A. Firm B does not have a dominant strategy.

Suppose the options to both firms are as illustrated in Figure 8 rather than Figure 7. Firm B chooses to advertise if firm A advertises (80 versus 60) and chooses not

Figure 8

Nondominant Strategy Game

The game indicated in Figure 7 is changed so that firm B does not have a dominant strategy. If firm A does not advertise, firm B earns 60 not advertising and 50 advertising; if firm A does advertise, firm B earns 60 not advertising and 80 advertising. Thus, what firm B does depends on what firm A does.

Firm A

	Advertise	Not Advertise
Advertise (Firm B)	Firm A 70 / Firm B 80	Firm A 40 / Firm B 50
Not Advertise	Firm A 100 / Firm B 60	Firm A 60 / Firm B 60

to advertise if firm A does not advertise (60 versus 50). Even though firm B does not have a dominant strategy, we can indicate what is likely to happen. Firm B is able to predict that firm A will advertise because that is a dominant strategy for firm A. Since firm B knows this, it knows that its own best strategy is also to advertise.

2.a.4. Sequential Games   The strategic situations we have considered so far have been ones in which both players must pick their strategies simultaneously. Each player had to choose a strategy knowing only the incentives facing the opponent, not the opponent's actual choice of strategy. But in many situations, one firm moves first, and the other is then able to choose a strategy based on the first firm's choice; this is known as a **sequential game.**

For years Volvo was known as the safest automobile on the road. This status enabled Volvo to command significantly higher prices than otherwise similar automobiles could. Now suppose that Daimler-Chrysler is considering whether to build an even safer car. Daimler-Chrysler knows that the firm known for producing the safest car will be able to earn a large profit but also fears the consequences if Volvo counters by building an even safer car.

Suppose that the situation facing Volvo and Daimler-Chrysler is as illustrated in Figure 9. Both firms start at point A, where Daimler-Chrysler must decide whether to enter with a car safer than those Volvo produces. If it does not, Volvo will receive a payoff of 120 and Daimler-Chrysler a payoff of 0, as noted by point C. If Daimler-Chrysler enters, however, they move to point B, where Volvo must decide whether to build an even safer car. The payoff to Volvo for building the even safer car is 50, but if Volvo does not build the safer car, its payoff will be 60. Volvo does not want Daimler-Chrysler to enter, but Daimler-Chrysler knows the payoffs facing Volvo and can conclude that the best option open to Volvo is not to produce the safer car. Thus, Daimler-Chrysler builds the safer car and Volvo does not counter. (Note that we are assuming there is no future beyond the decision to enter or not.)

sequential game: a situation in which one firm moves first and then the other is able to choose a strategy based on the first firm's choice

5. Why does cooperation among rivals occur most often in oligopolies?

2.b. Cooperation

If the firms in an oligopoly could come to some cooperative agreement, they could all be better off. For instance, Volvo and Daimler-Chrysler might spend no

Figure 9

Sequential Game

The game starts at point *A*, where Daimler-Chrysler must decide whether to enter with a safer car. If it does not, Volvo will receive a payoff of 120, Daimler-Chrysler a payoff of 0. If Daimler-Chrysler enters, however, the game moves to point *B*, where Volvo must decide whether to build an even safer car. Suppose that if Volvo builds the even safer car, its payoff will be 50 while Daimler-Chrysler will earn a payoff of −50 and that if Volvo does not build the even safer car, its payoff will be 60 while Daimler-Chrysler will get a payoff of 60. Daimler-Chrysler knows the payoffs facing Volvo and concludes that the best option open to Volvo is not to produce the even safer car.

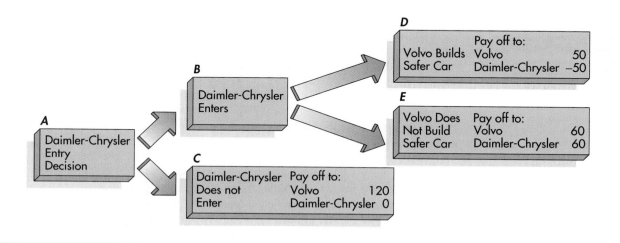

additional money and agree to share the market; the cigarette companies, discussed with Figures 7 and 8, might agree not to advertise. In each of these cases, the firms would earn greater profits. Cooperation is an integral part of oligopoly because there are only a few firms. The firms can communicate easier than the many firms in a perfectly competitive or monopolistically competitive industry.

2.b.1. Price-Leadership Oligopoly   One way for firms to communicate is to allow one firm to be the leader in changes in price or advertising activities. Once the leader makes a change, the others duplicate what the leader does. This action enables all firms to know exactly what the rivals will do. It eliminates a kink in the demand curve because both price increases and price decreases will be followed, and it avoids the situation where excessive expenses are made on advertising or other activities. This type of oligopoly is called a *price-leadership oligopoly*.

The steel industry in the 1960s is an example of a dominant-firm price-leadership oligopoly. For many years, steel producers allowed U.S. Steel to set prices for the entire industry. The cooperation of the steel companies probably led to higher profits than would have occurred with rivalry. However, the absence of rivalry is said to be one reason for the decline of the steel industry in the United States. Price leadership removed the need for the firms to compete by maintaining and upgrading equipment and materials and by developing new technologies. As a result, foreign firms that chose not to behave as price followers emerged as more-sophisticated producers of steel than U.S. firms.

For many years airlines also relied on a price leader. In many cases the price leader in the airlines was not the dominant airline but instead one of the weaker or new airlines. In recent years, airlines have communicated less through a price leader and more through their computerized reservation system, according to the Justice Department.

2.b.2. Collusion, Cartels, and Other Cooperative Mechanisms

Acting jointly allows firms to earn more profits than if they act independently or against each other. To avoid the destruction of strategic behavior, the few firms in an oligopoly can collude, or come to some agreement about price and output levels. Typically these agreements provide the members of the oligopoly higher profits and thus raise prices to consumers. Collusion, which leads to secret cooperative agreements, is illegal in the United States, although it is acceptable in many other nations.

A **cartel** is an organization of independent firms whose purpose is to control and limit production and maintain or increase prices and profits. A cartel can result from either formal or informal agreement among members. Like collusion, cartels are illegal in the United States. The cartel most people are familiar with is the Organization of Petroleum Exporting Countries (OPEC), a group of nations rather than a group of independent firms. During the 1970s, OPEC was able to coordinate oil production in such a way that it drove the market price of crude oil from $1.10 a barrel to $32 a barrel. For nearly eight years, each member of OPEC agreed to produce a certain, limited amount of crude oil as designated by the OPEC production committee. Then in the early 1980s, the cartel began to fall apart as individual members began to cheat on the agreement. Members began to produce more than their allocation in an attempt to increase profit. As each member of the cartel did this, the price of oil fell, reaching $12 per barrel in 1988. Oil prices rose again in 1990 when Iraq invaded Kuwait, causing widespread damage to Kuwait's oil fields. But, as repairs have been made to Kuwait's oil wells, it has increased production and oil prices have dropped.

Production quotas are not easy to maintain among different firms or different nations. Most cartels do not last very long because the members chisel on the agreements. If each producer thinks that it can increase its own production, and thus its profits, without affecting what the other producers do, all producers end up producing more than their assigned amounts; the price of the product declines and the cartel falls apart.

Economists have identified certain conditions that make it likely that a cartel will be stable. A cartel is likely to remain in force when:

- There are few firms in the industry.
- There are significant barriers to entry.
- An identical product is produced.
- There are few opportunities to keep actions secret.
- There are no legal barriers to sharing agreements.

The fact that sharing is possible, however, does not mean that successful sharing will occur. The incentive to cheat remains. There must be an ability to punish the cheaters if a cartel is to stick together. Typically a central authority or a dominant member of the cartel will enforce the rules of the cartel. In OPEC, the enforcer has been Saudi Arabia because it has the greatest supply of oil. In other cartels, a governing board acts as the enforcer. Even though cartels are illegal in the United States, a few have been sanctioned by the government. The National Collegiate Athletic Association (NCAA) is a cartel of colleges and universities. It sets rules of behavior and enforces those rules through a governing board. Member schools are placed on

cartel: an organization of independent firms whose purpose is to control and limit production and maintain or increase prices and profits

probation or their programs are dismantled when they violate the agreement. The citrus cartel, composed of citrus growers in California and Arizona, enforces its actions through its governing board. Sunkist Growers Inc., a cooperative of many growers, represents more than half of the California and Arizona production and also plays an important role in enforcing the rules of the cartel.

2.b.3. Facilitating Practices

Actions by firms can contribute to cooperation and collusion even though the firms do not formally agree to cooperate. Such actions are called **facilitating practices.** Pricing policies can leave the impression that firms are explicitly fixing prices, or cooperating, when in fact they are merely following the same strategies. For instance, the use of **cost-plus/markup pricing** tends to bring about similar if not identical pricing behavior among rival firms. If firms set prices by determining the average cost of an item and adding a fixed markup to the cost, they would be engaging in cost-plus pricing. If all firms face the same cost curves, then all firms will set the same prices. If costs decrease, then all firms will lower prices the same amount and at virtually the same time. Such pricing behavior is common in the grocery business.

Another practice that leads to implicit cooperation is the most-favored-customer policy. Often the time between purchase and delivery of a product is quite long. To avoid the possibility that customer A purchases a product at one price and then learns that customer B purchased the product at a lower price or benefited from product features unavailable to customer A, a producer will guarantee that customer A will receive the lowest price and all features for a certain period of time. Customer A is thus a **most-favored customer (MFC).**

The most-favored-customer policy actually gives firms an incentive not to lower prices even in the face of reduced demand. A firm that lowers the price of its product must then give rebates to all most-favored customers, which forces all other firms with most-favored-customer policies to do the same. In addition, the MFC policy allows a firm to collect information on what its rivals are doing. Customers will return products for a rebate when another firm offers the same product for a lower price.

Consider the behavior of firms that produced antiknock additives for gasoline from 1974 to 1979. Lead-based antiknock compounds had been used in the refining of gasoline since the 1920s. From the 1920s until 1948, the Ethyl Corporation was the sole domestic producer of the compounds. In 1948, DuPont entered the industry. The PPG Industries followed in 1961, and Nalco in 1964. Beginning in 1973, the demand for lead-based antiknock compounds decreased dramatically. However, because each company had most-favored-customer clauses, high prices were maintained even as demand for the product declined.

A most-favored-customer policy discourages price decreases because it requires producers to lower prices retroactively with rebates. If all rivals provide all buyers with most-favored-customer clauses, a high price is likely to be stabilized in the industry.

---

facilitating practices: actions by oligopolistic firms that can contribute to cooperation and collusion even though the firms do not formally agree to cooperate

cost-plus/markup pricing: a pricing policy that leads to similar if not identical pricing behavior among rival firms

most-favored customer (MFC): a customer who receives a guarantee of the lowest price and all product features for a certain period of time

---

RECAP

1. Oligopoly is a market structure in which there are so few firms that each must take into account what the others do, entry is difficult, and either undifferentiated or differentiated products are produced.
2. Interdependence and strategic behavior characterize an oligopolistic firm.
3. The shape of the demand curve and the marginal-revenue curve facing an oligopolist depends on how rival firms react to changes in price and product.

4. The kinked demand curve is one example of how oligopolistic firms might react to price changes. The kink occurs because rivals follow price cuts but not price increases.

5. Game theory provides a convenient way to describe behavior by oligopolistic firms. Such behavior includes the dominant strategy, as represented by the prisoner's dilemma; the nondominant strategy; and sequential decision making. In all of these games, the importance of the interdependence of firms is clear.

6. In a price-leadership oligopoly, one firm determines the price and quantity, knowing that all other firms will follow suit. The price leader is usually the dominant firm in the industry.

7. Oligopolistic firms have incentives to cooperate. Collusion, making a secret cooperative agreement, is illegal in the United States. Cartels, also illegal in the United States, rest on explicit cooperation achieved through formal agreement.

8. Facilitating practices implicitly encourage cooperation in an industry.

3. SUMMARY OF MARKET STRUCTURES AND THE INFORMATION ASSUMPTION

We have now discussed in some detail each of the four market structures. Table 2 summarizes the characteristics and the main predictions yielded by each model. The model of perfect competition predicts that firms will produce at a point where price and marginal cost are the same (at the bottom of the average-total-cost curve) and profit will be zero in the long run. The model of monopoly predicts that price will exceed marginal cost and that the firm can earn positive economic profit in the long run. With monopolistic competition, price will exceed marginal cost and the firm will not produce at the bottom point of the average-total-cost curve, but this is due to the consumer's desire for product differentiation. In the long run, the firm in monopolistic competition will earn a normal profit. In oligopoly, a firm may be able

Table 2

Summary of Perfect Competition, Monopoly, Monopolistic Competition, and Oligopoly

	Perfect Competition	Monopoly	Monopolistic Competition	Oligopoly
Number of firms	Many	One	Many	Few
Type of product	Undifferentiated	One	Differentiated	Undifferentiated or differentiated
Entry conditions	Easy	Difficult or impossible	Easy	Difficult
Demand curve for firm	Horizontal (perfectly elastic)	Downward sloping	Downward sloping	Downward sloping
Price and marginal cost	$MC = P$	$MC < P$	$MC < P$	$MC < P$
Long-run profit	Zero	Yes	Zero	Depends on whether entry occurs

to earn above-normal profit for a long time—as long as entry can be restricted. In oligopoly, price exceeds marginal cost, and the firm does not operate at the bottom of the average-total-cost curve.

Under perfect competition, consumers purchase products at the lowest possible price; there is no advertising, no excessive overhead, and no warranties or guarantees. Under monopoly, people purchase a single product and advertising is virtually non-existent. With monopolistic competition and oligopoly, advertising may occur but it provides information only. Consumers purchase different products because the products are, in fact, physically different, not because of images, feelings, or seeing some famous person endorse the product. Why, then, do we see and hear image advertising if the models do not account for it? Remember that a model is a simplification of reality. A model allows us to focus on one or more real-life aspects without getting bogged down in the details. Then, as we need to consider more or different aspects, we relax some of the assumptions of our model. The assumption we must relax now is the assumption that consumers and firms have perfect information.

Since information is costly to acquire, consumers and firms will not have complete or perfect information. This means that consumers will have to make decisions using incomplete information, and firms will have to ensure that consumers have information that will benefit the firms.

3.a. Brand Names

A firm can provide information to consumers by creating brand names. A brand name is a product that consumers associate with a specific firm: Vidal Sassoon hair care products, Guess clothes, Bayer aspirin, McDonald's, and Nike, rather than the names shampoo, jeans, aspirin, fast food, and athletic shoes. If consumers had perfect information, producers would have no incentive to create brand names or to differentiate products other than by actual physical characteristics. Brand names can thus serve as *signals*—indications of the quality of the product or of the firm producing and selling the product.

Consider the case of sidewalk vendors who sell neckties on the streets of any large city. If such a "firm" tells customers that it will guarantee the quality of its ties, customers will certainly question the validity of the guarantee since if the firm decides to go out of business, it can do so with virtually no losses. It has no headquarters, no brand name, no costly capital equipment, no loyal customers to worry about—indeed, no sunk, or unrecoverable, costs of any kind. In short, a firm with no obvious stake in the future has a difficult time persuading potential customers it will make good on its promises.

The incentives are different for a firm that has devoted significant resources to items that have no liquidation value, such as advertising campaigns or specific capital expenditures like McDonald's golden arches. Firms such as these have reputations to protect and want repeat business. And buyers, knowing that, can place greater trust in the promise of a high-quality product.

Businesses, then, purchase advertising time and space on television, on radio, and in the newspapers. They construct elaborate signs, build fancy storefronts, and attempt to locate in places where they are visible and accessible. They also package their products in carefully designed boxes and wrappings. All of these expenditures are intended to convince people that their products, identified by brand names, are quality products.

Consumers are often willing to pay a higher price for a brand-name product than for a similar product without a brand name. Consumers who purchase brand-name pharmaceuticals because they believe the brand name has some value may be right even if a brand-name pharmaceutical and a generic product are chemically identical. Drug companies that spend a great deal of money to create brand names may be less likely to create shoddy or dangerous products than firms that do not offer brand names. In the early 1990s, when President Clinton was describing the cause of high health-care costs, he blamed the drug companies. Supporting his contention, a congressional study pointed out that drug firms spend $10 billion per year on marketing and advertising, $2 billion more than they spend on developing new drugs. But this expenditure may be what is necessary to provide the information consumers want—the sunk costs necessary to provide quality assurance to consumers.[1]

3.b. Guarantees

Another way to inform consumers of the quality of the product is to provide a guarantee against product defects. Guarantees are difficult to fake. A low-quality product would break down frequently, making the guarantee quite costly for the firm. Thus, the higher the quality of the product, the better the guarantee offered by the firm.

Once the highest-quality product appears with its guarantee, consumers have some information about the quality of that product—and also about the quality of all remaining products. They know that products without guarantees are not of the highest quality. Without other information about a product that has no guarantee, consumers might assume the quality of that product to be no better than the average quality of all such products. This places the producer of the second-best product in a difficult position. If it continues to offer no guarantee, consumers will think its product is worse than it really is, but its guarantee cannot match that of the highest-quality product. Thus, the producer of the second-best product must offer a guarantee of its own, but the terms of its guarantee cannot be quite as good as those for the best product.

With the introduction of the guarantee on the highest-quality product, the competitive process is set in motion and in the end all producers must either offer guarantees or live with the knowledge that consumers rank their products lower in quality. The terms of the guarantees will in general be less liberal the lower a product's quality. Producers clearly do not want to announce their low-quality levels by offering stingy warranty coverage, but failure to offer something makes consumers think the quality level is even lower than it is.

RECAP

1. Brand names, guarantees, and sunk costs are ways firms can provide information to consumers.

SUMMARY

? What is monopolistic competition?

1. Monopolistic competition is a market structure in which many firms are producing a slightly different product and entry is easy. *§1*

2. Monopolistically competitive firms will earn a normal profit in the long run. *§1.a.2*

---

[1]Constance Sommer, "Drug Firms' 'Excess Profit': $2 Billion Yearly," *Los Angeles Times*, February 26, 1993.

? What behavior is most common in monopolistic competition?

3. Entry occurs in monopolistically competitive industries through the introduction of a slightly different product. *§1.a*

4. A monopolistically competitive firm will produce less output and charge a higher price than an identical perfectly competitive firm if demand and costs are assumed to be the same. *§1.b*

? What is oligopoly?

5. Oligopoly is a market structure in which a few large firms produce identical or slightly different products and entry is difficult but not impossible. *§2*

? In what form does rivalry occur in an oligopoly?

6. Strategic behavior characterizes oligopoly. Each oligopolist must watch the actions of other oligopolists in the industry. *§2.b*

7. The kinked demand curve results when firms follow a price decrease but do not follow a price increase. *§2.b.1*

8. Strategic behavior can be illustrated using game theory. A dominant strategy is when the strategy that makes the firm best off does not depend on what rivals do. A nondominant strategy occurs when a firm's behavior or strategy varies, depending on what its rivals do. *§2.b.2, 2.b.3*

9. A sequential game illustrates the situation where one firm selects a strategy before another firm does. *§2.b.4*

? Why does cooperation among rivals occur most often in oligopolies?

10. The small number of firms in oligopoly and the interdependence of these firms creates the situation where the firms are better off if they cooperate (as in the prisoner's dilemma). *§2.b.2, 2.c*

11. Price leadership is another type of strategic behavior. One firm determines price for the entire industry. All other firms follow the leader in increasing and decreasing prices. The dominant firm in the industry is most likely to be the price leader. *§2.c.1*

12. Practices like collusion and cartels minimize profit-reducing rivalry and ensure cooperation. Both are illegal in the United States but acceptable in many other nations. *§2.c.2*

13. Cost-plus pricing ensures that firms with the same costs will charge the same prices. The most-favored-customer policy guarantees a customer that the price he or she paid for a product will not be lowered for another customer. Cost-plus pricing and the most-favored-customer policy are facilitating practices. *§2.c.3*

14. Firms must ensure that consumers get information about the firm and its products that is beneficial. Brand names, guarantees, and certain (sunk cost) expenditures will indicate product quality. *§3.a*

KEY TERMS

strategic behavior *§2.a*

game theory *§2.a*

dominant strategy *§2.a.2*

sequential game *§2.a.4*

cartel *§2.b.2*

facilitating practices *§2.b.3*

cost-plus/markup pricing *§2.b.3*

most-favored customer (MFC) *§2.b.3*

EXERCISES

1. Disney, Universal, and MGM, among others, have movie studios in Hollywood. Each of these major studios also has one or several subsidiary studios. Disney, for example, has Touchstone. What market structure best describes these movie production companies? Why would each studio have subsidiary studios? Consider the movies that have come out under Disney and those under Touchstone. Are they different?

2. Suppose that Disney was experiencing above-normal profits. If Disney is a member of a monopolistically competitive industry, what would you predict would occur over time to its demand curve (the demand curve for Disney movies)? Suppose that Disney is a member of an oligopoly. How would this change your answer?

3. Why is the monopolistically competitive industry said to be inefficient? Suppose that you counted the higher price the consumer pays for the monopolistically competitive firm's product as part of consumer surplus. Would that change the conclusion regarding the efficiency of monopolistic competition?

4. Why might some people claim that the breakfast cereal industry is monopolistically competitive but the automobile industry is an oligopoly? In both cases, about eight to ten firms dominate the industry.

5. The graph that follows shows an individual firm in long-run equilibrium. In which market structure is this firm operating? Explain. Compare the long-run quantity and price to those of a perfectly competitive firm. What accounts for the difference? Is the equilibrium price greater than, equal to, or less than marginal cost? Why, or why not?

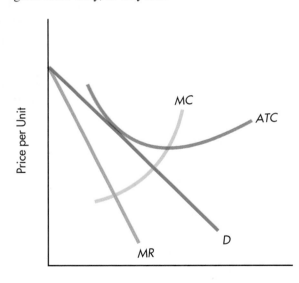

6. Explain what is meant by strategic behavior. How does the kinked demand curve describe strategic behavior?

7. What is the cost to a firm in an oligopoly that fails to take rivals' actions into account? Suppose the firm operates along demand curve D_1, shown below, as if no firms will follow its lead in price cuts or price

rises. In fact, however, other firms do follow the price cuts and the true demand curve below price P_1 lies below D_1. If the firm sets a price lower than P_1, what happens?

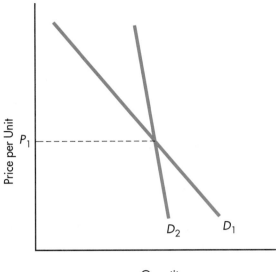

8. Suppose the following demand schedule exists for a firm in monopolistic competition. Suppose the marginal cost is a constant $70. How much will the firm produce? Is this a long- or short-run situation? Suppose the firm is earning above-normal profit. What will occur to this demand schedule?

Price	Quantity
$100	1
$ 95	2
$ 88	3
$ 80	4
$ 70	5
$ 55	6
$ 40	7
$ 22	8

9. The cement industry is an example of an undifferentiated oligopoly. The automobile industry is a differentiated oligopoly. Which of these two is most likely to advertise? Why?

10. The South American cocaine industry consists of several "families" that obtain the raw material, refine it, and distribute it in the United States. There are only about three large families, but there are several small families. What market structure does the

industry most closely resemble? What predictions based on the market-structure models can be made about the cocaine business? How do you explain the lack of wars among the families?

11. The NCAA is described as a cartel. In what way is it a cartel? What is the product being produced? How does the cartel stay together?

12. Almost every town has at least one funeral home even if the number of deaths could not possibly keep the funeral home busy. What market structure does the funeral home best exemplify? Use the firm's demand and cost curves and long-run equilibrium position to explain the fact that the funeral home can handle more business than it has. (*Hint:* Is the firm operating at the bottom of the average-total-cost curve?)

13. The payoff matrix below shows the profit two firms earn if both advertise, neither advertises, or one advertises while the other does not. Profits are reported in millions of dollars. Does either firm have a dominant strategy?

Firm 1

	Advertise	Not Advertise
Advertise	Firm 1 earns profit of 100.	Firm 1 earns profit of 50.
	Firm 2 earns profit of 20.	Firm 2 earns profit of 70.
Firm 2		
Not Advertise	Firm 1 earns profit of 0.	Firm 1 earns profit of 20.
	Firm 2 earns profit of 10.	Firm 2 earns profit of 60.

14. Use the payoff matrix below for the following exercises. The payoff matrix indicates the profit outcome that corresponds to each firm's pricing strategy.

Firm A's Price

		$20	$15
	$20	Firm A earns $40 profit. Firm B earns $37 profit.	Firm A earns $35 profit. Firm B earns $39 profit.
Firm B's Price			
	$15	Firm A earns $49 profit. Firm B earns $30 profit.	Firm A earns $38 profit. Firm B earns $35 profit.

a. Firms A and B are members of an oligopoly. Explain the interdependence that exists in oligopolies using the payoff matrix facing the two firms.

b. Assuming that the firms cooperate, what is the solution to the problem facing the firms?

c. Given your answer to part b, explain why cooperation would be mutually beneficial.

d. Given your answer to part c, explain why one of the firms might cheat on a cooperative arrangement.

15. What would occur if any maker of aspirin could put a Bayer Aspirin label on its product? Why must a signal between rivals be costly to fake and involve extensive sunk costs?

Internet Exercises/ Resources

For Internet exercises and web resources related to this chapter, go to **http://college.hmco.com.**

Poker Player's Game Theory Scoops Pounds 22bn for Treasury

The economist behind the Government's mobile phone windfall honed his skills in game theory by playing poker and Monopoly.

Prof Ken Binmore, 59, said they helped him develop a sense of strategy that was useful when he led the team that devised the auction for licenses to run the next generation of mobile telephones.

The bidding closed yesterday with the Treasury pounds 22.48 billion richer—five times more than the highest initial forecasts—thanks to intense rivalry between mobile phone companies.

Of his auction system, which took three years to develop, he said: "It's good for consumers, good for the Chancellor, and it will keep prices down as well. It's a triumph for economics."

Prof Binmore is director of the Centre for Economic Learning and Social Evolution at University College London, and author of 77 published papers and 11 books on evolutionary game theory, bargaining theory, experimental economics, political philosophy, mathematics and statistics.

At the heart of his work is the mathematical analysis of games first developed by the computer pioneer John von Neumann in the Twenties.

Game theory analyses successful strategies when the outcome is uncertain and, crucially, depends on the behaviour and strategies of others. Game theorists love auctions because the rules of the game are clearly defined. . . .

Prof Binmore, who said he used to do "pretty well" as a young poker player and claims he is "very good" at plotting strategies in Monopoly, had to design an auction that prevented bidders from adopting cunning tactics to swing the balance in their favour.

"We had to think of strategies they might adopt and then plan for them," he said. "One of the keys to it was offering all five licenses simultaneously."

He said Turkey had made a mistake when it offered two mobile phone licenses sequentially and then stipulated that bidding for the second license would start at whatever price the first license eventually sold for.

One company put in such a large initial bid that no one else followed. The company did not even bid for the second license because no one else could afford to, effectively giving it a monopoly.

"There are many pitfalls but I think we avoided them," said Prof Binmore. "In Spain and Finland they more or less gave their licenses away in a sort of 'beauty contest' in which a group of civil servants simply picked the business plan they thought was best.

"But who knows what's best? Not economists or civil servants. The ones who know are the guys who run the business, the bidders themselves. But they're not going to tell you which plan is best—they'll just tell you theirs is.

"The auction forces it out of them. As the price goes up, they have to revalue what they think the license is worth. You end up with the one bidder who still thinks they can make a profit, while all the others have dropped out. That final bidder's business plan is therefore presumably the best one."

Prof Binmore, a working class boy who grew up in a council flat in Kilburn, north London, after his family was bombed during the Blitz, uses his spare time to study moral and political philosophy.

Ironically, he admitted he hated using mobile phones, only carrying one in case his car broke down.

Source: "Poker Player's Game Theory Scoops Pounds," *Daily Telegraph* (London), April 28, 2000, p. 10. Copyright 2000 Telegraph Group Limited.

Daily Telegram (London)/April 28, 2000

Commentary

Strategic behavior involves the interdependence of actions; what one does affects and is affected by what others do. This is what game theory attempts to describe. It seems that game theory would be really useful for managers attempting to understand competition. All managers are absorbed in their own firm's situations. Putting themselves in the shoes of competitors and focusing on their competitors' probable reactions to various strategies is mind expanding. Although expressions like "game theory," "zero sum game," and "prisoner's dilemma" have become part of everyday language, game theory has not been used much by business.

Perhaps part of the problem is that people expect game theory to provide definitive answers to problems. Game theory doesn't necessarily provide a solution; it's a way of thinking about the future. Its value in this regard was emphasized in recent actions in the United Kingdom. The U.K. government rejected Sky's takeover bid for Manchester United because the merger would have given Sky the ability to influence the outcome of negotiations between all the soccer clubs and TV companies over match rights.

More often, game theory can identify potential problems. Consider the 1991 situation in Britain where licenses for Interactive TV franchises were auctioned off on a single-bid, franchise-by-franchise basis. The system generated wildly divergent results since competition for each franchise was uneven. Central TV, which knew it had no competition, got away with bidding just 2,000 pounds. Yorkshire Television was so worried about the competition that it bid 37.7 million pounds, an amount which later pushed it into financial difficulties. Game theory would have identified the potential problems if the number of players and the value each brought to the game had been identified. In another public auction, this one in Turkey, there were to be two auctions for broadcasting franchises. Only two licenses were to be sold and the auctions were to be held sequentially. The second auction would begin at the price paid for the first license. The problem was that the winner of the first auction bid so high that no one was interested in the second license. The first winner had purchased a monopoly. Again, game theory would have identified the potential problem: the auctions should have occurred simultaneously and should have had no end period; the auctions should have gone on until the winner in each had been determined.

Game theory can be a useful way to examine oligopoly and all the possible behaviors firms in an oligopolistic industry might undertake.

Chapter 13

The New Economy

Preview

Since about 1995 we have heard the term *New Economy.* Does the New Economy mean a new economics? Does it mean that conventional economics is dead? A headline in the *Wall Street Journal,* January 1, 2000, stated:

SO LONG SUPPLY AND DEMAND

In that same issue of the *Wall Street Journal* the editors argued that "products used in networks increase in value as supply rises, thereby contradicting the old economics of supply and demand."

The New Economy encompasses the results of the technological changes occurring in information processing. In this chapter we discuss technological change and its implications for economics. We examine what is different and what is the same in the New and Old Economies. ■

1. A NEW ECONOMICS?

1. What is the difference between the New Economy and the Old Economy?

The five best stock market performers in the 1980s are listed below along with the percentage change in the price of their stocks over the decade. Next to that list is a list of the top five performers for the 1990s.

1980's Top Performers		1990's Top Performers	
Company	*Change*	*Company*	*Change*
1. Circuit City	8,252%	1. AOL	79,630%
2. Limited	6,100%	2. Dell	72,445%
3. Hasbro	5,582%	3. EMC	69,638%
4. Home Depot	4,997%	4. Cisco	64,498%
5. Wal-Mart	4,032%	5. CMGI	61,187%

The difference in percentage changes between decades is staggering, 8,000 versus 80,000, but the greatest difference is that the top businesses in the 1980s were retailers while the top performers in the 1990s were the Internet—hi-tech companies. These differences are signs of the changes that have occurred since the 1980s. Other signs include the number of .com advertisements; the number of passwords you have to keep track of; the ease with which you can purchase items without entering a store; and the fact that you can register for classes, find out about your grades, and get a syllabus for a class on-line.

However, while the New Economy does mean many changes, it does not alter the fundamental truth that scarcity will always be with us. It is just human nature to want more than we have. This means we still have to make choices, compare costs and benefits, and realize there are opportunity costs involved in any decision. Let's discuss what the economics of the New Economy really are.

1.a. Technological Change

The New Economy is a world in which technological change, particularly that involving information, is occurring at a rapid pace. Technological change is nothing new, however. It has been occurring since the beginning of time. Technological change and innovation are necessary; for a country they increase standards of living, and for individual firms they increase shareholder wealth.

Where does technological change come from? It is primarily the result of research, the *R* in R&D (research and development). There are two kinds of research, **basic research,** which is aimed purely at the creation of new knowledge, and **applied research,** which is expected to have a practical payoff. **Development** is the *D* in R&D; it is the process of turning research findings into practical applications. Some firms are involved in all three activities, some in just one, and some firms do no research and development. Most businesses involved in R&D are interested in applied research since the return on R&D expenditures there is quicker than in basic research. Most basic research occurs at academic institutions (universities).

basic research: creation of new knowledge

applied research: finding applications for basic research results

development: turning research into viable products

The long-run effect of the adoption of technology typically means a reduction in the long-run cost curves—more output produced per dollar of expenditure—but may also affect economies and diseconomies of scale. For instance, in Figure 1(a) the shape of the long-run average cost curve remains the same but shifts down due to increased productivity. New methods of delivering vaccines (e.g., using fruits such as bananas to deliver the vaccine) have reduced the costs of vaccination but

Figure 1

Technological Change and Scale Economies

In Figure 1(a) the technological change has no effect on scale. Figure 1(b) illustrates the case in which technological change leads to an increase in economies of scale. Figure 1(c) reflects the case in which technological change reduces the scale economies.

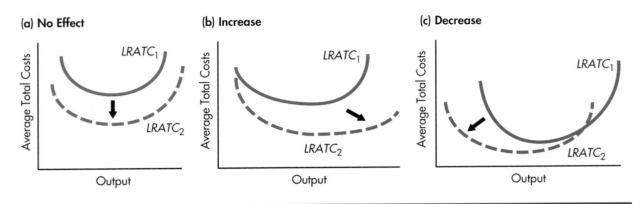

(a) No Effect

Average Total Costs

$LRATC_1$

$LRATC_2$

Output

(b) Increase

Average Total Costs

$LRATC_1$

$LRATC_2$

Output

(c) Decrease

Average Total Costs

$LRATC_1$

$LRATC_2$

Output

have not changed the economies of scale. This is an example of innovation without altering scale economies. Figure 1(b) illustrates the case in which the new technology increases the range of economies of scale. An example of this type of innovation is the basic oxygen furnace which quadrupled the range over which economies of scale occurred in steel manufacturing. Figure 1(c) illustrates the case in which the new technology reduces the range of economies of scale. Examples include fiber optics and satellites which reduced the economies of scale in communication, ATM machines which reduced the economies of scale in banking, and new power plants which reduced the scale economies in electricity generation.

1.b. Patent Races

Research and development is often referred to as a patent race in that firms compete to develop a new product or process and then obtain a patent on that product or process. The first firm successfully doing this is the winner.

Patents confer a property right—a right to the exclusive ownership of the patented product or process. Gaining that property right does not necessarily mean the patent holder is going to reap positive economic profits for 17 years (the length of a patent). In some cases, a patent allows rival firms to learn about the innovation and reverse-engineer it—take it apart and reconstruct it. In fact, the costs of duplicating a major new product are only about one-half of the original innovator's research and development costs and timely duplication of a major, patented new product is reported to be impossible in only a few industries. Nevertheless, the benefits from obtaining a patent can be substantial: brand names can be created or enhanced, new financing can be obtained, and relationships with other businesses can be created. In industries in which improvements in productivity are the result of learning and experience that occur as a firm produces more of a given item, a company that captures an initial advantage could have a long-term advantage.

When the semiconductor chips and electronic products industry was young, Texas Instruments priced its product at less than its then-current average costs in order to increase its output rate and its cumulative total output. Believing that the advantage of experience was large, it hoped that by increasing the speed at which it got experience it would quickly reduce its average costs. The strategy was successful and Texas Instruments was able to drive rivals from the market. An example of gaining a patent first is provided by Amazon.com. It gained an initial advantage over other booksellers and on-line retailers with its patented click-and-buy software.

1.c. Changing Business

As we discussed in previous chapters, in the Old Economy a company's sales force, system of branches, printing press, chain of stores, and delivery fleet could serve as barriers to entry to other companies and thus were assets to the company. In the New Economy, these could be liabilities rather than assets. The Encyclopaedia Britannica went from a peak in 1989 of $650 million in revenue and a sales force of 2,300 to a point where it won't release financial figures and has only about 300 employees. What happened? Technological change totally altered the encyclopedia business. The content of the encyclopedias is now provided on-line whereas it used to be sold by door-to-door salespeople. The sales force thus became obsolete. And encyclopedias are not alone; virtually every business has been and is being affected by the technological changes occurring in information processing and communication.

Nearly every product has both a physical aspect and an information content that goes along with the physical aspect. When the information content of a product can be separated from the physical product, the supply chain of the product may be fundamentally changed. A supply chain is the flow of resources from their original form through the steps that turn them into a final product. When the supply chain is torn apart or fundamentally altered, deconstruction of the supply chain is said to have occurred.

In some respects actions in the New Economy might more reflect markets in Adam Smith's time, 1770s, than what we know as markets today. Ebay has created a way that individual buyers and sellers can interact as buyers bid for products offered for sale by the sellers. The price is bid up as potential buyers try to acquire the product; if the price is too high, no one bids and the seller must decide whether to list again at a lower price.

Textbooks, for example, involve the physical book itself, the information contained in the book, and the bookstore at which the book can be examined and purchased. Are textbooks candidates for deconstruction? Yes. The authors could place the textbook material on a web site and allow the textbook, individual chapters, or parts of chapters to be downloaded for a price.

Consider the selling of automobiles. Currently, dealerships provide information in showrooms and at test drives, they hold inventory and distribute cars, they broker financing, they make a market in secondhand cars, and they operate maintenance and repair services. Each of these services could become a separate business. Some firms could specialize in test drives; customers could select autos to test-drive by going on-line to a web site and clicking the cars, models, options, and so on. Distributors could have a single warehouse from which the desired car would be shipped. Car purchasers could obtain financing via an auction on an electronic bulletin board.

1.d. Firm Size and the Adoption of Technology

Whenever a period of rapid technological change occurs, the question arises why it is the upstart firms that first innovate and the large dominant firms that lag behind. Business history contains many instances of companies with a wealth of assets, innovative products, strong reputations, financial resources, and powerful distribution channels whose market position was eroded or overtaken by companies with seemingly much smaller resource bases. Xerox versus Canon in copiers, Sony versus RCA in television, and CNN versus ABC, CBS, and NBC in news programming are examples.

Are small firms more nimble and less bureaucratic than large firms? Do large companies become fat and happy and fall asleep while small companies are hungry and awake to opportunities? Do the dominant firms keep innovations hidden away by buying the innovations of small upstart firms or even buying the small firms? Though superficially appealing, and thus often stated, these arguments fail to answer a fundamental question of why established firms would be systematically less able to innovate or break with established practice than new entrants or marginal firms. A more reasonable explanation is that by virtue of their well-established reputation, distribution channels, and other attributes, dominant firms are not as afraid of losing market share as small firms are and are less likely to take a chance on a new technology that could ruin their reputations than small firms are.

Another explanation given for the failure of incumbent firms to adopt new technology is called the sunk cost effect. In the early 1950s, a new steel-making technology, the oxygen furnace, became commercially viable. The furnace reduced milling time to 40 minutes as compared with the 6 to 8 hours in the open hearth technology that had been the industry standard since World War I. Despite the apparent superiority of the furnace, few U.S. steel-makers adopted it. Throughout the 1950s, U.S. steel-makers added nearly 50 million additional tons of the old furnace (open hearth, or OH) capacity, but they did not begin to replace their OH furnaces with the new furnaces until the late 1960s. Meanwhile steel-makers in the rest of the world were building new plants incorporating state of the art technology. The cost advantage afforded by this new technology was a key reason why Japanese and Korean steel-makers were able to penetrate the U.S. domestic market.

Why did U.S. steel-makers continue to invest in a seemingly inefficient technology? Their firms had developed a considerable amount of specific know-how related to the old technology, but the investment in this know-how was sunk. It should have made no difference to the decision to switch to new technology.

However, what is a sunk cost for the firm might not be a sunk cost for individuals involved with the firm. The CEO may have to justify costs to shareholders or the board of directors. Underlings may have vested interests in maintaining the current technology; their jobs may be based on it. There is, in these cases, a reluctance to adopt the newest technology not because of the failure to ignore sunk costs but because of the costs to individuals within the firm.

In the case of steel companies, because the new technology used relatively more pig iron as opposed to scrap iron than the old technology, new suppliers would have had to be arranged (pig iron instead of scrap) and in some cases new plants built at different locations. This could have been a considerable loss of income for suppliers working with the firm and for communities in which the plants were located. Thus, a great deal of pressure was placed on the U.S. steel firms not to change technologies.[1] The Japanese and Korean steel-makers could adopt the newest technology because they started from scratch. There were no special interest groups tied into the old technology.

Another example is IBM's failure to develop personal computers (PCs) after having invented them because of the active resistance of the "mainframe people" within IBM who were opposed to the growth of the PC group. The mainframe people saw the PC group as a potential threat to their internal power. In another case the maintenance engineers of a French cigarette manufacturer destroyed all the manuals and drawings of the highly specialized manufacturing equipment they were required to maintain. This made training new engineers much more difficult and the old engineers became irreplaceable and immensely powerful.

RECAP

1. The New Economy is the result of the technological changes that have occurred and are occurring in information processing.
2. Technological change involves the improvement of production and thus a reduction in costs.
3. In the New Economy, technological change has meant a change in many businesses. Specifically, the supply chains have been deconstructed as the information content of a product is separated from the physical aspect of the product.
4. There are many reasons that firms fail to adopt technology at the right time. One reason is a combination of optimism that market share will not be lost and fear that reputations and brand names could be hurt by adopting a new technology too rapidly. Another reason is called the sunk cost effect. It argues that what appears to be a sunk cost for a firm may be a nonsunk cost to people involved with the firm.

?

2. What are networks and what are the economics of networks?

2. NETWORKS

One way that firms have been dealing with the technological changes of the New Economy is by forming networks. A network can be an alliance of firms, such as with on-line purchasing auctions by major automobile manufacturers, or it can be a

---

[1]Sharon Oster, "The Diffusion of Innovation Among Steel Firms: The Basic Oxygen Furnace," *Bell Journal of Economics* 13 (Spring 1982): 45–68.

standard to which several businesses comply, such as high-definition television. Networks are not new in the New Economy but have become more important. Examples of existing networks include the use of alternating current in transporting electricity, local and long-distance telephone communication, television, railroad track gauges, computer operating systems, airline routes, and international mail.

Perhaps the most important aspect of networks is their connectedness. Networks are connected when a member of one network can communicate with a member of another network. Electricity is a connected network. Telephones are not connected in the sense that a telephone number is not portable; if you change carriers, you do not retain the same telephone number. Color television is a connected network; transmission occurs so that all brands of televisions can utilize the color. But HDTV is not a connected network; the United States is attempting to promote one system to transmit HDTV and Europe another system which is not compatible. Computer operating systems are not connected. The Internet is and is not; e-mail from one system can connect with other systems, but the connection is not perfect. International mail is connected; a letter can originate anywhere and be received anywhere.

2.a. Economics of Networks

positive feedback or **positive network externalities:** the benefits of one person's joining a network's being enjoyed by all its members.

When people refer to the New Economy, they are usually referring to the economics of networks. The economics of networks centers around **positive feedback,** or what economists call **positive network externalities.** Feedback means the benefits of an individual's joining a network go to every member of the network, not just the member joining. Recall from Chapter 5 that an externality occurs when the costs or benefits created by a private transaction spill over to people not involved in that private transaction. This is exactly what a network externality means; the costs or benefits of a private transaction (usually an individual joining the network) spill over to all members of the network. The positive network externality creates a situation where the value of a membership in a network rises increasingly rapidly as the network membership grows because each additional member provides increasingly larger benefits to all members.

Suppose that the value of a network is proportional to the number of users that can interconnect: then if there are n users, the value is proportional to $n(n - 1) =$

It seems that it is impossible to get away from the wireless phones. At restaurants, in movies, and along the highways, the phones are in constant use. The phones are examples of a network. It is possible to remain connected even when mountain climbing.

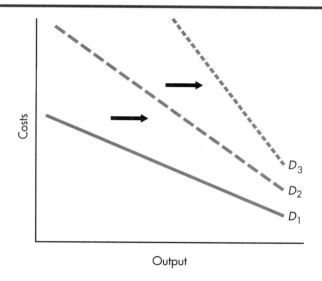

Figure 2

Positive Feedback

Positive feedback means that the value of being a member of a network rises more and more rapidly as the membership rises. Thus, the demand for membership shifts out as membership rises.

$n^2 - n$. If the value of a network to a single user is $1 for each other user on the network, then a network of size 20 has a value of $20 \times 20 - 20 = \$380$. If the value of a network to a single user is $1 for each other user on the network, then a network of size 200 has a value of $200 \times 200 - 200 = 40,000 - 200 = \$39,800$.

Why would the value of a network rise as the number of members of the network rose? Consider an Internet service provider such as AOL. Suppose AOL had 20,000 members who could communicate easily with each other but could not communicate with anyone else. The value of AOL would be quite small. However, with 100 million members, the value of membership would be much higher. In a similar vein, consider HDTV. There are several competing standards for transmitting high-definition television. If you purchase a television configured for one standard and then most transmission occurs on another standard, the value of your HDTV is very low.

Positive feedback means that the demand curve for membership in the network shifts out and becomes steeper as the network size increases, as illustrated in Figure 2. The value of the network rises as output rises; since the value increases, the quantity demanded at any given price rises as well. Thus, positive feedback means that as a network grows in membership, the demand for membership in that network rises as well. It also means that a member in a large network would have to give up a great deal (bear large switching costs) to join a different, smaller network.

2.b. Standards Wars

If positive feedback exists in a market, it is important for a firm or network to have the products and services that customers will use. If the use requires that the product/service of one firm connect with or communicate with those of another firm, then it may be necessary for the firms to comply with a standard. A standard is a product/service or a configuration of a product/service that ensures uniformity for all who comply with the standard. When two or more incompatible technologies struggle to become a standard, they are engaged in a **standards war.** Examples of wars include PC modems, video games, HDTV, and VCRs.

standards war: two or more incompatible technologies' being rivals for a standard

closed system: a standard's being available only to the innovator

open system: a standard's being available to everyone

One way that a firm might attempt to become the standard is to keep its system or innovation private, or proprietary. This is referred to as a **closed system.** An alternative approach is to open the system by offering to make the necessary interfaces and specifications available to others. Sony faced this problem with its Beta video cassette recorder system; it chose the closed approach and lost out to VHS, a more **open system.** Openness increases the chances of becoming a standard because it attracts allies and customers who fear being stuck with a network's having a very small membership. But openness means there are no profits directly obtainable from the system; all profits have to be derived from complementary products.

There are different degrees of openness; a full openness strategy provides the interconnections to everyone whereas a partial openness strategy provides the interconnection only to alliance members.

RECAP

1. Networks are an important element of the New Economy.
2. A network is an alliance of businesses or a standard to which several businesses comply in order to communicate.
3. The economics of a network centers around the existence of positive feedback (positive network externalities). Positive feedback means that each new member of a network adds additional value to the existing members. Thus, the greater the number of members, the greater the value of an individual membership.
4. The positive feedback of a network means that as a network grows, the cost to an individual member to leave that network and join another, smaller network rises.
5. Standards wars occur when two incompatible technologies compete to become the technology relied on in the marketplace.

❓

3. What do epidemics have to do with markets?

3. EPIDEMICS AND MARKET TIPPING

In the early 1990s, Wolverine, the company that makes Hush Puppies, was about to phase out the shoes that had made it famous. But then all of a sudden, sales exploded: the company sold 430,000 pairs of the shoes in 1995, four times that in 1996, and still more in 1997.[2]

In 1992, there were 2,154 murders in New York City and over 600,000 serious crimes. Within five years murders had dropped 64 percent, to 770, and total crimes had fallen by almost half, to 355,000.

In the mid-1990s, the city of Baltimore was attacked by an epidemic of syphilis. In just one year, from 1995 to 1996, the number of children born with the disease increased by 500 percent.

Sharp introduced the first low-priced fax machine in 1984. It sold only about 80,000 in that first year; sales rose very slowly until in 1987 they exploded.

The pattern followed by all these events is illustrated in Figure 3. Few people have the product (or disease) initially. Then some marginal change occurs, causing

---

[2]*The Tipping Point,* by Malcolm Gladwell (Boston: Little, Brown, 2000), is a very interesting view of tipping and provides many examples.

Figure 3

The Epidemic

Many economic data share the basic pattern of an epidemic as described by the curve shown here. The point at which the epidemic accelerates is called the tipping point.

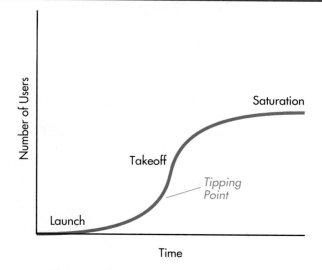

the takeoff. Finally, the epidemic reaches the saturation point, in which enough of the potential "victims" are affected that continued rapid growth is not possible. (The demand curve shifts slowly at first, then accelerates outward, and then moves more slowly once again as saturation occurs.)

The emergence of fashion trends, the ebb and flow of crime, the rise of teenage smoking, the adoption of technology, and many other everyday events share the basic pattern of an epidemic as described by the curve in Figure 3. While fashion trends and the Black Plague may not seem to have much in common, all such "epidemics" share two important elements. First, they are *contagious*. A few kids wearing the Hush Puppies infected others with the Hush Puppies "virus." Second, little changes have big effects; *marginal* matters. All the possible reasons that New York's crime rate dropped so precipitously in the 1990s are changes that happened at the margin—incremental changes. The crack trade leveled off; the population got a little older; the police force got a little better. But the result of these marginal changes was dramatic. Similarly, the HIV had been around for a long time but did not turn into an epidemic until one individual traveled to the west and set the epidemic off. These characteristics—contagiousness and the importance of marginal changes—are the same principles that define how measles moves through a grade school classroom, how the flu attacks every winter, and how the Pokémon cards and games spread among preadolescent children.

3.a. Tipping

tipping point: the point at which an event turns into an epidemic

The name given to that moment when an event turns into an epidemic is the **tipping point.** When the tipping point occurs in a market, the market is said to tip. Whether a market has the potential to tip depends on a tradeoff between positive feedback and variety. The existence of positive feedback effects means a market could tip. However, a tipped market is one in which a standardization has occurred; choices are reduced because there is only one network or one choice. Thus, if people have strong desires for variety in a market, that market is less likely to tip.

Who can explain how a fad or fashion trend gets started? When it does start, it seems we see evidence of it everywhere. In the late 1990s and early 2000s, the in-line scooter was a phenomenal fad. People used it for play, to commute to school or work, and as a means of urban transportation.

3.b. Winner-Takes-All

If a market tips, will just one firm or one network survive? Some business gurus and economists say yes, there is a winner-takes-all and the reason is the difference between the Old Economy and the New Economy. The Old Economy was driven by economies of scale while the New Economy is driven by the economics of networks. In reality, these differences are much exaggerated. Economies of scale on the supply side and a sufficient size on the demand side (such as caused by positive feedback) are both necessary for a winner-takes-all.

Figure 4 illustrates economies and diseconomies of scale; economies of scale occur from output level zero to output level *A* and diseconomies of scale occur thereafter. Only if economies of scale persisted throughout the entire market could one firm "own" the market. General Motors experienced economies of scale at the beginning of the twentieth century; yet GM was unable to take over the entire market. Why? The reason is that the economies of scale were not large enough to allow just one firm to supply the entire market. You can see in Figure 4 that a firm would not produce beyond point *A*, the bottom of the long run average cost curve. Thus,

Figure 4

Economies of Scale and Winner-Takes-All

Economies of scale must exist throughout the entire market for one firm to be the winner who takes it all. In this figure, no firm would produce beyond point *A* since its costs would be higher than a firm producing at point *A*. As a result, one firm can not supply the entire market.

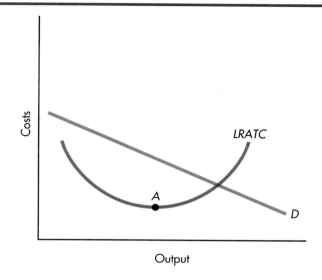

some other firm or firms would have to enter the market to satisfy demand. There would be no winner-takes-all.

In the case of a network, as the size of the membership increases, the demand for the output of the network, or membership, increases. In the previous example of 20 versus 200 members, the value of the network increases exponentially as users increase linearly. If this type of feedback situation does characterize a network, it implies that it is difficult for a small network to survive. For the same cost of connection, would you choose the smaller 20-person network or the larger 200-person network? Clearly, you would choose the larger network.

Another aspect of a network is that it is difficult (costly) for a member to switch to another network. The cost for any one user to switch to another network (the opportunity cost of not being connected to the large network) becomes increasingly large the larger the network is. As a result, it would seem that one network would dominate, that there would be a winner-takes-all.

In Figure 5(a) positive feedback and economies of scale both occur. In this case, there would be a winner-takes-all (just one network would survive). But in Figure 5(b), the network, represented by the curve *LRATC,* does not have sufficient economies of scale to satisfy demand. Thus, several networks would be required. This market would not have a winner-takes-all.

Figures 5(a) and 5(b) illustrate that both economies of scale and positive feedback effects are necessary for a winner-takes-all. Feedback effects alone are not sufficient for a winner-takes-all to emerge.

3.c. Pricing in the New Economy

What appears to be a striking difference between the New Economy and the Old Economy is how often things are given away free in the New Economy. For example, software is often given away for free; Internet access is given away; even

Figure 5

Winner-Takes-All

Figure 5(a) illustrates a case where positive feedback and economies of scale occur. In such a situation, a winner-takes-all could occur. In Figure 5(b), economies of scale do not exist throughout the market so that one firm can not supply the entire market.

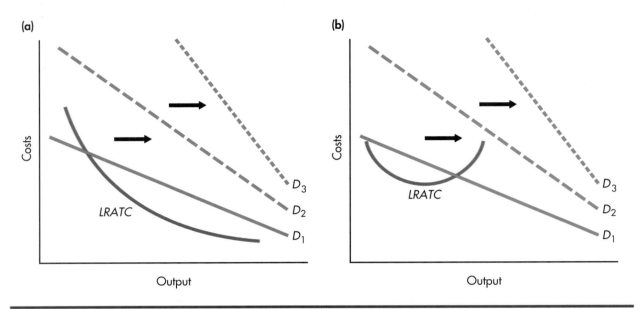

(a)

(b)

hardware such as computers has been given away. Why does this occur in the New but not in the Old Economy? Are prices set in a different way in the New Economy?

Firms set prices in the New Economy exactly as they did in the Old Economy; they find the quantity at which marginal revenue equals marginal cost and set the price according to demand. Why, then, would a firm give away its product? The reason depends on the existence of high fixed costs and very low marginal costs.

Recall that fixed costs are the costs that cannot be changed in the short run. In many instances these costs are the costs that were necessary to enter a business or to introduce a product. Marginal costs are the additional costs of producing one more unit of the good or service being supplied. Consider the production of a music CD. To produce the first CD, it is necessary to acquire and assemble the studio, the band, and the recording equipment. The band is paid a performance fee, the equipment is purchased, and the studio is rented. Thus, if the production company were only to create one CD, the cost of that CD would be very high. But none of these expensive items are necessary to produce the second CD. All those expensive items are fixed costs to the music producer; they won't change as additional CDs are produced. The only thing necessary for the second CD is the duplicating equipment and the plastic disk. Thus, each additional CD costs pennies to produce. This means that the marginal cost of the first CD is very high and that the marginal costs of the second and subsequent ones are near zero.

Winner-Takes-All and Market Inefficiency

Even though both economies of scale and increases in demand are necessary for a winner-takes-all, many people have claimed that these conditions are prevalent in the New Economy. One example widely used to support the winner-takes-all argument is the typewriter keyboard, called QWERTY. The first letter line on a typewriter or computer keyboard is QWERTYUIOP, or QWERTY for short. According to mythology, it is not the most efficient layout in terms of finger movement, but manufacturers had designed it to force typists to work more slowly on early typewriters because of the tendency of keys to jam. Several decades ago, jamming keys were no longer a problem, and it would have made sense to shift to an alternative, more efficient design. A rival layout, called the Dvorak keyboard, was available and purportedly more efficient. But the standard keyboard, the myth goes, was a network that had become locked in. People who had learned on the old keyboard were not about to change to a new one.

The QWERTY story says that markets are not likely to lead to the adoption of the most efficient technology. Once some historical accident or random event plays favor with some technology, it becomes the standard and is used thereafter even if it is not the most

efficient. The QWERTY story is employed to explain why VHS is used rather than the superior Beta, why Windows is used rather than the better Mac system, why gas-powered automobiles are used rather than steam-powered ones, and why light-water nuclear power plants are used rather than the better inert-gas nuclear power plants. All these examples are used to support the general view that free markets cannot be relied on to select the best technology.

According to many people, market winners will only by the sheerest of coincidences be the best of the available alternatives. The first technology that attracts development, the first standard that attracts adopters, or the first product that attracts consumers will tend to have an insurmountable advantage, even over superior rivals that happen to come along later. According to this argument, if DOS is the first operating system, then improvements such as the Macintosh will fail because consumers are so locked in to DOS that they will not make the switch to the better system. The success of Intel-based computers, in this view, is a tragic piece of bad luck.

The problem with this argument is that the QWERTY myth is wrong. The QWERTY keyboard was not an inferior structure designed to slow down typing. There were many competitive systems offered on

competing typewriters in the 1880s and 1890s, but none could perform better than the QWERTY system. Producers of alternative keyboards were motivated to cash in on any successes that alternative systems could generate. Other keyboards did compete with QWERTY; they just couldn't surpass QWERTY.

Similarly, to accept the idea of inefficient lock-in regarding DOS and Windows, we need to ignore the fact that DOS was not the first operating system, that consumers did switch away from DOS when they moved to Windows, that the DOS system was an appropriate choice for many users given the hardware of the time, and that the Mac system was far more expensive. Similarly, this was also the case for Beta and VHS. The problem with Beta was that Sony would not license it to other producers and that it was far more expensive than VHS. On the other hand, VHS was licensed to many manufacturers and was far less expensive; hence, VHS gained acceptance over Beta. Beta is still the format used for commercial and high-quality filming, when expenses are not as important.

Source: Stan Liebowitz and Stephen E. Margolis, "The Fable of the Keys," *Journal of Law and Economics* 33 (April 1990): 1; *Reason* 28, no. 2 (June 1996): 28.

This kind of high fixed costs and small marginal costs is illustrated in Figure 6. The first CD has very high costs (the fixed costs). The marginal cost curve drops rapidly from the level of the huge fixed costs to near zero as additional CDs are produced. Suppose that it costs ten million dollars to create that first music CD and that the cost of the second CD is one dollar while the cost of the third CD, the fourth, and

Figure 6

Huge Fixed Costs and Small Marginal Costs

The marginal cost curve drops rapidly from the level of the huge fixed costs to near zero. The price the firm will charge for the CDs is something close to its marginal cost. This price is so low that a firm might reason it is better off to give the CDs away.

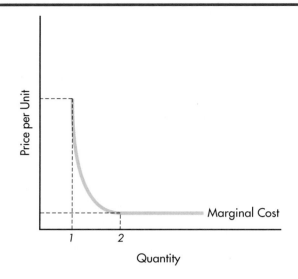

so on, is only five cents—the cost of the plastic. How much should the production firm charge for a CD? Should it charge a high price, say, the level of the fixed costs? If it does that and other firms are offering the same good or service for less, the firm will lose its market. The firm has to charge something close to its marginal cost in order not to lose out to rivals. Many firms reason that the price they can charge is so low, it is better to give the product away so as to entice consumers to purchase other goods or services from the firm that are more profitable. This is what Microsoft did, and this is what AOL and other Internet service providers do.

Another aspect of the New Economy is that price competition has become more pervasive. The reason consists of both the availability of information and the emergence of standards. A standard means uniformity, or nondifferentiation. Thus, a standard turns the product into a commodity; this means the products offered by different firms are identical. As the model of perfect competition tells us, when products are identical and entry is easy, price will be driven down to its lowest possible level.

Yet, because information about consumer buying habits is much more readily available in the New Economy than in the Old Economy, a firm can attempt to differentiate its goods and services or to treat each customer as a unique entity. When a customer purchases at Amazon.com, the customer's tastes in books or music are filed, and suggested complementary or substitute products offered the next time the customer logs in. At Peapod.com, customers may order groceries over the Internet; Peapod provides price per unit, ingredients, and nutritional information, thus enabling customers a means of comparison shopping. The customer selections are recorded and the information used to design marketing strategies. The customer becomes a single entity rather than a member of a group of customers. This is called **personalized selling.** Personalized prices were discussed under the name "price

personalized selling: the practice of customizing a good or service or price to each customer

discrimination" in the chapter "Elasticity." In essence, what the firm does is find out how much any given customer is willing and able to pay and attempt to set the price at that point for each customer.

3.d. The New and the Old Economies

There is no mistaking that the New Economy has altered the business landscape. Yet there also should be no mistaking that it has not altered the fundamental principles of economics. Scarcity is and always will be with us; people will always want more than they have. As a result, the concepts of opportunity costs, tradeoffs, and choices remain as important as ever. Technological change is not new; it has occurred since time began. Technological change in the New Economy has focused on information and has altered the structures of many businesses. What previously were assets have turned into liabilities in some cases. In other cases, businesses have formed networks and the economics of networks have been important aspects of the New Economy. Information about goods, services, and their prices and about consumer behavior is more readily available, and this has led to increased price competition and to personalized selling. Yet firms still attempt to maximize profit by setting price according to the rule: marginal revenue equals marginal cost.

RECAP

1. The New Economy is the result of the technological changes that have occurred and are occurring in information processing.

2. Networks are an important element in the New Economy. A network is an alliance of businesses or a standard to which several businesses comply in order to communicate.

3. While the combination of economies of scale and positive network externalities occur in many information industries, the New Economy is not necessarily a winner-takes-all economy. It is not sufficient for a winner-takes-all to occur for just positive feedback to occur. Economies of scale must be sufficiently large that the one network can supply the market.

4. Pricing in both the Old and the New Economies is carried out by finding the output level where $MR = MC$ and setting price according to demand at that point. Personalized pricing, or price discrimination, may be more prevalent in the New Economy due to the amount of information available about customers.

SUMMARY

? What is the difference between the New Economy and the Old Economy?

1. The New Economy describes the ongoing economic changes that have occurred as a result of the technological advances in information processing and communication. *§Preview*

2. Technological change involves the improvement of production and thus a reduction in costs. *§1.a*

3. In the New Economy, technological change has meant a change in the supply chains of many businesses because the information content and the physical product can be separated. This requires new configurations and new businesses. *§1.c*

4. There are many reasons that a firm fails to adopt technology at the right time. One reason is the firm's optimism that market share won't be lost; another is its fear that adopting too soon could harm its reputation; a third is called the sunk cost effect. It argues that individuals in the firm may lose out because of the new technology and therefore oppose its adoption. *§1.d*

? What are networks and what are the economics of networks?

5. Networks are alliances of firms or a standard to which many businesses conform. *§2*

6. The economics of networks refers primarily to positive feedback effects, called positive network externalities. A positive feedback occurs when the benefits of an individual's actions spill over and are received by other individuals. Such effects mean that when the membership of a network rises linearly, the value of membership rises exponentially. *§2.a*

7. Networks involve standards wars, situations in which two or more networks fight for the dominance of their products/services or standard. *§2.b*

8. Open networks are networks whose technology or interface is available to anyone. Closed networks are networks where only members of the network are able to interface with the network. *§2.b*

? What do epidemics have to do with markets?

9. Epidemics are set off when a contagious "disease" is in a few people and some marginal change causes a tipping; the epidemic ensues. *§3*

10. Firm strategies in the New Economy must take into account market tipping and incremental changes that can tip the market. *§3.a*

11. A firm or network may become the dominant or only firm if the market tips. This is called a winner-takes-all situation. A winner-takes-all requires economies of scale throughout the market and positive feedback effects. *§3.b*

12. When fixed costs are large and marginal costs very small, firms may find it more profitable to give away the product whose marginal cost is so small. *§3.c*

13. The New Economy enables more personalized selling—personalized pricing and personalized products—than was possible under the Old Economy. *§3.c*

KEY TERMS

basic research *§1.a*
applied research *§1.a*
development *§1.a*
positive feedback or positive network externalities *§2.a*
standards war *§2.b*

closed system *§2.b*
open system *§2.b*
tipping point *§3.a*
personalized selling *§3.c*

EXERCISES

1. If the downsizing trend of the late 1980s and early 1990s was due to technological change, what should it mean for individual firm cost curves? If the downsizing trend was a mistake—firms' cutting employees and increasing productivity in the short term only to suffer long-term reductions in productivity—what should it mean for individual firm cost curves?

2. Many analysts say that the infrastructure of eastern Europe resembles that of the United States in the 1800s. If so, what patterns of industrial development might be expected during the next few decades in eastern Europe?

3. Several cities are associated with specific industries: Akron-tires, Sunnyvale-computer chips, Orlando-tourism, and Hollywood-movies. Why do such centers emerge?

4. Two networks are vying for dominance in the HDTV network, the United States and Europe. It has been said that the winner is likely to be determined by

economies of scale in manufacturing televisions. Explain.

5. Amazon.com was the first mover in on-line book sales. It patented the one-click purchasing system. Barnes and Noble was a late entrant with BN.com. Is this a battle with a winner-takes-all outcome? Why or why not?

6. In early 1998, S3 was a small chip-design firm with a big problem. The company knew that Intel's patent wall would eventually stall its high-performance graphic chip business. So S3 hatched a plan to fix the problem. It outbid Intel to acquire the patents of bankrupt chip maker Exponential Technologies. In doing so, S3 acquired a patent that predated Intel's. Explain why S3 spent $10 million to purchase a bankrupt firm. What is the implication for the dominance of Intel?

7. In 1994, the $3.5 billion Avery Dennison Corporation developed a new film for use in product labeling. The film unit won a contract to provide the labels for Procter and Gamble shampoo bottles and appeared to have a huge growth potential. But an analysis of patent activity indicated that Dow Chemical was beginning to move into this business. Should Avery commit the huge resources needed to exploit the market opportunity for the film unit?

8. Explain why a firm might give away its product or service rather than sell it.

Internet Exercises/ Resources

For Internet exercises and web resources related to this chapter, go to **http://college.hmco.com.**

JLM Industries: Embracing the New Economy

JLM Industries has a simple motivation for its rush to offer customers an online forum to buy and sell chemicals and plastics.

It got tired of high-tech middlemen cutting in on its turf. John L. Macdonald, chief executive and founder of the Tampa manufacturer and distributor of chemicals, counts 47 e-commerce companies in his industry already. Most of them are run by companies with no hard assets, and therein lies JLM's advantage. "We believe as all of this shakes out, there will be a definite play for the bricks-and-mortar players like ourselves," said Walt Tarpley, president of JLM's marketing unit. "We have the ships. We have trucks. We have inventory. We don't have to rely on other people coming in and posting material on the site." With 500 employees in 15 countries and more than 5,000 customers, "We bring a ready-made customer base and liquidity . . . that other sites don't have," Macdonald said.

The story of JLM's push into electronic business-to-business is being repeated by different industries in different cities throughout the country: A traditional company in an "old-line" industry wakes up to the threat of a nimble competitor using the Internet, then tries to leverage its strengths

to catch up. In JLM's case, at least, it had time on its side. Unlike marketers of books and toys, chemical distributors were slow to embrace e-commerce, "stodgy" in Tarpley's words.

Until recently. One industry start-up, Chemdex.com, exploded on the Internet scene a couple of years ago. Enjoying the warm reception of all-things Web, Chemdex' stock jumped and its market capitalization approached $4-billion before recent sell-offs in the tech sector. JLM sensed trouble by mid-1999. It hired consultants and soon came up with a multitiered strategy for e-commerce: Revamp its Web site, which had been limited to information about the company. Sell its stockpile through the Web, emphasizing slow-moving and discontinued inventory that it could promote at a discount. Provide customers with real-time information concerning product bulletins and pricing changes. Create a virtual exchange, a supply house where its customers could buy and sell chemicals and plastics online in the new economy's version of a bartering system. "I think the longer you delay, the more chance there is for others to usurp you," Tarpley said. Nevertheless, the new jlmi.com is taking a while to gel. . . .

So far, the company says it has spent in the "high six figures" on its e-commerce initiative. The figure would have been in the seven figures if not for last year's purchase of ICI Chemical's South African distribution business. The purchase gave JLM licensing for an e-commerce software platform, saving about a half-million dollars, but delaying the rollout of online purchasing. The return on that investment, Tarpley predicts, will go far beyond building customer sales. By clearing an order electronically, the whole process speeds up so JLM cuts down on warehousing and distribution costs and the need for a large amount of working capital. Conservatively, the company expects to reap a 20 percent growth rate through its e-commerce efforts, adding as much as $7-million to its bottom line. After years of reluctance to embrace the new economy, the company's transformation is noticeable. JLM executives are learning to be nimble. They watch Web initiatives in the industry daily to gauge how to adapt their emerging game plan.

"We're trying to bridge that gap between the old and the new," Macdonald said. "We're riding two horses here."

St. Petersburg Times/April 17, 2000

Commentary

The article on JLM provides applications of several topics examined in the chapter. The first is the reluctance of old-line businesses to adopt technology, to become Internet literate. What makes the old-line businesses adopt a technology? A new entrant is able to enter because of the technological change. Without the Internet, the upstart would be at a significant disadvantage to the businesses with "brick and mortar," that is, the businesses with fixed places of business and large manufacturing capability. According to the chairman, JLM has an advantage over the 47 e-commerce firms in the industry. Because JLM has the hard assets—the ships, trucks, inventories—McDonald reasons JLM has an advantage. Under which conditions would these hard assets be an advantage, and conversely, under which would they be a disadvantage?

Chemicals and plastics have an information component that can be separated from the physical products; if nothing more, that information component is the qualities, types, and prices of the products. Thus, a New Economy firm could focus on the information and cause the brick and mortar business to change. Chemdex.com was such a firm. It provided a way that customers could buy and sell chemicals and plastics on-line. Now JLM thinks that because it can offer its own supplies and the distribution of those supplies on-line, it will win over the Chemdex.com-type companies.

The problem for JLM is whether its supplies and distribution lines are better than those of other firms. If a firm like Chemdex.com is able to post the information of several Old Economy chemical companies and let the customer comparison shop, then Chemdex.com is sure to be preferred over JLM.

Embracing technology is typically necessary for a firm to survive over the long term and is the case especially in this New Economy. But simply setting up a web site is not going to be a sufficient strategy for businesses faced with fundamental changes.

Chapter 14

Government Policy Toward Business

Fundamental Questions

1. What is antitrust policy?

2. What is the difference between economic regulation and social regulation?

3. Why does the government intervene in business activity?

The two main approaches the government uses to intervene in the activities of business are *antitrust policy* and *regulation*. The basis of antitrust policy is that businesses should compete "fairly." Guidelines of behavior and accepted types of behavior are defined, and firms that do not comply are sued. *Economic regulation* involves a larger role for government. It ranges from prescribing the pricing and output behavior of specific industries to the case where the government actually runs and operates the business. *Social regulation*, which applies generally across all businesses, involves health and safety standards for products and the workplace, standards for protecting the environment, and other government restrictions on the behavior of firms and individuals. ■

Preview

1. ANTITRUST POLICY

antitrust policy:
government policies and
programs designed to
control the growth of
monopoly and enhance
competition

Antitrust policy is the term used to describe government policies and programs designed to control the growth of monopoly and prevent firms from engaging in undesirable practices.

1.a. Antitrust and Business Activities

As noted in Table 1, three laws define the government's approach to antitrust policy—the Sherman, Clayton, and Federal Trade Commission Acts. These antitrust laws are intended to limit the creation and behavior of *trusts*, or combinations of independent firms. Today we refer to the process of combining firms as *mergers* and the resulting firms as large firms or corporations. Antitrust policy limits what these large firms can do. For instance, the firms cannot together decide to fix prices, they cannot restrict competition, and they cannot combine or become trusts if the resulting firm would have too great an influence in the market.

1.b. Interpretation

**1. What is antitrust
policy?**

Antitrust policy is the responsibility of two government agencies, the Antitrust Division of the Department of Justice and the Federal Trade Commission. These agencies try to distinguish beneficial from harmful business practices by focusing on *unreasonable* monopolistic activities. What is unreasonable? The answer has varied as the interpretation of the statutes by the courts and government authorities has changed. There have been several distinct phases of antitrust policy in the United States, as illustrated in Figure 1. The first began with passage of the Sherman Antitrust Act in 1890 and lasted until about 1914. In this period, litigation was infrequent. The courts used a **rule of reason** to judge firms' actions: being a monopoly or attempting to monopolize was not in itself illegal; to be illegal, an action had to be unreasonable in a competitive sense, and the anticompetitive effects had to be demonstrated.

rule of reason: to be illegal
an action must be
unreasonable in a
competitive sense and the
anticompetitive effects must
be demonstrated

Table 1

Antitrust Acts

Sherman Antitrust Act (1890)
Section 1 outlaws contracts and conspiracies in restraint of trade. *Section 2* forbids monopolization and attempts to monopolize.
Clayton Antitrust Act (1914)
Section 2, as amended by the Robinson-Patman Act (1936), bans price discrimination that substantially lessens competition or injures particular competitors. *Section 3* prohibits certain practices that might keep other firms from entering an industry or competing with an existing firm. *Section 7,* as amended by the Celler-Kefauver Act (1950), outlaws mergers that substantially lessen competition.
Federal Trade Commission Act (1914)
Section 5, as amended by the Wheeler-Lea Act (1938), prohibits unfair methods of competition and unfair or deceptive acts.

Figure 1

Phases of Antitrust Interpretation

The degree to which antitrust law has been enforced has varied over the years. With the Sherman Act of 1890, the government formally began antitrust policy. But enforcement was lax, based on a rule of reason, until about 1914. Between 1914 and the early 1980s, strict enforcement based on a per se rule was used. With the Reagan and Bush administrations, enforcement was relaxed again to the rule-of-reason standard. The Clinton Administration tightened enforcement.

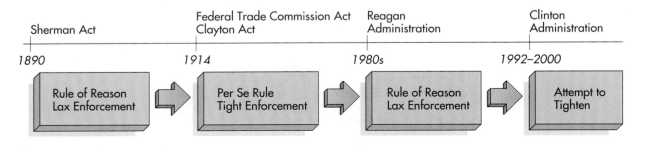

The second phase of antitrust policy began in 1914 with the passage of the Clayton Antitrust Act and the Federal Trade Commission Act. Operating under these two acts, the courts used the **per se rule** to judge firms' actions: activities that were potentially monopolizing tactics were illegal; the mere existence of these activities was sufficient evidence to lead to a guilty verdict.

per se rule: actions that could be anti-competitive are intrinsically illegal

Although the courts define the standard to be applied to antitrust cases, the administration in office appoints judges and defines the degree to which antitrust policy will be enforced. In the 1980s and through the Reagan and Bush administrations, the courts returned to the looser rule-of-reason standard. The only tactic deemed illegal was price fixing—rival firms could not determine prices by agreement; they had to allow prices to be set by demand and supply. Other than that, firms could do just about anything to enhance their profitability. When Clinton became president, an attempt was made to return to the tighter standards. More money was allocated to antitrust enforcement, more lawyers were hired, and more cases were brought.

1.c. Procedures

Action against alleged violators of the antitrust statutes may be initiated by the U.S. Department of Justice, by the Federal Trade Commission (FTC), or by private plaintiffs. The Justice Department focuses on the Sherman Antitrust Act. The FTC focuses on the Federal Trade Commission and Clayton Antitrust Acts. Private plaintiffs (consumers and businesses) may sue on the basis of any of the statutes except the Federal Trade Commission Act. Since 1941, the FTC and the Justice Department together have filed nearly 2,800 cases, and since 1970, private suits have far outnumbered those filed by the Justice Department and the FTC combined.

1.d. Remedies

Private plaintiffs who prove their injuries can receive compensation up to three times the damages caused by the action. The Justice Department and the FTC do not obtain treble damages but can impose substantial penalties. They can force firms to break up through dissolution or divestiture, and criminal actions can be filed by the Justice Department for violations of the Sherman Act. A guilty finding can result in fines and prison sentences.

1.e. Demonstration of Antitrust Violations

Price fixing is by definition illegal—there is no justification for it. Other aspects of the antitrust statutes are not as clear-cut and are, therefore, difficult to prove. For instance, Section 2 of the Sherman Act outlaws "monopolization" but does not forbid monopolies. Monopoly itself is allowed. *To monopolize* or *to attempt to monopolize* constitutes a violation. If the firm attempts to preserve its monopoly by activities that restrict entry, then the firm may be guilty of a Section 2 violation.

The first step in enforcing an antitrust policy is to define market concentration. Government regulations often apply only to large businesses, and antitrust policies are typically directed toward large firms. The basis for the focus on large firms comes from the four market structure models—perfect competition, monopolistic competition, oligopoly, and monopoly—which suggest that the fewer the number of firms controlling the production in an industry, the greater the chance of collusive activity and other behavior designed to monopolize a market. And under monopoly and oligopoly, it is likely that consumers pay more and firms produce less and earn greater profits than if the firms are small, perfect competitors. So the government focuses on larger firms and cases in which few firms dominate an industry. Measures of size and influence are intended to provide information about market structures.

Herfindahl index: a measure of concentration calculated as the sum of the squares of the market share of each firm in an industry

concentration: the degree to which a few firms control the output and pricing decisions in a market

The most commonly used measure of size and influence is called the **Herfindahl index.** The Herfindahl index is a measure of **concentration**—the degree to which a few firms control the output and pricing decisions in a market.[1] The Herfindahl index of concentration is defined as the sum of the squared market shares of each firm in the industry:

$$\text{Herfindahl index} = (S_1)^2 + (S_2)^2 + \cdots + (S_n)^2$$

where S refers to the market share of the firm, the subscripts refer to the firms, and there are n firms. The higher the Herfindahl index number, the more concentrated the industry.

An industry in which each of five firms has 20 percent of the market would have a Herfindahl index value of 2,000:

$$(20)^2 + (20)^2 + (20)^2 + (20)^2 + (20)^2 = 2,000$$

If the largest firm had 88 percent of the market and each of the others 3 percent, the Herfindahl index value would be 7,780:

$$(88)^2 + (3)^2 + (3)^2 + (3)^2 + (3)^2 = 7,780$$

The higher number indicates a much more concentrated market. As you can see from these examples, the Herfindahl index takes into account the size distribution of the firms in an industry. The idea is that an industry in which there is one dominant firm will be quite different from one in which there are several firms of equal size.

---

[1] The four-firm concentration ratio is another commonly used measured of concentration, but it has come under criticism because it does not account for the size distribution of firms. It merely divides the total output of the four largest firms by the total market output.

In 1982, 1984, and 1992, the Justice Department issued guidelines on market concentration and competition to inform businesses where the government would be especially likely to scrutinize activities. It stated that industries with Herfindahl indexes below 1,000 are considered *highly competitive*; those with indexes between 1,000 and 1,800 are *moderately competitive*; and those with indexes above 1,800 are *highly concentrated*.

Using the Herfindahl index to gauge the extent to which a few firms dominate a market sounds simple, but it is not. Before the concentration of an industry can be calculated, there must be some definition of the market. In a $100 billion market, an $80 billion firm would have an 80 percent market share. But in a $1,000 billion market, an $80 billion firm would have only an 8 percent market share. The Herfindahl index for the former would exceed 2,000, but for the latter it would be less than 1,000. Obviously, antitrust plaintiffs (those accusing a firm of attempting to monopolize a market) would want the market defined as narrowly as possible so that the alleged monopolizer would be seen to have a large market share. Conversely, defendants (those accused of monopolization) would argue for broadly defined markets in order to give the appearance that they possess a very small market share.

For example, Coca-Cola, Dr Pepper, PepsiCo, and Seven-Up are usually identified as producers of carbonated soft drinks (CSD). These firms provide bottlers with the concentrate that is used to make the drinks. Would CSD be the appropriate market in which to assess the competitive consequences of a merger, or should the market be more widely defined—perhaps to encompass all potable liquids (fruit juices, milk, coffee, tea, etc.)? In an actual merger case, the market definition was determined through interviews with CSD company executives. The executives indicated that they believed their primary competitors were other CSD producers. Their pricing and marketing strategies were made with other CSD producers in mind—not, as claimed by the defendant, by considering how the sellers of all potable drinks would react. The interviews also revealed that many CSD industry executives thought they could collectively raise the retail prices of carbonated soft drinks by as much as 10 percent with no fear of consumers switching to other beverages. That argument had implications for the definition of the market. If sellers can collectively raise the price by 10 percent without causing consumers to switch to other products, then those sellers represent the lion's share of the market. However, if consumers switch as a result of the price increase, then the market must be more broadly defined to include the substitutes consumers move to.

When the market and market shares have been defined, the next task is to establish intent. The ease or difficulty with which intent can be established depends on whether the per se rule or the rule-of-reason standard is being used.

1.f. Concentration and Business Policy from a Global Perspective

Concentration measures and the Justice Department guidelines are often defined for production only within the United States; this can present a misleading picture. For instance, the Herfindahl index in the United States for automobiles is very high, but if it took foreign competition into account, it would be significantly lower. In Sweden, two cars are produced, Volvo and Saab, and the Herfindahl index is greater than 5,000. That figure is also misleading, however, for Volvo and Saab account for only about 30 percent of all automobiles sold in Sweden. An appropriate policy measure must take into account all close substitutes whether domestically produced or not. In addition, it must account for firms producing in more than one nation, the multinationals. The Herfindahl index may not provide a good indication of the competitive situation prevailing in an industry if it does not account for these factors or for the different ways that governments treat their businesses—actions that are legal in one country may be illegal in another, for instance. Governments also restrict the imports of some goods and services, thereby affecting the number of substitutes available to domestic consumers. The definition of a market did not include worldwide factors until the early 1980s. From then until the early 1990s, market definition could include worldwide factors, but the United States would not apply antitrust sanctions against some action or restrict mergers unless they were deemed to harm U.S. consumers. In 1992, the United States extended its policies to include harm to either U.S. consumers or U.S. firms.

Compared to other countries, the United States is quite restrictive in terms of allowing certain types of business behavior and quite unrestrictive in placing limits on the importation of goods and services. When the per se rule was emerging in the United States during the 1920s and 1930s, most European nations had no antitrust laws at all, and cartels flourished. Today, many nations support cartels and cooperative behavior that is illegal in the United States. Some of these same nations are very restrictive in the importation of goods. Japan, for instance, allows, even supports, systems of cartels domestically while limiting the inflow of foreign-produced goods and services relative to the United States.

RECAP

1. Antitrust policy in the United States is based on the Sherman, Clayton, and Federal Trade Commission Acts.
2. The enforcement of antitrust policy has evolved through several phases. The first followed the Sherman Act in 1890 and extended to 1914. During this period, the rule-of-reason standard dictated policy. The second phase started with the Clayton and Federal Trade Commission Acts in 1914 and lasted through the 1970s. During this period, the per se rule dictated policy. In the 1980s, most practices were considered to be part of the competitive process. In the early 1990s, an attempt was made to return to stricter enforcement.
3. Antitrust policy encompasses business actions such as pricing, advertising, restraint of trade, supplier relationships, and mergers.
4. If two or more rivals combine, it is called a merger.
5. Antitrust policy in the United States is stricter than it is in other nations.

2. What is the difference between economic regulation and social regulation?

2. REGULATION

The justification given for antitrust policy is that it should enhance the competitive environment—to create a "level playing field" on which firms may compete. When the competitive environment cannot be enhanced, such as in the case with a natural monopoly where cost conditions lead to a sole supplier, then regulation is used to ensure that price and output are more beneficial for consumers than the levels the monopolist would set without government influence. Regulation of natural monopolies is far from the only type of government regulation that occurs, however. Regulation of industries that are not natural monopolies is also widespread in the

United States. This regulation has a number of different rationales, ranging from the protection of the health and safety of the general public to the health of a particular industry.

There are two categories of regulations, economic and social regulation. **Economic regulation** refers to the prescribing of prices and output levels for both natural monopolies and industries that are not natural monopolies. Economic regulation is specific, applying to a particular industry or line of business. **Social regulation** refers to prescribed performance standards, workplace health and safety standards, emission levels, and a variety of output and job standards that apply across several industries.

2.a. Regulation of Monopoly

Monopoly is inefficient; perfect competition, efficient. This comparison between monopoly and perfect competition has provided the basis for attempting to make monopolies behave more like perfectly competitive firms. Most natural monopolies are regulated by some level of government. In particular, the prices or rates that public utilities such as telephone companies, natural gas companies, and electricity suppliers can charge is determined by a federal, state, or local regulatory commission or board.

Figure 2 shows the demand, marginal-revenue, and long-run average-cost and marginal-cost curves for a natural monopoly. The huge economies of scale means it would be inefficient to have many small firms supply the product. Yet producing at $MR = MC$ and setting a price of P_m from the demand curve yield too little output

Figure 2

Natural Monopoly and Regulation

The demand, marginal-revenue, and long-run average-cost and marginal-cost curves for a natural monopoly are shown. The huge economies of scale mean it would be inefficient to have many small firms supply the product. Yet, producing at $MR = MC$ and setting a price of P_m from the demand curve yields too small an output and too much profit for the firm, in comparison to the perfectly competitive result. Too few resources are devoted to this product—too few because if more was produced, MC would equal price. To achieve allocative efficiency (giving consumers the goods they most want), the regulatory agency must attempt to have the monopolist set a price equal to marginal cost. This price would be P_r. The monopolist would then produce at quantity Q_r. The problem with the regulated price P_r is that the revenues do not cover average costs. The fair-rate-of-return price is set to allow the monopolist a normal profit. The price corresponding to the normal profit is one where demand and average total costs are equal, P_f.

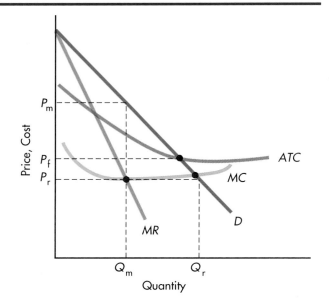

and too much profit for the firm, in comparison to the perfectly competitive result. In addition, since price is greater than marginal cost, resources are not being allocated efficiently. In fact, too few resources are devoted to this product—too few because if more was produced, *MC* would equal price. Can regulation solve this problem?

If the objective of the regulatory commission is to achieve allocative efficiency (giving consumers the goods they most want), it must attempt to have the monopolist set a price equal to marginal cost. This price would be P_r in Figure 2. The monopolist would then produce at quantity Q_r.

The problem with the regulated price P_r is that the regulated firm could actually make a loss. You can see in Figure 2 that revenues do not cover average costs. Figure 2 illustrates a fairly common situation with the public utilities because the costs of the public utility companies are large. Most public utilities must acquire sufficient resources (generating capacity or telephone-linking capacity, for example) to supply the *peak* demands. But because the peak periods are only a small portion of daily sales, the revenue generated overall is not sufficient to pay for the total resource required. For instance, air conditioning is used most heavily during the 5 to 9 P.M. time period during the months of the summer. To meet the demands during this peak period, the electric company has to acquire nearly double the generating capacity it would need to satisfy only the nonpeak demand. Thus, the regulated price equal to marginal cost is not sufficient to provide the revenue to pay for the large costs.

Regulatory commissions quickly moved away from setting price equal to marginal cost and have allowed for a **fair rate of return.** The fair-rate-of-return price is set to allow the monopolist a normal profit. The price corresponding to the normal profit is one where demand and average total costs are equal, P_f.

fair rate of return: a price that allows a monopoly firm to earn a normal profit

When price is set in order to achieve the most efficient allocation of resources ($P = MC$), the regulated firm is likely to suffer losses. Survival of the firm would then require subsidies from the public. On the other hand, the fair-return price ($P = ATC$) allows the monopolist to cover costs, but it does not solve the misallocation of resources problem since price is greater than marginal cost.

2.b. Regulation of Industries That Are Not Natural Monopolies

Let's briefly look at the historical reasons for the regulation of transportation and the airwaves. These industries provide good examples of the rationales for economic regulation. We will then discuss social regulation.

2.b.1. Transportation and Destructive Competition   For both railroads and air transport, equipment is extremely expensive and operating costs are relatively quite small—in other words, marginal costs are very low relative to fixed costs. This could mean that firms entering the industry have to set price equal to marginal cost to meet competition, but this is not high enough for them to be able to pay for their total costs—they might be covering their variable costs but not their huge fixed costs. Thus, competition between the firms could lead to the failure of the entire industry. In such cases, the government has often restricted entry, allowing only one firm or a few firms to provide a product. Restricting entry, however, allows existing firms to earn above-normal or monopoly profit. This monopoly profit provides a reason for the government to regulate the firms much as it would a natural monopoly.

The government has been involved in the railroad industry since its inception. Land was provided for construction, loans were provided for development, and transportation rates were defined in many cases. When technological change lowered the costs of some services and brought trucking in as a direct competitor to the railroad, the regulatory net spread from railroads into trucking. Trucking was regulated not because of self-destructive competition or because it was a natural monopoly, but because years of regulation had put railroads at a disadvantage relative to trucking. The Interstate Commerce Commission (ICC) was given jurisdiction over railroads in the last quarter of the nineteenth century. Trucking came under its umbrella in 1935.

Like railroads, the argument for regulating airlines was to create orderly growth and avoid self-destructive competition. From the mid-1930s to the mid-1970s, the Civil Aeronautics Authority and its successor, the Civil Aeronautics Board (CAB), controlled entry into airline markets by establishing boundaries between carriers. Each carrier was further restricted to specific routes. For example, United Airlines was authorized to serve north-south routes on the West Coast, and Delta and Eastern served such routes on the East Coast.

2.b.2. Airwaves and Private Property Rights In some cases the resource used to supply a product is available to anyone, so free entry and use could consume the resource and destroy the industry. For instance, if just anyone could broadcast radio or TV signals on any of the airwaves, the main broadcast spectrum could become so crowded that a clear signal could not be obtained. The problem is that there are no clear *private property rights* to the airwaves (no one owns a specific airwave frequency), and in the absence of specific property rights, chaos could result if government did not step in. Limiting entry and assigning airwave frequencies (assigning property rights) may create order, but it also creates a monopoly situation. The existence of the resulting monopoly then lends itself to regulation along the lines of a natural monopoly.

Television and broadcasting rights are granted by the Federal Communications Commission (FCC). The FCC also regulates the telecommunications industry; it controls entry and some prices.

2.c. Deregulation and Privatization in the United States

Whether or not the initial rationale justified regulation, sometimes the results were disastrous. Over time it became evident that many regulated companies lacked incentives to keep costs under control and to be responsive to consumer demands. The airlines competed in terms of schedules, movies, food, and size of aircraft because the CAB did not allow price competition. Nonprice competition led to a much more rapid increase in the number of flights and expansion of aircraft capacity than was demanded by passengers. As a result, the load factor (the average percentage of seats filled) fell to less than 50 percent in the early 1970s.

Price competition among truckers was also stifled by regulation. The ICC had a complex rate schedule and restrictions affecting whether trucks could be full or less than full and the routes trucks could take. As a result, by the mid-1970s, 36 percent of all truck-miles were logged by empty trucks.

These problems initiated a change. Trucking was deregulated in 1980. Trucks can now haul what they want, where they want, at rates set by the trucking companies. In air transportation, deregulation meant the end of government control of entry and prices. Deregulation of route authority and fares was completed by 1982, and the CAB was disbanded.

Much of the telecommunications industry was deregulated in 1984, when an antitrust suit against AT&T, filed by the Department of Justice in 1974, was finally settled. As part of the settlement, AT&T agreed to divest itself of the local portions of the 22 Bell operating companies. They were restructured into seven separate regulated monopolies known as the Baby Bells or Regional Bell Operating Companies (RBOCs). The seven new operating firms are excluded from long-distance service and from manufacturing terminal equipment. So AT&T continues to provide long-distance service and telephone equipment, but other suppliers may compete in both spheres, and customers can choose any supplier they wish.

The long-distance telephone market is deregulated. Although four firms have the dominant share of the market, there are about 500 providers of services and it is relatively easy for virtually anyone interested in entering the industry to do so. Prior to 1984, the long-distance telephone market was a monopoly. What has occurred since 1984 is illustrative of the benefits of moving from monopoly to competition. Prices have declined 72 percent since the creation of competition in the long-distance telephone market, from 52 cents per minute in 1985 to about 15 cents per minute in 1996. Services have risen significantly; consumer choice is widely expanded; innovation and technological change are increasing at extraordinary rates. People are changing long-distance carriers at a rate of about one per second; 50 million people changed long-distance carriers in 1996. From 1984 to 1996, AT&T's market share declined from nearly 100 to 53 percent of long-distance revenues. Where did the business go? A lot went to the facilities-based competitors; MCI, Sprint, and WorldCom got about one-third of the long-distance revenues. Hundreds of smaller companies more than doubled their market share, picking up 16 percent of the market.

The local market is essentially a set of monopoly markets, each market controlled by a Regional Bell Operating Company and GTE. The RBOCs and GTE have 99.5 percent of the market—97 million households versus 0.5 million households that are customers of competitive local exchange carriers.

privatization: transferring a publicly owned enterprise to private ownership

contracting out: the process of enlisting private firms to perform certain government functions

Another form of deregulation is privatization. **Privatization** is the term for changing from a government-run business to a privately owned and run business. Advocates of privatization claim that private firms could, in many instances, provide better services at reduced costs. Cities and local governments in the United States have **contracted out** (privatized) many services in recent years. Local governments are now allowing private firms to provide garbage services, water services, and even road building and maintenance. Rural/Metro Company in Scottsdale, Arizona, has been running a private fire department for several decades. It is now purchasing contracts to run fire departments and emergency medical services throughout Arizona. Corrections Corporation of America in Nashville, Tennessee, and California Private Transportation Company in Anaheim, California, are building prisons and toll roads. Many members of Congress are looking at the U.S. Postal Service and arguing that private firms could deliver mail better and less expensively.

2.d. Social Regulation

Although economists debate the costs and benefits of regulation, the amount of regulation has grown steadily since the Great Depression. Most of this growth has been due to social regulation.

Social regulation is concerned with the conditions under which goods and services are produced and the impact of these goods on the public. The following government agencies are concerned with social regulation:

- The Occupational Safety and Health Administration (OSHA), which is concerned with protecting workers against injuries and illnesses associated with their jobs
- The Consumer Product Safety Commission (CPSC), which specifies minimum standards for safety of products
- The Food and Drug Administration (FDA), which is concerned with the safety and effectiveness of food, drugs, and cosmetics
- The Equal Employment Opportunity Commission (EEOC), which focuses on the hiring, promotion, and discharge of workers
- The Environmental Protection Agency (EPA), which is concerned with air, water, and noise pollution

Social regulation is often applied across all industries. For instance, while the ICC focuses on trucking and railroads, the EPA enforces emission standards related to all businesses.

Social regulation has grown since the early 1970s as illustrated by the number of rules and regulations imposed by the federal government shown in Figure 3. Figure 3 shows the number of telephone-book-sized pages in the *Federal Register* required to list the rules and regulations of the federal government.

The annual administrative costs of federal regulatory activities exceed $15 billion. The costs of complying with the rules and regulations, which are imposed on businesses, shift their cost curves up. These costs have been estimated to exceed $300 billion per year. Complying with environmental regulations alone costs business more than $200 billion per year.[2]

Figure 3

The number of telephone-book-sized pages required to list the rules and regulations of the federal government number 80,000. The number of regulations grew until the Reagan years of 1980 to 1985 and then grew again during the Bush and Clinton administrations.

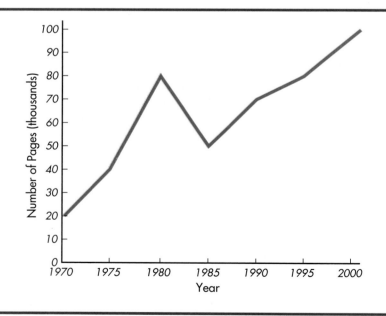

[2]William H. Miller, "Make It Rational," *Industry Week,* January 23, 1995, p. 25; and Judi Hasson, "Senate OKs Curbs on Regulations," *USA Today,* March 30, 1995, p. 6A.

Added to the direct costs of regulations are the opportunity costs. For instance, the lengthy FDA process for approving new biotechnology has stymied advances in agriculture. Regulatory restrictions on the telecommunications industry has resulted in the United States lagging behind Japan in the development of fiber optics and high-definition television. The total cost imposed on the U.S. economy from federal government regulations is estimated to be more than $600 billion a year, $6,000 per household.

A cost-benefit test for regulation would limit regulations designed to benefit a very few at the cost of many. However, the cost-benefit test also should include the opportunity costs implied by interfering with the free market, according to many economists. If labeling is desired by the public, won't the public voluntarily pay the higher price for it? Why, then, is regulation necessary unless it is to benefit some special interest group? If seat belts and antilock braking systems are desired by the public, won't the public voluntarily pay the price to have these safety systems? Why, if the market would ensure that what the public desires is produced at the lowest possible cost, is it necessary for the government to intervene in the economy and impose regulatory costs of $600 billion or more each year?

Many economists argue that regulations are the result of rent seeking—the attempt to get benefits for a few by imposing costs on others. Representative democracy provides an incentive to citizens to increase their wealth through government regulations, transfers, or direct expenditures without increasing the supply or ownership of resources. If special interest groups want to increase their wealth and are organized and politically powerful, politicians grant benefits that enable them to. Such benefits are called rents because, like economic rents, they represent a payment that is larger than necessary for the resource to be supplied. Activities undertaken to obtain special favors (rents) from government are called **rent seeking;** these activities produce zero output but use up resources.

Whether an action should be undertaken can be determined by comparing the costs of a certain action to the benefits of that action.

rent seeking: activities directed toward securing income without increasing output

2.e. Regulation and Deregulation in Other Countries

In most European nations, nationalization rather than regulation was the traditional solution to natural monopoly. Nationalization is where the government takes over and operates an industry. Privatization is the opposite of nationalization. Privatization, as discussed earlier, is the transfer of public-sector activities to the private sector. Privatization may take one of three forms: *wholesale privatization*, in which an entire publicly owned firm is transferred to private ownership; *contracting out,* in which a specific aspect of a government operation is carried out by a private firm; and *auctioning*, in which the rights to operate a government enterprise go to the highest private-sector bidder.

While the United States was deregulating, the rest of the world was privatizing. Chile, Argentina, Colombia, the United Kingdom, and 15 other nations now allow workers to invest their social security payroll deductions into privately managed funds. The Netherlands offered 25 percent of the Dutch postal and telephone system for private ownership in 1994. Britain has privatized its airlines, telephones, steel, and electric and gas utilities.

More than eighty countries have launched ambitious efforts to privatize their state-owned enterprises (SOEs) since 1980. More than 2,000 SOEs have been privatized in developing countries and more than 7,000 worldwide. State-owned enterprises are chronically unprofitable, partly because they are told to increase employment and locate so as to help the local population rather than to maximize efficiency. Governments provide SOEs with a variety of subsidies, such as reduced prices for resources and guarantees to cover operating losses. Privatization is intended to substitute the single objective of profit maximization for all these other objectives. Subjecting the newly privatized firm to the tests of the market and competition forces the companies to cut costs and increase efficiency or to get out of business altogether. At first glance, this would seem to indicate that the firms will have to cut employment. Interestingly, the experience has been that the privatized firms do perform much more efficiently but that they also increase output and employment relative to the SOEs. Employment in privatized firms has risen by about 10 percent relative to the SOEs.

2.f. Multinationals, International Regulation, GATT, and the WTO

International regulation occurs at two levels, one in which a specific government regulates the activities of individual firms operating within the country and the other in which several nations are involved. The General Agreement on Tariffs and Trade (GATT) is a form of the latter. In April 1947, delegates from the United States, Asia, Europe, and Latin America traveled to Geneva. All, aware of the effects of trade restrictions on economic health as experienced during the Great Depression, sought to liberalize trade, reduce barriers, and create an environment in which economies would prosper. The first global trade agreement resulted, called GATT. Today GATT is called the World Trade Organization (WTO). Its 132 member nations have agreed to settle trade disputes in the WTO courts rather than raise barriers, impose tariffs, or otherwise restrict trade. The WTO was created on January 1, 1995, and since has dealt with more trade disputes than GATT did during its entire fifty-year history. Another global regulatory agreement is currently being developed by the industrial nations. This one deals with multinational corporations. It is called the Multilateral Agreement on Investment (MAI). The principal aim of MAI is to have nations treat multinational companies exactly as they treat their own companies. There would be no investment required in local projects or companies, no uncompensated expropriation, no limit of capital movement, and all disputes would be settled by a global organization, either under the WTO or as a separate organization.

RECAP

1. The stated reason for regulation of industries such as railroads, trucking, and air transport was the potential for self-destructive competition. The stated reason for regulating airwaves was the lack of private property rights.

2. Since the mid-1970s, deregulation has occurred in airlines, trucking, railroads, and communications.

3. Social regulation deals with workplace safety, product safety, the environment, and other aspects of doing business; it applies to all industries.

4. In other countries, nationalization occurred instead of regulation. In those countries, deregulation means privatization.

5. Attempts to increase trade among nations has led to the creation of GATT and then the WTO.

3. GOVERNMENT AND BUSINESS

3. Why does the government intervene in business activity?

The government's role in business has risen over the years, primarily as a result of social regulation. Antitrust actions ebb and flow over time, and economic regulation has decreased during the past two decades or so. Nevertheless, the government has a huge role in the U.S. economy. Why does the government play such a big role when the U.S. economy is a capitalist system? The reason stems from the market survey we undertook in Chapter 3. The public's distrust of the price system and its feeling that "there ought to be a law" has induced politicians to call for just such a law. Whether such a law is justified depends on where you stand. Two general theories of why the government is a participant in economic activity are illustrative: the public interest theory and the capture theory.

3.a. Theories of Why the Government Intervenes in Business Activity

Why does the government intervene in the affairs of business? One explanation is that the government's intervention in the economy is for the public good. This is called the **public interest theory** of government intervention. According to this theory, the government carries out antitrust policy, regulates nuclear power, airlines, new pharmaceuticals, workplace safety, product safety, and the environment because the public's well-being depends on the government's actions. Without such intervention, according to this theory, unsafe drugs would be foisted off on an unwary public and unsafe nuclear power plants would be built. It is argued that the government must intervene in agriculture, trucking, airlines, and other industries to protect the public from competition that could destroy these industries. Moreover, the government must prevent large firms from destroying small ones. According to public interest theory, if the government did not intervene, the public would face many more monopolists.

In opposition to the public interest theory of government is the argument that government actions are simply ways to transfer wealth from one sector of the economy or one person to another. We might call this the "we don't like the market outcome" theory of government intervention. The market outcome says that those willing and able to pay for a good or service will get the good or service. If we want others to get the good or service or if we want the good or service to be free or provided at very low cost, we might join together and get the government to intervene in the market. One form of the "we don't like the market outcome" theory is called **capture theory.** According to capture theory, special interests, not the public, receive the benefits of antitrust policy and regulation. For instance, according to capture theory, the antitrust suit against Microsoft is an attempt to secure benefits for rival firms, not the general public; the group in charge of trucking regulations is composed of spokespeople from the trucking industry so that the regulations benefit truckers, not the general public; and the agency in charge of regulating nuclear power involves executives from the nuclear power industry, thereby ensuring that the regulations benefit the industry, not necessarily the general public. Capture theory claims that government intervention in business activities is like asking the fox to guard the henhouse.

How could Congress and the regulatory agencies create laws and regulations favorable to a special interest group at the expense of the general public? The

public interest theory: government intervenes in business activity to benefit the general public

capture theory: the government intervenes in business activity to transfer wealth from one group to another, to benefit a special interest

primary reason is that as a member of the general public you do not have as much concern over some activity that affects a special interest group as you would as a member of that special interest group. For instance, consider regulation that is favorable toward an industry group and unfavorable toward consumers. As a consumer you do not specialize in hiring moving companies, traveling by bus or air, or studying pharmaceuticals. You merely purchase the products that are offered. The industries concerned do specialize in their business and thus lobby intensely to guide the legislation and regulations that impact the industry. Another factor is that the legislation and regulations do not come with a label spelling out exactly who is benefited or harmed. Laws and rules that end up favoring special interest groups may have been originally intended to benefit or have been presented as benefiting the general public. For example, regulation of airport taxis occurred because of the claim that too many consumers were being ripped off. Thus, the taxi fares were fixed by law. This regulation reduced price competition, restricted entry, and provided stable revenue for the taxi firms—obviously benefiting the taxi firms. Similarly, legislation to increase the safety of new pharmaceuticals through years of testing may benefit the pharmaceutical firms at the expense of consumers, since the process of testing restricts entry and allows above-normal profits for a longer period of time.

So why does the government intervene in business activity? The theories say either because the public wants and needs the government's help or because private special interests use the government to get special benefits. There is another reason often given for the government's intervention in the private economy—inefficiency.

Voting is carried out in a technologically obsolete manner using card punches thereby creating the problem of hand counting in the past Presidential election. Here the vote counter is worrying about "chads" and "pregnant chads," the little pieces of paper created with the hole punch used to select the voters' choices.

It is argued that externalities and public goods (discussed in detail in the chapter "The Land Market: Natural Resources and Environmental Policy") and imperfect information lead to market inefficiencies that can only be resolved by the government.

An externality represents a case in which the costs or benefits of a transaction between two people spill over and affect others. An example is the pollution you create when you drive your automobile; you create it, but everyone bears the costs of that pollution. It is often argued that the externality can only be resolved by government intervention.

A second case of a market inefficiency is called a public good. A public good is a good or service for which exclusion does not occur and the consumption of the good by one person is not affected by the consumption by someone else. An example is national defense. With a private good like a pizza, the person who buys the pizza can choose who gets to eat it, and when some of it is consumed, less of it is available. If one person purchases a public good, that good would be available free to others. Also, if one person received the benefits of the public good, that would not limit anyone else from receiving those benefits as well. As a result, no one has an incentive to provide the public good. It is argued that if the public good is to be supplied, it must be supplied by the government.

A third possible market inefficiency is caused by imperfect information—a situation in which different people or firms have different information. Let's consider two cases of this, adverse selection and moral hazard.

3.b. Adverse Selection

When you purchase a used car, you are probably unsure of the car's quality. You could hire a mechanic to look at the car before you buy it, but because that procedure is quite expensive, you probably choose to forgo it. Most people assume that cars offered for sale by private individuals are defective in some way, and they are not willing to pay top dollar because they expect that the car will need expensive repairs. As a result, people who do have high-quality used cars for sale cannot obtain the high price they deserve.

adverse selection: the situation that occurs when higher-quality consumers or producers are driven out of the market because unobservable qualities are misvalued

Adverse selection occurs when unobservable qualities are misvalued because of a lack of information. The result of adverse selection is that low-quality consumers or producers drive higher-quality consumers or producers out of the market. People with high-quality used cars are most likely to trade their cars in to a dealer, leaving lower-quality used cars for sale by nondealers.

Adverse selection occurs in many markets. Banks do not always know which people applying for loans will default and which will pay on time. How can a bank distinguish among loan applicants? If the bank increases the interest rate in an attempt to drive high-risk applicants out of the market, adverse selection increases. As the bank raises the interest rate on loans, high-risk applicants continue to apply for loans but high-quality applicants do not. As a result, only high-risk applicants remain in the market.

Adverse selection occurs in insurance markets as well. People purchase automobile or health insurance even if they are excellent drivers and enjoy good health. As the cost of insurance rises, the good drivers and healthy people might reduce their coverage while the poor drivers and unhealthy people maintain their coverage. As a result, high-risk applicants take the place of more desirable low-risk applicants in the market for insurance.

Adverse selection explains why loan companies require down payments and why insurance companies require copayments or deductibles. Rather than increasing interest rates to eliminate high-risk applicants, a bank requests a higher down payment. Since only people who expect to pay off the loan and who have sufficient wealth or income to pay off the loan are willing to provide the down payment, adverse selection is reduced. Similarly, by requiring that a borrower provide collateral (a house or car or some other asset), a bank can separate high-risk from low-risk applicants. And an insurance company may require a policyholder to carry a deductible—the policyholder agrees to pay the first $300, say, of damage to his or her car. When an insurance company reduces the insurance charge and increases the deductible, good drivers and healthy people are more willing to purchase insurance, and poor drivers and less healthy people are less willing.

3.c. Moral Hazard

When information is costly to obtain, monitoring the behavior of the other party in an exchange may be difficult. When verification of trades or contracts is difficult and when people can change their behavior from what was anticipated when a trade or contract was made, a **moral hazard** exists.

moral hazard: when people alter their behavior from what was anticipated when a transaction was made

People who discover that they have a serious illness and then purchase health insurance are taking advantage of the insurance company's lack of information and creating a moral hazard. A person who drives much less carefully after obtaining car insurance is creating a moral hazard. A person who takes less care to be healthy after obtaining health insurance is creating a moral hazard.

Sometimes the moral hazard can be reduced when the person or firm creating the moral hazard and the person or firm being taken advantage of share in the costs. This is a reason insurance companies require a deductible, so that the company and the customer share in expenses and risks. You are more likely to drive carefully and safeguard your health if you have to pay some of the costs of an accident or illness.

3.d. Government Efficiency?

Economists do not unanimously agree that these cases of market inefficiency are sufficient arguments for government intervention. Some economists point to the fact that government inefficiency is far greater than the inefficiency of the market and that any government intervention will be worse than the market problem that led to the intervention. Many economists point out that inefficiency arguments are used when there is no inefficiency. For instance, the prisoner's dilemma discussed in the chapter "Monopolistic Competition and Oligopoly" is used as an argument of inefficiency, firms get bogged down in a result that is not the best for either firm. The counterargument is that firms finding themselves in a dilemma have an incentive to get out of the dilemma and would over time. The New Economy has brought forth a flurry of calls for government intervention to reduce the winner-takes-all results of the New Economy. Others are noting that there is no winner-takes-all in the long run; any firm or network making positive economic profit will entice other entrepreneurs to find ways around the standard or the monopoly. Even the Microsoft antitrust case was controversial. While some argued that Microsoft attempted to monopolize the market and acted unfairly in doing so, others argued that technology was already reducing the Microsoft dominance by the time the case was adjudicated.

1. According to economic theory, the government intervenes in the economy either as a benefit to the public interest or as a benefit to special interest groups. The arguments supporting the first reason are called the Public Interest theory. The arguments supporting the second approach are called the Capture Theory.

2. The Public Interest Theory rationale for the government's regulation and antitrust actions are that without such actions the general public would be harmed by business actions.

3. The Capture Theory argument might refer to government intervention as "We don't like the market outcome" rationale. Those not receiving benefits from the market outcome or not receiving as much of a benefit as they want, may argue that the government needs to step in and transfer resources from some other sector of the economy to them.

4. According to the Public Interest Theory, another rationale for government intervention is the inefficiencies created by externalities, public goods, and imperfect information.

5. Adverse selection occurs when low-quality consumers or producers force higher-quality consumers or producers out of the market.

6. Moral hazard exists when people alter their behavior in an unanticipated way after an agreement or contract has been defined.

7. The Capture Theory argument is that government actions create inefficiencies that are at least equal to those of the private market and that such actions do not resolve externalities, public goods problems, and imperfect information as well as private solutions would.

SUMMARY

❓ What is antitrust policy?

1. Antitrust policy is an attempt to enhance competition by restricting certain activities that could be anticompetitive. *§1.b*

2. The antitrust statutes include Sections 1 and 2 of the Sherman Antitrust Act, which forbids conspiracies and monopolization; Sections 2, 3, and 7 of the Clayton Antitrust Act, which prohibits anticompetitive pricing and nonprice restraints; and Section 5 of the Federal Trade Commission Act, which prohibits deceptive and unfair acts. *§1.b, Table 1*

3. The antitrust statutes have undergone several phases of interpretation. In the early years, a rule of reason prevailed; acts had to be unreasonable to be a violation of the statutes. Between 1914 and 1980, a per se rule applied more often. Under this policy, the mere existence of actions that could be used anticompetitively was a violation. In the early 1980s, the inter-

pretations returned to the rule-of-reason standard. In the early 1990s, another attempt to tighten enforcement was made. *§1.b*

4. The Herfindahl index is used to measure size and influence; industries with a Herfindahl index above 1,800 are considered highly concentrated. *§1.e*

5. Antitrust laws are more rigorously enforced in the United States than elsewhere. *§1.f*

❓ What is the difference between economic regulation and social regulation?

6. Economic regulation refers to the prescription of price and output for a particular industry. Social regulation refers to the setting of health and safety standards for products and the workplace, and environmental and operating procedures for all industries. *§2*

7. Because monopoly is inefficient and perfect competition efficient, governments have attempted to regulate the natural monopolies to make them more like perfect competitors. The huge economies of scale rule out breaking the natural monopolies up into small firms. Instead, price has been set at a fair rate of return, $P = ATC$. *§2.a*

8. Some industries have been regulated not because they are natural monopolies but because the government wants to limit entry in order to protect an industry from self-destructive competition and from the formation of a monopoly. Examples include airlines and railroads. *§2.b.1*

9. Some industries are regulated to prevent chaos because of the lack of private property rights. *§2.b.2*

10. Social regulation has increased even as economic regulation has decreased. *§2.d*

11. Deregulation in other developed countries took the form of privatization: the selling, auctioning, or contracting out of a government enterprise to private interests. *§2.e*

12. The WTO is intended to lower tariffs and increase trade. *§2.f*

(?) Why does the government intervene in business activity?

13. The public interest theory of regulation asserts that regulation is necessary to protect the public interest. The capture theory of regulation claims that regulation benefits only those who are regulated. *§3.a*

14. Market inefficiencies are given as reasons for government intervention. Such inefficiencies include adverse selection, moral hazard, externalities, and public goods. *§3.b, §3.c*

15. In contrast to the view that market inefficiencies require government intervention, it may be that the government is more inefficient than the private market. If left alone, the private market might resolve the market inefficiencies. *§3.d*

KEY TERMS

antitrust policy *§1*

rule of reason *§1.b*

per se rule *§1.b*

Herfindahl index *§1.e*

concentration *§1.e*

economic regulation *§2*

social regulation *§2*

fair rate of return *§2.a*

privatization *§2.c*

contracting out *§2.c*

rent seeking *§2.d*

public interest theory *§3.a*

capture theory *§3.a*

adverse selection *§3.b*

moral hazard *§3.c*

EXERCISES

1. Using demand and cost curves, demonstrate why a typical monopolistically competitive firm might want to create a barrier to entry.

2. Using the demand and cost curves of an individual firm in oligopoly, demonstrate what the effects of each of the following are:

   a. The Clean Air Act
   b. The Nutrition and Labeling Act
   c. A ban on smoking inside the workplace
   d. A sales tax

3. What is self-destructive competition? How does a natural monopoly differ from a firm that has large fixed costs and relatively small marginal costs?

4. Kodak has developed an important brand name through its advertising, innovation, and product quality and service. Suppose Kodak sets up a network of exclusive dealerships, and one of the dealers decides to carry Fuji and Mitsubishi as well as Kodak products. If Kodak terminates the dealership, is it acting in a pro- or anticompetitive manner?

5. Explain why auctioning broadcast licenses might be more efficient than having the FCC assign licenses on some basis designed by the FCC.

6. Which of the three types of government policies—antitrust, social regulation, economic regulation—is the basis for each of the following?

   a. Beautician education standards
   b. Certified Public Accounting requirements
   c. Liquor licensing
   d. Justice Department guidelines
   e. The Clean Air Act
   f. The Nutrition and Labeling Act

7. Provide the arguments for and against each of the rules or regulations listed in exercise 6 using public interest theory and capture theory.

8. In the chapter "Monopoly," we discussed the Glaxo-Wellcome monopoly on the AIDS drug AZT. As an active member of an AIDS prevention organization, argue that regulation by the FDA has been harmful. As an executive of Glaxo-Wellcome, argue that the FDA regulation has been beneficial.

9. Some airline executives have called for reregulation. Why might an executive of an airline prefer to operate under a regulated environment?

10. Suppose the Herfindahl index for domestic production of televisions is 5,000. Does this imply a very competitive or a noncompetitive environment?

11. Discuss the claim that social regulation is unnecessary. Does the claim depend on whether the industrial structure of an industry is composed primarily of perfect competition or primarily of oligopoly?

12. Suppose a monopolist is practicing price discrimination and a lawsuit against the monopolist forces an end to the practice. Is it possible that the result is a loss in efficiency? Explain.

13. The Justice Department sued several universities for collectively setting the size of scholarships offered. Explain why the alleged price fixing on the part of universities might be harmful to students.

14. Explain the often-heard statement "There ought to be a law" in terms of public interest theory and capture theory of government intervention in business activity. For instance, suppose a consumer hires Bekins moving company to transfer him from California to Utah and Bekins damages $3,000 worth of furniture and refuses to compensate the consumer. The consumer in frustration says, "There ought to be a law."

15. "The Japanese are beating us at every step. We must act as they do. We must allow and encourage cooperation among firms and we must develop partnerships between business and government. The first place we should begin is with the aerospace industry. Let's use the government to transfer the resources no longer employed in aerospace to nondefense industries such as the environment and health." Evaluate this industrial policy.

Internet Exercises/ Resources

For Internet exercises and web resources related to this chapter, go to **http://college.hmco.com.**

SO2 Emission Allowance Asset Report: Title IV of the 1990 Clean Air Act Amendments (CAAA)

CAAA established the Allowance Trading System (ATS), the system through which transactions in the market for allowance trading are conducted and tracked. To date, the tracking system indicates that trading activity has been much below the level anticipated at the outset. Prices for allowances have similarly been below expectations. The number of transactions reached a peak during the first quarter of 1996, then dropped off sharply, but has since rebounded somewhat. The chart below shows the prices associated with those transactions according to two different price indexes developed by allowance brokerage companies and published in the Allowance System Fact Sheet by the U.S. Environmental Protection Agency.

Three key reasons explain both the low volume of allowance trades and the associated low prices of those trades.

One of the most important developments contributing to the unexpected outcome of the allowance trading market has been the relatively inexpensive alternative that low sulfur coal now offers. A second important factor has been that the evolving market for compliance equipment, or scrubbers. Increased competition among contractors for compliance equipment and technological innovation in the industry have combined to reduce prices. A third factor that has influenced this market has been the uncertainty that impending deregulation of the electric utility industry has brought about. Confusion over cost recovery rules in general, and the evolving regulations surrounding gains and losses in the allowance trading market in particular, have caused utilities to be wary of active trading.

Thus far, compliance with the CAAA has been achieved in large part without the necessity of great volumes of allowance trading. Innovation, competition, and the discovery of better ways to comply have combined to reduce the overall cost of compliance. As the market evolves and as the century mark approaches, when all fossil fuel generating plants above 25 megawatts of generating capacity are required to comply with CAAA, the dynamics of the market could change considerably.

Source: Melissa Hardison, Donna Dart, and Chris Combe, "SO2 Emission Allowance Asset Report," January 9, 1998, Salt River Project Management Report. Reprinted with permission.

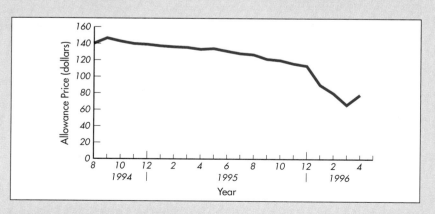

Salt River Project Management Report/January 9, 1998

Commentary

As discussed in the chapter, there are two general kinds of government regulations—social regulations and specific business regulations. Either kind of regulation can be implemented in many ways. Historically, regulation has been dictated by government or a government agency to a business or businesses. This command-and-control type of regulation has been criticized by many economists as being inefficient. Many economists would prefer to see some type of market-based regulation rather than command-and-control regulation.

How can a business be regulated and yet a market allowed to operate? What is occurring in the environmental area is an example of how a market can be used to regulate business activity. The electric utility industry has been regulated as far as the prices it can charge, the services it can provide, and its service areas. It also is socially regulated; for instance, the Environmental Protection Agency (EPA) dictates how a firm can dispose of its waste products. Both these areas of regulation are changing. The electric utility industry is in the process of being deregulated in terms of the service areas it can provide and the prices it can charge. In this article, the authors are discussing the results of the market-based approach the EPA has implemented toward reducing SO2 emissions by electric utilities. In 1995, the EPA implemented a trading allowance scheme. The EPA would dictate the total units of emissions that would be allowed in each area. It would then allocate allowances to each business. If a business wanted to emit up to its allowed amount of pollutants, it would have no excess allowance. If the business wanted to emit more than its allowance, it could purchase allowances from businesses that did not use their entire allowance. Thus, a market for allowances developed.

The price of the allowance depends on demand and supply. The more businesses that want to emit pollutants greater than their permits allow, the greater demand relative to supply and the higher the price of the allowance. Conversely, the more businesses with excess allowances, the greater supply relative to demand and the lower the price of the allowances.

In the article, it is clear that the price of allowances has fallen dramatically, from a high of about $149 to a low of about $60. Why would this occur, especially if the EPA is reducing allowed emissions each year? The authors correctly point out that it is the efficiency of the market that has led to lower prices.

A business will compare the cost of complying with the EPA—acquiring new capital and utilizing different resources—and the cost of purchasing additional emission allowances. If the business expects the EPA to continue reducing the allowable emissions and thus expects the price of allowances to rise in the future, it may decide that purchasing new, more efficient capital now makes sense. If many businesses do this, the demand for allowances will decline, the supply rise, and the price fall. This has occurred as many industries have acquired new, better scrubbers, the capital that reduces emissions from smokestacks.

In addition to the acquisition of new capital, utilities have been able to use the low-sulfur coal of the West rather than the higher-sulfur coal of the East at no higher or not much higher costs due to technological change in the acquisition of the coal and the deregulation of rail transport.

Part Four

Resource Markets

Chapter 15

Resource Markets

Fundamental Questions

1. **Who are the buyers and sellers of resources?**

2. **How are resource prices determined?**

3. **How does a firm allocate its expenditures among the various resources?**

Preview

Do you recycle? Are you concerned with global warming, saving the rain forest, and reducing pollution? Perhaps you've noted the number of homeless people on the streets and wondered why they are homeless and what can be done about homelessness. Have you ever been discriminated against because of your age, race, or sex? Have you been touched by illegal drugs—gang wars, drive-by shootings, crime? In the following chapters we discuss some aspects of these issues as we examine the resource markets. The resource markets involve labor, capital, and land in general terms, but more specifically they deal with people and their jobs, investments, and natural resources. ■

1. BUYERS AND SELLERS OF RESOURCES

There are three general classes of resources (*factors of production*, or *inputs*) and thus three resource markets: land, labor, and capital. The price and quantity of each resource are determined in its resource market. Rent and the quantity of land used are determined in the land market. The wage rate and the number of people employed are determined in the labor market. The interest rate and the quantity of capital used are determined in the capital market.

1.a. The Resource Markets

To understand the resource markets, you need to realize that the roles of firms and households are reversed from what they are in the product markets. Figure 1 is the simplest circular flow diagram you saw in Chapter 4. It illustrates the roles of firms and households in the product and resource markets. The product market is represented by the top lines in the figure. Households buy goods and services from firms, as shown by the line going from firms to households; and firms sell goods and services and receive revenue, as shown by the line going from households to firms. The resource market is represented by the bottom half of the diagram in Figure 1. Households are the sellers of resources, and firms are the buyers of resources. Households sell resources, as shown by the line going from households to firms; and firms pay households income, as shown by the line going from firms to households.

Resources are wanted not for themselves but for what they produce. A firm uses resources in order to produce goods and services. Thus, the demand for a resource by a firm depends on the demand for the goods and services that the firm produces. For this reason, the demand for resources is often called a **derived demand:** an automobile manufacturer uses land, labor, and capital to produce cars; a retail T-shirt store uses land, labor, and capital to sell T-shirts; a farmer uses land, labor, and capital to produce agricultural products.

derived demand: demand stemming from what a resource can produce, not demand for the resource itself

Figure 1

The Market for Resources

The buyers of resources are firms that purchase resources in order to produce goods and services. The sellers of resources are households that supply resources in order to obtain income with which to purchase goods and services.

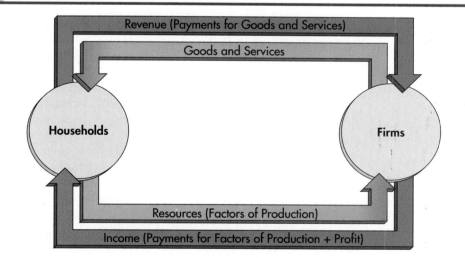

Households supply resources in order to earn income. By offering to work, individuals supply their labor; by purchasing stocks, bonds, and other financial capital, households supply firms with the ability to acquire capital; by offering their land and the minerals, trees, and other natural resources associated with it, households supply land.

RECAP

1. Resources are classified into three types: land, labor, and capital.
2. The price of each type of resource—rent, wages, and interest—and the quantity of each resource used are determined in the resource markets.
3. The buyers of resources are firms; the suppliers are households.

2. How are resource prices determined?

2. THE MARKET DEMAND FOR AND SUPPLY OF RESOURCES

Firms demand resources and households supply resources. Except for this reversal in buyers and sellers, the supply and demand curves for resource markets look just like the supply and demand curves for product markets. The market demand curve slopes downward and the market supply curve upward. In resource markets, as in product markets, equilibrium defines the price and quantity. Changes in demand or supply cause the equilibrium price and quantity to change.

2.a. Market Demand

A firm chooses inputs in order to maximize profits.

The demand curve for a resource slopes down, as shown in Figure 2, because as the price of the resource falls, everything else held constant, producers are more *willing* and more *able* to use (to purchase or rent) that resource. If the price of the resource falls, that resource becomes relatively less expensive than other resources that the firm could use. Firms will substitute this now relatively less expensive resource for other now relatively more expensive resources. Thus substitution occurs in production just as it does in consumption. Construction firms switch from copper tubing to plastic pipe as copper becomes relatively more expensive than plastic. Firms move from Manhattan to Dallas as land in Manhattan becomes relatively more expensive than land in Dallas. Economists may be hired to teach finance, management, and even accounting classes as the wages of professionals in those other fields rise relative to the wages of economists.

A lower price for a resource also increases a firm's *ability* to hire that resource. At a lower price, everything else held constant, firms can purchase more resources for the same total cost. If the price of a machine drops by 50 percent, the firm can buy two machines at the old cost of one. This means not that the firm will buy two machines but that it is able to buy the second machine. Thus, the demand curve for a resource slopes down because of income and substitution effects just as the demand curve for a product slopes down because of income and substitution effects, as you learned in the chapter on consumer choice.

2.a.1. The Elasticity of Resource Demand
The amount by which firms will alter their use of a resource when the price of that resource changes is measured by

Figure 2

Resource Market Demand and Market Supply

The demand curve for a resource slopes down, reflecting the inverse relation between the price of the resource and the quantity demanded. The supply curve of a resource slopes up, reflecting the direct relation between the price of the resource and the quantity supplied. Equilibrium occurs where the two curves intersect; the quantities demanded and supplied are the same at the equilibrium price. If the resource price is greater than the equilibrium price, a surplus of the resource arises and drives the price back down to equilibrium. If the resource price is less than the equilibrium price, a shortage occurs and forces the price back up to equilibrium.

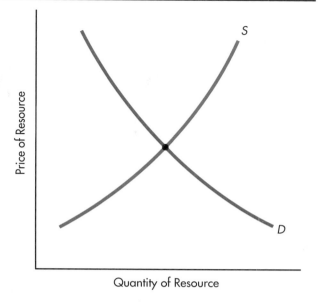

the price elasticity of resource demand. The price elasticity of the demand for a resource, e_r, is defined in exactly the same way as the price elasticity of demand—as the percentage change in the quantity demanded of a resource divided by the percentage change in the price of the resource:

$$e_r = \frac{\text{percentage change in quantity demanded of resource } j}{\text{percentage change in price of resource } j}$$

If the price of lumber rises by 10 percent and the quantity demanded falls by 5 percent, the price elasticity of demand for lumber is 0.5. If the rental rate of office space falls by 5 percent and the quantity demanded increases by 20 percent, the price elasticity of demand for office space is 4. The price elasticity of demand for a resource depends on:

- The price elasticity of demand for the product the resource is used to produce
- The proportion of total costs constituted by the resource
- The number of substitutes for the resource
- The time period under consideration

Price elasticity of the product The price elasticity of demand for a resource depends on the price elasticity of demand for the product the resource is being used to produce. For instance, if the price elasticity of demand for newspapers is very high and the price of newspapers increases, the quantity demanded of newspapers will fall by a "great deal." As a result, a similarly "great deal" fewer resources are needed. Suppose then that the price of one of these resources, ink, rises. If the higher ink cost leads to a rise in the price of newspapers, then the quantity of newspapers demanded will decline by a significant amount and cause the quantity of ink purchased to decline by a significant amount. Everything else the same, we can say that the larger the price elasticity of demand for a product, the larger the price elasticity of demand for resources used to produce that product. The reverse is true as well.

Proportion of total costs   The larger one resource's proportion of the total costs of producing a good, the higher the price elasticity of demand for that resource. If airplanes constitute 60 percent of the total costs of running an airline, the price elasticity of demand for airplanes will be high. A small increase in the price of an airplane will tend to raise the airline's costs significantly, and this is likely to increase the price of tickets. The higher price for tickets will reduce the quantity demanded and thereby reduce the number of airplanes demanded.

Number of substitutes   The number of substitutes for a resource affects the price elasticity of demand for a resource. For instance, if copper tubing, plastic tubing, steel tubing, or corrugated aluminum tubing can be used in construction equally well, the price elasticity of demand for any one of these types of tubing will be relatively high. Even a small increase in copper tubing would cause firms to switch immediately to other types of tubing.

Time period   The time period is also important in determining the price elasticity of demand. The longer the period of time under consideration, the greater the price elasticity of demand for a resource. A longer period of time enables firms to discover other substitutes and to move relatively immobile resources into or out of use.

The price elasticity of resource demand varies according to the four factors just mentioned. The price elasticity of resource demand also varies along a straight-line

Entrepreneurs must combine land, labor, and capital to produce the goods and services they hope to sell for a profit. Leo Lindy's on Broadway in New York City had to spend more on very specific capital, this neon-lighted sign, than if the deli was located off-Broadway since it is competing for the attention of theatergoers. The specific capital provides benefits to the firm in that it provides information to consumers about the stability of the firm and the type of service provided by the firm. Consumers can choose between the deli with the neon sign or a dark bistro down the street. A household supplies resources in order to maximize utility.

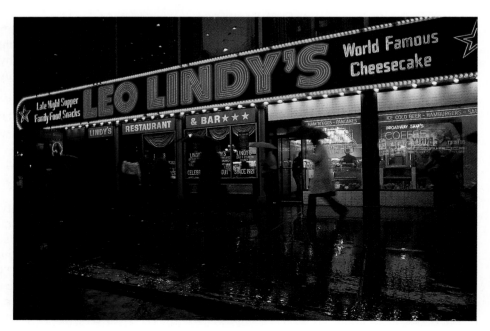

resource demand curve, going from elastic to inelastic as we move down the demand curve, just as is the case with a product demand curve (see the chapter on demand and supply elasticities).

2.a.2. Shifts in the Demand for a Resource
The demand curve for a resource will shift when one of the *nonprice* determinants of demand changes. Nonprice determinants of demand for a resource include:

- The prices of the product the resource is used to produce
- The productivity of a resource
- The number of buyers of the resource
- The prices of related resources
- The quantities of other resources

Price of the product When the price of copper rises, the demand for copper miners increases—the demand curve shifts out to the right. Mining firms hire more workers at each wage rate in order to produce more copper and earn the higher revenues.

Productivity When a resource becomes more productive—that is, when each unit of the resource can produce more output—the firm will use more of the resource. For instance, if new printing presses are able to produce twice as much in the same amount of time as existing presses, the demand for new printing presses will rise. The demand curve for printing presses will shift out to the right.

Number of buyers When new firms enter an industry, they require resources. The demand curve for resources will shift out to the right. For instance, when Wal-Mart builds a store in a small town, it must hire workers and acquire land, capital, buildings, and other supplies. The demand for workers, for capital, for land, and for the other supplies increases with the entry of Wal-Mart—the demand curves shift out to the right.

Substitutes A change in the price of substitute resources will affect the demand for a resource. For instance, if labor and machines are substitutes in the production of iron ore, then when the price of labor rises, the demand for machines increases— the demand curve for machines shifts out to the right. Conversely, if copper and plastic are substitutes in construction, then when the price of plastic declines, the demand for copper decreases—the demand curve for copper shifts in.

Quantity of other resources A restaurant using only 10 of its 60 tables requires only one waiter. If the other 50 tables are also used, the restaurant needs more waiters. With a bigger pot and more soil, the quantity of flowers grown with each additional amount of fertilizer applied will be larger than it would be with a smaller pot and less soil. More capital tends to increase the demand for labor; more land tends to increase the demand for tractors. In other words, the demand for a resource depends on how many of the other resources are available.

2.b. Market Supply

Individuals act so as to maximize their utility. They receive utility when they consume goods and services, but they need income to purchase the goods and services. To acquire income, households must sell the services of their resources. They must give up some of their leisure time and go to work or offer their other resources in order to acquire income. The quantity of resources that are supplied depends on the wages, rents, interest, and profits offered for those resources. If, while everything else is held constant, people can get higher wages, they will offer to work more hours; if they can obtain more rent for their land, they will offer more of their land for use, and so on. The quantity supplied of a resource rises as the price of the resource rises.

2.b.1. The Elasticity of Resource Supply The amount by which resource owners alter the quantity they offer for use when the price of the resource changes is measured by the price elasticity of resource supply, e_r^s. The price elasticity of supply for a resource is defined as the percentage change in the quantity supplied divided by the percentage change in the price of a resource:

$$e_r^s = \frac{\text{percentage change in quantity of resource supplied}}{\text{percentage change in price of resource}}$$

The price elasticity of resource supply depends on the number of substitute uses for a resource and the time period under consideration. Some resources have no substitutes. For instance, there are few if any substitutes for a rocket scientist; as a result, the price elasticity of supply for the rocket scientist is very low. Typically, the longer the period under consideration, the more likely that substitutes for a resource can be discovered. Given a few years, even an economist could be trained to be a rocket scientist. For a month or two, the quantity of oil that can be pulled from the ground is relatively fixed; given a year or so, new wells can be drilled and new supplies discovered. The price elasticity of resource supply increases as the time period increases.

When a resource has a perfectly inelastic supply curve, its pay or earnings is called **economic rent.** If a resource has a perfectly elastic supply curve, its pay or earnings is called **transfer earnings.** For upward-sloping supply curves, resource earnings consist of both transfer earnings and economic rent. Transfer earnings is what a resource could earn in its best alternative use (its opportunity cost). It is the amount that must be paid to get the resource to "transfer" to another use. Economic rent is earnings in excess of transfer earnings. It is the portion of a resource's earnings that is not necessary to keep the resource in its current use. A movie star can earn more than $1 million per movie but probably could not earn that kind of income in another occupation. Thus, the greatest share of the earnings of the movie star is economic rent.

There are two different meanings for the term *rent* in economics. The most common meaning refers to the payment for the use of something, as distinguished from payment for ownership. In this sense, you purchase a house but rent an apartment; you buy a car from Chrysler but rent cars from Avis. The second use of the term *rent* is to mean payment for the use of something that is in fixed—that is, perfectly inelastic—supply. The total quantity of land is fixed; payment for land is economic rent.

economic rent: the portion of earnings above transfer earnings

transfer earnings: the portion of total earnings required to keep a resource in its current use

2.b.2. Shifts in the Supply of a Resource

The supply of a resource will change—increase or decrease at every price—if:

- ▪ Tastes change.
- ▪ The number of suppliers changes.
- ▪ The prices of other uses of the resource change.

Suppose it suddenly becomes more prestigious to be a lawyer. The supply of people entering law schools will increase—the supply curve of lawyers will shift up or out to the right. The shift will occur because of a change in tastes (more prestige), not because of a change in the wage rate of lawyers.

An increase in the number of suppliers means that the supply curve shifts out to the right. For instance, discovery of oil in a country that is not currently an oil producer would mean an increase in the supply of oil—at each price a greater quantity of oil would be supplied. Immigration increases the supply of labor. More producers of bulldozers increase the supply of bulldozers.

The supply curve of a resource will shift if the price of related resources changes. If the wage rate of professionals in finance rises, economists and others may offer their services in the finance market. The supply curve of finance professionals will shift out. If the rental rate of land used for production of wheat rises, everything else held constant, land currently used to produce alfalfa will be switched over to wheat—the supply curve of land used in the production of wheat will shift out to the right.

2.c. Equilibrium

The intersection between the market demand and supply curves determines the price and quantity of a resource. If the demand curve shifts out, everything else held constant, the price rises; if the supply curve shifts out, everything else held constant, the price decreases. If the price rises above the equilibrium price, then a surplus exists and the price is forced back to equilibrium; if the price falls below the equilibrium level, then a shortage arises and the price is forced back up to equilibrium.

2.c.1. Price Ceilings and Floors

A resource market will move toward its equilibrium price and quantity as long as nothing interferes with the market adjustment. There are many instances where floors or ceilings are placed on the resource price, however. Consider the impact of a price floor in the labor market and a price ceiling in the steel market.

Figure 3(a) shows a labor market, with the quantity of labor in hours along the horizontal axis and the hourly wage rate along the vertical axis. The equilibrium wage determined in the market would be $W_e = \$3.50$. The minimum wage is $5.15 per hour, so the actual wage paid would be $W_m = \$5.15$, a price floor. At the minimum wage, the quantity of hours that people are willing and able to work is Q_s, while the quantity of hours that firms are willing and able to pay for is Q_d. The difference between Q_s and Q_d is the number of hours that people would like to work but for which there is no work.

A price ceiling works in just the opposite way of a price floor. The price ceiling creates a shortage. For instance, suppose the government requires foreign steel producers to sell their steel to U.S. manufacturers for no more than P_m in Figure 3(b). The quantity of steel demanded rises from Q_s to Q_d, whereas the quantity that the

Figure 3

Price Ceilings and Price Floors

Figure 3(a) is a labor market showing the quantity of labor in hours along the horizontal axis and the hourly wage rate along the vertical axis. The equilibrium wage determined in the market would be $W_e = \$3.50$, but because a minimum wage of $5.15 per hour has been imposed, the actual wage paid is $W_m = \$5.15$, a wage floor. At the minimum wage, the quantity of hours that people are willing and able to work is Q_s, while the quantity of hours that firms are willing and able to pay

for is Q_d. The difference between Q_s and Q_d is the number of hours that people would like to work but for which there is no work.

Figure 3(b) represents the market for steel. The equilibrium price is P_e, but because the government has implemented a program whereby foreign steel producers cannot sell their steel for more than P_m, the equilibrium price plays no role. A shortage is created equal to Q_d less Q_s.

(a) Labor Market

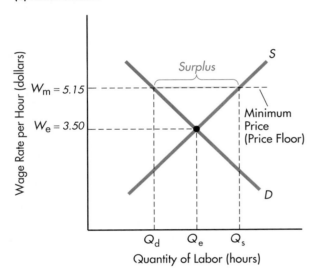

(b) Steel Market

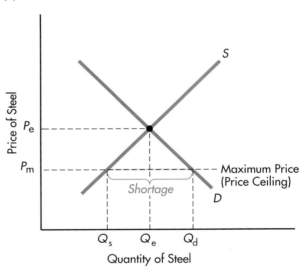

steel suppliers are willing to provide for sale at P_m is Q_s. The difference between Q_d and Q_s represents the shortage of steel.

RECAP

1. Firms purchase resources in such a way that they maximize profits. Households sell resources in order to maximize utility.

2. Transfer earnings is the portion of total earnings required to keep a resource in its current use.

3. Economic rent is earnings in excess of transfer earnings.

4. Equilibrium in a resource market defines the price (wages, rent, interest, profit) of that resource as long as the price and quantity are free to adjust. Price ceilings lead to shortages; price floors lead to surpluses.

3. HOW FIRMS DECIDE WHAT RESOURCES TO BUY

3. How does a firm allocate its expenditures among the various resources?

The market demand for a resource consists of the demands of each firm willing and able to pay for a resource. An electric utility firm in Iowa demands engineers, as does a construction firm in Minnesota. The market demand for engineers consists of demands of the Iowa utility and the Minnesota construction firm. Each firm's demand depends on separate and distinct factors, however. The electric utility firm hires more engineers to modernize its plant; the construction firm hires more engineers to fulfill its contracts with the state government to build bridges. Yet all firms have the same decision-making process for hiring or acquiring resources.

3.a. Individual Firm Demand: Marginal Revenue Product

How do you decide how much you are willing to pay for something? Don't you decide how much it is worth to you? This is what businesses do when they decide how much to pay a worker or to pay for a machine. A firm uses the quantity of each resource that will enable the firm to maximize profit. Firms maximize profit when they operate at the level where marginal revenue (*MR*) equals marginal cost (*MC*). Thus, firms acquire additional resources until *MR* = *MC*. If the acquisition of a resource will raise the firm's revenues more than it will increase its costs—that is, if *MR* will be greater than *MC*—the firm will hire the resource. Conversely, if the acquisition of a resource will raise costs more than it will raise revenue—that is, if *MR* will be less than *MC*—then the firm will not hire the resource.

A firm will purchase the services of another unit of a resource if that additional unit adds more to the firm's revenue than it costs. Recall from the chapter on the costs of doing business that the additional output an extra unit of a resource produces is called the marginal physical product (*MPP*) of that resource. The *MPP* of tax accountants for a CPA firm is the number of tax returns that additional tax accountant can complete; the *MPP* is listed in column 3 of the table in Figure 4, and the *MPP* curve is drawn in the accompanying graph. The *MPP* curve initially rises and then declines according to the law of diminishing marginal returns.

The value of this additional output to the firm is the additional revenue the output generates—the marginal revenue. Multiplying marginal physical product by marginal revenue yields the value of an additional unit of a resource to the firm, which is called the **marginal revenue product (*MRP*)**:

marginal revenue product (*MRP*): the value of the additional output that an extra unit of a resource can produce, *MPP* × *MR*; the value to the firm of an additional resource

$$MRP = MPP \times MR$$

The MRP of a resource, such as labor, is a measure of how much the additional output generated by the last worker is worth to the firm. The marginal-revenue-product curve is drawn in Figure 5. The information from Figure 4 is listed in columns 1 to 3 of Figure 5. Marginal revenue is calculated in column 6 of the table in Figure 5 and multiplied by the *MPP* to arrive at the *MRP* in column 7. You can see that after rising initially, the *MRP* curve slopes downward.

3.b. Marginal Factor Costs

The *MRP* measures the value of an additional resource to a firm. To determine the quantity of a resource that a firm will hire, the firm must know the cost of each additional unit of the resource. The cost of an additional unit of a resource depends on whether the firm is purchasing resources in a market with many suppliers or in a market with one or only a few suppliers.

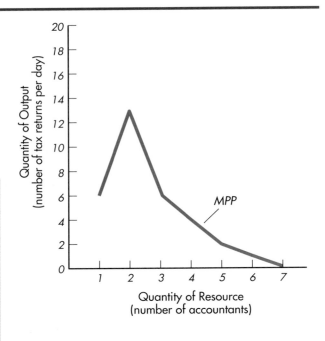

Figure 4

The MPP Curve

The value of a resource to a firm depends on the additional output that the resource produces. This additional output is the marginal physical product of the resource. The marginal physical product of accountants measured in number of tax returns per day is listed in the table. The marginal physical product is drawn as a curve in the graph.

(1) Number of Accountants	(2) Number of Tax Returns per Day	(3) MPP
1	6	6
2	19	13
3	25	6
4	29	4
5	31	2
6	32	1
7	32	0

3.b.1. Hiring Resources in a Perfectly Competitive Market If the firm is purchasing resources in a market where there is a very large number of suppliers of an identical resource—a perfectly competitive resource market—the price of each additional unit of the resource to the firm is constant. Why? Because no seller is large enough to individually change the price. A firm can hire as much of the resource as it wants without affecting either the quantity available or the price of that resource. This situation is shown in Figures 6(a) and 6(b) for the market for accountants. The market wage is defined by the market demand and market supply, as shown in Figure 6(a), and that wage translates to a horizontal supply curve for the individual firm, as shown in Figure 6(b).

Let's assume that the market wage for accountants is $150 per day. The firm can hire as many accountants as it wants at $150 per day without influencing the price. How many accountants will the firm hire? It will hire additional accountants as long as the additional revenue brought in by the last accountant hired is no less than the additional cost of that accountant.

Let's use the information in Figure 7, which combines Figures 5 and 6, to see how many accountants the firm would hire. The first accountant hired has a marginal revenue product of $600 per day and costs $150 per day. It is profitable to hire her. A second accountant, bringing in an additional $1,300 per day and costing $150 per day, is also profitable. The third accountant brings in $600 per day, the fourth $400 per day, the fifth $200 per day, the sixth $100 per day, and the seventh nothing. Thus,

Figure 5

The Marginal Revenue Product

The marginal physical product multiplied by the marginal revenue yields the marginal revenue product. The MPP curve from Figure 4 is multiplied by the marginal revenue and plotted in Figure 5 as the MRP curve. The information from Figure 4 is listed in columns 1 to 3 of Figure 5. The output price is listed in column 4, the total revenue, $P \times Q$, is listed in column 5, and marginal revenue is calculated in column 6. Multiplying column 6 by column 3 yields the MRP, listed in column 7.

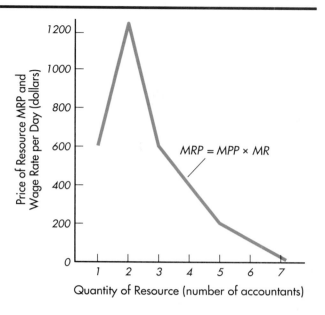

(1) Number of Accountants	(2) Number of Tax Returns per Day	(3) MPP	(4) Output Price (per tax return)	(5) Total Revenue	(6) Marginal Revenue	(7) MRP (MPP × MR)
1	6	6	$100	$ 600	$100	$ 600
2	19	13	$100	$1,900	$100	$1,300
3	25	6	$100	$2,500	$100	$ 600
4	29	4	$100	$2,900	$100	$ 400
5	31	2	$100	$3,100	$100	$ 200
6	32	1	$100	$3,200	$100	$ 100
7	32	0	$100	$3,200	$ 0	$ 0

the third, fourth, and fifth are profitable, but the sixth and seventh aren't. At $150 per day, the firm hires five accountants. You can see in the graph that the marginal revenue product lies above the wage rate until after the fifth accountant is hired.

The firm hires additional accountants until *MRP* is equal to the cost to the firm of another accountant. Remember, the *MRP* is the value of the additional resource to the firm; thus, the firm wants to be sure that the value of a resource exceeds its costs. The cost of an additional unit of a resource is the **marginal factor cost (*MFC*),** also known as the *marginal resource cost* or *marginal input cost*. The marginal factor cost for accountants is listed as column 3 in Figure 7.

The firm hires additional accountants until the marginal revenue product equals the marginal factor cost, *MRP* = *MFC*. This is a general rule; it holds whether the

marginal factor cost (MFC): the additional cost of an additional unit of a resource

Figure 6

The Perfectly Competitive Resource Market and the Individual Firm

The demand for and supply of a resource determine the price of the resource, as shown in Figure 6(a). This market price is the price the individual firm must pay to obtain any units of the resource. As shown in Figure 6(b), the individual firm is a price taker.

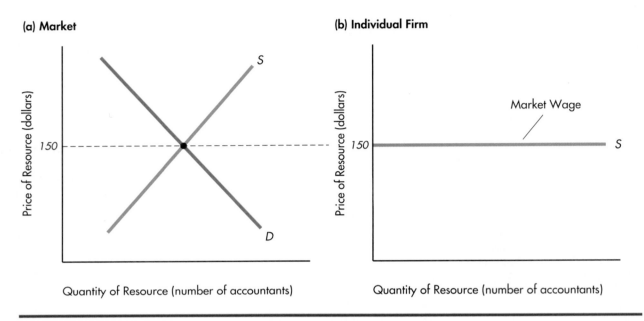

(a) Market

(b) Individual Firm

Resources will be employed up to the point at which MRP = MFC.

monopsonist: a firm that is the only buyer of a resource

firm sells its output in a perfectly competitive, monopoly, monopolistically competitive, or oligopoly market; and it holds for all resources, not just accountants.

3.b.2. Hiring Resources as a Monopoly Buyer   If only one firm is bidding for a resource or a product, that firm is called a **monopsonist.** In the early days of mining in the United States, it was not uncommon for firms to create entire towns in order to attract a readily available supply of labor. The sole provider of jobs in the town was the mining company. Thus, when the company hired labor, it affected the prices of all workers, not just the worker it recently hired. In the 1970s along the Alaskan pipeline, and in the 1980s in foreign countries where U.S. firms were hired to carry out specialized engineering projects or massive construction jobs, small towns dependent on a single U.S. firm were created. There are cases where a monopsony exists even though a company town was not created. For instance, many universities in small communities are monopsonistic employers—they are the primary employer in the town. When these universities hire a mechanic, they affect the wage rates of all mechanics in the town. Other examples of monopsonies are discussed in the Economic Insight "The Company Town."

A monopoly firm will pay resources less than their marginal revenue products. Suppose, for example, that a large semiconductor firm in a small town is the primary

Figure 7

The Employment of Resources

The marginal revenue product and the marginal factor cost (wage rate) together indicate the number of accountants the individual firm would hire. The *MRP* and the *MFC* for an individual firm are listed in the table. The *MRP* curve and the *MFC* curve are shown in the graph. The marginal revenue product exceeds the marginal factor cost (wage rate) until after the fifth accountant is hired. The firm will not hire more than five, for then the costs would exceed the additional revenue produced by the last accountant hired.

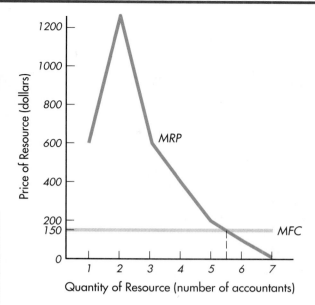

(1) Number of Accountants	(2) MRP	(3) MFC (wage per day)
1	$ 600	$150
2	$1,300	$150
3	$ 600	$150
4	$ 400	$150
5	$ 200	$150
6	$ 100	$150
7	$ 0	$150

employer in the town and that the firm is in the process of hiring accountants. As shown in the table in Figure 8, at a wage of $25 per day only 1 person is willing and able to work. If the firm pays $50 per day, it can hire 2 accountants. However, the firm isn't able to hire the first at $25 and the second at $50; it must pay both $50. Otherwise, the first will quit and then be rehired at $50 per day (only 2 were willing and able to work for $50). As a result, the total cost (called *total factor cost*) of two accountants is $100, not $75, and the additional, or marginal, factor cost is $75 rather than the $50 wage of the second accountant. If the firm offers $150 per day, it can hire 4 accountants; its total factor cost will be $600 and its marginal factor cost $300. This is shown in columns 8, 9, and 10 of the table. Column 8 is the wage per day, 9 is the total factor cost (column 1 times column 8), and 10 is the marginal factor cost.

The graph in Figure 8 shows the marginal factor cost and the supply curve of accountants in the small town. The *MFC* curve is plotted from data in column 10 of the table, and the supply curve is plotted from data in column 8. For a monopsonist, the *MFC* curve lies above the supply curve. The reason is the cost of each additional accountant to the firm is the additional accountant's wage *plus* the additional wages paid to all of the other accountants.

A firm buying in a perfectly competitive resource market will pay the marginal revenue product; a monopsonistic firm will pay less than the marginal revenue product.

The rising marginal factor cost means that the accountants would be paid less than their marginal revenue product. The firm would hire 4 accountants since the fifth accountant costs the firm $400 (*MFC*) but brings in only $200 (*MRP*). The fourth accountant produces $400 of additional revenue for the firm (*MRP*), costs the firm an additional $300 (*MFC*), but is paid only $150.

As long as resource services are purchased by other than a monopsonist, they are paid their marginal revenue products. A monopsonist pays less than the marginal revenue product.

3.c. Hiring When There Is More than One Resource

To this point we've examined the firm's hiring decision for one resource, everything else, including the quantities of all other resources, held constant. However, a firm uses several resources and makes hiring decisions regarding most of them all the time. How does the firm decide what combinations of resources to use? Like the consumer deciding what combinations of goods and services to purchase, the firm will ensure that the benefits of spending one more dollar are the same no matter which resource the firm chooses to spend that dollar on.

You may recall that the consumer maximizes utility when the marginal utility per dollar of expenditure is the same on all goods and services purchased:

$$MU_{CDs}/P_{CDs} = MU_{gas}/P_{gas} = \cdots = MU_n/P_n$$

A similar rule holds for the firm attempting to purchase resource services in order to maximize profit and minimize costs. The firm will be maximizing profit when its marginal revenue product per dollar of expenditure on all resources is the same:

$$MRP_{land}/MFC_{land} = MRP_{labor}/MFC_{labor} = \cdots = MRP_n/MFC_n$$

Figure 8

The Monopsonist

When the firm is a monopsonistic buyer of resources, it faces a marginal-factor-cost curve that lies above the supply curve. Each time the firm purchases a unit of the resource, the price of all units of the resource is driven up. As a result, the cost of one additional unit of the resource exceeds the price that must be paid for that additional unit of the resource. This is shown in columns 8 through 10 of the table; columns 8 and 10 are plotted in the graph. The firm hires resources until the marginal revenue product and marginal factor cost are equal. The firm pays resources the price given by the supply curve at the quantity determined by $MFC = MRP$. Thus, the resource receives less than its marginal revenue product.

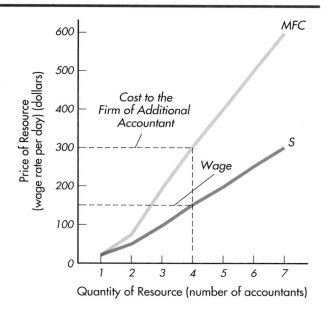

(1) Number of Accountants	(2) Number of Tax Returns per Day	(3) MPP	(4) Product Price (per tax return)	(5) Total Revenue	(6) MR	(7) MRP	(8) Wage per Day	(9) Total Factor Cost of Accountants	(10) MFC
1	6	6	$100	$ 600	$100	$ 600	$ 25	$ 25	$ 25
2	19	13	$100	$1,900	$100	$1,300	$ 50	$ 100	$ 75
3	25	6	$100	$2,500	$100	$ 600	$100	$ 300	$200
4	29	4	$100	$2,900	$100	$ 400	$150	$ 600	$300
5	31	2	$100	$3,100	$100	$ 200	$200	$1,000	$400
6	32	1	$100	$3,200	$100	$ 100	$250	$1,500	$500
7	32	0	$100	$3,200	$100	$ 0	$300	$2,100	$600

Note: Marginal revenue is the change in total revenue divided by the change in output. In this case, it is the change in total revenue divided by the change in the number of tax returns produced.

The last dollar spent on resources must yield the same marginal revenue product no matter which resource the dollar is spent on.

As long as the marginal factor cost of a resource is less than its marginal revenue product, the firm will increase profit by hiring more of the resource. If a dollar spent on labor yields less marginal revenue product than a dollar spent on capital, the firm will increase profit more by purchasing the capital than if it purchases the labor.[1]

---

[1]This equimarginal rule can also be written as $MPP_{land}/MFC_{land} = MPP_{labor}/MFC_{labor} = \cdots$, since $MRP = MFC$ or $MRP/MFC = 1$ and since $MRP = MPP \times MR$, $MPP/MFC = 1/MR$ for all resources.

If a resource is very expensive relative to other resources, then the expensive resource must generate a significantly larger marginal revenue product than the other resources. For instance, for a firm to remain in Manhattan, it must generate a significantly larger marginal revenue product than could be obtained in Dallas or elsewhere, because rents are so much higher in Manhattan. The price of land in Tokyo is so high that its use requires a very high marginal revenue product.

A firm will streamline its work force when the last dollar of expenditures on labor generates less marginal revenue product than if that dollar were spent on another resource; a firm will streamline by reducing its middle management if the last dollar spent on middle management generates less return (lower *MRP*) than if that dollar were spent on other labor or another resource. During the early 1990s, many U.S. firms decided that their expenditures on middle management particularly, but also on their entire labor force, were not generating the same return that expenditures on other resources would yield. As a result, firms reduced their work force; they dismissed many middle-management employees. The media referred to this process as downsizing, but it was part of the ongoing process by firms to ensure that the last dollar of expenditure on each resource generated the same *MRP.*

A firm in equilibrium in terms of allocating its expenditures among resources will alter the allocation only if the cost of one of the resources rises relative to the others. For instance, if government-mandated medical or other benefits mean that labor costs rise while everything else remains constant, then firms will tend to hire less labor and use more of other resources. Everything else the same, if the costs of doing business in the United States rise, firms will locate offices or plants in other countries.

3.d. Product Market Structures and Resource Demand

Firms purchase the types and quantities of resource services that allow them to maximize profit; each firm equates the *MRP* per dollar of expenditure on all resource services used. The *MRP* depends on the market structure in which the firm sells its output. A perfectly competitive firm produces more output and sells that output at a lower price than a firm operating in any other market, everything else the same. Since the perfectly competitive firm produces more output, it must use more resources. Thus, everything else the same, the demand curve for a resource by a perfectly competitive firm will lie above the demand curve for a resource by a firm selling in monopoly, oligopoly, or monopolistically competitive markets.

For the perfectly competitive firm, price and marginal revenue are the same, $P = MR$. Thus, the marginal revenue product, $MRP = MR \times MPP$, for the perfectly competitive firm can be written as $P \times MPP$. Sometimes this is called the value of the marginal product, *VMP*, to distinguish it from the marginal revenue product.

$$MRP = MR \times MPP$$
$$VMP = P \times MPP$$

The demand for a resource by a single firm is the *MRP* of that resource, no matter whether it sells its goods and services as a monopolist or as a perfect competitor (for the perfectly competitive firm, $VMP = MRP$, so that *MRP* is its resource demand as well). However, since for the firms not selling in a perfectly competitive market, price is greater than marginal revenue, *VMP* would be greater than *MRP,* which indicates that the perfectly competitive firm's demand curve for a resource lies above (or is greater than) the demand curve for a resource by a monopoly firm, oligopoly firm, or monopolistically competitive firm.

3.e. A Look Ahead

In the following chapters, we will examine aspects of the resource markets. In the labor market we discuss why different people receive different wages, why firms treat employees the way they do, the impact of labor laws, and the causes and results of discrimination. In the land market we'll look at problems of the environment and why the government is such a large player in the natural resources area. We will discuss the capital market and examine why firms carry out research and development and purchase robotics. Selling resource services creates income, so we'll examine who has income and why. These and other aspects of the resource markets will be examined within the framework discussed in this chapter.

RECAP

1. The *MRP* of a resource is a measure of how much the additional output generated by the last unit of the resource is worth to the firm.

2. Resources are hired up to the point at which $MRP = MFC$.

3. In a perfectly competitive resource market, resources are paid an amount equal to their marginal revenue product. In a monopsonistic resource market, resources are paid less than their marginal revenue product.

4. A firm will allocate its budget on resources up to the point that the last dollar spent yields an equal marginal revenue product no matter on which resource the dollar is spent.

5. A perfectly competitive firm will hire and acquire more resources than firms selling in monopoly, oligopoly, or monopolistically competitive product markets, everything else the same.

SUMMARY

? Who are the buyers and sellers of resources?

1. The term *resource markets* refers to the buyers and sellers of four classes of resources: land, labor, capital, and entrepreneurial ability. *§Preview*

2. The buyers of resources are firms that purchase resources in order to produce goods and services. *§1.a*

3. The sellers of resources are households that supply resources in order to obtain income with which to purchase goods and services. *§1.a*

? How are resource prices determined?

4. Equilibrium in each resource market defines the rate of pay of the resource and the quantity used. *§2*

5. The rate of pay of a resource consists of two parts: transfer earnings and economic rent. Transfer earnings are the rate of pay necessary to keep a resource in its current use. Economic rent is the excess of pay above transfer earnings. *§2.b.1*

6. A single firm's demand for a resource is the downward-sloping portion of the marginal-revenue-product curve for that resource. *§3.a*

7. A firm purchasing resources in a perfectly competitive resource market will hire resources up to the point that $MRP = MFC$. A firm that is one of only a few buyers or the only buyer of a particular resource (a monopsonist) will face a marginal-factor-cost curve that is above the supply curve for that resource.

As a result, the resource is paid less than its marginal revenue product. *§3.b.1, 3.b.2*

8. A firm will allocate its budget on resources in such a way that the last dollar spent will yield the same marginal revenue product no matter on which resource the dollar is spent. *§3.c*

KEY TERMS

derived demand *§1.a*

economic rent *§2.b.1*

transfer earnings *§2.b.1*

marginal revenue product (*MRP*) *§3.a*

marginal factor cost (*MFC*) *§3.b.1*

monopsonist *§3.b.2*

EXERCISES

1. What does it mean to say that the demand for resources is a derived demand? Is the demand for all goods and services a derived demand?

2. Using the information in the following table, calculate the marginal revenue product (*MRP* = *MPP* × *MR*).

Units of Resources	Total Output	Output Price	Resource Price
1	10	$5	$10
2	25	$5	$10
3	35	$5	$10
4	40	$5	$10
5	40	$5	$10

3. Using the data in exercise 2, determine how many units of resources the firm will want to acquire.

4. Suppose the output price falls from $5 to $4 to $3 to $1 in exercise 2. How would that change your answers to exercises 2 and 3?

5. Using the data in exercise 2, calculate the marginal factor cost.

6. Suppose the resource price rises from $10 to $12 to $14 to $18 to $20 as resource units go from 1 to 5. How would that change your answer to exercise 5? How would it change your answer to exercise 3?

7. Using exercise 6, calculate the transfer earnings and economic rent of the third unit of the resource when four units of the resource are employed. Do the same calculations when only three units of the resource are employed. How do you account for the different answers?

8. Do resources earn their marginal revenue products? Demonstrate under what conditions the answer is yes.

9. What is a monopsonist? How does a monopsonist differ from a monopolist?

10. Supposedly Larry Bird once said that he would play basketball for $10,000 per year. Yet he was paid over $1 million per year. If the quote is correct, how much were Bird's transfer earnings? How much was his economic rent?

11. In 1989 the Japanese spent more than $14 billion to buy 322 foreign companies, half of them in the United States, and $100 billion to buy foreign stocks and bonds. Why was Japanese money flowing so heavily out of Japan and into other parts of the world?

12. Early in her journalistic career, Gloria Steinem posed as a Playboy Bunny to examine the inside of a Playboy Club. Steinem discovered that the Bunnies had to purchase their costumes from the club, pay for the cleaning, purchase their food from the club, and so on. This "company store" exploited the employees (the Bunnies), according to Steinem. Explain what Steinem meant by exploitation.

13. Explain the idea behind the lyrics "You load 16 tons, and what do you get? You get another day older and deeper in debt. Saint Peter, don't you call me, 'cause I can't go. I owe my soul to the company store."

14. The Glaxo-Wellcome Company had a monopoly on AZT, a pharmaceutical that delays the onset of AIDS after someone has become HIV positive. The demand for that pharmaceutical was virtually perfectly price-inelastic. Explain how that might affect the demand for employees by the Glaxo-Wellcome Company.

Internet Exercises/ Resources

For Internet exercises and web resources related to this chapter, go to
http://college.hmco.com.

State Economy Will Feel Asia's Money Pains

Arizona's economy won't escape the fallout from the Asian financial crisis. Economists predict that Arizona businesses may lose about $50 million a year in exports to Asia, and the state's job growth rate may be trimmed by 0.5 percent as a result of the economic slowdown across the Pacific. High tech and commodity industries such as copper, cotton and citrus are likely to be the hardest hit, say trade experts. Still when you consider that Arizona sold more than $4.5 billion last year in Asia and that job growth has been more than 6 percent annually for the past four years, the damage is relatively mild, say economists.

Any impact from reduced exports could be offset by the benefits of lower prices in products coming back to the United States, said Elliot Pollack, a Scottsdale-based economist. "You have to weigh those various factors, and it's tough to do," he said. "It's like trying to hug Jell-O."

He added that international bankers have responded quickly to the crisis with bailout packages to the neediest countries and appear to have the situation under control. "Could this be the start of something major? It's possible, but I would say the probability is low," Pollack said.

One reason the damage has been light in Arizona is that the hardest hit countries—Thailand, the Philippines, Indonesia, Malaysia and South Korea—aren't major markets for Arizona exports, said Melissa Hardison, corporate economist for the Salt River Project.

She said a full one-third of Arizona's exports are destined for Asian countries. But the state's biggest partners in the Orient are Japan, which takes 13.4 percent of all Arizona exports; Taiwan, 7.7 percent; Hong Kong, 4.6 percent; and Singapore, 3.6 percent. None of those economies has been hard hit by the economic crisis, at least not yet, she said.

One industry that has felt the impact, however, is the state's $9.6 billion copper industry. . . .

The price of the metal has tumbled from $1.25 a pound in August to about 80 cents this month, pounded by fears that Asian weakness will slow demand for copper in construction and other industries that had figured to grow rapidly in the Far East.

The Arizona cotton industry also is vulnerable because 80 to 90 percent of the state's crop is sold in the Far East. But so far no contracts have been modified or canceled, said Rick Lavis, executive vice president of the Arizona Cotton Growers Association. The reason is that Arizona cotton is used primarily in textile plants to make clothing that is shipped back to the United States and American demand hasn't slowed, he said. "Also domestic mills are still running flat out," he said. "We are not seeing any diminishing of sales."

Source: Ed Taylor, "State Economy Will Feel Asia's Money Pains," *The Tribune*, December 31, 1997. Reprinted by permission.

The Tribune/**December 31, 1997**

Commentary

The demand for resources—land, labor, and capital—is often referred to as derived demand because these items are not wanted for themselves but for what they produce. When customers are purchasing products such as computers, telephone services, houses, and autos, the producers of these goods will provide the products. This means the producers must have the resources needed to produce the products. Capital, skilled and unskilled labor, and land will all be demanded by the producers.

Businesses must forecast what the demand for their products will be in coming weeks, months, and years. According to the article, one of the major uncertainties regarding the forecast for 1998 is what is occurring in Asia. The Asian economies have suffered serious recessions and financial service industry collapses. These economies, often called the Asian tigers, have grown at astounding rates over the past decade or so. But, in doing so, they have focused almost entirely on increasing exports and market share. This export focus combined with a rigid industry and market structure has created serious problems in these economies. Industries are dependent on the financial institutions that are at the center of the industry organizations known as Keiretsu in Japan and by other names in the other nations. The export growth has led to increasing flows of other currencies, notably dollars, into the Asian economies. The financial institutions supported the export strategy by providing loans to the companies, that is, increasing their debt. The institutions became so burdened by the debt that many could not continue to generate profit; many failed. This caused stock market collapses throughout Asia and declining currency values relative to the dollar.

The article is asking experts about the possible impacts of the Asian crisis on the United States, and on Arizona in particular. One of the economists points out that while Arizona exports may be affected negatively since U.S. prices are now higher, U.S. consumers will benefit because the Asian products will be less expensive. Another economist notes that even the exports won't be affected that much because Arizona businesses do not do much business with the affected Asian economies.

The demand for a resource depends on the price of the resource, the prices of related resources, the income of the consumers, the number of consumers, the size of the market, and the demand for the final product the resource is used to produce. In general, the Arizona economy will not be greatly affected because Asian consumers are not a large part of the market for products produced in Arizona. The demand for resources sold in Arizona depends on who the ultimate consumers are. The demand for copper has declined because the demand for firms to construct buildings, roads, and other items in the Asian countries has declined. The demand for the construction comes from the Asian countries, and their incomes have fallen and the prices of the resources (in U.S. dollars) have risen. In contrast, the demand for cotton may not be negatively affected because the demand for final products—the clothing that is created from the cotton—is coming not from Asia but from the United States.

Determining the outlook for the economy does seem something akin to "hugging Jell-O." You squeeze the Jell-O in your fist and it squeezes out between your fingers. You see growth in one aspect of the Asian situation but decline in another. However, the impact on the economy is a little more understandable than the results of squeezing Jell-O. Sales of cotton are not likely to decline as the buyers are U.S. buyers who are not dramatically affected by the Asian crisis. However, the copper industry is likely to feel the effects of the Asian economies situation because the product is dependent on Asian demand.

? **Fundamental Questions**

1. **Are people willing to work more hours for higher wages?**

2. **What are compensating wage differentials?**

3. **Why might wages be higher for people with more human capital than for those with less human capital?**

4. **What accounts for earnings disparities between males and females and between whites and nonwhites?**

5. **Are discrimination and freely functioning markets compatible?**

O lder workers tend to earn higher wages than younger workers; males earn more than females; whites earn more than African Americans and Hispanics; and unionized workers earn more than nonunionized workers. Yet, as we learned in the previous chapter, a worker will be paid his or her marginal revenue product (except in a monopsonistic firm). Does this mean that older workers are more productive than younger ones, males more productive than females, whites more productive than people of other ethnic backgrounds, and so on, or is there something missing in our theory of the labor market? In this chapter we delve more deeply into the labor market. ■

Preview

1. THE SUPPLY OF LABOR

1. Are people willing to work more hours for higher wages?

The supply of labor comes from individual households. Each member of a household must determine whether to give up a certain number of hours each day to work. That decision is the individual's labor supply decision and is called the *labor-leisure tradeoff*.

1.a. Individual Labor Supply: Labor-Leisure Tradeoff

People can allocate their time to work or leisure.

There are only twenty-four hours in a day, and people have to decide how to allocate this scarce time. They really have only two options: they can spend their time (1) working for pay or (2) not working. *Any* time spent not working is called *leisure time*. Leisure time includes being a "couch potato," serving as a volunteer coach for your daughter's first-grade soccer team, volunteering to serve food at St. Jude's food bank, or participating in any other activity except working at a paying job. People want leisure time. Although most people enjoy aspects of their jobs, most would rather have more leisure time and less work time. However, people must purchase the desired good, leisure, by forgoing the wages they could earn by working. As wages increase, the cost of leisure time increases, causing people to purchase less leisure. Purchasing less leisure means working more.

The number of hours that people are willing and able to work rises as the wage rate rises, at least until people say, "I have enough income; perhaps I'll enjoy a little more leisure." When the price of leisure increases—in other words, when the wage rate increases—people choose to work more. But, as the wage rate increases, some people choose to enjoy more leisure time. They now have more income with which they can purchase all goods and services, including leisure time. Thus, a wage increase has two opposing effects: one leads to increased hours of work and one leads to decreased hours. This means that the quantity of labor supplied may rise or fall as the wage rate rises.

The labor supply curve shown in Figure 1 is what the labor supply curve for an individual usually looks like. It rises as the wage rate rises until the wage is sufficiently high that people begin to choose more leisure; then the curve begins to turn backward. This is called the **backward-bending labor supply curve**.

backward-bending labor supply curve: a labor supply curve indicating that a person is willing and able to work more hours as the wage rate increases until, at some sufficiently high wage rate, the person chooses to work fewer hours

1.a.1. Do People Really Trade Off Labor and Leisure?
As discussed in the Economic Insight "The Overworked American?" not all economists agree with the idea that people trade off work and leisure. There is no doubt that few have the luxury of deciding each minute whether to work or to take leisure time. Some might be able to choose between part-time and full-time work, but full-time work usually means eight hours a day, and part-time work typically means lower-quality jobs and much less pay per hour than the full-time job. Most people, then, are unable to choose how much to work on a day-to-day basis depending on their preferences for leisure that day. But over a month, a year, or several years, people do choose to put in more or less time on the job. Some people choose occupations that enable them more flexibility; many prefer to be self-employed in order to be able to choose whether to put in more or less time on the job. People can also *moonlight*, work an additional job or put in extra hours after the full-time job is completed.

1.b. From Individual to Market Supply

When you enter the labor market, you offer various levels of services at various wage rates. The decision about whether to offer your labor services for employment

Figure 1

The Individual's Labor Supply Curve

As the wage rate rises, people are willing and able to supply more labor, at least up to some high wage rate. A higher wage rate means that the opportunity cost of leisure time increases so that people will purchase less leisure (will work more). Conversely, as the wage rate rises and people's incomes rise, more of all goods are purchased, including leisure time. As a result, fewer hours are supplied for work. Which of these opposing effects is larger determines whether the labor supply curve slopes upward or downward. The most commonly shaped labor supply curve is one that slopes upward until the wage rate reaches some high level and then, as people choose more leisure time, begins to bend backward.

labor force participation:
entering the work force

is a decision about **labor force participation,** joining the work force in the United States. People over the age of sixteen who are actively seeking a job are said to be members of the labor force. These are the people who have chosen to offer their labor services for employment at specific wage rates. As the wage rate increases, the number of people participating in the labor force increases.

Figure 2(a) shows the labor *market* supply curve. It consists of the horizontal sum of all individual labor supply curves, such as the sum of the individual labor supply curves shown in Figures 2(b) and 2(c). If the labor supply curve for each individual slopes upward, then the market supply curve, the sum of each individual supply curve, slopes upward. Even if the individual labor supply curve bends backward at some high wage, it is unlikely that all of the curves will bend backward at the same wage. Not everyone has the same tradeoffs between labor and leisure; not all offer to work at the same wage rate; not all want the same kind of job. As the wage rate rises, some people who chose not to participate in the labor market at lower wages are induced to offer their services for employment at a higher wage. You can see in Figure 2(b) that Mary chooses not to enter the labor force at wages below $20 per hour. Helen, in Figure 2(c), enters the labor force for any wage above $5 per hour. Thus, the labor market supply curve slopes up because the number of people willing and able to work rises as the wage rate rises and because the number of hours that each person is willing and able to work rises as the wage rate rises, at least up to some high wage rate.

1.c. Equilibrium

The labor market consists of the labor demand and labor supply curves. We've just discussed labor supply. Labor demand is based on the firms' marginal revenue product curves, as discussed in the previous chapter. The intersection of the labor demand and labor supply curves determines the equilibrium wage, W_e, and the quantity of hours people work at this equilibrium wage, Q_e, as shown in Figure 3.

The Overworked American?

The average employed person in the United States is now on the job an additional 163 hours, or the equivalent of an extra month a year, as compared to 1969.[1] What accounts for the increased hours devoted to work and thus the fewer hours devoted to leisure? The view of most economists is that people choose to work more in order to acquire more income. People trade off leisure for more work and thus more income.

Not all economists agree with the view that people can trade off work and leisure. Many argue that individuals have no choice, that leisure time is simply being squeezed out by the necessity of working and the demands of firms. A group of economists known as *institutionalists* argue that the modern industrial state does not give workers the flexibility economists seem to imply in their labor demand and labor supply model. The institutional economists argue that firms set the hours they require of their employees and that employees must accept them or accept significantly lower standards of living. They point to studies that have asked people about their work habits and found that people did not have a choice of hours; they had a choice of either no job or a job at hours that were not those they would choose.[2] In a popular book, *The Overworked American: The Unexpected Decline of Leisure,* author Juliet Schor argues that consumer-workers become indoctrinated by firms into consuming, which requires more income and thus more hours devoted to work. According to Schor, workers can't really trade off work and leisure, but if they could, their indoctrination to consume constrains them; they must work more and more to be able to consume more and more.[3]

The economists opposing the institutionalists' view point out that workers can change occupations or jobs because hours worked vary considerably from occupation to occupation and that workers can also moonlight (work extra jobs or hours) or retire in order to alter their hours.[4] They also point to surveys where it was found that people preferred their current number of hours and pay to working fewer hours at the same rate of pay or more hours at the same rate of pay.[5] Like most issues in economics, unanimity of opinion over this issue does not exist.

[1] Juliet B. Schor, *The Overworked American: The Unexpected Decline of Leisure* (New York: Basic Books, 1991).
[2] Shulamit Kahn and Kevin Lang, "Constraints on the Choice of Work Hours: Agency vs. Specific-Capital," *National Bureau of Economic Research Working Paper* 2238, May 1987, p. 14; Robert Moffit, "The Tobit Model, Hours of Work, and Institutional Constraints," *Review of Economics and Statistics* 64, August 1982, pp. 510–515.
[3] Schor, *The Overworked American.*
[4] Joseph Altonji and Christina H. Paxson, "Labor Supply Preferences, Hours Constraints, and Hour-Wage Tradeoffs," *Journal of Labor Economics* 6, no. 2 (1988), pp. 254–276.
[5] Susan E. Shank, "Preferred Hours of Work and Corresponding Earnings," *Monthly Labor Review,* November 1986, p. 41, Table 1.

The labor market pictured in Figure 3 suggests that as long as workers are the same and jobs are the same, there will be one equilibrium wage. In fact, workers are not the same, jobs are not the same, and wages are definitely not the same. College-educated people earn more than people with only a high school education, and people with a high school education earn more than those with only a grammar school education. Older workers earn more than younger workers. Men earn more than women. Whites earn more than nonwhites. Unionized workers tend to earn more than nonunionized workers.

The labor market model also suggests that workers will be paid their marginal revenue products. The more productive a worker is, the higher his or her compensation will be, and vice versa. This relationship does not always hold in the real world, however. There are large salary differences for people with similar levels of productivity, and people who are vastly different in terms of productivity are paid the same. Some explanations for these wage differentials are given in the remainder of this chapter.

Figure 2

The Labor Market Supply Curve

Figure 2(a) shows the labor market supply curve obtained by adding the individual labor supply curves of Figures 2(b) and 2(c). Figure 2(a) indicates that as the wage rate rises, the number of hours each person is willing and able to work increases, at least up to some high wage rate, and the number of people willing and able to supply hours of work increases.

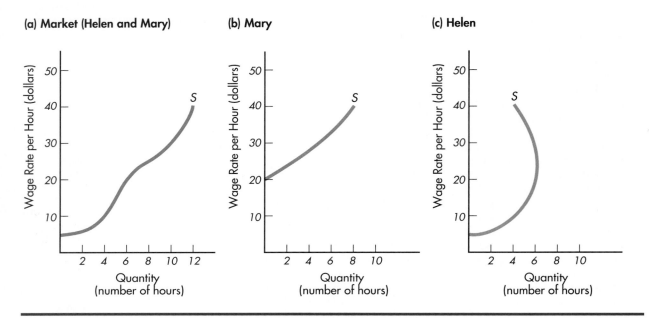

(a) Market (Helen and Mary) (b) Mary (c) Helen

Figure 3

Labor Market Equilibrium

If all workers are identical to firms—that is, if a firm doesn't care whether it hires Bob, Ray, Kate, or Allie—and if all firms and jobs are the same to workers—that is, if a worker doesn't care whether a job is with IBM or Ted's Hot Dog Stand— then one demand curve and one supply curve define the labor market. The intersection of the two curves is the labor market equilibrium at which the wage rate is determined.

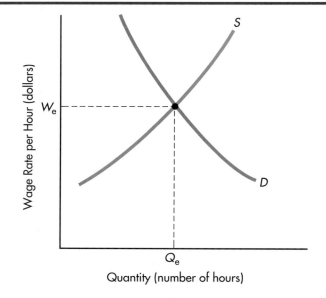

RECAP

1. An increase in the wage rate causes workers to increase the hours they are willing and able to work and reduce the hours of leisure; at the same time, the wage increase also means that income is higher and more leisure can be purchased. This causes the individual labor supply curve to be backward bending.

2. The labor market supply curve slopes upward because as the wage rate rises, more people are willing and able to work and people are willing and able to work more hours.

3. Equilibrium in the labor market defines the wage rate and the quantity of hours people work at that wage.

2. WAGE DIFFERENTIALS

If people were identical, if jobs were identical, and if information were perfect, there would be no wage differentials.

If all workers are the same to a firm—that is, if a firm doesn't care whether it hires Bob, Ray, Kate, or Allie—and if all firms and jobs are the same to workers—that is, if IBM is no different from Ted's Hot Dog Stand to individual workers—then the one demand for labor and the one supply of labor define the one equilibrium wage. However, if firms do differentiate among workers and if workers do differentiate among firms and jobs, then there is more than one labor market and more than one equilibrium wage level. In this case, wages may differ from job to job and from person to person. The reasons for wage differences include compensating wage differentials and differences in individual levels of productivity.

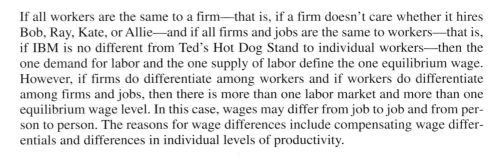

2. What are compensating wage differentials?

compensating wage differentials: wage differences that make up for the higher risk or poorer working conditions of one job over another

2.a. Compensating Wage Differentials

Some jobs are quite unpleasant because they are located in undesirable locations or are dangerous or unhealthy. In most market economies, enough people voluntarily choose to work in unpleasant jobs that the jobs get filled. People choose to work in unpleasant occupations because of **compensating wage differentials**—wage differences that make up for the high risk or poor working conditions of a job. Workers mine coal, clean sewers, and weld steel beams fifty stories off the ground because, compared to alternative jobs for which they could qualify, these jobs pay well.

Figure 4 illustrates the concept of compensating differentials. There are two labor markets, one for a risky occupation and one for a less risky occupation. At each wage rate, fewer people are willing and able to work in the risky occupation than in the less risky occupation. Thus, if the demand curves were identical, the supply curve of the risky occupation would be above (to the left of) the supply curve of the less risky occupation. As a result, the equilibrium wage rate is higher in the risky occupation ($10) than in the less risky occupation ($5). The difference between the wage in the risky occupation ($10 per hour) and the wage in the less risky occupation ($5 per hour) is an *equilibrium differential*—the compensation a worker receives for undertaking the greater risk.

Commercial deep-sea divers are exposed to the dangers of drowning and several physiological disorders as a result of compression and decompression. They choose this job because they earn about 90 percent more than the average high school graduate. Coal miners in West Virginia or in the United Kingdom are exposed to coal dust, black lung disease, and cave-ins. They choose to work in the mines because the pay is twice what they could earn elsewhere. Wage differentials ensure that deep-sea diving jobs, coal-mining jobs, and other risky occupations are filled.

Figure 4

Compensating Wage Differentials

Figure 4(a) shows the market for a risky occupation. Figure 4(b) shows the market for a less risky occupation. At each wage rate, fewer people are willing and able to work in the risky occupation than in the less risky occupation. Thus, the supply curve of the risky occupation is higher (supply is less) than the supply curve of the less risky occupation. As a result, the wage in the risky occupation ($10 per hour) is higher than the wage ($5

per hour) in the less risky occupation. The differential ($10 − $5 = $5) is an equilibrium differential—the amount necessary to induce enough people to fill the jobs. If the differential were any higher, more people would flow to the risky occupation, driving wages there down and wages in the less risky occupation up. If the differential were any lower, shortages would prevail in the risky occupation, driving wages there up.

(a) Risky Occupation

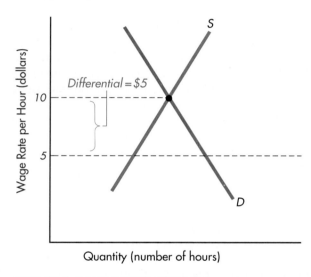

(b) Less Risky Occupation

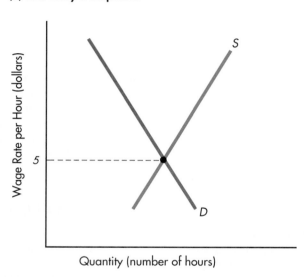

Any characteristic that distinguishes one job from another may result in a compensating wage differential. A job that requires a great deal of travel and time away from home usually pays more than a comparable job without the travel requirements because most people find extensive travel and time away from home to be costly. If people were indifferent between extensive travel and no travel, there would be no compensating wage differential.

2.b. Human Capital

3. Why might wages be higher for people with more human capital than for those with less human capital?

People differ with respect to their training and abilities. These differences influence the level of wages for two reasons: (1) skilled workers have higher marginal productivity than unskilled workers, and (2) the supply of skilled workers is smaller than the supply of unskilled workers because it takes time and money to acquire training and education. Because of greater productivity and smaller supply, then, skilled labor will generate higher wages than less-skilled labor. For instance, in Figure 5, the skilled-labor market generates a wage of $15 per hour, and the unskilled-labor market generates a wage of $8 per hour. The difference exists because the demand for skilled labor relative to the supply of skilled labor is greater than the demand for unskilled labor relative to the supply of unskilled labor.

Some jobs are more dangerous than others. Since fewer people are willing to work in the dangerous jobs if they pay the same as less dangerous jobs, it is necessary for the employers to pay more for the dangerous jobs. To induce people to climb tall buildings to wash windows, to construct skyscrapers, or to paint the Golden Gate Bridge, the pay must be increased. Some of the employees undertaking risky jobs earn more in two months than they could in a year undertaking a less risky job.

Figure 5

Human Capital

Two labor markets are pictured. Figure 5(a) shows the market for skilled labor. Figure 5(b) shows the market for unskilled labor. The smaller supply in the skilled-labor market results in a higher wage there. The equilibrium differential between the wages in the two markets is the return to human capital.

(a) Skilled-Labor Market

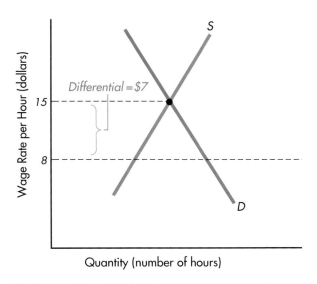

(b) Unskilled-Labor Market

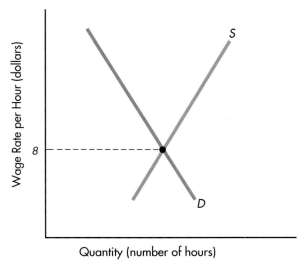

human capital: skills and training acquired through education and on-the-job training

The expectation of higher income induces people to acquire **human capital**—skills and training acquired through education and job experience. People go to college or vocational school or enter training programs because they expect the training to increase their future income. When people purchase human capital, they are said to be *investing in human capital*. Like investments in real capital (machines and equipment), education and training are purchased in order to generate output and income in the future.

2.b.1. Investment in Human Capital Individuals who go to college or obtain special training expect the costs of going to college or obtaining the training to be more than offset by the income and other benefits they will obtain in the future. Individuals who acquire human capital reap the rewards of that human capital over time. Figure 6(a) is an example of what the income profiles of workers with college degrees and workers without college degrees might look like. We might expect income of the worker without the degree to increase rapidly from the early working years until the worker gets to be about fifty; then income might rise more slowly, until the worker moves into retirement age. Until around age thirty, the worker without the college degree clearly enjoys more income than the college-educated worker. The shaded areas represent estimated income lost to the college-educated worker while he or she is attending classes and then gaining work experience. It may take several years after entering the labor market for a college-degree recipient to achieve and then surpass the income level of a worker without a degree, but on average a college-educated person does earn more than someone without a college education, as shown in Figure 6(b). Figure 6(b) shows the ratios of the median income of college- to high-school-educated workers. This is called the college income premium. As mentioned in Chapter 1, college-educated people earn more over their lifetimes than people without a college degree.

The decision about whether to attend college depends on whether the benefits exceed the costs.[1] Over the course of a lifetime, will the income and other benefits of a college degree offset the loss of income during the early years? Individuals who answer *yes* choose to attend college. This economic model of the decision to attend college does not suggest that every high school senior carries out a series of calculations regarding the expected costs and benefits of attending college. What it does suggest is that these people behave *as if* they carried out these calculations. As we discussed in Chapter 1, for many high school students, the decision to attend college was made long before they were in high school—there simply was no other alternative considered. For many, it was taken for granted by all friends and family members that college followed high school. This is the pattern for many families. Such patterns do not occur by accident. There is a reason why so many young adults go to college, and the economic model of labor suggests what that reason is: college-educated people have better-paying jobs and jobs with greater benefits and security than non-college-educated people.

2.b.2. Choice of a Major If you decide to attend college, you must then decide what field to major in. Your decision depends on the opportunity costs you face. If your opportunity costs of devoting a great deal of time to a job are high, you will choose to major in a field that is not overly time-consuming. For instance, for several years after college, men and women who have studied to become medical doc-

---

[1]In the chapter "The Capital Market," we discuss the concept of present value, which is the value today of benefits or costs that occur in the future. A person compares the present value of the benefits of college to the present value of the costs of college in deciding whether to attend college.

Figure 6

Income Profiles and Educational Level

Income rises rapidly until age fifty, then rises more slowly until retirement. Figure 6 compares the income earned by the worker without a degree with the income earned by a college graduate. Figure 6(a) suggests what the actual pattern looks like. Initially, the college graduate gives up substantial income in the form of direct costs and forgone earnings to go to college. Eventually, however, the income of the college graduate exceeds that of the high school-educated worker. Figure 6(b) illustrates the college income premium, the ratio of median income of college-educated to median income of non-college-educated individuals. Source: *Statistical Abstract of the United States, 2000; Economic Report of the President, 2001.*

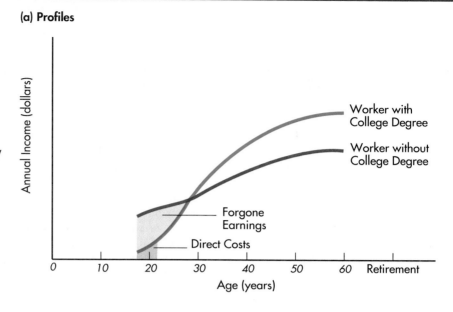

(a) Profiles

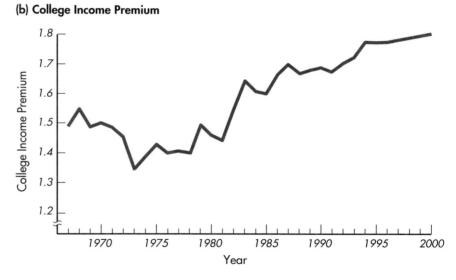

(b) College Income Premium

tors, lawyers, and accountants face long training periods and very long workdays, and they have to devote significant amounts of time each year to staying abreast of new developments in their profession. If you think that you are not likely to undertake and complete a four- or five-year apprenticeship after college in order to reap the rewards from your expenditure of time and money, then it would be very costly for you to be a premed student or to major in accounting or law. Your choice of a college major and an occupation reflects the opportunity costs you face. The greater the opportunity costs of any one occupation, the smaller the number of people who will select that occupation, everything else the same. For instance, it takes more time, money, and effort to become a medical doctor than to become a teacher in the K–12 schools. For this reason, many more people would choose to become teachers than doctors. As a result, a wage differential between the two fields exists that is sufficient to compensate them for the extra opportunity costs of the medical career.

2.b.3. Changing Careers   It is estimated that one in three people in the United States's labor force today will change careers at least once during their work lives. People choose a major and thus a career on the basis of information they have at their disposal, family influences, and other related factors. People acquire additional information once involved in their occupation, and sometimes their tastes change. They decide to embark on another career path. Who will make such a change? What types of occupations might see more changes?

Relying on the labor market model, we can suggest some answers to these questions. There might be a temptation to say that those who devoted the most effort, time, and money to their first occupation would be the least likely to change. But it is the marginal cost that matters; the effort, time, and money devoted to that first career are gone whether one remains in the first occupation or moves to another. In the words of the chapter on monopolistic competition and oligopoly, these are sunk, or unrecoverable, costs. Thus, we would expect people who have the greatest expected net gains to make a change. Those who see they are in dead-end positions or in occupations whose outlook for future income increases is not as good as other occupations would be more likely to move to a new career. We might expect people not to remain in or enter those professions where the marginal costs of remaining in the profession are high. For instance, those occupations that require continuous time and/or financial commitments if their members are to remain productive, such as the high-tech occupations, the hard sciences, engineering, accounting, or law, might lose relatively more people to areas that do not require similar time and money expenditures, such as management and administration.

RECAP

1. Compensating wage differentials are wage differences that make up for the higher risk or poorer working conditions of one job over another. Risky jobs pay more than risk-free jobs, and unpleasant jobs pay more than pleasant jobs.

2. Human capital is the education, training, and experience embodied in an individual.

3. An individual's choice of an occupation reflects a tradeoff between expected opportunity costs and expected benefits. An individual is likely to choose an occupation in which expected benefits outweigh expected opportunity costs.

3. DISCRIMINATION

4. What accounts for earnings disparities between males and females and between whites and nonwhites?

The United States is not alone in having differentials based on race and sex. In fact, there seem to be differentials among certain groups in nearly every country. "Colored" workers in Britain earn only about 60 percent of white workers' incomes. There are differentials in Israel between the Oriental Sephardic Jews and Ashkenazic Jews and in other nations between different groups based on color or religion. And in all countries women earn less than men. The Scandinavian countries, France, Australia, and New Zealand have female-to-male hourly pay ratios of 80 to 90 percent while other countries in western Europe have pay ratios of 65 to 75 percent.

3.a. Definition of Discrimination

Is discrimination present when there is prejudice or just when prejudice has harmful results? Consider a firm with two branch offices. One office employs only African Americans; the other, only whites. Workers in both branches are paid the same wages and have the same opportunities for advancement. Is discrimination occurring?

Is a firm that provides extensive training to employees discriminating when it prefers to hire young workers who are likely to stay with the firm long enough for it to recoup the training costs? Is an economics department that has no African American faculty members guilty of discrimination if African American economists constitute only 1 percent of the profession? Would your answer change if the department could show that it advertised job openings widely and made the same offers to African Americans and whites? Clearly, discrimination is a difficult subject to define and measure.

From an economist's viewpoint, a worker's value in the labor market depends on the factors affecting the marginal revenue product. When a factor that is unrelated to marginal revenue product acquires a positive or negative value in the labor market, **discrimination** is occurring. In Figure 7, if D_M is the demand for males and D_F is the demand for females, and males and females have identical marginal revenue products, then the resulting wage differences can be attributed to discrimination. Race, gender, age, physical handicaps, religion, sexual preference, and ethnic heritage may be factors that take on positive or negative values in the labor market and yet are unrelated to marginal revenue products.

discrimination: when factors unrelated to marginal revenue product affect the wages or jobs that are obtained

5. Are discrimination and freely functioning markets compatible?

3.b. Theories of Discrimination

Wage differentials due to race or gender pose a theoretical problem for economists because the labor market model attributes differences in wages to demand and supply differences that depend on productivity and the labor-leisure tradeoff. How can economists account for different pay scales for men and women, or for one race versus

Figure 7

Discrimination

The curve D_M is the demand for males, and D_F the demand for females. The two groups of workers are identical except in gender. The greater demand and the higher wage rate for males, even though males and females are equally productive, are due to discrimination.

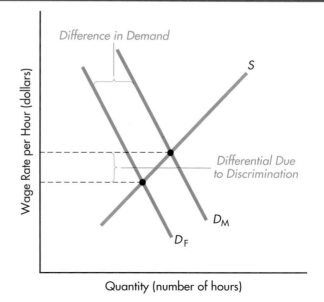

another, in the absence of marginal productivity differences between sexes or races? They identify discrimination as the cause of the differences even though they find discrimination difficult to rationalize because it is costly to those who discriminate.

In the freely functioning labor market, there is a profit to be made in *not* discriminating; therefore, discrimination should not exist. But, because discrimination does exist, economists have attempted to find plausible explanations for it. They have identified two sources of labor market discrimination. The first is *personal prejudice:* employers, fellow employees, or customers dislike associating with workers of a given race or sex. The second is *statistical discrimination:* employers project certain perceived group characteristics onto individuals. Economists tend to argue that personal prejudice is not consistent with a market economy but have acknowledged that statistical discrimination can coexist within a market economy.

3.b.1. Personal Prejudice

Certain groups in a society could be precluded from higher-paying jobs or from jobs that provide valuable human capital by personal prejudice on the part of employers, fellow workers, or customers.

Employer prejudice   If two workers have identical marginal revenue products and one worker is less expensive than the other, firms will want to hire the lower-cost worker. Otherwise, profits will be lower than they need to be. Suppose white males and others are identically productive, but managers prefer white males. Then the white males will be more expensive than women and minorities, and hiring white males will lower profits.

Discrimination might occur as employers attempt to hire only certain kinds of workers, as employees attempt to work only with certain kinds of coworkers or as customers attempt to purchase goods and services from certain kinds of workers.

Discrimination is costly in that less productive employees or more expensive but not more productive employees are used.

Under what conditions will lower profits as a result of personal prejudice be acceptable? Perhaps a monopoly firm can forgo some of its monopoly profit in order to satisfy the manager's personal prejudices (see the discussion of X-inefficiency in the chapter on monopoly), or perhaps firms that do not maximize profits can indulge in personal preferences. However, for profit-maximizing firms selling their goods in the market structures of perfect competition, monopolistic competition, or oligopoly, personal prejudice will mean a loss of profit unless all rivals also discriminate. Could firms form a cartel to discriminate? Recall from the discussion of oligopoly that cartels do not last long—there is an incentive to cheat—unless an entity like the government sanctions and enforces the cartel.

In the United States, well-meaning legislation intended to protect women actually created a situation in which women were denied access to training and education and thus were not able to gain the human capital necessary to compete for high-skill, high-paying jobs. Until the 1960s, women were barred from jobs because of legislation that attempted to protect them from heavy labor or injury. In reality, this legislation precluded women from obtaining certain kinds of human capital. Without the human capital, a generation or more of women were unable to obtain many high-paying jobs.

Worker prejudice   Workers may not want to associate with other races or sexes. White males may resist taking orders from females or sharing responsibility with a member of a minority group. White male workers who have these discriminatory preferences will tend to quit employers who employ women or minorities on a nondiscriminatory basis.

The worker prejudice explanation of discrimination assumes that white males are willing to accept lower-paying positions to avoid working with anyone other than a white male. Such discrimination is costly to those who discriminate.

Consumer prejudice   Customers may prefer to be served by white males in some situations and by minorities or women in others. If their preferences for white males extend to high-paying jobs such as physician and lawyer and their preferences for women and minorities are confined to lower-paying jobs like maid, nurse, and flight attendant, then women and minorities will be forced into occupations that work to their disadvantage.

The consumer prejudice explanation of discrimination assumes that consumers are willing to pay higher prices to be served by white males. In certain circumstances and during certain periods of time, this may be so; but over wide geographic areas or across different nations and over long periods of time, consumer prejudice does not appear to be a very likely explanation of discrimination.

3.b.2. Statistical Discrimination

Discrimination not related to personal prejudices can occur because of a lack of information. Employers must try to predict the potential productivity of job applicants, but rarely do they know what a worker's actual productivity will be. Often, the only information available when they hire someone is information that may be imperfectly related to productivity in general and may not apply to a particular person at all. Reliance on indicators of productivity such as education, experience, age, and test scores may keep some very good people from getting a job and may result in the hiring of some unproductive people. This is called **statistical discrimination.**

statistical discrimination: discrimination that results when an indicator of group performance is incorrectly applied to an individual member of the group

Suppose two types of workers apply for a word-processing job: those who can process 80 words per minute and those who can process only 40 words per minute. The problem is that these actual productivities are unknown to the employer. The employer can observe only the results of a five-minute word-processing test given to all applicants. How can the employer decide who is lucky or unlucky on the test and who can actually process 80 words per minute? Suppose the employer discovers that applicants from a particular vocational college, the DeVat School, are taught to perform well on preemployment tests but their overall performance as employees is the same as that of the rest of the applicants—some do well and some do not. The employer might decide to reject all applicants from DeVat because the good and bad ones can't be differentiated. Is the employer discriminating against DeVat? The answer is yes. The employer is using statistical discrimination.

Let's extend this example to race and gender. Suppose that, on average, minorities with a high school education are discovered to be less productive than white males with a high school education because of differences in the quality of the schools they attend. An employer using this information when making a hiring decision might prefer to hire a white male. Statistical discrimination can cause a systematic preference for one group over another even if some individuals in each group have the same measured characteristics.

3.c. Occupational Segregation

crowding: forcing a group into certain kinds of occupations

occupational segregation: the separation of jobs by sex

Statistical discrimination and imperfect information can lead to **crowding**—forcing women and minorities into occupations where they are unable to obtain the human capital necessary to compete for high-paying jobs. Today, even in the industrial nations, some occupations are considered women's jobs and different occupations are considered men's jobs. This separation of jobs by sex is called **occupational segregation.**

There is a substantial amount of occupational segregation in the United States and other industrialized nations.[2] One reason for occupational segregation is differences in the human capital acquired by males and females. Much of the human capital portion of the discrepancy between men and women is due to childbearing. Data suggest that marriage and children handicap women's efforts to earn as much as men. Many women leave the labor market during pregnancy, at childbirth, or when their children are young. These child-related interruptions are damaging to subsequent earnings because three out of four births occur to women before the age of thirty, the period in which men are gaining the training and experience that lead to higher earnings later in life. Second, even when mothers stay in the labor force, responsibility for children frequently constrains their choice of job: they accept lower wages in exchange for shorter or more flexible hours, location near home, limited out-of-town travel, and the like. Third, women have a disproportionate responsibility for child care and often have to make sacrifices that men do not make. For instance, when a young child is present, women are more likely than men to be absent from work, even when the men and women have equal levels of education and wages.

Perhaps most important of all, because most female children are expected to be mothers, they have been less likely than male children to acquire marketable human capital while in school. In the past, this difference was reflected in the choice of a curriculum in primary and secondary schools, in a college major, and in the reluctance of females to pursue graduate school training or to undergo the long hours and other rigors characteristic of apprenticeships in medicine, law, business, and other financially rewarding occupations. Females were channeled into languages, typing, and home economics, while males were channeled into mechanical drawing, shop, chemistry, and physics. This situation is changing, but the remnants of the past continue to influence the market. Since the late 1970s, about half of all law school classes and about one-third of medical school classes have been female. Nonetheless, mostly females major in languages, literature, education, and home economics, while mostly males major in physics, mathematics, chemistry, and engineering.

If new female entrants into the labor force have human capital equal to the human capital of new male entrants and thus greater than the human capital of females already in the labor force, then the average human capital and wages of females will rise. But even while the wage gap between males and females is decreasing, a gap will continue to exist because the average male in the labor force has more marketable human capital than the average female. The average rate of pay of males will continue to exceed that of females.

Statistical discrimination has a role in earnings disparities between men and women as well. Childless women earn less than men simply because it is the women who bear children. The human capital (training, education) women acquire will often be different, and less marketable, than that acquired by men. This occurs because many childless women did not know that they would be childless, and the subjects they studied in school as well as the jobs they took on leaving school did not provide the marketable training that most men received. Also, prospective employers were unlikely to know which young women would have children and which would not, which would leave their jobs and which would not, and this

---

[2]Victor R. Fuchs, "Women's Quest for Economic Equality," *Journal of Economic Perspectives* 3, no. 1 (Winter 1989), pp. 25–42, suggests that about half the occupations in the United States are gender biased, or "crowded." The ratios vary among the other industrialized nations, some having more and some having less occupational segregation. See Francine D. Blau and Lawrence M. Kahn, "The Gender Earnings Gap: Some International Evidence," NBER Working Paper No. 4224, December 1992.

affected the employers' willingness to provide training opportunities or to make other investments in job-related human capital. Because the odds are great that a woman will leave a job for some period of time to have a child, simply being a woman provides a signal to a firm. As a result of this signal, the wage offered a man might be higher than that offered a woman, or the job offered a man might contain better training than the one offered a woman.

Uncertainty about children does not end quickly for women or their employers. Even women who are childless at age thirty have a one in four chance of having at least one child by the time they are thirty-five. If females came into the world with a sign announcing the number of children that they would ultimately bear, the relationship between women's earnings and their number of children would be much stronger than the one we observe.

3.d. CEO Pay Packages

Chief executive officers (CEOs) commonly earn salaries and bonuses that far exceed the salaries and bonuses of the next person in charge. Steven Ross, the Time Warner boss, gathered $74.8 million in bonuses even as *Time* magazine laid off employees. J. F. O'Reilly of H. J. Heinz pulled in $74.8 million in compensation although Heinz had a rather average year. General Motors's former chairperson, Roger Smith, receives a $1.2 million annual pension even though GM lost both market share and money during his tenure. In the mid-1970s, CEOs earned about 34 times the pay of the average working person; by the 1990s they earned 110 times that average. Is this further evidence of discrimination?

One answer could be that the market for CEOs has failed. The owners of firms, thousands of shareholders, exert little influence over the day-to-day activities of the manager and have little influence over the manager's pay. As a result, CEOs basically do what they want, including getting paid huge salaries without regard to the desires of the owners. Another possible answer is that CEO pay is the result of a conspiracy involving other CEOs and friends of the CEO who, as members of the compensation board of a firm, fail to listen to investors or look to the firm's performance and simply provide the types of compensation they also want to receive. An alternative explanation to the market failure or conspiracy arguments claims that CEO pay makes sense from an economic efficiency basis. This explanation is built on an analogy with contests or tournaments.

High executive salaries could be the result of a tournament where the executive has won first prize; the pay increases the incentive for all employees to work harder and better.

In a tournament, the larger the first prize, and the larger the difference between the first prize and all other prizes, the more productive are the contestants. Thus, if we consider the labor market as a contest where the first prize is the CEO position, a large first prize induces more effort and higher productivity from all contestants. An extremely high pay package for the CEO induces that individual, and all employees (current and future), to exert extra efforts during their working lives.

3.e. The Economics of Superstars

Sometimes it appears that small differences in ability translate into huge differences in compensation. We saw how this phenomenon occurs in firms at the CEO level. It occurs in other situations as well, particularly in sports enterprises, which gave rise to its name—the **superstar effect.** Consider that the playing ability of the top ten tennis players or golfers is not much better than the playing ability of the players ranked between forty and fifty. Nonetheless, the compensation differences are incredibly large. The average income of the top ten tennis players and golfers is in the millions, while that of the lower-ranked ten players is in the thousands. If their productivity differences are so small, why are their compensation differences so large?

superstar effect: the situation in which people with small differences in abilities or productivity receive vastly different levels of compensation

Tiger Woods may turn out to be the greatest golfer of all time, surpassing Jack Nicklaus, Arnold Palmer, and Bobby Jones. For sure, Tiger Woods is a superstar. When he appears at a tournament, the crowds increase exponentially. The crowds do not disperse around the tournament watching each player but focus on Tiger. Hundreds of thousands struggle to get a glimpse of Tiger while other players are playing almost without anyone watching.

One explanation might be the limited time of those watching tennis or golf tournaments. Since most consumers have limited time, they choose to follow the top players. A tennis match between the fortieth and forty-first players might be nearly as good as that between the first and second. Yet, given the limited time to allocate between the two, nearly everyone would choose to watch the first and second players. At golf tournaments, huge throngs surround the top players, while lesser-known players play the game without the attention of adoring fans. These differences mean that the demand for the top players is huge relative to the demand for the lesser-ranked players. The sports franchises (the owners of the New York Yankees, for example) or the firms selling tickets to sporting events will be able to earn significantly higher prices if the ranked players are included in the activity; the marginal revenue product of the top-ranked players is thus much higher than that of the lesser-ranked players.

The superstar effect occurs outside of sports. You might, for example, observe two lawyers of relatively equal ability earning significantly different fees, or two economic consultants with apparently similar abilities earning vastly different consulting fees. When there is an all-or-nothing result in the market, the superstar effect might occur. Consider, for instance, the economist who offers advice to lawyers in cases involving firm behavior. A lawsuit filed against a firm might mean billions of dollars won or lost. Even if there are very small differences between economists, if the better economist means a win, then the better economist will receive huge compensation relative to the lesser economist. A $40 billion victory means that the marginal revenue product of the better economist is significantly greater than the marginal revenue product of the lesser economist, who has a $40 billion loss.

RECAP

1. Discrimination occurs when factors unrelated to marginal physical product acquire a positive or negative value in the labor market.

2. Earnings disparities may exist for a number of reasons, including personal prejudice, statistical discrimination, and human capital differentials. Human

capital differentials may exist because of occupational choice, statistical discrimination, or unequal opportunities to acquire human capital.

3. There are two general classes of discrimination theories: prejudice theory and statistical theory. Prejudice theory claims that employers, workers, and consumers express their personal prejudices by, respectively, earning lower profits, accepting lower wages, and paying higher prices. Statistical discrimination theory asserts that firms have imperfect information and must rely on general indicators of marginal physical product to pay wages and hire people and that reliance on these general indicators may create a pattern of discrimination.

4. Occupational segregation is the separation of jobs by sex. Some jobs are filled primarily by women, and other jobs are filled primarily by men.

5. Superstar effects occur when there is an all-or-nothing aspect to the market and result in cases where individuals with small productivity differences receive vastly different compensation.

4. WAGE DIFFERENTIALS AND GOVERNMENT POLICIES

Not until the 1960s did wage disparities and employment practices become a major public policy issue in the United States. In 1963 the Equal Pay Act outlawed separate pay scales for men and women performing similar jobs, and Title VII of the 1964 Civil Rights Act prohibited all forms of discrimination in employment.

4.a. Antidiscrimination Laws

Since the 1930s, about thirty states have enacted fair employment practice laws prohibiting discrimination in employment on the basis of race, creed, color, or national origin. Under state fair employment practice legislation, it is normally illegal for an organization to refuse employment, to discharge employees, or to discriminate in compensation or other terms of employment because of race.

These state laws did not apply to women, however. In fact, prior to the 1960s, sex discrimination was officially sanctioned by so-called protective labor laws, which limited the total hours that women were allowed to work and prohibited them from working at night, lifting heavy objects, and working during pregnancy.

With the Civil Rights Act of 1964, however, it became unlawful for any employer to discriminate on the basis of race, color, religion, sex, or national origin. Unions also were forbidden from excluding anyone on the basis of those five categories. Historically, it had been very difficult for racial minorities to obtain admission into unions representing workers in the skilled trades. This exclusion prevented minorities from obtaining the human capital necessary to compete for higher-paying jobs.

The Civil Rights Act applied only to actions after the effective date of July 1, 1965. It also permitted exceptions in cases where religion, sex, or national origin is a bona fide occupational qualification reasonably necessary to the normal operation of a business. This qualification might apply to certain jobs in religious organizations, for example. In addition, the act permits an employer to differentiate wages and other employment conditions on the basis of a bona fide seniority system, provided that such differences are not the result of an intention to discriminate. As a result of these exceptions, the Civil Rights Act has had neither as large nor as quick an impact on wage and job differentials as many had anticipated. It has, however, led to a clearer definition of discrimination.

disparate treatment: different treatment of individuals because of their race, sex, color, religion, or national origin

Two standards, or tests, of discrimination have evolved from court cases: disparate treatment and disparate impact. **Disparate treatment** means treating individuals differently because of their race, sex, color, religion, or national origin. The difficulty created by this standard is that personnel policies that appear to be neutral because they ignore race, gender, and so on, may nevertheless continue the effects of past discrimination. For instance, a seniority system that fires first the last person hired will protect those who were historically favored in hiring and training practices. Alternatively, a standard of hiring by word of mouth will perpetuate past discrimination if current employees are primarily of one race or sex.

disparate impact: an impact that differs according to race, sex, color, religion, or national origin, regardless of the motivation

The concern with perpetuating past discrimination led to the second standard, **disparate impact.** Under this standard it is the result of different treatment, not the motivation, that matters. Thus, statistical discrimination is illegal under the impact standard even though it is not illegal under the treatment standard.

4.b. Comparable Worth

The persistent wage gap between men and women in particular, but also between white males and minorities, has prompted well-meaning reformers to seek a new remedy for eliminating the gap—laws requiring companies to offer equal pay for jobs of comparable worth. **Comparable worth** is a catchword for the idea that pay ought to be determined by job characteristics rather than by supply and demand and that jobs with comparable requirements should receive comparable wages.

comparable worth: the idea that pay ought to be determined by job characteristics rather than by supply and demand and that jobs with comparable requirements should receive comparable wages

To identify jobs of comparable worth, employers would be required to evaluate all of the different jobs in their firms, answering questions such as these: What level of formal education is needed? How much training is necessary? Is previous experience needed? What skills are required? How much supervision is required? Is the work dangerous? Are working conditions unpleasant? By assigning point values to answers, employers could create job classifications based on job characteristics and could pay comparable wages for jobs with comparable "scores." A firm employing secretaries and steelworkers, for example, would determine the wages for these jobs by assessing job characteristics. If the assessment shows secretaries' work to be comparable to that of steelworkers, then the firm would pay secretaries and steelworkers comparable wages.

Proponents of comparable worth claim that market-determined wages are inappropriate because of the market's inability to assess marginal products as a result of statistical discrimination, team production, and personal prejudice. They argue that mandating a comparable worth system would minimize wage differentials that are due to statistical discrimination and occupational segregation, and they charge that a freely functioning market will continue to misallocate pay.

Opponents of comparable worth argue that interference with the functioning of the labor market will lead to shortages in some occupations and excess supplies in others. For instance, Figure 8 shows two markets for university professors, a market for computer science professors and a market for English professors. The supply and demand conditions in each market determine a wage for English professors that is less than the wage for computer science professors. The wage differential exists even though professors in both disciplines are required to have a Ph.D. and have essentially the same responsibilities.

Advocates of comparable worth would say that the two groups of professors should earn the same wage, the wage of the computer science professors, W_{CS}. But at this wage there would be a surplus of English professors, $QE_2 - QE_1$. The higher wage would cause the university to reduce the number of English professors it employs, from QE to QE_1. The net effect of comparable worth would be to

Figure 8

Comparable Worth

Two markets are shown, a market for computer science professors and a market for English professors. Demand and supply conditions determine that the wages for computer science professors are higher than the wages for English professors. Proponents of comparable worth might argue that the wages of both groups of professors should be equal to the higher wages of computer science professors since the requirements and responsibilities of the two jobs are virtually identical. However, the effect of imposing a higher wage in the market for English professors, W_{CS}, is to create a surplus of English professors, $QE_2 - QE_1$. In addition, the higher wage sends the signal to current college students that majoring in English will generate the same expected income as majoring in computer science. Students who might have studied computer science turn to English. In the future, an excess of English professors remains and even grows while the number of computer science professors shrinks.

(a) Market for Computer Science Professors

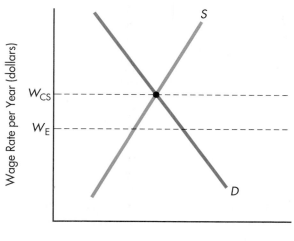

(b) Market for English Professors

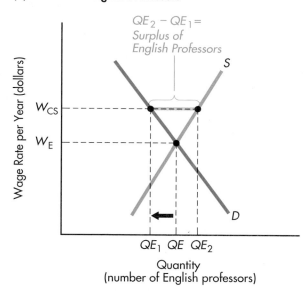

reduce the number of English professors employed but to increase the wages of those who are employed. The policy would also have a detrimental effect in the future. The wage would send the incorrect signal to current college students. It would tell students to remain in English instead of forgoing English for computer science.

Comparable worth has not fared well in the U.S. courtroom. On the whole, U.S. federal courts have not accepted the notion that unequal pay for comparable jobs violates existing employment discrimination law. Perhaps not surprisingly, therefore, the concept has made little headway in the private sector. Greater success has occurred in the public sector at the local and state levels. In Colorado Springs, San Jose, and Los Angeles and in Iowa, Michigan, New York, and Minnesota pay adjustments have been made on the basis of comparable worth. More than two-thirds of the state governments have begun studies to determine whether compensation of state workers reflects the worth of their jobs. Why has comparable worth had more success in the government sector? State governments suffer from the problem of team production, and if personal prejudice is to occur, it is more likely to occur in nonprofit organizations such as government where firms do not employ to the profit-maximizing point where $MFC = MRP$. Thus, it is in the state, local, and federal governments that comparable worth can be an effective policy. Comparable worth was adapted nationwide in Australia in the early 1970s and aspects of it have arisen in parts of the United Kingdom.

RECAP

1. The first national antidiscrimination law was the Civil Rights Act of 1964. It forbade firms from discriminating on the basis of sex, race, color, religion, or national origin.

2. Two tests of discrimination have evolved from court cases. According to the disparate treatment standard, it is illegal to intentionally treat individuals differently because of their race, sex, color, religion, or national origin. According to the disparate impact standard, it is the result, not the intention, of actions that is illegal.

3. Comparable worth is the idea that jobs should be evaluated on the basis of a number of characteristics and all jobs receiving the same evaluation should receive the same pay regardless of demand and supply conditions. Proponents argue that comparable worth is a solution to a market failure problem. Opponents argue that it will create surpluses and shortages in labor markets.

SUMMARY

? Are people willing to work more hours for higher wages?

1. The individual labor supply curve is backward bending because at some high wage, people choose to enjoy more leisure rather than to earn additional income. *§1.a*

? What are compensating wage differentials?

2. Equilibrium in the labor market defines the wage and quantity of hours worked. If all workers and all jobs were identical, then one wage would prevail. There are differential wages, however, because jobs and workers differ. *§1.c*

3. A compensating wage differential exists when a higher wage is determined in one labor market than in another due to differences in job characteristics. *§2.a*

? Why might wages be higher for people with more human capital than for those with less human capital?

4. Human capital is the training, education, and skills people acquire. Human capital increases productivity. Because acquiring human capital takes time and money, the necessity of obtaining human capital for

some jobs reduces the supply of labor to those jobs. *§2.b*

? What accounts for earnings disparities between males and females and between whites and nonwhites?

5. Earnings disparities may result from discrimination, occupational choice, human capital differences, educational opportunity differences, age, and immigration. *§3.a, 3.c, 3.d*

6. Discrimination occurs when some factor not related to marginal revenue product affects the wage rate someone receives. *§3.a*

? Are discrimination and freely functioning markets compatible?

7. There are two general types of discrimination—personal prejudice and statistical discrimination. *§3.b*

8. Personal prejudice is costly to those who demonstrate the prejudice and should not last in a market economy. For it to last, some restrictions on the functioning of markets must exist. *§3.b.1*

9. Statistical discrimination is the result of imperfect information and can occur as long as information is imperfect. *§3.b.2*

10. Occupational segregation exists when some jobs are held mainly by one group in society and other jobs by other groups. A great deal of occupational segregation exists between males and females in the United States. §3.c

KEY TERMS

backward-bending labor supply curve §1.a

labor force participation §1.b

compensating wage differentials §2.a

human capital §2.b

discrimination §3.a

statistical discrimination §3.b.2

crowding §3.c

occupational segregation §3.c

superstar effect §3.e

disparate treatment §4.a

disparate impact §4.a

comparable worth §4.b

EXERCISES

1. What could account for a backward-bending labor supply curve?

2. What is human capital? How does a training program such as Mrs. Fields Cookie College affect human capital? Is a college degree considered to be human capital?

3. Define equilibrium in the labor market. Illustrate equilibrium on a graph. Illustrate the situation in which there are two types of labor, skilled and unskilled.

4. Describe how people choose a major in college. If someone majors in English literature knowing that the starting salary for English literature graduates is much lower than the starting salary for accountants, is the English literature major irrational?

5. Explain what is meant by discrimination, and explain the difference between personal prejudice and statistical discrimination.

6. Explain why occupational segregation by sex might occur. Can you imagine any society in which you would not expect to find occupational segregation by sex? Explain. Would you expect to find occupational segregation by race in most societies?

7. Why are women's wages only 60 to 80 percent of men's wages, and why has this situation existed for several decades? Now that women are entering college and professional schools in increasing numbers, why doesn't the wage differential disappear?

8. Why do economists say that discrimination is inherently inefficient and therefore will not occur in general?

9. Demonstrate, using two labor markets, what is meant by comparable worth. What problems are created by comparable worth? Under what conditions might comparable worth make economic sense? Explain.

10. There is a great deal of talk in the United States about providing more job flexibility for families. Why is it necessary for the government to provide the flexibility through the Family and Medical Leave Act and other programs? Why doesn't the private market provide this flexibility?

11. Consider the decision of a working woman or man who has young children or elderly relatives to take care of. Explain in terms of the labor supply curve how this person's decision to work is affected by the presence of dependents. What happens to the opportunity cost of working? How is the labor supply curve affected?

Internet Exercises/ Resources

For Internet exercises and web resources related to this chapter, go to **http://college.hmco.com.**

Higher Apathy

A survey of college freshmen confirms what professors and administrators said they have been sensing, that students are increasingly disengaged and view higher education less as an opportunity to expand their minds and more as a means to increase their income.

The annual nationwide poll by researchers at the University of California at Los Angeles shows that two suggested goals of education—"to be very well off financially" and "to develop a meaningful philosophy of life"— have switched places in the last three decades.

In the survey taken at the start of the fall semester, 74.9 percent of freshmen chose being well off as an essential goal and 40.8 percent chose developing a philosophy. In 1968, the numbers were reversed, with 40.8 percent selecting financial security and 82.5 percent citing the importance of developing a philosophy.

It is using education more as a means to an end, rather than valuing what is being learned, said Linda Sax, director of the survey, first taken 32 years ago, at the Higher Education Research Institute at UCLA.

Now: Reasonable men can— and unreasonable men do— debate the nature and purposes of higher education. Cardinal Newman, for instance, had some ideas relating to the subject. And others might wonder if a year such as 1968 should serve as a benchmark for anything but rampant silliness. Nevertheless, the survey probably dismays the dwindling band believing colleges and universities ought to be devoted to higher education, not to mere training.

The researchers also found increased levels of "academic and political disengagement" among young scholars. (The less charitable might remark on the students' blasé ignorance.) Numerous rea-

sons could explain the survey's results. . . .

The colleges themselves have degraded the liberal arts. Deconstructionism (a.k.a. destructionism) and the others isms and fads to which the professoriat is prone generate indifference among students preferring knowledge to ideology. Russia and its former satellites have gotten the message; the academy has not. The enemies of the liberal arts lie within the ivied walls. If students consider history, English, and philosophy irrelevant, then perhaps it is because their professors treat the humanities as though they were. Why should students respect the so-called canon, when noisemakers inside the academy treat it with contempt? . . .

Source: Reprinted by permission of the *Richmond Times Dispatch*, January 25, 1998.

Richmond Times Dispatch/January 25, 1998

Commentary

Education and training account for a significant amount of the income differences among individuals. Generally the more education one has, the higher one's lifetime income. In recent years the importance of education in determining income has risen. While the average worker's real income has been broadly flat for most of the decade, those at the top have gained considerably. The factor generally credited with this widening inequality is the changing demand for labor. As globalization has sent lower-skilled jobs overseas, the U.S. economy has restructured toward higher-skilled, higher-paid jobs.

The transformation has been remarkable. Professional, technical, and managerial jobs accounted for just one-sixth of the U.S. work force in 1950. By 1995, that proportion had risen to one-third. This demand for skilled labor has placed a much higher premium on educational attainment. As a result, more people are going to college and acquiring the necessary skills. The following table summarizes the role of education and wages; it shows the change in wages for each level of education for males and females over the period 1984 to 1995 (from the Urban Institute, as reported in the *Financial Times,* January 12, 1998, p. 9).

Education	All	Male	Female
High school dropout	−1.5	−3.2	2.0
High school graduate	4.2	− .3	11.9
Some college	2.1	− .6	19.7
College graduate	8.5	7.0	18.4
Postcollege education	13.7	10.6	20.0

Given these facts, why should anyone be surprised that students are in school to acquire skills that translate into more income and a better life? The real surprise would be if people were attending college simply to develop a philosophy. The pressures of the labor market are such that quality education is necessary; the human capital developed must have value in the labor market. Firms will pay for the human capital acquired in college.

Chapter 17

The Capital Market

Fundamental Questions

1. **What role does saving play in the economy?**

2. **When is a dollar tomorrow better than a dollar today?**

3. **What is capital?**

4. **What is financial capital?**

5. **How are the values of stocks and bonds determined?**

6. **What is the relationship between the value of a stock and economic profit?**

Preview

Does a firm spend $100,000 today to acquire a machine that is expected to generate output for ten years? Do we extract more oil from the ground now or leave it for future generations? Does an individual obtain a college degree, which may provide benefits throughout life, when the cost of a four-year college education exceeds $100,000? The alternatives faced by these decision makers are similar to those confronting the employees of an aerospace company in suburban Los Angeles who offered to sell their winning California lottery ticket worth $3 million. The employees were willing to take $1.2 million cash. Three million dollars for only $1.2 million—that sounds like a good deal, but it's not as good as it sounds. A $3 million Lotto ticket is not $3 million: it is a promise that if the winner and the lottery survive 20 years, the winner will receive a check for about $150,000 each year before taxes (about $100,000 after taxes). "You're talking about money then versus money now," claimed one of the

ticket holders, who figured that lots of undesirable things could happen in the next twenty years: the lottery fund could go belly-up, the price of a loaf of bread could rise to $10, or nuclear disaster could make the annual payments worthless.

This issue is typical of a great deal of what occurs in the resource markets—comparing values over time. It is particularly common in the capital market because capital is often long lived; a piece of equipment may be usable for twenty or so years. ■

1. CAPITAL

Capital is the resource we refer to when we say that a production process is mechanized or when we talk about the capacity of a factory. *Capital* is buildings and machinery produced for the purpose of producing goods and services. *Financial capital* is the money with which physical capital is purchased.

1.a. Saving

1. What role does saving play in the economy?

Creating capital requires that saving take place. In some developing countries, farming is done solely by hand; in most nations, however, farming is quite mechanized. No doubt it has occurred to farmers in the developing countries that they could produce more if they had some capital—for instance, a plow and a horse. Unfortunately, the capital needed to make the switch to a more-mechanized operation can be obtained only by sacrificing current consumption. The construction of the plow requires that the farmer spend time away from the planting, care, or harvesting of the crops to build the plow, or she or he can use some of the crops to purchase the plow. Similarly, a horse can be obtained only by accumulating enough crops to purchase the horse; and the care and feeding of the horse, once acquired, would consume some of each year's crops. In order to obtain the capital, the farmer must forgo current consumption of the crops, and this sacrifice could be severe if the farmer's family depends on the crops for sustenance. Nevertheless, if the benefits of the additional production made possible by the plow and horse seem likely to be greater than the forgone consumption, the plow and horse will be acquired.

The process of sacrificing current consumption in order to accumulate capital (plows, horses) with which more output can be produced in the future, and thus more consumption enjoyed in the future, is called roundabout production. It is simply the process of **saving.** With saving, everything produced today is not consumed today. Some output, the amount saved, is used to create more production in the future. If the existing quantities of all resources were used today—if the forests were razed and every bit of timber were used, and if the world's supply of oil were extracted and used—living standards today might be higher but the future would be bleak. Forgoing some current consumption allows households, businesses, and society to obtain capital resources that can be used to increase future production and consumption. Any economy that grows—produces increasing amounts of goods and services and thus generates more income—must save and accumulate significant amounts of capital.

saving: not consuming all current production

1.b. The Capital Market

The capital market is the channel through which consumers and producers match their future plans with their behavior today. The demand for and supply of capital determine the equilibrium quantity and cost of capital.

Table 1

Present Value of an Annuity of $1 per Period

Period (n)	Interest (Discount) Rate (i)								
	1%	2%	3%	4%	5%	6%	7%	8%	9%
1	0.9901	0.9804	0.9709	0.9615	0.9524	0.9434	0.9346	0.9259	0.9174
2	1.9704	1.9416	1.9135	1.8861	1.8594	1.8334	1.8080	1.7833	1.7591
3	2.9410	2.8839	2.8286	2.7751	2.7232	2.6730	2.6243	2.5771	2.5313
4	3.9020	3.8077	3.7171	3.6299	3.5460	3.4651	3.3872	3.3121	3.2397
5	4.8534	4.7135	4.5797	4.4518	4.3295	4.2124	4.1002	3.9927	3.8897
6	5.7955	5.6014	5.4172	5.2421	5.0757	4.9173	4.7665	4.6229	4.4859
7	6.7282	6.4720	6.2303	6.0021	5.7864	5.5824	5.3893	5.2064	5.0330
8	7.6517	7.3255	7.0197	6.7327	6.4632	6.2098	5.9713	5.7466	5.5348
9	8.5660	8.1622	7.7861	7.4353	7.1078	6.8017	6.5152	6.2469	5.9952
10	9.4713	8.9826	8.5302	8.1109	7.7217	7.3601	7.0236	6.7101	6.4177
11	10.3676	9.7868	9.2526	8.7605	8.3064	7.8869	7.4987	7.1390	6.8052
12	11.2551	10.5753	9.9540	9.3851	8.8633	8.3838	7.9427	7.5361	7.1607
13	12.1337	11.3484	10.6350	9.9856	9.3936	8.8527	8.3577	7.9038	7.4869
14	13.0037	12.1062	11.2961	10.5631	9.8986	9.2950	8.7455	8.2442	7.7862
15	13.8651	12.8493	11.9379	11.1184	10.3797	9.7122	9.1079	8.5595	8.0607
16	14.7179	13.5777	12.5611	11.6523	10.8378	10.1059	9.4466	8.8514	8.3126
17	15.5623	14.2919	13.1661	12.1657	11.2741	10.4773	9.7632	9.1216	8.5436
18	16.3983	14.9920	13.7535	12.6593	11.6896	10.8276	10.0591	9.3719	8.7556
19	17.2260	15.6785	14.3238	13.1339	12.0853	11.1581	10.3356	9.6036	8.9501
20	18.0456	16.3514	14.8775	13.5903	12.4622	11.4699	10.5940	9.8181	9.1285
21	18.8570	17.0112	15.4150	14.0292	12.8212	11.7641	10.8355	10.0168	9.2922
22	19.6604	17.6580	15.9369	14.4511	13.1630	12.0416	11.0612	10.2007	9.4424
23	20.4558	18.2922	16.4436	14.8568	13.4886	12.3034	11.2722	10.3711	9.5802
24	21.2434	18.9139	16.9355	15.2470	13.7986	12.5504	11.4693	10.5288	9.7066
25	22.0232	19.5235	17.4131	15.6221	14.0939	12.7834	11.6536	10.6748	9.8226

1.b.1. Demand for Capital A firm acquires additional capital as long as the marginal revenue product of the additional capital exceeds the marginal factor cost of that additional capital. When a firm rents capital (where *rent* refers to payment for the use of capital), its calculations are identical to the calculations it made when deciding whether to hire another worker. Suppose a rock-crushing firm rents the trucks it uses to haul crushed rock. The firm will rent another truck only if the rental rate is less than the marginal revenue product generated by the rented truck.

Not all capital is rented, however. Firms also purchase capital: they buy buildings and machines that they might use for several years. And, of course, rental or leasing companies must own the capital that they rent to other firms. To decide how much

Period (n)	Interest (Discount) Rate (i)									
	10%	12%	14%	15%	16%	18%	20%	24%	28%	32%
1	0.9091	0.8929	0.8772	0.8696	0.8621	0.8475	0.8333	0.8065	0.7813	0.7576
2	1.7355	1.6901	1.6467	1.6257	1.6052	1.5656	1.5278	1.4568	1.3916	1.3315
3	2.4869	2.4018	2.3216	2.2832	2.2459	2.1743	2.1065	1.9813	1.8684	1.7663
4	3.1699	3.0373	2.9137	2.8550	2.7982	2.6901	2.5887	2.4043	2.2410	2.0957
5	3.7908	3.6048	3.4331	3.3522	3.2743	3.1272	2.9906	2.7454	2.5320	2.3452
6	4.3553	4.1114	3.8887	3.7845	3.6847	3.4976	3.3255	3.0205	2.7594	2.5342
7	4.8684	4.5638	4.2883	4.1604	4.0386	3.8115	3.6046	3.2423	2.9370	2.6775
8	5.3349	4.9676	4.6389	4.4873	4.3436	4.0776	3.8372	3.4212	3.0758	2.7860
9	5.7590	5.3282	4.9464	4.7716	4.6065	4.3030	4.0310	3.5655	3.1842	2.8681
10	6.1446	5.6502	5.2161	5.0188	4.8332	4.4941	4.1925	3.6819	3.2689	2.9304
11	6.4951	5.9377	5.4527	5.2337	5.0286	4.6560	4.3271	3.7757	3.3351	2.9776
12	6.8137	6.1944	5.6603	5.4206	5.1971	4.7932	4.4392	3.8514	3.3868	3.0133
13	7.1034	6.4235	5.8424	5.5831	5.3423	4.9095	4.5327	3.9124	3.4272	3.0404
14	7.3667	6.6282	6.0021	5.7245	5.4675	5.0081	4.6106	3.9616	3.4587	3.0609
15	7.6061	6.8109	6.1422	5.8474	5.5755	5.0916	4.6755	4.0013	3.4834	3.0764
16	7.8237	6.9740	6.2651	5.9542	5.6685	5.1624	4.7296	4.0333	3.5026	3.0882
17	8.0216	7.1196	6.3729	6.0472	5.7487	5.2223	4.7746	4.0591	3.5177	3.0971
18	8.2014	7.2497	6.4674	6.1280	5.8178	5.2732	4.8122	4.0799	3.5294	3.1039
19	8.3649	7.3658	6.5504	6.1982	5.8775	5.3162	4.8435	4.0967	3.5386	3.1090
20	8.5136	7.4694	6.6231	6.2593	5.9288	5.3527	4.8696	4.1103	3.5458	3.1129
21	8.6487	7.5620	6.6870	6.3125	5.9731	5.3837	4.8913	4.1212	3.5514	3.1158
22	8.7715	7.6446	6.7429	6.3587	6.0113	5.4099	4.9094	4.1300	3.5558	3.1180
23	8.8832	7.7184	6.7921	6.3988	6.0442	5.4321	4.9245	4.1371	3.5592	3.1197
24	8.9847	7.7843	6.8351	6.4338	6.0726	5.4510	4.9371	4.1428	3.5619	3.1210
25	9.0770	7.8431	6.8729	6.4642	6.0971	5.4669	4.9476	4.1474	3.5640	3.1220

2. When is a dollar tomorrow better than a dollar today?

capital to buy, a firm must compare the prices paid for the building or equipment today with the marginal revenue product generated by the capital over the lifetime of the capital.

The firm's problem is identical to the problem faced by the holders of the winning lottery ticket. To know whether a machine should be purchased, or whether the $3 million payoff over 20 years should be purchased for $1.2 million cash today, it is necessary to compare two values: a purchase price today and a return that occurs over several years. To make this comparison, it is necessary to take into account that people prefer to consume today instead of waiting until tomorrow and that there is a risk that future payoffs will not be made or that money in the future will not purchase as much as it does today. The value today of an amount to be paid or received

present value: the equivalent value today of some amount to be received in the future

future value: the equivalent value in the future of some amount received today

in the future is called the **present value.** The value at a future date of some amount to be paid or received today is called the **future value.**

How can the future and present values be calculated? If you have $100,000 today, you can deposit that $100,000 into an account that will yield the principal (the original amount, $100,000) plus the interest after some period of time. If the interest rate is 9 percent per year, you will get interest earnings of $9,000 after one year:

$$\$100,000 \times 0.09 = \$9,000$$

Thus, $109,000 one year in the future is the *future value* of $100,000 today at an interest rate of 9 percent, or $100,000 today is the *present value* of $109,000 one year in the future at a 9 percent interest rate. Let's express "one year in the future" as *FV* (future value) and "today" as *PV* (present value). Then we can write

$$FV = PV(1 + \text{interest rate})$$

If we divide both sides by (1 + interest rate), we have

$$PV = FV/(1 + \text{interest rate})$$

Thus, the present value, *PV*, is $100,000:

$$PV = \$109,000/(1.09) = \$100,000$$

Calculating present and future values is simple when you are looking only one year into the future. The calculations become more complicated when you are looking ahead several years. If there is a stream of values, such as with the Lotto ticket paying $100,000 per year for 20 years, you could calculate the present value of each payment and sum all the values to get the present value of the entire stream. Or you could use tables, such as Table 1, that have been constructed to show what the present value of some future amount is or what the future value of some current amount is.

Let's use Table 1 to see what a Lotto ticket that pays $100,000 per year (after taxes) over 20 years is worth today. To calculate the present value of $100,000 per year for 20 years at a specific rate of interest, find the row for 20 periods and then read across the columns until you reach the appropriate interest rate. For instance, at an 8 percent rate of interest, the number indicated is 9.8181. This number is the present value of payments of $1 per period for 20 periods at 8 percent. To get the present value of a stream of payments of $100,000 per year for 20 years at 8 percent, multiply $100,000 times 9.8181. The result is $981,810. You can see from the table that as the interest rate increases, the present value of the money to be received in the future declines. Look at a 10 percent rate of interest and 20 periods in the table; the value indicated is 8.5136, so $100,000 each year for 20 years is worth $851,360 today at a 10 percent rate of interest.

3. What is capital?

Now let's put this in the context of a firm that is deciding whether to purchase a unit of capital. Suppose a physician is contemplating the purchase of a new x-ray machine that will yield $100,000 per year for 20 years. As seen in Table 1, the present value of the marginal revenue product from the machine is $981,810 at an 8 percent interest rate. If the price of the machine is $900,000, the physician will buy the machine. As the interest rate rises, the present value of the machine's marginal revenue product declines. At a 10 percent interest rate, the present value of the marginal revenue product is $851,360. The physician will not purchase the machine in this case. As the interest rate rises, the quantity of capital purchased declines.

This same relationship holds for households as well. An individual deciding whether to purchase a college education compares the present value of the benefits generated by the degree with the purchase price of the degree. If the purchase price

Figure 1

The Market Demand for Capital

In Figure 1(a) the demand for capital is shown as a downward-sloping line with the quantity of capital measured on the horizontal axis and the price of capital measured on the vertical axis. As the price of capital changes, say from $80,000 to $100,000 per unit of capital (per machine), the quantity of capital demanded changes, from 350,000 to 300,000 machines. In Figure 1(b) the relationship between the demand for capital and the interest rate is illustrated. As the rate of interest rises, the demand for capital declines—the demand curve shifts in. The interest rate associated with each demand curve is in parentheses beside the curve.

(a) Change in Quantity Demanded

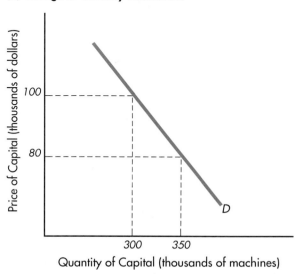

(b) Change in Demand

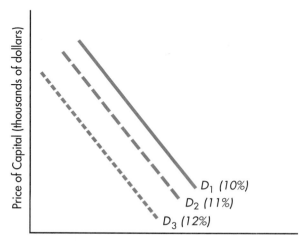

is less than the present value of the benefits, then the person goes to college. At a higher interest rate, the present value of the benefits will not exceed the purchase price. As a result, the human capital will not be purchased.

The market demand for capital is shown in Figure 1(a) as a downward-sloping curve with the quantity of capital measured along the horizontal axis and the price of capital measured along the vertical axis. An increase in the price of capital, say from $80,000 to $100,000 per machine in Figure 1(a), decreases the quantity of capital demanded, from 350,000 to 300,000 machines. This represents the case in which, for instance, a farmer will postpone the purchase of a new tractor or buy fewer tractors if the price increases, or an airline will postpone the purchase of a new airplane or purchase fewer airplanes as the price of airplanes increases.

As is the case for any demand curve, the demand curve for capital shifts when one of the nonprice determinants of demand changes. Perhaps the most important nonprice determinant of capital is the interest rate. You have seen how an increase in the interest rate decreases the present value of a future stream of income. In exactly the same manner, a higher interest rate lowers the present value of the marginal revenue product of capital, causing the demand curve for capital to shift in. Each time the interest rate increases, from 10 to 11 to 12 percent, the demand curve for capital shifts in, as shown in Figure 1(b) by the move from D_1 (10%) to D_2 (11%)

Figure 2

The Interest Rate, the Price of Capital, and the Rate of Return on Capital

The supply of capital is an upward-sloping curve. The demand for and supply of capital determine the price of capital as well as the quantity of capital produced and purchased. The rate of return on capital is the additional annual revenue generated by additional capital, divided by the purchase price of the capital. As the interest rate rises, the demand for capital declines (the demand curve shifts in) and the price of capital declines. As a result of the lower price, the rate of return rises.

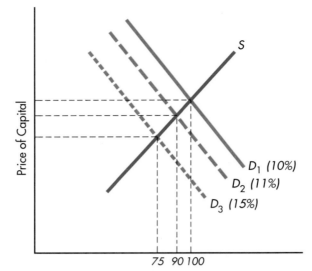

Quantity of Capital (thousands of units of capital)

to D_3 (12%). The number in parentheses next to each demand curve represents the interest rate associated with that demand curve.

The demand curve also shifts when any other determinant of demand changes. For instance, if a technological change increases the marginal physical product of capital, everything else held constant, the demand for capital increases. The invention of jet engines increased the demand for airplanes. The invention of small computers increased the overall demand for computers. Expectations and changes in income will also alter the demand for capital. For example, a business that expects strong demand for its goods purchases more capital now, causing the demand curve for capital to shift out.

1.b.2. Supply of Capital Some firms specialize in producing capital. John Deere supplies farm equipment, Boeing supplies airplanes, IBM produces computers, and so on. The quantity of capital supplied by these producers depends on the price of the capital. As the price of capital rises, the quantity that producers are willing and able to offer for sale rises, as shown in Figure 2 by the upward-sloping curve, *S*.

1.b.3. Equilibrium The demand for and supply of capital determine the price of capital, as well as the quantity produced and purchased. Changes in demand or supply change the equilibrium price and quantity. For example, changes in the interest rate affect the demand for capital and thus the price of capital. If the interest rate rises, the demand for capital decreases and the price of capital falls, shown in Figure 2 in the move from D_1 (10%) to D_2 (11%) to D_3 (15%). At an interest rate of 10 percent, 100,000 units of capital are demanded; at an 11 percent rate of interest, 90,000 units of capital are demanded; and at a 15 percent rate of interest, 75,000 units of capital are demanded. As the demand for capital shifts in, the price of capital falls.

Interest is the payment to the owners of capital for use of the capital services. Figure 2 illustrates the relationship among the price of capital, the interest rate, and the rate of return on capital. The rate of return on capital is the additional revenue generated by the capital each year (in present-value terms) divided by the price of the capital. For instance, if a $100,000 machine generates $10,000 of additional revenue each year (in present-value terms), the rate of return on that machine is 10 percent per year. With a lower price but the same marginal revenue product, the rate of return on the capital increases. The $10,000 per year divided by a $90,909 expenditure is an 11 percent per year return. Since the demand curve shifts in and the price of capital decreases each time the interest rate rises, the rate of return on capital must increase each time the interest rate rises. Similarly, the rate of return on capital must decrease each time the interest rate declines.

The interest rate represents the opportunity cost of capital, the annual rate of return available from alternative uses of the funds with which capital is acquired. A firm contemplating a $100,000 expenditure on a piece of equipment has many alternative uses for that $100,000. One alternative is to place the funds in an interest-earning account. Thus, the firm must expect to earn a rate of return on its capital that is at least equal to the interest rate if it is to purchase the capital in the first place. If the interest rate rises above the expected rate of return on capital, the demand for capital declines, the price of capital falls, and the rate of return on capital rises. For example, if the rate of return on a $100,000 piece of equipment is expected to be 10 percent to a firm but the interest rate that can be obtained from other uses of the $100,000 has risen to 11 percent, the firm is better off seeking other uses and not purchasing the piece of equipment. As many firms react this way, the demand for capital declines and the price of capital falls. The price continues to decline until the rate of return equals the interest rate, at a price of $90,909, since $10,000/$90,909 = 11 percent. Conversely, if the rate of return on the $100,000 equipment is expected to be 10 percent per year but the interest rate has fallen to 9 percent, the firm is better off purchasing the equipment. Thus, the demand for capital rises, the price of capital rises, and the rate of return on capital falls. The price will continue to rise until the rate of return equals the interest rate, at a price of $111,111, since $10,000/$111,111 = 9 percent.

The rate of return on capital and the interest rate will be equal in the long run. Any time the two are not equal, the price of capital will change; this in turn causes the rate of return on capital to change.

RECAP

1. Roundabout production is the process of saving and accumulating capital in order to increase production, and thus consumption, in the future.
2. Saving is the act of delaying consumption.
3. The capital market is the channel through which consumers and producers match their plans for the future with their behavior today.
4. Present value is the equivalent value today of some amount to be received in the future. Future value is the equivalent value in the future of some amount received today.
5. The demand for capital is represented by a downward-sloping curve, illustrating that the quantity of capital demanded rises as the price of capital falls.
6. The demand for capital shifts in when the interest rate rises.

7. The supply of capital is represented by an upward-sloping curve, illustrating that the quantity of capital supplied rises as the price of capital rises.

8. The demand for and supply of capital determine the price of capital. An increase in the price of capital lowers the rate of return on capital. Conversely, a decrease in the price of capital raises the rate of return on capital.

9. The rate of interest represents the rate of return on alternative uses of the funds with which capital is purchased. Thus, when the rate of interest rises above the rate of return on capital, the demand for capital declines, the price of capital declines, and the rate of return on capital rises. Conversely, when the rate of interest falls below the rate of return on capital, the demand for capital rises, the price of capital rises, and the rate of return on capital falls.

2. FINANCIAL CAPITAL

4. What is financial capital?

financial capital: the money used to purchase capital, stocks, and bonds

annual return: the dividend plus the capital gain per year

dividend: the amount returned to shareholders on each share of stock as a percent of the value of the stock

capital gain: an increase in the price of financial capital

Firms must obtain funds with which to purchase capital and carry out research and development. Corporations raise funds by taking out loans (debt or bonds) and selling the money from shares of ownership (equity or stocks). Stocks and bonds are called **financial capital.**

2.a. Stocks

The price of stocks for most firms can be found in daily newspapers. For example, Figure 3 shows the listing for the price of Coca-Cola and IBM stock on February 21, 2001. "Div" is the dividend, the amount paid to shareholders for each share of stock. For example, the dividend for IBM in 2001 was $.52 per share. "Yld" is the yield, the annual return. The **annual return** of a stock is the **dividend** the stock yields plus the **capital gain.** The capital gain is how much the price of the share of stock increases during the year. A capital loss is a negative capital gain. The "PE" is the price-to-earnings ratio: the price of the stock to the profit per share of the stock. "Vol" is the number of shares of the stock traded during the day. "Close" is the closing price and "Net Chg" is the change in the price of the stock during the day.

Figure 3

Typical Listing of Stocks in Daily Newspapers

This example lists Coca-Cola and IBM on February 21, 2001.

| 52 weeks | | Stock | Sym | Div | Yld % | PE | Vol 100s | Hi | Lo | Close | Net Chg |
Hi	Lo										
64	42.88	Coca-Cola	KO	.72	1.2	66	76233	60.98	58.40	58.47	−0.89
134.94	80.06	IBM	IBM	.52	.5	25	66985	115.60	110.78	111.50	−3.50

Figure 4

Typical Listing of Bonds in Daily Newspapers

The top part is a sample of Treasury bonds. The lower part is a sample of the list of corporate bonds traded on the New York Exchange.

Treasury Bonds, Notes, and Bills

Tuesday, February 21, 2001

Rate	Mo/Yr	Bid	Ask	Chg	Yld
5	Feb01n	99:30	100	....	4.88
$5\frac{5}{8}$	May01n	100:02	100:04	−1	5.00

New York Exchange Bonds

Bonds	Cur Yld	Vol	Close	Net Chg.
ATT $7\frac{1}{8}$ 02	7.1	20	101	$+\frac{1}{2}$
BellsoT $7\frac{5}{8}$ 35	7.6	122	$100\frac{1}{4}$	$+\frac{1}{4}$

2.b. Bonds

Bond prices for both corporate and government bonds can also be found in the financial pages of the newspaper. Figure 4 shows a typical listing of corporate bonds and government bonds. There are four aspects of a bond: coupon, maturity date, face value, and yield. The **coupon** is the fixed amount that the borrower agrees to pay the bondholder each year. The **maturity date** is the time when the coupon payments end and the principal is paid back. The **face value** is the amount of principal that will be paid back when the bond matures. The bond shown in Figure 4 has a maturity date of 2002 and a coupon equal to $7\frac{1}{8}$ percent of the face value of the bond. The **yield** or yield to maturity is defined as the annual rate of return on the bond if the bond were held to maturity. The other bonds mature in 2035.

Figure 4 also shows two government bonds. Their rate, month and year of maturity, bid price, asked price, and yield are noted.

There is an inverse relationship between the yield and the price. When price goes up, yield goes down, and vice versa. Suppose you bought a government bond for $100 that says the government will pay 5 percent of the face value, or $5, in interest and give you back the $100 at the end of the one-year period. Now suppose that just after you bought the bond, interest rates on bank deposits jump to 10 percent. Your bond pays you 5 percent, so your rate of return is less than you could get in a bank deposit. You decide to sell the bond. Unfortunately, everyone else realizes that the return is less than the bank deposit. To sell the bond, you have to lower the price. If you drop the price to $98, then the rate of return to the new bondholder will be ($105 − $98)/$98 = 7.1 percent. You still can't sell, so you lower the price some more. In fact, you have to lower the price until the $5 return is about the same rate as the bank deposit, 10 percent. That price is $95.45; if someone pays $95.45 now, then gets $105 at the end of the year, the rate of return for the year is 10 percent: ($105 − $95.45)/$95.45 = $9.545/$95.45.

coupon: fixed amount a borrower agrees to pay the bondholder each year

maturity date: the time when the coupon payments end and the principal is paid back

face value: amount of principal that will be paid back when a bond matures

yield: annual rate of return on a bond if the bond is held to maturity

5. How are the values of stocks and bonds determined?

2.c. Market for Financial Capital

The demand for stocks and bonds comes from investors. Investors are comparing potential rates of return and choosing to invest in those offering the greatest return. The supply of stocks and bonds comes from firms that want to raise money with which to purchase physical capital or other items. To sell their shares of stock, firms have to offer investors a return no worse than what investors could expect to obtain elsewhere. Thus, the cost of equity capital (money raised by selling shares of stock) to the firm is the return investors must receive in order not to take their money elsewhere. The supply of bonds comes from corporations and from the government, both of whom are issuing IOUs, or debt, in order to raise funds to purchase capital and other items. To sell the bonds, the interest rate on the bonds must be equal to or greater than the interest rate investors could get on comparable alternative investments.

2.c.1. Risk and the Cost of Capital
The cost of capital is the sum of the cost of bonds and the cost of shares of stock. The cost of bonds is the interest that has to be paid on those bonds. The cost of stocks is the amount that the investors would have to be paid not to move their funds to another firm, that is, the opportunity cost to investors of leaving their money with a particular firm. What is this cost? It depends on the firm. Kmart has to pay a higher cost of capital than Wal-Mart even though both are in the same business, Sequa a higher cost of capital than Boeing even though both build airplanes, Mesa a higher cost of capital than UAL even though both are airlines, and so on. In each case, the more risky firm has to pay a "risk premium."

What is risk? It is the possibility that some event, usually a bad event, will occur—the chance that an investment will do worse than alternatives. Suppose you have two alternative investments. In the first, you know with certainty you will get your money back plus an additional payment—the return on the investment. In the second, you may get a return but you may also get nothing. To be equally willing to give either alternative $20,000 of your money, you would require a higher possible return from the second than the first. For instance, suppose you are looking at a biotech start-up company as a possible investment. This investment could return several times the initial investment but it could also yield nothing. The other option you are considering is an established firm, Intel. Intel has been providing a return of about 25 percent per year during the past several years and it is very unlikely that the Intel investment will give you nothing back. Clearly, the biotech firm is a much more risky investment than Intel, and clearly the biotech firm will have to pay a substantial premium over Intel's cost of capital to entice investors to put their funds into the biotech company.

Rather than investing in the risky biotech firm or less risky Intel, investors could decide not to take any risk at all. They could purchase U.S. government bonds. Generally U.S. government bonds are considered risk-free because there is virtually no chance that the U.S. government would default on the bonds. Studies have shown that on average and over a long period of time, investors have to be paid about 6.5 percent per year more to invest in company stocks than in U.S. government securities. In other words, the long-term average cost of risk in the stock market (the risk premium) is about 6.5 percent per year. This means that a company of average risk would need to earn a rate of return about 6.5 percent more than the U.S. Treasury bond rate in order to reward its shareholders for the risks they had assumed. The interest rate on long-term U.S. bonds was about 6 percent in 2000. This means that a company of average risk would have a cost of capital of about 12.5 percent in 2000.

Figure 5

Intel Relative to the Market

Intel's stock price performance over a 20-year period is shown as the red line. The average firm's performance is shown as the blue line.

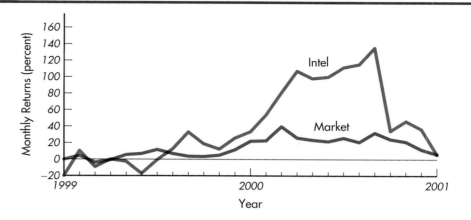

The riskiness of a firm is typically measured by comparing how much its stock price fluctuates compared to the average firm's. Figure 5 compares the returns on Intel stock to the average firm's over a two-year period. The red line is the Intel return, and it obviously, is more volatile than the market as a whole, illustrated by the blue line. This volatility means that Intel is more risky than the market on average. Suppose that Intel is about 1.5 percent more volatile than the market on average. This means Intel must compensate investors 14 percent to make them indifferent between keeping their shares of Intel or purchasing other stocks or U.S. government bonds. This is Intel's cost of capital. Similarly calculated estimates of the cost of capital for several other firms in 2000 are listed in Table 2.

? 6. What is the relationship between the value of a stock and economic profit?

2.d. Economic Profit

Recall once again that economic profit is accounting profit less the cost of equity capital. Economic profit tells us whether investors could do better putting their money into other activities. Consider the case of Coca-Cola. The firm had

Table 2

Cost of Capital, 2000

Company	Capital (millions)	Cost of Capital (percent)
Coca-Cola	$18,120	12.62
GE	$75,830	12.47
Merck	$29,553	10.72
Dell Computer	$ 1,330	14.79
e-bay	$ 1,038	13.55
Home Depot	$16,145	10.49
AOL	$ 4,482	15.53
Wal-Mart Stores	$54,013	10.99
The Gap	$ 6,720	11.21

$2.4 billion in accounting profits in 2000 and $18 billion of capital. A 12.62 percent cost of capital and $18 billion of capital means that the economic profit for Coca-Cola in 2000 was

$$Economic\ profit = \$2.4\ billion - \$18\ billion\ (0.1262)$$
$$= \$2.4\ billion - \$2.27\ billion$$
$$= \$.13\ billion$$

This is a positive economic profit; investors do not have an incentive to take their money out of Coca-Cola. In fact, other investors want to get in on the good thing. They would like to invest in Coca-Cola or in a competitor to Coca-Cola..

Does economic profit translate into high stock prices and increased shareholder value? The answer is yes, although it does not occur instantaneously. In any one year some of the top performing firms would have stock price gains that are greater than the average firm but some would have stock price gains that are less than the average firm. Over a longer period of time, say 5 or 10 years, the relationship between economic profit and share price performance is quite strong. The reason that the relationship is not perfect is that the stock market measures expectations—what investors expect to happen over the next day, month, year, or years. For example, because GE earns a significant economic profit investors expect its future profits to continue to be high and thus they expect its stock price to be high. For GE's stock price to climb further, its economic profit would have to be greater than expected.

Consider Glaxo-Wellcome's stock price experience when it announced a breakthrough medical treatment for HIV. In July 1996, the Eleventh International Conference on AIDS in Vancouver, British Columbia, reported on the successful effects of combining new AIDS drugs with the first AIDS drug, AZT. The *Wall Street Journal* reported that "prescriptions for AZT are surging as scientific evidence grows that using it in a cocktail with some of the newer drugs can make the presence of HIV virus in the blood undetectable."[1] Yet, when the announcement came out on July 11 about the AIDS cocktail, the stock of the pharmaceutical company owning AZT, Glaxo-Wellcome, hardly changed, trading for $22.25 per share rather than July 10's $22.5. It had traded for nearly $30 per share several months prior. The Glaxo experience indicates two things: first, the stocks reported in today's newspaper as the largest movers are not necessarily either the best or the worst companies in the market but instead are the companies about which new, unanticipated, information has become available; and second, information becomes available very quickly, much more quickly than a formal announcement at a conference. The Glaxo information had been reflected in stock prices at the time the studies were being completed, months before the July 11 conference. The conference just confirmed what had been anticipated.

Although stock prices are very volatile in the short-term, as the period over which we look back grows longer, firms that generated substantial economic profit are increasingly likely to have outperformed stock market expectations.

Stock price is the result of the demand for and supply of shares of the stock. If the demand increases while the supply remains about the same, then the price of the stock will rise. Why would demand increase? One reason is that investors expect the firm to perform better than other firms. Suppose an investor is considering two firms, A and B. The CEO for firm A is going to carry out an activity that will increase

---

[1]*Wall Street Journal,* July 11, 1996, p. B1.

profits next year but lead to losses in the following years. The CEO for firm B, on the other hand, is looking to the long term and wants to increase profits each year. The result of this is that firm B will not increase profits next year as much as firm A.

Investors, knowing the directions of the two CEOs, think to themselves, "I want to own firm A's stock only next year. I don't want to be holding it after that. But I don't want to be the last to sell. In fact, I want to be the first to sell and to own firm B as everyone else tries to buy firm B. So I should sell firm A's stock before the end of the year, perhaps in month 11. But others will expect me to do that and they will sell in month 10. So I will have to sell before that, in month 9, 8, . . ." The process of backing down the time of sale continues until the investor realizes that the only way she can gain is not to buy firm A but instead to buy firm B now. As other investors do the same, the stock price of A decreases now, not next year, and that of firm B rises now, not next year. *The stock price reflects the present value of the expected long-term economic profit stream.*

RECAP

1. Financial capital is the money acquired through taking out loans and selling shares of ownership in order to purchase physical capital.

2. Financial capital consists of the bonds a firm has issued and is acquired through the shares of stock that the firm has sold.

3. The return on a stock is the sum of the dividend on the stock and the capital gain. The dividend is the percentage of the price of the stock paid each year to shareholders. The capital gain is the increase in the price of the share of stock during the year.

4. The coupon on a bond is the fixed amount the borrower agrees to pay the bondholder each year. The maturity date is the time when the coupon payments end and the principal is paid back. The face value is the amount of principal that will be paid back when the bond matures.

5. There is an inverse relationship between the yield on a bond and its price. The yield is the annual rate of return on the bond if the bond is held to maturity.

6. The cost of capital consists of the cost of debt capital (interest on the bonds) and the cost of equity capital (the annual return necessary to keep investors from selling the shares of stock and putting their funds elsewhere).

7. There is a long-term link between economic profit and the value of shares of stock. During the long term, the more economic profit a firm earns, the better its stock market performance.

SUMMARY

❓ What role does saving play in the economy?

1. Saving is the process of using a portion of current production to acquire capital resources so that production can be increased in the future. *§1.a*

❓ When is a dollar tomorrow better than a dollar today?

2. Present value is the equivalent value today of some amount to be received in the future; future value is the equivalent value in the future of some amount received today. *§1.b.1*

? What is capital?

3. Capital is physical capital, the actual equipment and buildings used in production. *§1.b.1*

4. The demand for and supply of capital determine the price of capital and the quantity produced and purchased. A change in either demand or supply changes the price and quantity of capital. *§1.b.3*

5. When interest rates rises, the demand for capital decreases and the price of capital falls. This, in turn, raises the rate of return on capital. *§1.b.3*

6. The rate of return on capital and the interest rate tend toward equality. *§1.b.3*

? What is financial capital?

7. Financial capital is the funds used to aquire physical capital. These funds are raised by selling shares of stock (equity) and bonds (debt). *§2*

? How are the values of stocks and bonds determined?

8. The financial capital market determines the prices of stocks and bonds. *§2.c*

9. The price of a stock is determined by the demand for and supply of shares of that stock. The demand for stocks and bonds comes from investors who are seeking higher earnings than they are getting elsewhere. The supply comes from firms seeking funds with which to purchase physical capital or other resources. *§2.*

? What is the relationship between the value of a stock and economic profit?

10. Stock prices reflect the present value of the economic profit expected to be generated in the future. *§2.d*

KEY TERMS

saving *§1.a*
present value *§1.b.1*
future value *§1.b.1*
financial capital *§2*
annual return *§2.a*
dividend *§2.a*

capital gain *§2.a*
coupon *§2.b*
maturity date *§2.b*
face value *§2.b*
yield *§2.b*

EXERCISES

1. What is saving? Would seed be considered the savings of a gardener or farmer? Would expenditures on college be considered part of the savings of a household?

2. Financial capital refers to the stocks, bonds, and other financial instruments businesses use to raise money. What occurs to the present value of financial capital when the interest rate rises, everything else held constant?

3. You purchase a car for $2,000 down and $250 per month for five years. What is your total expenditure on the car? If the sticker price is $12,000, what is your total interest payment?

4. Calculate the present values of the following:

   a. $1,000 one year from today at interest rates of 5, 10, and 15 percent

   b. $1,000 per year for five years at interest rates of 5, 10, and 15 percent

5. Why are banks more willing to lend to a medical student than to a student in a vocational college?

6. Someone who expects to inherit a huge amount of income tends to be a borrower. Could an entire society expect future income to be much greater than current income and therefore borrow? If so, would the interest rate paid by that society tend to be higher or lower than the rate paid by a society that is not expecting future income growth? What would the change in the interest rate mean for capital accumulation?

7. Data appear to tell us that the saving rate in Japan is nearly three times the rate in the United States. If these data are correct, how might this difference affect the two economies?

8. Investors know for sure that the CEO of firm A will undertake an investment that yields $100 million profit next year and then $2 million each year after that for ten years. They also know for sure that the CEO of firm B will undertake an investment that yields nothing for two years and then a profit of $20 million per year for ten years. Which company will have the higher stock price today, next year, the second year, the third year?

9. The investors in exercise 8 are surprised by firm B's performance in year 5. Instead of $20 million, the profits are $40 million. What happens to firm B's stock price in years 1, 2, through year 7?

A Real Nail-Biter

TAMPA. It's one thing for a market to slide, but another thing for it to act as if it's bipolar.

That's the way it seemed Wednesday, when in the course of a single morning the Dow tumbled 433 points and then turned around. It closed down 114.69 at 9.975.02.

Experts call this seesawing "high intraday volatility."

It happens when the investors have been jittery anyway, making them extra vulnerable to more bits of bad news.

"Normal responses become magnified," said John P. Hussman, president of Hussman Econometrics Advisors in Cincinnati.

The market was already edgy over tension in the Mideast, the price of oil and the neck-and-neck presidential race, said Cheri Etling, assistant professor of finance at the University of Tampa's John H. Sykes College of Business.

Underlying all that, Hussman said, has been a nervousness among investors that the days of high stock prices—relative to earnings—soon may be over. Signs that the economy is slowing do not tend to support high prices.

Now, some individual investors are probably starting to suspect they paid too much for a stock, Hussman said. They feel like homeowners who bought a house at the top of the market, and then found out they won't get any price appreciation when they sell.

They're edgy and cranky.

Investors have been disappointed here and there over the past couple of weeks, Hussman said.

Intel, Apple and Home Depot all have said earnings are slowing.

"A lot of investors are starting to see catastrophes among individual stocks, so there's a temptation to get out or move to a more narrow strip of quality," he said.

Then along came the worrisome financial news from IBM, Hussman said, which meant even "that narrowing strip of quality was disappointing. That was why the market reacted so violently. It was IBM. It wasn't Priceline."

That accounts for the selling Wednesday morning. But not everybody was blue.

Some people were willing to buy—at lower prices—helping to push the market back up, creating the bipolar morning.

The market's optimists have been practically conditioned now to look at any price reduction as a chance to go out and buy some stocks on sale.

"The issue is," Hussman said, "who will win the day?"

Investors are still vulnerable to surprises. Hussman said many haven't accepted the idea the economy is slowing, and so have not adjusted their investing mentality to a more even keel.

Source: Copyright (Chart) Oh, that sinking feeling: The Dow Jones Industrial Average went into an early free-fall Wednesday morning and spent the rest of the day struggling to recover. Source: Bloomberg News Vaughn Hughes/Tribune chart.

The Tampa Tribune/October 19, 2000

Commentary

What does the term bipolar have to do with the stock market? The term describes a market that is high one hour and low the following hour. What makes a market manic-depressive? The simple answer is because the demand for stocks is fluctuating a great deal—the demand curve is shifting in and out. The reason that the demand is changing is investor expectations. If investors anticipate a future of positive economic profits for a firm, then the investors will want to invest in that firm by purchasing shares of the firm's stock. Conversely, if investors anticipate that economic profits will decline, then the investors will try to sell their shares of stock and purchase other shares or invest elsewhere. According to the article there is a "nervousness among investors that the days of high stock prices—relative to earnings—soon may be over. Signs that the economy is slowing do not tend to support high prices." Investors purchase a share of stock because they belive they will earn more from that investment than their other alternatives. If they begin to believe that the stock price will not rise in the future because the economy is slowing, investors may attempt to sell that stock. This leads to a stock price decline.

The article also notes that "some individual investors are probably starting to suspect they paid too much for a stock. They feel like homeowners who bought a house at the top of the market, and then found out they won't get any price appreciation when they sell." In other words, investors are think-ing that some other use of their funds will provide a greater return. When this occurs, funds are taken out of the stock market and placed elsewhere, driving stock prices down.

OK, so that explains why stock prices rise or fall, but what makes the stock market bipolar? The answer is that when investors are very uncertain as to whether the market will rise or fall, that is, whether firms will earn more or less economic profit, then they tend to react to any kind of news. If some firm announces it will have lower revenues than expected, sales of stock will occur. If a firm announces greater earnings than expected the stock will rise. In this environment, if the stock market experiences a rally and stock prices rise, then many investors begin to think that the firms will not be able to meet expectations about future economic profits and so will sell their stocks. This is called "profit taking." They attempt to take the profits they made from buying low and selling high and invest else-where. As investors take their profits, the stock market declines. This in turn leads other investors to sell in an attempt to avoid losses. The market decline gathers force until investors begin to expect that prices are low enough that firms will be able to generate sufficient economic profits in the future to justify the stock price. As these investors begin to purchase shares of stock, the market decline slows and a rally begins. Bipolar perhaps but quite logical; stock price movements are based on expectations of future economic profits.

Chapter 18

The Land Market: Natural Resources and Environmental Policy

? **Fundamental Questions**

1. **What is the difference between renewable and nonrenewable natural resources?**

2. **What is the optimal rate of use of natural resources?**

3. **Why might a market not result in the best use of the environment?**

4. **Why does the government get involved in environmental policy?**

5. **Why are global environmental problems so difficult to solve?**

Global warming, the destruction of the rain forest, the depletion of the ozone, the extinction of animal species, and other environmental issues are of great concern to many people. So are the costs that people have to pay in the name of the environment: higher prices on cars due to emission controls, annual fees to test for emissions from cars, higher gas prices due to refining requirements, higher taxes to pay for cleaning up the environment, and so on. In this chapter we examine the market for natural resources and discuss environmental issues and policy. ■

Preview

1. **What is the difference between renewable and nonrenewable natural resources?**

nonrenewable (exhaustible) natural resources: natural resources whose supply is fixed

renewable (nonexhaustible) natural resources: natural resources whose supply can be replenished

1. NATURAL RESOURCES

The category of resources we call "land" refers not just to land surface but to everything associated with the land—the natural resources. Natural resources are the nonproduced resources with which a society is endowed.

Nonrenewable (exhaustible) natural resources can be used only once and cannot be replaced. Examples include coal, natural gas, and oil. **Renewable (nonexhaustible) natural resources** can be used repeatedly without depleting the amount available for future use. Examples include the land, sea, rivers, and lakes. Plants and animals are classified as nonexhaustible natural resources because it is possible for them to renew themselves and thus replace those used in production and consumption activities. The prices of natural resources and the quantities used are determined in the market for natural resources.

1.a. The Market for Nonrenewable Resources

The market for nonrenewable natural resources consists of the demand for and supply of these resources. Supply depends on the amount of the resource in existence, and the supply curve is perfectly inelastic. Only a fixed amount of oil or coal exists, so the more that is used in any given year, the less that remains for future use. This means that an upward-sloping supply curve exists for a particular period of time, such as a year. The quantity that resource owners are willing to extract and offer for sale during any particular year depends on the price of the resource. The supply curve in Figure 1(a) is upward sloping to reflect the relationship between the price of the resource today and the amount extracted and offered to users today. Resource owners are willing to extract more of a resource from its natural state and offer it for sale as the price of the resource increases.

As some of the resource is used today, less is available next year. The supply curve of the resource in the future shifts up, as shown in Figure 1(b) by the move from S_1 to S_2. The shift occurs because the cost of extracting any quantity of the resource rises as the amount of the resource in existence falls. The first amounts extracted come from the most accessible sources, and each additional quantity then comes from a less accessible source. For instance, in the late 1800s, oil became an important resource. At first, it was extracted with small pumps that gathered up oil seeping out of the ground. Once that extremely accessible source was gone, wells had to be dug. Over time, wells had to be deeper and be placed in progressively more difficult terrain. From land, to the ocean off California, to the rugged waters off Alaska, to the wicked North Sea, the search for oil has progressed. As more and more is extracted, the marginal cost of extracting any given amount increases, and the supply curve shifts up.

If 200 billion barrels of crude oil are extracted this year, then in the future the extraction of another 200 billion barrels will be more difficult—more expensive—than the extraction of the 200 billion barrels was this year. This increase is illustrated by an upward shift of the supply curve in Figure 1(b). Figure 1(c) illustrates how the supply of a nonrenewable resource decreases over time as additional amounts of the resource are used. The curve S_1 is the supply in 1995, S_2 in 1996, S_3 in 1997, and so on, as more of the resource is used each year.

The demand for a nonrenewable natural resource is determined in the same way as the demand for any other resource. It is the marginal revenue product of the resource. Thus, anything that affects the *MRP* of the nonrenewable resource will affect the demand for that resource.

Figure 1

The Market for Nonrenewable Resources

The demand curve slopes down, and the supply curve slopes up. The intersection of demand and supply determines the quantity used today and the price at which the quantity was sold, as shown in Figure 1(a). As quantities are used today, less remains for the future. Because the available quantities come from increasingly more expensive sources, the supply curve shifts up over time, as shown in Figure 1(b). The curve S_1 represents the quantities supplied in 1890 at $1 per barrel, and S_2 represents the quantities supplied today at $17 per barrel. Figure 1(c) shows the effect on the supply of a resource over time as more of the resource is extracted. If 200 billion barrels of crude oil are extracted this year, then next year the extraction of 200 billion barrels will be more difficult—more expensive—than the extraction of 200 billion barrels was this year. The curve S_1 is the supply in 1995, S_2 the supply in 1996, and so on, as more of the resource is used each year.

(a) Demand and Supply

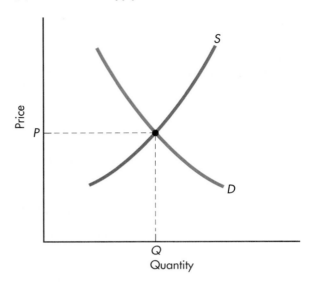

Equilibrium occurs in the market for a nonrenewable natural resource when the demand and supply curves intersect, as shown in Figure 2. The equilibrium price, $15, and quantity, 200 billion barrels, represent the price and quantity today. Extracting and selling the equilibrium quantity of 200 billion barrels today reduces the quantity available tomorrow by 200 billion barrels. This means that extracting the resource tomorrow is probably going to be more costly than extracting it today. Thus, the supply curve for the resource in the future lies above the supply curve for today, S_2 rather than S_1, if any of the resource is being consumed today. With a higher supply curve and the same demand, the price is higher, $20 rather than $15. Thus, the price in the future is likely to be higher than the price today if some of the resource is extracted and sold today.

The resource owner must decide whether to extract and sell the resource today or leave it in the ground for future use. Suppose that by extracting and selling the oil that lies below someone's land today, the landowner can make a profit of $10 per barrel after all costs of extraction have been paid. With that $10 the owner could buy stocks or bonds or put the money into a savings account or use it to acquire education or marketable skills. If the interest rate is 10 percent, the owner could realize $11 one year from now from the $10 profit obtained today. Should the oil be extracted today? The answer depends on how much profit the resource owner expects to earn on the oil one year from now, and this depends on what the price of oil and the cost of extraction are one year from now. In other words, the answer depends on whether the present value of extracting and selling the resources exceeds the present value of leaving the resource in the ground.

If the owner expects to obtain a profit of $13 a barrel one year from now, the present value of that $13 at a 10 percent rate of interest is $13/1.1 = $11.82. Clearly, the oil should be left in the ground. If the profit on the oil one year from now is expected to be only $10.50, the present value is $10.50/1.1 = $9.55. In this case, the oil should be extracted and the proceeds used to buy stocks, bonds, or savings accounts.

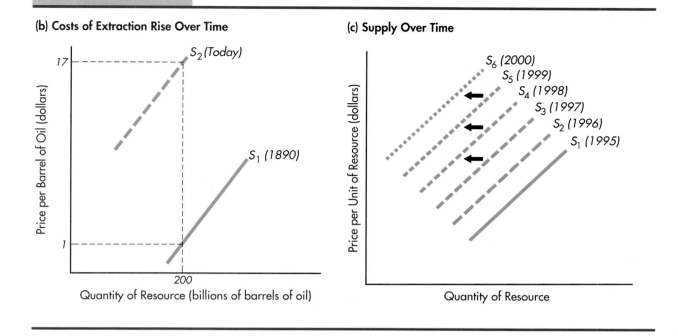

(b) Costs of Extraction Rise Over Time

Price per Barrel of Oil (dollars)

S_2 (Today)

17

S_1 (1890)

1

200

Quantity of Resource (billions of barrels of oil)

(c) Supply Over Time

Price per Unit of Resource (dollars)

S_6 (2000)
S_5 (1999)
S_4 (1998)
S_3 (1997)
S_2 (1996)
S_1 (1995)

Quantity of Resource

If the profit one year from now is $11 a barrel, the present value is $10; the same whether the oil is extracted today or next year.

As discussed in the previous chapter, the present value declines as the interest rate rises. Should the interest rate rise from 10 percent to 15 percent, then the present value of $11.50 one year from now is $10. A profit per barrel exceeding $11.50 next

Figure 2

Price Today and in the Future

Equilibrium occurs in the market for an exhaustible natural resource when the demand and supply curves intersect. The equilibrium price, $15, and quantity, 200 billion barrels, represent the price and quantity of the resource used today. Selling the equilibrium quantity of 200 billion barrels today reduces the quantity available tomorrow by 200 billion barrels. With a smaller and probably less accessible quantity, extracting the resource tomorrow is probably going to be more costly than extracting it today. Thus, the supply curve for the resource in the future lies above the supply curve for today, S_2 rather than S_1, if any of the resource is being consumed today. With a higher supply curve, the price is higher, $20 rather than $15. Thus, the price in the future is likely to be higher than the price today.

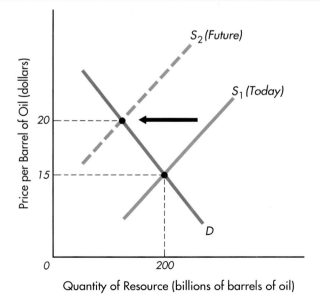

S_2 (Future)

S_1 (Today)

Price per Barrel of Oil (dollars)

20

15

D

0

200

Quantity of Resource (billions of barrels of oil)

2. What is the optimal rate of use of natural resources?

year would be necessary to leave the oil in the ground. As the interest rate rises, more is extracted and sold today and less is left for the future.

Because suppliers and potential suppliers continually calculate whether to extract now or in the future and how much to extract, an equilibrium arises where the present value of profit in the future just equals the value today; for this to occur, the year-to-year rate of increase in the price of the resource must equal the rate of interest on alternative uses of the funds. If the rate of interest is 10 percent a year, everything else held constant, the resource price will rise at a rate of about 10 percent a year.

If the present values of extracting and selling the resources now and of leaving them in the ground until a point in the future are to be equal, then the higher the interest rate, the greater the spread between present and future prices of an exhaustible resource must be. Suppose the interest rate rises above the current rate of return on the nonrenewable resource, oil. The higher interest rate means that producers looking to pump the oil out of the ground will pump more today and purchase stocks, bonds, or savings accounts with the money they get from selling the oil. More extraction means that the supply curve today shifts out and today's price falls. At the same time, the supply curve in the future shifts in (since less will be available in the future) and the future price rises. This will occur until the rate of return on leaving the oil in the ground equals the interest rate—that is, until the present value of pumping the oil and selling it is the same as the present value of the oil left in the ground. A higher interest rate implies the use of more resources today. Conversely, a lower interest rate implies the use of fewer resources today.

1.b. The Market for Renewable Resources

Renewable resources, unlike exhaustible, or nonrenewable, resources, can replenish themselves. Forests and wildlife can reproduce and renew their supplies. The role of the market for renewable resources is to determine a price at which the quantity of the resource used is just sufficient to enable the resource to renew itself at a rate that best satisfies society's wants.

Owners of forest lands could harvest all their trees in one year and reap a huge profit. But if they did so, several years would pass before the trees had grown enough to be cut again. The rate at which the trees are harvested depends on the interest rate. A large harvest one year means fewer trees available in the future and a longer time for renewal to occur. This would suggest a lower price today and a higher price in the future. If the interest rate rises, everything else held constant, owners will want to increase harvesting in order to get more money with which to purchase stocks and bonds. This would mean more trees now and fewer in the future, thereby driving up the price of the trees not cut today. If the interest rate falls, owners will want to harvest fewer trees today. This would mean that today's price will rise and the future price will fall. As was the case with the nonrenewable resources, the market adjusts so that the resources are allocated to their highest-valued use now and in the future. The timing of the use of resources depends on the rate of interest.

In summary, the markets for nonrenewable and renewable resources operate to ensure that current and future wants are satisfied in the least costly manner and that resources are used in their highest-valued alternative now and in the future. When a nonrenewable resource is being rapidly depleted, its future price rises and the present value of using the resource in the future rises so that less of the resource is used today. When a renewable resource is being used at a rate that does not allow the resource to replenish itself, the future price rises and the present value of the future use rises so that less of the resource is used today.

1. Nonrenewable natural resources are natural resources whose supply is fixed.

2. Renewable natural resources are natural resources that can be replenished.

3. The gap between the equilibrium price today and the equilibrium price at some point in the future generates a rate of return on nonrenewable resources that is equal to the interest rate on comparable assets.

4. Changes in the interest rate lead to different rates of use of nonrenewable resources.

5. The harvest rate of renewable resources is such that the rate of return on the resources is equal to the interest rate on comparable assets.

3. Why might a market not result in the best use of the environment?

market failure: occurs when consumers or producers do not have to bear the full costs of transactions they undertake

private costs: costs borne by the individual involved in the transaction that created the costs

2. ENVIRONMENTAL PROBLEMS

If the market for natural resources allocates resources to their most highly valued use today and in the future, why do we hear so much about the depletion of the ozone layer, the destruction of the rain forest, the pollution of the oceans and rivers, and the depletion of wildlife? Part of the answer may stem from problems created when private individuals and businesses lack incentives to take full account of the consequences of their actions. When consumers or producers do not have to bear the full costs of transactions they undertake, a **market failure** is said to have occurred. These market failures can be traced to two sources: externalities and public goods.

2.a. The Definition of Externalities

A business firm knows how much it costs to employ workers, and it knows the costs of purchasing materials or constructing buildings. An individual who buys a new car or pays for a pizza knows exactly what the cost will be. Such costs are **private costs:** They are costs borne solely by the individuals involved in the transaction that created the costs. Many environmental problems arise, however, because the costs of an individual's actions are *not* borne directly by that individual. When a firm pollutes the air or water or when a tourist leaves trash in a park, the cost of the action is not easily determined and is not borne by the individual or firm creating it. This situation represents a market failure because the price of the good and the equilibrium quantity produced and consumed do not reflect the full costs of producing or consuming the good. In this sense, "too much" or "too little" is produced.

Consider an oil tanker that runs aground and dumps crude oil into a pristine ocean area teeming with wildlife, or a public beach where people litter, or even your classrooms where people leave their cups, used papers, and food wrappers on the floor. A cost is involved in these actions: the crude oil may kill wildlife and ruin fishing industries, the trash may discourage families from using the beach, and the trash in the classroom may distract from the discussions and lectures. But in none of these cases is the cost of the action solely borne by the individuals who took the action. Instead, the cost is also borne by those who were not participants in the activity. The fishermen, the fish, and other wildlife did not spill the oil, yet they have to bear the cost. The beachgoers who encounter trash and broken bottles were not the litterers, yet they must bear the cost. Many students and professors do not litter and yet must wade through the trash. The cost is external to the activity and is thus called an

externality: a cost or benefit of an activity that is borne by parties not directly involved in the activity; an external cost or benefit

social costs: the sum of private costs and externalities

When social and private costs are not the same, then either too much or too little production occurs.

externality, specifically a *negative externality*. When externalities are added to private costs, the result is **social costs:**

$$\text{Social costs} = \text{private costs} + \text{externalities}$$

When private costs differ from social costs, individual decision makers ignore externalities. The full opportunity cost of using a scarce resource, for example, is borne not by the producer or the consumer but by society. The difference between the private cost and the full opportunity, or social, cost is the externality.

A *positive externality* may result from an activity in which benefits are received by consumers or firms not involved directly in the activity. For instance, inoculations for mumps, measles, and other communicable diseases provide benefits to all of society. The private costs of acquiring the inoculations exceed the social costs by the amount of the externality.

When there is a divergence between social costs and private costs, the result is either too much or too little production and consumption. In either case, resources are not being used in their highest-valued activity. For instance, those who pollute do not bear the entire costs of the pollution, and therefore pollute more than they otherwise would.

Consider a gas station selling gasoline with pumps that have no emission control equipment. Each time a consumer pumps gas, a certain quantity of pollutants is released into the air. The consumer demands gasoline at various prices as reflected by the demand curve. The gas station prices the gasoline in order to maximize profit—by equating marginal revenue and marginal cost and setting prices as given by the demand curve at the quantity where marginal revenue and marginal cost are equal, see Figure 3. The actual cost of the gasoline to society—including the private marginal cost and the externality—is given by the marginal-social-cost curve, *MSC*. Society would like the price to be set at P_{MSC} rather than P_{MC} and the quantity to be

Figure 3

Externalities

A firm selling a product whose consumption generates a social cost would sell the amount given by *MR = MC*, ignoring the social costs. Society would prefer the price and quantity given by *MR = MSC* in order to take into account the social costs.

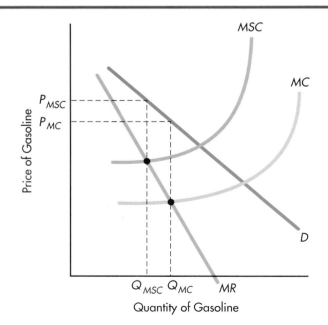

purchased to be Q_{MSC} rather than Q_{MC}. According to society's desires, "too much" gasoline is purchased.

In contrast to negative externalities, private costs exceed social costs when external benefits are created. From society's viewpoint, too few people would be vaccinated from communicable diseases if individuals bore all the costs of inoculations. In the case of a positive externality, the *MSC* curve would lie below the *MC* curve and "too little" of the good or service would be produced and purchased.

2.b. Private Property Rights and Externalities

private property right: the right to claim ownership of an item

Market failures may result because of the absence of well-defined **private property rights.** A private property right is the right to claim ownership of an item; it is well defined if there is a clear owner and if the right is recognized and enforced by society. Consider the pollution caused by auto emissions. Each driver of a car is imposing an externality on you. The problem is that neither you nor the driver owns the airspace in which the emissions occur. If you did, you could restrict the driving activity or you could charge the driver a price that would pay for the externality. If the driver owned the airspace, you would have to pay the driver not to drive and pollute. In either case, the externality would no longer be external; it would be part of the private costs.

Figure 4 shows the driver's demand (the marginal revenue product) for the driving and pollution, what we call the marginal benefits (*MB*) curve. The marginal benefits curve measures the additional benefits of consuming one more quantity of something. The first amount of driving—getting the driver to a job or necessary location—is very beneficial. As more and more driving occurs, the marginal benefits decline. The marginal costs (*MC*) to the driver of driving and polluting—additional time spent behind the wheel, additional frustration at not being at work or having fun, additional wear and tear on the car—rise as more driving occurs. The

Figure 4

Externalities

The marginal costs borne by the driver are shown by the rising curve *MC*. The costs the driver imposes on others exceed his private costs. As a result, the marginal-social-cost curve, *MSC*, lies above the marginal-cost curve. The marginal benefits from driving are indicated by the downward-sloping curve, *MB*. The amount of driving is given by the point where the *MC* curve and the *MB* curve intersect, Q_B. According to society, too much driving occurs. Society would choose the quantity Q_S, where marginal social costs and marginal benefits are equal. The solution to the externalities problem is to equate private costs and social costs.

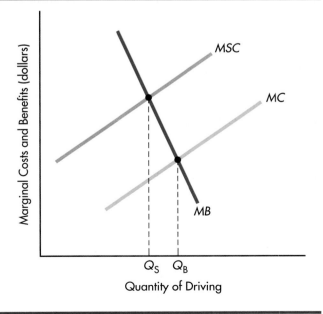

marginal cost of the driver does not measure the full costs of the driving; it does not include the additional pollutants created by the driving. The *full costs,* including the costs imposed on you and everyone else, are the **marginal social costs,** shown as the upward-sloping curve *MSC,* which lies above the *MC* curve.

marginal social costs: the additional private and external costs of producing or consuming one more unit of a good or service

The driver chooses the amount of driving indicated by the intersection of the *MC* and *MB* curves, quantity Q_B. This is an amount greater than is desired by society (you and others). The amount of activity you would desire is indicated by the intersection of the *MSC* curve and the *MB* curve, quantity Q_S. Thus, "too much" driving is provided because the *MC* curve does not take into account all costs. The market has failed to generate the "right" amount of pollution. The reason stems from the fact that no one owns the air; that is, no one has a private property right to the air.

The absence of a well-defined private property right may result in a market failure.

The lack of private property ownership or rights is a common one in the natural resources area. No one has a private property right to the ocean. No one owns the fish in the sea; no one owns the elephants that roam the African plains; and during the past one hundred years no one owned the American buffalo or bald eagle. Because no one owns these natural resources, a "too rapid" rate of use or harvest occurs.

The waters off New England once were among the world's most fertile fishing grounds. Now, fish are severely depleted in the area known as Georges Bank. Overfishing resulting from a lack of private property rights was fueled by the nation's increasing appetite for fish and by technological changes in fishing. A single fishing vessel using radar, sonar, spotter planes, sea-surface observations from satellites, advanced catching gear, onboard processing, and refrigeration can do the job of a hundred older boats and in less time. The Economic Insight "The Problems of Common Ownership" discusses some of the results of private and common ownership of resources.

The resource markets would solve the problem of harvesting now or in the future if someone owned the oceans or the fish. The prices would adjust until the present values of harvesting and not harvesting would be the same. Without private ownership, however, no one has the incentive to sell the resources at the profit-maximizing rate. A fishing crew has no incentive to harvest the "right" amount of fish, since leaving fish until the future simply leaves them for other fishing crews today. If someone owned the fish, that resource owner would sell the fish only up to the point that the present value of fish caught in the future would equal the present value of the revenue obtained from the fish caught today.

2.c. Public Goods

principle of mutual exclusivity: the owner of private property is entitled to enjoy the consumption of the property privately

public good: a good for which the principle of mutual exclusivity does not hold

According to the **principle of mutual exclusivity,** the owner of private property is entitled to enjoy the consumption of private property privately. The principle of mutual exclusivity refers to a well-defined private property right. It says that if you own a good, I cannot use it; and if I own a good, you cannot use it. When I purchase a pizza, it is mine to consume as I wish. You have absolutely no right to the pizza unless I provide that right. However, a good or service may also be a **public good,** a good for which the principle of mutual exclusivity does not apply. If you use a public good, I may also. Moreover, a public good is a good or service whose use by one consumer does not diminish the quantity available for other consumers.

The airwaves illustrate the characteristics of a public good quite well. A television station broadcasts on a certain frequency, and anyone can pick up that station. It doesn't matter whether one person or 1 million people tune in to the station, the signal is the same and additional users do not deprive others of any of the public good. If your neighbor tunes in to the channel you are watching, you don't receive a weaker signal.

The Problems of Common Ownership

Lured by the opportunity to earn a year's wages with one squeeze of the trigger, poachers have slaughtered elephants by the tens of thousands. A decade ago, Africa's elephant population was more than a million; it has now fallen to less than half of that. Environmentalists in the United States trying to save the flora and fauna of the ancient forests in the Pacific Northwest are battling local loggers, who see the trees as a means to feed their families. Thousands of acres of Amazon forest are burned each year to provide land for Brazil's ranchers and subsistence farmers, eliminating hundreds of species of plants and animals. The swordfish is being fished to extinction. These and other similar problems result from common ownership. When no one owns the land or the wildlife, no one has an incentive to harvest quantities that ensure reproduction and renewal.

Policies regarding forests illustrate the problem of common ownership. The government of Ontario, Canada, fights with small, private owners of forest lands over how to manage the trees. The Ontario government wants to cut the trees down and sell them, but private owners refuse to clear-cut their private forests (the process of cutting down all the trees in an area). Stories about deforestation and the degradation of Ontario's forest lands make the papers every

day in Ontario, but the private sector, which owns less than 10 percent of the timber, is not to blame. The deforestation is occurring on the government's land.

Sweden has more standing forest today than at any time in its past. Unlike Canada, most of the forest land in Sweden is privately owned. Neighboring Finland also has a huge forest industry and more forest than ever before. It too has mostly privately owned forest lands. In the less developed countries as well, common ownership encourages deforestation. In Brazil's Amazon basin, the government has subsidized the tearing down and burning of a forested area bigger than France. Deforestation has occurred in other regions of Latin America, several Asian nations, and much of Africa. In each case where there is common ownership, there is a problem with the rate of harvest. The difference is that private owners do not cut at a loss and do not cut to maintain employment levels or for other political reasons. They cut at a rate that yields them the greatest return—a rate of return that matches the rates of return earned on alternative assets.

The problems of the African elephant, the swordfish, and other species of plants and animals that are being depleted are no different from the problem of the forests.

Proposed solutions typically call for bans on the killing of the species. For example, Kenya, Tanzania, and several other African nations, with the support of most of the developed nations, are banning the trade of ivory in order to protect African elephants. The elephants' problem may stem partly from the demand for ivory, but it also stems from common ownership of the elephant and the low incomes of the African peoples. To a small farmer in Kenya whose crops are threatened by an elephant, the killing of the elephant means the survival of his family. If the farmer owned the elephants, had enough land to harvest food for them, and could then sell them, the plight of the elephant would change. Once in a while, someone proposes and implements a private ownership system. In South Africa, Zimbabwe, and Botswana, the government gives elephants to certain tribes to be harvested for ivory and for tourism. In those countries, elephants have not declined, and the living standards of the poorest tribes have improved. A ban on ivory in these countries would destroy the industry and lead to the destruction of the animals.

Sources: John H. Cushman, Jr., "World Group to Debate Plan to Protect Species by Numbers," *New York Times*, November 6, 1994, p. 44; Victoria Butler, "Is This the Way to Save Africa's Wildlife?" *International Wildlife*, March 1995, p. 38.

---

free rider: a consumer or producer who enjoys the benefits of a good or service without paying for it

When goods are public, an individual has an incentive to be a **free rider**—a consumer or producer who enjoys a good without paying for it. As an example, suppose that national defense was not provided by the government and paid for with tax money. Suppose that you would not be protected by the armed forces unless you paid a fee. A problem would arise because national defense is a public good; you would be protected whether or not you paid for it as long as others paid. Of course, since each person has an incentive not to pay for it, few voluntarily do and the

	Willingness to Pay		
Quantity	Jesse	Rafael	Total Willingness to Pay
1	$5	$3	$8
2	$4	$2	$6
3	$3	$1	$4
4	$2	$0	$2

Table 1

The Demand for a Public Good

quantity of the good produced is too small from society's viewpoint. Similarly, clean air and the ozone layer may be public goods. Each person has an incentive to use the good without paying for it, and many people can consume the good simultaneously. As a result, not enough people pay to improve the air quality or to protect the ozone layer, and the resulting environmental quality is lower than society would like.

2.c.1. The Demand for Public Goods

A private good comes in units that can be purchased by individuals, and once the good is purchased, the individual owns it and can decide how to consume it. The market demand curve is the *horizontal* summation of the individual demand curves. A public good, in contrast, is not divisible into units that can be purchased and owned by the buyers. Once the good is produced, the producer is unable to exclude nonpayers from consuming the good. Since they can enjoy the good without paying for it, many individuals will not pay for it. The demand curve for the public good may not exist.

Suppose there are two people in society, Jesse and Rafael, whose demands for a public good are shown in Table 1. The demands show how much each would be *willing* and *able* to pay per unit for the various quantities of the public good. Once the good is produced, however, neither Jesse nor Rafael has any incentive to pay for it. Jesse would be willing and able to pay $5 for one unit of the good, and Rafael would be willing and able to pay $3 for one unit. But neither has an incentive to actually pay anything. The last column in Table 1 shows the total amount society (Jesse and Rafael) would be willing and able to pay for various quantities of the public good. In contrast to the private good, where the market demand is the horizontal summation of the individual demands, the market demand for the public good is the *vertical* summation of the individual demand curves. The market demand for the public good shows how much society would be willing and able to pay for various quantities of a public good. Again, the problem is that the existence of this market demand curve does not mean that people will actually pay for the good; once produced, no one has an incentive to pay for it. There is, therefore, a market failure.

The market demand curve for a public good is derived by summing vertically all individual demand curves.

RECAP

1. Externalities occur when all of the costs of production or consumption are not borne by the private individuals involved in a transaction.

2. Externalities are market failures because the market does not determine the level of a good that society desires. A market failure occurs when social costs and benefits are not equal.

3. A market failure may result when private property rights are not well defined.

4. A public good is a good for which the principle of mutual exclusivity does not hold and thus free riding exists.

5. Free riding occurs when people can enjoy an activity without having to bear any costs for the activity.

6. Market failures may occur in the case of a public good. The demand for the public good may not exist because no one has an incentive to pay for the public good once it is produced.

The Botswana, Zimbabwe, and South African governments allow individuals to own elephants. These elephant "farmers" ensure that the elephants breed and reproduce so that they can be sold for their tusks, for hunting in special hunting parks, or to zoos in developed nations. This privatization has led to a revival of the elephant population in these nations. Most other nations have created national parks in which hunting is forbidden, and the results have not stemmed the tide of extinction of the species. These orphaned elephants are being cared for at a wildlife preserve in Kenya.

4. Why does the government get involved in environmental policy?

3. PUBLIC POLICIES

A market failure means too much of the rain forest is destroyed, too many emissions are spewed out into the ozone, too many fish are caught, or too many species are decimated by overuse of resources. If the market fails to correct these problems, what is the answer? Recall from earlier chapters that when people do not like the market outcome or when the market is inefficient, the government is often called on to intervene in the market. This is the case of environmental problems. The government has taken a huge role in environmental policy. In the United States, the Environmental Protection Agency (EPA) has grown more rapidly than any other agency in the last ten years. Faced with environmental problems, what does the EPA do?

3.a. Externalities

The government is called on to resolve market failures. It may levy taxes or subsidies, produce public goods, or assign private property rights.

Let's begin with the externality problem. Since the problem is that the marginal social cost (MSC) is not equal to the private marginal cost (MC), the solution requires that the two be made equal. How can the creators of the externality be required to take the externality into account, to *internalize* the externality? Externalities can be internalized through the imposition of regulations or taxes, the use of subsidies, or the assignment of private property rights.

3.a.1. Regulation

One form of environmental regulation is an **emission standard** that specifies the maximum level of pollution allowed from a specific source. Each automaker, for instance, must create a line of cars that meets fixed emission standards. Emission standards are also applied to steel factories, electric power plants, and many other industries.

The government defines an emission level and requires firms to meet the standards. Economists argue that the level should be determined by demand and supply—that is, by equating marginal benefits and marginal social costs. Figure 5 shows the market for pollution. (Alternatively, we could show the market for clean air, since the two, clean air and polluted air, add up to 100 percent.) The marginal costs and benefits of pollution are measured on the vertical axis. The horizontal axis measures the quantity of pollution, from perfectly clean air (0 on the graph) to totally polluted air (100 on the graph). Moving away from the origin along the horizontal axis, the percentage of polluted air rises (the particles of dirty air increase). When the air is perfectly clean (0 on the graph), the marginal benefit of a particle of pollutants emitted in the air is quite high. As the air becomes dirtier and dirtier, the marginal benefit of a few more polluted particles of air falls, as seen by the downward slope of the marginal-benefit curve, *MB*.

The marginal cost (*MC*) of dirty air rises at an accelerating rate because of diminishing marginal returns. The first 10 percent increase in pollutants occurs easily and is accomplished by not using the very expensive pollution abatement devices installed on automobiles and smokestacks. As the air gets dirtier and dirtier, the benefits a firm or individual might get from some additional pollution are quite small. The difference between the marginal cost and the marginal social cost (*MSC*) is that the marginal cost refers to the individual's private costs while the marginal social

---

Figure 5

The Optimal Amount of Pollution

The horizontal axis measures the quantity of pollution, from perfectly clean air (0 on the graph) to perfectly filthy air (100 on the graph). Moving away from the origin along the horizontal axis, the percentage of polluted air rises (the particles of dirty air increase). When the air is perfectly clean (0 on the graph), the marginal benefit of a particle of pollutants emitted in the air is quite high. As the air becomes dirtier and dirtier, the marginal benefit of a few more polluted particles of air falls, as seen by the downward slope of the marginal-benefit curve, *MB*. The optimal amount of pollution is determined by the intersection of the *MSC* and *MB* curves: 30 percent dirty air. This is a greater amount of clean air (less pollution) than is determined in the market, where private marginal costs, *MC (private)*, are equal to marginal benefits *(MB)*, or 50 percent dirty air. If a standard greater than 70 percent clean air is set by the government, the demand exceeds the marginal social costs. If a 100 percent clean air standard is set, the marginal benefits exceed the marginal social costs by the distance *AC*.

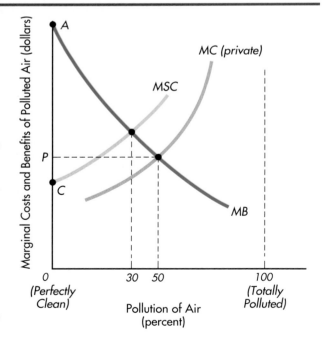

cost refers to society's marginal costs. When I drive my automobile, the costs of the pollution I create are borne by me in the sense that I have to purchase oxygenated fuels and maintain the quality of my car, but costs are also borne by others. Everyone has to breathe the polluted air I create.

The optimal amount of pollution for society is indicated by the intersection of the marginal-social-cost and marginal-benefit curves. This amount—30 percent in this example—is optimal because marginal social costs and marginal benefits are equalized, not because pollution is eliminated (it isn't). At 100 percent cleanliness, the demand for pollution (the marginal benefits) would greatly exceed the marginal costs, by the distance AC.

In reality, the emission level is seldom set at the optimal level. Moreover, the regulations may cause other problems. One hallmark of the standards approach is uniformity: standards apply to all firms and all areas. However, standards appropriate for small firms may be inappropriate for large firms, or standards appropriate for one area may be inappropriate for another. An emission standard for automobiles that is appropriate for Los Angeles would not necessarily be appropriate for Salem, Idaho. An emission standard applied to fishing might restrict the quantity of fish caught per shift. This might be appropriate in the mountain streams of Vermont, but not in Chesapeake Bay.

The regulatory approach also fails to account for private responses that tend to neutralize its impact. For example, a common regulatory practice is to impose standards for new products that are tougher than standards for existing products. This practice induces producers to remain with older products even though they may be environmentally damaging. As a result, the regulation may raise pollution levels higher than they would have been without regulation. Such was the case with the 1990 Clean Air Act. Standards for planned coal plants are tougher than for existing plants. The effect is that firms continue to use old plants even when more efficient or environmentally less damaging plants would be feasible.

Uniform standards can also be problematic if they aid large or existing firms in their attempts to keep smaller or new firms from competing. For instance, the Resource Conservation and Recovery Act, which covers the disposal of more than 450 substances, has 17,000 rulings related to it. These rulings mean that it can cost millions and take years to get approval to operate a business.[1] This is a fixed cost that makes it more difficult for new firms to enter the industry and begin competing with existing firms.

3.a.2. Taxes or Subsidies

An alternative to the problems caused by regulatory standards is to levy taxes or provide subsidies to resolve the market failure. Society might want to tax actions that cause a negative externality and subsidize actions that cause a positive externality, by the amount of the externality. In this way, social costs and private costs would be the same. A tax could be placed on automobiles or smokestacks or on products that create litter or damage the ozone layer. The tax would increase the price to the full cost—internal plus external costs—and consumers and producers would have to take the full cost into account in their decision making.

For instance, instead of mandating that automobile manufacturers install expensive pollution control equipment on all new cars (the costs of which would be paid by every car buyer nationwide), the government could impose a tax on drivers whose cars exceed federally set emission limits. That way the individual could

---

[1]David Brooks, "Saving the Earth from Its Friends," *National Review,* April 1, 1990, pp. 28–31.

Figure 6

The Effect of an Effluent Charge

The figure illustrates the demand for and supply of pollution. The amount of pollution that occurs in the absence of a tax is Q_1, at the intersection of S_1 and D_1. An emissions charge levied on waste tends to make pollution more expensive by the amount of the tax. In other words, producers can decide to pollute the same amount and pay the tax or pollute less and pay less tax. The supply curve shifts up to S_2, and the new amount of pollution is Q_2.

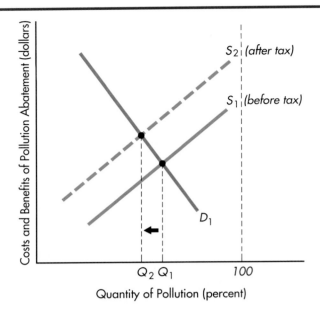

decide whether to drive an old junker that produces a lot of pollution. With the government mandate, new cars become relatively more expensive than the junkers and so people drive junkers longer than they otherwise would have.

A common use of taxes on externalities is the effluent charge—a charge on waste produced or emissions generated. With a tax on emissions, polluters can choose to install pollution abatement equipment, change production techniques so as to reduce pollution-causing activities, or pay the tax and continue to pollute.

Figure 6 illustrates the demand for and supply of pollution. The amount of pollution that occurs in the absence of a tax is Q_1, at the intersection of S_1 and D_1. An emissions charge levied on waste tends to make pollution more expensive by the amount of the tax. In other words, producers can decide to pollute the same amount and pay the tax or pollute less and pay less tax. The supply curve shifts up to S_2, and the new amount of pollution is Q_2.

Although the effluent tax enables individuals to decide whether to pollute and thus relies on self-interest to reduce pollution, the tax can be difficult to administer. A problem with effluent charges is discovering where the supply and demand curves are located and determining what charge is necessary to cover the externality.

3.a.3. The Coase Theorem In cases where the market failure results from a lack of private property rights, the problem can be corrected by the assignment of private property rights rather than by having the government regulate or impose taxes and subsidies.

To solve the problem of the destruction of the African elephant, each African country could assign individuals the ownership of the elephants. Suppose a government had the choice of assigning the right to an environmentalist or to a poacher. If the ownership were given to the poacher, then the environmentalist would have to decide how many elephants she could stand having killed. The environmentalist would then offer to pay the poacher some amount to refrain from any more killing. The environmentalist would be willing to pay the poacher enough so that the marginal cost just equaled the marginal benefit the environmentalist could get from additional killing. The poacher would accept a payment that would just offset his marginal cost of not poaching. If the *MSC* curve of Figure 7 represents the environmentalist's marginal costs and the *MC* curve represents the poacher's marginal costs, then the environmentalist would be willing to pay the poacher any amount up to the difference between the *MC* and *MSC* curves because that would induce the poacher to reduce poaching to the level the environmentalist desires. The poacher would be willing to accept any amount equal to or greater than the difference between the *MC* and *MSC* curves to reduce poaching to Q_S.

Conversely, if the government assigned the environmentalist the property right, the poacher would have to buy some of the elephants from the environmentalist. The poacher would pay up to the difference between the *MC* and *MSC* curves, and the environmentalist would accept anything equal to or greater than that difference.

Notice that no matter to whom the property rights are assigned, the quantity of elephants killed is the same. The only difference is that one of the parties provides payments to the other. When bargaining is costless and property rights can be assigned without difficulty, the amount of the externality-creating activity will be the same no matter who has the property right. This is known as the **Coase theorem,** named after Ronald Coase, the University of Chicago economist and 1991 Nobel Prize winner who discovered the principle.

In some cases where private property rights do not exist, it is not possible for the government to assign private property rights or to enforce them once assigned, and the Coase theorem does not hold. For instance, society cannot easily assign individual homeowners private rights to air and expect motorists to buy pollution rights from them. It would be virtually impossible for each motorist to speak with each

Coase theorem: when bargaining is costless and property rights can be assigned without difficulty, the amount of an externality-generating activity will not depend on who is assigned the property rights

---

Figure 7

The Assignment of Property Rights

The *MSC* curve of Figure 7 represents the environmentalist's marginal cost curve. The *MC* curve represents the poacher's marginal costs. If the government assigned ownership of the elephants to the poacher, the environmentalist would be willing to pay the poacher any amount up to the difference between the *MC* and *MSC* curves because that would induce the poacher to reduce poaching to the level the environmentalist desires. The poacher would be willing to accept any amount equal to or greater than the difference between the *MC* and *MSC* curves to reduce poaching to Q_S.

Conversely, if the government assigned the environmentalist the property right, the poacher would have to buy some of the elephants from the environmentalist. The poacher would pay up to the difference between the *MC* and *MSC* curves, and the environmentalist would accept anything equal to or greater than that difference.

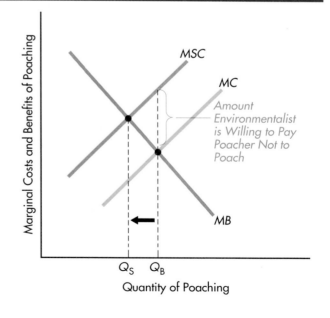

homeowner. In this case the transaction costs are too high. It is possible, in cases where the transaction costs are too high for the Coase theorem to work, that a market can be created for the property rights and that the market for property rights will reduce the externality problem.

3.a.4. A Market for the Property Rights

Economists have been able to create a new approach to applying government environmental policy in recent years. Under the old approach, the amount of pollution allowed from each generator, boiler, baking oven, or other piece of equipment was specified by the smog control agency. The new approach is to allow a company to choose the least expensive mix of new controls as long as total pollution does not exceed some assigned level. Each business gets a certificate indicating the amount of pollution it is permitted each year; each is given a property right to that amount of pollution. These permits can then be bought and sold in a market, which is referred to as a smog market. A firm easily meeting its standards can sell its excess to a firm having some difficulty meeting its standards. For example, Mobil Corporation purchased the permission to spew out an additional 900 pounds of noxious gas vapors each day, for about $3 million, from the city of South Gate, California. South Gate had acquired the credits from General Motors, which closed a plant there and sold the city the property and the pollution permits that went with the property.

In many regions of the country the Environmental Protection Agency uses an **emissions offset policy.** The EPA owns the air and sells permits to "use" the air. Companies with permits must not produce more pollution than their permits allow. But if they produce less pollution than their permits allow, they can "bank" the difference and use it later or they can sell it to other polluters. This creates a market for the right to pollute.

The amount of pollution wanted by the Environmental Protection Agency is indicated by the vertical supply curve of pollution rights in Figure 8. The demand for permits to pollute is shown by the downward-sloping curve, *MB*. With a price (*P*) for pollution rights determined, firms *internalize* the externality of polluting by using the price of the pollution rights to define the quantity (*Q*) of pollution they will undertake. If the EPA decides to reduce emissions further, it would shift the designated emission standard in, as illustrated in Figure 8. This would increase the price of the emission permits from P_1 to P_2. You might notice that a firm anticipating that the EPA would reduce emission standards and thus that the price would rise could make a profit by purchasing future permits. In fact, a futures market for emission permits has arisen and people do speculate both on the EPA standards and on the demand (*MB*) for emissions.

3.a.5. Global Problems

Global environmental problems are complicated by the fact that the individuals involved live in many nations. Sulfur dioxide and nitrogen dioxide emitted by factories in the United States are blown to Canada, where they mix with moisture and fall as acid rain. Manufacturing plants located along the Mexican side of the U.S.-Mexico border emit pollutants that flow across the border into the United States.

The ozone layer poses a major international challenge. Many scientists claim that the stratospheric ozone layer has been damaged by several chemical compounds, most notably chlorofluorocarbons and bromofluorocarbons (halons). The appearance of a major hole in the ozone layer over Antarctica, where no emissions originate, indicates the global nature of the externality. The problem is that no one government can claim ownership of the ozone. The standard approach has been to

emissions offset policy: an environmental policy wherein pollution permits are issued and a market in the permits then develops

5. Why are global environmental problems so difficult to solve?

Figure 8

The Value of Pollution Permits

The value of pollution permits depends on the demand for and supply of such permits. The vertical supply curve shows the amount of pollution allowed by EPA standards. The marginal benefits of polluting are shown by the downward-sloping curve, *MB*. With a price for pollution rights determined, firms internalize the externality of polluting by using the price of the pollution rights to define the quantity of pollution they will undertake.

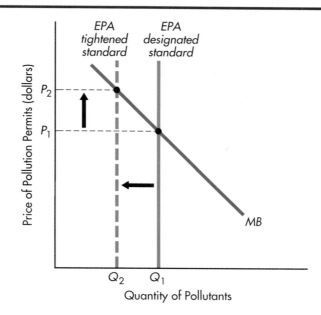

develop a nonbinding policy to which several countries will agree. In 1985, a convention of nations established a framework for international scientific and technical cooperation. In 1987, the Montreal Protocol committed signatories to freeze production levels of chlorofluorocarbons by 1989 and then cut their production in half by 1998. In 1989 in Paris, the world's seven biggest industrial economies agreed to begin major assaults on many environmental problems.

In November and December 1997, the representatives of most of the nations of the world met in Kyoto, Japan, to discuss global warming. Proposals for a solution included strict emissions control—reductions of something like 10 to 25 percent below 1990 levels—to the creation of an international market in emissions permits. No general agreement rose from the meeting except to meet again in November and December 1998. The U.S. proposal to create an international market in emission permits was not viewed favorably. One negotiator noted that many people have always had the government dictate results; they have no trust of the market. Others view the market with fear, believing that the larger nations will become a powerful cartel and dictate to the rest of the world.

You might imagine the difficulty of creating a new market. For a market to exist, private property rights must exist. Who is to assign property rights? For the market to function, those property rights must be enforced. One nation cannot take the property of another without compensation. Who is to ensure that those property rights are enforced? For those who do not like the market outcome, attempts will be made to alter the outcome. Who will monitor the activities in the market to minimize cheating? Creating a market is a difficult undertaking. But, the outcome of the market is a more efficient solution than any other, as we saw in Chapter 3.

3.b. Government Regulation of Public Goods

Public goods, as you learned earlier, are those goods or services for which the producer is unable to exclude nonpayers so that a free-rider problem emerges. Because users have no incentive to pay for the public good, the demand curve for the good will lie far below the demand that would exist if users had to purchase the good. As a result, "too little" of the public good is produced. Since too little is produced, too few resources flow to the production of the public good. How is the public good problem solved?

There have been attempts by private entrepreneurs to convert public goods into private goods. Large stadiums built around baseball or football fields restrict the viewing of the games outside of the stadiums; you have to purchase a ticket to see the contest. The Rural Metro Company of Scottsdale, Arizona, provides private subscription fire protection to residents of Scottsdale and surrounding communities. The company will put out fires at no cost to subscribers but will put out fires for nonsubscribers for a price that equals Rural Metro's average total cost. In general, however, the solution for the free-rider problems of public goods is to have the government produce the good. National defense, wildlife reserves in Kenya, wilderness areas in the United States, and the park systems in every country might not exist if a government did not provide them.

But a public good only requires a means of financing the production. It need not be the government that produces the good. Why the government produces the good rather than simply finances its production is a topic of some controversy. Many economists claim that that is part of the government failure, that whenever a government agency gets involved in anything, the objective is to increase that agency's responsibility and growth rather than to produce efficiently. Other economists argue that national defense and special industries require government production; to allow private companies to be responsible for national defense could lead to military unpreparedness.

How much of a public good should be provided? The optimal amount is the amount where the market-demand curve and the marginal-cost curve (supply curve) of producing the good intersect. If we could measure how much society would actually be willing and able to pay for a public good, we could determine the optimal quantity to produce very readily. For example, we know the marginal cost of producing a missile—all we have to do is equate it to the market demand for the missile to determine the number of missiles to produce. The problem is that we cannot easily determine the market demand. Surveys do not help because people have an incentive not to tell the truth—by indicating they would pay a lot when in reality they know they get it for free or by indicating they would pay nothing because they know their taxes will be set according to what they say. The only way that the public can register its demand for public goods is through the ballot box. But the ballot box does not measure the intensity of consumer preferences, and it too can fail to produce the optimal quantity of the public good.

RECAP

1. The solution to an externality is to ensure that those creating an externality internalize it.

2. Externalities may be internalized through the imposition of regulations or taxes, the use of subsidies, or the assignment of private property rights.

3. The Coase theorem illustrates the way private individuals can resolve externalities if property rights are assigned. Who has the property right does not matter; what matters is the assigning of the property right.

4. Global environmental issues are particularly difficult to solve because no one government can claim ownership of the property.

5. If a public good cannot be converted to a private good, the solution to providing the right amount of the public good is to have the government provide it.

SUMMARY

❓ What is the difference between renewable and nonrenewable natural resources?

1. Renewable natural resources are the wildlife, flora, and fauna that can regenerate. *§1*

2. Nonrenewable natural resources are the inert resources—coal, oil, and so on—that are fixed in supply. *§1.a*

❓ What is the optimal rate of use of natural resources?

3. The optimal rate of use of natural resources is not zero. It is the rate at which the renewable resource can satisfy society's wants now and in the future. *§1.a*

4. The optimal rate of use of renewable resources is the rate that equates the expected return from using the resources and the expected return from not using them. *§1.b*

❓ Why might a market not result in the best use of the environment?

5. A market failure occurs when the market fails to produce the right amount of output and to allocate the right amount of resources to alternative uses. The right amount refers to the amount that would occur in a world of perfect competition—the economically efficient amount. *§2*

6. When an externality occurs, private costs and benefits differ from social costs. Either too much or too little is consumed or produced relative to the quantities that would occur if all costs and benefits were included. *§2.a*

7. An externality may result from the lack of private property rights. *§2.a*

8. A public good is a good for which the principle of mutual exclusivity does not hold. *§2.b*

❓ Why does the government get involved in environmental policy?

9. The government is called on to solve environmental problems because of market failure and because people do not like the market outcome and believe they will benefit more with some other outcome. *§3*

10. Possible solutions to externalities include regulations, taxes, subsidies, and the assignment of private property rights. *§3*

11. The most common solution to public goods is for the government to supply the good. *§3.b*

❓ Why are global environmental problems so difficult to solve?

12. Global environmental problems are more difficult to resolve than domestic ones because of the lack of property rights. When no one government owns the resource being damaged by an externality, then the externality cannot be resolved by any one government. *§3.a*

KEY TERMS

nonrenewable (exhaustible) natural resources *§1*

renewable (nonexhaustible) natural resources *§1*

market failure *§2*

private costs *§2.a*

externality *§2.a*

social costs *§2.a*

private property right *§2.b*

marginal social costs (*MSC*) *§2.b*

principle of mutual exclusivity *§2.c*

public good *§2.c*

free rider *§2.c*

emission standard *§3.a.1*

Coase theorem *§3.a.3*

emissions offset policy *§3.a.4*

EXERCISES

1. The three following demand schedules constitute the total demand for a particular good.

    a. Determine the market demand schedule for the good if it is a private good.

    b. Determine the market demand schedule for the good if it is a public good.

Bob		Sally		Rafael	
P	**Q_d**	**P**	**Q_d**	**P**	**Q_d**
$6	0	$6	0	$6	1
$5	1	$5	0	$5	2
$4	2	$4	1	$4	3
$3	3	$3	2	$3	4
$2	4	$2	3	$2	5
$1	5	$1	4	$1	6

2. Using the public good described in exercise 1 and the following supply schedule, determine the optimal quantity of the good. Explain how you determined this quantity.

P	**Q_s**
$10	15
$ 9	11
$ 7	9
$ 6	8
$ 4	7
$ 2	4
$ 1	3

3. Use the following information to answer the questions listed below.

    a. What is the external cost per unit of output?

    b. What level of output will be produced?

    c. What level of output should be produced to achieve economic efficiency?

    d. What is the value to society of correcting the externality?

Quantity	MC	MSC	MB
1	$ 2	$ 4	$12
2	$ 4	$ 6	$10
3	$ 6	$ 8	$ 8
4	$ 8	$10	$ 6
5	$10	$12	$ 4

4. What level of tax would be appropriate to internalize the externality in exercise 3?

5. If, in exercise 3, the *MC* and *MSC* columns were reversed, you would have an example of what? Would too much or too little of the good be produced? How would the market failure be resolved, by tax or by subsidy?

6. What is meant by the term *overfishing*? What is the fundamental problem associated with overfishing of the oceans? What might lead to *underfishing*?

7. Explain why the optimal amount of pollution is not a zero amount. Use the same explanation to discuss the amount of health and safety that the government should require in the workplace.

8. Suppose the following table describes the marginal costs and marginal benefits of waste (garbage) reduction. What is the optimal amount of garbage? What is the situation if no garbage is allowed to be produced?

Percentage of Waste Eliminated	Marginal Costs (millions of dollars)	Marginal Benefits (millions of dollars)
10%	10	1,000
20%	15	500
30%	25	100
40%	40	50
50%	70	20
60%	110	5
70%	200	3
80%	500	2
90%	900	1
100%	2,000	0

9. Elephants eat 300 pounds of food per day. They flourished in Africa when they could roam over huge areas of land, eating the vegetation in one area and then moving on so that the vegetation could renew itself. Now, the area over which elephants can roam is declining. Without some action, the elephants will become extinct. What actions might save the elephants? What are the costs and benefits of such actions?

10. What could explain why the value of pollution permits in one area of the country is rising 20 percent per year while in another it is unchanged from year to year? What would you expect to occur as a result of this differential?

11. Smokers impose negative externalities on nonsmokers. Suppose the airspace in a restaurant is a resource owned by the restaurant owner.

   a. How would the owner respond to the negative externalities of smokers?
   b. Suppose that the smokers owned the airspace. How would that change matters?
   c. How about if the nonsmokers owned the airspace?
   d. Finally, consider what would occur if the government passed a law banning all smoking. How would the outcome compare with the outcomes described above?

12. Discuss the argument that education should be subsidized because it creates a positive externality.

13. If the best solution to solving the positive externality problem of education is to provide a subsidy, explain why education systems in all countries are nationalized, that is, are government entities.

14. Explain how a government policy to lower interest rates might influence the natural resource markets.

15. The government proposed higher taxes on the use of nonrenewable resources. If implemented, what would be the likely impact of these taxes? How would the taxes affect saving? Would future generations be better off as a result of the taxes?

Boulder Targets Traffic Congestion

What if driving at rush hour cost you lots more money, not just more time? What if parking put such a dent in your pocketbook it made you want to take the bus? Boulder wants to spend $897,000 on a "traffic-congestion pricing study" to get your answers. The aim is to discover new ways to manipulate market demand for car travel and cut driving to and in Boulder. City leaders and federal sponsors say the study may uncover futuristic ways to blunt traffic growth.

"In my opinion, it would be money well spent," said Joe McDonald, who sits on Boulder's transportation advisory board. "Building more highways to fight congestion is like fighting obesity by getting a bigger belt." Councilman Tad Kline isn't sure the study is the wisest use of money. "Y'know, we could deliver a lot of service for that much money," he said. He would prefer another "Hop," Boulder's successful new shuttle between downtown, the University of Colorado campus and Crossroads Mall.

Some of the options for congestion pricing are simple. Others rely on new technology. The ideas include:

A variable toll that would increase at rush hours. The money could be collected electronically, similar to the E-470 toll road, where lasers read windshield bar codes and bills are mailed to car owners.

A mileage tax. Drivers would pay the tax based on their odometer readings when they register their cars.

Hiking parking prices. Charges would be highest during rush hours.

The pricing options are intended to "be in people's faces," said Boulder transit projects manager Debra Baskett, who organized the study. "We want something that's going to modify behavior."

"The whole concept makes a lot of sense. The whole premise is that users pay the way. Those who drive more pay more."

Councilman Kline, who said he is undecided but leaning toward the study, is troubled by equity and privacy issues. If driving becomes more expensive, only the more affluent will drive, he said. "And after you get through with the laser readers and the bar codes and the myriad taxing schemes, you get down to the fact that all those things involve a very large data base that is held by the government," Kline said.

Source: Mary George, "Boulder Targets Traffic Congestion," *Denver Post*, February 5, 1995, p. 1c. Reprinted by permission.

Denver Post/February 5, 1995

Commentary

Congestion on the roads is a problem plaguing many cities. The source of the problem is that to the individual, the marginal cost of entering the highway or road is less than the marginal social cost the driver imposes. When deciding whether to enter a highway, you consider the time you will spend on the highway versus the time spent driving some other way or some other time. If the marginal cost exceeds the marginal benefit, you do not enter the highway or you do not drive. Conversely, if the marginal benefit exceeds the marginal cost you do enter the highway or you do drive. Your calculation of marginal costs does not include the additional congestion you add to the highway.

Suppose there are 50,000 cars on the highway when you are deciding whether to enter the highway. You carry out your calculations, determining that entering the highway will save you 10 minutes over taking another approach and will only cost you 15 minutes more of driving time than if you wait an hour until rush hour is over. Thus, you decide to drive now and to drive on the highway.

For you, the decision to enter the highway now made sense. However, your addition to the road causes an additional slowdown of 10 seconds for each of the 50,000 cars or 500,000 seconds total. You have imposed a significant social cost but you did not use that social cost in your calculation. This externality is referred to as a market failure—the additional social costs were not included in your calculation. Since everyone makes the same calculation, the roads become highly congested during rush hours. How can the market failure be corrected?

One approach might be to assign property rights. Suppose that the roadways were privately owned. Then the owners would want to maximize profit. They would do this by raising the price when demand rose and by price discriminating according to the price elasticity of demand. Suppose that the price elasticity of demand is lower during rush hour than during off-peak times. Then, by raising the price of entering the highway during rush hour relative to that during off-peak times, total revenue would rise. This would also induce some people to shift their driving to off-peak times. Many of the pricing schemes being considered by the Boulder City Council simulate the assignment of property rights and profit maximization.

According to Councilman Kline, "If driving becomes more expensive, only the more affluent will drive." This statement indicates the difference between assigning private property rights and having the government act as if it were a private owner. The private owner will behave so as to maximize profits—internalize externalities and operate and price efficiently. The government will not maximize profits. The government will have other objectives—ensuring a more equitable distribution of the scarce resource or, perhaps, its members' being reelected. Perhaps the Boulder City Council will decide to tax only those with new cars or those with incomes above a certain level or to exempt older cars or people with incomes below a certain level from the higher price.

Another approach Boulder is considering is to impose a tax on mileage. The tax imposes a penalty on total driving. It does nothing about driving during rush hour. If someone drives many miles each year but always drives off-peak, then that person would pay a higher tax than someone who drives fewer miles but only during rush hour. While reducing total driving, the proposal does nothing for reducing rush hour driving.

Part Five

Current Issues Involving the Public Sector and the Market Economy

Chapter 19 | Aging, Social Security, and Health Care

Fundamental Questions

1. Why worry about social security?

2. Why is health care heading the list of U.S. citizens' concerns?

Preview

The population of the United States is aging rapidly. Currently, more than 12 percent of the population is retired—living off pensions, savings, and social security. By the year 2030, 21 percent of the population will be older than 65. The aging of the population is likely to have a dramatic effect on living standards. For instance, the types of goods and services produced will increasingly be influenced by the elderly. In particular, expenditures on health care will continue to rise. Already, people in the United States allocate more than 14 percent of their income to medical care. Is there a limit to how much they are willing to commit? The aging of the population also means that an increasing percentage of people will be retired and a smaller percentage will be producing goods and services and paying taxes. What are the implications for social security and for productivity? In this chapter, we look at the impact of an aging population on medical care and social security. ■

Part Five / Current Issues Involving the Public Sector and the Market Economy

1. AGING AND SOCIAL SECURITY

The oldest population of the United States, persons 65 years or older, numbered 36 million in 1999 and represented more than 12.5 percent of the U.S. population, about one in every eight Americans. The oldest group itself is getting older. In 1999, the 65 to 74 age group was 8 times larger than in 1900, but the 75 to 84 group was 12 times larger and the 85-plus group was 22 times larger. The median age in 1850 was 18.9. It is now 40.

The pattern of aging is clearly visible in Figure 1, which shows the age of the U.S. population at three points of time, 1970, 1990, and what is anticipated for 2010. The pattern has been described as a python swallowing a pig: the pig represents the baby boom generation working its way up the age scale, the python.

The growth of the older population in the United States has brought several issues to the forefront of political debate. Among them are social security and health care.

1.a. Social Security

1. Why worry about social security?

An aging population means that the concerns of the aged will dominate national concerns. Retirement and security for the aged is one such concern. Old-Age, Survivors, and Disability Insurance (OASDI), also known as social security, had

---

Figure 1

Aging Patterns in the United States

The age distribution of the U.S. population at three points of time: 1970, 1990, and what is anticipated for 2010. The pattern has been described as a python

swallowing a pig. The pig represents the baby boom generation working its way up the age scale, the python. Source: U. S. Bureau of the Census.

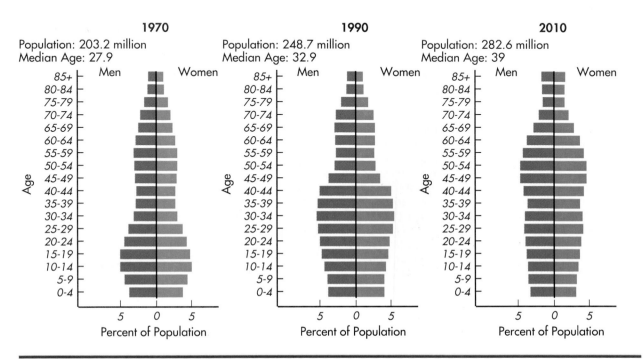

been established in 108 countries by the beginning of 1975. Some of the oldest plans are those of Germany (1889), the United Kingdom (1908), France (1910), Sweden (1913), and Italy (1919). The United States did not enact a national retirement program until 1935.

The social security system in the United States, which covers both Old-Age, Survivors, and Disability Insurance (commonly referred to as social security) and hospital insurance (Medicare), is financed by a payroll tax Federal Insurance Corporation of America (FICA), levied in equal portions on the employer and the employee. The initial FICA tax rate was 1 percent of the first $3,000 of wage income paid by both parties. By 2000, this had risen to a tax rate of 7.65 percent (6.2 percent on the first $72,600 of earnings for the social security contribution and 1.45 percent on all earnings for the Medicare contribution), for each employee and employer.

1.b. The Viability of Social Security

Social security was intended to supplement the retirement funds of individuals.

The social security taxes the working population pays today are used to provide benefits for current retirees. As a result, the financial viability of the system depends on the ratio of those working to those retired. The age distribution of the United States population has affected this viability. The consequence is a change in the ratio of workers to social security beneficiaries, see Figure 2. The ratio has declined from 16.5 in 1950 to about 3 today and is expected to decline to 2 by 2030. The situation in the United States is not any different from that in other parts of the world, as noted in the Economic Insight "The World Is Aging." This trend means that the source of social security benefits is getting relatively smaller. The viability of the system depends on whether the trends of recent years continue. If birthrates remain low and if people continue to live longer, then the obligations to people who will retire in twenty-five years will be large relative to the income of the working population at that time.

The social security tax has risen more rapidly in the past two decades than any other tax. Social security tax revenues were less than 5 percent of personal income

Figure 2

Social Security Viability

The ratio of workers to social security beneficiaries is shown. The ratio has declined from 16.5 in 1950 to about 3 today and is expected to decline to 2 or less by 2030. This trend means that the source of social security benefits is getting relatively smaller. The viability of the system depends on whether the trends of recent years continue. Sources: *Statistical Abstract of the United States, 1994*; Joseph E. Stiglitz, *Economics of the Public Sector* (New York: W. W. Norton, 1986), p. 277; Henry J. Aaron, Barry P. Bosworth, and Gary T. Burtless, *Can America Afford to Grow Old?* (Washington, D.C.: Brookings Institution, 1989), p. 38.

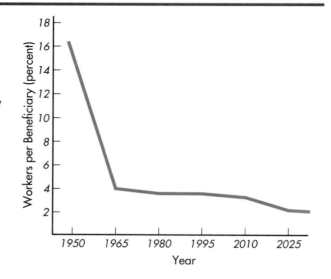

The World Is Aging

The United States is not the only country whose population is growing older. Most of the developed nations in the world are experiencing the same aging of their populations. As seen in the accompanying figure, the elderly population constituted about 12 percent in the United States in 1985 but nearly 17 percent in Sweden. Although three-quarters of the world's population resides in developing areas, these areas contain only about 50 percent of the world's elderly. The developed countries are aging because the birthrates in these countries have decreased and life expectancy has increased. Japan's life expectancy of 77 years is the highest among the major countries, but most developed nations approach 75 years. In contrast, Bangladesh and some African nations south of the Sahara have life expectancies of 49 years.

As longevity has increased and families have had fewer children, the ratio of persons 65 and older to persons age 20 to 64 has risen in most of the developed countries. These elderly support ratios will rise modestly over the next fifteen years because the large number of people born between 1946 and 1961 will still be in the labor force. But as the large working-age population begins to retire after 2005, the elderly support ratio will rise sharply.

Source: U.S. Department of Commerce, U. S. Bureau of the Census, *International Population Reports.*

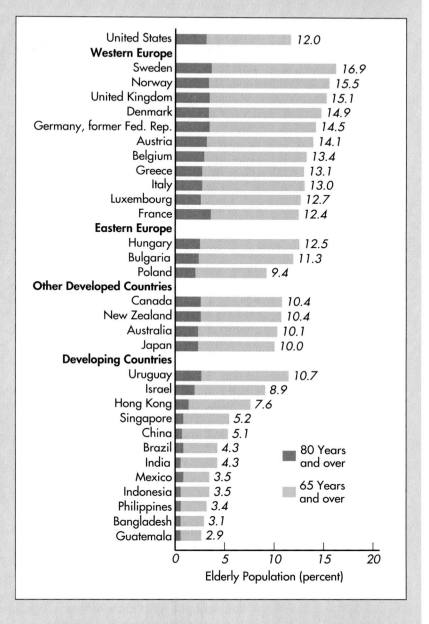

in 1960 and currently exceed 11 percent of personal income. The revenues from the personal income tax were 3.4 percent of personal income in 1940 and rose to the current amount of more than 15 percent in the early 1980s. Social security expenditures also have risen more rapidly than any other government program. Social security outlays currently constitute 7 percent of GDP, whereas national defense is less than 5.5 percent, and education and training expenditures are less than 1 percent. From 1979 to 1990, national defense expenditures rose 53.6 percent, education and training expenditures rose 0.8 percent, GDP grew 30.2 percent, and social security grew 70.9 percent, adjusted for inflation.

If the system was funded solely by the revenues collected from the social security tax and if those revenues could be used for no other purpose than to provide benefits to social security recipients, then the worries about the system's viability would be much smaller. However, the social security system is included in the federal government's budget, and its revenues are used to pay for general government expenditures. This means that the excess of social security taxes over social security benefits is used pay for other government programs; the funds are not deposited in a trust fund and allowed to accumulate for future years.

If the amount paid into the social security system by an individual was equal, on average, to the amount received by that individual in retirement benefits, the worries about the viability of the system would also be less. But people who retired in the 1980s, after working since the age of 21 at the minimum wage level, will recover all social security taxes paid, including employer and employee shares, in less than 4 years; at the maximum taxable amount each year, the employee would have recovered the total contributions in only 5 years. Retirees in the 1990s recover the total contributions and interest earnings in 7 years. At an age of 82, the average worker who retired at age 65 will have received more than twice his and his employer's contributions to social security. Other social security issues are noted in the Economic Insight "Myths About Social Security."

So what's the alternative? There have been many proposals—increasing taxes, increasing the eligibility age, means testing, and holding down cost-of-living increases. The eligibility age, the age when individuals can start collecting Social Security, is to begin rising in 2000 until it reaches age 67 for those born in 1960 or later. Means testing has been resisted but is under serious consideration. Means testing would put a limit on the income one could earn and still collect Social Security.

One of the more controversial proposals has been to privatize the system. This is what Chile, Australia, Turkey, Sweden, Italy, Argentina, Mexico, the Philippines, Great Britain, and several other nations have done. Privatization allows individuals to choose among an approved list of possible investments rather than giving the money to the government. What the individual earns on those investments would be the individual's retirement funds. Unlike the government program, which is a pay-as-you-go system and which provides defined benefits for contributors, the private system will pay what individual investments earn. Some systems, like Chile's, are fully privatized: workers are required to save a portion of their own salary for retirement but give no money directly to the government. Others, like Great Britain's, are partially privatized: workers still contribute payroll taxes, but only part of this money is used to support a government-run system of basic pensions; the rest may be used for a private plan chosen by the worker. In Australia, workers are required to contribute 9 percent of their income to a fund of their choice.

Those critical of privatization note that with private investments there's no guaranteed return. Who would want to risk their life savings in the stock market? Social

Myths About Social Security

The first recipient of social security in the United States was Ida Mae Fuller in 1940. Her check was for $22.45. By the time she died, shortly after her one hundredth birthday, she had collected about $20,000 in benefits, a large return considering that she had paid in a total of $22.

We've contributed to that fund all our lives! It's our money! It's not the government's money!

This is one of the most strongly and widely held myths about the social security system. In fact, the typical retiree collects more than twice the amount represented by employer and employee contributions plus interest.

The benefits of the system are determined by a scientific formula designed to ensure that the fund remains viable.

This is another myth about social security. The system of annually adjusting social security benefits as the cost of living increases dates only from 1975, and it came about as the result of political machinations, not foresight. In 1975, the annual benefits were about $7,000. Attempting to hold the line on federal spending, President Nixon proposed a 5 percent increase in social security benefits and threatened a veto of anything higher. Democrats saw an opportunity to embarrass the president. They decided to pass a 10 percent increase and force Nixon to make an unpopular veto. The 10 percent increase was introduced in the Senate, but then rumors that Nixon would doublecross them and sign the bill anyway began circulating. So

Congress increased the benefits to 20 percent, knowing that this huge increase would be vetoed. Nixon, however, signed the bill and proudly boasted of how well he had taken care of the elderly. Congress, irritated at being outflanked, passed the cost-of-living adjustment program to show that it, too, cared about the elderly.

Social Security ensures that only the elderly poor are cared for.

In fact, there are at least a million individuals currently collecting social security benefits who also have incomes exceeding $100,000 per year.

Sources: Jack Anderson, "Why Should I Pay for People Who Don't Need It?" *Parade Magazine,* February 21, 1993, p. 4; Eric Blac, "Social Security: Myths, Facts," *Arizona Republic,* February 21, 1993, p. F1.

---

security, in contrast, is a sure thing. Most of the privatization plans have met this criticism by ensuring that no one contributing to the new plan will earn less than what they would have received under the former government-run plan.

The form of privatization differs from country to country, but the results have been uniformly positive. In every case, the returns individuals have received exceed those of the government system. In addition, the national savings rates have increased and government borrowing and debt creation decreased.

RECAP

1. The U.S. population is aging due to lower birthrates, higher life expectancy, and the impact of the baby boom generation.

2. Social security, otherwise known as Old-Age, Survivors, and Disability Insurance, is financed by a tax imposed on employers and employees.

3. Social security is funded to provide benefits to the current retirees by the current working population's contributions. As the population ages, the ratio of contributors to beneficiaries declines.

4. Solutions to the social security problem include means testing, increasing eligibility age, and privatization.

2. HEALTH ECONOMICS

Spending for health care in the United States is nearly $1 trillion. Figure 3 shows that in 1965 health-care expenditures were only 5.9 percent of GDP but were 13 percent in 2000. Per capita spending in 2000 was $3,925. Why have health-care expenditures risen so dramatically?

2.a. Overview

Figure 4 shows where the nation's health-care dollar is spent and where the money comes from. Figure 4(a) shows that expenditures for hospital services constitute 39 cents of every dollar, or 39 percent of the nation's health-care bill; nursing-home expenditures, 8 percent; spending for physicians' services, 20 percent; and spending for other personal health-care services (dental care, other professional services, drugs and other nondurables, durable medical products, and miscellaneous personal-care services), 21 percent. The remaining 12 percent of national health expenditures goes for medical research, construction of medical facilities, government public health services, and the administration of private health insurance.

Figure 4(b) shows the sources of payment for these expenditures. Of the $1 trillion spent on health care, 54 percent comes from private sources: private insurance and direct payments. Private health insurance, the single largest payer for health care, accounts for 33 cents of every dollar of national health expenditures, or 33 percent. Private direct payments account for 21 percent. Direct payments consist of out-of-pocket payments made by individuals, including copayments and deductibles required by many third-party payers (third-party payers are insurance companies and government).

Government spending on health care constitutes 45 percent of the total; the federal government pays about 70 percent of this. **Medicare,** the largest publicly sponsored health-care program, funds health-care services for about 35 million aged and disabled enrollees. The Medicare program pays for 20 percent of all national health expenditures. **Medicaid,** a jointly funded federal and state program, finances 16 percent of all health care covering the costs of medical care for poor families, the need-

Medicare: a federal health-care program for the elderly and disabled

Medicaid: a joint federal-state program that pays for health care for poor families, the neediest elderly, and disabled persons

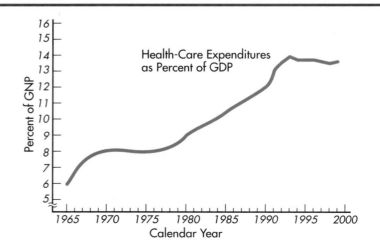

Figure 3

The Growth of U.S. Health-Care Spending

As a percentage of gross domestic product, health-care expenditures have risen from about 6 percent in 1965 to over 13 percent in 1999. Sources: *Health Care Financing Review,* 1999; Office of National Health Statistics, Office of the Actuary. www.hcfa.gov/.

Figure 4

The U.S. Health Dollar

Figure 4(a) shows expenditures on health care by source; Figure 4(b) shows sources of payment for health expenditures. Source: *Health Care Financing Review,* 2000. www.hcfa.gov/stats.

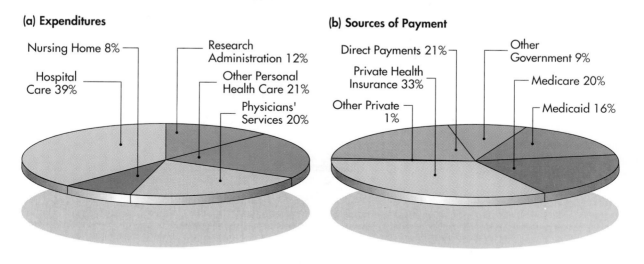

(a) Expenditures

Nursing Home 8% — Research Administration 12%

Hospital Care 39% — Other Personal Health Care 21%

Physicians' Services 20%

(b) Sources of Payment

Direct Payments 21% — Other Government 9%

Private Health Insurance 33% — Medicare 20%

Other Private 1% — Medicaid 16%

iest elderly, and disabled persons who are eligible for social security disability benefits. Other government programs pay for 9 percent.

Health-care spending varies tremendously among various groups in the U.S. population. Figure 5 illustrates how health-care expenditures vary across the economy. If each person spent the same amount on health care, the line of perfect equality shown in Figure 5 would describe the distribution of spending. In fact, the distribution of health expenditures is heavily skewed. The top 1 percent of persons ranked by health-care expenditures account for almost 30 percent of total health expenditures, and the top 5 percent incur 55 percent of all health expenditures. The bottom 50 percent of the population account for only 4 percent of all expenditures, and the bottom 70 percent account for only 10 percent of costs.

The high-cost segment of the population is older now than it was in the 1970s. Figure 6 shows that the distribution of spending for hospital care and for nursing homes is heavily dominated by the elderly. The top curve in Figure 6 represents the cumulative percentage of the population in each age group. As the age rises from under 5 to 10 to 20, and so on, there are increasing numbers of people. Eventually 100 percent of the population has been accounted for. The bottom curve represents the cumulative percentage of nursing home expenditures accounted for by people in each age group. Similarly, the middle line represents the cumulative percentage of expenditures on hospitals accounted for by each age group.

2.b. The Market for Medical Care

Health-care costs have risen because the demand for health care has risen relative to supply.

Rising costs or expenditures mean that the demand for medical care has risen relative to supply (Figure 7). The initial demand for medical care is D_1, and the supply of medical care is S_1. The intersection determines the price of medical care, P_1, and

Figure 5

The Inequality of U.S. Health-Care Spending

High-cost users of health care account for most health-care spending. The top 1 percent account for 30 percent of expenditures, and the top 5 percent for 55 percent of expenditures, while the bottom 70 percent account for only 10 percent of health-care expenditures. Source: Steven A. Garfinkel et al., "High-Cost Users of Medical Care," *Health Care Financing Review*, Summer 1988, pp. 41–50.

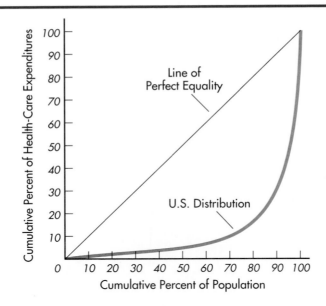

the total expenditures, P_1 times Q_1. An increase in demand relative to supply is shown as the outward shift of the demand curve, from D_1 to D_2. As a result, the price of medical care rises, from P_1 to P_2, as do the total expenditures on medical care, from P_1 times Q_1 to P_2 times Q_2. What accounts for the rising demand relative to supply?

Figure 6

Age and Health-Care Spending

The high-cost users are increasingly the elderly. Nursing-home expenditures are predominantly made for people older than 70. The use of hospitals is also primarily by the aged. Source: *Health Care Financing Review*, www.hcfa.gov/ (various issues).

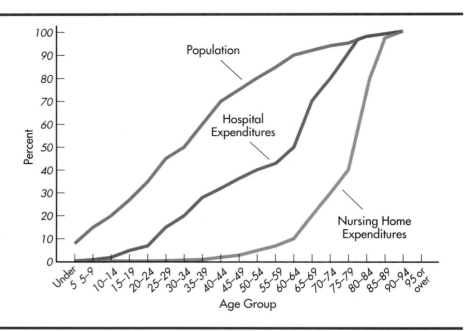

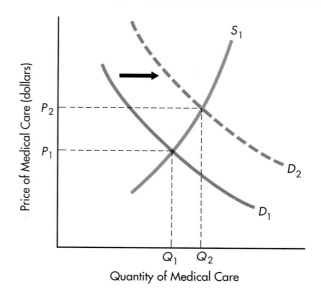

Figure 7

The Market for Medical Care: A Demand Shift

The demand for and supply of health care determine the price of medical care, P_1, and the total expenditures, P_1 times Q_1. Rising health-care expenditures may be due to increased demand. A larger demand, D_2, means a higher price and a greater total quantity of expenditures, P_2 times Q_2.

2.b.1. Demand Increase: The Aging Population

The aging of the population stimulates the demand for health care. The elderly consume four times as much health care per capita as the rest of the population. About 90 percent of the expenditures for nursing home care are for persons 65 or over, a group that constitutes only 12 percent of the population. The aged (65 or older) currently account for 35 percent of hospital expenditures. In contrast, the young, although they constitute 29 percent of the population, consume only 11 percent of hospital care. Per capita spending on personal health care for those 85 years of age or over is 2.5 times that for people age 65 to 69 years. For hospital care, per capita consumption is twice as great for those age 85 or over as for those age 65 to 69; for nursing home care, it is 23 times as great.

2.b.2. Demand Increase: The Financing Mechanism

For demand to increase, the aged must be both *willing* to buy medical care and *able* to pay for it. The emergence of Medicare and Medicaid in 1966 gave many elderly the ability. Medicare covers the cost of the first 100 days of hospital or nursing-home care for the elderly and disabled, providing benefits to 32 million people. Like social security, Medicare is funded by payroll taxes and is available on the basis of age (or disability), *not* need. By contrast, Medicaid helps only the neediest people, including many elderly people whose Medicare benefits have run out. As a result, Medicaid is considered the program most associated with long-term health care (such as for people living in nursing homes).

The effect of the Medicare and Medicaid programs has been to increase the demand for services and to decrease the price elasticity of demand because individuals do not pay for much of their health care. Private sources pay for about 59 percent of personal health care for the general population, and Medicare and Medicaid pick up most of the remainder. Private sources, however, pay for 74 percent of care for people under age 65. For the elderly, the private share of spending is only

15 percent for hospital care, 36 percent for physicians' services, and 58 percent for nursing-home care.[2] Medicaid spending for those 85 or over is seven times the spending for people age 65 to 69 and three times greater than the spending for people age 75 to 79. This difference is attributable to the heavy concentration of Medicaid money in nursing-home care, which those 85 or over use much more than others. Medicare spending for the oldest group is double that for the 65 to 69 group.

2.b.3. Demand Increase: New Technologies   New medical technologies provide the very sick with increased opportunities for survival. Everyone wants the latest technology to be used when their life or the lives of their loved ones are at stake. But because these technologies are cost-increasing innovations and because costs are not paid by the users, the increased technology increases demand.

2.b.4. Supply   Even if the demand curve for medical care was not shifting out rapidly, the cost of medical care could be forced up by an upward shift of the supply curve, as shown in Figure 8. The supply curve, composed of the marginal-cost curves of individual suppliers of medical care, shifts up, from S_1 to S_2, if the cost of producing medical care is rising—that is, if resource prices are rising or if diseconomies of scale are being experienced. The three largest resources in the medical industry in terms of total expenditures are hospitals (39 percent), physicians (20 percent), and nursing homes (8 percent).

Hospitals   The original function of hospitals was to provide the poor with a place to die. Not until the twentieth century could wealthy individuals who were sick find more comfort, cleanliness, and service in a hospital than in their own homes. As technological changes in medicine occurred, the function of the hospital changed: the hospital became the doctor's workshop.

The cost of hospital care is attributable in large part to the way current operations and capital purchases are financed. Only a small fraction of the cost of hospital care is paid for directly by patients; the bulk comes from *third parties*, of which the government is the most important. The term *third-party payers* refers to insurance companies and government programs: neither the user (the patient) nor the supplier (the physician or hospital) pays.

Hospital size is typically measured in numbers of beds; efficiency, in expenditures per case or expenditures per patient-day. To make precise determinations of the effect of size on efficiency is difficult because hospitals that differ in size are likely to differ also with respect to location, kind of patient admitted, services provided, and other characteristics. Hospitals that do not provide a large number of complex services need not be very large to be efficient. But if hospitals do provide a large number of services, it is very inefficient for them to be small. A hospital of 200 beds can efficiently provide most of the basic services needed for routine short-term care. If that hospital grows to 600 beds yet still provides only the same basic services, inefficiencies are likely to develop because of increasing difficulties of administrative control. What is more likely to happen, however, is that specialized services will be introduced—services that could not have been provided at a reasonable cost when the hospital had only 200 beds.

In the past twenty years, the average number of beds per hospital increased by 50 percent, inpatient days declined by about 10 percent, lengths of stay declined by about 10 percent, and occupancy rates declined by nearly 20 percent. The problem

---

[2]*Health Care Financing Review,* various issues.

Figure 8

The Market for Medical Care: A Supply Shift

The rising cost of medical care may be caused by an increase in the costs of supplying medical care. The supply curve shifts up, from S_1 to S_2, and the price of medical care rises, from P_1 to P_2.

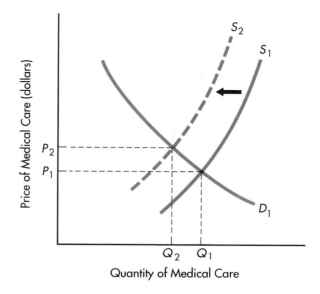

that more beds per hospital and shorter stays creates for the hospital is that the occupancy rate is only about 66 percent while the efficient occupancy rate is between 80 and 88 percent.

Physicians   Physicians affect the cost of medical care not only through their impact on the operation of the hospital but also through their fees. Expenditures on physicians' services rose more rapidly than any other medical-care expenditure category in the 1980s and 1990s. Is the increased cost of physicians due to a shortage of doctors? The answer is not necessarily yes. From 1966 to 1997, the supply of physicians increased 100 percent while the U. S. population increased about 25 percent. As a result, the ratio of active physicians per 100,000 people increased substantially, from 169 in 1975 to 240 in 1997.

The factors that have led to rising physicians' fees include an increase in demand relative to the supply of certain types of physicians, the ability of physicians to restrict price competition, and the payment system. The number of physicians per population has risen in many areas of the country. Yet, because the American Medical Association restricts advertising by physicians, consumers are unable to obtain complete information about prices or professional quality, and physicians are less likely to compete through advertising or lower prices. Moreover, the restrictions on advertising enable established physicians to keep new, entering physicians from competing for their customers by charging lower prices.

The payment system influences physicians' fees and the supply of physicians. Over 31 percent of all physicians' fees are set by the government. More than 75 percent are set by third-party providers. The physicians are reimbursed on the basis of procedures and according to specialty. A gynecologist would have to examine 275 women a week to achieve the income earned by one cardiac surgeon doing two operations per week. The rates of return from medical education by specialty are shown in Table 1, but most specialists do better than the general practitioner. In fact, more than 60 percent of all physicians in the United States are specialists. You can see that

Specialty	Rate of Return (percent)
Pediatrics	9
General practice/family practice	11
Psychiatry	13
Internal medicine	14
Obstetrics-gynecology	16
Pathology	17
Surgery	19
Radiology	20
Anesthesiology	22
Total, all physicians	16

Table 1

Rates of Return from Medical Education

Sources: Steven R. Eastaugh, *Financing Health Care* (Dover, Mass.: Auburn House, 1987), p. 57; *Statistical Abstract of the United States, 1994,* p. 123.

the rate of return varies tremendously among specialties. The payment system has induced more physicians to specialize in those areas than would have occurred otherwise.

The costs of doing business have risen for physicians. For instance, the cost of malpractice insurance has increased about 25 percent a year during the past two decades. Although only about 1 percent of health-care expenditures can be directly attributed to malpractice suits, there are some implicit costs associated with the fear of malpractice suits. The threat of malpractice suits has caused an increase in both the number of tests ordered by physicians and in the quantity of medical equipment purchased by them.

The United States has the most technologically advanced medical care in the world. Partly due to this, the cost of medical care is also the highest.

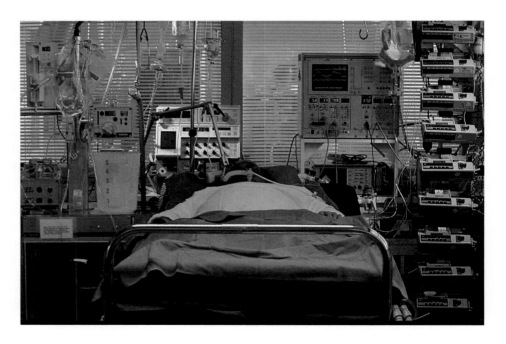

2.c. HMOs and PPOs

health maintenance organization (HMO): an organization that provides comprehensive medical care to a voluntarily enrolled consumer population in return for a fixed, prepaid amount of money

The increased costs of medical care and the increased supply of physicians have led to new medical-care delivery systems, the health maintenance organization and the preferred provider organization. A **health maintenance organization (HMO)** provides comprehensive medical care, including preventive, diagnostic, outpatient, and hospital services, in return for a fixed, prepaid amount of money from the enrollees.

There are four basic types of HMOs: staff, medical group, independent practice associations (IPAs), and networks. *Staff HMOs*, such as the Group Health Cooperative of Puget Sound in Seattle and ANCHOR Health Plan in Chicago, hire physicians as salaried employees. *Group HMOs* function as a medical group practice. Several physicians operating as a partnership or corporation contract with HMO management and an insurance plan to provide services and pool and redistribute income according to a predetermined formula. *Independent practice associations* are separate legal entities that contract with individual physicians practicing in a traditional office setting. *Networks* are organizations that franchise operations, in the same way that McDonald's and Pizza Hut are franchised operations. For instance, Blue Cross/Blue Shield is the main company, and local HMOs are franchises of Blue Cross/Blue Shield.

preferred provider organization (PPO): a group of physicians who contract to provide comprehensive medical services

A **preferred provider organization (PPO)** is a group of physicians who contract with a firm to provide services at a price discount in hopes of increasing their volume of business or a firm that contracts with a group of physicians. A general practitioner serves as a member's primary-care provider and refers patients to specialists as needed. Instead of contacting a specialist directly, a patient must be referred to a specialist by the primary-care provider. Specialists are reimbursed out of the fees paid to the PPO plan by the firms that contract with it. The general practitioners have an incentive to reduce total costs because they split a portion of the fixed fees that remain at the end of the year. As a result, the use of specialists and special tests is lower than in health-care plans that permit patients to select the specialists. Many hospitals are organizing PPOs in hopes of better managing hospital utilization and offsetting declining revenues.

Because HMOs and PPOs provide comprehensive coverage, they alter incentives for the patient. Patients who belong to an HMO or PPO are less likely to seek hospitalization for diagnostic work and other care that can be provided on an outpatient basis than are patients whose health insurance coverage is limited to care provided in the hospital. An HMO also alters incentives for physicians. Because their income is determined by annual payments, they are not likely to provide or order unnecessary care as a way of boosting their incomes.

2.d. National Comparisons

Historically, as per capita national income has risen, the proportion of that income that is spent on health has grown: a 10 percent increase in gross domestic product (GDP) per capita is associated with a 4.4 percent increase in the share of GDP going for health. (Gross domestic product, you will recall, is a measure of the total income created in an economy during one year.) Figure 9 shows the health-to-GDP ratios of the 24 members of the Organization for Economic Cooperation and Development (OECD). The share of health expenditures in GDP varied from 4.0 percent in Turkey to 13.7 percent in the United States.

Per capita expenditures for health range from $377 in Turkey to $4,080 in the United States, as shown in Figure 10. The U.S. per capita spending exceeded spending in Canada by 47 percent and other countries by more than 50 percent.

Figure 9

Total Health Expenditures as a Share of Gross Domestic Product

Total health expenditures are divided by gross domestic product to provide a comparison among countries. The United States allocates a higher percentage of its gross output to medical care than does any other country. Sources: OECD Health Data; 1999 *Statistical Abstract of the United States; Economic Report of the President, 1999.*
www.oecd.org
www.cdc.gov

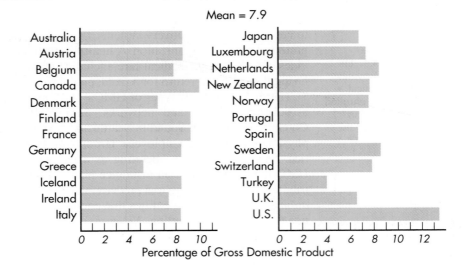

Mean = 7.9

Percentage of Gross Domestic Product

Figure 10

Per Capita Health Spending

The per capita expenditures of several countries are shown. The U.S. expenditures are the highest. Sources: *Measuring Health Care, 1960–1983* (Paris: Organization for Cooperation and Development, 1985); OECD Health Data 1991; *OECD Health Systems: Facts and Trends,* various issues; *World Development Report, 2000; Economic Report of the President, 2000.*

U.S.	$4,080
Switzerland	$2,573
Germany	$2,264
Canada	$2,158
France	$2,026
Norway	$1,996
Denmark	$1,931
Austria	$1,896
Netherlands	$1,874
Australia	$1,866
Sweden	$1,773

Belgium	$1,759
Japan	$1,757
Italy	$1,539
Finland	$1,520
U.K.	$1,391
New Zealand	$1,357
Ireland	$1,293
Greece	$1,226
Spain	$1,182
Portugal	$1,142
Turkey	$377

Per Capita Expenditures

Increases in health-care expenditures and the widening gap between the United States and other countries have led to a consideration of how medical care is provided in various countries. The comparison considered most often is between the United States and Canada because the two are neighbors with not too dissimilar economic and political systems and yet very different medical systems.

The U.S. and Canadian payment systems differ considerably. In the United States, physicians are paid more for doing more, and the return on their time is higher if they perform a procedure than if they use their cognitive skills. Because procedures often require hospital care, this approach translates into higher expenditures for hospital care. In Canada, by contrast, physicians operate under a system of fee schedules and overall provincial limits on health spending, and they have no incentive to increase the number of procedures.

Canadian patients are virtually fully insured. There are no deductibles or copayments. Canadian physicians are mostly reimbursed on a fee-for-service basis. Canada has a significantly lower ratio of specialists to general practitioners than the United States has.

Canadians receive fewer health services than Americans, yet there is no discernible difference in the infant mortality and life expectancy statistics of the two nations. Do Americans enjoy the diversity, the extra services, and the choice that they pay extra for even if there are no discernible differences in measures of health? For instance, the average stay in a hospital is shorter in the United States than it is in Canada, but the tests and procedures are more numerous. Would Canadians pay more for a shorter stay and more tests and procedures if they had the choice? If the answer to these questions is no, can we say that the system in the United States is less desirable than the system in Canada?

2.e. Do the Laws of Economics Apply to Health Care?

Rising health-care costs have led many people to claim that or act as if health care is different, that the laws of economics do not apply to it. People tend to look at health care as a right, something everyone is entitled to regardless of costs. You may recall our survey and discussion about allocation mechanisms in Chapter 3; most people look on health care as something different from other goods and services. They do not want the market system to determine who gets the health care and who doesn't.

Is health care a scarce good? The answer is a clear yes; at a zero price more people want health care than there is health care available, the definition of a scarce good. Scarcity means that choices must be made, that there is an opportunity cost for choosing to purchase the scarce good. The choice is made on the basis of rational self-interest. These principles of economics suggest that health care is an economic good and subject to the laws of economics.

The demand curve for medical care looks like any other demand curve; it slopes down because the higher the price, the lower the quantity demanded. The demand curve is probably quite inelastic, but it does slope downward. There also is a standard-looking supply curve. Physicians, hospitals, and medical firms offer an increasing quantity of medical care for sale as the price rises. As shown in Figures 7 and 8 and repeated in Figure 11, the demand and supply curves look no different than the curves representing a market in any other economic good.

In Figure 11, the price for medical care is the level at which the demand and supply curves intersect, the point of equilibrium. At price P_1, the quantity of medical care demanded is equal to the quantity supplied. Those people willing and able to pay price P_1 (all those lying along the demand curve from A to B) get the medical

Figure 11

Do the Laws of Economics Apply to Health Care?

The price of medical care is the level at which the demand and supply curves intersect, the point of equilibrium. At price P_1, the quantity of medical care demanded is equal to the quantity supplied. Those people willing and able to pay price P_1 (all those lying along demand curve D_1 from A to B) get the medical care. Those not willing and able to pay the price (all those lying along the demand curve from B to C) do not get the health care.

The third-party payment system allows many who would not be willing and able to purchase the health care (those lying along the demand curve from B to C) to be able to purchase the care. This shifts the demand curve out and drives health-care costs up, as shown by the shift in the demand curve from D_1 to D_2.

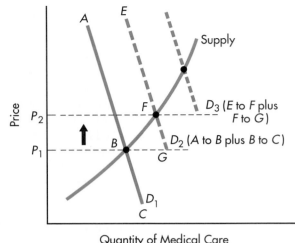

care. Those not willing and able to pay the price (all those lying along the demand curve from B to C) do not get the health care.

The problems that arise in the health-care market are due not to a repeal of the laws of economics but instead to the nature of the product. People believe they and others have an inalienable right to medical care, that it is not right to ignore those people making up the demand curve from B to C. As a result, government programs to provide medical insurance have been created. These programs, along with private insurance programs, mean that most of the payments for medical care are made by third parties, as described earlier in this chapter. The third-party payment system allows many of those who would not be willing and able to purchase the health care, those lying along the demand curve from B to C, to be able to purchase the care. This shifts the demand curve out, which drives health-care costs up, as shown by the shift from D_1 to D_2 in Figure 11.

The government and private insurance programs thus face ever-rising health-care costs; each new equilibrium means some are unable to afford the care; if their demand is covered, the demand curve shifts out again, to D_3. This continues as long as someone is willing and able to pay the price. That someone has been the government, principally through Medicare, and private employers through employee benefit plans. The result has been double-digit price increases for health care for over a decade.

"Repealing the laws of economics" in the case of health care means that the demand for and supply of health care do not determine the price or quantity and that not just those willing and able to pay get the care.

2.e.1. Managed Care: Changes in the Health-Care Industry   Managed competition refers to the use of large buying groups to purchase medical care and pharmaceuticals, thereby using monopsony power to force lower prices. The Canadian system, wherein each province has control over the hospital and medical care budgets, is an example of the monopsony approach of managed competition.

managed competition: government intervention in the health-care market to guide competition so that costs are reduced

managed care: comprehensive medical care provided within one firm

The large buyer, the provincial government, purchases services for the citizens in the province.

Managed care refers to the situation where patients purchase membership in a medical firm—the HMO or PPO—that provides physicians, pharmaceuticals, tests, hospitals, and any other medical treatment. The HMO may contract with pharmaceutical companies, hospitals, and physicians or it may hire the physicians, own the hospitals, and dispense pharmaceuticals itself whereas the PPO contracts with individual physicians, hospitals, and pharmacies.

Enrollment in HMOs has risen from 19 million people in 1990 to over 60 million today, while enrollment in PPOs has risen from 28 million to more than 90 million. Employers generally pay HMOs and PPOs a flat monthly fee per employee—called a capitation fee. The HMOs and PPOs earn revenue only by enrolling members—the more members, the more revenue. To increase profit, the HMOs and PPOs must control costs. The HMOs want to reduce the demand for the most costly types of medical services, thereby reducing their costs. Some HMOs and PPOs have provided full coverage for the less costly or routine services and have required copayments when patients seek specialty services. Having to pay a portion of costs, the patient is less likely to seek the service. The HMOs have also discovered that there are significant economies of scale—many have merged—and their minimum efficient scale (MES) point is becoming increasingly large. Thus, the medical care industry is rapidly changing from one dominated by small firms—the individual physician—to an oligopoly. As the efficient size of an HMO is rising, it is becoming increasingly more difficult to start a new HMO. With very large fixed costs and small marginal costs, entry is restricted. Since the industry is becoming an oligopoly, we should expect to observe the same types of behaviors in the health-care market that we observe in other oligopoly markets.

RECAP

1. Health care is the fastest-growing portion of total national expenditures. It is rising primarily because of the rising cost of physician services, nursing homes, and hospital services.

2. The demand for medical care has risen at a very rapid rate. One reason for the increase is the introduction of Medicare and Medicaid and private insurance plans that make demand relatively inelastic. The aging of the population has also increased the demand for medical care.

3. The cost of providing medical care has risen because of increases in hospital costs and physicians' fees. Rising hospital costs are partly a result of the reimbursement plans of third-party providers and partly a result of the control of the operation of hospitals by physicians.

4. Physicians' fees have risen even though the supply of physicians has risen. The demand for medical services does not match the supply; reimbursement methods have led to higher rates of return in certain specialties and thus have drawn an increasing number of physicians to those specialties.

5. In some nations, nearly all medical care is provided by the government; in others, most medical care is purchased by patients. In all, the scarce good, health care, must be rationed, either by price or by some other mechanism.

6. The laws of economics do apply to the medical arena. The difficulty is that people do not like the outcome of those laws.

SUMMARY

❓ Why worry about social security?

1. Social security is a government-mandated pension fund. In the United States it is funded by a tax on employer and employee. The current tax collections are used to provide benefits to current retirees. *§1.a*

❓ Why is health care heading the list of U.S. citizens' concerns?

2. The rapidly rising costs of medical care result from increases in demand relative to supply. *§2.a*

3. The increasing demand results from the aging of the population and from payment systems that decrease the price elasticity of demand. *§2.b.1, 2.b.2*

4. The reduced supply (higher costs of producing medical care) results from inefficiencies in the allocation of physicians among specialties and inefficiencies in the operation and organization of hospitals. *§2.b.4*

5. The health industry is changing in response to rapidly rising costs. Alternative methods of providing health care have arisen. Both HMOs and PPOs provide health care at a lower cost. *§2.c*

6. The percentage of income allocated to health care varies tremendously from country to country. The United States spends more per capita for health care than any other nation. The United States provides medical care through a combination of government programs (Medicare and Medicaid) and private purchases, insurance, and direct payments. Some nations have primarily government-provided systems; others have primarily private systems. *§2.d*

KEY TERMS

Medicare *§2.a*

Medicaid *§2.a*

health maintenance organization (HMO) *§2.c*

preferred provider organization (PPO) *§2.c*

managed competition *§2.e.1*

managed care *§2.e.1*

EXERCISES

1. What is social security? What is Medicare? What is the economic role of these government policies?

2. Why have medical-care expenditures risen more rapidly than expenditures on any other goods and services?

3. Explain how both the supply of physicians and physicians' fees can increase.

4. Why are there more medical specialists and fewer general practitioners in the United States than in Canada?

5. What is the economic logic of increasing social security benefits?

6. What does it mean to say people have a right to a specific good or service? Why do people believe they have a right to medical care but do not believe they have a right to a 3,000-square-foot house?

7. Suppose the objective of government policy is to increase an economy's growth and raise citizens' standards of living. Explain in this context the roles of retirement, social security, Medicare, and mandatory retirement.

8. Explain why the U.S. system of payment for medical procedures leads to higher health costs than a system of payment for physicians' services.

9. Analyze the following solutions to the problem of social security.

   a. The retirement age is increased to 70.
   b. The FICA tax is increased.
   c. The income plus social security payments cannot exceed the poverty level.
   d. The total amount of social security benefits received cannot exceed the amount paid in by employer and employee plus the interest earnings on those amounts.

10. Oregon proposed a solution to the health costs problem that was widely criticized. The solution would

allow the state to pay only for common medical problems. Special and expensive problems would not be covered. Using the market for medical care, analyze the Oregon plan.

11. What would be the impact of a policy that did away with Medicare and Medicaid and instead provided each individual with the amounts they contributed during their working lives to the Medicare program?

12. Why is a third-party payer a problem? Private insurance companies are third-party payers and yet they want to maximize profit. So wouldn't they ensure that the allocation of dollars was efficient?

13. "We must recognize that health care is not a commodity. Those with more resources should not be able to purchase services while those with less do without. Health care is a social good that should be available to every person without regard to his or her resources." Evaluate this statement.

Internet Exercises/ Resources

For Internet exercises and web resources related to this chapter, go to
http://college.hmco.com.

Chapter 19 / Aging, Social Security, and Health Care   **437**

Many Travel a Painful Circuit for Their Managed Health Care

Some hobble with injured legs across town for X rays before returning to their doctor, who could have taken the pictures in the first place. Others find themselves pressured to leave one hospital for another, even when their conditions are fragile. And some are referred back to their doctor's office for blood tests, tests that could have been done at the same lab where they had just undergone other screenings. Consumers in the Philadelphia area have discovered that health care under managed care can be a frustrating experience. While some patients are paying less out-of-pocket for well-coordinated care, others are finding unanticipated quirks and limitations that seem to complicate treatment rather than ease it. Managed care is not supposed to be a maze. Its goals include making medical care more accessible for consumers and less expensive for employers by overseeing who receives treatment, how much they get, and where they go for it. Until now, the Philadelphia area has lagged in replacing traditional indemnity plans—patients pick doctors, insurers pay bill—with

managed care. But, that's changing, as employers and consumers alike face rising health-care costs. One estimate indicates that nearly 4 to 10 people in the region belong to a health maintenance organization, one type of managed care. Among them are Sonya and Gus Pappas of Swarthmore, whose experiences under managed care could not have been more different, even though both were treated last year under the same insurance plan.

Gus Pappas, 32, an accountant, said he had been swaddled in the best health care imaginable from the moment he collapsed on his way to his doctor's office last March, through surgery for colon cancer, and nearly a year of follow-up chemotherapy. And he never saw a bill. By contrast, his wife, 28, a fund-raiser, encountered a bureaucratic morass as she sought treatment for infertility. Rather than travel to the lab to which the insurer directed her for tests, she paid hundreds of dollars a month out-of-pocket to use the lab at her doctor's office.

"You feel trapped," said Sonya Pappas, who sees patients as

caught in a riptide of change racing through health care. "It is almost like you don't know what everyone's role is and where they stand."

Some observers say the insurers seem to use their advantage to direct patients to services with low rates, even if they weren't user-friendly. Consequently, doctors and patients complain about inefficiencies, delays, higher costs, and even compromised care. "In searching for the best price, they fragment the system," said Alan Zuckerman, executive vice president in Philadelphia for Chi Systems, a health-care consulting firm.

"Our position is that we have more comprehensive benefits, high-quality delivery systems and better prices," said John Daddis, the Philadelphia insurer's senior vice president for managed care. "There are some trade-offs on choice. But that's inherent in the whole concept."

Source: Marian Uhlman, "Many Travel a Painful Circuit for Their Managed Health Care," *Philadelphia Inquirer*, February 1, 1995, p. 1. Reprinted by permission.

Philadelphia Inquirer/**February 1, 1995**

Commentary

Rationing of one kind or another is inevitable with a scarce good. For the vast majority of goods, people have chosen rationing by price. Many have difficulty with applying that same choice to medical care. Moreover, because of the way that firms have provided medical care benefits to employees, there has been little regard to the price of medical care over the past twenty years. Since patients do not pay directly for care, the patients have no incentive to be price conscious. They encourage doctors to carry out additional tests and to provide the most technologically advanced medical care. This, combined with the government provision of medical care for the elderly, drove the prices of medical care and medical insurance up at accelerating rates during the 1970s and 1980s.

To reduce their costs, firms began to look for alternative ways to provide their employees medical insurance benefits. What evolved is managed care—a firm enlists physicians and all medical experts to provide services to enrollees. Some firms hire the physicians directly while others contract with the physicians to provide services at a certain fee. Most physicians accept the conditions because the demand for their services on a fee-for-service basis is rapidly declining. To reduce costs, the managing firm allocates patients among doctors so that workloads are about equal. The managing firm also provides only the basic types of medical procedures. Fertility, plastic surgery, and certain high-technology or experimental procedures, like bone-marrow transplants, are not covered by the managed care. If enrollees want to go outside of the firm or network for care, then they must pay out of pocket. This is what Sonya Pappas decided to do.

The demand curve for medical care looks like any other demand curve; it slopes down because the higher the price, the lower the quantity of medical care demanded. There also is a standard-looking supply curve; physicians, hospitals, and medical firms offer an increasing quantity of medical care for sale as the price rises. As shown in the diagram below, with demand's rising—the demand curve's shifting out—the price of medical care rose. Managed care is an attempt to reduce the rate at which the demand curve shifts out—shown as the smaller shifts from D_3 to D_4 to D_5. It also is an attempt to reduce the cost of supplying medical care—causing the supply curve to shift down—shown as the shift from S_1 to S_2. If successful, the managed care approach would lead to an equilibrium at a lower price and higher quantity.

As the article noted, there are tradeoffs involved. If people are willing and able to pay the price, then they can get any medical care they want. If they are not willing or able to pay the price, they must take what is available at the lower price. In other words, rationing the care in some way other than price occurs. In some cases, services are not available—are not supplied. In other cases, it is a first-come, first-served basis; those coming into the office first get served first. Lines and waiting in offices result. In still other cases, the patient is shuffled from place to place and medical facility to medical facility—time and convenience allocate the scarce goods.

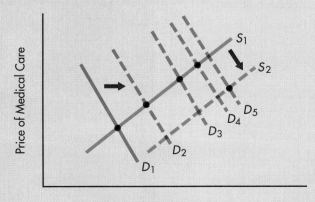

Income Distribution, Poverty, and Government Policy

? Fundamental Questions

1. Are incomes distributed equally in the United States?

2. How is poverty measured, and does poverty exist in the United States?

3. Who are the poor?

4. What are the determinants of income?

5. How does the government try to reduce poverty?

Preview

Half a million Americans will spend today living on city streets or in temporary shelters, and more than a million will do so over the next year. The trickle of people surviving on city streets a decade ago has become a steady stream—men, women, children, white, African American, Hispanic, mentally healthy, mentally ill. *Homeless* used to describe people who were transient, poor, socially isolated, and living in the cheap hotels and flophouses on skid row. They had housing, but they didn't have homes. Today, the homeless are "houseless" too.

Even the poor in the United States are better off than the entire populations of other nations, however. In Bolivia, the average life expectancy is only 53 years, a full 20 years less than in the United States. In Burma, only about one-fourth of the population has access to safe water. In Burundi, less than one-fourth of the urban

houses have electricity. In Chad, less than one-third of the children reach the sixth grade. In Ethiopia, the per capita income is $120, sixty times lower than in the United States.

What accounts for the inequality among nations and among households within a nation? Who are the poor and the rich? Is the inequality of incomes something that can or should be corrected? These questions are the topic of this chapter. Previous chapters have discussed how the market system works to ensure that resources flow to their highest-valued uses, that output is produced in the least-cost manner, and that people get what they want at the lowest possible price—in other words, the efficiency of the market system. Efficiency and equity do not necessarily go together, however. Efficiency implies that goods and services are allocated to those with the ability to pay, not necessarily to those with needs. ■

1. INCOME DISTRIBUTION AND POVERTY

In a market system, incomes are distributed according to the ownership of resources. Those who own the most highly valued resources have the highest incomes. One consequence of a market system, therefore, is that incomes are distributed unequally.

1.a. A Measure of Income Inequality

1. Are incomes distributed equally in the United States?

Lorenz curve: a curve measuring the degree of inequality of income distribution within a society

In the United States, as in every country, there are rich and there are poor. Incomes are not distributed equally and the degree of inequality varies widely from country to country. In order to compare income distributions, economists need a measure of income inequality. The most widely used measure is the **Lorenz curve,** which provides a picture of how income is distributed among members of a population.

Equal incomes among members of a population can be plotted as a 45-degree line that is equidistant from the axes (see Figure 1). The horizontal axis measures the total population in cumulative percentages. As we move along the horizontal axis, we are counting a larger and larger percentage of the population. The numbers end at 100, which designates 100 percent of the population. The vertical axis measures total real GDP in cumulative percentages. As we move up the vertical axis, the percentage of total real GDP being counted rises to 100 percent. The 45-degree line splitting the distance between the axes is called the *line of income equality.* At each point on the line, the percentage of total population and the percentage of total real GDP are equal. The line of income equality indicates that 10 percent of the population earns 10 percent of the income, 20 percent of the population earns 20 percent of the income, and so on, until we see that 90 percent of the population earns 90 percent of the income and 100 percent of the population earns 100 percent of the income.

Points off the line of income equality indicate an income distribution that is unequal. Figure 1 shows the line of income equality and a curve that bows down below the income-equality line. The bowed curve is a Lorenz curve. The Lorenz curve in Figure 1 is for the United States. The bottom 20 percent of the population receives 3.6 percent of total real GDP income, seen at point *A*. The second 20 percent accounts for another 9.6 percent of real GDP income, shown as point *B*, so the bottom 40 percent of the population has 12.8 percent of the real GDP income (3.6 percent owned by the first 20 percent of the population plus the additional

Figure 1

The U.S. Lorenz Curve

The farther a Lorenz curve lies from the line of income equality, the greater the inequality of the income distribution. The bottom 20 percent of the U.S. population receives 4.6 percent of total real GDP income, seen at point *A*. The second 20 percent accounts for another 9.6 percent of real GDP income, shown as point *B*, where the bottom 40 percent of the population has 12.8 percent of the real GDP income (3.6 percent owned by the first 20 percent of the population plus the additional 9.6 percent owned by the second 20 percent). The third 20 percent accounts for another 15.2 percent of real GDP income, so point *C* is plotted at a population of 60 percent and an income of 28.4 percent. The fourth 20 percent accounts for another 23.4 percent of the real GDP income, shown as point *D*, where 80 percent of the population owns 51.8 percent of the income. The richest 20 percent accounts for the remaining 48.2 percent of real GDP income, shown as point *E*. With the last 20 percent of the population and the last 48.2 percent of real GDP income, 100 percent of population and 100 percent of real GDP income are accounted for. Point *E*, therefore, is plotted where both income and population are 100 percent. Source: Data are from "A Brief Look at Postwar U.S. Income Inequality," "The Changing Shape of the Nation's Income Distribution, 1947–98" (P60-204).
http://www.census.gov/hhes/www/incineq.html
http://ferret.bls.census.gov

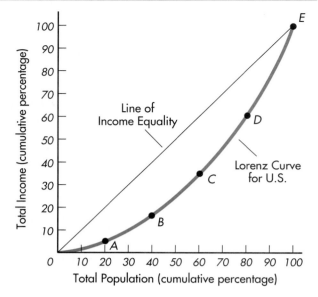

9.6 percent owned by the second 20 percent). The third 20 percent accounts for another 15.7 percent of real GDP income, so point *C* is plotted at a population of 60 percent and an income of 28.4 percent. The fourth 20 percent accounts for another 23.4 percent of the national income, shown as point *D*, where 80 percent of the population receives 51.8 percent of the income. The richest 20 percent accounts for the remaining 48.2 percent of real GDP income, shown as point *E*. With the last 20 percent of the population and the last 48.2 percent of real GDP income, 100 percent of population and 100 percent of real GDP income are accounted for. Point *E*, therefore, is plotted where both income and population are 100 percent.[1]

The farther the Lorenz curve bows down, away from the line of income equality, the greater the inequality of the distribution of income. In Chapter 4 it was noted that

---

[1]A Lorenz curve for wealth could also be shown. It would bow down below the Lorenz curve for income, indicating that wealth is more unequally distributed than income. Wealth and income are different and should be kept distinct. Wealth is the stock of assets. Income is the flow of earnings that results from the stock of assets.

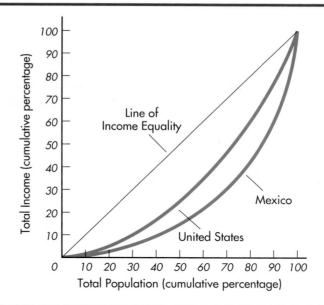

Figure 2

Lorenz Curves for Mexico and the United States

Based on data for the United States and Mexico, the two Lorenz curves show that total real GDP income in Mexico is distributed among Mexican citizens much more unequally than total real GDP income in the United States is distributed among citizens of the United States. Source: Data are from *World Development Report, 1997,* Table 5.

on average, in developed countries, the richest 20 percent of households receive about 40 percent of household income and the poorest 20 percent receive only about 5 or 6 percent of household income. That distribution, however, is much more equal than the distribution found in developing countries. In developing countries the richest 20 percent of the population receives more than 50 percent of total household income, and the poorest 20 percent receives less than 4 percent of total household income. Figure 2 shows two Lorenz curves, one for the United States and one for Mexico. The curve for Mexico bows down far below the curve for the United States, indicating the greater inequality in Mexico.

1.b. Income Distribution Among Nations

Incomes differ greatly from one nation to another as well as within nations. Mexico's income distribution is less equal than in the United States, but income levels in Mexico are also significantly lower than in the United States. The per capita annual income in Mexico is $4,265, while in the United States it exceeds $28,000. Figure 3 shows the per capita incomes of several countries. The figure illustrates how great the differences in per capita income are. The Economic Insight "Economic Development and Happiness" suggests that the feeling of well-being of a population generally depends on the levels of per capita income.

The distribution of total world income among nations is very unequal, as shown in Figure 4. Three-fourths of the world's population lives in developing countries, but the income earned by the people in these countries—the lowest 90 percent of the population in terms of income—is only about 20 percent of the total world income, shown as point *A*. The richest countries, earning nearly 80 percent of total world income, have only 10 percent of the world's population, the difference between *A* and *B*.

Figure 3

Per Capita Real Gross Domestic Product

Levels of income vary tremendously among nations; for instance, per capita income in Switzerland is the highest; Ethiopia the lowest. Source: www.un.org/pubs/cyberschoolbus.

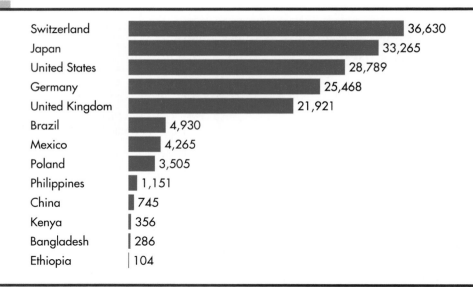

Switzerland	36,630
Japan	33,265
United States	28,789
Germany	25,468
United Kingdom	21,921
Brazil	4,930
Mexico	4,265
Poland	3,505
Philippines	1,151
China	745
Kenya	356
Bangladesh	286
Ethiopia	104

Figure 4

World Lorenz Curve

The Lorenz curve is typically used to illustrate the income distribution within countries. In this figure a Lorenz curve is drawn to compare how world income is distributed across countries. The bottom 90 percent of the world's population, residing in the less developed countries, accounts for 20 percent of the world's income, shown as point A. The richest 10 percent of the population, residing in the developed countries, accounts for 80 percent of total income, shown as point B. Source: Data are from World Development Report, 1999 and 2000.

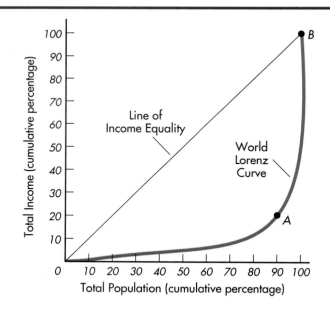

Economic Development and Happiness

A nation's standard of living influences the attitudes of the nation's population toward life in general, although it is not the only factor. Year after year, the Danes, Swiss, Irish, and Dutch feel happier and more satisfied with life than do the French, Greeks, Italians, and Germans. Regardless of whether they are German-, French-, or Italian-speaking, the Swiss rank very high on life satisfaction— much higher than their German, French, and Italian neighbors. People in the Scandinavian countries generally are both prosperous and happy. However, the link between national affluence and well-being isn't consistent. Germans, for instance, average more than double the per capita income of the Irish, but the Irish are happier. Similarly, although the developed nations all had higher per capita incomes than the Mexicans, the Mexicans stated a higher satisfaction with life than the populations of many of the developed nations. The overall pattern does show that wealthier nations tend to show higher levels of life satisfaction than poorer ones, but income and wealth are not the only factors influencing happiness. Related to wealth is the type of government under which citizens live. The most prosperous nations have enjoyed stable democratic governments, and there is a link between a history of stable democracy and national well-being. The thirteen nations that have maintained democratic institutions continuously since 1920 all enjoy higher life satisfaction levels than do the eleven nations whose democracies developed after World War II.

Sources: Ronald Inglehart, *Culture Shift in Advanced Industrial Society* (Princeton, N.J.: Princeton University Press, 1990); David G. Myers, *The Pursuit of Happiness* (New York: William Morrow and Company, 1992).

2. How is poverty measured, and does poverty exist in the United States?

1.c. Measuring Poverty

A Lorenz curve does not indicate who the poor are or what their quality of life is. It is a relative measure. On the other hand, an absolute measure such as per capita income does not necessarily indicate how people feel about their income status or whether they enjoy good health and a decent standard of living. Those who are comfortable in one country could be impoverished in another. The poverty level in the United States would represent a substantial increase in living standards in many other nations. Yet members of a poor family in the United States would probably not feel less poor if they knew that their income level exceeded the median income in other countries.

1.d. The Definition of Poverty

If income or per capita income is to be used as a measure of poverty, then the proper definition of *income* must be used. Economists can measure income before any government intervention affecting the distribution of income, after accounting for government cash transfers, or after accounting for government cash transfers and assistance like food or shelter.

The first of these measurements indicates what people would earn from the market system in the absence of government intervention. To obtain a good measure of this income figure is virtually impossible because the government is such an important part of the economic system in almost all countries, including the United States. The U.S. government transfers over $400 billion annually from taxpayers to various groups.

Table 1

Year	Poverty Level	Year	Poverty Level
1959	$ 2,973	1985	$10,989
1960	$ 3,022	1986	$11,203
1966	$ 3,317	1987	$11,611
1969	$ 3,743	1988	$12,090
1970	$ 3,968	1989	$12,675
1975	$ 5,500	1990	$13,359
1976	$ 5,815	1991	$13,924
1977	$ 6,191	1992	$13,950
1978	$ 6,662	1993	$14,764
1979	$ 7,412	1994	$15,200
1980	$ 8,414	1995	$15,600
1981	$ 9,287	1996	$16,036
1982	$ 9,862	1997	$16,400
1983	$10,178	1998	$16,660
1984	$10,609	1999	$16,895
		2000	$17,463

Average Income Poverty Cutoffs for a Nonfarm Family of Four in the United States, 1959–1999

Sources: www.census.gov/hhes/www/poverty.html.

cash transfers: money allocated away from one group in society to another

in-kind transfers: the allocations of goods and services from one group in society to another

Poverty statistics published by the federal government are based on incomes that include earnings from cash transfers but often not in-kind transfers. **Cash transfers** are unearned funds given to certain sectors of the population. They include social security retirement benefits, disability pensions, and unemployment compensation to those who are temporarily out of work. **In-kind transfers,** or non-cash transfers, are services or products provided to certain sectors of society. They include food purchased with food stamps and medical services provided under Medicaid. Although economists agree that these in-kind transfers increase the economic well-being of those who receive them, there is much debate over how they should be accounted for and the extent to which they should be added to money income for the purpose of defining *poverty*. The official poverty rate measure does not account for in-kind transfers. If it did, the official poverty rate would be significantly lower.

The U.S. government uses after-transfers income to measure poverty, but does not include all such transfers. It adds market earnings, the cash equivalent of non-cash transfers, and cash transfers to calculate family incomes. But it does not include food stamps, aid to families with dependent children (AFDC), or housing subsidies. In sum, the poverty measure is arbitrary. It is an arbitrary level of income, and income is an arbitrary measure of the ability to purchase necessities.

Table 1 lists the average poverty levels of income for a nonfarm family of four since 1959. Families with incomes above the cutoffs would be above the poverty level, in the eyes of the federal government.

Where does the arbitrary poverty income level come from? A 1955 study found that the average family in the United States spent about one-third of its income on food, so when the government decided to begin measuring poverty in the 1960s, it

Figure 5

The Trends of Poverty Incidence

The number of people classified as living in poverty is measured on the left vertical axis. The percentage of the population classified as living in poverty is measured on the right vertical axis. The number and the percentage declined steadily throughout the 1960s, rose during the recessions of 1969, 1974, 1981, and 1990 and fell between 1982 and 1990 and again from 1992 to 2000. Sources: www.census.gov/ hhes/www/poverty.html.

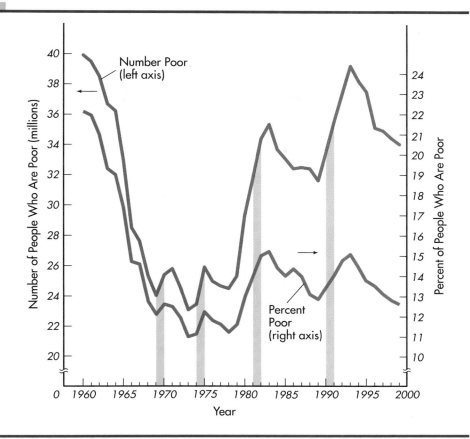

calculated the cost to purchase a meal that met a predetermined nutritional standard and multiplied that cost by 3. That is where it drew the poverty line. Since then, the official poverty-line income has been adjusted for inflation each year.

1.e. Poverty Distribution and Economic Trends

How many Americans fall below the poverty line? Figure 5 compares the number of people living in poverty and the percentage of the total population living in poverty (the incidence of poverty) for each year. From 1960 to the late 1970s, the incidence of poverty declined rapidly. From the late 1970s until the early 1980s, the incidence of poverty rose; it then began to decline again after 1982. Small upswings in the incidence of poverty occurred in 1968 and 1974, and a large rise occurred between 1978 and 1982. It then fell until 1990, when the U.S. once again dipped into recession. It continued to rise even as the economy grew in 1993 and then declined through 1997.

The health of the economy is a primary determinant of the incidence of poverty.

A major factor accounting for the incidence of poverty is the health of the economy. People are generally made better off by economic growth. Economic stagnation and recession throw the relatively poor out of their jobs and into poverty. Economic growth increases the number of jobs and draws people out of poverty and into the mainstream of economic progress.

Four recent recessions have had important impacts on the numbers of people thrown into poverty. The recession of 1969–1970 was relatively mild. Between 1969 and 1971, the unemployment rate rose from 3.4 to 5.8 percent, and the total number of people unemployed rose from 2,832,000 to 5,016,000. This recession halted the decline in poverty rates for two years. When the economy once again began to expand, the poverty rates dropped. The 1974 recession brought on another bout of unemployment that threw people into poverty. The 1974 recession was relatively serious, causing the unemployment rate to rise to 8.3 percent by 1975 and the number of unemployed to rise to 7,929,000. Once again, however, the poverty rate declined as the economy picked up after 1975. The recession of 1980–1982 threw the economy off track again. In 1979, the total number of people unemployed was 6,137,000; by 1982, a whopping 10,717,000 were without jobs. As the economy came out of this recession, the poverty rate began to decline, and it continued to decline as the economy grew throughout the 1980s. However, the poverty rate rose as the economy fell into recession in 1990 and struggled into 1992. The poverty rate of 14.2 percent in 1991 was the highest level in nearly three decades; the number of people living in poverty grew to 35.7 million. Somewhat surprising was that the number of people in poverty and the incidence of poverty both grew in 1993 and 1994, years of economic growth. Some people point to this as evidence that the poverty measure is flawed, that it does not give an accurate indication of who and how many do not get proper nutrition and health care. Some argue that the poverty rate is really not nearly as high as these figures indicate; that government transfers and programs are not properly taken into account. Others argue that it is an indication that government programs must be increased, that not enough care is taken to provide for the poor.

There are many controversies over the poverty measure. The measure makes no distinction between the needs of a 3-month-old and a 14-year-old or between a rural

Incomes are unequally distributed in every nation. In developing countries, the distinction between rich and poor is greater than in the industrial nations, although the per capita income is significantly less in the developing countries. For instance, although the per capita income in Nigeria is only 7 percent of the per capita income in the United States, the wealthy in Lagos, Nigeria live very well, with large houses, servants, expensive clothes, and other accouterments of wealth. During the 1970s, many Nigerians became very wealthy as the price of oil surged and Nigerian oil production rose. Economic crisis and the collapse of oil prices since the late 1970s has led to a decline in Nigeria that wiped out the gains of the previous twenty years.

family in a cold climate and an urban family in the subtropics. It draws no distinction between income and purchasing power. A welfare mom living on $400 a month is treated identically to a graduate student who earns $400 a month at a part-time job and borrows an additional $1,500 from her parents. Nor does it consider the problem of income from the underground economy—the income not reported or measured in income statistics. Nevertheless, the measure is used to determine how federal government money is to be allocated among states and regions.

RECAP

1. The Lorenz curve shows the degree to which incomes are distributed equally in a society.
2. The Lorenz curve bows down below the line of equality for all nations. It is less bowed for developed nations than for developing countries, because income is more equally distributed in developed than in developing countries.
3. There are two ways to measure poverty: with an absolute measure and with a relative measure. The Lorenz curve is a relative measure. Per capita income is an absolute measure.
4. Per capita income after cash and in-kind transfers is used by the U.S. government to define poverty.
5. Recessions increase the incidence of poverty; economic growth reduces the incidence of poverty.

3. Who are the poor?

2. THE POOR

Poverty is not a condition that randomly strikes women and men, and white, African American, and Hispanic families equally. Nor does it strike the educated and well trained in the same way it strikes the uneducated. The incidence of poverty itself is unequally distributed among sectors of the society.

2.a. Temporary and Permanent Poverty

If those who are poor at any one time are poor only temporarily, then their plight is only temporary. If people in poverty are able to improve their situation while others slip into poverty temporarily, the problem of poverty for society is not as serious as it is if poverty is a permanent condition once a person has slipped into it.

Studies indicate that approximately 25 percent of all Americans fall below the poverty line at some time in their lives. Many of these spells of poverty are relatively short; nearly 45 percent last less than a year. However, more than 50 percent of those in poverty at a particular time remain in poverty for at least ten years.

One major determinant of an individual's income is age. A young person or a senior citizen has a much greater chance of suffering a low income than a person who is between 30 and 60 years old. Figure 6 shows the percentage of the population below the poverty level by race and age in 1995. The highest incidence of poverty by age occurs among those under 18 years. The second highest occurs among those between 18 and 24. The third highest occurs among those 25 to 34.

Figure 6

Age, Race, and Poverty

The young and old constitute most of the poverty group: 24 percent of the children under age six live in poverty. And 12.9 percent of people 65 or older also live in poverty. The poverty rate among whites is 11.2 percent; among African Americans, 28.4 percent; and among Hispanics, 29.4 percent. Source: *Statistical Abstract of the United States, 1999.* www.census.gov/hhes/ www/poverty/.

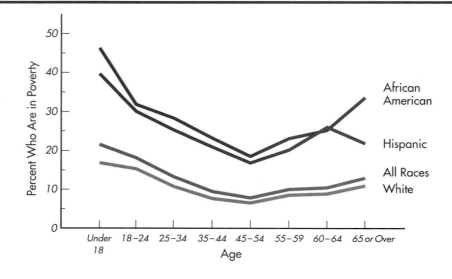

Poverty does not affect all racial and all age groups equally. As Figure 7 shows, the percentages of the population of different groups that fall below the poverty level each year are not equal. African Americans and Hispanics carry a much heavier burden of poverty relative to the size of their populations than do whites.

Poverty does not affect races, sexes, or different age groups equally.

Poverty does not affect males and females equally either. Approximately 35 percent of all families headed by a female have poverty-level incomes. Only 8 percent

Figure 7

The Incidence of Poverty by Race and Hispanic Origin

The incidence of poverty is higher for African Americans and Hispanics than it is for whites. Good times help whites more than they help other races, and bad times harm whites less than they harm other races. Sources: *Current Population Reports,* 1999 and *Statistical Abstract of the United States, 1999.* www.census.gov/hhes/ www/poverty/.

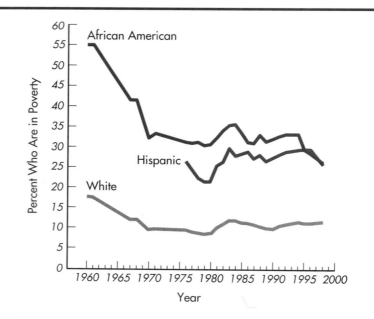

of all families headed by a male have incomes so low. More than 55 percent of households with a female head and children are living in poverty.

2.b. Causes of Poverty

4. What are the determinants of income?

The primary characteristic of those who fall below the poverty line is the lack of a job.

The less education a person has, the greater his or her chance of experiencing poverty.

The primary characteristic of those who fall below the poverty line is the lack of a job—elderly, young, and nonworking students. People who fall below the poverty line may have jobs but work less than full-time, or their jobs may pay so little that their income does not exceed the poverty cutoff. For instance, a job paying the minimum wage for 40 hours a week and 50 weeks a year yields an income that is more than $6,000 below the poverty level.

Place of residence also affects a person's ability to earn income. A little over half of the poor live in big cities, where they tend to be concentrated downtown. The remainder live in rural areas.

The less education an individual has, the lower the income that individual earns. The less education an individual has, the greater the chance that individual will experience poverty. A significant percentage of those in poverty have less than eight years of education. Fully 25 percent of the people with less than eight years of education fall below the poverty level of income. Only 4 percent of those with one or more years of college fall below the poverty cutoff. Lack of education prevents people from securing well-paying jobs. Without the human capital obtained from education or training programs, finding a job that is stable and will not disappear during a recession is very difficult. Even someone who has the desire to work but has no exceptional abilities and has not acquired the skills necessary for a well-paying job is unlikely to escape poverty completely. Minorities and women, the young, the disabled, and the old have disproportionately less education than the rest of the population and as a result have a higher likelihood of falling into poverty.

1. Many people experience poverty only temporarily. Nearly 45 percent of the spells of poverty last less than a year. However, nearly 50 percent of those in poverty remain there for at least ten years.
2. The highest incidences of poverty occur among those who are under 21 or over 65.
3. The incidence of poverty is much higher among African Americans and Hispanics than it is among whites.
4. A poor person may be poor because of age, lack of a job, lack of education, or place of residence.

3. GOVERNMENT ANTIPOVERTY POLICIES

5. How does the government try to reduce poverty?

Why are economists and others concerned with income inequality and poverty? One reason might be normative. People might have compassion for those who have less than they do, or people might not like to see the squalid living conditions endured by some in poverty. In other words, the existence of poverty may mean lower levels of utility for members of society not in poverty. If increases in poverty mean decreases in utility, then people will want less poverty. They will be willing and able to purchase less poverty by allocating portions of their income or their time to alleviating the problem.

Another reason for concern about income inequality and poverty might be positive, or not dependent on value judgments. Perhaps the inequality is a result of inefficiency, and a correction of the situation that creates the inefficiency will improve the functioning of the economy. For instance, if education provides benefits for society that are not taken into account in individual decisions to acquire education, then too few people acquire education. People who would have acquired education if the positive benefits for society had been subsidized but did not are wasted resources. These people would have earned more income, fewer would have fallen into poverty, and the distribution of income might have been more equal. In this sense, the number of people in poverty and the existence of income inequality provide indications that allocative efficiency has failed to occur.

The government is often called on to resolve market failures. If poverty is distasteful to society, then citizens, by paying taxes and through their votes, may ask the government to reduce poverty. Whatever the rationale, positive or normative, the fact is that the government is involved in antipoverty programs and in the attempt to reduce income inequality. Having accepted this fact, several questions arise. For instance, is the government carrying out its antipoverty programs efficiently? What are the ramifications of the government programs? Have the programs reduced poverty?

3.a. Tax Policy

One approach to reducing poverty is to provide people with enough income to bring them above the poverty level. Funds used to supplement the incomes of the poor must come from somewhere. Many societies adopt a Robin Hood approach, taxing the rich to give to the poor. Income taxes can influence income distribution through their impact on after-tax income. Taxes may be progressive, proportional, or regressive.

progressive income tax: a tax whose rate increases as income increases

A **progressive income tax** is a tax that rises as income rises—the marginal tax rate increases as income increases. If someone with an annual income of $20,000 pays $5,000 in taxes while someone else with an annual income of $40,000 pays $12,000 in taxes, the tax rate is progressive. The first person is paying a 25 percent rate, and the second is paying a 30 percent rate.

proportional tax: a tax whose rate does not change as the tax base changes

A **proportional tax** is a tax whose rate does not change as the tax base changes. The rate of a proportional income tax remains the same at every level of income. If the tax rate is 20 percent, then individuals who earn $10,000 or $100,000 pay 20 percent.

regressive tax: a tax whose rate decreases as the tax base changes

A **regressive tax** is a tax whose rate decreases as the tax base increases. The social security tax is regressive; a specified rate is paid on income up to a specified level. On income beyond that level, no social security taxes are paid. In 2000, cutoff level of income was $76,200 and the tax rate was 6.2%. A person earning $300,000 paid no more social security taxes than someone earning $80,000.

A progressive tax rate tends to reduce income inequality; a proportional tax does not affect income distribution; and a regressive tax increases inequality. The progressive tax takes larger percentages of income from high-income members of society than it takes from low-income members. This tends to equalize after-tax incomes. In the United States, the federal income tax is progressive. The tax rate rises from zero to 36 percent as income rises (39 percent for incomes above $1 million).

3.b. Transfers

The main transfer programs are social insurance, cash welfare or public assistance, in-kind transfers, and employment programs. Social security—officially known as

Old Age, Survivors, and Disability Insurance (OASDI) and listed as FICA on your paycheck stubs—is the largest social insurance program. It helps a family replace income that is lost when a worker retires in old age, becomes severely disabled, or dies. Coverage is nearly universal, so the total amount of money involved is immense—nearly $200 billion annually. Two-thirds of the aged rely on social security for more than half of their income.

Unemployment insurance provides temporary benefits to regularly employed people who become temporarily unemployed. Funded by a national tax on payrolls levied on firms with eight or more workers, the system is run by state governments. Benefits normally amount to about 50 percent of a worker's usual wage.

Aid to Families with Dependent Children (AFDC) is the second largest cash welfare program. The average AFDC family is headed by a mother with two small children and receives about $400 per month. In 1996 the federal government required each state to develop its own welfare program, one that contained a system for creating work for recipients who were able.

Supplemental Security Income (SSI) ranks first among cash welfare programs. Fully 65 percent of the SSI population is blind or otherwise disabled. The rest are over age 65. Unlike social security recipients, who are *entitled* to receive benefits because they are a certain age or otherwise qualify, recipients of SSI must meet certain disability requirements or be of a certain age and must have incomes below about $4,500 per year.

About 60 percent of all poor households receive in-kind transfers. The largest of these programs is Medicaid (for a discussion of Medicaid and the medical-care industry, see the chapter "Aging, Social Security, and Health Care"). Medicaid provides federal funds to states to help them cover the costs of long-term medical and nursing-home care. Second in magnitude is the food stamp program, which gives households coupons that are redeemable at grocery stores. The amounts vary with income and household size. Other programs include jobs and training directed toward disadvantaged workers and the Head Start program, an education program available to poor children. Total government outlays for social service (welfare) programs run more than $700 billion annually.

3.c. The Effectiveness of Welfare Programs

In 1964, President Lyndon Johnson declared "unconditional war on poverty." In 1967, total transfers were about $10 billion. After nearly a quarter-century of increasing outlays to reduce poverty, is the war being won? Unfortunately, there is no easy or straightforward answer to that question. In fact, there is disagreement about whether antipoverty programs have reduced or increased poverty. Some people maintain that without the programs, income inequality and poverty would have been much more severe. Others argue that welfare has been a drag on the economy and may have made poverty and inequality worse than they otherwise would have been.

It is impossible to compare what did happen with what would have happened in the absence of the government's programs. All economists can do is look at what actually occurred. The distribution of money income among families in 1929, 1992, and 1998 is shown in Figure 8. The Lorenz curve has shifted in toward the line of income equality since 1929. In 1929, the lowest 20 percent of the population had 4 percent of the income and the top 5 percent had 30 percent of the income. In 1992, the lowest 20 percent had about 4 percent and the top 5 percent had about 18 percent.

Another measure of income distribution is provided by a **Gini ratio.** The Gini ratio is a measure of the dispersion of income that ranges between 0 and 1. The Gini

Gini ratio: a measure of the dispersion of income ranging between 0 and 1; 0 means all families have the same income; 1 means one family has all of the income

Figure 8

Income Distribution over Time

Income distribution in the United States is more equal now than in 1929 but less equal than in 1994. This is shown by the movement of the Lorenz curve in toward the line of income equality. Sources: *World Development Report, 1999* and *2000*; *Current Population Reports.* www.census.gov/hhes/www/poverty/.

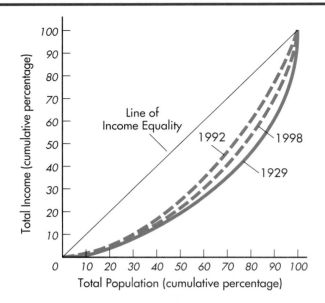

ratio measures the deviation between the Lorenz curve and the line of perfect equality; it is a measure of the area between the Lorenz curve and the line of perfect equality divided by the total area if one family had all of the income. A lower Gini value indicates less dispersion in the income distribution: a Gini of 0 would occur if every family had the exact same amount of income; a Gini of 1 would occur if all income accrued to only one family. Figure 9 shows that from 1947 to 1968 the dispersion of income fell gradually but has risen since.

Figure 10 shows the annual expenditures on poverty programs along with the incidence of poverty from 1960. The incidence-of-poverty curve is taken from Figure 5. During the 1960s, as transfers and spending increased, the incidence of poverty fell. Since the early 1970s, transfers and spending has increased much more rapidly than in the previous decade, but the incidence of poverty has changed little, and in fact, it rose during the recessions of the early 1980s and the early 1990s.

3.c.1. Disincentives Created by the Welfare System

Those who argue that welfare programs are a drag on the economy and may make poverty and income inequality worse typically focus on the disincentives created by the transfers. Incentives for both the rich and the poor to work hard and increase their productivity may be reduced by programs that take from the rich and give to the poor. Those paying taxes may ask themselves, "Why should I work an extra hour every day if all the extra income does is pay additional taxes?" Someone who gets to keep only 60 cents out of the next dollar earned has less incentive to earn that dollar than if he or she gets to keep it all.

Those who receive benefits may lose the incentive to change their status. Why should someone take a job paying $6,000 per year when he or she can remain unemployed and receive $8,000? Someone out of work might wonder, "Why should I spend eight hours a day in miserable working conditions when I can relax every day

Figure 9

The Gini Ratio

The Gini ratio is a measure of the dispersion of income that ranges between 0 and 1. A lower value indicates less dispersion in the income distribution: a Gini of 0 would occur if every family had the exact same amount of income, while a Gini of 1 would occur if all income accrued to only one family. Figure 9 shows that from 1947 to 1968 the dispersion of income fell gradually. Since then the dispersion has risen slowly. Source: *Economic Report of the President, 2000.*

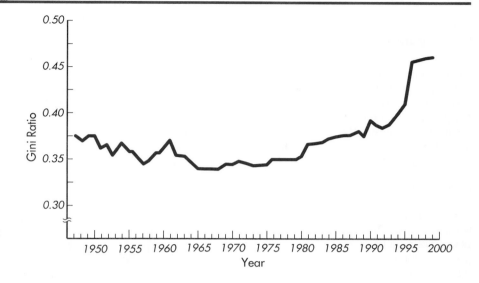

and bring home nearly the same amount of income?" If incentives to work are weak, then the total income created in the economy is less than it otherwise would be. Less income and lower economic growth mean more people in poverty.

3.c.2. Welfare Dependency   Some have argued that the welfare system causes welfare dependency—that children who grow up on welfare are likely to become welfare recipients as adults and to have children who eventually become dependent on welfare. Evidence that such a situation occurs is not strong, but the incentives for it to occur do exist. Society tries to provide families with decent living standards but does not want transfers to go to those who do not need them. As a result, transfer programs are designed to provide the greatest benefits to the people with the lowest incomes. As incomes rise, benefits decrease.

Transfer programs are designed much like a progressive income tax. The higher the person's income, the fewer benefits he or she gets. A family of four with no earned income can receive about $400 worth of food stamps per month. A family of four with $100 of income per month can receive only about $250 worth of food stamps per month. For earning $100, the second family received food stamps worth $50 less than the stamps received by the nonworking family. This is a 30 percent marginal penalty on working. Eventually, as earned income rises, benefits are reduced dollar for dollar—there is a 100 percent marginal penalty on working.

3.d. Equity and Efficiency

Efficiency requires that goods and services go to those willing and able to pay the price. The allocation of goods and services on the basis of equity would provide

Figure 10

Spending and Poverty

Curves representing total government spending in real (1987) billions of dollars on poverty programs since 1960 and the incidence of poverty since 1960 are shown. Total expenditures on antipoverty programs in equal purchasing power terms (real terms) are measured on the left vertical axis, and the percent of population in poverty is shown on the right vertical axis. During the 1960s, the incidence of poverty decreased as spending increased. Since then, spending has continued to increase, but the incidence of poverty has not declined. Source: Department of Commerce, 1999. www.census.gov/hhes/www/poverty/.

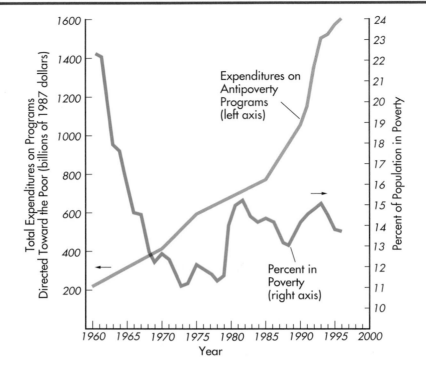

goods to those who meet the definition of *equity*. For instance, if *equity* means "equality," then all persons would receive the same goods and services whether or not they had the ability to pay. If *equity* means "goods and services go to those with the greatest need," then some definition of *need* must be created. *Equity* requires a definition.

There are two general definitions of *equity*: the means test and the ends test. The *ends test* examines the existing situation, the results of whatever has gone on in the past. For instance, the distribution of income is more equal now than it was fifty years ago. This is an end result of whatever occurred during the past fifty years. The *means test* considers the means to achieve the end. If the opportunity to earn income were equally distributed, then according to the means definition, equity would occur even if the existing distribution of income were unequal.

Policymakers who rely on the ends test tend to support policies directed toward changing the existing distribution of income, such as providing assistance to the poor by taking from the rich. A problem with the ends test is that it may be antithetical to efficiency. Policies intended to create a more equal distribution of income can reduce incentives to earn income and thereby reduce the efficiency with which the economy functions.

Policymakers who advocate a means test of equity look not at whether income is distributed equally but instead at whether the opportunity to earn income is distributed equally. To them, *equity* means "equal opportunities to earn, to accumulate wealth, to obtain human capital, and to be an entrepreneur." There need be no trade-off between efficiency and equity if the means definition is used. Efficiency is achieved when entry and exit are free and there are no market failures. Once barriers are erected, efficiency is decreased. Thus, policies that tear down the barriers and resolve the market failures increase the efficiency of the market.

3.e. The Negative Income Tax and Family Allowance Plans

negative income tax (NIT): a tax system that transfers increasing amounts of income to households earning incomes below some specified level as their income declines

The solution to the welfare system problems most often proposed by economists is the **negative income tax (NIT)**—a tax system that transfers increasing amounts of income to households earning incomes below some specified level. The lower the income, the more that is transferred. As income rises above the specified level, a tax is applied. Economists like the NIT because, at least in theory, it attacks the distribution of income and reduces poverty without reducing efficiency.

Suppose policymakers determine that a family of four is to be guaranteed an income of $10,000. If the family earns nothing, then it will get a transfer of $10,000. If the family earns some income, it will receive $10,000 less a tax on the earned income. If the tax rate is 50 percent, then for each dollar earned, $.50 will be taken out of the $10,000 transfer.

The top 20 percent of household income earners in the United States earn 44.6 percent of total household income while the bottom 20 percent earn just 4.6 percent. The government provides assistance to the lowest rungs of income recipients through food stamps, Aid to Families with Dependent Children, Medicare, Medicaid, and public housing. In urban areas, public housing known as the projects are multistory buildings housing hundreds of families. In rural areas, the government-provided housing often takes the form of wide trailers located on the outskirts of small towns.

With a 50 percent tax rate, there would always be some incentive to work under the NIT system because each additional dollar of earnings would bring the recipient of the transfer $.50 in additional income. At some income level, the tax taken would be equal to the transfer of $10,000. This level of income is referred to as the *break-even income level*. The break-even income level in the case of a $10,000 guaranteed income and a 50 percent tax rate is $20,000. Once a family of four earns more than $20,000, its taxes exceed the transfer of $10,000.

The break-even level of income is determined by the income floor and the tax rate:

$$\text{Break-even income} = \frac{\text{income floor}}{\text{negative income tax rate}}$$

If the guaranteed income floor is $13,000 and the tax rate is 50 percent, then the break-even income would be $26,000. If the guaranteed income floor is $13,000 but the tax rate is 33 percent, then the break-even income would be $39,000.

In order for the negative income tax to eradicate poverty, the guaranteed level of income has to be equal to the poverty level, $16,036 in 1996. But if the tax rate is less than 100 percent, the break-even income level will be above the poverty level and families who are not officially considered "poor" will also receive benefits. At a guaranteed income level of $16,036 and a 33 percent tax rate, the break-even income level is $48,108. All families of four earning less than $48,108 would receive some income benefits.

For people now covered by welfare programs, the negative income tax would increase the incentive to work, and that is what proponents of the negative income tax like. However, for people who are too well off to receive welfare but would become eligible for NIT payments, the negative income tax might create work disincentives. It provides these families with more income, and they may choose to buy more leisure.

The possibility of disincentive effects worried both social reformers and legislators, so in the late 1960s the government carried out a number of experiments to estimate the effect of the negative income tax on the supply of labor. Families from a number of U.S. cities were offered negative-income-tax payments in return for allowing social scientists to monitor their behavior. A matched set of families, who were not given NIT payments, were also observed. The idea was to compare the behavior of the families receiving NIT payments with that of the families who did not receive them. The experiments lasted about a decade and showed pretty clearly that the net effects of the negative income tax on labor supply were quite small.

Even though disincentive effects did not seem to occur to any great extent, the negative income tax has not gained political acceptability. One reason is the high break-even income level. Politicians are not very supportive of programs that may provide income transfers to a family earning significantly more than the poverty income level. Another reason is the transfer of dollars rather than in-kind benefits (food and medical care). Policymakers do not look favorably on the idea of giving a family cash that the family can use as it pleases.

RECAP

1. Tax policies can affect the distribution of income. A progressive income tax has a rate that increases as income increases. Thus, a progressive tax reduces

income inequality. A proportional tax has a rate that is the same no matter the income level. A regressive tax has a rate that declines as income increases.

2. The federal income tax in the United States is slightly progressive, with rates rising from zero to 36 percent as income increases.

3. Spending programs used by the government to fight poverty include social insurance, cash welfare, in-kind transfers, and employment programs.

4. Incomes in the United States have become more equally distributed since 1929.

5. *Equity* can be defined as an end or as the means to an end. Defined as an end, *equity* means "equal distribution of income." Defined as the means to an end, *equity* means "equal opportunities to earn income."

6. Economists often propose the negative income tax as a way to resolve the welfare issue. It has not gained political acceptability, however.

SUMMARY

❓ Are incomes distributed equally in the United States?

1. The Lorenz curve illustrates the degree of income inequality. *§1.a*

2. If the Lorenz curve corresponds with the line of income equality, then incomes are distributed equally. If the Lorenz curve bows down below the line of income equality, then income is distributed in such a way that more people earn low incomes than earn high incomes. *§1.a*

3. As a rule, incomes are distributed more unequally in developing countries than in developed countries. *§1.b*

❓ How is poverty measured, and does poverty exist in the United States?

4. Poverty is a measure of how well basic human needs are being met. Poverty is both a relative and an absolute concept. *§1.c*

5. Income consists of resource earnings and transfers. Transfers may be in cash or in kind. The distribution of income in the United States is more unequal when only market earnings are considered than it is when transfers as well as market earnings are considered. *§1.d*

6. The incidence of poverty decreases as the economy grows and increases as the economy falls into recession. *§1.e*

❓ Who are the poor?

7. Many people fall below the poverty line for a short time only. However, a significant core of people remain in poverty for at least ten years. *§2.a*

8. The poor are primarily those without jobs (the youngest and oldest members of society), those residing in the centers of large cities and in rural areas, and those without education. *§2.b*

❓ What are the determinants of income?

9. Age, a lack of education, and a lack of a full-time or well-paying job are the primary determinants of income. *§2.b*

❓ How does the government try to reduce poverty?

10. Tax policies can be used to alter income distribution. A progressive tax takes a higher rate from higher-income groups than from lower-income groups, thus reducing income inequality. *§3.a*

11. Transfer programs are used to fight poverty. The main transfer programs are social insurance, cash welfare or public assistance, in-kind transfers, and employment programs. *§3.b*

12. Welfare systems may reduce incentives to work and thereby harm the economy and cause more poverty. *§3.c.1*

13. *Equity* can be defined as an end or as the means to an end. *Equity* defined as an end is judged on the basis of actual income distributions. *Equity* defined as the means to an end is judged on the basis of equal opportunities to earn income, not on the existing income distribution. *§3.d*

14. The negative income tax is often proposed as a solution to the disincentives created by welfare. The neg- ative income tax would provide income to the lowest-income families. The lower the income, the greater the benefit received by the family. As family income rose, the amount of income transferred to the family would decrease until it reached some break-even level of income. *§3.e*

KEY TERMS

Lorenz curve *§1.a*

cash transfers *§1.d*

in-kind transfers *§1.d*

progressive income tax *§3.a*

proportional tax *§3.a*

regressive tax *§3.a*

Gini ratio *§3.c*

negative income tax (NIT) *§3.e*

EXERCISES

1. What is a Lorenz curve? What would the curve look like if income were equally distributed? Could the curve ever bow upward above the line of income equality?

2. Why does the health of the economy affect the number of people living in poverty?

3. What would it mean if the poverty income level of the United States were applied to Mexico?

4. What is the difference between a means and an ends definition of *equity*? What policies in force today would not be used under the means test of equality?

5. What positive arguments can be made for reducing income inequality? What normative arguments are made for reducing income inequality?

6. What does it mean to say that poverty is a luxury good?

7. Are people who are poor today in the United States likely to be poor for the rest of their lives? Under what conditions is generational poverty likely to exist?

8. Use the following information to plot a Lorenz curve.

Percent of Population	Percent of Income
20	5
40	15
60	35
80	65
100	100

9. If the incidence of poverty decreases during periods when the economy is growing and increases during periods when the economy is in recession, what government policies might be used to reduce poverty most effectively?

10. If the arguments for reducing income inequality and poverty are normative, why rely on the government to reduce the inequality? Why doesn't the private market resolve the problem?

11. How could transfer programs (welfare programs) actually increase the number of people in poverty?

12. What is the difference between in-kind and cash transfers? Which might increase the utility of the recipients the most? Why is there political resistance to the negative income tax?

13. Is it possible to eradicate poverty? The government's definition of poverty is a family of four with reported income less than $16,036. According to a recent study by the Heritage Foundation, this figure does not include the housing that 40 percent of those in poverty own or the cars that 62 percent own. Nor does it consider how the poorest 20 percent of house-holds manage to consume twice as much as they earn. Is poverty a relative concept or an absolute concept?

14. Consider the following three solutions offered to get rid of homelessness and discuss whether any would solve the problem. First, provide permanent housing for all who are homeless. Second, provide free hospital care for the one-third of homeless who are mentally ill. Third, provide subsidies for the homeless to purchase homes.

15. What is the relationship between the Gini coefficient and the Lorenz curve? Illustrate your answer using exercise 8.

Internet Exercises/ Resources

For Internet exercises and web resources related to this chapter, go to
http://college.hmco.com.

America's Income Inequality Is Not Inequity

The economic expansion that began in 1991 will soon become the longest in our history, yet last week Americans may have been distracted by two reports reminding them of a widening gap between the rich and poor.

The Center on Budget and Policy Priorities and the Economic Policy Institute, two liberal research groups, put out a state-by-state breakdown of Census Bureau data, which found nine states (led by New York) in which the richest 20 percent of households now earn at least 11 times the income of the poorest 20 percent. This indicated a much sharper disparity between the top and bottom than existed two decades ago.

Then the Federal Reserve Bank released its latest survey of consumer finances. It showed that the average net worth of families earning less than $10,000 a year had fallen by $6,600 over the past three years, while households earning more than $100,000 a year had seen their wealth jump by more than $300,000.

Our response is: So what?

Few of us should be surprised—or threatened—by statistics on inequality. Some Americans believe the more equality the better, but the fact is that the distribution of income and wealth isn't arbitrary. It emerges from broad trends in the economy and is a byproduct of a decade that created 17 million jobs and added 20 percent to median household net worth.

The unstated implication of the state-by-state report was that the states where income disparities are lower are somehow "fairer" than the states with high disparities. But the truth is that among communities, states and regions, income and wealth will vary for many reasons, several of them unavoidable and laudable.

Education, immigration

Consider, for example, that income varies with education. According to census data, high school dropouts in the work force earn an average of $26,207, while workers with a professional degree average $127,499. Census figures show that many of the states with the widest income gaps have greater diversity in education levels than states with smaller income gaps.

Twenty-six percent of those over the age of 24 in New York—the state with the greatest income disparity—have at least a bachelor's degree, whereas in Indiana, which was among the seven states with the lowest income disparity, only 16 percent do. Should we be lamenting that so many New Yorkers went to college?

Another nonnefarious cause of increasing income disparity may be our ever-higher immigration rates. Immigrants tend to cluster in low- and high-income groups. Thus it is no surprise that in the seven most unequal states—New York, Arizona, New Mexico, Louisiana, California, Rhode Island, and Texas—about 13 percent of the population is foreign-born (in California, it's 25 percent). Among the seven states with the smallest income disparities, the immigrant population is only 3.8 percent.

The shift away from manufacturing is also a factor. Service workers span the gamut from hotel maids to brain surgeons, while the pay range is generally narrower in the manufacturing sector. States that are industrial tend to have more equal distributions of income.

Data from the Bureau of Labor Statistics show that about 10 percent of workers in Arizona, Louisiana and New York have manufacturing jobs, whereas in more equal states like Indiana and Wisconsin the figure is 23 percent.

Also, in the seven states with the greatest income inequality, more than 80 percent of the population lives in or near metropolitan areas. In states with the most equality, only about half does. If we were to turn back the clock 100 years and again become a largely rural nation, we might not see such large income disparities, but that's because America's cities are our engines of wealth and offer greater prospects for those who succeed.

Up from the bottom

And what of the poorest Americans' loss of ground compared to the richest, as reported by the Fed? The apostles of equality consider the rising inequality kindling for social unrest. But while that would be true if most workers on the bottom rungs were trapped there for generations, America isn't a caste society, and studies that track individuals' incomes over time show that Americans have a remarkable ability to propel themselves upward.

A 17-year study of lifetime earnings by the Federal Reserve Bank of Dallas found that only 5 percent of people in the economy's lowest 20 percent failed to move to a higher income group. In a similar study by the Treasury Department covering 1979 to 1988, 86 percent of Americans in the bottom fifth of income earners improved their status.

Inequality is not inequity. Artificial efforts to try to curb wealth gaps invariably do more harm than good. Heavier taxation might narrow the division between rich and poor, but it would be a hollow triumph if it stifled the economy. What Americans ought to care most about is maintaining our growth, not the red herring of gaps in income and wealth.

Source: "America's Income Inequality Is Not Inequity," *Star Tribune* (Minneapolis, MN), January 25, 2000, p. 13A.

Star Tribune (Minneapolis, MN)/January 25, 2000

Commentary

In the United States, incomes are rising and income inequality is rising. The article notes that in several states, the richest 20 percent of households now earn at least eleven times the income of the poorest 20 percent. This reflects a Lorenz curve that is moving further away from the line of equality—a Gini coefficient that is rising. Very few doubt that income inequality is rising, in the United States and in other nations as well. The question many have is, What to do about the inequality?

The authors of this article argue that nothing should be done. The inequality in the result of differential income levels, immigration, and a shift away from manufacturing. Service workers span the gamut from hotel maids to brain surgeons, while the pay range is generally narrower in the manufacturing sector. States that are industrial tend to have more equal distributions of income. The authors note that inequality is not inequity, and that 86 percent of Americans in the bottom fifth of income earners improved their status between 1979 and 1988.

The question of income inequality is not whether there is inequality but whether inequality is bad. What causes inequality? Many studies have shown that differential levels of education tend to be a primary factor in differential levels of income. The value of a college degree is substantial—and is rising at a very rapid rate. Those without college degrees tend to earn nearly $100,000 less per year than those with a professional degree. This differential will induce more and more people to attend college—to gain the skills valued in the marketplace. What would occur if the government were to place a high tax on high incomes and redistribute incomes to those with low incomes? The incentive to acquire a college degree or the valued skills would decline. As a result, the growth of national income would decline, and while inequality might be reduced, so would overall standards of living.

Part Six

Issues in International Trade and Finance

Chapter 21

World Trade Equilibrium

? Fundamental Questions

1. **What are the prevailing patterns of trade between countries? What goods are traded?**

2. **What determines the goods a nation will export?**

3. **How are the equilibrium price and the quantity of goods traded determined?**

4. **What are the sources of comparative advantage?**

Preview

he United States's once-dominant position as an exporter of color television sets has since been claimed by nations like Japan and Taiwan. What caused this change? Is it because Japan specializes in the export of high-tech equipment? If countries tend to specialize in the export of particular kinds of goods, why does the United States import Heineken beer at the same time it exports Budweiser? This chapter will examine the volume of world trade and the nature of trade linkages between countries. As you saw in Chapter 2, trade occurs because of specialization in production. No single individual or country can produce everything better than others can. The result is specialization of production based on comparative advantage. Remember that comparative advantage is in turn based on relative opportunity costs: a country will specialize in the production of those goods for which its opportunity costs of production are lower than costs in other countries. Nations then trade what they produce in excess

of their own consumption to acquire other things they want to consume. In this chapter, we will go a step further to discuss the sources of comparative advantage. We will look at why one country has a comparative advantage in, say, automobile production, while another country has a comparative advantage in wheat production.

The world equilibrium price and quantity traded are derived from individual countries' demand and supply curves. This relationship between the world trade equilibrium and individual country markets will be utilized in the chapter on "International Trade Restrictions" to discuss the ways that countries can interfere with free international trade to achieve their own economic or political goals. ■

1. AN OVERVIEW OF WORLD TRADE

1. What are the prevailing patterns of trade between countries? What goods are traded?

Trade occurs because it makes people better off. International trade occurs because it makes people better off than they would be if they could consume only domestically produced products. Who trades with whom, and what sorts of goods are traded? These are the questions we first consider before investigating the underlying reasons for trade.

1.a. The Direction of Trade

Table 1 shows patterns of trade between two large groups of countries: the industrial countries and the developing countries. The industrial countries include all of western Europe, Japan, Australia, New Zealand, Canada, and the United States. The developing countries are, essentially, the rest of the world. Table 1 shows the dollar values and percentages of total trade between these groups of countries. The vertical column at the left lists the origin of exports, and the horizontal row at the top lists the destination of imports.

Trade between industrial countries accounts for the majority of international trade.

As Table 1 shows, trade between industrial countries accounts for the bulk of international trade. Trade between industrial countries is a little less than $2.7 trillion in value and amounts to 48 percent of world trade. Exports from industrial countries to developing countries represent 18 percent of total world trade. Exports from developing countries to industrial countries account for 20 percent of total

Table 1

The Direction of Trade (in billions of dollars and percentages of world trade)

| | Destination | |
Origin	Industrial Countries	Developing Countries
Industrial countries	$2,691	$993
	48%	18%
Developing countries	$1,108	$746
	20%	13%

Source: *Direction of Trade Statistics Quarterly,* June 2000. Reprinted by permission of International Monetary Fund.

trade, while exports from the developing countries to other developing countries currently represent only 13 percent of international trade.

Table 2 lists the major trading partners of selected countries and the percentage of total exports and imports accounted for by each country's top ten trading partners. For instance, 23 percent of U.S. exports went to Canada, and 13 percent of U.S. imports came from Japan. From a glance at the other countries listed in Table 2, it is clear that the United States is a major trading partner for many nations. This is true because of the size of the U.S. economy and the nation's relatively high level of income. It is also apparent that Canada and Mexico are very dependent on trade with the United States: about seven-eighths of Canadian exports and 67 percent of its imports, and about three-quarters of Mexican exports and almost 60 percent of its imports involve the United States. The dollar value of trade among the three North American nations is shown in Figure 1.

Table 2
Major Trading Partners of Selected Countries

United States				Canada			
Exports		Imports		Exports		Imports	
Canada	23%	Canada	20%	U.S.	87%	U.S.	67%
Mexico	12%	Japan	13%	Japan	2%	Japan	5%
Japan	8%	Mexico	10%	U.K.	1%	U.K.	3%
U.K.	6%	China	8%	Germany	1%	China	3%
Germany	4%	U.K.	5%	China	1%	Mexico	3%
Germany				**Mexico**			
Exports		Imports		Exports		Imports	
France	11%	France	10%	U.S.	73%	U.S.	58%
U.S.	10%	Netherlands	8%	Canada	5%	Japan	3%
U.K.	8%	U.S.	8%	Japan	1%	Germany	3%
Italy	7%	Italy	7%	Germany	1%	Korea	1%
Netherlands	6%	U.K	7%	Spain	1%	Italy	1%
Japan				**United Kingdom**			
Exports		Imports		Exports		Imports	
U.S.	31%	U.S.	44%	U.S.	15%	U.S.	13%
Korea	6%	China	14%	Germany	11%	Germany	12%
China	6%	Korea	5%	France	9%	France	8%
Hong Kong	5%	Australia	4%	Netherlands	7%	Netherlands	6%
Germany	4%	Indonesia	4%	Ireland	6%	Japan	5%

Source: Data for all countries from International Monetary Fund, Direction of Trade Statistics Quarterly, June 2000.

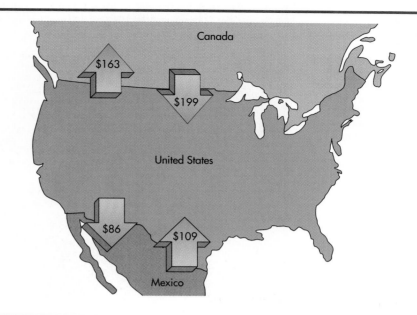

Figure 1

Merchandise Trade Flows in North America (billions of dollars)

In 1999, the United States exported $163 billion worth of goods to Canada and imported $199 billion of goods from Canada. The same year, U.S. merchandise exports to Mexico were $86 billion, while merchandise imports from Mexico were $109 billion.

1.b. What Goods Are Traded?

The volume of trade in motor vehicles exceeds that of any other good.

Because countries differ in their comparative advantages, they will tend to export different goods. Countries also have different tastes and technological needs, and thus tend to differ in what they will import. Some goods are more widely traded than others, as Table 3 shows. Motor vehicles is the most heavily traded good in the world, accounting for 4.87 percent of the total volume of world trade.

Table 3

Top Ten Exported Products (in millions of dollars and percentages of world exports)

Product Category	Value	Percentage of World Trade
Motor vehicles	$217,906	4.87%
Crude petroleum	$194,115	4.34%
Transistors, valves, etc.	$147,393	3.26%
Data processing equipment	$113,106	2.51%
Motor vehicle parts	$112,572	2.51%
Special transactions	$108,677	2.40%
Telecom equipment, parts	$102,957	2.29%
Petroleum products	$ 85,187	1.91%
ADP machine parts	$ 82,865	1.84%
Electrical Machinery	$ 69,109	1.54%

Source: Data from U.N. Conference on Trade and Development, *Handbook of International Trade and Development Statistics, 1996–1997* (TD/STAT.24), p. 162.

Comparative advantage is based on what a country can do relatively better than other countries. This photo shows a woman in Sri Lanka picking tea leaves. Sri Lanka is one of the few countries that export a significant amount of tea. Due to favorable growing conditions (a natural resource), these countries have a comparative advantage in tea production.

Motor vehicles is followed by crude petroleum, transistors and valves, automatic data processing equipment, motor vehicle parts, and special transactions. The top ten exported products, however, represent only 27 percent of world trade. The remaining 73 percent is distributed among a great variety of products. The importance of petroleum and motor vehicles in international trade should not obscure the fact that international trade involves all sorts of products from all over the world.

RECAP

1. Trade between industrial countries accounts for the bulk of international trade.
2. The most important trading partners of the United States are Canada, Mexico, and Japan.
3. Motor vehicles are the most heavily traded good in the world, in terms of value of exports.
4. World trade is distributed across a great variety of products.

2. AN EXAMPLE OF INTERNATIONAL TRADE EQUILIBRIUM

The international economy is very complex. Each country has a unique pattern of trade, in terms both of trading partners and of goods traded. Some countries trade a great deal and others trade very little. We already know that countries specialize and trade according to comparative advantage, but what are the fundamental determinants of international trade that explain the pattern of comparative advantage?

The answer to this question will in turn provide a better understanding basic questions about how international trade functions: What goods will be ? How much will be traded? What prices will prevail for traded goods?

2.a. Comparative Advantage

2. What determines the goods a nation will export?

Comparative advantage is found by comparing the relative costs of production in each country. We measure the cost of producing a particular good in two countries in terms of opportunity costs—what other goods must be given up in order to produce more of the good in question.

Table 4 presents a hypothetical example of two countries, the United States and India, that both produce two goods, wheat and cloth. The table lists the amounts of each good that could be produced by each worker. This example assumes that labor productivity differences alone determine comparative advantage. In the United States, a worker can produce either 8 units of wheat or 4 units of cloth. In India, a worker can produce 4 units of wheat or 3 units of cloth.

absolute advantage: an advantage derived from one country having a lower absolute input cost of producing a particular good than another country

The United States has an **absolute advantage**—greater productivity—in producing both wheat and cloth. Absolute advantage is determined by comparing the absolute productivity in different countries of producing each good. Since one worker can produce more of either good in the United States than in India, the United States is the more efficient producer of both goods.

It might seem that since the United States is the more efficient producer of both goods, there would be no need for trade with India. But absolute advantage is not the critical consideration. What matters in determining the benefits of international trade is comparative advantage, as originally discussed in Chapter 2. To find the **comparative advantage**—the lower opportunity cost—we must compare the opportunity cost of producing each good in each country.

comparative advantage: an advantage derived from comparing the opportunity costs of production in two countries

The opportunity cost of producing wheat is what must be given up in cloth using the same resources, like one worker per day. Look again at Table 4 to see the production of wheat and cloth in the two countries. Since one worker can produce 8 units of wheat or 4 units of cloth, if we take a worker from cloth production and move him to wheat production, we gain 8 units of wheat and lose 4 units of cloth. The opportunity cost of producing wheat equals 4/8, or 1/2, unit of cloth:

$$\frac{\text{Output of cloth given up}}{\text{Output of wheat gained}} = \begin{array}{l} \text{opportunity cost of} \\ \text{producing 1 unit of wheat} \\ \text{(in terms of cloth given up)} \end{array}$$

$$4/8 = 1/2$$

Applying the same thinking to India, we find that one worker can produce 4 units of wheat or 3 units of cloth. The opportunity cost of producing 1 unit of wheat in India is 3/4 unit of cloth.

Table 4	Output per Worker per Day in Either Wheat or Cloth	
An Example of Comparative Advantage	U.S.	India
wheat	8	4
cloth	4	3

A comparison of the domestic opportunity costs in each country will reveal which one has the comparative advantage in producing each good. The U.S. opportunity cost of producing 1 unit of wheat is 1/2 unit of cloth; the Indian opportunity cost is 3/4 unit of cloth. Because the United States has a lower domestic opportunity cost, it has the comparative advantage in wheat production and will export wheat. Since wheat production costs are lower in the United States, India is better off trading for wheat rather than trying to produce it domestically.

The comparative advantage in cloth is found the same way. Taking a worker in the United States from wheat production and putting her in cloth production, we gain 4 units of cloth but lose 8 units of wheat per day. So the opportunity cost is

$$\frac{\text{Output of wheat given up}}{\text{Output of cloth gained}} = \begin{array}{l}\text{opportunity cost of} \\ \text{producing 1 unit of cloth} \\ \text{(in terms of wheat given up)}\end{array}$$

$$8/4 = 2$$

In India, moving a worker from wheat to cloth production means that we gain 3 units of cloth but lose 4 units of wheat, so the opportunity cost is $4/3$, or $1\frac{1}{3}$ units of wheat for 1 unit of cloth. Comparing the U.S. opportunity cost of 2 units of wheat with the Indian opportunity cost of $1\frac{1}{3}$ units, we see that India has the comparative advantage in cloth production and will therefore export cloth. In this case, the United States is better off trading for cloth than producing it since India's costs of production are lower.

In international trade, as in other areas of economic decision making, it is opportunity cost that matters—and opportunity costs are reflected in comparative advantage. Absolute advantage is irrelevant, because knowing the absolute number of labor hours required to produce a good does not tell us if we can benefit from trade. We benefit from trade if we are able to obtain a good from a foreign country by giving up less than we would have to give up to obtain the good at home. Because only opportunity cost can allow us to make such comparisons, international trade proceeds on the basis of comparative advantage.

2.b. Terms of Trade

On the basis of comparative advantage, India will specialize in cloth production and the United States will specialize in wheat production. The two countries will then trade with each other to satisfy the domestic demand for both goods. International trade permits greater consumption than would be possible from domestic production alone. Since countries trade when they can obtain a good more cheaply from a foreign producer than they can at home, international trade allows all traders to consume more. This is evident when we examine the terms of trade.

The **terms of trade** are the amount of an exported good that must be given up to obtain one unit of an imported good. The Economic Insight "The Dutch Disease" provides a popular example of a dramatic shift in the terms of trade. As you saw earlier, comparative advantage dictates that the United States will specialize in wheat production and export wheat to India in exchange for Indian cloth. But the amount of wheat that the United States will exchange for a unit of cloth is limited by the domestic tradeoffs. If a unit of cloth can be obtained domestically for 2 units of wheat, the United States will be willing to trade with India only if the terms of trade are less than 2 units of wheat for a unit of cloth.

India in turn will be willing to trade its cloth for U.S. wheat only if it can receive a better price than its domestic opportunity costs. Since a unit of cloth in India costs

terms of trade: the amount of an exported good that must be given up to obtain one unit of an imported good

The terms of trade are the amount of an export that must be given up for a certain quantity of an import. The price of an import will be equal to its price in the foreign country of origin multiplied by the exchange rate (the domestic-currency price of foreign currency). As the exchange rate changes, the terms of trade will change. This can have important consequences for international trade.

A problem can arise when one export industry in an economy is booming relative to others. In the 1970s, for instance, the Netherlands experienced a boom in its natural gas industry. The dramatic energy price increases of the 1970s resulted in large Dutch exports of natural gas. Increased demand for exports from the Netherlands caused the Dutch currency to appreciate, making Dutch goods more expensive for foreign buyers. This situation caused the terms of trade to worsen for the Netherlands. Although the natural gas sector boomed, Dutch manufacturing was finding it difficult to compete in the world market.

The phenomenon of a boom in one industry causing declines in the rest of the economy is popularly called the Dutch Disease. It is usually associated with dramatic increases in the demand for a primary commodity and can afflict any nation experiencing such a boom. For instance, a rapid rise in the demand for coffee could lead to a Dutch Disease problem for Colombia, where a coffee boom would be accompanied by decline in other sectors of the economy.

$1\frac{1}{3}$ units of wheat, India will gain from trade if it can obtain more than $1\frac{1}{3}$ units of wheat for its cloth.

The limits of the terms of trade are determined by the opportunity costs in each country:

1 unit of cloth for more than $1\frac{1}{3}$ but less than 2 units of wheat

Within this range, the actual terms of trade will be decided by the bargaining power of the two countries. The closer the United States can come to giving up only $1\frac{1}{3}$ units of wheat for cloth, the better the terms of trade for the United States. The closer India can come to receiving 2 units of wheat for its cloth, the better the terms of trade for India.

Though each country would like to push the other as close to the limits of the terms of trade as possible, any terms within the limits set by domestic opportunity costs will be mutually beneficial. Both countries benefit because they are able to consume goods at a cost less than their domestic opportunity costs. To illustrate the *gains from trade*, let us assume that the actual terms of trade are 1 unit of cloth for $1\frac{1}{2}$ units of wheat.

Suppose the United States has 2 workers, one of whom goes to wheat production and the other to cloth production. This would result in the U.S. production of 8 units of wheat and 4 units of cloth. Without international trade, the United States can produce and consume 8 units of wheat and 4 units of cloth. If the United States, with its comparative advantage in wheat production, chooses to produce only wheat, it can use both workers to produce 16 units. If the terms of trade are $1\frac{1}{2}$ units of wheat per unit of cloth, the United States can keep 8 units of wheat and trade the other 8 for $5\frac{1}{3}$ units of cloth (8 divided by $1\frac{1}{2}$). By trading U.S. wheat for Indian cloth, the United States is able to consume more than it could without trade. With no trade and half its labor devoted to each good, the United States could consume 8 units of wheat

Table 5	Without International Trade
Hypothetical Example of U.S. Gains from Specialization and Trade	1 worker in wheat production: produce and consume 8 wheat 1 worker in cloth production: produce and consume 4 cloth
	With Specialization and Trade
	2 workers in wheat production: produce 16 wheat and consume 8; trade 8 wheat for $5\frac{1}{3}$ cloth
	Before trade: consume 8 wheat and 4 cloth
	After trade: consume 8 wheat and $5\frac{1}{3}$ cloth; gain $1\frac{1}{3}$ cloth by specialization and trade

The gain from trade is increased consumption.

and 4 units of cloth. After trade, the United States consumes 8 units of wheat and $5\frac{1}{3}$ units of cloth. By devoting all its labor hours to wheat production and trading wheat for cloth, the United States gains $1\frac{1}{3}$ units of cloth. This is the gain from trade—an increase in consumption, as summarized in Table 5.

2.c. Export Supply and Import Demand

The preceding example suggests that countries all benefit from specialization and trade. Realistically, however, countries do not completely specialize. Typically, domestic industries satisfy part of the domestic demand for goods that are also imported. To understand how the quantity of goods traded is determined, we must construct demand and supply curves for each country and use them to create export supply and import demand curves.

The proportion of domestic demand for a good that is satisfied by domestic production and the proportion that will be satisfied by imports are determined by the domestic supply and demand curves and the international equilibrium price of a good. The international equilibrium price and quantity may be determined once we know the export supply and import demand curves for each country. These curves are derived from the domestic supply and demand in each country. Figure 2 illustrates the derivation of the export supply and import demand curves.

Figure 2(a) shows the domestic supply and demand curves for the U.S. wheat market. The domestic equilibrium price is $6 and the domestic equilibrium quantity is 200 million bushels. (The domestic no-trade equilibrium price is the price that exists prior to international trade.) A price above $6 will yield a U.S. wheat surplus. For instance, at a price of $9, the U.S. surplus will be 200 million bushels. A price below equilibrium will produce a wheat shortage: at a price of $3, the shortage will be 200 million bushels. The key point here is that the world price of a good may be quite different than the domestic no-trade equilibrium price. And once international trade occurs, the world price will prevail in the domestic economy.

export supply curve: a curve showing the relationship between the world price of a good and the amount that a country will export

If the world price of wheat is different than a country's domestic no-trade equilibrium price, the country will become an exporter or importer. For instance, if the world price is above the domestic no-trade equilibrium price, the domestic surplus can be exported to the rest of the world. Figure 2(b) shows the U.S. **export supply curve.** This curve illustrates the U.S. domestic surplus of wheat for prices above the

Figure 2

The Import Demand and Export Supply Curves

Figures 2(a) and 2(c) show the domestic demand and supply curves for wheat in the United States and India, respectively. The domestic no-trade equilibrium price is $6 in the United States and $12 in India. Any price above the domestic no-trade equilibrium prices will create domestic surpluses, which are reflected in the export supply curves in Figures 2(b) and 2(d). Any price below the domestic no-trade equilibrium prices will create domestic shortages, which are reflected in the import demand curves in Figures 2(b) and 2(d).

(a) U.S. Domestic Wheat Market

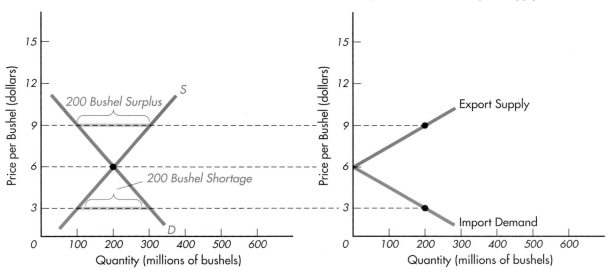

(b) U.S. Import Demand and Export Supply

(c) Indian Domestic Wheat Market

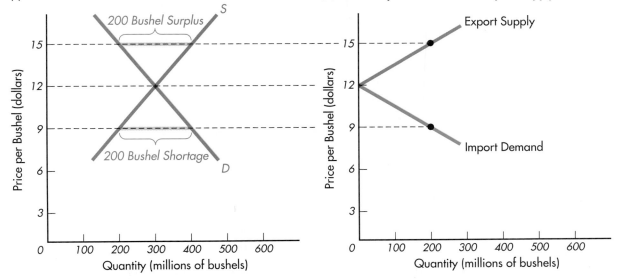

(d) Indian Import Demand and Export Supply

domestic no-trade equilibrium price of $6. At a world price of $9, the United States would supply 200 million bushels of wheat to the rest of the world. The export supply is equal to the domestic surplus. The higher the world price above the domestic no-trade equilibrium, the greater the quantity of wheat exported by the United States.

If the world price of wheat is below the domestic no-trade equilibrium price, the United States will import wheat. The **import demand curve** is the amount of the U.S. shortage at various prices below the no-trade equilibrium. In Figure 2(b), the import demand curve is a downward-sloping line, indicating that the lower the price below the domestic no-trade equilibrium of $6, the greater the quantity of wheat imported by the United States. At a price of $3, the United States will import 200 million bushels.

The domestic supply and demand curves and the export supply and import demand curves for India appear in Figures 2(c) and (d). The domestic no-trade equilibrium price in India is $12. At this price, India would neither import nor export any wheat because the domestic demand would be satisfied by domestic supply. The export supply curve for India is shown in Figure 2(d) as an upward-sloping line that measures the amount of the domestic surplus as the price level rises above the domestic no-trade equilibrium price of $12. According to Figure 2(c), if the world price of wheat is $15, the domestic surplus in India is equal to 200 million bushels. The corresponding point on the export supply curve indicates that, at a price of $15, 200 million bushels will be exported. The import demand curve for India reflects the domestic shortage at a price below the domestic no-trade equilibrium price. At $9, the domestic shortage is equal to 200 million bushels: the import demand curve indicates that at $9, 200 million bushels will be imported.

import demand curve: a curve showing the relationship between the world price of a good and the amount that a country will import

?

3. **How are the equilibrium price and the quantity of goods traded determined?**

2.d. The World Equilibrium Price and Quantity Traded

The international equilibrium price of wheat and the quantity of wheat traded are found by combining the import demand and export supply curves for the United States and India, as in Figure 3. International equilibrium occurs if the

Figure 3

International Equilibrium Price and Quantity

The international equilibrium price is the price at which the export supply curve of the United States intersects with the import demand curve of India. At the equilibrium price of $9, the United States will export 200 million bushels to India.

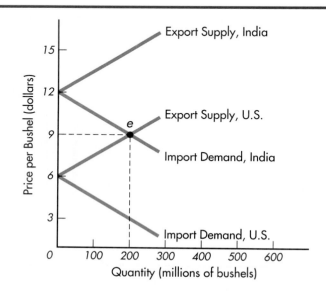

quantity of imports demanded by one country is equal to the quantity of exports supplied by the other country. In Figure 3, this equilibrium occurs at the point labeled *e*. At this point, the import demand curve for India indicates that India wants to import 200 million bushels at a price of $9. The export supply curve for the United States indicates that the United States wants to export 200 million bushels at a price of $9. Only at $9 will the quantity of wheat demanded by the importing nation equal the quantity of wheat supplied by the exporting nation. So the equilibrium world price of wheat is $9 and the equilibrium quantity of wheat traded is 200 million bushels.

International equilibrium occurs at the point where the quantity of imports demanded by one country is equal to the quantity of exports supplied by the other country.

RECAP

1. Comparative advantage is based on the relative opportunity costs of producing goods in different countries.
2. A country has an absolute advantage when it can produce a good more efficiently than can other nations.
3. A country has a comparative advantage when the opportunity cost of producing a good, in terms of forgone output of other goods, is lower than that of other nations.
4. The terms of trade are the amount of an export good that must be given up to obtain one unit of an import good.
5. The limits of the terms of trade are determined by the domestic opportunity costs of production in each country.
6. The export supply and import demand curves measure the domestic surplus and shortage, respectively, at different world prices.
7. International equilibrium occurs at the point where one country's import demand curve intersects with the export supply curve of another country.

4. What are the sources of comparative advantage?

3. SOURCES OF COMPARATIVE ADVANTAGE

We know that countries specialize and trade in accordance with comparative advantage, but what gives a country a comparative advantage? Economists have suggested several theories of the source of comparative advantage. Let us review these theories.

3.a. Productivity Differences

The example of comparative advantage earlier in this chapter showed the United States to have a comparative advantage in wheat production and India to have a comparative advantage in cloth production. Comparative advantage was determined by differences in the labor hours required to produce each good. In this example, differences in the *productivity* of labor accounted for comparative advantage.

For over two hundred years, economists have argued that productivity differences account for comparative advantage. In fact, this theory of comparative advantage is often called the *Ricardian model*, after David Ricardo, a nineteenth-century English

Comparative advantage due to productivity differences between countries is often called the Ricardian model of comparative advantage.

economist who explained and analyzed the idea of productivity-based comparative advantage. Variation in the productivity of labor can explain many observed trade patterns in the world.

Although we know that labor productivity differs across countries—and that this can help explain why countries produce the goods they do—there are factors other than labor productivity that determine comparative advantage. Furthermore, even if labor productivity were all that mattered, we would still want to know why some countries have more productive workers than others. The standard interpretation of the Ricardian model is that technological differences between countries account for differences in labor productivity. The countries with the most-advanced technology would have a comparative advantage with regard to those goods that can be produced most efficiently with modern technology.

3.b. Factor Abundance

Goods differ in terms of the resources, or factors of production, required for their production. Countries differ in terms of the abundance of different factors of production: land, labor, capital, and entrepreneurial ability. It seems self-evident that countries would have an advantage in producing those goods that use relatively large amounts of their most abundant factor of production. Certainly countries with a relatively large amount of farmland would have a comparative advantage in agriculture, and countries with a relatively large amount of capital would tend to specialize in the production of manufactured goods.

Comparative advantage based on differences in the abundance of factors of production across countries is described in the Heckscher-Ohlin model.

The idea that comparative advantage is based on the relative abundance of factors of production is sometimes called the *Heckscher-Ohlin model*, after the two Swedish economists, Eli Heckscher and Bertil Ohlin, who developed the original argument. The original model assumed that countries possess only two factors of production: labor and capital. Thus, researchers have examined the labor and capital requirements of various industries to see whether labor-abundant countries export goods whose production is relatively labor-intensive, and capital-abundant countries export goods that are relatively capital-intensive. In many cases, factor abundance has served well as an explanation of observed trade patterns. However, there remain cases in which comparative advantage seems to run counter to the predictions of the factor-abundance theory. In response, economists have suggested other explanations for comparative advantage.

3.c. Other Theories of Comparative Advantage

New theories of comparative advantage have typically come about in an effort to explain the trade pattern in some narrow category of products. They are not intended to serve as general explanations of comparative advantage, as do factor abundance and productivity. These supplementary theories emphasize human skills, product cycles, and preferences.

Human skills This approach emphasizes differences across countries in the availability of skilled and unskilled labor. The basic idea is that countries with a relatively abundant stock of highly skilled labor will have a comparative advantage in producing goods that require relatively large amounts of skilled labor. This theory is similar to the factor-abundance theory, except that here the analysis rests on two segments (skilled and unskilled) of the labor factor.

The human-skills argument is consistent with the observation that most U.S. exports are produced in high-wage (skilled-labor) industries and most U.S. imports are products produced in relatively low-wage industries. Since the United States has a well-educated labor force, relative to many other countries, we would expect the United States to have a comparative advantage in industries requiring a large amount of skilled labor. Developing countries would be expected to have a comparative advantage in industries requiring a relatively large amount of unskilled labor.

Product life cycles   This theory explains how comparative advantage in a specific good can shift over time from one country to another. This occurs because goods experience a *product life cycle*. At the outset, development and testing are required to conceptualize and design the product. For this reason, the early production will be undertaken by an innovative firm. Over time, however, a successful product tends to become standardized, in the sense that many manufacturers can produce it. The mature product may be produced by firms that do little or no research and development, specializing instead in copying successful products invented and developed by others.

Manufactured goods have life cycles. At first they are produced by the firm that invented them. Later, they may be produced by firms in other countries that copy the technology of the innovator.

The product-life-cycle theory is related to international comparative advantage in that a new product will be first produced and exported by the nation in which it was invented. As the product is exported elsewhere and foreign firms become familiar with it, the technology is copied in other countries by foreign firms seeking to produce a competing version. As the product matures, comparative advantage shifts away from the country of origin if other countries have lower manufacturing costs using the now-standardized technology.

The history of color television production shows how comparative advantage can shift over the product life cycle. Color television was invented in the United States, and U.S. firms initially produced and exported color TVs. Over time, as the technology of color television manufacturing became well known, countries like Japan and Taiwan came to dominate the business. Firms in these countries had a comparative advantage over U.S. firms in the manufacture of color televisions. Once the technology is widely available, countries with lower production costs, due to lower wages, can compete effectively against the higher-wage nation that developed the technology.

Preferences   The theories of comparative advantage we have looked at so far have all been based on supply factors. It may be, though, that the demand side of the market can explain some of the patterns observed in international trade. Seldom are different producers' goods exactly identical. Consumers may prefer the goods of one firm to those of another firm. Domestic firms usually produce goods to satisfy domestic consumers. But since different consumers have different preferences, some consumers will prefer goods produced by foreign firms. International trade allows consumers to expand their consumption opportunities.

Consumers who live in countries with similar levels of development can be expected to have similar consumption patterns. The consumption patterns of consumers in countries at much different levels of development are much less similar. This would suggest that firms in industrial countries will find a larger market for their goods in other industrial countries than in developing countries.

As you saw earlier in this chapter, industrial countries tend to trade with other industrial countries. This pattern runs counter to the factor-abundance theory of comparative advantage, which would suggest that countries with the most dissimilar endowments of resources would find trade most beneficial. Yet rich countries, with large supplies of capital and skilled labor forces, trade more actively with other rich countries than they do with poor countries. Firms in industrial countries tend to produce goods that relatively wealthy consumers will buy. The key point here is that we do not live in a world based on simple comparative advantage, in which all cloth is identical, regardless of the producer. We inhabit a world of differentiated products, and consumers want choices between different brands or styles of a seemingly similar good.

intraindustry trade: simultaneous import and export of goods in the same industry by a particular country

Another feature of international trade that may be explained by consumer preference is **intraindustry trade,** a circumstance in which a country both exports and imports goods in the same industry. The fact that the United States exports Budweiser beer and imports Heineken beer is not surprising when preferences are taken into account. Supply-side theories of comparative advantage rarely provide an explanation of intraindustry trade, since they would expect each country to export only those goods produced in industries in which a comparative advantage exists. Yet the real world is characterized by a great deal of intraindustry trade.

We have discussed several potential sources of comparative advantage: labor productivity, factor abundance, human skills, product cycles, and preferences. Each of these theories, summarized in Figure 4, has proven useful in understanding certain trade patterns. Each has also been shown to have limitations as a general theory applicable to all cases. Once again we are reminded that the world is a very complicated place. Theories are simpler than reality. Nevertheless, they help us to understand how comparative advantage arises.

RECAP

1. Comparative advantage can arise because of differences in labor productivity.

2. Countries differ in their resource endowments, and a given country may enjoy a comparative advantage in products that intensively use its most abundant factor of production.

3. Industrial countries may have a comparative advantage in products requiring a large amount of skilled labor. Developing countries may have a comparative advantage in products requiring a large amount of unskilled labor.

4. Comparative advantage in a new good initially resides in the country that invented the good. Over time, other nations learn the technology and may gain a comparative advantage in producing the good.

5. In some industries, consumer preferences for differentiated goods may explain international trade flows, including intraindustry trade.

SUMMARY

What are the prevailing patterns of trade between countries? What goods are traded?

1. International trade flows largely between industrial countries. *§1.a*

2. International trade involves many diverse products. *§1.b*

What determines the goods a nation will export?

3. Comparative advantage is based on the opportunity costs of production. *§2.a*

4. Domestic opportunity costs determine the limits of the terms of trade between two countries—that is, the

Figure 4

Theories of Comparative Advantage

Several theories exist that explain comparative advantage: labor productivity, factor abundance, human skills, product life cycles, and preferences.

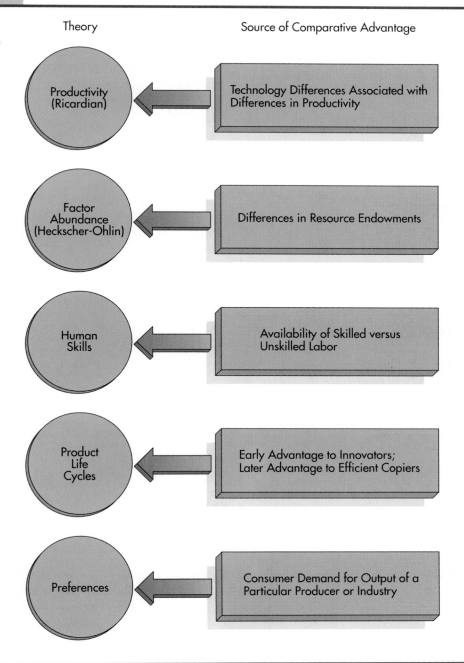

Theory	Source of Comparative Advantage
Productivity (Ricardian)	Technology Differences Associated with Differences in Productivity
Factor Abundance (Heckscher-Ohlin)	Differences in Resource Endowments
Human Skills	Availability of Skilled versus Unskilled Labor
Product Life Cycles	Early Advantage to Innovators; Later Advantage to Efficient Copiers
Preferences	Consumer Demand for Output of a Particular Producer or Industry

amount of exports that must be given up to obtain imports. *§2.b*

5. The export supply curve shows the domestic surplus and amount of exports available at alternative world prices. *§2.c*

6. The import demand curve shows the domestic shortage and amount of imports demanded at alternative world prices. *§2.c*

How are the equilibrium price and the quantity of goods traded determined?

7. The international equilibrium price and quantity of a good traded are determined by the intersection of the export supply of one country with the import demand of another country. *§2.d*

What are the sources of comparative advantage?

8. The productivity-differences and factor-abundance theories of comparative advantage are general theo-ries that seek to explain patterns of international trade flow. *§3.a, 3.b*

9. Other theories of comparative advantage aimed at explaining trade in particular kinds of goods focus on human skills, product life cycles, and consumer preferences. *§3.c*

KEY TERMS

absolute advantage *§2.a*

comparative advantage *§2.a*

terms of trade *§2.b*

export supply curve *§2.c*

import demand curve *§2.c*

intraindustry trade *§3.c*

EXERCISES

1. Why must voluntary trade between two countries be mutually beneficial?

Use the following table for exercises 2–6.

Amount of Beef or Computers Produced by One Worker in a Day

	Canada	Japan
Beef	6	5
Computers	2	4

2. Which country has the absolute advantage in beef production?

3. Which country has the absolute advantage in computer production?

4. Which country has the comparative advantage in beef production?

5. Which country has the comparative advantage in computer production?

6. What are the limits of the terms of trade? Specifically, when is Canada willing to trade with Japan, and when is Japan willing to trade with Canada?

7. Use the following supply and demand schedule for two countries to determine the international equilibrium price of shoes. How many shoes will be traded?

Demand and Supply of Shoes (1,000s)

	Mexico		Chile	
Price	Qty. Demanded	Qty. Supplied	Qty. Demanded	Qty. Supplied
$10	40	0	50	0
$20	35	20	40	10
$30	30	40	30	20
$40	25	60	20	30
$50	20	80	10	40

8. How would each of the following theories of comparative advantage explain the fact that the United States exports computers?
   a. Productivity differences
   b. Factor abundance
   c. Human skills
   d. Product life cycle
   e. Preferences

9. Which of the theories of comparative advantage could explain why the United States exports computers to Japan at the same time that it imports computers from Japan? Explain.

10. Developing countries have complained that the terms of trade they face are unfavorable. If they voluntarily engage in international trade, what do you suppose they mean by "unfavorable terms of trade"?

11. If two countries reach equilibrium in their domestic markets at the same price, what can be said about their export supply and import demand curves and about the international trade equilibrium?

Economically Speaking

China Trade Will Come Back to Haunt Us

I don't know who came first in the recent race in Buffalo, but the winner, clearly, was China. Practically all of the people who ran were clad in footwear that was "Made in China."

The soaring trade deficit with China, more than $68 billion in 1998, can only be ascribed to President Clinton's "most favored nation" trade policy.

It is increasingly difficult to find hard goods that are not made in China. The list would include all toys, nearly all hand tools, kitchen utensils, small kitchen appliances, some furniture, cameras, TV sets and air conditioners.

Barbie, the little girls' icon, used to be an American. No longer. Barbie is now a natural-ized American—an immigrant from China. But "the unkindest cut of all" was my discovery that Lionel electric trains, as American as apple pie, are now being made in China. Is nothing sacred?

In the recent fuss at the World Trade Organization meeting in Seattle, organized labor was a prominent portion of the opposition to China's admission to the WTO. Isn't there a bit of hypocrisy here? How did all those boxes from China get unloaded from the ships onto the wharves? Then how did they move into tractor-trailers and into the distribution warehouses in the nation's interior? The answer: The "almighty buck" rules. So long as the price is right, merchants will stock these items and consumers will take them from the shelves. And China will flourish at the expense of American workers.

I've been through this before. I suppose it's useless to tell people to take a long look at the consequences of their actions. It seems it's the immediate future that counts most.

China is a threat. Let's not fund that nation. It's too late to boycott the stores that sell items "made in China"—there are practically no alternatives. An embargo is the only real solution.

Source: "China Trade Will Come Back to Haunt Us," *Buffalo News,* August 15, 2000, p. 3B. Copyright 2000. *Buffalo News.*

Buffalo News/August 15, 2000

Commentary

There is no lack of stories in the U.S. media on the threat of foreign economic domination. As this article indicates, many people point to the large U.S. trade deficit with China as evidence that a problem exists.

However, the bilateral trade accounts provide little, if any, information on such issues. Indeed, it is easy to think of an example in which a country has a persistent trade deficit with one of its trading partners but has its overall trade account in balance. Suppose there are three countries that trade among themselves, which we will call countries A, B, and C. The people of each country produce only one type of good and consume only one other type of good. The people of country A produce apples and consume bananas, the people of country B produce bananas and consume cucumbers, and the people of country C produce cucumbers and consume apples. Even when the trade account of each country is balanced, each has a deficit with one of its trading partners and a surplus with the other. Furthermore, a larger trade deficit between countries A and B (with each country retaining balanced trade) implies that the people of country A are better off since they are consuming more. If the government of country A tried to impose a law forcing bilateral trade balance with country B, citizens of country A could not consume as many bananas as before and would be forced to attempt to sell apples to the uninterested citizens of country B.

This simple example demonstrates that the U.S. trade deficit with China should not in itself be a

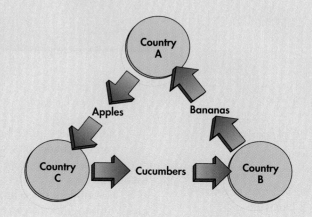

cause for concern, especially if the overall trade deficit is shrinking. The United States could have a persistent trade deficit with China and yet maintain an overall balanced trade account. In fact, any country would be expected to have a trade deficit with some countries and a trade surplus with others. This reflects comparative advantage. Trade between countries makes both the exporting and the importing countries better off.

This is not to say that concern about the overall trade deficit is not well founded. An overall trade deficit indicates that a country is consuming more than it is producing. At any particular time, a country may want to run a trade deficit or a trade surplus, depending on the circumstances it faces. But regardless of the overall trade account of a country, we should expect bilateral trade imbalances among trading partners.

Chapter 22

International Trade Restrictions

Fundamental Questions

1. Why do countries restrict international trade?

2. How do countries restrict the entry of foreign goods and promote the export of domestic goods?

3. What sorts of agreements do countries enter into to reduce barriers to international trade?

The Japanese government once announced that foreign-made skis would not be allowed into Japan because they were unsafe. Japanese ski manufacturers were active supporters of the ban. The U.S. government once imposed a tax of almost 50 percent on imports of motorcycles with engines larger than 700 cc. The only U.S.-owned motorcycle manufacturer, Harley-Davidson, produced no motorcycles with engines smaller than 1,000 cc and so did not care about the small-engine market. In the mid-1980s, Britain began replacing the distinctive red steel telephone booths that were used all through the country with new booths. Many U.S. residents were interested in buying an old British phone booth to use as a decorative novelty, so the phone booths were exported to the United States. However, when the phone booths arrived, the U.S. Customs Service impounded them because there was a limit on the amount of iron and steel products that could be exported from Britain to the United States. The

Preview

phone booths would be allowed to enter the country only if British exports of some other iron and steel products were reduced. The British exporters protested the classification of the phone booths as iron and steel products and argued that they should be considered antiques (which have no import restrictions). The phone booths were not reclassified, so as a result, few have entered the United States, and prices of old British phone booths have been in the thousands of dollars. There are many examples of government policy influencing the prices and quantities of goods traded internationally.

International trade is rarely determined solely by comparative advantage and the free market forces of supply and demand. Governments often find that political pressures favor policies that at least partially offset the prevailing comparative advantages. Government policy aimed at influencing international trade flows is called **commercial policy.** This chapter first examines the arguments in support of commercial policy and then discusses the various tools of commercial policy employed by governments. ◼

commercial policy: government policy that influences international trade flows

1. Why do countries restrict international trade?

1. ARGUMENTS FOR PROTECTION

Governments restrict foreign trade to protect domestic producers from foreign competition. In some cases the protection may be justified; in most cases it harms consumers. Of the arguments used to promote such protection, only a few are valid. We will look first at arguments widely considered to have little or no merit, and then at those that may sometimes be valid.

International trade on the basis of comparative advantage maximizes world output and allows consumers access to better-quality products at lower prices than would be available in the domestic market alone. If trade is restricted, consumers pay higher prices for lower-quality goods, and world output declines. Protection from foreign competition imposes costs on the domestic economy as well as on foreign producers. When production does not proceed on the basis of comparative advantage, resources are not expended on their most efficient uses. Whenever government restrictions alter the pattern of trade, we should expect someone to benefit and someone else to suffer. Generally speaking, protection from foreign competition benefits domestic producers at the expense of domestic consumers.

Protection from foreign competition generally benefits domestic producers at the expense of domestic consumers.

1.a. Creation of Domestic Jobs

If foreign goods are kept out of the domestic economy, it is often argued, jobs will be created at home. This argument holds that domestic firms will produce the goods that otherwise would have been produced abroad, thus employing domestic workers instead of foreign workers. The weakness of this argument is that only the protected industry would benefit in terms of employment. Since domestic consumers will pay higher prices to buy the output of the protected industry, they will have less to spend on other goods and services, which could cause employment in other industries to drop. If other countries retaliate by restricting entry of U.S. exports, the output of U.S. firms that produce for export will fall as well. Typically, restrictions to "save domestic jobs" simply redistribute jobs by creating employment in the protected industry and reducing employment elsewhere.

Table 1 shows estimates of consumer costs and producer gains associated with protection in certain Japanese and U.S. industries. The first column lists the total cost to domestic consumers, in terms of higher prices paid, for each industry. For

Table 1

Benefits and Costs of Protection from Foreign Competition in Japan and the United States

	Consumer Costs		Producer Gains
	Total (million U.S. dollars)	Per Job Saved (U.S. dollars)	(million U.S. dollars)
Japan			
Food and beverages	58,394	762,000	43,210
Textiles and light industry	8,979	485,000	3,341
Metals	5,162	974,000	2,546
Chemical products	15,500	2,385,000	8,466
Machinery	21,587	287,000	12,286
United States			
Food and beverages	2,947	488,000	1,775
Textiles and light industry	26,443	148,000	12,242
Chemical products	484	942,000	222
Machinery	542	348,000	157

Sources: Data are drawn from Yoko Sazanimi, Shujiro Urata, and Hiroki Kawai, *Measuring the Costs of Protection in Japan* (Institute for International Economics, Washington, D.C., 1995); Gary C. Hufbauer and Kimberly Ann Elliott, *Measuring the Costs of Protection in the United States* (Institute for International Economics, Washington, D.C., 1994).

Saving domestic jobs from foreign competition may cost domestic consumers more than it benefits the protected industries.

instance, the consumer cost of protecting the U.S. food and beverage industry is $2,947 million. The second column lists the cost to consumers of saving one job in each industry (found by dividing the total consumer cost by the number of jobs saved by protection). In food and beverages, each job saved costs U.S. consumers $488,000. The gain to U.S. producers appears in the third column. Government protection of food and beverage firms allowed them to gain $1,775 million. This gain is less than the costs to consumers of $2,947 million.

Table 2 shows the annual cost to the United States of import restrictions in terms of reduced GDP as estimated by an agency of the U.S. government. The total estimated amount of $12,402 million means that U.S. GDP would be over $12 billion higher without import restrictions.

Tables 1 and 2 demonstrate the very high cost per job saved by protection. If the costs to consumers are greater than the benefits to protected industries, you may wonder why government provides any protection aimed at saving jobs. The answer, in a word, is politics. Protection of the U.S. textile industry means that all consumers pay a higher price for clothing. But individual consumers do not know how much of the price they pay for clothes is due to protection, and consumers rarely lobby their political representatives to eliminate protection and reduce prices. Meanwhile, there is a great deal of pressure for protection. Employers and workers in the industry know the benefits of protection: higher prices for their output, higher profits for owners, and higher wages for workers. As a result, there will be active lobbying for protection against foreign competition.

Table 2

**Annual Gain in U.S. GDP
if U.S. Import Restrictions
Were Eliminated**

Sector	GDP Gain (million dollars)
Simultaneous liberalization of all restraints	12,402
Individual liberalization	
Textiles and apparel	10,376
Maritime transport (Jones Act)	1,324
Dairy	152
Sugar	986
Peanuts	8
Nonrubber footwear	501
Ball and roller bearings, and parts	49
Pressed and blown glass	34
Costume jewelry and costume novelties	19
Frozen fruit, fruit juices, and vegetables	28
Ceramic wall and floor tile	9
Personal leather goods	14
Leather gloves and mittens	16
China tableware	12

Source: *The Economic Effects of Significant U.S. Imports Restraints* (U.S. International Trade Commission, Washington, D.C., 1999), p. xvi.

1.b. Creation of a "Level Playing Field"

Special interest groups sometimes claim that other nations that export successfully to the home market have unfair advantages over domestic producers. Fairness, however, is often in the eye of the beholder. People who call for creating a "level playing field" believe that the domestic government should take steps to offset the perceived advantage of the foreign firm. They often claim that foreign firms have an unfair advantage because foreign workers are willing to work for very low wages. "Fair trade, not free trade" is the cry that this claim generates. But advocates of fair trade are really claiming that production in accordance with comparative advantage is unfair. This is clearly wrong. A country with relatively low wages is typically a country with an abundance of low-skilled labor. Such a country will have a comparative advantage in products that use low-skilled labor most intensively. To create a "level playing field" by imposing restrictions that eliminate the comparative advantage of foreign firms will make domestic consumers worse off and undermine the basis for specialization and economic efficiency.

Calls for "fair trade" are typically aimed at imposing restrictions to match those imposed by other nations.

Some calls for "fair trade" are based on the notion of reciprocity. If a country imposes import restrictions on goods from a country that does not have similar restrictions, reciprocal tariffs and quotas may be called for in the latter country in order to stimulate a reduction of trade restrictions in the former country. For instance, it has been claimed that U.S. construction firms are discriminated against in Japan, because no U.S. firm has had a major construction project in Japan since the 1960s. Yet Japanese construction firms do billions of dollars' worth of business in the United States each year. Advocates of fair trade could argue that U.S. restrictions should be imposed on Japanese construction firms.

One danger of calls for fairness based on reciprocity is that calls for fair trade may be invoked in cases where, in fact, foreign restrictions on U.S. imports do not exist. For instance, suppose the U.S. auto industry wanted to restrict the entry of imported autos to help stimulate sales of domestically produced cars. One strategy might be to point out that U.S. auto sales abroad had fallen and to claim that this was due to unfair treatment of U.S. auto exports in other countries. Of course, there are many other possible reasons why foreign sales of U.S. autos might have fallen. But blaming foreign trade restrictions might win political support for restricting imports of foreign cars into the United States.

1.c. Government Revenue Creation

Developing countries often justify tariffs as an important source of government revenue.

Tariffs on trade generate government revenue. Industrial countries, which find income taxes easy to collect, rarely justify tariffs on the basis of the revenue they generate for government spending. But many developing countries find income taxes difficult to levy and collect, while tariffs are easy to collect. Customs agents can be positioned at ports of entry to examine all goods that enter and leave the country. The observability of trade flows makes tariffs a popular tax in developing countries, whose revenue requirements may provide a valid justification for their existence. Table 3 shows that tariffs account for a relatively large fraction of government revenue in many developing countries, and only a small fraction in industrial countries.

1.d. National Defense

Industries that are truly critical to the national defense should be protected from foreign competition if that is the only way to ensure their existence.

It has long been argued that industries crucial to the national defense, like shipbuilding, should be protected from foreign competition. Even though the United States does not have a comparative advantage in shipbuilding, a domestic shipbuilding industry is necessary since foreign-made ships may not be available during war. This is a valid argument as long as the protected industry is genuinely critical to the national defense. In some industries, like copper or other basic metals, it might make more sense to import the crucial products during peacetime and store them for use in the event of war; these products do not require domestic production to be useful. Care must be taken to ensure that the national-defense argument is not used to protect industries other than those truly crucial to the nation's defense.

Table 3

Tariffs as a Percentage of Total Government Revenue

Country	Tariffs as Percentage of Government Revenue
United Kingdom	0.1%
Japan	1.2%
United States	1.1%
Costa Rica	8.4%
Ghana	26.8%
Dominican Republic	36.4%
Lesotho	53.2%

Source: International Monetary Fund, *Government Finance Statistics Yearbook*, Washington, D.C., 1998.

1.e. Infant Industries

Countries sometimes justify protecting new industries that need time to become competitive with the rest of the world.

Nations are often inclined to protect new industries on the basis that the protection will give those industries adequate time to develop. New industries need time to establish themselves and to become efficient enough that their costs are no higher than those of their foreign rivals. An alternative to protecting young and/or critical domestic industries with tariffs and quotas is to subsidize them. Subsidies allow such firms to charge lower prices and to compete with more-efficient foreign producers, while permitting consumers to pay the world price rather than the higher prices associated with tariffs or quotas on foreign goods.

Protecting an infant industry from foreign competition may make sense but only until the industry matures. Once the industry achieves sufficient size, protection should be withdrawn, and the industry should be made to compete with its foreign counterparts. Unfortunately, such protection is rarely withdrawn, because the larger and more successful the industry becomes, the more political power it wields. In fact, if an infant industry truly has a good chance to become competitive and produce profitably once it is well established, it is not at all clear that government should even offer protection to reduce short-run losses. New firms typically incur losses, but they are only temporary if the firm is successful.

1.f. Strategic Trade Policy

strategic trade policy: the use of trade restrictions or subsidies to allow domestic firms with decreasing costs to gain a greater share of the world market

increasing-returns-to-scale industry: an industry in which the costs of producing a unit of output fall as more output is produced

Government can use trade policy as a strategy to stimulate production by a domestic industry capable of achieving increasing returns to scale.

There is another view of international trade that regards as misleading the description of comparative advantage presented in the previous chapter. According to this outlook, called **strategic trade policy,** international trade largely involves firms that pursue economies of scale—that is, firms that achieve lower costs per unit of production the more they produce. In contrast to the constant opportunity costs illustrated in the example of wheat and cloth in the chapter on "World Trade Equilibrium," opportunity costs in some industries may fall with the level of output. Such **increasing-returns-to-scale industries** will tend to concentrate production in the hands of a few very large firms, rather than many competitive firms. Proponents of strategic trade policy contend that government can use tariffs or subsidies to allow domestic firms with decreasing costs an advantage over their foreign rivals.

A monopoly exists when there is only one producer in an industry and no close substitutes for the product exist. If the average costs of production decline with increases in output, then the larger a firm is, the lower its per unit costs will be. One large producer will be more efficient than many small ones. A simple example of a natural-monopoly industry will indicate how strategic trade policy can make a country better off. Suppose that the production of buses is an industry characterized by increasing returns to scale and that there are only two firms capable of producing buses: Volkswagen in Germany and General Motors in the United States. If both firms produce buses, their costs will be so high that both will experience losses. If only one of the two produces buses, however, it will be able to sell buses at home and abroad, creating a level of output that allows the firm to earn a profit.

Assume further that a monopoly producer will earn $100 million and that if both firms produce, they will each lose $5 million. Obviously, a firm that doesn't produce earns nothing. Which firm will produce? Because of the decreasing-cost nature of the industry, the firm that is the first to produce will realize lower costs and be able to preclude the other firm from entering the market. But strategic trade policy can alter the market in favor of the domestic firm.

Suppose Volkswagen is the world's only producer of buses. General Motors does not produce them. The U.S. government could offer General Motors an $8 million subsidy to produce buses. General Motors would then enter the bus market, since the

$8 million subsidy would more than offset the $5 million loss it would suffer by entering the market. Volkswagen would sustain losses of $5 million once General Motors entered. Ultimately, Volkswagen would stop producing buses to avoid the loss, and General Motors would have the entire market and earn $100 million plus the subsidy.

Strategic trade policy is aimed at offsetting the increasing-returns-to-scale advantage enjoyed by foreign producers and at stimulating production in domestic industries capable of realizing decreasing costs. One practical problem for government is the need to understand the technology of different industries and to forecast accurately the subsidy needed to induce domestic firms to produce new products. A second problem is the likelihood of retaliation by the foreign government. If the U.S. government subsidizes General Motors in its attack on the bus market, the German government is likely to subsidize Volkswagen rather than lose the entire bus market to a U.S. producer. As a result, taxpayers in both nations will be subsidizing two firms, each producing too few buses to earn a profit.

RECAP

1. Government restrictions on foreign trade are usually aimed at protecting domestic producers from foreign competition.

2. Import restrictions may save domestic jobs, but the costs to consumers may be greater than the benefits to those who retain their jobs.

3. Advocates of "fair trade," or the creation of a "level playing field," call for import restrictions as a means of lowering foreign restrictions on markets for domestic exports.

4. Tariffs are an important source of revenue in many developing countries.

5. The national-defense argument in favor of trade restrictions is that protection from foreign competition is necessary to ensure that certain key defense-related industries continue to produce.

6. The infant-industries argument in favor of trade restriction is to allow a new industry a period of time in which to become competitive with its foreign counterparts.

7. Strategic trade policy is intended to provide domestic increasing-returns-to-scale industries an advantage over their foreign competitors.

?

2. How do countries restrict the entry of foreign goods and promote the export of domestic goods?

2. TOOLS OF POLICY

Commercial policy makes use of several tools, including tariffs, quotas, subsidies, and nontariff barriers like health and safety regulations that restrict the entry of foreign products. Since 1945, barriers to trade have been reduced. Much of the progress toward free trade may be linked to the *General Agreement on Tariffs and Trade*, or *GATT*, that began in 1947. In 1995, the *World Trade Organization (WTO)* was formed to incorporate the agreements under GATT into a formal permanent international organization that oversees world trade. The WTO has three objectives: to help global trade flow as freely as possible, to achieve reductions in trade restrictions gradually through negotiation, and to provide an impartial means of settling disputes. Nevertheless, restrictions on trade still exist, and this section will review the most commonly used restrictions.

2.a. Tariffs

tariff: a tax on imports or exports

A **tariff** is a tax on imports or exports. Every country imposes tariffs on at least some imports. Some countries also impose tariffs on selected exports as a means of raising government revenue. Brazil, for instance, taxes coffee exports. The United States does not employ export tariffs, which are forbidden by the U.S. Constitution.

Tariffs are frequently imposed in order to protect domestic producers from foreign competition. The dangers of imposing tariffs are well illustrated in the Economic Insight "Smoot-Hawley Tariff." The effect of a tariff is illustrated in Figure 1, which shows the domestic market for oranges. Without international trade, the domestic equilibrium price, P_d, and quantity demanded, Q_d, are determined by the intersection of the domestic demand and supply curves. If the world price of oranges, P_w, is lower than the domestic equilibrium price, this country will import oranges. The quantity imported will be the difference between the quantity Q_1 produced domestically at a price of P_w and the quantity Q_2 demanded domestically at the world price of oranges.

When the world price of the traded good is lower than the domestic equilibrium price without international trade, free trade causes domestic production to fall and domestic consumption to rise. The domestic shortage at the world price is met by imports. Domestic consumers are better off, since they can buy more at a lower price. But domestic producers are worse off, since they now sell fewer oranges and receive a lower price.

Suppose a tariff of T (the dollar value of the tariff) is imposed on orange imports. The price paid by consumers is now $P_w + T$, rather than P_w. At this higher price, domestic producers will produce Q_3 and domestic consumers will purchase Q_4.

Smoot-Hawley Tariff

Many economists believe that the Great Depression of the 1930s was at least partly due to the Smoot-Hawley Tariff Act, signed into law by President Herbert Hoover in 1930. Hoover had promised that, if elected, he would raise tariffs on agricultural products to raise U.S. farm income. Congress began work on the tariff increases in 1928. Congressman Willis Hawley and Senator Reed Smoot conducted the hearings.

In testimony before Congress, manufacturers and other special interest groups also sought protection from foreign competition. The resulting bill increased tariffs on over 12,000 products. Tariffs reached their highest levels ever, about 60 percent of average import values.

Only twice before in U.S. history had tariffs approached the levels of the Smoot-Hawley era.

Before President Hoover signed the bill, 38 foreign governments made formal protests, warning that they would retaliate with high tariffs on U.S. products. A petition signed by 1,028 economists warned of the harmful effects of the bill. Nevertheless, Hoover signed the bill into law.

World trade collapsed as other countries raised their tariffs in response. Between 1930 and 1931, U.S. imports fell 29 percent, but U.S. exports fell 33 percent. By 1933, world trade was about one-third of its 1929 level. As the level of trade fell, so did income and prices. In 1934, in an effort to correct the mistakes of Smoot-

Hawley, Congress passed the Reciprocal Trade Agreements Act, which allowed the president to lower U.S. tariffs in return for reductions in foreign tariffs on U.S. goods. This act ushered in the modern era of relatively low tariffs. In the United States today, tariffs are about 5 percent of the average value of imports.

Many economists believe the collapse of world trade and the Depression to be linked by a decrease in real income caused by abandoning production based on comparative advantage. Few economists argue that the Great Depression was caused solely by the Smoot-Hawley tariff, but the experience serves as a lesson to those who support higher tariffs to protect domestic producers.

Figure 1

The Effects of a Tariff

The domestic equilibrium price and quantity with no trade are P_d and Q_d, respectively. The world price is P_w. With free trade, therefore, imports will equal $Q_2 - Q_1$. A tariff added to the world price reduces imports to $Q_4 - Q_3$.

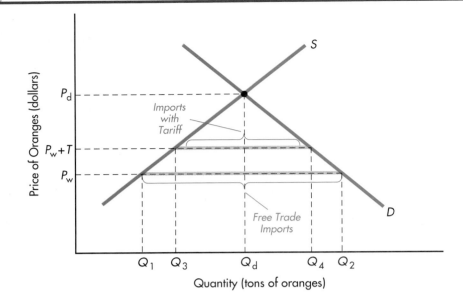

The tariff has the effect of increasing domestic production and reducing domestic consumption, relative to the free trade equilibrium. Imports fall accordingly, from $Q_2 - Q_1$ to $Q_4 - Q_3$.

Domestic producers are better off, since the tariff has increased their sales of oranges and raised the price they receive. Domestic consumers pay higher prices for fewer oranges than they would with free trade, but they are still better off than they would be without trade. If the tariff had raised the price paid by consumers to P_d, there would be no trade, and the domestic equilibrium quantity, Q_d, would prevail.

The government earns revenue from imports of oranges. If each ton of oranges generates tariff revenue of T, the total tariff revenue to the government is found by multiplying the tariff by the quantity of oranges imported. In Figure 1, this amount is $T \times (Q_4 - Q_3)$. As the tariff changes, so does the quantity of imports and the government revenue.

2.b. Quotas

quantity quota: a limit on the amount of a good that may be imported

value quota: a limit on the monetary value of a good that may be imported

Quotas are limits on the quantity or value of goods imported and exported. A **quantity quota** restricts the physical amount of a good. For instance, through 2000 the United States allowed only 1.5 million tons of sugar to be imported. Even though the United States is not a competitive sugar producer compared to other nations like the Dominican Republic or Cuba, the quota allowed U.S. firms to produce about 6 percent of the world's sugar output. A **value quota** restricts the monetary value of a good that may be traded. Instead of a physical quota on sugar, the United States could have limited the dollar value of sugar imports.

Quotas are used to protect domestic producers from foreign competition. By restricting the amount of a good that may be imported, they increase its price and allow domestic producers to sell more at a higher price than they would with free trade. Figure 2 illustrates the effect of a quota on the domestic orange market. The domestic equilibrium supply and demand curves determine the equilibrium price and

Figure 2

The Effects of a Quota

The domestic equilibrium price with no international trade is P_d. At this price, 250 tons of oranges would be produced and consumed at home. With free trade, the price is P_w and 300 tons will be imported. An import quota of 100 tons will cause the price to be P_q, where the domestic shortage equals the 100 tons allowed by the quota.

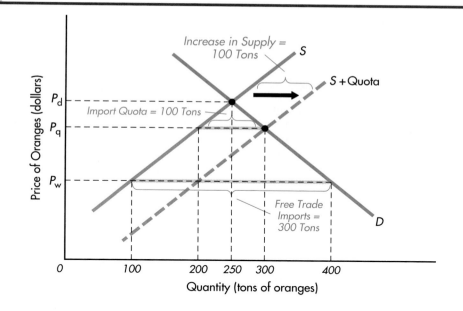

quantity without trade to be P_d and 250 tons, respectively. The world price of oranges is P_w. Since P_w lies below P_d, this country will import oranges. The quantity of imports is equal to the amount of the domestic shortage at P_w. The quantity demanded at P_w is 400 tons, and the quantity supplied domestically is 100 tons, so imports will equal 300 tons of oranges. With free trade, domestic producers sell 100 tons at a price of P_w.

But suppose domestic orange growers convince the government to restrict orange imports. The government then imposes a quota of 100 tons on imported oranges. The effect of the quota on consumers is to shift the supply curve to the right by the amount of the quota, 100 tons. Since the quota is less than the quantity of imports with free trade, the quantity of imports will equal the quota. The domestic equilibrium price with the quota occurs at the point where the domestic shortage equals the quota. At price P_q, the domestic quantity demanded (300 tons) is 100 tons more than the domestic quantity supplied (200 tons).

Quotas benefit domestic producers in the same way that tariffs do. Domestic producers receive a higher price (P_q instead of P_w) for a greater quantity (200 instead of 100) than they do under free trade. The effect on domestic consumers is also similar to that of a tariff: they pay a higher price for a smaller quantity than they would with free trade. A tariff generates government tax revenue; quotas do not (unless the government auctioned off the right to import under the quota). Furthermore, a tariff only raises the price of the product in the domestic market. Foreign producers receive the world price, P_w. With a quota, both domestic and foreign producers receive the higher price, P_q, for the goods sold in the domestic market. So foreign producers are hurt by the reduction in the quantity of imports permitted, but they do receive a higher price for the amount they sell.

2.c. Other Barriers to Trade

Tariffs and quotas are not the only barriers to the free flow of goods across international borders. There are three additional sources of restrictions on free trade:

subsidies, government procurement, and health and safety standards. Though often enacted for reasons other than protection from foreign competition, a careful analysis reveals their import-reducing effect.

Before discussing these three types of barriers, let us note the cultural or institutional barriers to trade that also exist in many countries. Such barriers may exist independently of any conscious government policy. For instance, Japan has frequently been criticized by U.S. officials for informal business practices that discriminate against foreigners. Under the Japanese distribution system, goods typically pass through several layers of middlemen before appearing in a retail store. A foreign firm faces the difficult task of gaining entry to this system to supply goods to the retailer. Furthermore, a foreigner cannot easily open a retail store. Japanese law requires a new retail firm to receive permission from other retailers in the area in order to open a business. A firm that lacks contacts and knowledge of the system cannot penetrate the Japanese market.

In the fall of 1989, the U.S. toy firm Toys "R" Us announced its intent to open several large discount toy stores in Japan. However, local toy stores in each area objected to having a Toys "R" Us store nearby. The U.S. government has argued that the laws favoring existing firms are an important factor in keeping Japan closed to foreign firms that would like to enter the Japanese market. Eventually, Toys "R" Us opened stores in Japan.

subsidies: payments made by government to domestic firms to encourage exports

2.c.1. Subsidies Subsidies are payments by a government to an exporter. Subsidies are paid to stimulate exports by allowing the exporter to charge a lower price. The amount of a subsidy is determined by the international price of a product relative to the domestic price in the absence of trade. Domestic consumers are harmed by subsidies in that their taxes finance the subsidies. Also, since the subsidy diverts resources from the domestic market toward export production, the increase in the supply of export goods could be associated with a decrease in the supply of domestic goods, causing domestic prices to rise.

Subsidies may take forms other than direct cash payments. These include tax reductions, low-interest loans, low-cost insurance, government-sponsored research funding, and other devices. The U.S. government subsidizes export activity through the U.S. Export-Import Bank, which provides loans and insurance to help U.S. exporters sell their goods to foreign buyers. Subsidies are more commonplace in Europe than in Japan or the United States.

2.c.2. Government Procurement Governments are often required by law to buy only from local producers. In the United States, a "buy American" act passed in 1933 required U.S. government agencies to buy U.S. goods and services unless the domestic price was more than 12 percent above the foreign price. This kind of policy allows domestic firms to charge the government a higher price for their products than they charge consumers; the taxpayers bear the burden. The United States is by no means alone in the use of such policies. Many other nations also use such policies to create larger markets for domestic goods. The World Trade Organization has a standing committee working to reduce discrimination against foreign producers and open government procurement practices to global competition.

2.c.3. Health and Safety Standards Government serves as a guardian of the public health and welfare by requiring that products offered to the public be safe and fulfill the use for which they are intended. Government standards for products sold in the domestic marketplace can have the effect (intentional or not) of protecting domestic producers from foreign competition. These effects should be considered in evaluating the full impact of such standards.

As mentioned in the Preview, the government of Japan once threatened to prohibit foreign-made snow skis from entering the country for reasons of safety. Only Japanese-made skis were determined to be suitable for Japanese snow. Several western European nations announced that U.S. beef would not be allowed into Europe because hormones approved by the U.S. government are fed to U.S. beef cattle. In the late 1960s, France required tractors sold there to have a maximum speed of 17 miles per hour; in Germany, the permissible speed was 13 miles per hour, and in the Netherlands it was 10 miles per hour. Tractors produced in one country had to be modified to meet the requirements of the other countries. Such modifications raise the price of goods and discourage international trade.

Product standards may not eliminate foreign competition, but standards different from those of the rest of the world do provide an element of protection to domestic firms.

RECAP

1. The World Trade Organization works to achieve reductions in trade barriers.
2. A tariff is a tax on imports or exports. Tariffs protect domestic firms by raising the prices of foreign goods.
3. Quotas are government-imposed limits on the quantity or value of an imported good. Quotas protect domestic firms by restricting the entry of foreign products to a level less than the quantity demanded.
4. Subsidies are payments by the government to domestic producers. Subsidies lower the price of domestic goods to foreign buyers.
5. Governments are often required by law to buy only domestic products.
6. Health and safety standards can also be used to protect domestic firms.

3. PREFERENTIAL TRADE AGREEMENTS

? **3. What sorts of agreements do countries enter into to reduce barriers to international trade?**

In an effort to stimulate international trade, groups of countries sometimes enter into agreements to abolish most barriers to trade among themselves. Such arrangements between countries are known as preferential trading agreements. The European Union and the North American Free Trade Agreement (NAFTA) are examples of preferential trading agreements.

3.a. Free Trade Areas and Customs Unions

free trade area: an organization of nations whose members have no trade barriers among themselves but are free to fashion their own trade policies toward nonmembers

customs union: an organization of nations whose members have no trade barriers among themselves but impose common trade barriers on nonmembers

Two common forms of preferential trade agreements are **free trade areas** (FTAs) and **customs unions** (CUs). These two approaches differ with regard to treatment of countries outside the agreement. In an FTA, member countries eliminate trade barriers among themselves, but each member country chooses its own trade policies toward nonmember countries. Members of a CU agree to eliminate trade barriers among themselves and to maintain common trade barriers against nonmembers.

The best-known CU is the European Union (EU), formerly known as the European Economic Community (EEC), created in 1957 by France, West Germany, Italy, Belgium, the Netherlands, and Luxembourg. The United Kingdom, Ireland, and Denmark joined in 1973, followed by Greece in 1981 and Spain and Portugal in 1986. In 1992 the EEC was replaced by the EU with an agreement to create a single market for goods and services in western Europe. Besides free trade in goods,

The North American Free Trade Agreement stimulates trade among Mexico, Canada, and the United States. In coming years, there will be more and more container ships from Mexico unloading their cargo at U.S. docks. Similarly, freight from Canada and the United States will increase in volume at Mexican ports.

European financial markets and institutions will eventually be able to operate across national boundaries. For instance, a bank in any EU country will be permitted to operate in any or all other EU countries.

In 1989, the United States and Canada negotiated a free trade area. The United States, Canada, and Mexico negotiated a free trade area in 1992 which became effective on January 1, 1994. Under the North American Free Trade Agreement (NAFTA), tariffs are lowered on 8,000 different items, and each nation's financial market is opened to competition from the other two nations. The NAFTA does not eliminate all barriers to trade among the three nations but is a significant step in that direction.

3.b. Trade Creation and Diversion

Free trade agreements provide for free trade among a group of countries, not worldwide. As a result, a customs union or free trade area may make a nation better off or worse off compared to the free trade equilibrium.

Figure 3 illustrates the effect of a free trade area. With no international trade, the U.S. supply and demand curves for oranges would result in an equilibrium price of $500 per ton and an equilibrium quantity of 425 tons. Suppose there are two other orange-producing countries, Israel and Brazil. Israel, the low-cost producer of oranges, is willing to sell all the oranges the United States can buy for $150 per ton, as represented by the horizontal supply curve S_I. Brazil will supply oranges for a price of $200 per ton, as represented by the horizontal supply curve S_B.

With free trade, the United States would import oranges from Israel. The quantity demanded at $150 is 750 tons, and the domestic quantity supplied at this price is 100 tons. The shortage of 650 tons is met by imports from Israel.

Now suppose a 100 percent tariff is imposed on orange imports. The price domestic consumers pay for foreign oranges is twice as high as before. For oranges from Israel the new price is $300, twice the old price of $150. The new supply curve for Israel is represented as S_I + Tariff. Oranges from Brazil now sell for $400, twice the old price of $200; the new supply curve for Brazil is shown as S_B + Tariff. After the 100 percent tariff is imposed, oranges are still imported from Israel. But at the new

Figure 3

Trade Creation and Trade Diversion with a Free Trade Area

With no trade, the domestic equilibrium price is $500 and the equilibrium quantity is 425 tons. With free trade, the price is $150, and 650 tons would be imported, as indicated by the supply curve for Israel, S_I. A 100 percent tariff on imports would result in imports of 350 tons from Israel, according to the supply curve S_I + Tariff. A free trade agreement that eliminates tariffs on Brazilian oranges only would result in a new equilibrium price of $200 and imports of 550 tons from Brazil, according to supply curve S_B.

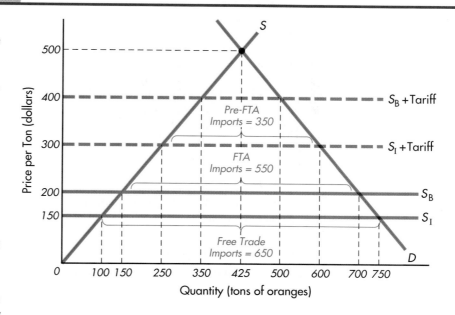

trade diversion: an effect of a preferential trade agreement, reducing economic efficiency by shifting production to a higher-cost producer

trade creation: an effect of a preferential trade agreement, allowing a country to obtain goods at a lower cost than is available at home

price of $300, the domestic quantity demanded is 600 tons and the domestic quantity supplied is 250 tons. Thus only 350 tons will be imported. The tariff reduces the volume of trade relative to the free trade equilibrium, at which 650 tons were imported.

Now suppose that the United States negotiates a free trade agreement with Brazil, eliminating tariffs on imports from Brazil. Israel is not a member of the free trade agreement, so imports from Israel are still covered by the 100 percent tariff. The relevant supply curve for Brazil is now S_B, so oranges may be imported from Brazil for $200, a lower price than Israel's price including the tariff. At a price of $200, the domestic quantity demanded is 700 tons and the domestic quantity supplied is 150 tons; 550 tons will be imported.

The effects of the free trade agreement are twofold. First, trade was diverted away from the lowest-cost producer, Israel, to the FTA partner, Brazil. This **trade-diversion** effect of an FTA reduces worldwide economic efficiency, since production is diverted from the country with the comparative advantage. Oranges are not being produced as efficiently as possible. The other effect of the FTA is that the quantity of imports increases relative to the effect of a tariff applicable to all imports. Imports rise from 350 tons (the quantity imported from Israel with the tariff) to 550 tons. The FTA thus has a **trade-creation** effect, resulting from the lower price available after the tariff reduction. Trade creation is a beneficial aspect of the FTA: the expansion of international trade allows this country to realize greater benefits from trade than would be possible without trade.

Countries form preferential trade agreements because they believe FTAs will make each member country better off. The member countries view the trade-creation effects of such agreements as benefiting their exporters by increasing exports to member countries and as benefiting consumers by making a wider variety of goods available at a lower price. From the point of view of the world as a whole, preferential trade agreements are more desirable the more they stimulate trade creation to allow the benefits of trade to be realized and the less they emphasize trade diversion, so that production occurs on the basis of comparative advantage. This principle suggests that the most successful FTAs or CUs are those that increase trade volume but do not change the patterns of trade in terms of who specializes and exports each good. In the case of Figure 3, a more successful FTA would reduce tariffs on Israeli as well as Brazilian oranges, so that oranges would be imported from the lowest-cost producer, Israel.

RECAP

1. Countries form preferential trade agreements in order to stimulate trade among themselves.
2. The most common forms of preferential trade agreement are free trade areas (FTAs) and customs unions (CUs).
3. Preferential trade agreements have a harmful trade-diversion effect when they cause production to shift from the nation with a comparative advantage to a higher-cost producer.
4. Preferential trade agreements have a beneficial trade-creation effect when they reduce prices for traded goods and stimulate the volume of international trade.

SUMMARY

? Why do countries restrict international trade?

1. Commercial policy is government policy that influences the direction and volume of international trade. §Preview
2. Protecting domestic producers from foreign competition usually imposes costs on domestic consumers. §1
3. Rationales for commercial policy include saving domestic jobs, creating a fair-trade relationship with other countries, raising tariff revenue, ensuring a domestic supply of key defense goods, allowing new industries a chance to become internationally competitive, and giving domestic industries with increasing returns to scale an advantage over foreign competitors. §1.a–1.f

? How do countries restrict the entry of foreign goods and promote the export of domestic goods?

4. Tariffs protect domestic industry by increasing the price of foreign goods. §2.a

5. Quotas protect domestic industry by limiting the quantity of foreign goods allowed into the country. §2.b
6. Subsidies allow relatively inefficient domestic producers to compete with foreign firms. §2.c.1
7. Government procurement practices and health and safety regulations can protect domestic industry from foreign competition. §2.c.2, 2.c.3

? What sorts of agreements do countries enter into to reduce barriers to international trade?

8. Free trade areas and customs unions are two types of preferential trade agreements that reduce trade restrictions among member countries. §3.a
9. Preferential trade agreements have harmful trade-diversion effects and beneficial trade-creation effects. §3.b

KEY TERMS

commercial policy *§Preview*

strategic trade policy *§1.f*

increasing-returns-to-scale industry *§1.f*

tariff *§2.a*

quantity quota *§2.b*

value quota *§2.b*

subsidies *§2.c.1*

free trade area *§3.a*

customs union *§3.a*

trade diversion *§3.b*

trade creation *§3.b*

EXERCISES

1. What are the potential benefits and costs of a commercial policy designed to pursue each of the following goals?

   a. Save domestic jobs.
   b. Create a level playing field.
   c. Increase government revenue.
   d. Provide a strong national defense.
   e. Protect an infant industry.
   f. Stimulate exports of an industry with increasing returns to scale.

2. For each of the goals listed in exercise 1, discuss what the appropriate commercial policy is likely to be (in terms of tariffs, quotas, subsidies, etc.).

3. Tariffs and quotas both raise the price of foreign goods to domestic consumers. What is the difference between the effects of a tariff and the effects of a quota on the following?

   a. The domestic government
   b. Foreign producers
   c. Domestic producers

4. Would trade-diversion and trade-creation effects occur if the whole world became a free trade area? Explain.

5. What is the difference between a customs union and a free trade area?

6. Draw a graph of the U.S. automobile market in which the domestic equilibrium price without trade is P_d and the equilibrium quantity is Q_d. Use this graph to illustrate and explain the effects of a tariff if the United States were an auto importer with free trade. Then use the graph to illustrate and explain the effects of a quota.

7. If commercial policy can benefit U.S. industry, why would any U.S. resident oppose such policies?

8. Suppose you were asked to assess U.S. commercial policy to determine whether the benefits of protection for U.S. industries are worth the costs. Do Tables 1 and 2 provide all the information you need? If not, what else would you want to know?

9. How would the effects of international trade on the domestic orange market change if the world price of oranges were above the domestic equilibrium price? Draw a graph to help explain your answer.

10. Suppose the world price of kiwi fruit is $20 per case and the U.S. equilibrium price with no international trade is $35 per case. If the U.S. government had previously banned the import of kiwi fruit but then imposed a tariff of $5 per case and allowed kiwi imports, what would happen to the equilibrium price and quantity of kiwi fruit consumed in the United States?

Internet Exercises/ Resources

For Internet exercises and web resources related to this chapter, go to **http://college.hmco.com.**

Imports and Competition in Domestic Markets

Foremost among the asserted benefits of reducing trade barriers is competition: firms that operate in an economy with relatively weak domestic competition are supposed to be forced by the onslaught of foreign goods to improve their quality and service and to keep costs and prices down. The benefits of trade liberalization are assumed to be particularly great in developing countries, where a relatively few firms may control a given industry. But while the theoretical benefits of freer trade are well understood, do businesses actually respond in that way? After studying the effects of trade liberalization in Turkey, NBER researcher James Levinsohn concludes that the answer is "yes."

Until 1984, the Turkish economy was highly protected against imports, with tariffs averaging 49 percent and an array of nontariff barriers including quotas, import licenses, and foreign exchange regulations. In 1984, however, tariffs were reduced to an average of 20 percent and restrictions on many types of imports were eliminated. . . . Levinsohn investigated the impact of this sweeping liberalization by using detailed data on individual firms from the Turkish manufacturing census. . . .

Prior to the change in trade policy, Levinsohn finds, firms in six of the eleven industries studied were pricing at marginal cost, indicating a high level of competition. In three industries, companies were pricing above marginal cost, indicating the existence of imperfect competition, while in two industries, including the largely government-owned steel industry, firms were losing money on each unit of output. The 1984 trade liberalization reduced the level of protection enjoyed by nine of the eleven industries. In the three high-margin industries, miscellaneous chemicals, pottery, and electrical machinery, price markups declined as import competition increased. For two of the previously competitive industries, transport equipment and scientific equipment, the trade reform resulted in higher levels of import protection, and price mark-ups in those industries increased. Of the six previously competitive industries that had their protection reduced by the trade reform, three had lower markups and one was unchanged; one of the two industries in that category with higher mark-ups was the steel industry.

Levinsohn warns that the price markups reported by companies to census officials may not be completely accurate. Firms with high profits may be inclined to understate their revenues or overstate costs in case tax officials learn of their reports, while firms with losses may exit the industry and not report. Nonetheless, Levinsohn writes, the Turkish data indicate that imports increase competition and restrict the ability of domestic firms to exercise market power.

Source: From *NBER Digest*, July–August 1991. Used by permission of the National Bureau of Economic Research.

NBER Digest/July–August 1991

Commentary

Consider the following hypothetical situation: The legislature of the state of Maine considers a tax to support the pineapple farmers of the state. Of course, Maine's climate is not conducive to growing pineapples, but it is possible, at great cost, to grow a few pineapples in greenhouses. The tax on pineapples brought into the state raises the price of Hawaiian pineapples by enough to make pineapples grown in Maine competitive. Thus Maine's pineapple industry is saved from competitors whose price reflects their unfair climactic advantage, though the consumers of the state must pay exorbitant prices for their pineapples.

This scenario, with its absurd distortion of the workings of the market, differs in degree but not in kind from the description of the effects of import competition in the accompanying article. The protectionist measure of imposing quotas or tariffs on imports saves jobs in the domestic import-competing industries but at a great cost to consumers. It is estimated that the cost of protecting the U.S. domestic textile industry is $238 per family in the United States.

The effect of reducing domestic competition with quotas can be understood using supply and demand analysis. Let's analyze the case of quotas on textile imports into the United States. In the diagram, S_1 is the domestic supply of textiles, S_2 is the sum of the domestic supply and the foreign supply allowed in by the quotas, and D is the demand for textiles. Under the quota system, the price of textiles in the United States is represented by P_q and the quantity of textiles consumed is Q_q. If the quotas were removed, the price of textiles in the United States would equal the world price of P_w, and this lower price would be associated with an increase in the consumption of textiles to Q_w. The quota represents a cost to society in terms of a loss of consumer welfare as well as a loss from the inefficient use of

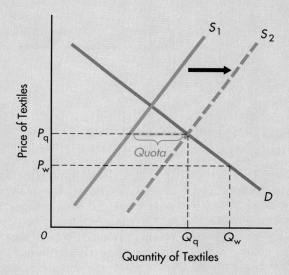

resources in an industry in which this country has no comparative advantage, just as Maine has no comparative advantage in the production of pineapples.

Given the costs to society of these quotas, why is there such strong support for them in Congress? An important political aspect of protectionist policies is that their benefits are concentrated among a relatively small number of people while their costs are diffuse and spread across all consumers. Each individual import-competing producer faces very large losses from free trade while the cost to each consumer of a protectionist policy is less dramatic. It is also easier to organize a relatively small number of manufacturers than to mobilize a vast population of consumers. These factors explain the strong lobby for the protection of industries like textiles and the absence of a legislative lobby that operates specifically in the interest of textile consumers.

Industrial arguments for trade protection should be seen for what they are: an attempt by an industry to increase its profits at the expense of the general public.

Chapter 23

Exchange-Rate Systems and Practices

? **Fundamental Questions**

1. **How does a commodity standard fix exchange rates between countries?**

2. **What kinds of exchange-rate arrangements exist today?**

3. **How is equilibrium determined in the foreign exchange market?**

4. **How do fixed and floating exchange rates differ in their adjustment to shifts in supply and demand for currencies?**

5. **What are the advantages and disadvantages of fixed and floating exchange rates?**

6. **What determines the kind of exchange-rate system a country adopts?**

Preview

Exchange-rate policy is an important element of macroeconomic policy. An exchange rate is the link between two nations' monies. The value of a U.S. dollar in terms of Japanese yen or European euro determines how many dollars a U.S. resident will need to buy goods priced in yen or euro. Thus changes in the exchange rate can have far-reaching implications. Exchange rates may be determined in free markets, through government intervention in the foreign exchange market, or even by law.

In the early 1990s, one U.S. dollar was worth about 125 Japanese yen. By spring of 1995, the dollar was worth 83 yen. By early 1998, a dollar was worth 125 yen again and by January 2001, 114 yen would buy 1 dollar. Why does the dollar fluctuate in value relative to the yen? What are the effects of such changes? Should

governments permit exchange rates to change? What can governments do to discourage changing exchange rates? These are all important questions, which this chapter will help to answer.

The chapter begins with a review of the history of exchange-rate systems. It follows with an overview of exchange-rate practices in the world today and an analysis of the benefits and costs of alternative exchange-rate arrangements. Along the way, it introduces terminology and institutions that play a major role in the evolution of exchange rates. ■

1. PAST AND CURRENT EXCHANGE-RATE ARRANGEMENTS

1.a. The Gold Standard

1. How does a commodity standard fix exchange rates between countries?

gold standard: a system whereby national currencies are fixed in terms of their value in gold, thus creating fixed exchange rates between currencies

In ancient times, government-produced monies were made of precious metals like gold. Later, when governments began to issue paper money, it was usually convertible into a fixed amount of gold. Ensuring the convertibility of paper money into gold was a way to maintain confidence in the currency's value, at home and abroad. If a unit of currency was worth a fixed amount of gold, its value could be stated in terms of its gold value. The countries that maintained a constant gold value for their currencies were said to be on a **gold standard.**

Some countries had backed their currencies with gold long before 1880; however, the practice became widespread around 1880, so economists typically date the beginning of the gold standard to this period. From roughly 1880 to 1914, currencies had fixed values in terms of gold. For instance, the U.S. dollar's value was fixed at $20.67 per ounce of gold. Any other currency that was fixed in terms of gold also had a fixed exchange rate against the dollar. A simple example will illustrate how this works.

Suppose the price of an ounce of gold is $20 in the United States and £4 in the United Kingdom. The pound is worth five times the value of a dollar, since it takes five times as many dollars as pounds to buy one ounce of gold. Because 1 pound buys five times as much gold as 1 dollar, the exchange rate is £1 = $5. Since currency values are linked by gold values, as the supply of gold fluctuates, there will be pressure to alter prices of goods and services. The gold standard fixes only the current price of gold. As the stock of gold increases, everything else held constant, the gold and currency prices of goods and services will tend to rise (as would occur when the money supply increases).

A commodity money standard exists when exchange rates are fixed based on the values of different currencies in terms of some commodity.

A gold standard is only one possible *commodity money standard.* Any other highly valued commodity (silver, for instance) could serve as a standard linking monies in a fixed exchange-rate system.

The gold standard ended with the outbreak of World War I. War financing was partially funded by increases in the money supplies of the hostile nations. A gold standard would not permit such a rapid increase in the money supply unless the stock of gold increased dramatically, which it did not. As money supplies grew faster than gold supplies, the link between money and gold had to be broken. During the war years and the Great Depression of the 1930s, and on through World War II, there was no organized system for setting exchange rates. Foreign trade and investment shrunk as a result of the war, obviating the need for a well-functioning method of determining exchange rates.

1.b. The Bretton Woods System

At the end of World War II, there was widespread political support for an exchange-rate system linking all monies in much the same way as the gold standard had. It was believed that a system of fixed exchange rates would promote the growth of world trade. In 1944, delegates from 44 nations met in Bretton Woods, New Hampshire, to discuss the creation of such a system. The agreement reached at this conference has had a profound impact on the world.

gold exchange standard: an exchange-rate system in which each nation fixes the value of its currency in terms of gold, but buys and sells the U.S. dollar rather than gold to maintain fixed exchange rates

The exchange-rate arrangement that emerged from the Bretton Woods conference is often called a **gold exchange standard.** Each country was to fix the value of its currency in terms of gold, just as it had under the gold standard. The U.S. dollar price of gold, for instance, was $35 an ounce. However, there were fundamental differences between this system and the old gold standard. The U.S. dollar, rather than gold, served as the focal point of the system. Instead of buying and selling gold, countries bought and sold U.S. dollars to maintain a fixed exchange rate with the dollar. Since the United States was the major victor nation, its currency was the dominant world currency. The United States had the productive capacity to supply much-needed goods to the rest of the world, and these goods were priced in dollars.

reserve currency: a currency that is used to settle international debts and is held by governments to use in foreign exchange market interventions

The U.S. dollar was the **reserve currency** of the system. International debts were settled with dollars, and international trade contracts were often denominated in dollars. In effect, the world was on a dollar standard following World War II.

1.c. The International Monetary Fund and the World Bank

International Monetary Fund (IMF): an international organization that supervises exchange-rate arrangements and lends money to member countries experiencing problems meeting their external financial obligations

Two new organizations also emerged from the Bretton Woods conference: the International Monetary Fund and the World Bank. The **International Monetary Fund (IMF)** was created to supervise the exchange-rate practices of member countries and to encourage the free convertibility of any national money into the monies of other countries. The IMF also lends money to countries that are experiencing problems meeting their international payment obligations. The funds available to the IMF come from the annual membership fees (called *quotas*) of the 182 member countries of the IMF. The U.S. quota, for instance, is almost $48 billion. (The term *quota* has a different meaning in this context than it does in international trade.)

World Bank: an international organization that makes loans and provides technical expertise to developing countries

The **World Bank** was created to help finance economic development in poor countries. It provides loans to developing countries at more favorable terms than are available from commercial lenders and also offers technical expertise. The World Bank obtains the funds it lends by selling bonds. It is one of the world's major borrowers. See the Economic Insight "The IMF and the World Bank" for an explanation of how these institutions work.

1.d. The Transition Years

The Bretton Woods system of fixed exchange rates required countries to actively buy and sell dollars to maintain fixed exchange rates when the *free market equilibrium* in the foreign exchange market differed from the fixed rate. The free market equilibrium exchange rate is the rate that would be established in the absence of government intervention. Governmental buying and selling of currencies to achieve a target exchange rate is called **foreign exchange market intervention.** The effec-

foreign exchange market intervention: buying or selling of currencies by a government or central bank to achieve a specified exchange rate

tiveness of such intervention was limited to situations in which free market pressure to deviate from the fixed exchange rate was temporary. For instance, suppose a country has a bad harvest and earns less foreign exchange than usual. This may only be a temporary situation if the next harvest is plentiful and the country resumes its typical export sales. During the period of reduced exports, it will be necessary for

The IMF and the World Bank

The International Monetary Fund (IMF) and the World Bank were both created at the Bretton Woods conference in 1944. The IMF oversees the international monetary system, promoting stable exchange rates and macroeconomic policies. The World Bank promotes the economic development of the poor nations. Both organizations are owned and directed by their 182 member countries.

The IMF provides loans to nations having trouble repaying their foreign debts. Before the IMF lends any money, however, the borrower must agree to certain conditions. The IMF *conditionality* usually requires that the country meet targets for key macro-economic variables like money-supply growth, inflation, tax collections, and subsidies. The conditions attached to IMF loans are aimed at promoting stable economic growth.

The World Bank assists developing countries by providing long-term financing for development projects and programs. The Bank also provides expertise in many areas in which poor nations lack expert knowledge: agriculture, medicine, construction, and education, as well as economics. The IMF primarily employs economists to carry out its mission.

The diversity of World Bank activities results in the employment of about 6,500 people. The IMF has a staff of approximately 1,700. Both organizations post employees around the world, but most work at the headquarters in Washington, D.C.

World Bank funds are largely acquired by borrowing on the international bond market. The IMF receives its funding from member-country subscription fees, called quotas. A member's quota determines its voting power in setting IMF policies. The United States, whose quota accounts for the largest fraction of the total, has the most votes.

devaluation: a deliberate decrease in the official value of a currency

equilibrium exchange rates: the exchange rates that are established in the absence of government foreign exchange market intervention

2. What kinds of exchange-rate arrangements exist today?

the government of this country to intervene to avoid a depreciation of its domestic currency. In the 1960s, however, there were several episodes of permanent rather than temporary changes that called for changes in exchange rates rather than government foreign exchange market intervention. The problems that arise in response to permanent pressures to change the exchange rate will be discussed further in section 2, when we analyze the benefits and costs of alternative exchange-rate systems.

The Bretton Woods system officially dissolved in 1971, at a meeting of the finance ministers of the leading world powers at the Smithsonian Institution in Washington, D.C. The Smithsonian agreement changed the exchange rates set during the Bretton Woods era. One result was a **devaluation** of the U.S. dollar. (A currency is said to be devalued when its value is officially lowered.) If a dollar is worth 1/35 oz. of gold, then gold costs $35 an ounce.

Under the Smithsonian agreement, countries were to maintain fixed exchange rates at newly defined values. It soon became clear, however, that the new exchange rates were not **equilibrium exchange rates** that could be maintained without government intervention and that government intervention could not maintain the disequilibrium fixed exchange rates forever. The U.S. dollar was devalued again in February 1973, when the dollar price of gold was raised to $42.22. This new exchange rate was still not an equilibrium rate, and in March 1973 the major industrial countries abandoned fixed exchange rates.

1.e. Today

When fixed exchange rates were abandoned by the major industrial countries in March 1973, the world did not move to purely free-market-determined floating exchange rates. Under the system in existence since that time, the major industrial

In March 1973, the major industrial countries abandoned fixed exchange rates for floating rates.

countries intervene to keep their currencies within acceptable ranges, while many smaller countries maintain fixed exchange rates.

The world today consists of some countries with fixed exchange rates, whose governments keep the exchange rates between two or more currencies constant over time; other countries with floating exchange rates, which shift on a daily basis according to the forces of supply and demand; and still others whose exchange-rate systems lie somewhere in between. Table 1, which lists the exchange-rate arrangements of over 180 countries, illustrates the diversity of exchange-rate arrangements currently in effect.

We provide a brief description of each:

Crawling pegs   The exchange rate is adjusted periodically in small amounts at a fixed, preannounced rate or in response to certain indicators (such as inflation differentials against major trading partners).

Crawling bands   The exchange rate is maintained within certain fluctuation margins around a central rate that is periodically adjusted at a fixed, preannounced rate or in response to certain indicators.

Managed floating   The monetary authority (usually the central bank) influences the exchange rate through active foreign exchange market intervention with no preannounced path for the exchange rate.

Independently floating   The exchange rate is market determined, and any intervention is aimed at moderating fluctuations rather than determining the level of the exchange rate.

No separate legal tender   Either another country's currency circulates as the legal tender, or the country belongs to a monetary union where the legal tender is shared by the members (like the euro).

Currency board   A fixed exchange rate is established by a legislative commitment to exchange domestic currency for a specified foreign currency at a fixed exchange rate. New issues of domestic currency are typically backed in some fixed ratio (like one-to-one) by additional holdings of the key foreign currency.

Fixed peg   The exchange rate is fixed against a major currency or some basket of currencies. Active intervention may be required to maintain the target pegged rate.

Horizontal bands   The exchange rate fluctuates around a fixed central target rate. Such target zones allow for a moderate amount of exchange rate fluctuation while tying the currency to the target central rate.

Under "Exchange Rates with No Separate Legal Tender" in Table 1 we see the euro area. The countries listed in this section all use a common currency, the *euro*. The new European currency, the euro, made its debut on January 1, 1999. The symbol is a €. Table 2 lists the exchange rates at which each of the member currencies is converted into euro. These are supposed to be forever fixed. Of course, once the national monies disappear, these exchange rates will only be of historical interest as there will be no more Belgian francs, German marks, and so on.

Euro notes and coins will begin circulating January 1, 2002. In the transition years, people use the euro as a unit of account, denominating financial asset values and transactions in euro amounts. Bank accounts are available in euros and credit transactions may be denominated in euros. However, actual cash transactions cannot be made with euros until euro cash starts circulating in 2002.

There is a six-month period, from January 1 until July 1, 2002, when euro currency will circulate jointly with national monies and both may be used for cash transactions. During this period, the euro cash will slowly take over cash business and the national monies will be slowly withdrawn from circulation. After July 1, 2002 the national monies (like the German mark, French franc, and Italian lira) will no longer be a legal tender and only the euro may be used.

Table 3 lists the end-of-year exchange rates for several currencies versus the U.S. dollar from the 1950s. For most of the currencies, there was little movement in the 1950s and 1960s, the era of the Bretton Woods agreement. In the early 1970s, exchange rates began to fluctuate. More recently, there has been considerable change in the foreign exchange value of a dollar, as Table 3 illustrates.

2. FIXED OR FLOATING EXCHANGE RATES

Is the United States better off today with floating exchange rates than it was with the fixed exchange rates of the post–World War II period? The choice of an exchange-rate system has multiple implications for the performance of a nation's economy and, therefore, for the conduct of macroeconomic policy. As is true of many policy issues in economics, economists often disagree about the merits of fixed versus flexible exchange rates. Let us look at the characteristics of the different exchange-rate systems.

2.a. Equilibrium in the Foreign Exchange Market

3. How is equilibrium determined in the foreign exchange market?

An exchange rate is the price of one money in terms of another. Equilibrium is determined by the supply of and demand for the two currencies in the foreign exchange market. Figure 1 contains two supply and demand diagrams for the U.S. dollar–euro foreign exchange market. The downward-sloping demand curve indicates that the higher the dollar price of euro, the fewer euro will be demanded. The upward-sloping supply curve indicates that the higher the dollar price of euro, the more euro will be supplied.

Table 1

Exchange Rate Arrangements (as of January 1, 2000)

Crawling Pegs (6)	Exchange Rates Within Crawling Bands (9)	Managed Floating with No Preannounced Path for Exchange Rate (25)	Independently Floating (48)
Angola	Chile	Algeria	Afghanistan, Islamic State of
Bolivia	Colombia	Azerbaijan	Albania
Costa Rica	Honduras	Belarus	Armenia
Nicaragua	Hungary	Cambodia	Australia
Tunisia	Israel	Czech Rep.	Brazil
Turkey	Poland	Dominican Rep.	Canada
	Sri Lanka	Ethiopia	Congo, Dem. Rep. of the
	Uruguay	Jamaica	Ecuador
	Venezuela	Kenya	Eritrea
		Kyrgyz Rep.	Gambia, The
		Lao P.D.R.	Georgia
		Malawi	Ghana
		Mauritania	Guatemala
		Nigeria	Guinea
		Norway	Guyana
		Pakistan	Haiti
		Paraguay	India
		Romania	Indonesia
		Russia	Japan
		Singapore	Kazakhstan
		Slovak Rep.	Korea
		Slovenia	Liberia
		Suriname	Madagascar
		Tajikistan	Mauritius
		Uzbekistan	Mexico
			Moldova
			Mongolia
			Mozambique
			New Zealand
			Papua New Guinea
			Peru
			Philippines
			Rwanda
			São Tomé and Principe
			Sierra Leone
			Somalia
			South Africa
			Sudan
			Sweden
			Switzerland
			Tanzania
			Thailand
			Uganda
			United Kingdom
			United States
			Yemen
			Zambia
			Zimbabwe

Exchange Arrangements with No Separate Legal Tender (37)	Currency Board Arrangements (8)	Other Conventional Fixed Peg Arrangements (Including De Facto Peg Arrangements Under Managed Floating) (44)	Exchange Rates Within Horizontal Bands (8)
Another currency as legal tender	Argentina	*Against a single currency (30)*	*Within a cooperative arrangement ERM II (2)*
Kiribati	Bosnia and	Aruba	Denmark
Marshall Islands	Herzegovina	Bahamas	Greece
Micronesia	Brunei Darusalam	Bahrain	*Other band*
Palau	Bulgaria	Barbados	*arrangements (6)*
Panama	Djibouti	Belize	Croatia
San Marino	Estonia	Bhutan	Cyprus
CFA franc zone	Hong Kong SAR	Cape Verde	Iceland
WAEMU	Lithuania	China	Libya
Benin		Comoros	Ukraine
Burkina Faso		Egypt	Vietnam
Côte d'Ivoire		El Salvador	
Guinea-Bissau		Iran, Islamic Rep. of	
Mali		Iraq	
Niger		Jordan	
Senegal		Lebanon	
Togo		Lesotho	
CAEMC		Macedonia, FYR	
Cameroon		Malaysia	
Central African Rep.		Maldives	
Chad		Namibia	
Congo, Rep. of		Nepal	
Equatorial Guinea		Netherlands Antilles	
Gabon		Oman	
Euro Area		Qatar	
Austria		Saudi Arabia	
Belgium		Syrian Arab Republic	
Finland		Swaziland	
France		Trinidad and Tobago	
Germany		Turkmenistan	
Ireland		United Arab Emirates	
Italy		*Against a composite (13)*	
Luxembourg		Bangladesh	
Netherlands		Botswana	
Portugal		Burundi	
Spain		Fiji	
		Kuwait	
		Latvia	
		Malta	
		Morocco	
		Myanmar	
		Samoa	
		Seychelles	
		Solomon Islands	
		Tonga	
		Vanuatu	

Sources: IMF staff reports; International Monetary Fund, *Annual Report of the Executive Board of Directors for the Fiscal Year Ended April 30,1999*

Table 2	Currency	Units of National Currency for € 1
Euro Exchange Rates for Member Currencies	Belgian franc	40.3399
	Deutsche mark	1.95583
	Spanish peseta	166.386
	French franc	6.55957
	Irish pound	0.787564
	Italian lira	1936.27
	Luxembourg franc	40.3399
	Dutch guilder	2.20371
	Austrian schilling	13.7603
	Portuguese escudo	200.482
	Finnish markka	5.94573

Equilibrium in the foreign exchange market occurs at the point where the foreign exchange demand and supply curves intersect.

In Figure 1(a), the initial equilibrium occurs at the point where the demand curve D_1 intersects the supply curve. At this point, the equilibrium exchange rate is $1.00 (1 euro costs $1.00) and the quantity of euro bought and sold is Q_1.

Suppose U.S. residents increase their demand for French wine. Because euro are needed to pay for the wine, the greater U.S. demand for French wine generates a greater demand for euro by U.S. citizens, who hold dollars. The demand curve in Figure 1(a) thus shifts from D_1 to D_2. This increased demand for euro causes the euro

Table 3

Exchange Rates of Selected Countries (currency units per U.S. dollar)

Year	Canadian Dollar	Japanese Yen	French Franc	German Mark	Italian Lira	British Pound	Euro
1950	1.06	361	3.50	4.20	625	.36	—
1955	1.00	361	3.50	4.22	625	.36	—
1960	1.00	358	4.90	4.17	621	.36	—
1965	1.08	361	4.90	4.01	625	.36	—
1970	1.01	358	5.52	3.65	623	.42	—
1975	1.02	305	4.49	2.62	684	.50	—
1980	1.19	203	4.52	1.96	931	.42	—
1985	1.40	201	7.56	2.46	1,679	.69	—
1990	1.16	134	5.13	1.49	1,130	.52	—
1995	1.36	103	4.90	1.43	1,584	.65	—
1997	1.43	130	5.95	1.78	1,744	.60	—
1998	1.53	116	5.62	1.67	1,653	.60	—
1999	1.44	102	—	—	—	.62	1.00
2000	1.49	114	—	—	—	.67	1.06

Source: End-of-year exchange rates from International Monetary Fund, *International Financial Statistics,* Washington, D.C., various issues.

Figure 1

The Supply of and Demand for Foreign Exchange

This figure represents the foreign exchange market for euro traded for dollars. The demand curve for euro is based partly on the U.S. demand for French products, and the supply curve of euro is based partly on the French demand for U.S. products: an increase in demand for French wine causes demand for euro to increase from D_1 to D_2. This shift causes an increase from Q_1 to Q_2 in the equilibrium quantity of euro traded and causes the euro to appreciate to $1.03 from the initial equilibrium exchange rate of $1.00. A decrease in demand for French wine causes the demand for euro to fall from D_1 to D_3. This shift leads to a fall in the equilibrium quantity traded to Q_3 and a depreciation of the euro to $.97. If the French demand for U.S. tractors falls, fewer euro are supplied for exchange for dollars, as illustrated by the fall in supply from S_1 to S_3. This shift causes the euro to appreciate to $1.03 and the equilibrium quantity of francs traded to fall to Q_3. If the French demand for U.S. tractors rises, then more francs are supplied for dollars and the supply curve increases from S_1 to S_2. This causes the euro to depreciate and the equilibrium quantity of euro traded to rise to Q_2.

(a) A Change in the U.S. Demand for French Wine

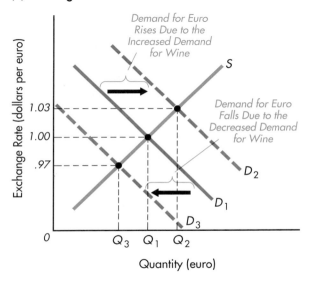

(b) A Change in the French Demand for U.S. Tractors

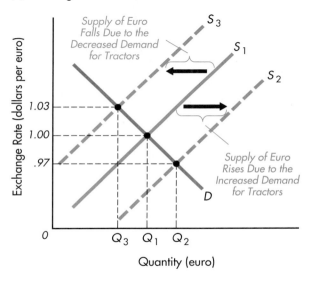

to appreciate relative to the dollar. The new exchange rate is $1.03, and a greater quantity of euro, Q_2, is bought and sold.

If the U.S. demand for French wine falls, the demand for euro also falls, as illustrated by the shift from D_1 to D_3 in Figure 1(a). The decreased demand for euro causes the euro to depreciate relative to the dollar, so that the exchange rate falls to $.97.

So far, we have considered how shifts in the U.S. demand for French goods affect the dollar-euro exchange rate. We can also use the same supply and demand diagram to analyze how changes in the French demand for U.S. goods affect the equilibrium exchange rate. The supply of euro to the foreign exchange market partly originates with French residents who buy goods from the rest of the world. If a French importer buys a tractor from a U.S. firm, the importer must exchange euro for dollars to pay for the tractor. As French residents' demand for foreign goods and services rises and falls, the supply of euro to the foreign exchange market changes.

Suppose the French demand for U.S. tractors increases. This brings about a shift of the supply curve: as euro are exchanged for dollars to buy the U.S. tractors, the supply of euro increases. In Figure 1(b), the supply of euro curve shifts from S_1 to S_2. The greater supply of euro causes the euro to depreciate relative to the dollar, and the exchange rate falls from $1.00 to $.97. If the French demand for U.S. tractors decreases, the supply of euro decreases from S_1 to S_3, and the franc appreciates to $1.03.

Foreign exchange supply and demand curves are affected by changes in tastes and technology and by changing government policy. As demand and supply change, the equilibrium exchange rate changes. In fact, continuous shifts in supply and demand cause the exchange rate to change as often as every day, on the basis of free market forces. Now let us consider how fixed exchange rates differ from floating exchange rates.

2.b. Adjustment Mechanisms Under Fixed and Flexible Exchange Rates

4. How do fixed and floating exchange rates differ in their adjustment to shifts in supply and demand for currencies?

Figure 2 shows the dollar-euro foreign exchange market. The exchange rate is the number of dollars required to buy 1 euro; the quantity is the quantity of euro bought and sold. Suppose that, initially, the equilibrium is at point A, with quantity Q_1 euro traded at $1.00 per euro.

Suppose French wine becomes more popular in the United States, and the demand for euro increases from D_1 to D_2. With flexible exchange rates (as in Figure 1), a new equilibrium is established at point B. The exchange rate rises to $1.03 per euro, and the quantity of euro bought and sold is Q_2. The increased demand for euro has caused the euro to **appreciate** (rise in value against the dollar) and the dollar to **depreciate** (fall in value against the euro). This is an example of a freely floating exchange rate, determined by the free market forces of supply and demand.

Figure 2

Foreign Exchange Market Equilibrium Under Fixed and Flexible Exchange Rates

Initially, equilibrium is at point A; the exchange rate is $1.00 and Q_1 euro are traded. An increase in demand for French wine causes the demand for euro to increase from D_1 to D_2. With flexible exchange rates, the euro appreciates in value to $1.03 and Q_2 euro are traded; equilibrium is at point B. If the government is committed to maintaining a fixed exchange rate of $1.00, the supply of euro must be increased to S_2 so that a new equilibrium can occur at point C. The government must intervene in the foreign exchange market and sell euro to shift the supply curve to S_2.

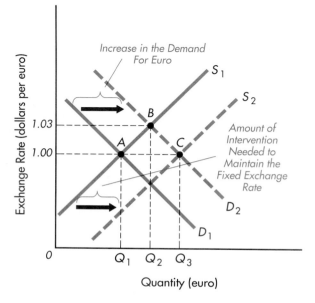

5. What are the advantages and disadvantages of fixed and floating exchange rates?

Now suppose the Federal Reserve is committed to maintaining a fixed exchange rate of $1.00 per euro. The increase in demand for euro causes a shortage of euro at the exchange rate of $1.00. According to the new demand curve, D_2, the quantity of francs demanded at $1.00 is Q_3. The quantity supplied is found on the original supply curve S_1, at Q_1. The only way to maintain the exchange rate of $1.00 is for the Federal Reserve to supply euro to meet the shortage of $Q_3 - Q_1$. In other words, the Fed must sell $Q_3 - Q_1$ euro to shift the supply curve to S_2 and thus maintain the fixed exchange rate.

If the increased demand for euro is temporary, the Fed can continue to supply euro for the short time necessary. However, if the increased demand for euro is permanent, the Fed's intervention will eventually end when it runs out of euro. This situation—a permanent change in supply or demand—is referred to as a **fundamental disequilibrium.** The fixed exchange rate is no longer an equilibrium rate. Under the Bretton Woods agreement, a country was supposed to devalue its currency in such cases.

Suppose that the shift to D_2 in Figure 2 is permanent. In this case, the dollar should be devalued. A devaluation to $1.03 per euro would restore equilibrium in the foreign exchange market without requiring further intervention by the government. Sometimes, however, governments try to maintain the old exchange rate ($1.00 per euro, in this case) even though most people believe the shift in demand to be permanent. When this happens, **speculators** buy the currency that is in greater demand (euro, in our example) in anticipation of the eventual devaluation of the other currency (dollars, in Figure 2). A speculator who purchases euro for $1.00 prior to the devaluation and sells them for $1.03 after the devaluation earns $.03 per euro purchased.

Speculation puts greater devaluation pressure on the dollar: the speculators sell dollars and buy euro, causing the demand for euro to increase even further. Such speculative activity contributed to the breakdown of the Bretton Woods system of fixed exchange rates. Several countries intervened to support exchange rates that were far out of line with free market forces. The longer a devaluation was put off, the more obvious it became that devaluation was forthcoming and the more speculators entered the market. In 1971 and 1973, speculators sold dollars for yen and German marks. They were betting that the dollar would be devalued; both times they were correct. The speculative activity of the early 1970s drew attention to the folly of efforts to maintain fixed exchange rates in the face of a change in the fundamental equilibrium exchange rate.

2.c. **Constraints on Economic Policy**

Fixed exchange rates can be maintained over time only between countries with similar economic policies and similar underlying economic conditions. As prices rise within a country, the domestic value of a unit of its currency falls, since the currency buys fewer goods and services. In the foreign exchange market too, the value of a unit of domestic currency falls, since it buys relatively fewer goods and services than the foreign currency does. A fixed exchange rate thus requires that the purchasing power of the two currencies change at roughly the same rate over time. Only if two nations have approximately the same inflation experience will they be able to maintain a fixed exchange rate. This condition was a frequent source of problems in the Bretton Woods era of fixed exchange rates. In the late 1960s, for instance, the U.S. government was following a more expansionary macroeconomic policy than was Germany. U.S. government expenditures on the war in Vietnam and domestic antipoverty initiatives led to inflationary pressures that were not matched in

Germany. Between 1965 and 1970, price levels rose by 23.2 percent in the United States but only by 12.8 percent in Germany. Since the purchasing power of a dollar was falling faster than that of the mark, the fixed exchange rate could not be maintained. The dollar had to be devalued.

One of the advantages of floating exchange rates is that countries are free to pursue their own macroeconomic policies without worrying about maintaining an exchange-rate commitment. If U.S. policy produces a higher inflation rate than Japanese policy, the dollar will automatically depreciate in value against the yen. The United States can choose the macroeconomic policy it wants, independently of other nations, and let the exchange rate adjust if its inflation rate differs markedly from that of other nations. If the dollar were fixed in value relative to the yen, the two nations couldn't follow independent policies and expect to maintain the exchange rate.

It became obvious in the late 1960s that many governments considered other issues more important than maintenance of a fixed exchange rate. A nation that puts a high priority on reducing unemployment will typically stimulate the economy to try to increase income and create jobs. This initiative may cause the domestic inflation rate to rise and the domestic currency to depreciate relative to other currencies. If one goal or the other—lower unemployment or a fixed exchange rate—must be given up, it is likely that the exchange-rate goal will be sacrificed.

Floating exchange rates allow countries to formulate their macroeconomic policies independently of other nations. Fixed exchange rates require the economic policies of countries linked by the exchange rate to be similar.

Floating exchange rates allow countries to formulate domestic economic policy solely in response to domestic issues; attention need not be paid to the economic policies of the rest of the world. For residents of some countries, this freedom may be more of a problem than a benefit. The freedom to choose a rate of inflation and let the exchange rate adjust itself can have undesirable consequences in countries whose politicians, for whatever reason, follow highly inflationary policies. In these countries a fixed-exchange-rate system would impose discipline, since maintenance of the exchange rate would not permit policies that diverged sharply from those of its trading partner.

RECAP

1. Under a fixed-exchange-rate system, governments must intervene in the foreign exchange market to maintain the exchange rate. A fundamental disequilibrium requires a currency devaluation.
2. Fixed exchange rates can be maintained only between countries with similar macroeconomic policies and similar underlying economic conditions.
3. Fixed exchange rates serve as a constraint on inflationary government policies.

6. What determines the kind of exchange-rate system a country adopts?

3. THE CHOICE OF AN EXCHANGE-RATE SYSTEM

Different countries choose different exchange-rate arrangements. Why does the United States choose floating exchange rates while Barbados adopts a fixed exchange rate? Let us compare the characteristics of countries that choose to float with those of countries that choose to fix their exchange rates.

3.a. Country Characteristics

The choice of an exchange-rate system is an important element of the macroeconomic policy of any country. The choice seems to be related to country size, openness, inflation, and diversification of trade.

3.a.1. Size
Large countries (measured by economic output or GDP) tend to be both independent and relatively unwilling to forgo domestic policy goals in order to maintain a fixed exchange rate. Because large countries have large domestic markets, international issues are less crucial to everyday business than they are in a small country.

3.a.2. Openness
Closely related to size is the relative openness of the economy. By openness, we mean the degree to which the country depends on international trade. Because every country is involved in international trade, openness is very much a matter of degree. An **open economy,** according to economists, is one in which a relatively large fraction of the GDP is devoted to internationally tradable goods. In a closed economy, a relatively small fraction of the GDP is devoted to internationally tradable goods. The more open an economy, the greater the impact of variations in the exchange rate on the domestic economy. The more open the economy, therefore, the greater the tendency to establish fixed exchange rates.

open economy: an economy in which a relatively large fraction of the GDP is devoted to internationally tradable goods

3.a.3. Inflation
Countries whose policies produce inflation rates much higher or lower than those of other countries tend to choose floating exchange rates. A fixed exchange rate cannot be maintained when a country experiences inflation much different from that of the rest of the world.

3.a.4. Trade Diversification
Countries that trade largely with a single foreign country tend to peg their currency's value to that of the trading partner. For instance, South Africa accounts for the dominant share of the total trade of Swaziland. By pegging its currency, the lilangeni, to the South African rand, Swaziland enjoys more stable lilangeni prices of goods than it would with floating exchange rates. Trade with South Africa is such a dominant feature of the Swaziland economy that a fluctuating lilangeni price of the rand would be reflected in a fluctuating price level in Swaziland. If the lilangeni depreciated against the rand, the lilangeni prices of imports from South Africa would rise: this would bring about a rise in the Swaziland price level. Exchange-rate depreciation tends to affect the domestic price level in all countries, but the effect is magnified if a single foreign country accounts for much of a nation's trade. Countries with diversified trading patterns find fixed exchange rates less desirable, because price stability would prevail only in trade with a single country. With all other trading partners, prices would still fluctuate.

Table 4 summarizes the national characteristics associated with alternative exchange-rate systems. Many countries do not fit into the neat categorization of Table 4, but it is nonetheless useful for understanding the great majority of countries' choices.

3.b. Multiple Exchange Rates

Most countries conduct all their foreign exchange transactions at a single exchange rate. For instance, if the dollar-pound exchange rate is $1.80, residents of the United States can purchase British pounds at $1.80, no matter what use they make of the pounds. However, some countries have **multiple exchange rates**—different exchange rates for different types of transactions. A typical arrangement is a dual exchange-rate system, consisting of a free-market-determined floating exchange rate for financial transactions and a fixed exchange rate that overvalues the domestic currency for transactions in goods and services. Some countries adopt even more elaborate arrangements, with special exchange rates for a variety of different transactions. For example, Venezuela once had a four-tier system. The central bank

multiple exchange rates: a system whereby a government fixes different exchange rates for different types of transactions

Table 4	Fixed-Rate Countries	Floating-Rate Countries
Characteristics of Countries with Fixed and Floating Exchange Rates	Small size	Large size
	Open economy	Closed economy
	Harmonious inflation rate	Divergent inflation rate
	Concentrated trade	Diversified trade

traded dollars for bolivars (Bs) at the following rates: sell dollars for Bs4.30 for interest payments on foreign debt; sell dollars for Bs6.00 for national petroleum and iron-ore companies; and sell dollars for Bs7.50 for other government agencies. All other transactions took place at the free market floating exchange rate of Bs14.40.

Countries with multiple exchange rates use them as an alternative to taxes and subsidies. Activities that the policymakers want to encourage are subsidized by allowing participants in them to buy foreign exchange at an artificially low price or sell foreign exchange at an artificially high price. Participants in activities that policymakers want to discourage are forced to pay an artificially high price to buy foreign exchange and to receive an artificially low price to sell foreign exchange. For instance, firms that manufacture goods for export but import some of the resources used in production may be permitted to buy foreign exchange at an artificially low price. This allows them to pay a lower domestic currency price for their imported resources and consequently to charge a lower price for their output, which increases exports. In Venezuela, as you just saw, petroleum companies could buy dollars from the central bank for Bs6.00 even though the free market rate was Bs14.40. In order to encourage greater production and export of Venezuelan petroleum, the central bank subsidized the dollars the petroleum companies needed for imports.

In an effort to discourage imports, developing countries often charge an artificially high price for foreign exchange that will be used to import consumer goods. Such multiple-exchange-rate systems have the same effects as direct government subsidies to exporting manufacturers and taxes on the importation of consumer goods: exports are stimulated and consumer-goods imports are reduced.

The IMF has tried to discourage multiple exchange rates, because they cause the domestic prices of internationally traded goods to differ from the international prices. The result is inefficient resource utilization in consumption and production, since domestic residents respond to the contrived relative prices rather than the true prices set on world markets. Monitoring and administering compliance with multiple exchange rates create additional costs, and people devote resources to avoiding the unfavorable aspects of multiple exchange rates (for example, by getting their transactions classified to the most favorable exchange rate).

3.c. Overvalued Exchange Rates

Developing countries often establish an official exchange rate—the exchange rate set by law—that differs from the equilibrium exchange rate. Figure 3 illustrates an overvalued exchange rate. Assume that a developing country whose currency is called the peso fixes an official peso-dollar exchange rate of 150 pesos per dollar, while the free market equilibrium exchange rate is 200 pesos per dollar. Since the

Figure 3

Overvalued Exchange Rate

The official exchange rate is 150 pesos per dollar, while the free market equilibrium exchange rate is 200 pesos per dollar. Since the official peso price of a dollar is below the equilibrium, the peso is said to be overvalued.

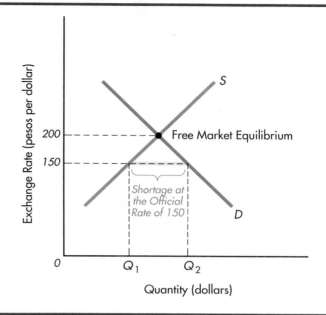

Overvalued exchange rates are used to subsidize favored transactions.

official rate is less than the equilibrium rate, a dollar shortage results. Then Q_2 dollars are demanded at 150 pesos per dollar, but only Q_1 are supplied.

When the official peso-dollar rate is less than the free market rate, the peso is overvalued. To support the official rate, the country must impose tariffs or other restrictions on trade to reduce the demand for dollars. Overvaluing the domestic currency subsidizes favored activities or groups: if everyone had access to the official rate, there would be a dollar shortage. In addition to imposing quotas or tariffs on international trade in goods or financial assets, the country can use multiple exchange rates to ensure that only favored groups buy dollars at the official rate. In fact, a typical feature of multiple-exchange-rate regimes is the availability of an overvalued domestic currency rate for favored transactions. Other residents are forced into the free market, where in this case they pay 200 pesos for their dollars.

RECAP

1. Countries with fixed exchange rates tend to be small, open economies with inflation rates similar to those of their trading partners. Their currencies are typically pegged to that of their main trading partner.

2. Some countries adopt multiple exchange rates for different kinds of transactions.

3. Multiple exchange rates resemble a system of subsidies for favored activities and taxes for activities that are discouraged.

4. An exchange rate is overvalued when the official domestic currency price of foreign currency is lower than the equilibrium price.

SUMMARY

? How does a commodity standard fix exchange rates between countries?

1. Between 1880 and 1914, a gold standard provided for fixed exchange rates among countries. *§1.a*

2. The gold standard ended with World War I, and no established international monetary system replaced it until after World War II, when the Bretton Woods agreement created a fixed-exchange-rate system. *§1.b*

? What kinds of exchange-rate arrangements exist today?

3. Today some countries have fixed exchange rates, others have floating exchange rates, and still others have managed floats or other types of systems. *§1.e*

? How is equilibrium determined in the foreign exchange market?

4. Foreign-exchange-market equilibrium is determined by the intersection of the demand and supply curves for foreign exchange. *§2.a*

? How do fixed and floating exchange rates differ in their adjustment to shifts in supply and demand for currencies?

5. Under fixed exchange rates, central banks must intervene in the foreign exchange market to keep the exchange rate from shifting. *§2.b*

? What are the advantages and disadvantages of fixed and floating exchange rates?

6. Floating exchange rates permit countries to pursue independent economic policies. A fixed exchange rate requires a country to adopt policies similar to those of the country whose currency it pegs to. A fixed exchange rate may serve to prevent a country from pursuing inflationary policies. *§2.c*

? What determines the kind of exchange-rate system a country adopts?

7. The choice of an exchange-rate system is related to the size and openness of a country, its inflation experience, and the diversification of its international trade. *§3.a*

8. Multiple exchange rates are used to subsidize favored activities and raise costs for other activities. *§3.b*

KEY TERMS

gold standard *§1.a*

gold exchange standard *§1.b*

reserve currency *§1.b*

International Monetary Fund (IMF) *§1.c*

World Bank *§1.c*

foreign exchange market intervention *§1.d*

devaluation *§1.d*

equilibrium exchange rates *§1.d*

appreciate *§2.b*

depreciate *§2.b*

fundamental disequilibrium *§2.b*

speculators *§2.b*

open economy *§3.a.2*

multiple exchange rates *§3.b*

EXERCISES

1. Under a gold standard, if the price of an ounce of gold is 400 U.S. dollars and 500 Canadian dollars, what is the exchange rate between U.S. and Canadian dollars?

2. What were the three major results of the Bretton Woods conference?

3. What is the difference between the IMF and the World Bank?

4. How can Mexico fix the value of the peso relative to the dollar when the demand for and supply of dollars and pesos changes continuously? Illustrate your explanation with a graph.

5. Draw a foreign-exchange-market supply and demand diagram to show how the yen-dollar exchange rate is determined. Set the initial equilibrium at a rate of 100 yen per dollar.

6. Using the diagram in exercise 5, illustrate the effect of a change in tastes prompting Japanese residents to buy more goods from the United States. If the exchange rate is floating, what will happen to the foreign-exchange-market equilibrium?

7. Using the diagram in exercise 5, illustrate the effect of the change in Japanese tastes if exchange rates are fixed. What will happen to the foreign-exchange-market equilibrium?

8. When and why should exchange rates change under a fixed exchange-rate system?

9. Other things being equal, what kind of exchange-rate system would you expect each of the following countries to adopt?

   a. A small country that conducts all of its trade with the United States

   b. A country that has no international trade

   c. A country whose policies have led to a 300 percent annual rate of inflation

   d. A country that wants to offer exporters cheap access to the imported inputs they need but to dis-courage other domestic residents from importing goods

   e. A large country like the United States or Japan

10. Illustrate and explain the meaning and likely effects of an overvalued exchange rate.

11. When did the euro appear? Which currencies are in the euro area and what are the exchange rates between each of the currencies and the euro?

12. Suppose you just returned home from a vacation in Mazatlán, Mexico, where you exchanged U.S. dollars for Mexican pesos. How did your trip to Mexico affect the supply and demand for dollars and the exchange rate (assume that all other things are equal)?

13. What does it mean to say that a currency appreciates or depreciates in value? Give an example of each and briefly mention what might cause such a change.

14. If you were an economic policy czar with total power to choose your country's economic policy, would you want a fixed or floating exchange rate for your currency? Why?

15. How does a currency speculator profit from exchange-rate changes? Give an example of a profitable speculation.

E.U. Extends Invitations to 6 Countries: Turkey on Hold

The European Union threw open its doors Friday to six new nations, expanding the list of active applicants for its vast zone of prosperity to encompass nearly all of Eastern and Central Europe.

The invitations went to Bulgaria, Romania, Slovakia, Latvia and Lithuania, plus Malta. The E.U.'s 15 current members also made Turkey a candidate for its rich free-trade club, but more tentatively.

Turkey, which would be the E.U.'s second most populous member after Germany, would not begin discussions until it makes progress instituting democratic practices and protecting human rights.

In Ankara, Prime Minister Bulent Ecevit acknowledged that "there may be details that are hard for us to digest," but he called the invitation "a great success for Turkey."

"This is a historical step toward a united Europe," said E.U. Commissioner Gunter Verheugen. "The Iron Curtain has been definitely removed and the period of uncertainty ends."

Friday's invitations were another step toward a Europe that is becoming more united and, its members hope, more of a power on the world stage.

Eleven E.U. countries already have their own single currency, the euro, and all of them will put the finishing touches on their own defense force, a rapid-reaction contingent of some 60,000 troops expected to become operational in 2003.

Source: "E.U. Extends Invitations to 6 Countries; Turkey on Hold," *Star Tribune* (Minneapolis, MN), December 11, 1999, p. 7A.

Star Tribune **(Minneapolis, MN)/December 11, 1999**

Commentary

The expansion of the European Union to include the countries from eastern Europe holds much promise for the economic development of these countries. Once in the EU, these countries would be able to trade freely with the other EU countries just as the states of the United States trade freely with one another. Just as the U.S. states all share a common money to help facilitate interstate trade, it is likely that the eastern European countries would also welcome the adoption of the euro as their money to further solidify the links between their economies and those of the rest of the EU.

A fixed exchange-rate system represents an agreement among countries to convert their individual currencies from one to another at a given rate. The adoption of one money for Europe is the strongest possible commitment to fixed exchange rates among the EU countries. If every nation uses the same currency, the euro, then all would be linked to the same inflation rate and there would be no fluctuation of the value of the currency across the EU nations using the currency—just as each state in the United States uses the same money, the U.S. dollar. The adoption of a single currency requires that economic policies be similar across EU countries. This means that individual countries must subjugate their monetary policies to the goals of the European Central Bank. If each nation insists on exercising its own monetary and fiscal policies and chooses different interest and inflation rates, there can never be one money.

A convergence in inflation rates is necessary for the smooth operation of any fixed exchange rate. Persistent inflation differentials across the members of a fixed-exchange-rate system affect the competitiveness of each member's exports in the world market. Though a fixed-exchange-rate system maintains stable *nominal exchange rates* (the rate observed in the foreign exchange market), the competitiveness of a currency is represented by the *real exchange rate*. The real exchange rate is the nominal exchange rate adjusted for the price level at home compared to the price level abroad:

$$\text{Real exchange rate} = \frac{\text{nominal exchange rate} \times \text{foreign price level}}{\text{domestic price level}}$$

The disruptive changes in competitiveness caused by persistent inflation differentials require a realignment of a fixed-exchange-rate system that adjusts nominal exchange rates to keep real exchange rates from drifting too far from their correct value. For instance, if the Italian price level starts to rise faster than German prices, Italian goods will be priced out of the German market unless there is an Italian currency that depreciates on the foreign exchange market. According to the equation just presented, if Italy is the domestic country and its price level rises, the real exchange rate falls and Italian goods are, therefore, relatively more expensive unless the nominal exchange rate rises to offset the higher domestic price level. The need for similar inflation rates within a fixed exchange-rate system indicates that a country could successfully join the fixed-exchange-rate system or a region with one money only when its inflation rate fell to a level closer to that of other European countries.

Any countries seeking to join the euro area must align their economic policies with those of other member countries.

absolute advantage   an advantage derived from one country having a lower absolute input cost of producing a particular good than another country (21)

accounting measure of costs   the direct costs that can be measured (9)

accounting profit   total revenue less total costs except for the opportunity cost of capital (9)

adding value   creating output that is more valuable than the resources used to create the output (9)

adverse selection   the situation that occurs when higher-quality consumers or producers are driven out of the market because unobservable qualities are misvalued (14)

annual return   the dividend plus the capital gain per year (17)

antitrust policy   government policies and programs designed to control the growth of monopoly and enhance competition (14)

applied research   finding applications for basic research results (13)

appreciate   to increase the value of a currency under floating exchange rates, that is, exchange rates determined by supply and demand (23)

arc elasticity   the price elasticity of demand measured over a price range using the midpoint, or average, as the base (6)

association as causation   the mistaken assumption that because two events seem to occur together, one causes the other (1)

assumptions   statements that are taken for granted without justification (1)

average fixed cost (AFC)   total fixed cost divided by the quantity produced (8)

average physical product (APP)   output per unit of resource (8)

average total cost (ATC)   total cost divided by the total output (8)

average variable cost (AVC)   total variable costs divided by the quantity produced (8)

backward-bending labor supply curve   a labor supply curve indicating that a person is willing and able to work more hours as the wage rate increases until, at some sufficiently high wage rate, the person chooses to work fewer hours (16)

barrier to entry   anything that impedes the ability of firms to begin a new business in an industry in which existing firms are earning positive economic profits (11)

barter   the direct exchange of goods and services without the use of money (3)

basic research   creation of new knowledge (13)

break-even price   a price that is equal to the minimum point of the average-total-cost curve (10)

budget line   a line showing all the combinations of goods that can be purchased with a given level of income (7 App.)

budget deficit   the shortage that results when government spending is greater than revenue (5)

budget surplus   the excess that results when government spending is less than revenue (5)

business cycle   the recurrent pattern of rising real GDP followed by falling real GDP (5)

business firm   a business organization controlled by a single management (4)

capital   products such as machinery and equipment that are used in production (1)

capital account   the record in the balance of payments of the flow of financial assets into and out of a country (7)

capital consumption allowance   the estimated value of depreciation plus the value of accidental damage to capital stock (6)

capital gain   an increase in the price of financial capital (17)

capture theory   government actions benefit some special-interest group that has captured control of regulations, legislation, or governing authority (14)

cartel   an organization of independent firms whose purpose is to control and limit production and maintain or increase prices and profits (12)

cash transfers   money allocated away from one group in society to another (20)

centrally planned economy   an economic system in which the government determines what goods and services are produced and the prices at which they are sold (5)

ceteris paribus   other things being equal, or everything else held constant (1)

circular flow diagram   a model showing the flow of output and income from one sector of the economy to another (4)

closed system   a standard's being available only to the innovator (13)

Coase theorem   when bargaining is costless and property rights can be assigned without difficulty, the amount of an externality-generating activity will not depend on who is assigned the property rights (18)

commercial policy   government policy that influences international trade flows (22)

comparable worth   the idea that pay ought to be determined by job characteristics rather than by supply and demand and that jobs with comparable requirements should receive comparable wages (16)

comparative advantage   the ability to produce a good or service at a lower opportunity cost than someone else (2, 21)

compensating wage differentials   wage differences that make up for the higher risk or poorer working conditions of one job over another (16)

complementary goods   goods that are used together (as the price of one rises, the demand for the other falls) (3)

concentration   the degree to which a few firms control the output and pricing decisions in a market (14)

constant returns to scale   unit costs remain constant as the quantity of production is increased and all resources are variable (8)

consumer equilibrium   the point at which the marginal utilities per dollar of expenditure on the last unit of each good purchased are equal (7)

consumer sovereignty   the supreme authority of consumers to determine, by means of their purchases, what is produced (4)

consumer surplus   the difference between what the consumer is willing to pay for a unit of a good and the price that the consumer actually has to pay (7)

consumption   household spending (4)

contracting out   hiring a private firm to provide a product or service for a government entity (14)

corporation   a legal entity owned by shareholders whose liability for the firm's losses is limited to the value of the stock they own (4)

cost-plus pricing or **markup pricing**   a pricing policy whereby a firm computes its average cost of producing a product and then sets the price at some percentage above this cost (12)

coupon   fixed amount a borrower agrees to pay the bondholder each year (17)

cross-price elasticity of demand   the percentage change in the demand for one good divided by the percentage change in the price of a related good, *ceteris paribus* (6)

crowding   forcing a group into certain kinds of occupations (16)

customs union   an organization of nations whose members have no trade barriers among themselves but are free to fashion their own trade policies toward nonmembers (22)

deadweight loss   the reduction of consumer surplus without a corresponding increase in monopoly profit when a perfectly competitive firm is monopolized (11)

debt   loans (9)

demand   the quantities of a well-defined commodity that consumers are willing and able to buy at each possible price during a given period of time, *ceteris paribus* (3)

demand curve   a graph of a demand schedule that measures price on the vertical axis and quantity demanded on the horizontal axis (3)

demand schedule   a list or table of the prices and the corresponding quantities demanded of a particular good or service (3)

dependent variable   the variable whose value depends on the value of the independent variable (1 App.)

depreciate (a currency)   to decrease the value of a currency under floating exchange rates (23)

derived demand   demand stemming from what a good or service can produce, not demand for the good or service itself (15)

determinants of demand   factors other than the price of the good that influence demand—income, tastes, prices of related goods and services, expectations, and number of buyers (3)

determinants of supply   factors other than the price of the good that influence supply—prices of resources, technology and productivity, expectations of producers, number of producers, and the prices of related goods and services (3)

devaluation   a deliberate decrease in the official value of a currency (23)

development   turning research into viable products (13)

diminishing marginal utility   the principle that the more of a good that one obtains in a specific period of time, the less is the additional utility yielded by each additional unit of that good (7)

direct or **positive relationship**   the relationship that exists when the values of related variables move in the same direction (1 App.)

discrimination   prejudice that occurs when factors unrelated to marginal productivity affect the wages or jobs that are obtained (16)

diseconomies of scale   the increases of unit costs as the quantity of production increases and all resources are variable (8)

disequilibrium   a point at which quantity demanded and quantity supplied are not equal at a particular price (3)

disparate impact   an impact that differs according to race, sex, color, religion, or national origin, regardless of the motivation (16)

disparate treatment   different treatment of individuals because of their race, sex, color, religion, or national origin (16)

disutility   dissatisfaction (7)

diversification   producing more than one product in order to enhance profits or reduce risk of loss (13)

dividend   the amount returned to shareholders on each share of stock as a precent of the value of the stock (17)

dominant strategy   a strategy that produces better results no matter what strategy the opposing firm follows (12)

double coincidence of wants   the situation that exists when A has what B wants and B has what A wants (3)

dumping   selling goods at a lower price in foreign markets than at home (11)

economic bad   any item for which we would pay to have less (1)

economic costs   total costs including explicit costs and the full opportunity costs of the resources that the producer does not buy or hire but already owns (9)

economic efficiency   a situation where no one in society can be made better off without making someone else worse off (5, 10)

economic good   any good that is scarce (1)

economic profit   total revenue less total costs including all opportunity costs (9)

natural monopoly a monopoly that emerges because of economies of scale (11)

negative economic profit total revenue that is less than total costs when total costs include all opportunity costs (9)

negative income tax (NIT) a tax system that transfers increasing amounts of income to households earning incomes below some specified level as their income declines (20)

net exports exports minus imports (4)

nonrenewable (exhaustible) natural resources resources that cannot be replaced or renewed (18)

normal accounting profit zero economic profit (9)

normal goods goods for which the income elasticity of demand is positive (6)

normative analysis analysis of what ought to be (1)

occupational segregation the separation of jobs by sex (16)

open economy an economy in which a relatively large fraction of the GDP is devoted to internationally tradable goods (23)

open system a standard's being available to everyone (13)

opportunity costs the highest-valued alternative that must be forgone when a choice is made (2)

partnership a business with two or more owners who share the firm's profits and losses (4)

per se rule actions that could be anticompetitive are intrinsically illegal (14)

perfectly elastic demand curve a horizontal demand curve indicating that consumers can and will purchase all they want at one price (6)

perfectly inelastic demand curve a vertical demand curve indicating that there is no change in the quantity demanded as the price changes (6)

personalized selling the practice of customizing a good or service or price to each customer (13)

positive analysis analysis of what is (1)

positive economic profit total revenue that is greater than total costs when total costs include all opportunity costs (9)

positive feedback or **positive network externalities** the benefits of one person's joining a network's being enjoyed by all its members (13)

potential competition possible entry or rivalry capable of forcing existing producers to behave as if the competition actually existed (11)

predatory dumping dumping to drive competitors out of business (11)

preferred provider organization (PPO) a group of physicians who contract to provide services at a price discount (19)

present value the equivalent value today of some amount to be received in the future (17)

price ceiling a situation where the price is not allowed to rise above a certain level (3)

price discrimination charging different customers different prices for the same product (6, 11)

price elasticity of demand the percentage change in the quantity demanded of a product divided by the percentage change in the price of that product (6)

price elasticity of supply the percentage change in quantity supplied divided by the percentage change in price, *ceteris paribus* (6)

price floor a situation where the price is not allowed to decrease below a certain level (3)

price maker a firm that sets the price of the product it sells (9)

principle of mutual exclusivity the rule that the owner of private property is entitled to enjoy the consumption of the property privately (18)

private costs costs borne by the individual in the transaction that created the costs (18)

private property right the limitation of ownership to an individual (5, 18)

private sector households, businesses, and the international sector (4)

privatization transferring a publicly owned enterprise to private ownership (14)

producer surplus the difference between the price firms would have been willing to accept for their products and the price they actually receive (10)

production possibilities curve (PPC) a graphical representation showing the maximum quantity of goods and services that can be produced using limited resources to the fullest extent possible (2)

productivity the quantity of output produced per unit of resource (3)

progressive tax (progressive income tax) a tax whose rate rises as income rises (20)

proportional tax a tax whose rate does not change as the tax base changes (20)

public choice the use of economics to analyze the actions and inner workings of the public sector (5)

public goods goods whose consumption cannot be limited only to the person who purchased the good (5, 18)

public interest theory the theory that government should intervene in business actions to improve the well-being of the general public (14)

public sector the government (4)

quantity demanded the amount of a product that people are willing and able to purchase at a specific price (3)

quantity quota a limit on the amount of a good that may be imported (22)

quantity supplied the amount sellers are willing and able to offer at a given price, during a given period of time, everything else held constant (3)

rational self-interest the term economists use to describe how people make choices (1)

regressive tax a tax whose rate decreases as the tax base changes (20)

regulated monopoly a monopoly firm whose behavior is monitored and prescribed by a government entity (11)

relative price the price of one good expressed in terms of the price of another good (3)

renewable (nonexhaustible) natural resources resources that can be replaced or renewed (18)

rent seeking the use of resources simply to transfer wealth from one group to another without increasing production or total wealth (5, 14)

reserve currency a currency that is used to settle international debts and is held by governments to use in foreign exchange market interventions (23)

resources goods used to produce other goods, i.e., land, labor, capital, and entrepreneurial ability (1)

rule of reason the rule that to be illegal, an action must be unreasonable in a competitive sense and the anticompetitive effects must be demonstrated (14)

saving not consuming all current production (17)

scale size; all resources change when scale changes (8)

scarcity the shortage that exists when less of something is available than is wanted at a zero price (1)

scientific method a manner of analyzing issues that involves five steps: recognition of the problem, assumptions, model building, predictions, and tests of the model (1)

sequential game a situation in which one firm moves first and then the other firm is able to choose a strategy based on the first firm's choices (12)

short run a period of time short enough that the quantities of at least some of the resources cannot be varied (6)

short-run average total cost (*SRATC*) the lowest-cost combination of resources with which each level of output is produced when the quantity of at least one resource is fixed (8)

shortage a quantity supplied that is smaller than the quantity demanded at a given price (3)

shutdown price the minimum point of the average-variable-cost curve (10)

slope the steepness of a curve, measured as the ratio of the rise to the run (1 App.)

social costs the private and external costs of a transaction (18)

social regulation the prescribing of health, safety, performance, and environmental standards that apply across several industries (14)

sole proprietorship a business owned by one person who receives all the profits and is responsible for all the debts incurred by the business (4)

speculators people who seek to profit from an expected shift in an exchange rate by selling the currency expected to depreciate and buying the currency expected to appreciate, then exchanging the appreciated currency for the depreciated currency after the exchange rate adjustment (23)

standards war two or more incompatible technologies' being rivals for a standard (13)

statistical discrimination discrimination that results when an indicator of group performance is incorrectly applied to an individual member of the group (16)

strategic behavior behavior that occurs when what is best for B depends on what A chooses and what A chooses depends on what B is most likely to do (12)

strategic trade policy the use of trade restrictions or subsidies to allow domestic firms with decreasing costs to gain a greater share of the world market (22)

subsidies payments made by government to domestic firms to encourage exports (22)

substitute goods goods that can be used in place of each other (as the price of one rises, the demand for the other rises) (3)

substitution effect the tendency of people to purchase less expensive goods that serve the same purpose as a good whose price has risen (7)

superstar effect the situation where people with small differences in abilities or productivity receive vastly different levels of compensation (16)

supply the amount of a good or service that producers are willing and able to offer for sale at each possible price during a period of time, *ceteris paribus* (3)

supply curve a graph of a supply schedule that measures price on the vertical axis and quantity supplied on the horizontal axis (3)

supply schedule a list or table of prices and corresponding quantities supplied of a particular good or service (3)

surplus a quantity supplied that is larger than the quantity demanded at a given price (3)

tariff a tax on imports or exports (22)

tax incidence a measure of who pays a tax (6)

technical efficiency producing at a point on the *PPC* (5)

terms of trade the amount of exports that must be exchanged for some amount of imports (21)

tests trials or measurements used to determine whether a theory is consistent with the facts (1)

theory (or model) a simplified, logical story based on positive analysis that is used to explain an event (1)

tipping point the point at which an event turns into an epidemic (13)

total costs (TC) the sum of total variable and total fixed costs (8)

total fixed costs (TFC) costs that must be paid whether a firm produces or not (8)

total physical product (TPP) the maximum output that can be produced when successive units of a variable resource are added to fixed amounts of other resources (8)

total revenue (TR) $TR = P \times Q$ (16)

total utility a measure of the total satisfaction derived from consuming a quantity of some good or service (7)

total variable costs (*TVC*) costs that rise or fall as production rises or falls (8)

trade creation an effect of a preferential trade agreement, allowing a country to obtain goods at a lower cost than is available at home (22)

trade deficit the situation that exists when imports exceed exports (4)

economic regulation   the prescription of price and output for a specific industry (14)

economic rent   the portion of earnings above transfer earnings; the payment for use of a resource whose supply is fixed (15)

economies of scale   the decrease of unit costs as the quantity of production increases and all resources are variable (8)

emission standard   a maximum allowable level of pollution from a specific source (18)

emissions offset policy   an environmental policy wherein pollution permits are issued and a market in the permits then develops; an increase in pollutants by one source is acceptable if met by a decrease by another source (18)

equilibrium   the point at which quantity demanded and quantity supplied are equal at a particular price (3)

equilibrium exchange rates   the exchange rates that are established in the absence of government foreign exchange market intervention (23)

equimarginal principle or **consumer equilibrium**   to maximize utility, consumers must allocate their scarce incomes among goods so as to equate the marginal utilities per dollar of expenditure on the last unit of each good purchased (7)

equity   shares of stock (9)

exchange rate   the price of one country's money in terms of another country's money (3)

export supply curve   a curve showing the relationship between the world price of a good and the amount that a country will export (11)

exports   products that a country sells to other countries (4)

externalities   the costs or benefits of a transaction that are borne by someone not directly involved in the transaction (5, 18)

face value   the amount of principal that will be paid back when a bond matures (17)

facilitating practices   actions by oligopolistic firms that can contribute to cooperation and collusion even though the firms do not formally agree to cooperate (12)

factors of production   goods used to produce other goods (1)

fair rate of return   a price that allows a monopoly firm to earn a normal profit (14)

fallacy of composition   the mistaken assumption that what applies in the case of one applies to the case of many (1)

Federal Reserve   the central bank of the United States (5)

financial capital   the money used to purchase capital; stocks and bonds (17)

financial intermediaries   institutions that accept deposits from savers and make loans to borrowers (4)

fiscal policy   the policy directed toward government spending and taxation (5)

foreign exchange market intervention   the buying and selling of currencies by a government or central bank to achieve a specified exchange rate (23)

free good   a good for which there is no scarcity (1)

free ride   the enjoyment of the benefits of a good by a producer or consumer without having to pay for them (5)

free rider   a consumer or producer who enjoys the benefits of a good or service without paying for them (18)

free trade area   an organization of nations whose members have no trade barriers among themselves but are free to fashion their own trade policies toward nonmembers (22)

fundamental disequilibrium   a permanent shift in the foreign exchange market supply and demand curves such that the fixed exchange rate is no longer an equilibrium rate (23)

future value   the equivalent value in the future of some amount received today (17)

game theory   a description of oligopolistic behavior as a series of strategic moves and countermoves (12)

Gini ratio   a measure of the dispersion of income ranging between 0 and 1: 0 means all families have the same income; 1 means 1 family has all of the income (20)

gold exchange standard   an exchange-rate system in which each nation fixes the value of its currency in terms of gold, but buys and sells the U.S. dollar rather than gold to maintain fixed exchange rates (23)

gold standard   a system whereby national currencies are fixed in terms of their value in gold, thus creating fixed exchange rates between currencies (23)

health maintenance organization (HMO)   an organization that provides comprehensive medical care to a voluntarily enrolled consumer population in return for a fixed, prepaid amount of money (19)

Herfindahl index   a measure of concentration calculated as the sum of the squares of the market share of each firm in an industry (14)

household   one or more persons who occupy a unit of housing (4)

human capital   skills, training, and personal health acquired through education and on-the-job training (16)

import demand curve   a curve showing the relationship between the world price of a good and the amount that a country will import (21)

imports   products that a country buys from other countries (4)

income elasticity of demand   the percentage change in the demand for a good divided by the percentage change in income, *ceteris paribus* (6)

increasing-returns-to-scale industry   an industry in which the costs of producing a unit of output fall as more output is produced (22)

independent variable   the variable whose value does not depend on the value of other variables (1 App.)

indifference curve   a curve showing all combinations of two goods that the consumer is indifferent among (7 App.)

indifference map   a complete set of indifference curves (7 App.)

indifferent   lacking any preference (7 App.)

inferior goods goods for which the income elasticity of demand is negative (6)

in-kind transfers allocations of goods and services from one group in society to another (20)

inputs goods used to produce other goods (1)

International Monetary Fund (IMF) an international organization that supervises exchange-rate arrangements and lends money to member countries experiencing problems meeting their external financial obligations (23)

intraindustry trade the simultaneous import and export of goods in the same industry by a particular country (21)

inverse or **negative relationship** the relationship that exists when the values of related variables move in opposite directions (1 App.)

investment spending on capital goods to be used in producing goods and services (4)

labor the physical and intellectual services of people, including the training, education, and abilities of the individuals in a society (1)

labor force participation entering the work force (16)

land all the natural resources, such as minerals, timber, and water, as well as the land itself (1)

law of demand as the price of a good or service rises (falls), the quantity of that good or service that people are willing and able to purchase during a particular period of time falls (rises), *ceteris paribus* (3)

law of diminishing marginal returns when successive equal amounts of a variable resource are combined with a fixed amount of another resource, marginal increases in output that can be attributed to each additional unit of the variable resource will eventually decline (8)

law of supply as the price of a good or service that producers are willing and able to offer for sale during a particular period of time rises (falls), the quantity of that good or service supplied rises (falls), *ceteris paribus* (3)

local monopoly a monopoly that exists in a limited geographic area (11)

long run a period of time long enough that the quantities of all resources can be varied (16)

long-run average total cost (*LRAC*) the lowest-cost combination of resources with which each level of output is produced when all resources are variable (8)

Lorenz curve a curve measuring the degree of inequality of income distribution within a society (20)

macroeconomics the study of the economy as a whole (1)

managed care comprehensive medical care provided within one firm (19)

managed competition government intervention in the health-care market to guide competition so that costs are reduced (19)

marginal benefit additional benefit (2, 18)

marginal cost (MC) the additional costs of producing one more unit of output (2, 8)

marginal factor cost (MFC) the additional cost of an additional unit of a resource (15)

marginal opportunity cost the amount of one good or service that must be given up to obtain one additional unit of another good or service (2)

marginal physical product (MPP) the additional quantity that is produced when one additional unit of a resource is used in combination with the same quantities of all other resources (8)

marginal revenue product (MRP) the value of the additional output that an extra unit of a resource can produce, $MPP \times MR$ (15)

marginal social cost the additional social cost that results from a one-unit increase in production (18)

marginal utility the extra utility derived from consuming one more unit of a good or service (7)

market a place or service that enables buyers and sellers to exchange goods and services (3)

market failure the failure of the market system to achieve economic and technical efficiency (18)

market imperfection a lack of efficiency that results from imperfect information in the market place (5)

maturity date the time when the coupon payments end and the principal is paid back (17)

median voter theorem candidates or parties select positions on issues that reflect the median voter's positions on those issues (22)

Medicaid a joint federal-state program that pays for health care for poor families, the neediest elderly, and disabled persons (19)

Medicare a federal health-care program for the elderly, and the disabled (19)

microeconomics the study of economics at the level of the individual (1)

minimum efficient scale (MES) the minimum point of the long-run average cost curve; the output level at which the cost per unit of output is the lowest (8)

model see *theory* (1)

monetary policy the policy directed toward the control of the money supply (5)

monopoly a market structure in which there is a single supplier of a product (5, 11)

monopoly firm (monopolist) a single supplier of a product for which there are no close substitutes (11)

monopoly power market power, the ability to set prices (11)

monopsonist a firm that is the only buyer of a resource (15)

moral hazard the chance that people will alter their behavior in unanticipated ways after an agreement or contract has been defined (14)

most-favored customer (MFC) a customer who receives a guarantee of the lowest price and all product features for a certain period of time (12)

multinational business a firm that owns and operates producing units in foreign countries (4)

multiple exchange rates a system whereby a government fixes different exchange rates for different types of transactions (23)

trade diversion an effect of a preferential trade agreement, reducing economic efficiency by shifting production to a higher-cost producer (22)

tradeoff the act of giving up one good or activity in order to obtain some other good or activity (2)

trade surplus the situation that exists when imports are less than exports (4)

transaction costs the costs involved in making an exchange (3)

transfer earnings the portion of total earnings required to keep a resource in its current use (15)

transfer payment the income transferred from one citizen, who is earning income, to another citizen (5)

unlimited wants boundless desires for goods and services (1)

utility a measure of the satisfaction received from possessing or consuming goods and services (7)

value quota a limit on the monetary value of a good that may be imported (22)

World Bank an international organization that makes loans and provides technical expertise to developing countries (23)

X-inefficiency the tendency of a firm not faced with competition to become inefficient (11)

yield the annual rate of return on a bond if the bond is held to maturity (17)

zero economic profit the result when total revenue equals total costs where total costs include all opportunity costs (9)

Text Credits

Economically Speaking

CHAPTER

1   "Pumped Up Over Cheap Gas," from *The Arizona Republic,* January 22, 1995, p. B1. Used with permission. Permission does not imply endorsement.

2   "Car Sector Braces for Stiffer Competition," by Fadzil Ghazali, Section: Automotive, p. 4, July 4, 2000, *Berhad Business Times,* Malaysia.

3   Excerpts from "A Slueth for Landlords with Eviction in Mind," by Corey Kilgannon from the *New York Times,* March 26, 2000, p. 4. Copyright © 2000 by the New York Times Co. Reprinted with permission.

4   "Zooming in on Wills," by Andrew Pierce, June 16, 2000. *The Times.* Reprinted by permission of © The Times Newspapers Limited.

5   "A Big 'Nein' to Deutsche Telekom; Telecommunications: Germany Still Doesn't Have a Completely Open Market," by A. Michael Noll. *The Los Angeles Times,* July 26, 2000, Wednesday, Home Edition, Metro Part B. p. 9, Op Ed Desk. Reprinted by permission of A. Michael Noll.

6   "Equal-Pricing Bill Passed," by Pete Bowles. *Newsday* (New York), December 18, 1997, A85. Newsday, Inc. © 1997. Reprinted with permission.

7   "Too Much Too Young," by Andy Goldberg. *The Daily Telegraph* (London) June 8, 2000, Thursday, p. 6. © Telegraph Limited 2000. Reprinted by permission.

8   "Old Concept in a New Era," by Jerry Heaster. *The Kansas City Star,* June 14, 2000, Wednesday, Metropolitan Edition, Business, p. 1. Reprinted by permission of The Kansas City Star.

9   "The Cutting Edge: Focus on Technology," by Jube Shiver, *Los Angeles Times,* February 7, 2000, Monday, Home Edition, Business, Part C, p. 1. Reprinted by permission of the Los Angeles Times Syndicate.

10 "Food Marketers Show a Taste for Video Growth" from Moira McCormick, *Billboard,* May 23, 1992, p. 49 © 1995 BPI Communications, Inc. Used with permission of *Billboard Magazine.*

11 "Conflict Diamonds: Americans Can Stop the Damage They Do," *Star Tribune,* June 12, 2000, Monday, Metro Edition, p. 10A. Reprinted by permission Star Tribune.

12 "Poker player's game theory scoops . . ." by Roger Highfield. *The Daily Telegraph* (London), April 28, 2000, Friday, p. 10. © Telegraph Limited 2000. Reprinted by permission.

13 "JLM Industries Embracing the New Economy," by Jeff Harrington, *St. Petersburg Times, Business,* Cover Story, p. 10. Dateline: Tampa. Reprinted by permission.

14 "S02 Emission Allowance Asset Report," by Melissa Hardison, Donna Dart and Chris Combe, January 9, 1998. Salt River Project Management Report. Reprinted with permission.

15 "State Economy Will Feel Asia's Money Pains," by Ed Taylor. From *The Tribune,* December 31, 1997. Reprinted by permission.

16 "Higher Apathy," from the *Richmond Times Dispatch,* January 25, 1998. Reprinted by permission of the *Richmond Times Dispatch.*

17 "A real nail-biter," by Jo-Ann Johnston, October 19, 2000. Thursday, Final Edition, Business & Finance, pg. 1. Reprinted by permission of The Tampa Tribune.

18 "Boulder Targets Traffic Congestion," by Mary George, *The Denver Post.* February 5, 1995, p. 1C. Reprinted by permission.

19 "Many Travel a Painful Circuit for Their Managed Health Care," by Marian Uhlman. *The Philadelphia Inquirer,* February 1, 1995, p. 1. Reprinted by permission.

20 "America's Income Inequality is Not Inequity," by W. Michael Cox and Richard Alm. *Star Tribune,* January 25, 2000, Tuesday, Metro Edition, p. 13A. Reprinted by permission of the author.

21 "China Trade Will Come Back to Haunt," *The Buffalo News,* August 15, 2000. Tuesday, Final Edition, Viewpoints, p. 3B. Reprinted by permission of Morton Weinberg.

22 From NBER Digest, July/August 1991. Used by permission of the National Bureau of Economic Research.

23 "E. U. Extends Invitations to 6 Countries; Turkey on Hold," *Washington Post,* December 11, 1999, Saturday, Metro Edition, News, p. 7A. Reprinted by permission.

Economic Insights

CHAPTER

4   Excerpt from *An Inquiry into the Nature and Causes of the Wealth of Nations,* edited and with an introduction, notes, marginal summary, and index by Edward Cannan, with a preface by George Stigler. (Chicago University Press, 1976), Reprinted by permission of the publisher.